D1215452

Robert Frost

CRITICAL COMPANION TO

Robert Frost

A Literary Reference to His Life and Work

DEIRDRE FAGAN

Facts On File

An imprint of Infobase Publishing

For Paul, Maureen, Frank, Sean

Critical Companion to Robert Frost: A Literary Reference to His Life and Work

Facts On File, Inc.
An imprint of Infobase Publishing
132 West 31st Street
New York NY 10001

ISBN-10: 0-8160-6182-3
ISBN-13: 978-0-8160-6182-2

Library of Congress Cataloging-in-Publication Data

Fagan, Deirdre.
Critical companion to Robert Frost: a literary reference to his life and work / by Deirdre Fagan.
p. cm.
Includes bibliographical references and index.
ISBN 0-8160-6182-3 (hc : alk. paper)
1. Frost, Robert, 1874–1963—Handbooks, manuals, etc. I. Title.
PS3511.R94Z6425 2007
811'.52—dc22   2006013269

Facts On File books are available at special discounts when purchased in bulk quantities for businesses, associations, institutions, or sales promotions. Please call our Special Sales Department in New York at (212) 967-8800 or (800) 322-8755.

You can find Facts On File on the World Wide Web at http://www.factsonfile.com

Text design by Erika K. Arroyo
Cover design by Cathy Rincon

Printed in the United States of America

VB Hermitage 10 9 8 7 6 5 4 3 2 1

This book is printed on acid-free paper.

CONTENTS

INTRODUCTION

This volume seeks to explicate for the student, the scholar, and the public various aspects of Robert Frost's life and work. It contains a number of useful features, but by far the most important is the series of entries in Part II of the book covering each of Frost's published poems, plays, and masques. Each entry is designed to be a beginning rather than an ending in the study of a particular work. The consistency of expression across each entry, especially in the discussion of the interrelationships of significant details, is designed to aid readers in using the book and getting started on their own explorations. No entry was written with the intention of its becoming a definitive reading or even of providing an accumulation of readings. Further reading sections are included to support the readings contained herein but more often to make available additional and even contradictory readings. They are also meant to suggest other possibilities for beginning or ending an interpretation.

The volume selected as the most definitive for Frost's poetry and prose was the Library of America edition (1995), and all interpretations rely on the versions presented there. The dates following the titles of poems are those of first publication in a collection. If the poem was published earlier in a periodical, that date is often included in the entry. Dates following the titles of prose works indicate the date of the first publication. Dates following lecture titles indicate the year the lecture was given.

All the published poems, plays, and masques included in the Library of America edition have entries in Part II of this book. The most prominent and lengthy prose pieces have entries as well. Letters, extraordinarily brief pieces, tributes to other now largely unknown writers, and other pieces that hold little relevance to an understanding of Frost's work or life have been excluded.

Part I of the book contains a concise biography of the poet. Part III contains entries on topics in the study of Frost's life and work. They highlight some of the most important people and places in his life and also treat some of the most prominent themes and symbols in his poetry. References to topics covered in Part III are given in SMALL CAPITAL LETTERS to indicate a cross-reference to an entry.

In writing this book, I have kept in mind lessons learned from my experience of teaching college English for more than a decade. The readings of the poems do not always arrive at firm conclusions, because Frost himself rarely does and poetry analysis is as organic as is the writing of poetry. Frost is often wry, satirical, tongue-in-cheek, ambiguous, and even contradictory; the entries in this book are not intended to be.

ACKNOWLEDGMENTS

A daughter's gratitude goes to my foremost editor, a most exacting teacher, and a remarkable poet and person, my father, Frank Fagan. I thank in a daily mantra my husband and best friend, Robert Seltzer, for his constant devotion and support of mind and spirit. Theirs is a work of love, and I will fondly remember talking about poems with them both, forever grateful for their hard work as first readers, for my father's insights as a poet and Bob's as a philosopher. I thank my young son Liam for not deleting any files and for providing frequent moments of comic relief. I wish to recognize my brother Sean Fagan for his brilliance and guidance, Mary Spagnoli Seltzer and Leslie Seltzer for their assistance in the selection of photographs, and Laura, Dan, Vincent, Anthony, and Cassandra Grucza for helping me meet deadlines. My dear friend Linda Gordon, always an inspiration, who encouraged me to take some photographs of my own, will not be forgotten. For their endless emotional support and encouragement, I am grateful to my sisters and colleagues Suzanne Ferriss, Kate Waites, and Lynn Wolf. For my education, I recognize the influence of the estimable Helen Regueiro Elam, the passionate and inspiring Richard M. Goldman, and the necessary corrective of Josiah B. Gould's humor and wit. Theodore Arapoglou aided my research, and he and Lisa DeJesus helped preserve my sanity. I wish also to thank my editor Jeff Soloway, Joshua B. Shaw at the Rauner Special Collections Library at Dartmouth College, the Library of Congress, Courtney Loy at the United States Postal Service, and Time Life Books. I respectfully acknowledge the work of the scholars who preceded me. I am particularly indebted to Jay Parini's intimate and illuminating biography, Jeffrey Cramer's companion to biographical associations, and Richard Poirier and Mark Richardson's informative notes in the Library of America edition (1995) of Frost's poems.

PART I

Biography

Robert Frost

(1874–1963)

Robert Frost, who once described himself as a bastard Vermonter, was born in SAN FRANCISCO, California. He was the son of the spiritual and mystical Isabelle (Belle) Moodie Frost and the rough and impetuous William (Will) Prescott Frost, Jr. His early life was as tumultuous and unstable as the relationship between his parents, causing him to seek stability in his adult life, which he found in his relationship with his wife Elinor Miriam White Frost and his children. Frost was a teacher, a poet-philosopher, and a philosopher-poet. He was a husband. He was a father, grandfather, and great-grandfather. He was a tall, large-framed man with piercing blue eyes and a friendly but corrective manner. He was insecure but driven, proud and patient. He did not publish his first book of poetry until he was 39 years old, but his career lasted nearly 50 years. He was the first poet to read at a presidential inauguration, John F. Kennedy's, and one of the first to hold a poet-in-residence position at a college. He transformed the poetic landscape. He remains the most publicly celebrated American poet.

William Prescott Frost (1823–1901) was Frost's paternal grandfather. He was working as a farmer in Kingston, New Hampshire, when his son, Frost's father, Will, Jr. (1850–85), was born. Will was raised in Lawrence, Massachusetts, where his father was a foreman in one of the Lawrence cotton mills. Will was "a wild and unmanageable rebel" when young, so much so that "in their attempts to keep the boy off the streets at night, his parents tried to lock him in his bedroom." He was a "good scholar" and a Phi Beta Kappa graduate of Harvard, but his ease with academics also afforded him time to become a "poker player, heavy drinker, and frequenter of brothels" while in college (Thompson, *Early Years*, 2). After he graduated from Harvard, his adventurous spirit made him eager to move west to San Francisco. But Will needed money, and a teaching position as principal of Lewistown Academy in Lewistown, Pennsylvania, would provide that.

Robert Lee Frost in 1963, at age 87. *(Photo by David H. Rhinelander, Courtesy Library of Congress)*

Isabelle (Belle) Moodie (1844–1900), Frost's mother, was the only other teacher at Lewistown Academy. She was a native of Leith, a seaport town in Scotland, the daughter of a sea captain, Thomas Moodie, who died shortly after her birth, and an irresponsible mother, Mary, who sent Belle at age 11 to the United States to be raised by a prosperous uncle, also named Thomas Moodie, of Columbus, Ohio. Belle arrived from Scotland in 1856. She was beautiful, spirited, and spiritual.

Will fell in love with Belle almost immediately upon meeting her, and in an effort to be nearer to her responded to an ad she had placed offering lessons in phonography, a system of stenography. After five months of lessons he wrote her a letter of proposal, part of which read: "As I became better acquainted with you, I saw in you a nearer approach to my ideal of a true woman, joined with the native cultivation and refinement of a lady, than I had ever chanced upon among any of my lady friends" (Thompson, *Early Years*, 4–5). Will expressed that he was aware of reasons why they should not be wed, such as their difference in age (Belle was six years his senior) and their difference in religion (Belle was Christian and Will described himself as lacking belief). But as Robert Frost's biographer Lawrance Thompson describes, "Importunate and persuasive as a lover, he conducted his courtship so well that he very quickly won the hand of Miss Moodie" (*Early Years*, 6).

Will and Belle were married in Lewistown in March only six months after they had met. At the end of the school year, Will and Belle resigned their positions and made their way to San Francisco, as Will had originally intended, only now he would bring with him a bride. On their way, the two stopped in Columbus to visit Belle's friends and family. Belle remained in Columbus until Will gained work in San Francisco and found a home for them, and then she joined him.

Belle and Will's first child, Robert Lee Frost, named by his father after Confederate general Robert E. Lee, was born on March 26, 1874. Throughout the family's time in California, Will worked as a newspaperman at San Francisco Bay area papers now long defunct: the *Post* and the *Bulletin*. Life with Will was tumultuous, passionate, and unstable. From 1879 to 1884 the family moved frequently between apartments and hotels, taking trips to Napa Valley and the California countryside. The relationship between Belle and Will was strained. Will's impetuosity, temper, and rough ways caused him to play forcefully with the young Frost and was a point of contention between Belle and Will. Frost later wrote about the harrowing experience of watching his reckless father swim in the Pacific Ocean in "Once by the Pacific." Thompson describes Will as a "punisher," a "hero," and a "companion" to his son Robert.

Belle had a profound influence on Frost as well, taking the role of comforter and protector. Frost listened to his mother's stories of fairies and goblins and used such worlds as images in his poems, sometimes dark, as in "The Demiurge's Laugh," and sometimes like glitter dust, as in "Waiting." Belle's impression that she had the gift of second sight and could see into the future affected Frost. Like the romantic poet William Blake, Frost, according to one account, believed that he, too, could communicate with the spirit world. Belle also homeschooled the children. The young Frost was sensitive and often had nervous stomach cramps that kept him from attending public grade school. He attempted to go to school on several occasions but ended up withdrawing and being homeschooled through the third grade. Later Frost would tell his good friend Louis Untermeyer that when he was a

child he "played sick to get out of going to school" (Parini, 16).

Frost's "On Emerson" says that "A melancholy dualism is the only soundness," and he begins to describe his "own unsoundness" as coming from his family history and teachings, primarily his mother's. His mother was Presbyterian turned Unitarian, as well as a Swedenborgian. (Emanuel Swedenborg (1688–1772) was a Swedish scientist and theologian whose vision and writings posthumously inspired the establishment of the Church of the New Jerusalem.) Frost said he was not sure if he was "baptized in them all" but says he was largely "under the auspices of Emerson."

Will's fondness for whiskey and his hot temper put strains on his relationship with his wife and caused Belle to take young Robert east with her to Lawrence in 1876 to meet Will's parents for the first time. Frost's sister, Jeanie Florence, was born in Lawrence on June 25 of that year. Belle would not stay long before taking the children and heading to a farm in Greenfield, Massachusetts, the family home of a friend. While Belle and the children were away, Will became heavily involved in Democratic politics.

In "A Poet's Boyhood," which appeared in a brochure announcing a Frost reading to be held at the Berkeley Community Theater on November 6, 1960, in Berkeley, California, Frost speaks of politics; of his father's role in nominating the popular Democratic candidate for the presidency in 1880, Winfield Scott Hancock; and of his father's disappointment when Hancock was narrowly beaten by James Garfield, and his "even greater disappointment when Hancock as an old friend and fellow soldier of Garfield's went to Garfield's inauguration and shook hands with him in public right on the platform." At age 86 Frost was returning to the region of his birth as an esteemed poet and was reminiscing about his San Francisco childhood. He describes the family as "Democrats and very intense ones" and recalls accompanying his father to work when Will was chairman of the Democratic City Committee, since Frost was kept from school for his health. Frost "absorbed from his father a great deal, including a feral drive to make something of himself, to exercise influence, to feel the world bending to his will. Frost's lifelong love of competitive sports, and his passion to excel and win in whatever he did, were also a legacy from his father. But Frost also learned the price of failure from Will Frost, and how easily one's ambitions may be thwarted, by others and oneself" (Parini, 19). Frost once said of his father that he was a "bad boy who never stopped being one," a trait that Frost clearly did not inherit (Gerber, 21).

Belle and the children returned to San Francisco in late November 1876 to find Will in the hospital with tuberculosis. On May 5, 1885, Will died of tuberculosis at age 34 in San Francisco, Frost's first tragic loss. He would suffer many. Belle and the children, financed by Will's parents, returned to Lawrence with the coffin by train, the "longest, loneliest train ride" Frost ever took, to bury Will and live with the parents: "Belle Frost's openness of manner, her liberal idea of child rear-

ing, and her Swedenborgian serenity did not settle well with the elder Frosts, who may have blamed her on some unspoken level for the early death of their beloved Willie" (Parini, 19–21).

Although Belle and the children did not live with Frost's grandparents for long, the family remained in the region, and Frost's growing attachment and lifelong love affair with the mountains and the people began: "I'd sometimes complain or run off to go swimming, but on the whole I guess I liked to try myself out in a job—helping a man load a wagon, pile firewood, rake or hoe. It was all odd jobs in those days. I liked working with the characters, listening to them, their stories, the way they had to tell a story—the country was full of characters" (Parini, 21).

In 1886, Belle secured a teaching position and moved with the children to Salem Depot, New Hampshire, to teach in the district school. Frost

Frost playing baseball at the Homer Noble Farm, Ripton, Vermont. *(Courtesy Dartmouth College Library)*

liked going to school in Salem, Massachusetts, where his mother held one of her first teaching jobs, as his mother was his teacher. He liked playing baseball and was quite good at it, a skill he would maintain throughout his adult life. He would later impress his colleagues at the BREAD LOAF SCHOOL OF ENGLISH with his pitching ability and determination. He swung birches on an aunt's farm, the source for his famous poem "Birches," in which he speaks of a boy too far from town to learn baseball. He once told an audience that "It was almost sacrilegious climbing a birch tree till it bent, till it gave and swooped to the ground," adding "but that's what boys did in those days" (Parini, 22).

In 1888 Frost passed entrance examinations and entered Lawrence High School. Belle resigned the Salem Depot position to take a teaching job in Methuen, Massachusetts. Frost finished the school year at the head of his class. The family spent the summer working at a hotel in Maine, Belle and Jeanie as chambermaids and Frost doing odd jobs such as collecting mail and groceries and carrying suitcases. Belle was hired to teach at Methuen the following year, and the family returned to Lawrence.

The loss of his father and the struggles of his mother and sister affected Frost. His younger sister Jeanie had physical and mental illnesses throughout her life. Jeanie was bright, bookish, and troubled, and their relationship was often strained. Although he was older than Jeanie, Frost entered the third grade and she the fourth after testing. Frost and Jeanie entered the fifth grade together, and Frost would eventually surpass Jeanie in high school. Jeanie was described by her mother as a "healthy, pretty, and good" baby, but from the time she was three she suffered from "ailments which the doctors of San Francisco had not satisfactorily diagnosed or alleviated" including "prolonged periods of crying and hysteria" and a "nervous disorder" (Thompson, *Early Years,* 47). She was also hospitalized her senior year of high school with typhoid fever. She nearly died, was forced to withdraw from school, and never graduated. She later underwent an operation for curvature of the spine.

In 1920 Frost was forced to commit his sister to the state mental hospital at Augusta, Maine, fol-

lowing her earlier arrest and diagnosis of insanity in Portland, Maine. From the hospital, Jeanie once wrote to her brother that "she could see into and through another person's mind, that it was difficult to do so when there were two heads in a straight line from her; but that even then she could do it—with both" (Thompson, *Early Years,* 496). Jay Parini describes her mental state as "bordering on schizophrenia" (42). Jeanie died on September 27, 1929, in the mental hospital. Frost's daughter Irma would have a mental illness similar to Jeanie's.

In a letter to Louis Untermeyer dated April 12, 1920, Frost wrote about Jeanie:

> She has always been antiphysical and a sensibilitist. I must say she was pretty well broken by the coarseness and brutality of the world before the war was thought of. This was partly because she thought she ought to be on principle. She has had very little use for me. I am coarse for having had children and coarse for having wanted to succeed a little. She made a birth in the family the occasion for writing us once of the indelicacy of having children. Indelicacy was the word. Long ago I disqualified myself from helping her through a rough world by my obvious liking for the world's roughness.... "I suppose I am a brute in that my nature refuses to carry sympathy to the point of going crazy just because someone else goes crazy, or of dying just because someone else dies. As I get older I find it easier to lie awake nights over other people's troubles. But that's as far as I go to date. In good time I will join them in death to show our common humility. (*Selected Letters* 247–248)

Frost once said of his sister, "She and I always had unhappy times together, poor thing" (Thompson, *Early Years,* 519). But Parini does report one good visit upon Frost's return from ENGLAND when Frost played the "role of big brother more generously and thoughtfully than he had in the past" (160).

Frost's childhood was not idyllic, but Frost's love of Mother Goose, of his family, and of nature, baseball, and language would set the stage for his character and his poetry. He inherited his father's competitive and passionate personality, but other than a few early bouts of masculinity and tough-ness, he managed to keep himself at least somewhat subdued once he created and settled his own family.

Of all the relationships Frost had to his mother, father, grandparents, and sister, his relationship to his mother was the most positive. But the greatest family influences in his later life were his wife Eli-nor Miriam Frost and their children. Elinor was the daughter of Henrietta Ada Cole White and Edwin White, who was a Universalist minister who became a carpenter, to Henrietta's chagrin, when he decided he did not share the beliefs of the Univer-salist Church or any other church.

Elinor had a chronic illness that kept her from school, so it was not until she qualified for member-ship in the class of 1892 that she and Frost met at Lawrence High School. Frost began to fall in love with Elinor immediately. He was impressed with her mind and with the interests they shared. He was the editor of the school periodical, the *Bulletin*, in which he published his first poems, and some of the couple's shared literary ideals can be found in an essay Elinor published in the *Bulletin* titled "A Phase of Novel Writing." Frost's fascination with Elinor took on a cosmic cast when it was announced that they would share valedictorian honors upon graduation:

> To the superstitious young man, thus paired with his beloved, the decision seemed prophetic. He knew that his love for Elinor had been growing throughout the year. He had entered passion-ately into all the preliminaries of courtship— walking home with her after school, carrying her books, escorting her to evening functions, consulting her about her editorial problems, jeal-ously admiring her poems, showing her what he had written, and reading aloud to her recently from [Edward Rowland] Sill and Emily Dickin-son. (Thompson, *The Early Years,* 125)

Frost had given Elinor books by the latter two poets as a romantic gesture during their courtship. The summer after graduation was the height of their courtship.

Because both Frost and Elinor planned to attend college, Frost at Dartmouth and Elinor at Lawrence

Elinor Miriam White Frost, 1892. *(Courtesy Dartmouth College Library)*

University, they knew they would be parted in the fall, so they seized the day as young lovers do and spent every possible waking moment together, tak-ing nature walks and talking. They secretly wed in their own whimsical ceremony, pledging their undying love to one another. Frost would later say when his son Carol married quickly and young that he "like[d] children to be terribly in love," and it is likely that he had himself and Elinor in mind. Frost was passionate for Elinor, and Elinor had to resist his advances. "The Subverted Flower" would char-acterize those early encounters, and Frost withheld it from publication until four years after Elinor's death, for modesty's sake.

Elinor and Frost were physically but not emo-tionally parted by college in the fall, but Frost dropped out of Dartmouth and returned home. "None of my relatives wanted me to write. Grand-father wanted me to be a lawyer. My mother was very fond of poetry, and, while she never said so, I always felt that underneath she wanted me to write," Frost once said (Lathem, 36). Around this time, however, Frost's paternal grandfather offered to support him for a year while Frost tried his hand at being a poet. Frost rejected the offer, arguing that it would take him 20 years to become a recognized poet, which it did. He taught at the Salem District School and at his mother's school in Methuen, where he took over an unruly class of hers. In the summer of 1894, when Elinor returned home from college, Frost was eager to marry her publicly, but she insisted they wait until she finished college and Frost was employed in a promising line of work. He had been holding various jobs, but nothing reliable.

Frost's first poem, "My Butterfly: An Elegy," was published in the November 8, 1894, issue of the *Independent.* That same year, in a manner reminiscent of his father, Frost printed two copies of a chapbook, *Twilight,* and impetuously visited Elinor with a copy in hand. She responded coolly to his passionate outburst, causing Frost to destroy his own copy, and shortly thereafter he began a dangerous sojourn into the Dismal Swamp on the Virginia-North Carolina border.

Frost was young, in love with Elinor, and threatened by her being away in college and the possibility that there might be a competitor for her affections, which caused him to fall into a depression that made him seek "a place that would mirror his bleak mood exactly, in the name as well as the character." The locale had been "regarded by poets from [Henry Wadsworth] Longfellow to Thomas More as a place where those who have lost hope run away from the world" (Parini, 48). As a young aspiring poet, this area connected him to his predecessors and gave him a place to embrace his quixotic emotions. In some sense, the sojourn was a turning point for him. He would write about the physical and emotional journey in various poems, among them the first poem of his first book, "Into My Own," drawing on this harrowing and enlightening experience.

This reckless behavior only further enforced Elinor's view that they should delay their marriage plans, but her love for Frost bound her to him. The adventure also sobered him a bit. In 1895 he began working as a reporter for the Lawrence *Daily American* and *Sentinel.* Despite their tumultuous courtship and Elinor's father's objections (he found Frost unreliable and irresponsible and his behavior emo-

tional and adolescent), Frost and Elinor were officially married on December 19, 1895. Elinor's constant presence matured him: "Elinor encouraged and loved him, and served as a permanent muse until her death in 1939. The scenes of their courtship were branded on Frost's unconscious, and would recur frequently in dreams and poems—a perpetual source of inspiration and anxiety" (Parini, 54). When Frost married Elinor, she became quite literally his other half, to his betterment. Frost said of her that she was the "unspoken half of everything [he] ever wrote," and it is not difficult to see her as the unspoken half of everything he ever felt or lived. (Thompson, *Selected Letters,* 450). Their marriage was a lifelong love affair, but it was not without its challenges.

Elinor and Robert Frost had six children: Elliott, Lesley, Carol, Irma, Marjorie, and Elinor Bettina. Of the six, two died in childhood, one in childbirth, and one of suicide, and Irma would end up in a mental hospital. Elinor also had at least one miscarriage, in 1915. They faced financial and family struggles as a team, however, and were also a team in homeschooling their children, each taking on the tasks to which he or she was most suitable. Elinor was supportive of Frost when he tried his hand as a farmer and a teacher before he published his first book and his career took off, even advocating to Frost's paternal grandfather for the Derry Farm, in Derry, New Hampshire. Throughout her lifetime, each book Frost published would be dedicated to her (except *New Hampshire,* which was dedicated "To Vermont and Michigan"), and she was instrumental in managing his career. The two were challenged in all ways imaginable, and the tensions that are inevitable in such a lifelong friendship and partnership are alluded to in the poems and in letters and conversations.

Frost and Elinor at first lived with his mother and sister while he taught his mother's older students. Their first child, their son Elliott, was born on September 25, 1896, only 10 months after they married. The summer of 1897 Frost spent with Elinor and Elliott in Amesbury, Massachusetts. He then entered Harvard University in September, with the help of his paternal grandfather, and moved to Cambridge, Massachusetts; he visited his family weekly. Frost was awarded a prize for excellence in classical studies his first semester and was later awarded the Sewall Scholarship for academic excellence. After spending the summer in Amesbury he returned to Harvard the following fall. In 1899, Frost left Harvard to return to Lawrence, and this was the end of his career as a college student.

Frost and Elinor's second child, their daughter Lesley, was born April 28, 1899, and they moved to the Derry Farm. Belle was diagnosed with advanced cancer and came to live with Elinor and Frost. She died the same year as Frost and Elinor's first child, Elliott. Elliott died just months before his fourth birthday, on July 8, 1900, of typhoid fever. Frost's mother died on November 2. Frost and Elinor's third child, their son Carol, was born May 27, 1901. Frost's grandfather, William Prescott Frost, died on July 10 of the same year.

Elliott's death was a huge blow to the Frosts. When he took ill, Elinor's mother "argued with her daughter that a doctor could not help the boy; they must all pray for God's help." This caused Frost to delay in taking action, and by the time he called the doctor, it was too late. Frost and Elinor were at his bedside all night; he died at 4 A.M. Frost would later say that he felt as guilty over not having called the doctor as if he had "murder[ed] his own child" (Parini, 68). He would also write "Home Burial," about a young couple who lose their first and only child and their inability to communicate to one another their grief.

Frost's paternal grandparents were the source of significant financial help throughout his adult life. While the Derry Farm was given to the couple, the transfer of ownership was, much to Frost's chagrin, carried out on certain conditions. When his paternal grandfather died in 1901, Frost felt "oddly liberated." He also was freed from immediate financial worries: "In his will, the good feelings he harbored toward his grandson were made explicit; Frost was left five hundred dollars per annum for ten years, then eight hundred per annum in subsequent years," and the Derry Farm would become his property in 1911 (Parini, 80).

Frost and Elinor's fourth child, Irma, was born on June 27, 1903, and their fifth child, Marjorie, was born on March 28, 1905. In 1906, Frost took a teaching position at Pinkerton Academy in Derry,

New Hampshire. He published another poem, "The Tuft of Flowers," in the Derry *Enterprise* in March. In 1907, their sixth child, Elinor Bettina, was born on June 18 but died on June 21. In May 1909 "Into My Own" appeared in the *New England* magazine.

Frost was a playful father who was involved in his children's homeschooling, reading to them frequently and taking long botanical walks with them. Lesley Frost recalled that "the children would follow their father into the woods, through the cranberry bog, or along a stream, listening to his tales of goblins and fairies, absorbing his detailed botanical expositions, taking in stories meant to inform them about historical figures and epochs" (Parini, 85). The children also were required to memorize English and American poetry and to learn to identify various plant life they encountered on their walks. Elinor taught the children reading, writing, geography, and spelling; Frost taught botany and astronomy. Parini writes that Frost "engaged them throughout their lives with loving consistency, engaging them

Young Frost in England, 1913, around the time of the publication of *A Boy's Will. (Courtesy Library of Congress)*

emotionally and advising them with care and thoughtfulness" (445). In Parini's judgment, Frost was a bit too involved in the children's later lives, at least financially. He continued to be the children's supporter well into their adult lives, partly because of the various physical and emotional difficulties his children faced.

Carol suffered from respiratory problems and at one time was urged to move to Colorado for his health. He married Lillian LaBatt Frost on November 3, 1923, and they had one child, William Prescott Frost, born on October 15, 1924. Frost wrote to Lincoln MacVeagh, his editor at Holt that

> Carol's marriage was only a little of a surprise. He and Lillian had been engaged for some time. They were such children that I didn't want to commit them to each other by taking much notice of the affair or saying much about it. I doubt if I thought it would survive.... I may be frosty, but I rather like to look on at such things. And I like children to be terribly in love. They are a nice pair.

He described Lillian as "pretty, quiet and practical" and explained that she had been a good friend of the girls in the family for a number of years (Thompson, *Years of Triumph*, 258–259).

Carol had health, financial, and emotional problems throughout his life. Frost was a great support, even giving Carol and Lillian the Stone House in Shaftsbury, Vermont. Carol suffered depression throughout his life and committed suicide on October 9, 1940. He shot himself, and his son Prescott discovered the body. Frost had stayed with Carol for several days prior to the incident. Carol had been speaking of suicide and Frost was called to keep him company. A day after he left his son's side, he received the call from Prescott. Frost wrote in a letter to his close friend Louis Untermeyer on October 26, 1940,

> I took the wrong way with [Carol]. I tried many ways and every single one of them was wrong. Some thing in me is still asking for the chance to try one more. There's where the greatest pain is located. I am cut off too abruptly in my plans and efforts for his peace of mind. ... Well then

I'll be brave about this failure as I have meant to be about my other failures before (*Selected Letters* 491).

Irma married John Paine Cone on October 15, 1926. She gave birth to a son, Harold, and she and her husband divorced in 1946. Irma was suffering from a mental illness similar to Frost's sister Jeanie's, and Frost, having "recently experienced the suicide of Carol, . . . dreaded a similar turn in Irma's life (Parini, 366). He purchased a home for Irma in Acton, Massachusetts, in 1927. Her health deteriorated over time, however, and within a few years it was clear that she could no longer care for herself: "One day she left her house in Acton and wandered aimlessly around Cambridge, confused and anxious" (Parini, 375). She was placed in a state mental hospital in Concord, New Hampshire. Frost was one of the people who took her to the hospital.

Marjorie suffered various illnesses throughout her life. She was hospitalized with pneumonia, a pericardiac infection, chronic appendicitis, and nervous exhaustion in 1925. In 1927 she spent 10 weeks at Johns Hopkins Hospital for treatment. In 1930 she was hospitalized in Baltimore with tuberculosis, and in 1931 she entered a sanatorium in Boulder, Colorado. She married Willard Fraser in Billings, Montana, on June 3, 1933. Frost was unable to attend because of exhaustion from delivering public lectures and readings. In 1934, following the birth of her daughter Marjorie Robin Fraser on March 16, Marjorie developed puerperal fever. The Frosts arranged to have her treated at the Mayo Clinic in Rochester, Minnesota. Although she received intensive serum injections and blood transfusions, she died on May 2, 1934.

Lesley attended Wellesley College, Barnard College, and the University of Michigan at various points. She worked in an airplane factory, and she and Marjorie opened a bookstore in Pittsfield, Massachusetts, in 1924. She married James Dwight Francis in September 1928. Like Irma, but for different reasons, Lesley suffered marital difficulties. She had two daughters with Dwight, Elinor Frost Francis and Lesley Lee Francis, but shortly thereafter they divorced. Lesley and her offspring would make contributions to the study of Frost and his poetry.

Frost sold the Derry farm and moved the family to an apartment in Derry Village in 1911. He took a teaching job in Plymouth, New Hampshire. Frost's career as a poet officially began when he resigned the Plymouth position and used the proceeds of the sale of the Derry Farm to sail to England on August 23, 1912.

Upon arrival, the family lived in a cottage in Beaconsfield, Buckinghamshire, called The Bungalow, but it "lacked the full charm of rural England." Soon afterward the family rented a home called Little Iddens in Dymock, Gloucestershire, which reminded them of the Derry Farm (Parini, 144). They would later rent a thatched-roof home near Little Iddens.

While in England Frost felt brave among strangers, and though he had never before approached a book publisher with his poetry, only the editors of periodicals, he prepared *A Boy's Will* and sent it to David Nutt and Company of London, which, much to his surprise, accepted it for publication. And "[s]uddenly, with the arrival of [a] brief note, so many hopes deferred seemed realized or at least realizable" (Thompson, *Early Years*, 401). Frost had

Frost at Pinkerton Academy, Derry, New Hampshire, 1910. *(Courtesy Library of Congress)*

waited 39 years for his first real recognition as a poet. The time had finally arrived, and he was giddily beside himself. His book was published April 1, 1913, six days after his birthday. His second book, *North of Boston*, was published May 15, 1914.

Frost described his "coverless book," taken to be *A Boy's Will*, in a February 26, 1913, letter to friend John Bartlett as coming "pretty near being the story of five years of [his] life" (*Selected Letters*, 66). *A Boy's Will* was Frost's first triumph, though not his greatest, but without it he could not have gone on to publish the large number of lasting poems of the later books. He had headed to England an unknown in 1912, and by 1913 his first book had captured the praise of reviewers. One of the more significant reviews of his first book came from fellow poet Ezra Pound, whom he met in London.

Frost was introduced to Pound through the poet Frank F. S. Flint, whom Frost had met by chance at the opening of Henry Monro's Poetry Bookshop on Devonshire Street in London. Flint told Pound about Frost, and Pound was immediately eager to meet him. He invited Frost to visit him in Kensington with a curt note that read "at home, sometimes," and several months later (just before his first publication) Frost took him up on it (Parini, 127). Pound was eager to get hold of *A Boy's Will*, which had not yet gone to press, so their first meeting took them to the office of Frost's publisher, David Nutt, to get a copy of the book. Later that day Pound wrote a favorable review for *Poetry*, Harriet Monro's magazine. In a letter to Alice Corbin Henderson, assistant of Harriet Monro, he wrote, "Have just discovered another Amur'kn. Vurry Amurk'n, with, I think, the seeds of grace" (Parini, 128). Frank F. S. Flint also offered a favorable review. He admired Frost's "direct observation of the object and immediate correlation with the emotion—spontaneity, subtlety in the evocation of moods, humour" and his "ear for silence" (Meyers, 102). Flint had thought that each poem was the expression of one mood, or one emotion, or one idea. Norman Douglas of the *English Review* wrote that there was a "wild, racy flavour" to Frost's poems and that "they sound that inevitable response to nature which is the hall-mark of true lyric feeling" (Thornton, 21).

To Frost's mind, Pound's review would come at a cost. Pound had asserted that Frost was yet another great artist who had been rejected by American editors and had to seek refuge and recognition in Europe. Because of this, Frost feared he was "going to suffer a good deal at home by the support of Pound" (Meyers, 109). But this was not the result. Within weeks Pound introduced Frost to William Butler Yeats, and Frost's European success was assured. His American recognition would come later, but not much.

The most significant friendship of Frost's lifetime was likely that with Edward Thomas, whom he met while in England, though it was short lived. Himself a critic, journalist, and poet, Thomas met Frost in a restaurant in London in 1913, and the two spent the next four years either taking long talking walks together or exchanging letters. Their families also grew close. When Thomas enlisted in the British Army and was killed in the Battle of Arras on April 9, 1917, it was a huge blow to Frost. Frost would write a poem titled "To E. T." for Thomas and include it in *New Hampshire* (1923). (*See* LITERARY FRIENDS AND ACQUAINTANCES.)

Frost learned in 1914 that Henry Holt of New York would publish his books in the United States. On February 13, 1915, the Frost family returned to the United States, arriving on February 23, and lived on a farm in Franconia, New Hampshire. *North of Boston* would be published first, on February 20, 1915; *A Boy's Will* would follow in April. Frost's third book, *Mountain Interval,* was published on November 27, 1916, by Holt.

Donald J. Greiner writes that when Frost returned to the United States from England, a "multiedged dispute" about his poetry ensued: "Some

Frost at his desk in Franconia, New Hampshire. *(Courtesy Dartmouth College Library)*

Frost looks at his Dartmouth honorary degree. *(Courtesy Dartmouth College Library)*

critics used Frost to comment upon the sorry state of American publishing, lamenting that native artists of exceptional merit had to find publication in a foreign country because American publishers and editors were blind and deaf to the newer movements in poetry"; others "attack[ed] Frost for his so-called British-made reputation, these critics used the poet's work as a transition to a more general argument that the American public should not patronize an American artist just because the English think well of him" (66–67).

After returning to the U.S. and being published by Holt, now credentialed, Frost secured a position at Amherst College in 1916. He was also elected to the National Institute of Arts and Letters. The relationship with Amherst would likely be the most meaningful college association of his career. It continued throughout his lifetime, and Frost held various positions at different times.

The family moved to Amherst in 1917. At the college, Frost taught courses in poetry appreciation and pre-Shakespearean drama. In 1918 Frost was awarded his first honorary M.A. degree by Amherst. He would accumulate more than 40 honorary graduate degrees in his lifetime, despite his never having completed one as a student, including ones from the two schools he attended: Dartmouth and Harvard.

The Frost family moved piecemeal to the Stone House in South Shaftsbury, Vermont, in 1920. In 1921 Frost read for the first time at the newly established Bread Loaf School of English in Vermont, which began in 1920 and is affiliated with Middlebury College. He returned each summer, and the Bread Loaf School would be a significant mainstay in his public life.

In 1921 also for the first time, Frost accepted a one-year fellowship at the University of Michigan. The position was renewed and he taught again the following year. In 1923 he resigned to return to Amherst College. In 1924 he was awarded a lifetime appointment at the University of Michigan as a fellow in letters, with no teaching obligations. He resigned from Amherst to take the position. He stayed with Michigan until the fall of 1925, but he returned to Amherst in January, 1926. In 1924 he also won his first Pulitzer Prize for *New Hampshire*. He would win three more Pulitzers, for *Collected Poems* in 1931, for *A Further Range* in 1936, and for *A Witness Tree* in 1943.

In 1936 Frost became the Charles Eliot Norton Professor of Poetry at Harvard University, another meaningful moment in his career, as he had attended Harvard. The following year would be one of the most trying of his life. Elinor was diagnosed with breast cancer and underwent surgery. Frost wrote to his close friend Louis Untermeyer on October 4, 1937:

> I tried two or three times yesterday to tell you that Elinor had just been operated on for a growth in her breast. I doubt if she fully realizes her peril. . . . You can see what a difference this must make in any future we have. She has been the unspoken half of everything I ever wrote, and both halves of many a thing from My November Guest down to the last stanzas of Two Tramps in Mud Time—as you may have divined. I don't say it is quite up with us. We shall make the most of such hope as there is in such cases. . . . Her unrealization is what makes it hard for me to keep from speaking to somebody for sympathy. I have had almost too much of her suffering in this world. (*Selected Letters*, 450)

Elinor died on March 20, 1938, while they were wintering, for rest, in Gainesville, FLORIDA. Elinor was climbing stairs in their home when she had a severe heart attack and collapsed. She suffered seven more attacks in the next two days. Frost, highly agitated, was kept from her but "could hear her muffled responses to the doctor through the closed door" (Parini, 310). Frost lost his friend and partner of 43 years: "[T]he death of Elinor is a major curtain that fell in the play of Frost's life, signaling the final act. The conditions, even the setting, for his life changed significantly from this point on" (Parini, 314).

In the introduction to the *Family Letters of Robert and Elinor Frost*, Lesley writes, "With all their

play of mind, they shared a deep innocence, a naivete common to genius, at once wide and sad, that heartbreaking insight that recognizes the hairsbreadth between joy into pain, pain into joy." She notes that while the children were away, Elinor wrote letters to them two or three times a week and that after she died "the family correspondence was immeasurably reduced and we were to discover that what we had assumed was a patriarchy had actually been matriarchal" (*Family Letters*, x).

Frost journeyed to the Derry Farm, hoping to bury Elinor's ashes there, since she had wished that they be spread along the Hyla Brook, but he was not received warmly by the new owners, so Elinor was buried in Old Bennington, Vermont. Under her name, the family stone reads, "Together wing to wing and oar to oar," a line from Frost's "The Master Speed," and that they were.

Frost bought the Homer Noble Farm in Ripton, Vermont, near Bread Loaf in 1939. Friends Theodore and Kathleen (Kay) Morrison, the latter of whom became Frost's secretary, lived in the main house, and Frost lived in a three-room cabin on the property. Frost's *A Witness Tree* (1942) was dedicated to Kay: "To K. M. for her part in it." After Elinor's death it was Morrison who came to Frost's aid. Frost once told Louis Mertins, "I owe everything in the world to her. She found me in the gutter, hopeless, sick, run down. She bundled me up and carted me to her home and cared for me like a child, sick child. Without her I would today be in my grave. If I have done anything since I came out of the hospital, it is all due to her" (Cramer, 123).

In 1939 Frost accepted a two-year appointment as Ralph Waldo Emerson Fellow in Poetry at Harvard, and in 1941 as Fellow in American Civilization there. In 1943 he became the George Ticknor Fellow in Humanities at Dartmouth College. It was as though all the colleges of his past were in a tug of war over him.

In 1948 Frost chose to leave Dartmouth to resume a post at Amherst, this time as Simpson Lecturer in Literature, a position he held until his death. Frost also spent several winters in Florida. In 1940 he purchased five acres of land in South Miami. He built two small houses there and named the property Pencil Pines. In 1949 Frost's *Complete Poems* was published by Holt.

In 1959 Frost was appointed to a three-year term as Honorary Consultant in the Humanities at the Library of Congress. Frost also read at President Kennedy's inauguration in 1962. Kennedy and Frost had a friend in common, Congressman Steward L. Udall, whom Frost had gotten to know while poetry consultant for the Library of Congress. It was Udall who suggested to Kennedy that Frost read a poem at his inauguration. Kennedy liked poetry and in particular liked Frost. During his campaign, he would often conclude a speech by quoting the final lines of "Stopping by Woods on a Snowy Evening" about having promises to keep: "And miles to go before I sleep." When Udall first suggested it, Kennedy is quoted as having said "Oh no! You know Frost always steals any show he is a part of." But the politician in him knew it was a good idea, and he later had a telephone conversa-

tion with Frost to discuss the invitation. As poet William Meredith later recalled in an interview, "It was a novel idea, and one that focused attention on Kennedy as a man of culture, as a man interested in culture."

During their conversation about the inauguration, Kennedy, as Parini puts it, "gingerly" suggested that Frost write a poem for the occasion. Frost did not particularly welcome the idea. Feeling obligated, however, he did write a poem specifically for the inauguration, but he began to draft it only days before the event. He worked on it until the night before, treating it as a "preamble to his reading of 'The Gift Outright,'" but the result, partly because of Frost's advanced age and partly because of his limited enthusiasm for the chore, was a poem written more out of duty than inspiration (Parini, 414).

The poem, "For John F. Kennedy His Inauguration," now treated as a preface to "The Gift Outright," was never read at the inauguration. On that cold, windy day the sun's reflection on the glaring white paper made it impossible for Frost to read the print. Recovering well, he recited "The Gift Outright" from memory, improvising on the last line: "Such as she was, such as she *would* become, *has* become, and I—and for this occasion let me change that to—what she *will* become" (Parini, 414).

In 1962 Frost received the Congressional Gold Medal and was also invited by President Kennedy to travel to the Soviet Union as part of a cultural exchange program. The highlight of the trip was his meeting with Soviet Premier Nikita Khrushchev. For Frost, who was a deep nationalist and whose career was affected by his politics, the trip held great meaning. He was essentially, if only momentarily, in a key political position and spoke with Khrushchev for more than 90 minutes: The "most powerful figure in the Soviet Union had met with an American cultural icon, and they had freely talked about matters of huge cultural import" (Parini, 434)

The trip to Russia was a crowning moment in Frost's life. F. D. Reeve, who accompanied Frost on the trip, wrote:

I don't wish to seem either sentimental or pretentious but, you know, I'd had a feeling a

Frost's 85th birthday celebration. *(Photo by Walter Albertin. Courtesy Library of Congress)*

number of times on that trip that Frost was prefiguring his own death. He had long worried about his health. He had been sick. And he kept reading his latest poems, including 'Away.' It seemed then, as one would like to think it actual now, that this was a fillip to his life, the last and greatest play of wit. (135)

One of the last letters Frost ever wrote was to his daughter Lesley Frost Ballantine on January 12, 1963. At his death, Lesley was the sole remaining healthy child of Elinor and Robert. He wrote:

I am not hard to touch but I'd rather be taken for brave than anything else. A little hard and stern in judgment, perhaps, but always touched by the heroic. You have passed muster. So has Prescott. You have both found a way to make

shift. You can't know how much I have counted on you in family matters. It is no time yet to defer a little to others in my future affairs but I have deferred not a little in my thoughts to the strength I find in you. (*Selected Letters*, 596)

Frost died shortly after midnight on January 29, 1963, in Boston, Massachusetts. A private memorial service was held in Appleton Chapel in Harvard Yard on January 31; a public service was held at Johnson Chapel, Amherst College, on February 17. He was buried among family on June 16 in the Old First Congregational Church in Old Bennington, Vermont. He lived to see great-grandchildren born, finding "himself at mid-twentieth century as close to the first of the New Hampshire Frosts as he was to the farthest removed of his lineal descendents born 155 years later" (Mertins, 305). Kennedy wrote

Frost family burial plot. Old First Congregational Church, Old Bennington, Vermont. *(Photo by Deirdre Fagan)*

of his death, "His death impoverishes us all; but he has bequeathed his nation a body of imperishable verse from which Americans will forever gain joy and understanding" (Woolley and Peters).

In "Remarks on Receiving the Gold Medal" Frost expresses that the "sensible and healthy live somewhere between self-approval and the approval of society. They make their adjustment without too much talk of compromise." In many ways, he was speaking of himself. He was insecure until the end, always a bit surprised by the awards and prizes heaped on him, but he did well to strike a balance between public recognition and private satisfaction.

Frost hid behind his poems. He did not want to show his hand. He spoke straightforwardly and in metaphors, a contradiction but a true one. He was a great constructor of his own myth; he had all the tools to become an icon, and he did. He had fierce determination and enormous ambition and he put great energy into his myth making.

In his *Introduction to King Jasper,* Frost wrote of his poetry, "If I wanted you to know, I should have told you in the poem," and that he did. His poetry has been commented on, studied, and criticized by numerous critics over the decades, each shedding light on the nuances in his work. Early in his career critics considered Frost an uncomplicated NEW ENGLAND nature poet. His simple language, use of the vernacular, and emphasis on tones and natural speech patterns made his poetry accessible and, at times, widely misunderstood. Simplicity in language, however, did not equal simplicity in thought. There are tensions and contradictions in his poetry, and it is often dark.

Frost might be said to be one of the great poet-philosophers, as the poet, like the philosopher, is a type of truth seeker. Much of Frost's poetry conveys philosophical views of life, death, and the unknown. He shares a desire to find meaning where it is at best obscured. His poetry is an expression of artistic will—the willing of understanding when there is little that can be fully understood, including Frost himself.

FURTHER READING

Adams, Frederick B., Jr. *To Russia with Frost.* Boston: Club of Odd Volumes, 1963.

Anderson, Margaret Bartlett. *Robert Frost and John Bartlett: The Record of a Friendship.* New York: Holt, 1963.

Burnshaw, Stanley. *Robert Frost Himself.* New York: George Braziller, 1986.

Cook, Reginald. *The Dimensions of Robert Frost.* New York: Rinehart, 1958.

Cox, Sidney. *Robert Frost: Original "Ordinary Man."* New York: Holt, 1929.

———. *A Swinger of Birches: A Portrait of Robert Frost.* New York: New York University Press, 1957.

Cramer, Jeffrey S. *Robert Frost among His Poems: A Literary Companion to the Poet's Own Biographical Contexts and Associations.* Jefferson, N.C.: MacFarland, 1996.

Evans, William R., ed. *Robert Frost and Sidney Cox: Forty Years of Friendship.* Hanover: University Press of New England, 1981.

Francis, Lesley Lee. *The Frost Family's Adventure in Poetry: Sheer Morning Gladness at the Brim.* Columbia: University of Missouri Press, 1994.

Francis, Robert. *Robert Frost: A Time to Talk.* Amherst: University of Massachusetts Press, 1972.

Frost, Lesley. *New Hampshire's Child: The Derry Journals of Lesley Frost.* Albany: State University of New York Press, 1969.

Frost, Robert. *The Letters of Robert Frost to Louis Untermeyer.* Edited by Louis Untermeyer. New York: Holt, Rinehart and Winston, 1963.

———. *Robert Frost on Writing.* Edited by Elaine Barry. New Brunswick: Rutgers University Press, 1973.

———. *Selected Letters of Robert Frost.* Edited by Lawrance Thompson. New York: Holt, Rinehart and Winston, 1964.

Frost, Robert, and Elinor Frost. *The Family Letters of Robert and Elinor Frost.* Edited by Arnold Grade. Albany: State University of New York Press, 1972.

Gerber, Philip L. *Robert Frost.* New York: Twayne, 1966.

Gould, Jean. *Robert Frost: The Aim Was Song.* New York: Dodd, Mead, 1964.

Grade, Arnold, ed. *The Family Letters of Robert and Elinor Frost.* Albany: State University of New York Press, 1972.

Greiner, Donald J. *Robert Frost: The Poet and His Critics.* Chicago: American Library Association, 1974.

Katz, Sandra L. *Elinor Frost: A Poet's Wife.* Westfield: Institute for Massachusetts Studies, 1988.

Kennedy. John F. "Statement by the President on the Death of Robert Frost." The American Presidency Project, edited by John Woolley and Gerhard Peters. Available online. URL: http://www.presidency.ncsb.edu/ws/index.php?pid=9476&st=&st1=

Lathem, Edward Connery, ed. *The Poetry of Robert Frost.* New York: Henry Holt, 1969.

Mertins, Louis. *Robert Frost: Life and Talks-Walking.* Norman: University of Oklahoma Press, 1965.

Meyers, Jeffrey. *Robert Frost: A Biography.* New York: Houghton Mifflin, 1996.

Munson, Gorham B. *Robert Frost: A Study in Sensibility and Good Sense.* New York: Dorham, 1927.

Newdick, Robert S. *Newdick's Season of Frost: An Interrupted Biography.* Edited by William A. Sutton. Albany: State University of New York Press, 1976.

Parini, Jay. *Robert Frost: A Life.* New York: Holt, 1999.

Reeve, Franklin D. *Robert Frost in Russia.* Boston: Little, Brown, 1963.

Sergeant, Elizabeth Shepley. *Robert Frost: The Trial by Existence.* New York: Holt, 1960.

Smythe, Daniel. *Robert Frost Speaks.* New York: Twayne, 1964.

Thompson, Lawrance. *Fire and Ice: The Art and Thought of Robert Frost.* New York: Russell & Russell, 1942.

———. *Robert Frost: The Early Years.* New York: Holt, Rinehart and Winston, 1966.

———. *Robert Frost: The Years of Triumph, 1915–1938.* New York: Holt, Rinehart and Winston, 1970.

———, and R. H. Winnick. *Robert Frost: The Later Years: 1938–1963.* New York: Holt, Rinehart and Winston, 1976.

Thornton, Richard. *Recognition of Robert Frost: Twenty-fifth Anniversary.* New York: Henry Holt, 1937.

Walsh, John Evangelist. *Into My Own: The English Years of Robert Frost, 1912–1915.* New York: Grove, 1988.

PART II

Works A–Z

"Acceptance" (1928)

First appearing in *West-Running Brook*, this sonnet represents a sense of both yielding to nature and exhibiting a healthy respect for it. Near the beginning of the poem the speaker points out that no voice in nature gives a cry when the sun goes down. He says that nothing is disturbed by "what has happened." Frost's choice of "happened" almost suggests that the sun's going down is something that has happened *to* someone or something. It is not merely that it occurred, but that there should be some reason and concern for it. The idea is that nature ought to see the sunset as some sort of death or some sort of sad event, but without mourning. It is as if the speaker were accounting for nature's inability to reason and suggesting that since it should not know why the sun has gone down, it ought to be fearful when it does, since fear often is rooted in ignorance. In some way, lack of knowledge ought to cause trepidation among birds, but it does not.

The speaker seems almost to envy nature's unconcern for the passing of light or the passing of time, and he recognizes that human beings cannot be so indifferent. We do mourn the falling of leaves and the setting of the sun, and we do lament the passing of time, but among these birds there is an acceptance of the inevitable that does not question. There is a willingness simply to allow nature to do its duty. Juxtaposed with this, however, is the speaker's assessment that "Birds, at least, must know." The idea that nature is not knowledgeable is reconsidered, and instead the narrator asserts that nature must be aware of itself. (These sorts of contradictions often appear in Frost; a similar contradiction can be found in "The Road Not Taken.") That the bird does know and can accept that the sun has gone and will return again is what the poem hinges on. Other creatures are able to accept in nature what occurs naturally. For humankind, this is a much more difficult task.

The ending of the poem provides a sentient bird who "At most he thinks or twitters softly, 'Safe!'" There is a sense of almost human fear ascribed to the bird, and yet the bird, despite his exclamation, "Safe!," goes on to accept the darkness and his inability to see into the future. Indeed, he says, "Let what will be, be." This acceptance is something the speaker desires, because just letting be is not something humans can fully do. This poem ends on a note both resigned and hopeful—a tone of acceptance. The scheme of things, life and the world, has been reduced to one nightfall, which is accepted as a natural occurrence that can be yielded to without subjugation.

But nothing is ever as simple as it seems in Frost. The title, "Acceptance," alerts the reader that the poem is about anything but. While it seems that the bird is accepting of the darkness, he too is haunted by it. There is a touch of sarcasm in the phrase, "Let what will be, be." The bird says, "Now let the night be dark for all of me. / Let the night be too dark for me to see." This darkness is unpleasant and enveloping. It is not so much acceptance that is being witnessed, but a sort of repression. Ultimately, the bird is no better equipped to accept the scheme of things than humans are, and the irony of the title is that the poem is really about the inability to accept.

In "Acceptance," nature's power is evident, but so is the desire to accept that power as a given and not to resist it. Frost is, however, uncomfortable with nature's powers, despite the assertion in the poem that those powers should not be challenged. The speaker is observing what nature does and wondering what importance it has for him, and he is trying to diminish its power by denying how unsettling it can be. *See* NATURE and NIGHT.

FURTHER READING

Bagby, George F. *Frost and the Book of Nature.* Knoxville: University of Tennessee Press, 1993.

Faggen, Robert. *Robert Frost and the Challenge of Darwin.* Ann Arbor: University of Michigan Press, 1997.

"Accidentally on Purpose" (1962)

See CLUSTER OF FAITH.

"Acquainted with the Night" (1928)

This terza rima sonnet (see FORM) from *West-Running Brook* features a very different narrator from the country poet who is so familiar to us through such poems as "Birches" and "Stopping by Woods on a Snowy Evening." Here the narrator is uncharacteristically urban. Some critics have drawn parallels to Dante's *Inferno*, also written in tercets with interlocking rhymes, but the urban setting and images, speculated to be based on Ann Arbor, where Frost was living at the time of composition, seem more reminiscent of William Blake's "London." Frost writes, "I have outwalked the furthest city light / I have looked down the saddest city lane," while Blake writes, "I wander thro' each charter'd street, / Near where the charter'd Thames does flow. / And mark in every face I meet / Marks of weakness, marks of woe."

The poem shares something in common with Frost's other journey poems, such as "Into My Own." He once again finds himself alone, only this time the setting is very different. The speaker, in a sort of soliloquy, reveals that more than once he has been "acquainted with the night." The choice of acquainted is intriguing because it suggests a certain knowledge and familiarity without intimacy. An acquaintance is not a friend.

When the speaker says that he "has walked out in rain—and back in rain" he expresses an all-encompassing awareness of the night, darkness, and what they hold. He has "outwalked the furthest city light" and "looked down the saddest city lane," suggesting that night is associated with unexplainable sadness, but it is yet unclear whether this sadness is the speaker's or is witnessed by the speaker. The question is whether the sadness is inherent in the lane or is the perception of the speaker. When he walks past the "watchman on his beat" and drops his eyes, "unwilling to explain," he reflects Frost's often coy persona. He does not say that he cannot explain but rather that he is unwilling to. The speaker's unwillingness suggests that the sadness comes from within, not from outside, himself.

In the third stanza the speaker stands still, and the sound of feet stops. It is the sound of his own feet that is stopped, and when he hears from far away an "interrupted cry," the poem grows more complicated. Is the cry from within or outside? The call is not meant to summon the speaker "back" or "say good-by," writes Frost, but then, what is the cry for? Is it a cry of help? A cry of sadness, as alluded to in stanza two?

The poem's trodding metrical feet become harder to understand between this fourth stanza and the ending couplet. The break indicated by the semicolon following "good-by" indicates a strange shift. The speaker begins to acquaint his readers with the night when he moves from the present to an "unearthly height" and a "luminary clock against the sky." The clock is illuminated for the speaker, and its "unearthly height" suggests that it is Time, not time, with which the poem is concerned. That is, while he might be preoccupied with what seems to be earthly time, it is unearthly, transcendental time that vexes him.

When the proclamation comes from on high that "the time was neither wrong nor right," Frost leaves his readers in the night he has created and begins again by returning to the poem's title and first line: "I have been one acquainted with the night."

The figure of night suggests the night that shrouds one in darkness, sadness, and contemplation in the darkest of hours. Night for Frost represents the innermost loneliness, a loneliness that keeps him isolated from those who cry out, but not for him, and from the watchman, who may or may not be aware of his presence. The speaker has scared himself with his "desert places." Like Emily Dickinson in poems such as "I heard a Fly buzz—when I died—" and "I felt a Funeral, in my Brain," he seems to have experienced a figurative death, as if he had been to the other side and returned to tell us about it. And now it seems that it is his own cries that are heard.

The repetition of "I have" and of "acquainted with the night" echo footfalls, suggesting that the reader accompanies the speaker into the night and must also determine whether the time is wrong or right. Jay Parini writes that Frost once said the clock "was in the tower of the old Washtenaw County Courthouse" in Ann Arbor, which would clearly indicate that there is a literal clock depicted in the poem (246). But the clock, like the night, is also symbolic. There may be an actual clock observed by the speaker, but what it represents goes beyond time as we know it.

Frost is often thought of as simply a poet of country matters, but he is much more than that. Here he places himself in a city setting. The poem flows smoothly but the speaker is ill at ease, and perhaps that is why it is a setting to which Frost does not often return. John Cunningham asserts that "One does well in Frost's universe to be acquainted with the night, to know what it is like, but values and meaning are existential in the one who carries out his errands and keeps his promises. They are not transcendental" (270). *See* NATURE and NIGHT.

FURTHER READING

Brady, Patrick. "From New Criticism to Chaos and Emergence Theory: A Reinterpretation of a Poem by Robert Frost," *Synthesis: An Interdisciplinary Journal* 1, no. 1 (Spring 1995): 41–57.

Cunningham, John. "Human Presence in Frost's Universe." In *The Cambridge Companion to Robert Frost,* edited by Robert Faggen, 261–272. Cambridge: Cambridge University Press, 2001.

Murray, Keat. "Robert Frost's Portrait of a Modern Mind: The Archetypal Resonance of 'Acquainted with the Night,'" *Midwest Quarterly* 41, no. 4 (June 2000): 370–384.

Pack, Robert. *Belief and Uncertainty in the Poetry of Robert Frost.* Hanover, N.H.: Middlebury College Press, 2003.

Parini, Jay. *Robert Frost: A Life.* New York: Holt, 1999.

Timmerman, John H. *Robert Frost: The Ethics of Ambiguity.* Lewisburg, Pa.: Bucknell University Press, 2002.

"Address to the Amherst Alumni Council" (1920)

This address was given to the Amherst College Alumni Council in 1920. The text comes from the proceedings dated November 7–9. In his brief remarks Frost reveals his philosophy of teaching and his attitudes toward college as a place of learning. He opens by distinguishing between language and literature. Language is "for scholarship" and literature "for art." Frost then proceeds to discuss the "ancient institution of poverty" that people with all their "Bolshevism, and syndicalism, and anarchism, and socialism" are interested in losing. Frost's antisocialist politics find their way in, but only briefly. What he chiefly is concerned with is poverty as necessary for cultivating the spirit of the poet, painter, inventor, or musician. Such people must live frugally so they can get "the thing done and . . . show it to the world." He imagines that abolishing poverty would land the artist in the "only place left for him": college.

Frost describes college not only as a place where people "think for themselves" but more significantly where "they make projects for themselves; where the believing and the desiring part of their nature has a chance." He relates this to his own aspirations as a teacher. He wants to give his students a chance. He "like[s] to stand aside entirely" and let his students command their own wills. He wants to be "gentle enough and unassuming enough simply to stand aside to let the man who will have his chance." The address closes with Frost saying that the role of the Language and Literature Group is to create a "numerous" American audience of readers and the great American writer who "won't be very numerous."

John Meiklejohn was president of Amherst College at the time and is described by Jay Parini as "a maverick in American education." Meiklejohn first invited Frost to teach at the college in Amherst, Massachusetts, for the spring semester in 1917 for the then princely sum of $2,000 (Parini, 175).

FURTHER READING

Parini, Jay. *Robert Frost: A Life.* New York: Holt, 1999.

Thompson, Lawrance. *Robert Frost: The Years of Triumph, 1915–1938.* New York: Holt, Rinehart and Winston, 1970.

"After Apple-Picking" (1914)

Louis Untermeyer describes this poem as "so vivid a memory of experience that the reader absorbs it physically" (244). One of Frost's most anthologized poems, it first appeared in his second book, *North of Boston*. Whereas "Birches" was not printed until *Mountain Interval*, which followed *North of Boston*, the notion of climbing trees toward heaven is established here. "After Apple-Picking" appeared first, but it might be considered the later voice of "Birches." The narrator is not the swinger of birches here but rather a mature speaker who is much like the weary poet who wanted to "get away from earth awhile / And then come back to it and begin over."

The poem opens with the image of a ladder sticking through a tree, but it quickly moves to a barrel that was not filled and apples that were not picked. The essence of difficult rural life is illustrated through the descriptions of hard work and work that is never done. But there is also a mystical element. The narrator is strangely altered by the "scent of apples"—they seem to have the effect of poppies on his psyche. He cannot "rub the strangeness" from his sight. He has looked "through a pane of glass," which seems to be a thin coating of ice formed overnight in the "drinking trough," and, as if gazing into Alice's looking glass, he has seen something that was "held against the world of hoary grass." The world described here is as worn, tired, and old as the speaker feels, and a world brighter and more magical can be seen only as a mirage, momentarily held before it melts. But again the speaker is at fault: He has "let" the image "fall and break."

The speaker seems to be having a dream within a dream: While the image falls away, he finds himself growing more and more full of sleep. As his body aches with the work left undone and his arches ache from time spent perched upon a ladder, he visualizes apples magnified; seemingly beautiful apples "appear and disappear" in his mind's eye. The poem begins to lull the reader with the dreamy imagery and the distant, repetitive, "rumbling sound / Of load on load of apples coming in." The apple farmer desired a "great harvest," surely for his livelihood, but is exhausted by the magnitude of the work, which is as magnified as the apples in his view. Once again he embraces full responsibility, as his "desire" has brought something more than he can manage.

The poem seems straightforward: a description of a tired apple farmer growing heavy with sleep and dozing off to the sound in his memory of a hard day's work. But as is typical in Frost, the reader never gets off quite so easily. Just when it seems as though the poem will draw to a dreamy close, the reader is thrust back to what has been left undone. Just as the barrel remained unfilled, the farmer is reminded of the "ten thousand fruit to touch" and of the apples that "struck the earth" and "[w]ent surely to the cider-apple heap / As of no worth."

The trance is interrupted by the present-tense breaking in of "[o]ne can see what will trouble / This sleep of mine, whatever sleep it is," and the reader is forced to question what it is that will trouble the speaker's sleep. The work left undone seems a likely cause, but so does the matter of the apples left to the cider heap. They were treated as if of no worth, simply for having "struck the earth." But the apple farmer, too, has struck the earth. He is no longer climbing toward heaven, perched on a ladder, up above the earth at an untouchable height. He has, in his fatigue, struck the earth, and it is there that he is reminded of the work left undone and the possibility that he, while idle, is of no worth. Marie Borroff speculates that apples "constitute any series of things—or persons—with which one is responsibly concerned, each of which must be not merely handled but handled with love. This is the source of the kind of tiredness that is peculiarly human, the kind . . . that leads to a troubled, not a dreamless, sleep" (26–28).

The return to earth late in the poem is highlighted by a consideration of nature. The speaker questions what sort of sleep he might have, some "human sleep," or a "long sleep"—which one the woodchuck, if he were around, might be able to determine. This places nature in a more knowledgeable role than the narrator. Or as one critic put it, the narrator seems to have been "duped by a woodchuck." The woodchuck, otherwise known as a groundhog, hibernates for all of winter, beginning in late fall. The reference to the absent woodchuck suggests further that the farmer's work, which should have been completed by late fall, has grown all the more heavy on his mind.

Frost moves in and out of traditional forms with his rhymes here, weaving in and out of weariness and in and out of sleep. As in "Acquainted with the Night" and other poems, the structure of the poem mimics its message, and here the end rhymes lull the reader to succumb to the dreamy quality of the poem.

Frost's use of a long sleep seems metaphorically suggestive of the long sleep of death or of the shift into the afterlife, as it differs from a human sleep. But Laurence Perrine argues that "whatever sleep it is," it presents "a continuation of earthly activity" (89). Either way, this farmer is "done with apple-picking now" as the "Essence of winter sleep is on the night." *See* FARMER, FROST AS.

FURTHER READING

Baker, Christopher. "Frost's 'After Apple-Picking' as Hypnagogic Vision," *Robert Frost Review* (Fall 1994): 28–32.

Beacham, Walton. "Technique and the Sense of Play in the Poetry of Robert Frost." In *Frost: Centennial Essays II,* edited by Jac Tharpe, 246–261. Jackson: University Press of Mississippi, 1976.

Borroff, Marie. "Robert Frost: To Earthward." In *Frost: Centennial Essays II,* edited by Jac Tharpe, 21–39. Jackson: University Press of Mississippi, 1976.

Brooks, Cleanth and Robert Penn Warren. *Understanding Poetry.* 3rd ed. New York: Holt, Rinehart and Winston, 1960.

Conder, John J. "'After Apple Picking': Frost's Troubled Sleep." In *Frost Centennial Essays,* edited by Jac Tharpe, 171–181. Jackson: University Press of Mississippi, 1974.

Doreski, William. "Meta-Meditation in Robert Frost's 'The Wood-Pile,' 'After Apple-Picking,' and 'Directive'" *A Review of International English Literature* 23, no. 4 (October 1992): 35–49.

Kozilkowski, Stan. "Frost's 'After Apple-Picking' and God's Judgment," *Robert Frost Review* (Fall 1997): 39–43.

Monteiro, George. *Robert Frost and The New England Renaissance.* Lexington: University Press of Kentucky, 1988.

Pack, Robert. *Belief and Uncertainty in the Poetry of Robert Frost.* Hanover, N.H.: Middlebury College Press, 2003.

Perrine, Laurence. "Robert Frost and the Idea of Immortality." In *Frost: Centennial Essays II,* edited by Jac Tharpe, 87–89. Jackson: University Press of Mississippi, 1976.

Sanders, David A. "Looking through the Glass: Frost's 'After Apple-Picking' and Paul's 1 Corinthians," *Robert Frost Review* (Fall 1996): 12–22.

Untermeyer, Louis. *The Road Not Taken: An Introduction to Robert Frost.* New York: Holt, 1951.

"Afterflakes" (1936)

"Afterflakes" was first published in the autumn 1934 printing of the *Yale Review,* and later collected in the section "Taken Singly" of *A Further Range.* The term *afterflakes* is reminiscent of afterlife, afterglow, afterthought, or afterbirth. That is, the selection of *afterflakes* must certainly be meant to suggest other such "after" words, which indicate not only something that comes after another thing but also what remains—the persistence of what preceded in the initial life, glow, thought, birth, or flakes. In this instance it is his own shadow on the snow that halts him and makes him look to the sky with questions. He wonders if his shadow reveals something about himself: "If I shed such a darkness, / If the reason was in me, / That shadow of mine should show in form / Against the shapeless shadow of storm, / How swarthy I must be."

Here a principle of physics is turned on its head. Surely during a "teeming snowfall" one would be unable to cast a shadow. But for some reason, in this case, the shadow has appeared, causing the narrator to question how. Is it his own "swarthy" nature? The reason for the shadow must be "in" him, as it is clearly not an aspect of the natural world—it is, after all, occurring so unnaturally.

One interesting feature of the poem is its perplexing movement. In the first stanza the speaker "look[s] back up at the sky," in the second he contemplates, and in the third he "look[s] back upward" again. This is striking because it seems that from the moment he seeks guidance, he remains looking upward. And yet there is a movement in the poem from a "teeming snowfall" to "the whole sky was blue." One considers how abruptly the snowstorm shifted, but one also wonders how one turns "back" when one has not before turned away.

Seeing his own shadow here causes the narrator to become deeply reflective. It seems that Frost intended the sky's response to be that the shadow was not "in" him, since the sun comes "shining through" in the end. But it is unclear what to make of the misstep in time. Ultimately there may have been no teeming snowfall after all, instead simply the perception of the speaker, a reflection of his "frost knots" (one of only several instances where Frost puns his name), whatever they may be. Since the sun shines through in the final line, and since sun is required for a shadow to be cast, it appears that the sun has been shining all along. The darkness "shed" may have come from within but was also seen only from within. It was the perception of the speaker, perhaps brought on by the melancholy of a day of snowfall. Frost's afterflakes may be the afterthoughts of snowflakes.

FURTHER READING

Bagby, George F. *Frost and the Book of Nature.* Knoxville: University of Tennessee Press, 1993.

Timmerman, John H. *Robert Frost: The Ethics of Ambiguity.* Lewisburg, Pa.: Bucknell University Press, 2002.

"Aim Was Song, The" (1923)

In this lyric in iambic tetrameter, fittingly given its subject matter, first published in the magazine the *Measure* in March 1921 before later being collected in *New Hampshire*, Frost seizes on both human gifts and human egoism while celebrating his own poetic abilities. He begins the poem with "Before man" but is largely concerned with after man, rather than before. He asserts that in a prehistoric time the wind "once blew itself untaught" and, with his tongue in cheek, applauds humans' ability to rein in the wind and give it not only focus but value.

According to the poem, part of the reason behind man's coming to Earth was to tell nature, in this case the wind, "what was wrong." The wind was blowing without purpose and apparently was an aimless wanderer that needed to be both controlled and trained. In this way, Frost develops a creation myth, but in this instance it is not the wind that is created but rather the song and perhaps poetry. When Frost writes that man "took a little in his mouth, And held it long enough for north / To be converted into south," an image of a Greek god is summoned to mind. Not only does man become supernaturally graceful and powerful as he blows, but he also becomes godlike in his ability to convert one thing to its seeming opposite. As the air is drawn inward and outward an image of a compass with its points facing north and south at once comes to mind, as does the notion that a change from north to south wind may replace a cold breath with a warm one.

Frost's choice of the word "measure" is calculated, as the term can be applied to both music and poetry. To measure is to bring order and provide an overlay of human organization to the barbaric and uncivilized wind. In a sense, man is shown to have colonized the wind. As Charles Berger explains, "Frost stands the Wordsworthian model of nature as pedagogue on its head, by having man become the instructor" (152). In man's attempt to control the universe and natural law, he crafts the "wind the wind had meant to be." He, the teacher, causes the wind to "see" what it was capable of all along. Paradoxically, however, the aim was "song" even when the wind "blew too hard."

Berger points out that "[s]cattered throughout the poem are teasingly moral terms, such as 'right,' 'wrong,' and 'ought'" (151). There is an attempt to highlight the morality or immorality of the colonization. But the poem may be largely symbolic: It could be concerning itself with itself. Frost's flawless "measure" may metaphorically be about the creation of poetry. We do not blow a song, so whistling first comes to mind, but whatever is created, in the end it joins both "word and note." While this creation myth may hold that whistling was the first harness of the wind, it also emphasizes that an individual genius and a leap of imagination are needed to make whistling poetry. Here poets become gods by making poetry with just "[a] little through the lips and throat."

Katherine Kearns states that "[h]ere is the poet as revenant, as ventriloquist's dummy, the poet who fears that his open mouth will spill out laughter and screams, the poet as everything . . . and the poet as nothing" (44). Frost casts a creation myth that makes poetry egotistical, easeful, and beautiful all at once, through whistling by measure.

FURTHER READING

Berger, Charles. "Echoing Eden: Frost and Origins." In *Robert Frost,* Modern Critical Views, edited by Harold Bloom, 147–165. Philadelphia: Chelsea House, 2003.

Doyle, John Robert, Jr. *The Poetry of Robert Frost.* New York: Hafner Press, 1962, 145–146.

Hoffman, Tyler. *Robert Frost and the Politics of Poetry.* Hanover, N.H.: Middlebury College Press, 2001, 181–182.

Kearns, Katherine. "Frost on the Doorstep and Lyricism at the Millennium." In *Roads Not Taken: Rereading Robert Frost,* edited by Earl J. Wilcox and Jonathan N. Barron, 32–51. Columbia: University of Missouri Press, 2000.

———. *Robert Frost and a Poetics of Appetite.* Cambridge: Cambridge University Press, 1994.

Richardson, Mark. *The Ordeal of Robert Frost: The Poet and his Poetics.* Chicago: University of Illinois Press, 1997.

"All Revelation" (1942)

"All Revelation" is a complicated poem that causes us to thrust our heads in "for the view." Frost's "Cyb'laean" refers to Cybele, the goddess of Earth in its primitive state, of caverns, nature, and fertility. Words such as "geode," "crystals," and "ray cathode" give this poem a scientific feel more similar to Frost's later poems, such as those from *In the Clearing,* than to others in *A Witness Tree.* The poem was first published as "Geode" in a 1938 issue of the *Yale Review.*

In the first stanza there is an image of a head thrusting into something, yet "where it is it thrusts in from / Or what it is it thrusts into" is unclear. There arises the question of what can come of its thrusting

"[b]y that Cyb'laean avenue." The suggestion here, of course, is of disorder and chaos. In stanza two, the question of withdrawing the head, and what will be withdrawn with it is raised: The lines "What take hence or leave behind, / These things the mind has pondered on / A moment and still asking gone" seem to refer to the brevity of the thought and the possible fruitlessness of the journey.

At the end of stanza two there is an exclamatory gesture: "Strange apparition of the mind!" This indicates a break midway through the poem and an epiphanic flash, though of what we do not know. And the "impervious geode" of stanza three seems to refer back to the initial head that was thrust in. It is as though the epiphany of the inquiry caused "every point and facet" to radiate, as it "glowed" in "answer to the mental thrust."

The poem ends with "All revelation has been ours," and we realize that revelation, which is generally considered to be divine and coming from outside, has been our own, "So none need be afraid of size."

This poem is modern in its inclusion of scientific terms, and this lends it well to a variety of interpretations, both literal and metaphorical. A strictly literal interpretation, stemming largely from the use of the term *ray cathode,* an inversion of *cathode ray tube,* is that the poem reflects on the effects television has on the mind, as Peter Hays has demonstrated. Cathode ray tubes would have been used in all television sets when this poem was written. After all, heads thrust in for the view, seeking the response of eyes, and they "[b]ring out the stars, bring out the flowers." Certainly the first televisions must have seemed "strange apparition[s]" of the mind.

But to take the poem only literally is to move away from its esoteric but philosophical underpinnings. It seems to assure that while human beings may seek divine revelation, investigations demonstrate there can be revelations of only one kind: our own. There may also be a playful jab at divinity in the line "[s]o none need be afraid of size."

Richard Poirier and Jeffrey Meyers have put forth the interesting though somewhat questionable possibility, given Frost's usual topics, that the poem is a description of sexual intercourse. *See* STARS.

FURTHER READING

Hass, Robert. *Going by Contraries: Robert Frost's Conflict with Science.* Charlottesville: University Press of Virginia, 2002.

Hays, Peter L. "Frost and the Critics: More Revelation on 'All Revelation,'" *English Language Notes* 18, no. 4 (June 1981): 283–290.

Kearns, Katherine. *Robert Frost and a Poetics of Appetite.* Cambridge: Cambridge University Press, 1994.

Meyers, Jeffery. *Robert Frost: A Biography.* New York: Houghton Mifflin, 1996.

Poirier, Richard. *Robert Frost: The Work of Knowing.* New York: Oxford University Press, 1977.

Timmerman, John H. *Robert Frost: The Ethics of Ambiguity.* Lewisburg, Pa.: Bucknell University Press, 2002.

"America Is Hard to See" (1962)

This poem was titled "Columbus Day" when Frost first read it at Amherst College in December 1950. Frost claimed to have written "the whole eighty-four lines of it without consulting a single book in one night" but also said that it was "true in a sense that [he] had been all [his] life writing it" (Cramer, 162). It was first published in the June 1951 issue of the *Atlantic Monthly* as "And All We Call American," 11 years before being collected in *In the Clearing.*

Making numerous geographical references, this poem criticizes Columbus by derisively pointing out that it is not that there "had been something strangely wrong / With every coast he tried along" but instead that "The trouble was with him the mariner," because his "reckoning" "wasn't off a mere degree" but an entire "sea." The speaker admits that when he was young he had a different perception of Columbus and would then have had him "sung / As a god," but that with age came wisdom and the knowledge that Columbus was a conqueror who did nothing but "spread the room / Of our enacting out the doom / Of being in each other's way." After all, the more we "spread" and pop-

ulate, the more we must learn "how to crowd but still be kind."

The speaker goes on to describe Columbus as ill-willed and almost hateful in his desire to "discover." Depicting his rivalry with other explorers, the speaker points out that "High purpose makes the hero rude." He imagines Columbus forever at sea, forever working to colonize, and eventually finding that the colonized are tired of "being looted" and having their "beliefs disputed." The poem minimizes Columbus's historical relevance by presenting as foolish having "a town, / A holiday" named after him.

The title of the poem, found in stanza 11, has historical and contemporary significance. The poem was written when the country was less than two centuries old, yet even now it is hard to see "from inside" or "outside" what American will become.

FURTHER READING

Cramer, Jeffrey S. *Robert Frost among His Poems: A Literary Companion to the Poet's Own Biographical Contexts and Associations.* Jefferson, N.C.: MacFarland, 1996.

"Answer, An" (1942)

This couplet was collected in *A Witness Tree.* It appears in a grouping called "Quantula," along with other pithy poems, which suggests that Frost intended them to be together because of their small "quantity" and presumed force. (In Latin, *quantula* means "How little?" or "How small?") The reference in this heroic couplet is to Hesiod, in his *Works and Days:* "And they live untouched by sorrow in the islands of the blessed along the shore of deep swirling Ocean." Frost shares with us either a father's or some other elder's response to his son, but what has been asked he chooses to keep to himself. Playing on "blessed," he thrice blesses in his couplet, but his conclusion is rueful: The father, conversant with classical literature, never has come across such a utopian setting as that celebrated by Hesiod.

William Pritchard has suggested that "[s]urrounded by much white space, occupying one page of the old *Complete Poems,* the utterance took on an added point" (239). The volume *Complete Poems* to which he refers was published in 1949.

FURTHER READING

Frost, Robert. *Complete Poems of Robert Frost.* New York: Holt, 1949.
Pritchard, William H. *Frost: A Literary Life Reconsidered.* Amherst: University of Massachusetts Press, 1993.

"Any Size We Please" (1947)

A poem of playful hope from *Steeple Bush,* "Any Size We Please" provides an omniscient view of a man who, half-wishing to be any size he pleases, could somehow curve the universe into his embrace. In a dramatic effort, when no one is paying attention, he throws his arms out, reaching as far as he can into the "dark of space."

The first part of the poem expresses a frantic desire to accept that space is not what the man thought it was, that is, it is not a three-dimensional Newtonian space. Frost writes that "like a half-mad outpost sentinel, / Indulging an absurd dramatic spell," the man wants to hold his arms absolutely parallel and think that they will never meet—that they will have "infinite appeal." But Einstein's theory of curved space does not guarantee this anymore, describing instead a universe foreign to our perceptions, a universe that not only has more than three dimensions but is curved.

The man says "Hell" because he recognizes that his desires are in vain. Despite his recognition that he is wrong, he embraces that he exists and accepts that what he was hoping for is not possible. To feel safe, he hugs at himself. "His science needn't get him so unnerved," since he can comfort himself; "[h]e thought," after all, to curve his arms about himself.

He is a "lonely case," first, because he is one of the few still holding on to the old belief system and, second, because he is made aware that he is, as we all are, alone in a foreign universe. In this way he becomes the Everyman for humanity's position.

The title can be read two ways, either pessimistically or optimistically. Pessimistically it shows that regardless of how small or large we think we are, the universe will always be foreign and cold. Optimistically, however, we can offer ourselves our own warmth, and that which is within reach can be made familiar, regardless of how foreign or cold it may seem. The characterization and formulation of the Universe will always have a human element, or for at least as long as we are able to conceive of it. "Any Size We Please" questions the importance of size in a universe whose size is inconceivable.

In *Steeple Bush* the poem was published under the heading "Editorials." *See* SCIENCE.

FURTHER READING

Hass, Robert. *Going by Contraries: Robert Frost's Conflict with Science.* Charlottesville: University Press of Virginia, 2002.
Kearns, Katherine. *Robert Frost and a Poetics of Appetite.* Cambridge: Cambridge University Press, 1994.

"Armful, The" (1928)

Frost focuses on being overburdened: "For every parcel I stoop down to seize, / I lose some other off my arms and knees." The speaker wants to hold onto everything but has little to hold with, in hand, mind, or heart. The pile keeps building, however, and the reader, too, feels the heft of the objects in the poem. The speaker has to use his full body to hold it all, employing all his strength to carry the load.

Later in the poem a succumbing, a giving in, is described. His exhaustion bears down on him, and he sits down in the "middle of them all." He drops the "armful in the road" and begins again. But what is it to try to build a "better load"? What is it to be so overburdened as to be forced to the ground? So unable to hold what he has that he must drop an armful in the road?

The scene could be interpreted as comical, but the exasperation reflected in a desire to start anew, like the speaker's desire in "Birches" "to get away from earth awhile / And then come back to it and begin over," seems to undermine such a reading.

Frost's struggles with his family and in his personal life are easily read into this poem, as it seems he was always trying to "stack them in a better load."

The poem was first published in the February 8, 1928, issue of the *Nation* and was included in *West-Running Brook* later that year.

FURTHER READING

Cook, Reginald. *Robert Frost: A Living Voice.* Amherst: University of Massachusetts Press, 1974.

McCoy, Joan D. "Frost's 'The Armful,'" *Explicator* 47, no. 1 (Fall 1988): 21–23.

"Assurance" (1942)

This brief quatrain was collected in *A Witness Tree.* It appears in a grouping called "Quantula," along with other pithy poems, which suggests that Frost intended them to be together because of their small "quantity" and presumed force. (In Latin, *quantula* means "How little?" or "How small?")

In this poem, once again, as is typical in Frost, nature is depicted as dangerous, and humans are at the whim of the wind, sea, rain, and whatever else the elements choose to bring. Frost describes the porthole in a ship and explains how what is outside the porthole, not even an inch away, is dangerous. And yet the position of the observer and the strength of the "slab of glass" and the "double ring of fitted brass" defies the danger (through trust). The porthole is manmade and therefore subject to human faultiness, yet it still provides just enough assurance to make the speaker feel momentarily at ease (for at least as long as the trip may last). The speaker cannot deny that assurance is not guaranteed; he may feel assurance, but that does not mean he has it. The danger still looms large; the poem does not necessarily mean that the danger is "properly" defied; it is simply temporarily defied. The speaker "trust[s]" that it feels defied, though he does not know how it feels. The personification of danger is not uncommon in Frost, nor is the importance of protection

from nature as a theme, but Frost's keeping nature on the other side of the glass is.

Jeffrey Cramer notes that this poem "may have been written on or been a memory of any one of Frost's sea voyages." Then he notes that in a letter from one such voyage from Cherbourg to New York in November 1928, Frost wrote, "We ran right out of Cherbourgh [sic] into a hundred-and-fifty mile gale that knocked her nose in and brought us to a standstill for three hours a thousand miles from anywhere among some of the biggest waves they say you ever see" (141).

FURTHER READING

Cramer, Jeffrey S. *Robert Frost among His Poems: A Literary Companion to the Poet's Own Biographical Contexts and Associations.* Jefferson, N.C.: MacFarland, 1996.

"Astrometaphysical" (1947)

The first stanza is filled with praise, as the speaker has loved the sky whether it be "against or for" him; he says he has loved it in both clear and stormy weather. In the second stanza, he demonstrates his humbleness. The speaker looks up and it seems that, in awe, he loses his balance and stumbles. But the seeming reverence paid in these first two stanzas is undone by the third, where the speaker conceives of the Lord as one who lords over, and by the fourth and fifth, where the speaker expresses a lack of hope and a demand for what he feels he is owed in an afterlife.

When reread from the beginning, it is evident in the first stanza that what the Lord brings, in this case the weather, is not always welcomed. And in the second stanza, when the speaker looks up and stumbles, it may be his belief that trips him and causes him to end up on a "crutch." Perhaps he is stunned not by what he "sees" in looking up, but from "looking up too much." That is, from losing focus on the here and now, on the only real world he knows. There seems to be a suggestion that in seeking the afterworld, people lose sight of what is in this one.

The speaker expresses his love for every heaven, all seven of them, and makes a pitch for his own reward in the third stanza. (Jeffrey Cramer notes that "in Muslim and cabalist doctrines, there are seven heavens, of which the seventh is the highest" [151]). The speaker then speaks of death and the transition from this to another life as being "translated," suggesting that something of himself will continue into the beyond. But he also talks of his scalp "in the cope" being "constellated." This is trademark Frost: He is, as always, noncommittal. Translation into immortality does not give him total hope. There is something withheld, something uncertain. To be constellated would suggest that his energy would continue as a constellation, as something unlike him, so he questions "if that seems to tend" to his "undue renown." "If" he is transformed (always the questioning and less-than-trusting poet), then he holds that he should go up, not down. But the speaker is never certain what is going to happen to him, what he will be granted—will it be "astrometaphysical"? And he is not certain that even if what is supposed to happen does happen, he should have hope. It "may not" give him hope, he says.

It is unclear just what relationship to the Lord is being presented. The poem is written as a prayer, but the speaker ultimately seems to be talking to himself. After all, he appears uncertain as to just what type of Lord he is dealing with. In the end Frost seems to be denying that immortality should entail hope, or that the quest for immortality should be hopeful. He is, once again, noncommittal about his religious beliefs.

The poem was collected in *Steeple Bush* but first appeared in a 1946 issue of the *Virginia Quarterly*. See BELIEF.

FURTHER READING

Cramer, Jeffrey S. *Robert Frost among His Poems: A Literary Companion to the Poet's Own Biographical Contexts and Associations.* Jefferson, N.C.: MacFarland, 1996.

"Atmosphere" (1928)

Aptly first published in the October 1928 issue of *Ladies Home Journal* (it was later collected in *West-Running Brook*), the poem's subtitle is "Inscription for a Garden Wall." Quite unlike "Mending Wall," but similar in its questioning of a wall's purpose, "Atmosphere" looks closely at the specific effects of a wall in nature. The human tendency to "wall up" nature and to surround it causes effects in nature, positive or negative.

The poem explains that away from the wall, where all is open field, the tall grasses are so flattened by the wind that the fields appear to be barren. But at the wall the currents of the wind "eddy" over it and lose force; they are no longer strong enough to clear a space, to disperse anything, and the atmosphere gradually thickens in the light of the burning sun, which draws out moisture, color, odor. The wall serves a purpose; by breaking the will of the wind it helps concentrate the warmth, which draws "atmosphere."

See WALLS.

FURTHER READING

Thorson, Robert J. The Stone Wall Initiative. Available online. URL: http://stonewall.uconn.edu/. Accessed June 29, 2006.

"At Woodward's Gardens" (1936)

"On warm Sundays in spring," the Frosts "often went to the botanical displays at Woodward's Gardens in the old mission district," Jay Parini writes (13). Woodward's Gardens, in operation from 1854 to 1927, occupied six acres in San Francisco's Mission District. The admission fee was 25 cents, and the gardens housed the largest marine aquarium in the country at the time, zoological gardens, greenhouses, and a restaurant. Frost was born in San Francisco in 1874 and lived there until 1885. While Parini notes that "Frost was most impressed by the aquatic merry-go-round at the gardens," here we discover "a boy, presuming on his intellect" who is mystified by monkeys (13).

The boy, presumably Frost, shows two caged monkeys what appears to be a magnifying glass, feeling quite superior in his knowledge of its capabilities.

Words are useless for him to explain the object to the animals, so "presuming on his intellect" he believes that they "never could be made to understand." In his human superiority, he makes the glass a weapon, to show them how it works. He makes the glass reflect on each monkey's nose, and a "puzzled dimness" comes to their eyes "[t]hat blinking could not seem to blink away." The attitude of the boy seems less than pleasant, as he seems in his pride to be toying with the monkeys' ignorance.

As the monkeys stand "laced together" behind the bars, they react in what Robert Faggen calls a "decidedly human way" when they exchange "troubled glances over life" (90). One puts his hand up to his nose, and Frost writes that perhaps he is "[w]ithin a million years of an idea"—presumably a reference to Darwin's theory of EVOLUTION (Faggen wrote extensively on the connection between Frost and Darwin). The "weapon" stings the monkey's little "knuckles," and what was "already known" is once more confirmed by "psychological experiment." Frost again pokes fun at the boy's feeling of authority, before leading up to the monkey's takeover of the object. The boy, in all his superiority, is not quite as smart as he thinks he is. In a "sudden flash of arm, a snatch," the glass "was the monkeys', not the boy's."

The monkeys, though, are in some sense just as inquisitive, if not more so, than the boy. They use all of their senses to discover the object: "[t]hey bit the glass and listened for the flavor. / They broke the handle and the binding off it," and still they are "none the wiser." They eventually give up and hide it in their bedding straw, away from the boy, who ultimately seems to have had no more knowledge than they. While the monkeys' way of approaching the object might seem to have a mocking element to it, in some sense it is also more sincere than the boy's.

"Against the day of prisoners' ennui" the monkeys come forth and "answer" the boy "for themselves": "Who said it mattered / What monkeys did or didn't understand?" they seem to ask the boy back. They might not "understand a burning-glass" or "the sun itself," but the poem concludes, with Frostian epigrammatic grace, that "It's knowing what to do with things that counts."

Frost seems to end by embracing Darwin and of the simple life, the day-to-day. He seems to say that we are not so different from monkeys, and he embraces the similarities between us and them. He even seems to suggest that they might be better off than we are, because they are interested in how things work rather than in how to use them as weapons to harm one another.

The poem first appeared in the April 1937 issue of *Poetry* and was collected later that year in *A Further Range* with the subtitle "or, Resourcefulness Is More Than Understanding." *See* SAN FRANCISCO.

FURTHER READING

Faggen, Robert. *Robert Frost and the Challenge of Darwin.* Ann Arbor: University of Michigan Press, 1997.

Hass, Robert. *Going by Contraries: Robert Frost's Conflict with Science.* Charlottesville: University Press of Virginia, 2002.

Parini, Jay. *Robert Frost: A Life.* New York: Holt, 1999.

Turrill, Charles Beebe. "Woodward's Gardens." The Virtual Museum of the City of San Francisco. Available online. URL: http://www.sfmuseum.org/hist9/woodward.html. Accessed June 29, 2006.

"Auspex" (1962)

Jay Parini points out that "Frost's lifelong love of competitive sports, and his passion to excel and win in whatever he did," were "a legacy from his father" (19). In this poem the speaker is at odds with how he is perceived and how he perceives of himself. Frost was always insecure and constantly striving for confirmation. Like many people, he fluctuated between enormous self-pride and great self-doubt. He received so many doctoral hoods that a quilt was made of them as a gift, and yet he continued to seek outside validation for his work. In the end, he was very much disappointed not to receive the ultimate accolade: the Nobel Prize.

Parini notes that when the poet was young, the Frost family took regular weekend ventures into the California countryside; this poem offers a glimpse of one memory of those excursions. In

"Auspex" (which, Jeffrey Meyers has explained, is Latin for one who watches birds for purposes of divination) the young speaker is eyed by nature but is spared (14). Two themes are prevalent in the poem: (1) humans' vulnerability in nature and (2) human self-perception. After all, the speaker says, "Such auspices are very hard to read." In one sense, the boy is spared by the great eagle; in another, he is discarded and rejected because he is unworthy. The question is, which interpretation of the omen is accurate?

Reflecting Frost's knowledge of Greek and Roman mythology, the parents in the poem declare that the boy was rejected by the royal bird as "one who would not make a Ganymede." In Greek mythology, Ganymede was a Trojan boy of great beauty whom Zeus carried away to be cupbearer to the gods. Here the eagle is likened to Zeus but also to Jove, who in Roman mythology, is the equivalent to Zeus, so the boy asks why his parents do not "find a barkeep unto Jove" in him. (The story of Ganymede can be found in Ovid's *Metamorphoses* and in Virgil's *Aeneid*.)

The young boy remains "resentful" of his playful and literary parents because they make him feel as though he does not have the power to be anything he wants to be. But he says that only he has the power to determine what he can and cannot be—a jab at the notion that gods have any say in the behavior of human beings. The poem strongly reflects an embracing of free will as opposed to predestination, but it also reflects Frost's self-image, his desire to be a great and remembered poet, and his late recognition.

The poem was collected in *In the Clearing* but first appeared in Elizabeth Shepley Sergeant's *Robert Frost: The Trial by Existence* (1960). *See* SAN FRANCISCO.

FURTHER READING

Meyers, Jeffrey. *Robert Frost: A Biography*. New York: Houghton Mifflin, 1996.
Parini, Jay. *Robert Frost: A Life*. New York: Holt, 1999.
Sergeant, Elizabeth Shepley. *Robert Frost: The Trial by Existence*. New York: Holt, Rinehart and Winston, 1960.

"Away!" (1962)

Randall Jarrell says that Frost occasionally writes with a "bare sorrow with which, sometimes, things are accepted as they are, neither exaggerated nor explained away," and in "Away!" we find Frost's strongest expression of this disposition (28). "Away!," a poem Frost himself called a "little death" poem, begins with a familiar walk out of town and into open land. As in "Vantage Point," he is again seeking a different view from which to observe the world, and he leaves others behind as he does in "Into My Own."

There is bite to his depiction of his friends when he says, "Let them get well-wined / And go lie down," as if to say, this is not a journey for everyone. This time he is not going into the dark: "Don't think I leave / for the outer dark," he insists; "There is no one I / Am put out with / Or put out by." Frost distinguishes between "outer dark" and, presumably, inner dark, and it is the inner dark that the speaker cannot shake here any more than he could in "Tree at My Window," where the weather is a metaphor for struggle.

"Away!" also reiterates the beliefs presented in "Too Anxious for Rivers." There is no divine hand orchestrating this speaker's life. He is going it alone; he takes full responsibility for his choices. But he is not entirely sure of his agnosticism: "Unless I'm wrong / I but obey / The urge of song: / "I'm— bound—away!" / And I may return / If dissatisfied / With what I learned / From having died."

This journey seems to be a final one, Frost's version of Dickinson's carriage ride with death. Laurence Perrine points out that the speaker "does not know what he will 'learn / From having died.' But his thought is focused on a possible return to earth, not an elevation to some realm of heavenly bliss" (95).

The speaker boasts that if he should find the answers he has been seeking in this deserted death and is unsatisfied, he will return with what he has learned. But will he be more sure of all he thought was true?

The poem was Frost's 1958 Christmas poem and was later included in *In the Clearing*. *See* FUGITIVE.

FURTHER READING

Hoffman, Tyler. *Robert Frost and the Politics of Poetry.* Hanover, N.H.: Middlebury College Press, 2001.

Jarrell, Randall. "The Other Frost." In *Poetry and the Age,* 28. New York: Vintage, 1955.

Kau, Joseph. "Frost's 'Away!': "Illusions and Allusions," *Notes on Modern American Literature* 7, no. 3 (Winter 1983): 17.

Meyers, Jeffrey. *Robert Frost: A Biography.* New York: Houghton Mifflin, 1996.

Perrine, Laurence. "Robert Frost and the Idea of Immortality." In *Frost: Centennial Essays II,* edited by Jac Tharpe, 85–98. Jackson: University Press of Mississippi, 1976.

"A-Wishing Well" (1962)

Frost's Christmas poem for 1959, "A-Wishing Well," which later appeared in *In the Clearing,* begins "a poet would a-wishing go," and immediately calls into question who the poet is—whether the poet is Frost or some other poet. A. R. Ferguson has named the American poet Edward Rowland Sill, of whom Frost was quite fond: When Frost first met his wife Elinor he presented a book of Sill's poems to her, along with a book of Emily Dickinson's. But it also seems possible that Frost had no specific poet in mind (or was even referring to himself), despite his assertion that he "quote[s] him with respect verbatim." It would not be unlike Frost, and it would be in keeping with the playfulness of the rhyme scheme, which seems to mimic a nursery rhyme, with its jog-trot rhythms: "A poet would a-wishing go, / and he wished love were thus and so. / 'If but it were' he said, said he," and so on.

Some "quaint dissatisfaction" eats at the poet, and Frost wonders what it is. He says he would give anything to learn "the one thing more of his concern." The move from the playfulness of the opening lines to a more serious tone occurs when the poet seems to whisper, "But listen to me register / The one thing more I wish there were." By line 11, "one thing" has already been repeated three times, and yet its meaning is still ambiguous.

The poet calls himself a "confirmed astronomer" and says that he is "always for a better sky"—that he does not "care how the world gets by." This image of Frost is of someone concerned with abstract ideas and poetic thought rather than the everyday of simple life. Getting by is not what it is about, he seems to say. But the poem does not bear this out: It is precisely about finding what will best help us get by, even if it means a loss of life in procuring another moon.

The speaker wants to "let go restraint" and fully embrace possibility. When he lets go, he is impish and childlike, "splashing phosphorescent paint" and filling the sky "full of moons / As circus day of toy balloons." Then the mature poet says satirically, "That ought to make the Sunday Press." His sense breaks through as he says, "But that's not like me," and his childish side is stopped in its tracks; the poet goes on to say quite seriously that "[o]n much less / And much much easier to get / From childhood has my heart been set."

The poet goes on making childhood wishes, trying to be foolhardy but always failing at it. He says that some planets, "the unblinking four"—presumably referring to Mars, Venus, Saturn, and Jupiter—"Are seen to juggle moons galore." He would like the power to add many moons, but he says he only asks for "an extra one." He wants Earth to have "another satellite." The poet sends wishes to the moon, echoing "Twinkle, Twinkle, Little Star," written by poet Jane Taylor (1783–1824) in the lines "I wish I may I wish I might, / give earth another satellite." But "Where would we get another?" he asks. A movement from innocence to hope then occurs, reminiscent of William Blake's *Songs of Innocence and Experience.* This poet has gone a-wishing and is brought back to earth by the inquiries of clever people who ask where he "get[s] a poem." Suddenly poems are likened to moons, to satellites, to the birth of all things.

In responding to questions about where he gets a poem, Frost "despair[s]." First he flippantly says "New York," and then he plays on childhood myths about where babies come from: brought by storks or grown in pots. He says some claim to remember when the first moon (or poem?) was born, and he recalls that it "cost the Earth as fierce a pang / As

Keats (or was it Milton?) sang." Frost certainly would have known whether he was referring to John Keats or John Milton, so his questioning here is only further indication of his ironic wit. He is referring to the following lines from Keats's Hyperion, Book II: "Nearest him / Asia, born of most enormous Caf, / who cost her mother Tellus keener pangs, / Though feminine, than any of her sons" (1.52–55). (Keats took the word *Caf* from William Beckford's novel *Vathek* [1784]). Asia was the child of Oceanus and Tethys, who, Homer claimed, were responsible for the birth of all the other gods. This poem, like many others, demonstrates Frost's education in Greek and Roman classics and mythology. In Frost's rendition of the myth, Asia was "torn from [Earth's] Pacific side."

When the moon was first born, "All the sea water in one tide / And all the air rushed to the spot." The poet tells us that "Believe the Arcadians or not, / They saved themselves by hanging on / To a plant called the silphion." The silphion was an herb, thought to be a kind of giant fennel, that had medicinal and contraceptive properties. Here it is a plant that cannot be uprooted. The tone of the poem again shifts, telling a ghost story in keeping with "Witch of Coös." Frost writes that those men who did not let go of the silphion but were swept away by the gale nonetheless left their "desperately clutching hand[s]" behind, so that "In branches of the silphion / Is sometimes found a skeleton," which "[s]cience has failed to understand."

Again, Frost's playfulness returns when he writes that one of the hands "has been lately all the talk / in the museum of Antioch." Antioch was one of the most beautiful ancient cities and was located on one of the trade routes between the East and the Greco-Roman world. The city lay buried for nearly 2,000 years before a team of scholars excavated it in the 1930s. And "that's how it was from the Pacific," the poet concludes. He asserts that it "needn't be quite so terrific" to get another moon, or satellite, "from the Atlantic," finding his wish suitably reasonable to fulfill, even if some "[g]ood liberals will object."

Frost ends on a hopeful note, assuring that the human race is "practically inexterminate" and, as such, will always find another place to "start the world all over at." The poem makes many allusions, and in some ways it may be seen as overwrought with them, but the poet's wishes are clear. Adopting a childlike persona, he wishes on the stars to supply Earth with another satellite, should the one we have ever blink and go out. He uses childhood rhymes, such as *moons* and *balloons*, but the innocence he presents is not without experience; this wish is plenty grown up.

See STARS.

FURTHER READING

Parini, Jay. *Robert Frost: A Life.* New York: Holt, 1999.

"Ax-Helve, The" (1923)

One of Frost's best narrative poems, "The Ax-Helve" first appeared in the September 1917 issue of the *Atlantic* and was later collected in *New Hampshire*. Despite the title's focus on an object, the ax-helve, the poem is more concerned with relationships between people, between neighbors.

Frost with an ax in winter. "The Ax-Helve": "[W]hat he thought of—not me, but my ax, / Me only as I took my ax to heart." *(Photo by Eric Schaal. Courtesy Getty Images)*

The poem begins with a familiar rural scene: a man (significantly, a "Yankee") chopping wood in his yard. The speaker recalls how his hand was once "held," or rather caught by an alder branch, when he was chopping wood. Presumably, when he raised the blade, a branch caught it to keep him from "striking at another alder's roots." He is clearly inferring the intention of the alder tree. This time the intentions are just as unclear, when Baptiste, his French-Canadian neighbor, halts his hand from chopping. The speaker speculates again and considers that Baptiste's reasoning cannot be the same as the alder tree's, since the tree he is chopping has already been cut down. It is important to note that Baptiste caught his "ax expertly on the rise," since it would be a careful enterprise to halt a man's chopping. Baptiste demonstrates his knowledge of chopping and of axes, as well as his stealth, in this gesture.

Baptiste sneaks up on the speaker, and in doing so he must allow the man to become "calm" before retrieving the ax. The speaker states clearly that he let Baptiste take the ax from him, even though he "didn't know him well enough to know / What it was all about." Being interrupted while chopping wood in the country would seem to be an unsettling experience, but this narrator acquiesces quite easily to someone else's taking charge. There is a sense of ease in this country setting, as well as the speaker's insecurity in his own skill with an ax. The narrator refers to himself as "a bad neighbor" and suggests that the intrusion might have been a way of disarming him before having at him. Much to his surprise, all his neighbor was concerned with was his ax. Nonetheless, what Baptiste thinks of his ax is of some concern, "only as I took my ax to heart," he says.

Much to the speaker's surprise, it is the ax-helve that is "bad," not himself. Baptiste criticizes it for being "made on machine" rather than by hand, and in this there is some criticism of industrialization, which is clearly contrasted to rural agricultural life. Baptiste is described as "plowing the grain" of the handle, and the imagery contributes to the setting. Baptiste invites the speaker to his home, so that he can "put [him] one in" by replacing the handle with one of "good hick'ry." The speaker, ever-cautious, wonders why Baptiste cares, wonders if Baptiste has something to sell, though it does not appear that way.

When he arrives at the house, he finds that his "welcome differed from no other welcome" and that "Baptiste knew best why I was where I was." This self-analysis is somewhat puzzling, as it suggests that the speaker is still passively involved. He is not sure why he is there, and he seems to be frequently second-guessing himself. The speaker wonders if Baptiste is overjoyed at having gotten him there and says that as long "as he would leave enough unsaid" all would be well. There seems to be an inherent distrust of neighbors, reminiscent of Frost's statement in "Mending Wall" that "good fences make good neighbors." The speaker's speculations turn to Baptiste, and he realizes that he "must judge" if what he knows about an ax "was to count / For nothing in the measure of a neighbor." Just as he wondered if he was being judged by what he knew about an ax, here he wonders if he must judge Baptiste in the same way.

In the meantime Mrs. Baptiste, who does not "spick too much Henglish," is rocking herself about the room, sometimes dangerously close to the stove. Rocking chairs are a staple in country homes, and they do have a tendency, when rocked, to put those rocking unknowingly into compromising positions. Mrs. Baptiste, silently and possibly knowingly, makes the speaker "afraid" that she is aware of what is passing between him and her husband. What is passing between them, however, is not entirely clear, as it is passing in silence. It is passing in the way they use an axe and make an axe, and in the conversations people have with others and themselves about their neighbors, rather than with the neighbors themselves.

As Baptiste starts to fashion a new handle for his neighbor, his love for his work is made clear. He has a "quiverful to choose from," though the speaker does not presume to "ask which" handle he should have. The descriptions that follow are expressed with love: "he liked to have it slender as a whipstock, / Free from the least knot, / equal to the strain / Of bending like a sword across the knee." As Baptiste shows "the lines of a good helve," the speaker marvels at Baptiste's ability to make "a short job long / For love of it, and yet not waste time either." Baptiste is slow and passionate about his work, savoring every moment, but working all the while.

While Baptiste is at work, the two neighbors chat, and oddly Baptiste starts to defend his choice to homeschool his children. Frost also homeschooled his children, and his frequent criticisms of formal education are hinted at in this second-to-last stanza. "Doubts" about "laid-on education" are the important topic of discussion between the two. As they share their views, the speaker again wonders why he is there: "Was I desired in friendship[?]" he speculates.

When all is finished, the conversation and the ax, Baptiste presents an ax that the speaker likens to the snake that "stood up for evil" in the garden of Adam and Eve. Frost commented in an interview in the *Atlantic* in the year the poem was published that "Canadian woodchoppers whittle their axe-handles, following the curve of the grain, and they're strong and beautiful. Art should follow the lines in nature, like a grain of an ax-handle. False art puts curves on things that haven't any curves." This comment and his note in the margins of a friend's book that "This is as near as I like to come to talking about art, in a work of art—such as it is" have caused many to interpret the ax as a metaphor for poetry. Robert Faggen complicates this reading by asserting that "Frost plays out questions of whether intellect, artistic proclivity, or moral sympathy are the best or even the dominant forces in the survival and success of individuals or groups" (122).

FURTHER READING

Borroff, Marie. "Robert Frost: To Earthward." In *Frost: Centennial Essays II*, edited by Jac Tharpe, 21–39. Jackson: University Press of Mississippi, 1976.

Doyle, John Robert, Jr. *The Poetry of Robert Frost: An Analysis*. New York: Hafner Press, 1962.

Faggen, Robert. *Robert Frost and the Challenge of Darwin*. Ann Arbor: University of Michigan Press, 1997.

Hoffman, Tyler. *Robert Frost and the Politics of Poetry*. Hanover, N.H.: Middlebury College Press, 2001.

Meyers, Jeffrey. *Robert Frost: A Biography*. New York: Houghton Mifflin, 1996.

Monteiro, George. *Robert Frost and the New England Renaissance*. Lexington: University Press of Kentucky, 1988.

Parini, Jay. *Robert Frost: A Life*. New York: Holt, 1999.

"Bad Island—Easter, The" (1962)

From *In the Clearing*, this poem, which was first published in the September 17, 1954, issue of the *Times Literary Supplement*, concerns itself with Easter Island, now typically known as Rapa Nui, one of the most isolated islands on Earth. The island is 2,300 miles from the coast of Chile and 2,400 miles from Tahiti. In 1722, the first European reached Easter Island, a Dutchman named Captain Jacob Roggeveen.

When Frost begins, "That primitive head / So ambitiously vast," he is calling attention to the fascinating moai of Easter Island—human heads carved in hardened volcanic ash. They stand 13 feet high and weigh 14 tons, and there is a concentration of them along the island's southeast coast. The backs of the heads face the sea (in contrast to the people in "Neither Out Far nor In Deep" who "turn their back on the land") and are thought to represent the spirits of ancestors, chiefs, or other high-ranking males. Scientists have estimated that they were carved, transported, and erected between 1400 and 1600 A.D. Frost describes this primitive culture as "rude" in their "art," revealing a Eurocentric artistic taste. But he is intrigued by the statues and uses them as a way of speculating about the island's indigenous people and culture.

Frost points out that it is as hard to read and understand the statues as it is "a clinical chart." He reflects that the ancient carvers must have been "days on that stone . . . Till it flaked from the ledge." Frost is intrigued by the faces of these ancestors, whose lips seem "scornfully curled," and he questions whether the faces on these stone heads reveal something of the scorn the race had for "having been born." But he also calls into question the idea of being ruled as a form of being "cajoled," "coerced," "cozened," and "fooled," unless it was by "guile," "fraud," "force," punishment, or bribery. If these enormous heads are meant to pay tribute to chiefs, the speaker wonders, then is the scorn demonstrated on their faces the scorn the carvers had for their rulers?

Frost cynically imagines that to be induced to put forth the great amount of effort that is evident in their work, these ancients may have been "persuaded to see / Something in it for them." But he arrives at no solid conclusion. While he continues to speculate throughout the poem, he admits that all is "in vain" and concludes that "Some mistake had been made / No book can explain," so that the culture did not survive.

Frost selects the German word for culture, *kultur*, apparently to draw a similarity between the regime he describes and the Nazi regime. He is playful when, partly to rhyme with *kultur*, he creates the word "altrur-ian" out of altruism. Tyler Hoffman points out that this also "invokes the utopian land of William Dean Howells's socialist novel *A Traveler to Altruria* (1984), in which altruism replaces competition as the engine of the economy" (153).

Frost has a motive: to highlight the deficiencies of this old culture in order for us to recognize the same in our own. He finishes by saying that "not a trace" of the culture is left, and then offers that "the gospel of sharing" ... "has decayed" into "being a thief." Frost offers irony in his subtitle when he writes that perhaps the island was called "Easter" because it "may have risen once."

FURTHER READING

Hoffman, Tyler. *Robert Frost and the Politics of Poetry.* Hanover, N.H.: Middlebury College Press, 2001.
PBS.org. "Secrets of Easter Island." Available online. URL: http://www.pbs.org/wgbh/nova/easter/civilization/. Accessed June 30, 2006.

"Bear, The" (1928)

The last poem of the first edition of *West-Running Brook*, and made up almost entirely of rhyming couplets, "The Bear" makes a certain distinction between man and other animals. As in Frost's description of nature in "Acceptance," here Frost's description of a bear highlights the key to the difference between man and bear—that the bear "does not cry aloud" about his position in the world as man does. The poem begins with the image of a bear being a bear, eating cherries from a tree and taking a "cross-country in the fall." But as with all things in nature, the speaker, being a man, cannot observe the bear's behavior without personal reflection. Here the speaker realizes that the "world has room to make a bear feel free" while "the universe feels cramped to you and me."

Man must always have a "telescope at one end of his beat, / And at the other a microscope." Never satisfied with his existence alone, man must always be looking inward or to the sky for some understanding of his existence. "He paces back and forth" like the Greeks, philosophizing and moving from "one extreme" to "the other." Frost asserts that these two extremes are the difference between "agreeing with one Greek" and "agreeing with another Greek"—the difference between agreeing with Plato or with Aristotle. Plato is known for articulating that the transcendent is the only place where humans can find the realm of being that contains permanent unchanging ideas and the true forms of beauty, truth, and so on. Aristotle, Plato's pupil, in contrast, argued that "forms" exist only in the things themselves, as they are perceived in this world. By summoning the two ideas to mind, Frost plays on man's constant "back and forth" and his "sway[ing] from cheek to cheek" between this world and the transcendental.

People's ability to reason and seek answers causes them to feel "caged" in this vast universe. Jay Parini notes that "people are, in effect, caged—by each other, and by conventions of one kind or another; our mode of vision is limited," but it seems that they are even more caged by themselves (247). Unlike the bear, who without a care "flings over and off down through the maples" and then presumably takes a long winter's rest, people are found pacing "back and forth" without rest, constantly troubled over the human condition.

Frost closes by providing an image of man as a "baggy figure, / equally pathetic / When sedentary and when peripatetic." The term *peripatetic* derives from Aristotle's constant pacing while conducting discussions and therefore is also the word for an Aristotelian (one who follows the philosophy of Aristotle). In this term, Frost suggests that Aristotle's pacing led to no more enlightenment or satisfaction than a sedentary and baggy fellow's would.

Frost offers a bit of criticism of what man considers his "plight." The description he offers is somewhat pathetic. And when he writes that "Man acts more like the poor bear in a cage / That all day fights a nervous inward rage," it is clear that he disapproves of this behavior. Even while he includes himself by saying that the universe is cramped to "you and me," he finds something silly in man's nervousness and rage.

See PHILOSOPHY.

FURTHER READING

Hass, Robert. *Going by Contraries: Robert Frost's Conflict with Science.* Charlottesville: University Press of Virginia, 2002.

Parini, Jay. *Robert Frost: A Life.* New York: Holt, 1999.

Reed, Richard. "The Animal World in Robert Frost's Poetry." In *Frost: Centennial Essays II*, edited by Jac Tharpe, 159–169. Jackson: University Press of Mississippi, 1976.

"Bearer of Evil Tidings, The" (1936)

When first published in *A Further Range*, this ballad bore the subtitle "The Himalayas" (which Frost had a pet peeve about pronouncing correctly—Himal-yas; at a reading he once shared that he partly learned about language from poetry, and he used the word *Himalayas* as an example). The "bearer of evil tidings" of the title never quite completes his mission. Halfway to "tell Belshazzar / What soon enough he would know," he remembers that evil tidings are "a dangerous thing to bear." As in "The Road Not Taken," here two roads diverge, and the traveler chooses the one that "went off to the mountains / And into the wild unknown."

The bearer goes through the "Vale of Cashmere" until he comes to the "land of Pamir," which alludes to Thomas More's *Lalla Rookh* (1817) and also to Kashmir, a historical region of northwest India and northeast Pakistan. (Pamir is a mountainous region of northern Kashmir that is sometimes called "the roof of the world.") More's poem tells of a princess's trip from Delhi to Cashmere to meet her betrothed, the king of Bucharia: "Who has not heard the Vale of Cashmere, / With its roses the brightest, the earth ever gave, / Its temples and grottos, and fountains, as clear, / As the love-lighted eyes that hang over their wave?" In Frost's poem, the bearer meets a girl who brings him home with her and teaches him her tribe's religion. Her "religion" tells the story of a virgin girl who, while on her way to marry a Persian prince, is impregnated by a god, causing her army to "come to a troubled halt" and found a village. Frost holds that this is why there are people "On one Himalayan shelf."

The bearer of evil tidings had something "in common" with the "race he chose to adopt": "They had both of them had their reasons / For stopping where they had stopped." The villagers' reason, it seems, was that "it had seemed discreet to remain there / And neither go on nor back." But this suggests that they had stayed for discretion's sake, when they had actually each stayed because evil tidings are a "dangerous thing to bear."

The final stanza mentions the name Belshazzar, who was the son of Nebuchadnezzar II and the last king of Babylon; in the Bible he was warned of his doom by "handwriting on the wall." Frost spares the bearer in this poem and ends with a suggestion that the bearer would have had little effect on the outcome, even if he were to have followed through on his mission. The messenger would have likely been killed for his message, but he has chosen survival over responsibility. Frost seems, if not to commend the choice, at least to find it reasonable.

The poem was first published in the winter 1936 issue of the *Yale Review*.

FURTHER READING

Cook, Marjorie. "Acceptance in Frost's Poetry: Conflict as Play." In *Frost Centennial Essays II*, edited by Jac Tharpe, 229–230. Jackson: University Press of Mississippi, 1976.

Doyle, John. *The Poetry of Robert Frost.* New York: Hafner Press, 1962.

"Beech" (1942)

"Beech," the first poem in *A Witness Tree,* "Sycamore" being the second, seems intended to set the mood for the rest of the book. The tree that the poem refers to is the tree that marked the boundaries of the Homer Noble Farm in Ripton, Vermont, a short distance from the Bread Loaf Writer's Conference, where Frost spent many summers (*see* BREAD LOAF SCHOOL OF ENGLISH). Jay Parini points out that the actual tree was an "old sugar maple marred by a spike, situated near a rock cairn" (340).

Frost creates an "imaginary line" that "bends square in woods" around the property, and in doing so he proceeds to consider his own imaginary lines and deep wounds. The speaker calls this beech "Witness Tree," and suggests that it has borne witness and "commit[ed] to memory" its wounds, just as the speaker has his own. The speaker expects the tree to remember as well as bear witness to his "being not unbounded." He says that in this way the "truth's established."

The notion of truth presented here is complex, as it seems that truth is established through a marking of boundaries, that what we call truth is just an identification of that which we can mark off from the rest. The poem is existential in that it is concerned with truth and with the speaker's being. In a similar sense, Frost puts forth that the circum-

Frost's cabin at Homer Noble Farm, Ripton, Vermont. "Beech": "Where my imaginary line / Bends square in the woods, an iron spine / And pile of real rocks have been founded." *(Photo by Deirdre Fagan)*

stances are not without "dark and doubt," because we are surrounded "by a world of doubt." The tree is only a boundary, he recognizes, just as his own boundaries are recognizable only to him.

The poem is signed, "The Moodie Forester," which offers a double meaning, since Frost's mother's maiden name was Moodie.

FURTHER READING

Cook, Marjorie E. "Dilemmas of Interpretation: Ambiguities and Practicalities." In *Robert Frost: The Man and the Poet,* edited by Earl J. Wilcox, 125–141. Rock Hill, S.C.: Winthrop College, 1990.

Lakritz, Andrew. "Frost in Transition." In *Roads Not Taken: Rereading Robert Frost,* edited by Earl J. Wilcox and Jonathan N. Barron, 198–216. Columbia: University of Missouri Press, 2000, 198–216.

Miller, David L. "Dominion of the Eye in Frost." In *Frost: Centennial Essays II,* edited by Jac Tharpe, 141–158. Jackson: University Press of Mississippi, 1976.

Parini, Jay. *Robert Frost: A Life.* New York: Holt, 1999, 339–340.

Will, Norman P. "Robert Frost's 'Beech': Faith Regained," *Notes on Modern American Literature* 6, no. 1 (Spring–Summer 1982): 2.

"Bereft" (1928)

The speaker in this poem is at the whim of nature, and the nature presented is not one to be welcomed. There is a keen and frightening recognition of what nature can bring and will, as seasons pass and winter grows nearer. The speaker wonders where he has "heard this wind before / Change like this to a deeper roar," but it is clear that he has heard it a season before.

The speaker is standing in the doorway of his home, thinking about the conditions outside. He observes the passing of summer and sees the "massed" and "somber clouds," and the mood of the poem seems to darken with daylight in each line. Unlike the leaves "trodden underfoot" in "A Leaf-Treader," here the leaves are like snakes, coiling, hissing, and striking at the speaker's legs. The speaker feels vulnerable and defensive as he perceives "[s]omething sinister in the tone" of the wind.

As the poem draws to its close, the "secret" of the speaker is revealed: He is in his "life alone" and has "no one left but God." The irony of the last line is compelling. If the speaker has God left, then he should not feel so vulnerable at the whim of nature, which is controlled by God; therefore, as Robert Faggen puts it, the poem evokes "the torment of blind faith before a terrible God" (246). Frost seems to poke fun at those who can find God in a nature that is so disagreeable. As in other poems, the speaker feels unsafe and uneasy with nature, even when in his house.

The poem first appeared in the February 9, 1927, issue of the *New Republic* and was later included in *West-Running Brook.*

FURTHER READING

Faggen, Robert. *Robert Frost and the Challenge of Darwin.* Ann Arbor: University of Michigan Press, 1997.

"Beyond Words" (1947)

In "An Old Man's Winter Night," the old man has "icicles along the wall to keep," but here, the only other place where icicles appear in Frost's poetry, the "icicles along the gutter" feel like an "armory of hate." Appearing in *Steeple Bush,* the brief four-line poem works with a single rhyme, *gutter* with *utter,* and the repetition of the word "you" five times. The poem's meaning largely comes from the first two lines, and the last two explain how to read the first two.

Icicles have long held a position as a great murder weapon, since they melt after the act. Here they are the speaker's armory, and in this way the speaker suggests that either he is protected by them or he will use them as weapons. The underlying threat of the last two lines is that the listener must "wait" for what is to come. There is tension in the poem, but the reader is left mostly uninformed. Clearly the speaker is in some sort of an argument, and the repetition of "you" signals that he is at a loss for words in retaliation; he is "beyond words." Instead, like a child in the schoolyard, all that he can summon to defend himself is a feeble "you wait!" While the speaker claims to be without words or beyond them, he ironically expresses this loss through words, through poetry.

According to Jeffrey Meyers, Frost said the poem was about his wife Elinor, and Meyers suggests that there are two voices in the poem, the last two lines being the woman's (77). Several critics have also drawn a connection to "Home Burial" and the woman's similar repetition of "don't." As Katherine Kearns expresses, in "Beyond Words," "Frost also makes an oblique comment on the paradox of lyricism: that when emotion is at its purest, language fails."

FURTHER READING

Kearns, Katherine. "Frost on the Doorstep of Lyricism at the Millennium." In *Roads Not Taken: Rereading Robert Frost*, edited by Earl J. Wilcox and Jonathan N. Barron, 32–51. Columbia: University of Missouri Press, 2000.

Meyers, Jeffrey. *Robert Frost: A Biography*. New York: Houghton Mifflin, 1996.

"Birches" (1916)

One of Frost's most anthologized poems, originally titled "Swinging Birches," "Birches" was first collected in *Mountain Interval*, along with several of his other best-known poems, including "The Road Not Taken," "An Old Man's Winter Night," "Meeting and Passing," "The Oven Bird," and "Out, Out—." "Birches" had been written several years before, while the family was in Beaconsfield, ENGLAND, and had first been published in the *Atlantic Monthly* in August 1915. Frost often claimed that he wrote the poem quickly in one sitting, but later commentators believe that this is not accurate. Drafts have been discovered, along with a comment in a letter to Robert Penn Warren that the poem was made of two separate fragments pieced together.

Frost had a particular fondness for birches. In *Fifty Poets: An American Auto-Anthology* (1953) he wrote that if an ark were sailing and he were allowed to bring a single plant on board for seed, he would select a birch tree. "Don't ask me why at a time of doom and confusion like this," he wrote; "my reasons might be forced and unreal. But if I defend my choice, I will say I took it for its vocality and ulteriority."

Karen Kilcup maintains that the poem was inspired by another on the same subject by the American poet Lucy Larcom (who was a teacher of Frost's friend Susan Hayes Ward), "Swinging on a Birch-Tree," but it was also clearly inspired by Frost's own experiences as a boy. His first experience with swinging on birch trees was in Amherst, New Hampshire, on his Aunt Sarah's farm. He once told an audience that "It was almost sacrilegious climbing a birch tree till it bent, till it gave and swooped to the ground," and he admitted, "but that's what boys did in those days" (Parini, 22).

In blank verse the speaker imagines a better explanation for how the birch trees were bent. He is empathetic to how they got that way and opens by comparing them to "straighter darker trees," which he sees as stronger and more able to withstand nature's buffets. He'd prefer to "think some boy's been swinging them," but he is quickly reminded that swinging "doesn't bend them down to stay as ice-storms do." The poem continues to move from reverie to reflection and from the view of youth to one of maturity. It can be read as a carefully choreographed dance between two visions. The fluidity of the form creates the impression of improvisational speaking or dancing, which is perhaps why Frost wanted to create the impression that the poem had been written easily.

The first shift in the poem is between the third line and fourth, where the speaker moves from imaginative telling to the reality of ice storms. This is followed by some of Frost's greatest descriptives: the way the trees "click upon themselves" and "shed crystal shells," and the comparison of the ice breaking and crashing to the ground to "the inner dome of heaven" having fallen. These lines are a reminder of the supple strength of birch trees; no matter how much they bend and are unable to "right themselves," they "seem not to break." (Frost in a lecture once drew attention to his choice of the word *crazes* in the line, "As the stir cracks and crazes their enamel," where he describes the birch twigs encased in ice. As illustration he drew a pattern of "crackly china" on the board [Barry 148].)

The speaker is almost stopped short by "Truth" breaking in. He is impatient with this interruption and truth's matter-of-factness. He suggests that he was just about to say something when he was suddenly distracted from his reverie. He goes on to describe how some country boy might have bent the trees, a boy "too far from town to learn baseball" and who had to play "alone." The images of a boy "riding" birch trees is fairytale-like. The boy learned through repetition how not to launch out too soon and therefore not bend the trees all the way to the ground. The boy practiced mindfully, taking the same care one might in pouring liquid all the way to the top of a container or cup. The speaker addresses his readers directly as he makes this unlikely comparison. Certainly most people would prefer to take care with a leisurely activity than with a task that requires taking pains. The boy, fully engaged, is full of life and "kick[s] his way down through the air" like a dancer. But then truth breaks in again, and the speaker says resignedly, "So was I once a swinger of birches." It is a regret of age: The speaker dreams of "going back." This statement interrupts the dream the poem has created, just as truth has interrupted the speaker's dream (and much as it does in "After Apple-Picking").

There is an abrupt shift at this point, because the truth that breaks in this time is dark and foreboding. The speaker is "weary of considerations, / And life is too much like a pathless wood"—that is, there is no clear road to take; he longs to "get away from earth awhile," but that's not all. He explains what life does to a man: "your face burns and tickles with the cobwebs / Broken across it, and one eye . . . weeping." These are dark, stinging images. They are disturbing when compared with the beauty of girls leaning forward with their hair tossed over their heads to dry in the sun, or the boy kicking his way to the ground with almost balletic grace and glee.

The speaker backs off a bit, as if afraid that he has revealed too much. He prays, "May no fate willfully misunderstand me / And half grant what I wish and snatch me away / Not to return." Here fate is unforgiving, and the speaker suggests that she will, to spite his somewhat contentious attitude toward real life, grant him his wish and remove him from life altogether. But he does not want to die. He merely wants to start again, to remove the stiffness from his bones so he can once again be a swinger of birches. He knows well that Earth is, if not the best place, the "right place for love," and he does not know "where it's likely to go better." The love expressed here is for life, for swinging birch trees, and for filling his own cup to the brim. These lines reflect Frost's agnostic side: He is not convinced enough of what lies in heaven to be so willing to go there; heaven is a fragile concept, as the speaker observes earlier in the poem, when he describes the "inner dome of heaven" falling.

Just as in "After Apple-Picking," when the "ladder's sticking through a tree / Toward heaven," the speaker is willing to climb toward heaven, but not to it. Just when the tree can "bear no more"—when he has filled the cup "to the brim, and even above the brim," he wants to be set down again to start over. He concludes, "That would be good both going and coming back. / One could do worse than be a swinger of birches."

The birch tree, in a sense, is the speaker. His branches have been weighed down by life, and this old white birch is no longer as strong as the "straighter darker trees."

Frost once said, "Susan Hayes Ward my first discoverer (1893) said I must write for her a girls companion piece to 'Birches' which she took to be for boys; and she would furnish me with the materials. Some years afterward to my own great surprise I found myself doing as she commanded" (Cramer, 70). (*See also* "Wild Grapes.")

FURTHER READING

Bagby, George F. "The Promethean Frost," *Twentieth Century Literature* 38, no. 1 (Spring 1992): 1–19.

Barry, Elaine. *Robert Frost on Writing.* New Brunswick, N.J.: Rutgers University Press, 1973.

Cramer, Jeffrey S. *Robert Frost among His Poems: A Literary Companion to the Poet's Own Biographical*

Contexts and Associations. Jefferson, N.C.: MacFarland, 1996.

Frost, Robert. "On 'Birches.'" In *Robert Frost Collected Poems, Prose, & Plays,* edited by Richard Poirier and Mark Richardson New York: Library of America.

Hass, Robert. *Going by Contraries: Robert Frost's Conflict with Science.* Charlottesville: University Press of Virginia, 2002.

Isitt, Larry. "Dark Climber: Robert Frost's Spiritual Ambivalence in 'Birches,'" *Robert Frost Review* (Fall 1994): 13–16.

Kilcup, Karen. "Something of a Sentimental Sweet Singer: Robert Frost, Lucy Larcom, and 'Swinging Birches.'" In *Roads Not Taken: Rereading Robert Frost,* edited by Earl J. Wilcox and Jonathan N. Barron, 11–31. Columbia: University of Missouri Press, 2000.

Monteiro, George. *Robert Frost and the New England Renaissance.* Lexington: University Press of Kentucky, 1988.

Parini, Jay. *Robert Frost: A Life.* New York: Holt, 1999.

"Birthplace, The" (1928)

In "The Birthplace" Frost describes a mountaintop where "my father built" and the family made a home. The human tendency to subdue and enclose nature is described in pleasant patriarchal terms. The father's job is to rein in nature and to make it amenable to the family's presence in it. In this instance, the feminine mountain is an even greater parent to the family, generously allowing them to situate themselves temporarily in her lap. Katherine Kearns points out that the "human mother is simply absent from the poem, so that the dozen children seem raised up from the cultivated ground" (19). In this way the poem can be read as not only patriarchal but dismissive of women's role in parenting. But the poem seems less concerned with relationships between men and women than with the relationship between human and nature, the ultimate matriarchal force, which is greater than any human patriarchy. Here the mountain, like any parent, when she has had enough of the rough

housing of a "dozen girls and boys," pushes them "off her knees." While the mountain seemed to "like the stir" for "a little while," with "always something in her smile," she ultimately returns to herself and is once again "full of trees."

The descriptions here are pleasant: Nature is not rough on us, and we are kind to her, even when we are attempting to control her. Our attempts at control have only temporary value in a world where we are transient and nature seems eternal, however. The poem is a reminder that we are simply passing through. Houses last only as long as nature allows. And nature's memory, apparently unlike ours, is fleeting. Once we are gone, there is little trace of what, in the grand scheme of things, was our brief time. If asked today, the speaker reminds us, the mountain "wouldn't know our name." While he playfully points out that of course a woman's name would have changed with marriage, revealing yet again a patriarchal approach and placing the poem in a somewhat historical context, he largely is recording our transience. Frost reflects in a similar way to the poet Horace Smith, who wrote in his "Ozymandias," "What powerful but unrecorded race / Once dwelt in that annihilated place."

Mark Richardson argues that in Frost "There is a hatred of being controlled disciplined, managed—in a word, a hatred of being made, apparently, 'feminine' . . . [and] by the same token an admiration for those who control, discipline, and manage—whether mowers and plowers, poets, or politicians." Richardson demonstrates that "The Birthplace" is a keen example of such admiration (218). Ironically, the patriarchal poet resumes control by writing in poetry the memory of the birthplace and recording it for at least a bit longer than the place on the mountaintop. Perhaps this is how there is "ever any hope."

The poem was first published in June 1923 in the *Dartmouth Bema* and was later collected in *West-Running Brook.*

FURTHER READING

Kearns, Katherine. "The Serpent's Tale." In *Robert Frost,* Modern Critical Views, edited by Harold Bloom, 179–180. Philadelphia: Chelsea House, 2003.

Richardson, Mark. "Frost's Poetics of Control." In *The Cambridge Companion to Robert Frost*, edited by Robert Faggen, 197–219. Cambridge: Cambridge University Press, 2001.

"Black Cottage, The" (1914)

One of Frost's many narrative poems appearing in his second book, *North of Boston,* which opens with "Mending Wall" and "Death of the Hired Man," "The Black Cottage" presents a scene that is more complex than it might at first appear. The poem has much in common with William Wordsworth's "Ruined Cottage," including similarities in form as well as content. In Frost's poem the narrator and a minister are out walking, a familiar image in Frost, though the narrator is usually unaccompanied, when they happen upon a little cottage of which they were apparently already speaking. It seems that a discussion of the cottage had arisen in the form of a sermon and was already half through at the start of the poem.

The conversation that follows takes up the family who inhabited the place: originally a woman, her husband, and two boys. The cottage has since been abandoned, first by the father, then by the boys, and then by the woman when she died, but speculation about the life they led remains. The minister asserts "how forsaken / A little cottage" it has always seemed by the "world's having passed it by," and possibilities as to the sermon's veiled purpose begin to emerge. While the focus seems to be on the family, the poem is far more philosophically inclined: The minister asks the narrator to sit down on the stoop if he is in "no haste" so that they might "measure how far fifty years ha[s] brought [them]." The minister speculates that they, too, might have passed the little cottage by, just as they were about to at the start of the poem, and so there is an attempt to slow the world down a bit and allow time for reflection not only on the family but on themselves and life.

Earlier in the poem the minister confuses Gettysburg and Fredericksburg, recognizing that it "makes a difference which" but neglecting to clarify at which battle the patriarch of the family "fell." The geography of the cottage is hard to discern because of this, since Gettysburg is the site of a major Union Army Civil War victory, whereas Fredericksburg is the site of one of the bloodiest Union defeats by the Confederates. The minister later says that the old woman had seen Garrison or Whittier. (William Lloyd Garrison was an abolitionist leader, whereas John Greenleaf Whittier was an American poet whose work reflected his opposition to slavery as well as his nostalgia about New England.) The minister seems to set this information aside and instead points out that "One wasn't long in learning that [the old woman] thought / Whatever else the Civil War was for, / It wasn't just to keep the States together, / Nor just to free the slaves, though it did both." He shares that she would not or, more appropriately, could not believe "those ends enough / To have given outright for them all she gave," evoking the memory of the countless soldiers who have died for America's progress.

The minister points out that we are "so removed / From the world's view today of all those things" and that Thomas Jefferson's Declaration of Independence is a "hard mystery"—"What did he mean?" he asks. There is a question here of what all the fighting has been for. What is it to be independent, and what is the worth of equality? The minister says, "Each age will have to reconsider it" and "it will trouble us a thousand years." But after this reflection, he returns to the old woman and her philosophy. First, she could not be told what the West or the South was saying because she "had some art of hearing and yet not / Hearing the latter wisdom of the world." She knew only white folks, having seen only a few black ones and no "yellow," presumably Asian, ones ever. Like Zora Neale Hurston's image of God as the "Great Stuffer of Bags" from her essay "How It Feels to Be Colored Me," here the minister demonstrates the old woman's reasoning about race: "how could they be made so very unlike / By the same hand working in the same stuff?" The minister oddly wonders what can be done with such a person, saying that it is "strange how such innocence gets its own way."

The minister comes off as oddly critical of the woman's innocence, but at the same time he embraces it. He says that he "wouldn't be surprised" if in the end innocence would be the "force that would at last prevail," suggesting that he thinks it should not be. He goes on to speculate about the younger churchgoers and nonchurchgoers, "Whom we all have to think of nowadays" (an allusion to the decrease in religiously inclined people in the modern world), and begins talking about changing "the Creed." He suggests that the woman kept him from changing it, even though the words "descended into Hades" seem "too pagan to our liberal youth." The minister is caught between moving forward with new ideas and hanging back with old ones. He seems to be inclined toward the former but resigned to the latter, if only for that "bonnet in the pew" (certainly not for any religious conviction, as Robert Faggen points out).

Ultimately the minister resolves that he is glad the old woman kept him from making a change, and this is where the import of the poem comes clear. Frost's poems are rarely without a philosophical element, and here the philosophy is plain enough: "Why abandon a belief / Merely because it ceases to be true. / Cling to it long enough, and not a doubt / It will turn true again, for so it goes. / Most of the change we think we see in life / Is due to truths being in and out of favor." These lines may explain why it did not matter to the minister whether it was Fredericksburg or Gettysburg, Garrison or Whittier. As Blanford Parker notes, the minister uses the discussion of the old lady as a "pretext for ruing the loss of the moral and religious values of the old abolitionist Protestants who were then almost extinct" (192).

Frost does not embrace the minister's view of truth, even while he reports it; instead, he calls attention to tradition and the weakness of holding tradition as its own argument, whether it be in relation to human sacrifice, war, equality, or religion, as described in the poem. The minister holds that he would prefer to be "a monarch of a desert land" if only because it would be so "walled" that no one would come along to "force change on." In this way the narrator's sermon begins to override the minister's. What is it to be master of no one? If one needs to gain dominion over an uninhabited land in order to bear "truth," then how true can that

truth be? Certainly an unquestioning populace, an innocent populace, is not the most discerning.

Perhaps the minister, as religious representative, is meant to be synecdochically a representation of God, wishing to be master to the ignorant who ask no questions. In this interpretation the "babe born to the desert" at the end of the poem could be in some way connected to Jesus, and the poem could be an example of Frost's questioning of his own faith. The poem is complex in its use of the black cottage, possibly as a symbol for an abandoned church. The sons do not return to where they "were boys" and innocently embraced religion, and what 50 years has brought in human history, meaning, and truth remains obscure at the end of the poem.

The sermon ends when unaccommodating nature interferes. The narrator and minister are forced away by the threat of the bees in the wall. The "fierce heads" look out, much as those who question the truth do, and time goes on as the sunset continues to blaze on abandoned windows, leaving an image of material things that withstand time, maybe more than progress.

That the minister's sentiment also shares something with Frost's lines from "Into My Own": "They would not find me changed from him they knew—Only more sure of all I thought was true"; the woman's sacrifice, which she gave "outright," can be compared to "we gave ourselves outright" from "The Gift Outright."

FURTHER READING

Allen, Margaret. "'The Black Cottage': Robert Frost and the Jeffersonian Ideal of Equality." In *Frost Centennial Essays,* edited by Jac L. Tharpe, 221–229. Jackson: University Press of Mississippi, 1974.

Barron, Jonathan N. "A Tale of Two Cottages: Frost and Wordsworth." In *Roads Not Taken: Rereading Robert Frost,* edited by Earl J. Wilcox and Jonathan N. Barron, 132–152. Columbia: University of Missouri Press, 2000.

Faggen, Robert. *Robert Frost and the Challenge of Darwin.* Ann Arbor: University of Michigan Press, 1997.

Parker, Blanford. "Frost and the Meditative Lyric." In *The Cambridge Companion to Robert Frost,* edited by

Robert Faggen, 179–196. Cambridge: Cambridge University Press, 2001.

Schiffbauer, Judith P. "Three Poems by Robert Frost: A Jamesian Reading," *Kentucky Philological Review* 8 (1993): 46–52.

"Blueberries" (1914)

First appearing in *North of Boston*, "Blueberries" is an anthropological study of New England characters who spy, gossip, and conspire together against their neighbor Patterson. Frost masters dialogue in the piece, moving smoothly between a speaker and listener. The voices discuss the blueberries "as big as the end of your thumb / Real sky-blue, and heavy" that can be found in Loren Patterson's pasture. The listener is not quite sure what part of the pasture the speaker means, and the speaker has a hard time explaining exactly where the plump berries can be found. The speaker describes the blueberry's heartiness and its ability to grow just about anywhere. He speculates that they "fatten their fruit" on charcoal and suggests that perhaps that is why they are ebony skinned. The subtle shade of blue that makes them a blueberry and not a blackberry, Frost writes, is simply a "mist from the breath of the wind."

The speaker and listener question whether Patterson knows what he has, and they resolve that a chewink, or a ground robin, will gather the berries for him if he does not know. Soon the speculation turns from the blueberries to Loren, his polite but wary way, and his many children. Loren "thought a big thought" and said "I have left those there berries, I shrewdly suspect, / To ripen too long. I am greatly to blame." Rather than accuse his neighbor of stealing his berries or plotting to steal them, Loren simply points out that they are overripe and in need of picking and that he is to blame if they are plucked by someone else. Loren's social position is highlighted: He has many children and apparently is not well off. He feeds his children wild berries "they say," and those they do not eat they sell "and buy shoes for their feet."

The listener asserts that it is no matter what "they say," dismissing gossip and hearsay and putting a fine spin on the berry eating and lack of work in the lines "taking what Nature is willing to give, / Not forcing her hand with harrow and plow." There is an appreciation for living off the land, but these two gossipers are most aware that they do not have the same skills as Loren Patterson. They are envious; they want to know what half "the flock of them know" about finding berries in "bogs" and elsewhere. That Patterson lives off the land without much trouble or effort spites those to whom berry finding and picking does not come so easily.

The neighbors assume that Patterson is covert, intentionally hiding his berry-picking places. They call him a "rascal," and the speaker says he managed to "keep a straight face" once when asked "if he knew any fruit to be had / For the picking." The New England portrait is further refined by the use of colloquialisms and dialect in Patterson's repetition of "I'm sure—I'm sure" and his reference to his wife as Mame.

With each stanza the neighbors work themselves up a bit more. All their speculation has caused them to imagine Patterson undercutting them, so they decide they will pick in his pasture to prove he is mistaken if he "thinks all the fruit that grows wild is for him."

But these two do not regularly pick berries; indeed it has been so long that they do not quite remember how, but they are going to do it nonetheless, just to show they can, just to compete with Patterson.

Berry picking has an ethereal quality in this poem. In the penultimate stanza the two recall a time when they temporarily lost themselves, and each other, while berry picking (suggesting that the two voices are husband and wife). They are assured that this time they will not get lost, since they will have company, Patterson's children, but they "won't complain."

The poem concerns itself with borders between neighbors and property rights in much the same way that "Mending Wall" does, but it also has a playfulness and absurdity that gives the poem a less serious tone. The allusions to two kinds of jewels (the drops glistening on the berries and the berries themselves) and earlier to berries springing up as unexplainably as a "conjuror's trick" create a magical undertone.

The "vision for thieves" with which the poem ends is a reminder of what the poem has been: a vision of thieves. It introduces co-conspirators, a husband and wife trying to outsmart their neighbor, who is said, absurdly, to live and raise a large family on wild berries alone. This image of New England characters and of what it means to live off the land flies in the face of the hard work that Frost, a not very successful farmer, knew all too well farming and rural life to be. Although there are themes of distrust, conspiracy, and conniving in the poem, it becomes by its end more of a farce than a drama.

Jeffrey Cramer reports that, according to Frost, the poem was written in 1912 and was probably inspired by Frost's childhood memories of being on his father's aunt and uncle's farm in Amherst, New Hampshire. His great-aunt and great-uncle supplemented their income by picking and selling wild berries; Frost and his sister Jeanie helped them pick and accompanied them on the ride by wagon to the neighboring town of Milford to sell the berries.

FURTHER READING

Cramer, Jeffrey S. *Robert Frost among His Poems: A Literary Companion to the Poet's Own Biographical Contexts and Associations.* Jefferson, N.C.: MacFarland, 1996.
Goede, William. "The 'Code-Hero' in Frost's 'Blueberries.'" *Discourse* 11 (1968): 33–41.

"Blue-Butterfly Day" (1923)

Possibly an updated version of William Wordsworth's "To a Butterfly," "Blue-Butterfly Day" is a lyric that celebrates, though not without reserve, the first hint of spring. The first stanza juxtaposes such "sky-flakes" with the snowflakes of winter, and states that there is "more unmixed color on the wing" of these early butterflies than on any of the flowers in early spring. The spring azure butterfly, also known as *Celastrina ladon,* is blue and may be the butterfly Frost describes; they are common in early spring in the Northeast and are commonly found on roadsides.

In the second stanza, Frost, like the haiku poet Matsuo Bashō (1644–94), who makes red pepper pods into dragonflies by adding wings to them, makes these butterflies "flowers that fly and all but sing." These lines suggest the transient lives of butterflies, whose brief lifespans allow them to ride out their "desire" only through propagation. The poem also evokes the fleeting quality of spring: The constant threat in April in New England that spring will not be without several more frosty nights is apparent. The soggy ground of a recent winter's thaw becomes Frost's "April mire."

In the final two lines, the butterflies "lie closed over in the wind and cling, / Where wheels have freshly sliced the April mire," and truth breaks in, as it does in "Birches." The desperately clinging butterflies, whose wings close to preserve warmth, are seemingly at the end of their short lives. The image of wheels in the final line also casts a dark shadow on the intrusion of technology on what was initially an idyllic nature scene.

The poem was first published in the March 16, 1921, issue of the *New Republic* and was later included in *New Hampshire. See* TECHNOLOGY.

FURTHER READING

Faggen, Robert. *Robert Frost and the Challenge of Darwin.* Ann Arbor: University of Michigan, 1997.
Henderson, Harold G. *An Introduction to Haiku.* New York: Doubleday & Co., 1958.
Monteiro, George. *Robert Frost and the New England Renaissance.* Lexington: University Press of Kentucky, 1988.

"Blue Ribbon at Amesbury, A" (1936)

First appearing in the *Atlantic Monthly* in April 1936, and then later that year in *A Further Range* with the subtitle, "Small Plans Gratefully Heard Of," this poem depicts a prize-winning "pullet," a young hen who won the blue ribbon, the top prize, at Amesbury. Jeffrey Meyers says the poem "celebrates the appearance" of Frost's own "prizewinner at a poultry show northeast of Lawrence" (53). Amesbury, Massachusetts, is roughly 20 miles northeast of Lawrence, Massachusetts, and it has been holding its annual "Amesbury Days" celebration since the turn of the 20th century, so the biographical connection is likely.

The prize hen of the poem is well "coiffured" with all her "fluff of plumage," but there is something to her character as well, and in her we "make ourselves acquainted / With one a Sewell might have painted." Franklane Sewell (d. 1945), an illustrator of fowl whose work appeared in *The Eastern Poultryman* and *Farm-Poultry,* is the source for this reference. The painter Robert Van Vorst Sewell (1860–1924) may not be an unlikely candidate either.

When the hen returns home she is "common with the flock again," and while she "lingers at the feeding trough" her keeper "lingers too," meditating on the "breeder's art." He is enthralled with his hen and considers starting with her "a race" so grand "That shall all living things displace." The description of the hen's character that follows is humanized. She works for the biblical six days and rests one, during which she may even "score" one of her "egg-success[es]" that is a most remarkable "vehicle of seed." This hen is the "last to mount" the roost, not letting the "night drive her off." Although she is kept and flying to her roost is "her extent of flight," she has the spirit to move the "whole flock along," and in this way she is the shepherd.

Frost considers the eminence of a winning hen by humanizing her and questioning what winning has done to change her plight, as well as reflecting on the hen keeper's scheming. The "lowly pen" still contains the hen, prize-winning or not, and while it protects her from the night and the snow, she is not contented, as she is without a "complacent chirr." At the same time, the keeper, much like the greatest shepherd of his flock, God, concerns himself with his "plan" for a perfect design. The religious references cannot be ignored, from "Mother Eve" to the design of a race.

FURTHER READING

Meyers, Jeffrey. *Robert Frost: A Biography.* New York: Houghton Mifflin, 1996.

"Boeotian" (1942)

"Boeotian" first appeared in *A Witness Tree.* Boeotia was an ancient region of Greece, north of Attica and the Gulf of Corinth, and was the home of the poet Hesiod. Just as in "The Bear," here Frost evokes Plato. This time, rather than pacing back and forth between "agreeing with one Greek" and "agreeing with another," Frost instead "toys" with the "Platonic notion / That wisdom need not be of Athens Attic." Frost also toys with the word *attic,* since it is used as a synonym for Athens and also refers to the dialect of Attica, in which the bulk of classical Greek literature is written.

The four-line poem appears in a grouping called "Quantula," along with other pithy poems, which suggests that Frost intended them to be together because of their small "quantity" and presumed force. (In Latin, *quantula* means "How little?" or "How small?") In it, Frost asserts that if wisdom is practical then it cannot also be transcendental, as Plato supposes, and that if it is not laconic and practical, then he at least does not want it to be systematic (for Plato, wisdom was completely systematic). Frost seems to push his assertion further by asserting that wisdom could "even [be] "Boeotian." By saying that he likes to "toy" with the Platonic notion, he dismisses the idea of the transcendental as a basis for wisdom as rubbish, but it is something that can amuse him the way a mouse does a cat.

See PHILOSOPHY.

FURTHER READING

Pritchard, William H. *Frost: A Literary Life Reconsidered.* New York: Oxford University Press, 1984.

"Bond and Free" (1916)

In "Bond and Free" a clear distinction is drawn between love and thought, heart and mind. At the start, love appears to be the weaker of the two. Love is described as clinging and having walls: "wall within wall to shut fear out." It is vulnerable and self-protective. Thought, however, is strong and does not have to protect itself; its substance is its own protection. While love is a bond, "with hills and circling arms about," thought is free and can soar on its "pair of dauntless wings."

Regardless of where the speaker wanders, snow or sand or turf, he finds that love has made an imprint and left a "trace." This imprint is seen as "straining in the world's embrace." Thought, in contrast, is not shackled; it is able to shake its "ankles free." Love is seemingly not described in positive terms, then. It is confining and restraining. And thought is superior to love as it provides freedom that takes us out of this world in the third stanza, when it "cleaves the interstellar gloom / And sits in Sirius' disc all night." (Sirius is the "dog" star that follows Orion.) But, oddly, thought only cleaves in the night. In the day it must "retrace [its] flight." And in doing so it returns with the "smell of burning on every plume," like Icarus, the son of Daedelus. In mythology Icarus flew too close to the sun, despite his father's warning, and caused his wax wings to melt, plunging him into the sea.

The closing stanza, not uncharacteristically, contradicts the first part of the poem. Love, by staying close to home, by being earthly, fares better than thought. Thought seeks "in another star" what can apparently be found right here on Earth—namely, love—and love is "glad to be" found here. This reflects the same sentiment that can be found in "Birches," the poem that follows "Bond and Free" in *Mountain Interval*, where Frost asserts that "Earth's the right place for love." In "Bond and Free," while thought's "gains in heaven are what they are" (the speaker does not tell us what they are), Frost is still more comfortable with what he knows.

The poem suggests a dichotomy between love and thought in which love holds the inferior position at the start of the poem but by the end gains the upper hand. Thought is made masculine in the poem, while love is feminine. The superiority of thought to love that is expressed early on perhaps reflects a misogynistic viewpoint, but this is complicated and even turned on its head by the end of the poem. If love is considered irrational and needy and thought is considered reasonable and free, then thought is likely to be embraced over love. But if

love is what is known here on Earth and thought is indicative of otherworldly concerns that cannot be "known," then love becomes transcendent. It is also possible that the kind of love that exceeds earthly boundaries is not equal to, as strong as, or as gainful as the love people can have for one another. One way to interpret the unflattering allusion to Icarus in the description of thought is that the kind of thought that embraces the transcendent will suffer similar consequences.

The poem first appeared in *Mountain Interval*. See MYTHOLOGY AND FOLKLORE, STARS, and WALLS.

FURTHER READING

Bagby, George F. "The Promethean Frost," *Twentieth Century Literature* 38, no. 1 (Spring 1992): 1–19.

Doyle, John Robert, Jr. *The Poetry of Robert Frost.* New York: Hafner Press, 1962.

Marcus, Mordecai. "Robert Frost's 'Bond and Free': Structure and Meaning," *Concerning Poetry* 8, no. 1 (1975): 61–64.

"Bonfire, The" (1916)

One of two poems read before the Phi Beta Kappa Society at Harvard's commencement in 1916 (the other was "The Ax-Helve"), this ghost story frightens the narrator as much as the children. "Oh, let's go up the hill and scare ourselves," he says, and this is not the first time the poet has scared himself. In "Desert Places," he admits that he has it in him "so much nearer home / To scare [him]self with [his] own desert places." Lawrance Thompson writes in his biography of Frost that in April 1905, the "best bonfire of all . . . got away." While Frost was performing the ritual of burning dead leaves and branches in Derry, a bonfire was blown out of control, only contained partly by a stone wall and dirt road, and Frost ended up putting it out with his coat and pails of water from Hyla Brook. The bonfire here seems to draw on that experience and on the fear it must have instilled.

The narrator wants to do all but "bring to life this old volcano," so he talks about building a bonfire so large that people will be brought to their windows.

The children, looking up at and to him, wonder if such a bonfire will scare him, too. He admits that it will, and this clearly does not offer reassurance to the children, nor does it to the speaker. He admits that of course a fire that only "itself can put out" is a frightening prospect, and this leads him to recall a time, "upon an April," when playing with fire, "[t]here came a gust," and control was lost. But the gust was no mere coincidence: "Something or someone watching made that gust," and there is a suggestion that an omnipotent force had a hand in the "black that spread like black death." Nature is never without purpose in Frost; it is a constant palpable threat, and its gestures are frequently presented as both thoughtful and intentional. The narrator mentions Hyla Brook, a brook by Frost's old farm in Derry, which provides the title of another of his poems, while juxtaposing fire with water, water being the only trusted barrier to the fire.

The children inquire, "If it scares you, what will it do to us?" and the narrator offers no comfort: "Scare you," he says. But he soon reveals that he needs comforting, too, and that he would like to know what the children would "say to war if it should come." The children are quick to respond that "war's not for children, it's for men," and this launches the narrator into a lecture. He haunts the children and the reader with the italicized, emphatic words *War is for everyone, for children too.*" The narrator ends up scaring the children long before they get to the bonfire by pointing out that war itself is a conflagration: It starts up unexpectedly, spreads, and is soon beyond anyone's control, leaving behind nothing but scorched earth.

The poem is a fireside ghost story, but it is preemptive: It occurs before the fire, and it talks of war's effects on children, not just on men. It is a frightening tale, but, like war, it is not make-believe. Frost offers a critique of war and observes that adults are no more knowledgeable than children: "your mistake was ours," he says. It seems that his scaring is meant to impart wisdom. He is the grown child facing the possibility of war, and he wants to prepare the children somehow for that same reality. He wants them to know that everybody is harmed in war, not only adults, and that war is no more controllable than fire. He haunts the children with

images of bombers "opening clouds at night with droning speed." People do not need ghost tales to frighten them; humanity can scare itself with itself, and does so repeatedly. War is not new and war for children is not new, but human memory is short, and people easily forget. Frost writes that he "mustn't" tell the children about reality, but he already has. Like the fire and war, the speaker is uncontrolled in his telling. The truth is blurted out before he knows it, and before he and the children have gone up the hill.

"The best way is to come up hill with me / And have our fire and laugh and be afraid" says the narrator, and we realize that he wants to remove reality and hold it at arm's length. He wants to be able to laugh at the fire, at war, at humanity and its horrors, but in the end he is afraid, for himself and for the children.

The poem was first published in November 1916 in *The Seven Arts* and was collected later that year in *Mountain Interval.*

FURTHER READING

Kearns, Katherine. *Robert Frost and a Poetics of Appetite.* Cambridge: Cambridge University Press, 1994.

Monteiro, George. *Robert Frost and the New England Renaissance.* Lexington: University Press of Kentucky, 1988.

Thompson, Lawrance. *Robert Frost: The Early Years.* New York: Holt, Rinehart, and Winston, 1966.

"Boundless Moment, A" (1923)

"He" and "I," out walking in March, suspect they see a "Paradise-in-bloom." Frost's capitalizing and hyphenating suggest that the term is the name of a flower. It is more likely that he is playfully creating a new term, referring to spring as a sort of paradise, as close as possible to the paradise of Adam and Eve. This apparition appears out of a desire for winter's end on one of those March days that are "fair enough for flowers" but still halt us in the wind. March is the month when winter in New England has overstayed its welcome and residents are ready for spring. These two fellows are "too ready to believe the most" when they see something "far in the maples." It is a "boundless moment" because their imaginations take them beyond seasonal boundaries to the possibility of "a strange world," where in March "such white luxuriance of May" as a paradise-in-bloom can be theirs.

These two characters have deceived themselves for the moment, but truth breaks in, as it does with the ice storm in "Birches," and they must move on, fully aware that the "ghost" was simply a "young beech clinging to its last year's leaves." In Frost, we are consistently reminded, as we are here, that it is not we but nature making the decisions, in command.

The poem was first published in the October 24, 1923, issue of the *New Republic* and was later included in *New Hampshire.*

FURTHER READING

Poirier, Richard. *Robert Frost: The Work of Knowing.* New York: Oxford University Press, 1977.

Boy's Will, A (1913)

Frost's first commercially published book was printed in 1913 by David Nutt of London and was dedicated to his wife Elinor. Frost was so exhilarated that he wrote to friend and former student John Bartlett on January 30, 1913, and included a set of page proofs of the not-yet-printed book. The note accompanying it talked about how the book was "pretty near being the story of five years" of his life. He felt that the first poem of the book, "Into My Own" represented how he "went away from people (and college)," and "Tuft of Flowers" showed how he "came back to them." The book was to "plot a curved line of flight," as he wrote in his "Preface to Poems in *This Is My Best.*" Frost had used "Tuft of Flowers" to get his job at Pinkerton Academy, he once said, just as "little Tommy Tucker sang for his supper."

One of the first responses to the book was Ezra Pound's, which can be found in a letter to Alice Corbin Henderson, assistant of Harriet Monro of *Poetry* magazine: "Have just discovered another Amur'kn. Vurry Amurk'n, with, I think, the seeds of grace" (Parini, 128). Pound's declaration was something akin to Emerson's of Whitman: "I greet you at the beginning of a great career." Frank F. S. Flint also offered a favorable review. He admired Frost's "direct observation of the object and immediate correlation with the emotion—spontaneity, subtlety in the evocation of moods, humour" and his "ear for silences" (Meyers, 102). Flint had thought that each poem was the expression of one mood, or one emotion, or one idea, and it seems that he may have had such poems as "Into My Own," "Waiting," and "Reluctance," in mind. Norman Douglas of the *English Review* wrote that there was a "wild, racy flavour" to Frost's poems and that "they sound that inevitable response to nature which is the hall-mark of true lyric feeling" (Thornton, 21).

The first edition of the book included glosses, or explanatory epigraphs, accompanying each poem. They were not included in later editions. An American edition of the book was not available until 1915, when Henry Holt and Company of New York issued it simultaneously with *North of Boston.* The title was derived from the refrain in Henry Wadsworth Longfellow's "My Lost Youth": "'a boy's will is the wind's will, / And the thoughts of youth are long, long thoughts.'" The nod to Longfellow demonstrated the kinship Frost felt with earlier American writers who also had made the American landscape and its themes central to their work.

Mark Richardson writes that *A Boy's Will* should be regarded "as an effort on Frost's part to find a voice among his poetic predecessors, not only of the nineteenth century but of earlier ones as well." Many of the poems in this first volume, perhaps more so than any of Frost's later collections, allude to the poems of the poets who preceded Frost, among them William Shakespeare, William Wordsworth, Thomas Hardy, Emily Dickinson, and others.

The book, while indicative of many of the themes associated with Frost, such as rural life, nature, individuality, philosophy, and others, does not contain many of his most anthologized poems, but it does hold some gems, such as "Into My Own,"

"The Vantage Point," and "Reluctance." The book has many strengths as it establishes Frost's voice (if a somewhat more youthful and indebted one), his subject matter, and his skill. Lewis H. Miller, Jr., describes the design of the book as "thematic and dramatic" and holds that it "is unique to the Frost canon in its portrayal of a young, often immature speaker who develops and ripens as the poems unfold" (351). An unsigned review from September 20, 1913, read, "We do not need to be told that the poet is a young man: the dew and the ecstasy—the audacity, too—of pristine vision are here" (Greenberg and Hepburn, 45).

A Boy's Will was Frost's first triumph, and without it he could not have gone on to publish the large number of immortal poems of the later books.

FURTHER READING

Haynes, Donald T. "The Narrative Unity of A Boy's Will," Publications of the Modern Language Association of America 87, no. 3 (May 1972): 452–464.

Meyers, Jeffrey. Robert Frost: A Biography. New York: Houghton Mifflin, 1996.

Miller, Lewis H., Jr. "Design and Drama in A Boy's Will." In Frost: Centennial Essays, edited by Jac Tharpe, 351–368. Jackson: University Press of Mississippi, 1974.

Parini, Jay. Robert Frost: A Life. New York: Holt, 1999.

Richardson, Mark. The Ordeal of Robert Frost: The Poet and his Poetics. Chicago: University of Illinois Press, 1997, 104–109.

Sanders, David. "Frost's North of Boston, Its Language, Its People, Its Poet," Journal of Modern Literature 27, nos. 1–2 (Fall 2003): 70–78.

Thornton, Richard, ed. Recognition of Robert Frost: Twenty-fifth Anniversary. New York: Holt, 1937.

"Unsigned Review of A Boy's Will." In Robert Frost: An Introduction, edited by Robert A. Greenberg, and James G. Hepburn, 45–46. New York: Holt, Rinehart and Winston, 1961.

"Bravado" (1947)

See "FIVE NOCTURNES."

"Broken Drought, The" (1947)

This poem first appeared in the April 1947 issue of the Atlantic Monthly with the title "But He Meant It" and was later included in Steeple Bush in a grouping called "Editorials." The sonnet exposes a prophet who has been predicting a "disaster": a serious drought. But the rain begins to fall "outside the hall," causing the prophet to cease his "shout[ing]." While the rainfall is "stingy" and not a downpour, it still clearly hurts the prophet's "theory of the drought." The crowd cheers loudly for the rain, and Frost writes that the prophet "did as Shakespeare says . . . / Good orators will do when they are out," and that is "spit"; he is alluding to act 4, scene 1, from As You Like It, where Rosalind says, "Very good orators, when they are out, they will spit."

The prophet, while flustered, maintains his ground, holding that "no spit of rain" could cure the drought he was predicting, for it "was the drought of deserts." He is unconvinced that there is salvation in the rain because he still believes that Earth will soon be as "uninhabitable as the moon." The closing couplet does not resolve matters; rather, the poem closes with questions: "What for that matter had it ever been? / Who advised man to come and live therein?"

The poem moves from the embarrassment of the prophet to the question of who thought to come to Earth in the first place—as if to suggest that human beings came from somewhere else. It also suggests that Earth, perhaps because it is subject to such environmental strains as droughts, has always been somewhat uninhabitable. And if humans were indeed "advised" to come to Earth, that advice was hardly good. It seems that once again Frost is questioning the notion of a benevolent creator.

The Shakespearean sonnet has an AB/AB, CD/CD, EF/EF, GG rhyme scheme. Here Frost employs an AB/BA, CC/DD, EF/FE, GG rhyme scheme, and some of the rhymes are "eye rhymes," such as "been" and "therein."

FURTHER READING

Maxson, H. A. *On the Sonnets of Robert Frost: A Critical Examination of the 37 Poems.* Jefferson, N.C.: McFarland, 1997.

"Brook in the City, A" (1923)

When houses were first given numbers, it was a clear indication of population growth and industrialization. There was no need for house numbers when towns were made up of a few families and when everyone in a town knew the names of all the members of each family. In "A Brook in the City" the poet questions that shift from an agricultural to an industrial nation and the shift from rural life to city life with the displacement of a farmhouse and a country brook.

The poem opens with the image of a farmhouse that was once held in the "elbow-crook" of a brook, but a city has now grown around it. The brook, too, has been affected; it has been transformed into a city sewer. The speaker is "one who knew the brook" and once "dipped a finger length" in it. He wonders how a brook with such "strength" and "impulse," how such "an immortal force" could be so controlled and tamed as a city brook. And he speculates that no one will ever know "except for ancient maps" that the brook once ran free, as a part of nature. In this T. S. Eliot sort of wasteland, the grass is "cemented down," the apple trees have become firewood, and the brook is trapped in a "dungeon under stone."

The speaker speculates whether keeping the city brook "forever under" makes thoughts rise like water and "keep / This new-built city from both work and sleep."

The poem was first published in the March 9, 1921, issue of *New Republic* and was later collected in *New Hampshire.* Frost once wrote that the brook was partially based on a brook in Greenwich Village.

FURTHER READING

Cramer, Jeffrey S. *Robert Frost among His Poems: A Literary Companion to the Poet's Own Biographical Contexts and Associations.* Jefferson, N.C.: MacFarland, 1996.

"Brown's Descent (Or the Willy-Nilly Slide)" (1916)

Written in iambic tetrameter quatrains and originally read as "The Story of Brown and the Winter Wind," this comical poem appeared first in *Mountain Interval* and is about Brown, who "lived at such a lofty farm" that when he slipped on "the icy crust / That cased the world" he was "gone!" Frost evokes the childish side of us, that part of us that forever laughs at the man who slips on the banana peel and goes bumbling, tripping, and fumbling along "'cross lots, 'cross walls, 'cross everything." Brown is a figure who all can see "for miles," so when he makes his "wild descent" one night, with his lantern in hand, the speaker imagines him visible to all like a falling star. Brown goes "willy-nilly" down the hill, reeling, lurching, and bobbing, but manages, farcically, to keep his lantern from going out. Both the rhyme scheme and the subject are reminiscent of Wee-Willy Winkle, who ran through the town in his nightgown. Frost once said that he was heavily influenced by Mother Goose, and that influence is never more evident than here.

When Brown comes down "like a coasting child" to the bottom of the "slippery slope" he realizes that he is two miles away from home. Frost uses this as an opportunity to assert the hearty quality of the Yankee, whose "stock" never peters out: They "are what they always were." It is also a moment to reflect on nature and on the human being's capacity to overcome nature. As in "A Tree Fallen across the Road," where nature blocks the sleigh's way, here nature gets in the way, but Brown finds a way around it; he simply cannot get back the way he came. Nature provides constraints and occasionally takes us out of our way, but she does not stop us or interfere with our resolve. Brown never gave up hope: He "bowed with grace to natural law" and then went around nature, "[b]y road."

The speaker reveals that he's "kept Brown standing in the cold / While [he] invested him with reasons," but Brown "snaps his eyes three times" the way Dorothy clicks her slippers in the *Wizard of Oz,* and then he is off. At some point the talking must stop, and then one has to get up and go, the poem seems to say. Talking becomes futile and trivial. The importance of human action when dealing with nature's calamities is highlighted, as is the strength of Yankee character.

According to Jeffrey Cramer, the poem was based on a story Frost had been told of a similar descent made by a man named Goss in Ashland, New Hampshire. Frost wrote in a letter that he did not think it was a "good poem." He claimed that he "sort of did it on purpose to please a few people who gave [him] the subject." See WALLS.

FURTHER READING

Cramer, Jeffrey S. *Robert Frost among His Poems: A Literary Companion to the Poet's Own Biographical Contexts and Associations.* Jefferson, N.C.: MacFarland, 1996.

"Build Soil—A Political Pastoral" (1936)

"Build Soil—A Political Pastoral" was presented at Columbia University in New York City in May 1932, before the political conventions of that year, when the Democrats would nominate Franklin Delano Roosevelt for the first time to run against Herbert Hoover, and in the midst of the Great Depression. It was later collected in *A Further Range,* according to Stanley Burnshaw, against his wife Elinor's advice and because "he wanted to make his position known."

The pastoral, a literary work that idealizes rural life, parodies Virgil's *Eclogue I* (40 B.C.), in which the shepherds Tityrus and Meliboeus, the latter of whom has just lost his farm (Virgil's farm was confiscated in 42 B.C.), discuss the difficulties of city and country life.

In Frost's poem, Meliboeus, the first to speak, talks about being "done forever with potato crops" and moving on to sheep, not because he is planning to sell wool but simply for his own sake—it is clearly a forced move. He will "dress up in sheep's clothing and eat sheep." Frost's sly reference to the muse, the ancient Greeks' mythological inspiration for poetry and the other arts, does not include the conventional epic invocation of her. Instead, Meliboeus makes the tongue-in-cheek, almost matter-of-fact comment that "The Muse takes care of you."

Meliboeus is envious of Tityrus, even if he says, "I don't blame you," because he recognizes a difference between those who "have to work" and those who do not. He urges Tityrus, who can loaf about and live by writing, to have "some pity" and use his "talents as a writer" to "improve food prices" or at least "[g]et in a poem toward the next election."

In this opening stanza, several financial terms such as "interest," "nothing down," and "calculate" evoke overriding concerns of Frost's time. Later in the piece Meliboeus wonders, "Why should I / Have to sell you my apples and buy yours?" and this questioning of what is the "good of commerce" will be prevalent throughout.

Meliboeus comes as the shepherd to Tityrus, who is presented as the philosopher, and the dialogue takes on a Socratic cast. When Meliboeus says of Tityrus, "You live by writing / Your poems on a farm and call that farming," it is quite clear Frost is poking a little fun at himself as poet-farmer.

When Tityrus first speaks, he warns that he has "half a mind / To take a writing hand in politics," which is precisely what Frost is doing. Tityrus wonders whether politics is a fit subject for poetry, and by drawing an analogy between war and politics, he says that politics must be, since war is a popular poetic subject. Meliboeus thinks the "times seem revolutionary bad," and therefore Tityrus wonders if they may have quite possibly "reached a depth / Of desperation that would warrant [poetry]." Tityrus ponders universal poetic themes, such as "joy and grief" and "summer and winter" and whether topical subjects such as who is "guilty" are appropriate to the genre. He holds that "Life may be tragically bad" and that he may "sing it so," but that does not mean that he should "dare / Name names." He makes an example of a political poem. "Whittier's luck with Skipper Ireson awes me," he says, referring to John Greenleaf Whittier's "Skipper Ireson's Ride," a poem about the well-known Captain Floyd Ireson, who in 1808 refused to aid a fishing boat disabled by a nor'easter. The fisherman perished, and justice came to Ireson in the form of tar and feathers. "Build Soil" is an example of how politics and poetry might merge, but Tityrus feels that poetry should steer clear of politics, and "[l]et newspapers profess to fear the worst!" The topical is the enemy of the universal, and yet this is a topical poem.

Before long, however, the conversation turns to socialism, which has been a kind of subtext from the start, when Meliboeus inquires whether it is really a needed reform. Tityrus informs Meliboeus that "we have it now. / For socialism is an element in any government." "There's no such thing as socialism pure," he points out; "there's only democratic socialism."

Once again an analogy to poetry is drawn with a discussion of love, which occurs only between individuals (men and women, friends, parents and children, and so on), and in Socratic style, the conversation wanders a bit before returning to the original question of socialism.

There is an attempt to define what "socialized" means, and Frost's criticisms are quite clear, for "the worst one of all to leave uncurbed, / Unsocialized, is ingenuity." In socialism "none shall be as ambitious as he can. / None should be as ingenious as he could." In his view, socialism, by promoting equality in the distribution of resources, creates a cap on the development of native abilities and individual industriousness. It is suggested that only ill can come of it, and Frost coyly implicates "some chemist at Columbia," his host institution, as a potential threat.

Frost is worried about socialism and wary of foreign entanglements, and this apprehension is expressed throughout. The crux of the poem is contained in the lines in which the speaker declares what has to happen if society is to be set right again: "We're always too much out or too much in / . . . We're so much out that the odds are against our ever getting inside again. / But inside in is where we've got to get." Frost advocates tilling one's own soil, as a farmer and as a nation, when he says that Americans need to be national before they are international, personal before they are interpersonal. He is Virgilian not only in his manner but in his view.

Tityrus resolves, however, that "To market 'tis our destiny to go," but he well knows that some things should never be bought or sold; the land is one of these things. There are poets who "fall all over each other to bring soil" to the market (this appears a criticism of other, supposedly lesser poets), but Tityrus preaches against this. Frost exposes himself here by admitting to his preaching; he is fully aware of what he is up to, and he would not want to give the impression that he is preaching without knowing it. Meliboeus playfully says to Tityrus, "I thought you were already preaching. / But preach on and see if I can tell the difference."

Tityrus does not want to "lure the city to the country," and this echoes to some degree the sentiment of "Christmas Trees." Tityrus believes, and probably Frost did too, that those who should possess the land are "only those, / Who love it." He says the best are those who no matter how abused they are by "business, law, art . . . still hang on." A true love is "strong and stupid." The poem is, to some extent, about the universal theme of love here, even if it claims to be simply a political pastoral. Again the weaving of the two subjects allows for a discussion of poetry as well as politics.

"All reasoning is in a circle," Tityrus concludes, saying matter-of-factly, "that's why the universe is round." While this is flawed reasoning, it makes for a clear explanation of the circular nature of this discussion. The dialogue returns to the idea that only farmers should till the land. Meliboeus is urged to be a "poor castaway of commerce" and to avoid the market at nearly all costs. Our job is to "build the soil" and to "Turn the farm in upon itself / Until it can contain itself no more." We are too much out, because we are losing, through commerce, our own soil. We have to hold on to our roots, keep turning the soil, and nurture and replenish what is ours.

Tityrus was "brought up a state-rights free-trade Democrat," and he calls that "an inconsistency." There cannot be both. People also should not join too many "gangs," outside of nation, family, and perhaps a college. Frost sings "Let me be the one / To do what is done—", and he satirizes current politics and comments on poetry along the way. The poem ends with Meliboeus embracing Tityrus's advice, agreeing that Americans are "too unseparate," and returning to the farm to cut posts or mend fences—typical Frostian rural images.

Roosevelt would use a kind of socialism in an effort to bring the nation out of the Depression, and just as Frost lampoons Roosevelt's New Deal in "An Equalizer," he reveals his conservative bias through the voices of Tityrus and Meliboeus. *See* POLITICS and FARMER, FROST AS.

FURTHER READING

Burnshaw, Stanley. *Robert Frost Himself.* New York: George Braziller, 1986, 60–65.

Claassen, Jo-Marie. "Robert Frost's 'Build Soil': A Modern Text Based on an Ancient Mode, the Pastoral," *Theoria: A Journal of Studies in the Arts, Humanities, and Social Sciences* 65 (October 1985): 1–13.

Hoffman, Tyler. *Robert Frost and the Politics of Poetry.* Hanover, N.H.: Middlebury College Press, 2001, 228–289.

Parini, Jay. *Robert Frost: A Life.* New York: Holt, 1999, 278–283.

Perrine, Laurence. "The Meaning of Frost's 'Build Soil.'" In *Frost Centennial Essays,* edited by Jac Tharpe, 230–235. Jackson: University Press of Mississippi, 1974.

"Bursting Rapture" (1947)

The speaker is sick with worry in this Italian sonnet. He goes to the "physician to complain," but the physician offers little comfort and a stark solution. The shift in American society from an agricultural to an industrial nation is of concern at the start, as it is pointed out that "now 'twas there as elsewhere" a greater societal respect for science and intellectual pursuits than for physical labor and living off the land. There is, as in "A Brook in the City," a worry about this shift, but it is a lesser concern than the possibility that industrialization will lead to self-destruction.

It becomes clear that the speaker is sick with worry not so much about industrialization as about what it brings. Art does not make bombs, science does, and the movement away from farming is what is blamed for the creation of the atomic bomb. The physician's "answer" to the complaint makes up the bulk of the poem. He is at first patronizing with his "There, there," the way a mother might attempt to comfort a small child. Then he is dismissive, suggesting that what the speaker complains of, "all the nations share." But the physician's words take a turn when he says that the "effort is a mounting ecstasy," as if to suggest that there is pleasure to be taken from the bleak possibility of war. There is a mounting fervor that is somehow exquisite and makes one ecstatic. The reality is that, like much pleasure, when it reaches its peak, relief is found "in one burst," and it will be no different in the case of nuclear war.

The cold war concerns expressed place the poem in a particular historical context but are clearly not without relevance today or for the future. The poem demonstrates a significant dispute between humanists and scientists that was indicative of the modern period. Poetry does not kill, and ultimately everyone is worried about where human intelligence is leading.

The cold war concerns also reflect a modest degree of indifference; after all, we "shall see. / That's what a certain bomb was sent to be." And over atomic bombs, we seem to have little control.

This poem first appeared in *Steeple Bush* in a group titled "Editorials." *See* SCIENCE.

FURTHER READING

Thompson, Lawrance. *Robert Frost: The Early Years.* New York: Holt, Rinehart and Winston, 1966, 301.

"[But Outer Space . . .]" (1962)

The six-line poem "[But Outer Space . . .]" satirically takes on the subject of outer space. Frost playfully italicizes the third syllables of three "popul" words, questioning the decision to explore outer space by poking fun at "all the fuss" that the population has made for doing so and holding that outer space is more "pop*ul*ar" than "pop*ul*ous." He suggests that unless outer space is going to offer humanity another place to root itself and thrive, it has significantly less importance than all the fuss over it suggests.

The poem was originally titled "The Astronomer" and was included in a chapbook titled, *A Remembrance Collection of New Poems* (1959) that was created for Frost's 85th birthday celebration at the Waldorf Astoria in New York. The poem was later included in *In the Clearing. See* SCIENCE.

FURTHER READING

Marcus, Mordecai. *The Poems of Robert Frost: An Explication.* Boston: G. K. Hall, 1991.

"Cabin in the Clearing, A" (1962)

This was Frost's 1951 Christmas poem, and it later appeared in *In the Clearing,* its title apparently the inspiration for the book's title. Mist and Smoke are personified and are discussing the inhabitants of an isolated cabin. The poem reads something like a play, and the voices are distinct. Mist is concerned for the people's well-being. While Smoke points out that they have been there "long enough" to clear a space and a path, Mist worries that they do not "know where they are" and fears "they never will." Mist appears as a priestlike figure, worrying existentially for these country folk. Although they are isolated from their neighbors, Mist holds that they are near them "in plight" and that they are all "equally bewildered," drawing attention to the shared position of all human beings and the universal conundrum. Smoke, who is the smoke wafting from the cabin's chimney, is protective of the inhabitants, not wanting their "happiness despaired of." The poet has taken these apparent opposites and juxtaposed their positions, highlighting their similarities as well. The garden Mist is smoke made of water; it is the "damper counterpart of smoke."

Mist, while concerned, is not pessimistic and will not "give them up for lost." Mist points out that it is "no further from their fate" than Smoke, being garden mist just below with smoke just above,

and through this commonality Mist hopes to demonstrate that they share a similar interest in these folks. Smoke suggests that the people turn to Native Americans to ask where they are, apparently because Native Americans are supposed to have a greater connection to nature and a better understanding of humanity's existence. The cabin's inhabitants are apparently neighbors with Native Americans, since Smoke suggests that they have been inhabitants here long enough to learn the "native tongue." But Mist is steadfast in his conclusion that whether looking to Native Americans, nature, or philosophers at the pulpit, humans will be "none the wiser." While we will ask "anyone there is to ask" for an answer as to our existence, we are reminded in this conversation that there is no one who truly knows. Still we have "fond faith" that appears to be "accumulated fact" and that in itself can "take fire and light the world up."

The poem is Darwinian. Smoke says that if we can ever figure out who we are we will know "better" where we are, but finding out who we are "is too much to believe" for we are "too sudden to be credible." If we have evolved, rather than appeared, it will be too much for us "or the on looking world." Human beings are too sudden to feel comfortable with their existence. There is not enough history, so people seek answers everywhere and anywhere they are offered. Mist and Smoke, absences of being, are presented as better able to assess our value and worth, our being, than we are. They also represent the haze that we find ourselves in when contemplating such subjects.

The drops on the eaves "eavesdrop," and this clever turn of phrase makes for much fun in the final lines. The poem closes with Mist and Smoke playing a game of attempting to tell which is "bass," or man, from "soprano," or woman, while listening to the couple talk in the dark, in bed. Mist is pleased that the turning off of the light has "not put their thought out" and is enjoying the groping for answers in the dark.

The poem closes with a grand assertion that none could better appraise than Smoke and Mist the "kindred spirit of an inner haze," recalling the haunting "kindred spider" of "Design."

FURTHER READING

Monteiro, George. *Robert Frost and the New England Renaissance.* Lexington: University Press of Kentucky, 1988, 87–88.

Richardson, Mark. "Frost and the Cold War: A Look at the Later Poetry." In *Roads Not Taken: Rereading Robert Frost,* edited by Earl J. Wilcox and Jonathan N. Barron, 55–77. Columbia: University of Missouri Press, 2000.

Timmerman, John H. *Robert Frost: The Ethics of Ambiguity.* Lewisburg, Pa.: Bucknell University Press, 2002, 125–127.

"Canis Major" (1928)

First published as "On a Star-Bright Night." Like Carl Sandburg's "Fog" that "comes on / little cat feet" and then "sits looking / over harbor and city / on silent haunches," here the constellation "Canis Major" is animated. Canis Major is translated "Greater Dog," and the brightest star in the constellation is Sirius, often called "the dog star," a star that Frost mentions in a few other poems, including "Bond and Free." Here the constellation becomes the "great Overdog" who never stops his dancing. The speaker says that he is himself "a poor underdog," but at least for this night he will bark with the great Overdog, and his bark will be just as strong, even if only human and small. The poem unites human beings with the stars of the universe, making us equal in our "romps through the dark."

The poem was first published in the books section of the *New York Herald Tribune* on March 22, 1925, as "On a Star-Bright Night" and was later collected in *West-Running Brook. See* NIGHT and STARS.

FURTHER READING

Doyle, John Robert, Jr. *The Poetry of Robert Frost: An Analysis.* New York: Hafner Press, 1962, 154–155.

"Carpe Diem" (1942)

In unrhymed iambic trimeters, Frost makes a direct allusion to English poet Robert Herrick's "To the Virgins, to Make Much of Time," whose opening lines read, "Gather ye rosebuds while ye may, / Old Time is still a-flying, / And this same flower that smiles to-day, / To-morrow will be dying." *Carpe diem* is Latin for "seize the day," and, like Herrick, Frost contemplates youth and age and what it is to make much of time. In contrast he concludes that Herrick's "gather-roses" is an "imposed" burden.

"Age" encourages "two quiet children" to be "happy, happy, happy, / And seize the day of pleasure." And the speaker implies how old the theme is while offering a new twist on that same old theme. He questions whether it is better to seize the present after all, or whether life is more lived in the future or the past than in the present. To him the present is "too much for the senses, / Too crowding, too confusing— / Too present to imagine." The present overwhelms us, it is more than we can handle, and he proposes that it is not until we can have some distance from experience that we can begin to "imagine," and make much of those experiences. Imagination is given a higher position than experience, as imagination is what allows for what might have been and what will be.

The children may "go loving," but if they are "overflooded" with happiness they may not know what they have—their minds will be, as Dickinson says, too "near" themselves "to see." Not until they are able to reflect on what they have gained or what they have lost will their experience become valuable. Age is an onlooker: The children are strangers, and he cannot predict whether they will separate or marry, but Age has gained wisdom and knows that whatever the outcome may be, it will be seen as better or worse with time. Jay Parini points out that the poem was written shortly after his wife Elinor's death.

The poem was first published in the September 1938, issue of the *Atlantic Monthly* and was later included in *A Witness Tree.*

FURTHER READING

Parini, Jay. *Robert Frost: A Life.* New York: Holt, 1999, 317.

"Case for Jefferson, A" (1947)

First appearing in *Steeple Bush*, "A Case for Jefferson" criticizes a man named Harrison and says that if he loved this country, he would not want it "made over new." Frost is at his most patriotic here, taking the position that if a person criticizes his country, he is not a true American. Frost makes regional references and references to radical thinkers in order to demonstrate how off-track Harrison is and to show how Harrison changes from "night" to "day." He is "Freudian" and "Marxian," and these are not appropriate positions for an American democrat to take. Frost calls him a "Puritan Yankee through and through" and scoffs at his adopting characteristics not in keeping with his background. He suggests that Harrison is juvenile in his approach, having a "mind hardly out of [its] teens."

It is a political poem that has little merit except to show how patriotic and blind Frost was capable of being, as in his suggestion that change equals "[b]lowing it all to smithereens."

FURTHER READING

Cook, Reginald. *Robert Frost: A Living Voice.* Amherst: University of Massachusetts Press, 1974.

"Case of the United States of America versus Ezra Pound" (1958)

In July, 1943, poet Ezra Pound was indicted for treason for making radio broadcasts in support of the Axis powers in World War II. He was living in Italy at the time but was returned to the United States in November 1945. In February 1946 he was sent to St. Elizabeth's federal psychiatric hospital in Washington, D.C., considered unfit to plead by reason of insanity. In April 1958 the indictment against him was dismissed. Frost was a key figure in the case, advocating on Pound's behalf. This document was read in court by Thurman Arnold on April 18, 1958. In it Frost defends Pound and

speaks on behalf of fellow writers Archibald MacLeish, Ernest Hemingway, and T. S. Eliot. He wrote that none of them could "bear the disgrace" of letting Pound die institutionalized. He wrote that the Department of Justice's decision would "have to be reached more by magnanimity than by logic." Some 50 years earlier, in London, the influential Pound had befriended the young Frost and helpfully championed his poetry. *See also* LITERARY FRIENDS AND ACQUAINTANCES.

FURTHER READING

Jackson, Sarah R. "Made in London: The Robert Frost and Ezra Pound Connection," *Worcester Review* 15, nos. 1–2 (1994): 108–121.

Sokol, B. J. "What Went Wrong between Robert Frost and Ezra Pound," *New England Quarterly* 49, no. 5 (December 1976): 521–541.

"Caveat Poeta" (1955?)

A caveat is a warning (in Latin, "let him beware") or qualification. "Caveat Poeta" cautions that while there may be no better place than academia for a poet to "mew his youth," the young poet must "kee[p] one leg out of the grave" and "look out for himself" because "much goes on in college that is against the spirit" of the poet. The ordinariness of the college mill is a threat to the ingenuity of the poet and the cultivation of his art.

Frost is insightful about academia, advising English departments to treat all students as though they were going to "wind up as scholars." Not much has changed, as first-year English still remains in most colleges the last course in which students are "allowed," or rather required, "to read books like men and women of the world." It is also, as Frost puts it, the course many English professors seize on as their last opportunity to "at least impose a respect for scholarship on the business men." An English department is often the only one at a university that comes in contact with all first-year students. It is not only responsible for teaching students about reading and writing in college but also often attempts to instill in them a lifelong interest in literature.

Frost satirically says that we have to "admit that there aren't enough poets and other artists around to be worth much consideration" and in this way highlights a primary flaw of the academy in regard to artists. Universities are no longer about fostering literary talents if ever they were; they are about a utilitarian appeal to the common denominator. The poet must watch out for himself, because the academy, if it has the chance, will rob him of what is true. "He has less to fear perhaps if what he is out for is writing epics," Frost adds derisively.

Frost turns to conventions and how one cannot help but encounter them. He resolves that they have to "be locked horns with somewhere" and that it "may as well be in school as anywhere." The poet is outside of the academy and outside of convention, but with no better place for him to cultivate his or her art, college will do. He holds that he has always encountered convention with "ironical detachment." The piece closes with Frost stating a personal desire as a way of reflecting on poets in general: "I want, I am expecting everything and everybody in on me and my art, but as much as possible with a force tempered on my terms. There is always the chance it will be on their terms more than on mine and then I shall go down writing."

"Caveat Poeta" was not published during Frost's lifetime but is a resource for his mature views about the academic world he resisted as a student but learned to embrace as a poet, since it had become one of the few settings in which a poet could actually earn a living.

"Census-Taker, The" (1923)

As in "The Black Cottage," in "The Census Taker" the speaker, this time alone, happens upon an abandoned logging camp, which becomes a source for reflection. The "black-paper-covered house" is a reminder that, as in his nature poem of the same title, "nothing gold can stay." The absence of life fills him with sorrow; the emptiness of the house is not its to bear alone; it fills the speaker with emptiness as well.

It is autumn, the season that represents loss but not death, and the speaker notes that no one would know it is autumn since "every tree / That could have dropped a leaf was down itself / And nothing but the stump of it was left." The scene appears more like winter, and in an odd way, it suggests that nature without humanity has no life, instead of the other way around.

The lack of leaves and branches to inhibit the wind makes the scene all the more forceful and causes the speaker to imagine the many "rude men" who would have passed in and out of the doors of this house, which has been abandoned for only one year. He envisions 10 men total in his "dreamy unofficial counting" and imagines them returning from a hard day's work hungry, demanding supper. Frost makes their absence felt when he describes in detail the absence that is the house's: The men "were not on the table with their elbows, . . . not sleeping in the shelves of bunks."

Inanimate objects outlive us. They go on, seemingly forever, and here the house and the ax handle picked up off the floor are reminders of hard work and hard living.

It is a surprise that the house has "fallen to decay" in only one year. The absence described is so present that it is hard to imagine its coming so suddenly, but it is to that fleeting quality that the poem alludes. The speaker says he feels no less sorrow than he does for the houses "fallen to ruin in ten thousand years," and the meaning of the title becomes ironically clear: The speaker is the census-taker of the dead.

He offers the dead a last chance to speak if they are "aggrieved," and in this he offers something of a burial. It is a sort of unofficial declaration of death and an opportunity for laying to rest. His melancholy is at its greatest when he speaks of having to "count souls / Where they grow fewer and fewer every year" and then "shrink to none at all."

The closing line, "It must be I want life to go on living," expresses a universal desire and the speaker's resolve. The poem suggests that if we live long enough, we all become census-takers of the dead, and it concludes by sharing that ultimately we want all lives, including our own, to go on without end.

The poem was first published in the April 6, 1921, issue of the *New Republic* and was later included in *New Hampshire*.

FURTHER READING

Bagby, George F. "The Promethean Frost," *Twentieth Century Literature* 38, no. 1 (Spring 1992): 1–19.

Doreski, William. "Robert Frost's 'The Census-Taker' and the Problem of Wilderness," *Twentieth Century Literature* 34, no. 1 (Spring 1988): 30–39.

children's stories and a children's poem: "Schneider and the Woodchuck," "Schneider and the Little Bird," "The Wise Men," "Old Stick-in-the-Mud," and "The Blue Bird to Lesley"

The two Schneider stories and "The Wise Men" are the only children's stories included in the Library of America's *Frost Collected Poems, Prose, and Plays* (1995). In *The Robert Frost Reader* (1972) "Schneider and the Woodchuck" is printed along with "The Wise Men," "Old Stick-in-the-Mud," and the poem "The Blue Bird to Lesley." The editors of *The Robert Frost Reader*, Edward Connery Lathem and Lawrance Thompson, report that Frost wrote 16 children's stories, possibly with a view to publication, which are now in a manuscript volume of the C. Waller Barrett Collection of the University of Virginia Library. A limited edition including 18 stories, *As Told to a Child: Stories from the Derry Notebook* (2000), was recently published in ENGLAND. The book includes illustrations by Frost's children from "The Bouquet," a magazine they compiled in September 1914.

In the woodchuck story the dog Schneider is duped by a woodchuck, and in the little bird story he is a furry resource for building a nest. Both fables are brief and end ironically: In the first Schneider says, "woodchucks can't talk"; the

woodchuck replies, "[n]either can dogs"; and the narrator asserts, "That's so: they can't." In the second Schneider suggests that the bird use his own feathers for a nest since he is "full of them," and the bird replies, "Do you mean full like a pillow?" The two fables are indicative of Frost's poetic style, as each builds toward an ironic conclusion.

"Schneider and the Little Bird" uses Frost's daughter Lesley's name and "The Wise Men" refers to his son Carol and daughters Lesley, Margy, and Irma. "The Wise Men" is longer than the Schneider stories but takes the same approach. Carol climbs a nut tree on the farm and disappears for two days and nights. Then three little old men who look like magicians—with white beards, cloaks, and pointed red hats decorated with stars—emerge one by one from the tree, but there is still no sign of Carol. When Carol does appear, he explains that he had dropped his cap so that his family would not worry about him. But now his family wants to know about the men. Carol explains that he met them at the top of the tree, where they were trying to figure out how "high the sky is." Carol wanted to know what the sky was going to do tomorrow if the little men knew everything, but they did not answer him. They just left the tree one by one. The poem closes with Carol saying, "But the funniest thing is about that cap," which remains missing at the end of the tale.

In "Old Stick-in-the-Mud" a fence post is anthropomorphized into a berry picker who helps Irma collect checkerberries while she takes his place in the fence. With a wire in her mouth, she holds the fence together so that the cows cannot get out. When she returns home with a can of berries, she tells the whole story to her Mama and Papa.

"The Blue Bird to Lesley" has a simple rhyme and language and tells the story of a blue bird that had to fly south for winter and did not have time to bring the message to Lesley itself. But he would every day "wonder about her / And cry some without her" and think of her "[e]very time he began a / Coconut or banana."

Biographer Jay Parini describes Frost's relationship with his children and "his playfulness and inventiveness" as "vital to their imaginative development." He goes on to declare that "One can hardly imagine a father more accessible to his children" (445). Frost and his wife Elinor home-schooled the children for a period, teaching them to read and write. Frost also was known for taking the children for long walks in the woods and for playing games with them. These children's stories are a testament to his love for his children. They also reveal, however, the characteristic tongue-in-cheek style of Frost the man and the poet. As Frost's granddaughter Lesley Lee Francis writes of the stories published in *As Told to a Child: Stories from the Derry notebook,*

> Besides providing a view of the farm that parallels the children's journals, RF's little prose stories, for and about his own children, reflect the poet's developing poetic idiom. Jotted down casually to amuse the children—perhaps also to allay their fears on a cold winter's night—the stories represent the trusting view of life, in sharp contrast to the often grim themes of the *North of Boston* blank verse narratives.

She also says that "Always the poet, RF worked through these stories to catch the tones, strategies, and expressions of living speech: colloquial double negatives, hesitations, what he came to call 'the sound of sense.'" Frost leaves his readers wondering about Carol's cap in "The Wise Men" just as he leaves them speculating at the end of his poems.

FURTHER READING

Francis, Lesley Lee. "Robert Frost and the Child: *Mother Goose* and 'The Imagination Thing,'" *Massachusetts Review* 45, no. 2 (Summer 2004): 256–268.

Frost, Robert. *The Robert Frost Reader: Poetry and Prose.* Edited by Edward Connery Lathem and Lawrance Thompson. New York: Henry Holt, 1972.

Parini, Jay. *Robert Frost: A Life.* New York: Holt, 1999.

"Choose Something like a Star" (1943)

"Choose Something like a Star" is the first poem listed in "An Afterword" in the *Steeple Bush* section of *The Complete Poems of Robert Frost* (1949), followed by "Closed for Good" and "From Plane to Plane." It was first published in *Come In and Other Poems* (1943) and also appeared as "Take Something like a Star" in *Selected Poems* (1963), where in the final line "choose" was also changed to "take." Jeffrey Cramer reports that Frost once remarked at a reading at BREAD LOAF SCHOOL OF ENGLISH that the poem "was written as much to himself as to anyone else, for fluctuating through fifty years of politics." Cramer added, "He said that you need to focus on something far enough away, like a star or an ancient poet" (158).

Frost opens with an apostrophe, a literary technique in which a personified abstraction is addressed; "O Star, (the fairest one in sight)." The speaker addresses the star forcefully, holding that while "mystery becomes the proud," full "reserve is not allowed." He wants the star to impart knowledge to him in some way, so he blurts out impatiently, "Say something!" as one might to a silent lover during a quarrel. The star's response is brief, cool, and straightforward: "I burn."

This is not a satisfactory response. The speaker holds that at the very least, the star ought to share to what degree it burns. But the star offers no additional information. Like the lover in a quarrel, the speaker, holding tightly to what the star has imparted, makes the most of the minimalist gesture by saying that it "does tell something in the end" and even "asks a little of us here."

The speaker calls the star "as steadfast as Keats' Eremite." The reference is to the romantic poet John Keats's sonnet of that name, which was written to his lover Fanny Brawne in 1818 or 1819. It opens, "Bright star, would I were stedfast as thou art—" and expresses a desire to "live ever—or else swoon to death" over a "fair love's ripening breast." In Frost's poem the appeal is to be steadfast not by living forever but rather by keeping our minds from being "swayed" by "the mob." Instead we are to seek a state of being as high as a star, and avoid carrying "praise or blame too far."

Frost described the poem as one he "like[d] to say" and one that he had a "fancy" for. He liked its "Horatian" ending and the "two ways of spelling 'staid.'" He said he "mingle[d] science and spirit here" ("On 'Choose Something like a Star,'" 899).

In "On Extravagance: A Talk," Frost introduces "Choose Something like a Star," and then says, "by that star I mean the Arabian Nights or Catullus or something in the Bible or something way off or something way off in the woods, and when I've made a mistake in my vote." He says that the line "Some mystery becomes the proud" comes from his "long efforts to understand contemporary poets." "[L]et them be mystery," he says and then adds, "that's my generosity—call it that."

Frost begins the poem deferentially but quickly takes control by attempting to assert his will on the fair star. As is evident from his comments in "On Extravagance," his attitude stems from the poem's being at least partly about other poets and poetry itself. The "star" that comes out at night may be poetry, asking us to rise to the occasion. Frost believes a little mystery is acceptable, but he often quibbles with the poets who do not "[u]se language we can comprehend."

FURTHER READING

Bagby, George F. *Frost and the Book of Nature*. Knoxville: University of Tennessee Press, 1993, 136–137.

Cramer, Jeffrey S. *Robert Frost among His Poems: A Literary Companion to the Poet's Own Biographical Contexts and Associations*. Jefferson, N.C.: MacFarland, 1996.

Faggen, Robert. *Robert Frost and the Challenge of Darwin*. Ann Arbor: University of Michigan Press, 1997.

Frost, Robert. "On Choose Something like a Star." In *Frost Collected Poems, Prose and Plays*. Edited by Richard Poirier and Mark Richardson, 899. New York: Library of America, 1995.

Kearns, Katherine. *Robert Frost and a Poetics of Appetite*. Cambridge: Cambridge University Press, 1994, 65–67.

Timmerman, John H. *Robert Frost: The Ethics of Ambiguity*. Lewisburg, Pa.: Bucknell University Press, 2002, 144–145.

"Christmas Trees" (1916)

Subtitled "A Christmas Circular Letter," "Christmas Trees" was sent as a Christmas message in 1915, is the second poem of *Mountain Interval*, and has also been published as a children's book.

In this poem the city withdraws into itself, much like the poet does in other poems, such as "Into My Own" and "Acquainted with the Night." The city leaves the "country to the country," but just as the poet returns from his journeys, the city returns to the country to "look for something it ha[s] left behind." Frost provides an interesting twist on Christmas trees by pointing out that city dwellers still need something from the country: those trees, chopped down to be placed in living rooms rather than left in the woods behind a house.

A city man is interested in purchasing the trees in the speaker's pasture. The speaker says that he is not "tempted for a moment / To sell them off their feet to go in cars," but it turns out he is. He "dallie[s] so much," in fact, that he finds himself in the position of letting the city buyer look at his trees and consider whether there are "enough to be worthwhile" to purchase. The fellow sees "a thousand" and offers a mere $30 for them. A country boy who originally did not want to "strip" his pasture bare, the speaker is suddenly willing to sell—not to this man but possibly to another. He says that he will "be writing . . . within the hour" to others who are willing to pay more per tree. The poem comes down to "the trial by market everything must come to," and it becomes clear that, while the setup suggests that the poem is about city and country life, it is more about marketing and profitability and the inability to refuse commerce, even when it runs the risk of eliminating what we cherish.

By the end of the Christmas letter, the poet is offering to "lay one in a letter"—roll up a tree and send it as a Christmas wish. He has resolved that they are something of value, insomuch as he can give them away or sell them, and he no longer seems to hold the same commitment to letting them be. The poem suggests that the country will eventually be no more, given the speaker's easy calculations and his general willingness to succumb to trade. *See* COUNTRY VERSUS CITY.

FURTHER READING

Sergeant, Elizabeth Shepley. *Robert Frost: The Trial by Existence*. New York: Holt, Rinehart and Winston, 1960.

"Clear and Colder" (1936)

Not to be confused with "Clear and Colder: Boston Common," one of Frost's uncollected poems, "Clear and Colder" appeared in *A Further Range*.

Frost uses witches in various poems: In "Design" he gives the "ingredients of a witches' broth," "Clear and Colder" appears three poems later in *A Further Range*, and later in the volume the witch who "[w]as once the beauty Abishag" is described in "Provide, Provide."

The title "Clear and Colder" is a phrase from a weather forecast and suggests that the weather and the poem are immanent, something to be looked forward to. Weather of this sort is a witches' brew, as seasons encroach on one another and the elements mix. The recipe for this "Fall Elixir" comes from the "Witches' Weather Primer" and could be taken from a Julia Child cookbook. First summer is allowed to simmer, left alone—no need to stir or skim—until it is just about the right consistency. There is no need for human intervention as all is fated, and the augers can be read as astrologers read the stars to reckon outcomes. Stars of the second magnitude are not as bright as stars of the first magnitude, but Frost's choice here seems to have more to do with rhyme scheme than meaning.

The recipe then calls for adding some "left-over winter" and a dash of "snow for powder." Leftover winter from Canada is heading south, stripping the leaves of autumn and splintering branches as the winds pick up. Bring them on, the speaker declares exultantly—and the chill rains too, harbingers of the snows to come, colder than seems seasonable. Throw in a dash of snow, as well, he allows, as he might season a sauce with a spice.

Now the "witches' chowder" that is cooked up needs to brew and ferment—"Wait and watch the liquor settle." As always in Frost, nature is rarely altogether benign. This concoction resembles a witches' brew of apparent infelicity. By "[a]ll my eye and Cotton Mather," he exclaims, conjuring up the infamous 17th-century minister and witch hunter and reaffirming the place of the poem in his most familiar landscape. The New England connection to witchcraft makes for fantastical material that here and in "Design" is used to explain nature, which sometimes seems like a form of witchcraft.

The speaker, for one, welcomes the "chowder" the elements have provided and can stand "whole dayfuls" of it, in fact. What is brewed in the "kettle" of this often harsh environment is "heady," and those familiar with it "love it." The repetition of "love it" reinforces just how much the speaker enjoys the power of the season.

The poem's final line tells us that "Gods are not above it," and presumably by "it" Frost means witchcraft. There is an interesting juxtaposition of gods and witches, each having their supernatural powers. Dragging the gods into all this activity of nature's witchcraft reinforces Frost's often-stated view that fate must be fatalistically accepted. Nothing happens that the gods do not approve. Fate is what is to come, and upon its arrival it becomes what is. In this case, the fullest form of acceptance is simply to savor what comes.

See STARS.

FURTHER READING

Poirier, Richard. *Robert Frost: The Work of Knowing.* New York: Oxford University Press, 1977.

"Cliff Dwelling, A" (1947)

In "A Cliff Dwelling," which first appeared in *Steeple Bush*, Frost equates the sky with the plain, as they both appear "sandy" in the seemingly far-off setting, a barren desert. He notes that "no habitation meets the eye" there and that little life remains. As in other poems, such as "A Census-Taker," here the speaker reflects on inhabitants from "years ago—ten thousand years" who have long since died. There is little evidence of their existence, only a "spot of black," "a cavern hole" that indicates that at one time cliff dwellers inhabited the place. He imagines in Darwinian terms the species from which humans might have evolved, a being who "used to climb and crawl." It seems that the figure disappeared into the hole in the wall and perhaps died somewhere inside the cliff, since the last image the speaker can summon is of a calloused foot disappearing within.

Frost frequently dwells on lives lost, whether human lives of the past, as here; lives in nature such as the leaves that fall from the trees each autumn; or young lives recently lost, as in "Home Burial."

FURTHER READING

Hill, William Thomas. "'Oh Years Ago—Ten Thousand Years': The Sound of Sense and Iconography in 'A Cliff Dwelling' by Robert Frost," *Gakuen* (August–September 1995): 36–43.

Poirier, Richard. *Robert Frost: The Work of Knowing.* New York: Oxford University Press, 1977.

"Closed for Good" (1949)

Appearing in "An Afterword" to *Steeple Bush*, "Closed for Good" is an earlier version of a poem that bears the same name in *In the Clearing*. In the *Complete Poems* 1949 edition, the first and last stanza are removed, the word "brush" is replaced with "spread," and the opening stanza then begins with "They" instead of "And."

The speaker considers what he owes to the "passers of the past" who have built the road on which he now makes his way. He recognizes that they let him be and do not return with "steed" and "chariot" to shove him to "one side." They cleared the road, but they have left him to his own path.

As in "The Census-Taker" and other poems that are homages to the past, the speaker is grateful and thoughtful, wishing not to forget but to pay "some sweet share." He is paying his debt to those who have come before him and thereby made his road much easier. As in "Carpe Diem," where he says that the present cannot be experienced until it is in the past, here he experiences the present through the past.

Ultimately Frost is reflecting on his poetic life and on how his predecessors have forged a path for his poetry. Similar to Ezra Pound's "Pact" with Walt Whitman, Frost seeks to demonstrate through the metaphor of the road that he and his predeces-

sors share "one sap and one root" and that while they "broke the new wood," or created the road, it is now his "time for carving." Unlike Pound, he does not "detest" the "passers of the past" but is still grateful that "they've gone away" and not haunted him for his "slowness."

The speaker knows that eventually he will cease his role as a "foot printer," and "some slight beast / So mousy or so foxy" will take his place. By paying homage to those who came before him, he also indicates that those who follow him should not forget him, either, but should instead "print there" as his "proxy."

FURTHER READING

Richardson, Mark. "Frost's 'Closed for Good': Editorial and Interpretive Problems," *Robert Frost Review* (Fall 1996): 22–35.

"Cloud Shadow, A" (1942)

In this poem from *A Witness Tree*, Frost teasingly writes that a poem on spring would be a foolish endeavor, as if to suggest that the only poems of real worth are on weightier subjects. To write on spring is to write of cheery, bright, and flowery subjects that are not sufficient for serious poetry: "For whom would a poem on Spring be by?" The unanswered question leaves the reader to wonder, as the "breeze disdain[s] to make reply."

The speaker tries to tell the breeze that "There's no such thing!" as a poem on spring and suggests that poems that deal with spring themes, if they are to be good, must go beyond being uplifting and be more profound. For example, "Blue-Butterfly Day," one of Frost's poems that comes closest to being a "Spring poem," takes a turn at the end, leaving the butterflies "closed over in the wind and cling[ing]" to life.

In the concluding lines a "cloud shadow" crosses the breeze's face, casting a dark shadow across the open pages of the speaker's book (nature in Frost so often conveys at least some hint of the ominous). The breeze fears the speaker will "make her miss the place" where the poem on spring might be. The breeze, spring's envoy, knows something, perhaps, that the speaker does not.

FURTHER READING

Marcus, Mordecai. *The Poems of Robert Frost: An Explication.* Boston: G. K. Hall, 1991.

Cluster of Faith: "Accidentally on Purpose," "A Never Naught Song," "Version," "A Concept Self-Conceived," "[Forgive, O Lord, my little jokes on Thee]" (1962)

What Robert Hass calls "Frost's final word on his long struggle with evolution," "Accidentally on Purpose" postulates existence as a purposeful accident. "The Universe is but the Thing of things," Frost writes in the opening line. Respect for its vastness is highlighted in the thrice repeated, almost liturgical, "mighty." Whereas the opening stanza reflects on the universe as a series of "balls all going round in rings," something like a child's toy, the second stanza focuses on the time when human beings were but "albino monkey[s] in a jungle."

With Darwin, EVOLUTION has been explained, and the speaker questions whether evolution had "no real purpose till it got to us." He is concerned with thought and humanity, and our "purpose," but he says it is a mistake to believe that there was no purpose before. There must have always been a purpose, he believes, and we are that "purpose coming to a head," its culmination.

The poem is only cautiously Darwinian; its speaker is agnostic. He does not know whose purpose the universe was, admits he has no ability to discern, and suggests that sort of speculation be left to "the scientific wits." He does not need divinity, however; all he wants is "intention, purpose, and design." His "head and brain" do not help him understand why we are here any more than the monkey in the jungle does. Yet we remain just as "hap-

pily instinctive," embracing such earthly delights as "love at sight," for that is our "best guide upward further to the light." As Frost writes in "Birches," "Earth's the right place for love." *See* SCIENCE.

"A Never Naught Song," continues the theme that there has always been a "purpose" when it proposes that there was never "naught," or nothing: "There was always thought." The speaker imagines the Big Bang as a "burst" of matter and the bursting forth of the universe as an "atomic One." When the bang occurred, "everything was there, every single thing . . . Clear from hydrogen / All the way to men." This bang was the creation of all things; it was even the first evidence of thought. The speaker's explanation eliminates the need for the "whole Yggdrasil," which is, in Norse mythology, the world tree, a giant ash that connects and shelters all known worlds. This song, then, replaces the tree myth with matter that is "[c]unningly minute" and yet possessed of the "force of thought."

"Version" suggests yet another approach to making something of nothing: that an archer comedically shot his arrow at "non-existence." This version of a creation myth is more mythological than the earlier two, which present scientific concepts. It also in many ways contradicts "Accidentally on Purpose," as it focuses less on the notion of a purpose and more on the possibility of a humorous accident. This poem has an unusual textual history: It is considered to have first been published incompletely in *In the Clearing,* and Edward C. Lathem altered and lengthened the poem from manuscript evidence (Library of America, 1987).

"A Concept Self-Conceived" faults the notion that God is in all things by pointing out that such a concept is of our own making and therefore is "no more good than old Pantheism." He suggests that a monotheistic approach is not at all superior to a pantheistic approach—both are childish. The speaker points out that we reassure ourselves, as children do in the dark, and we perpetuate our own belief. He criticizes the religious raising of children when he asserts that such indoctrination "never give[s] a child a choice."

This five-poem "cluster" is, at the last, presented as a joke on God, closing with the couplet "Forgive, O Lord, my little jokes on Thee / And I'll forgive

Thy great big one on me." But the speaker is only half in jest, as he clearly feels he has been wronged. The cluster is a comment on faith, and it is unclear at times whether it is the poet or some other voice doing the criticizing. The cluster seems to say that we must either grant design and talk about the designer or do what Darwin did and grant the design but deny its source.

Robert Faggen calls the cluster a "clever reference to the inextricable relationship between the material of stars and the impulses of religion," a "cartoon history of cosmology and a caricature of ideas of evolution."

"Accidentally on Purpose" was originally published as Frost's 1960 Christmas poem; "Forgive, O Lord" was originally published in 1959 as "The Preacher" in *A Remembrance Collection of New Poems,* created for Frost's 85th birthday celebration at the Waldorf Astoria in New York. These and the others later appeared together in *In the Clearing.* See BELIEF.

FURTHER READING

Faggen, Robert. *Robert Frost and the Challenge of Darwin.* Ann Arbor: University of Michigan Press, 1997, 307–312.

Hass, Robert. *Going by Contraries: Robert Frost's Conflict with Science.* Charlottesville: University Press of Virginia, 2002, 86–88.

"Cocoon, The" (1928)

Some "women-folk" are cast as butterflies spinning a cocoon in time for winter. The cocoon is the smoke that wafts from their chimney, and since "no one for hours has set a foot outdoors" the speaker imagines the smoke enveloping them and the "poor house" for all of winter. The cocoon will keep "its life so close and out of sight." The women are described as lonely inmates who are, in their loneliness and perhaps vulnerability, clinging to the house and prudently "anchoring" themselves to "earth and moon."

The speaker begins "As far as I can see," so there is an awareness that his sight, or vision, may

be limited and possibly even obscured by the "autumn haze." He criticizes the women's choice to stay indoors and isolated, however. It seems to him that their loneliness will be "more lonely ere it will be less," since they have chosen to confine themselves, without human interaction or community. The speaker regards their loneliness "[f]rom which no winter gale can hope to blow it,—" because he is so familiar with it himself, an idea also expressed in "Desert Places."

The poem was first published in the February 9, 1927, issue of *New Republic* and was later included in *West-Running Brook.*

"Code, The" (1914)

One of Frost's dramatic narratives set in New England farm country, "The Code" concerns itself with the accepted behavior among farmers. Frost juxtaposes city and country life and folk as he does in other poems, such as "Christmas Trees" and "An Unstamped Letter in Our Rural Letter Box."

In this instance there are three men "piling cocks of hay" together when "[s]uddenly / One helper," James, "thrusting pitchfork in the ground, / March[es] himself off the field and home." The two remaining men, one city farmer and one hired hand, discuss why James left, and the hand quickly points out to the farmer that it was something that he said, "About [their] taking pains." It soon becomes clear that the "average farmer" would not have said as much, in order to avoid the suggestion that there was fault to be found in James's work. Frost highlights that it takes James roughly a half an hour to act on the comment, because he has to "chew it over." Such subtle descriptions of country folk lend themselves to overall impressions of languor and simplicity.

The hired hand who remains explains how the insult came from the farmer's not "understand[ing]" their ways and tells a story intended to offer insight. His story involves an occurrence at Sanders's place, where he had been hired to do some haying. None of the men liked Sanders, and while Sanders was hard on himself, he was also quite hard on the men he hired. He would "keep at their heels and threaten to mow their legs off." The storyteller ended up "paired off" with Sanders at some point and, taking some advantage of Sanders, managed to bury him under a "rackful" of hay. The other men, when they discovered what happened, thought that he had killed Sanders but found out that Sanders had simply made his way back to his house, where he kept out of the way for the remainder of the day. The hired hands' "just trying / To bury him had hurt his dignity," much in the same way the city farmer has hurt James's, and thus comes the meaning of the story.

The city farmer inquires, with a tone of self-concern, "Weren't you relieved to find he wasn't dead?" And startlingly the hand responds, "No! and yet I don't know—it's hard to say. / I went about to kill him fair enough." This admission is striking since, in the correlation to the original tale, the animosity and threat linger uncomfortably in the air. The farmer inquires, "Did he discharge you?" and the hand responds, "Discharge me? No! He knew I did just right," and "The Code" is returned to as the primary theme.

"The Code" sets protocols and behaviors among men, and being unfamiliar with it, the farmer runs the risk of causing insult but also the risk of suffering harm. And yet, oddly, part of the code is that it is right to behave in such ways. This embracing of tradition and accepted behaviors highlights a strange simplicity in country life, but it also casts a dark shadow on what is often considered idyllic, uncomplicated rural living.

The poem appeared in the collection *North of Boston* after being published first in the February 1914 issue of *Poetry* under the title "The Code—Heroics." *See* COUNTRY VERSUS CITY and FARMER, FROST AS.

FURTHER READING

Feaster, John. "Robert Frost's 'The Code': A Context and a Commentary," *Cresset* 55, no. 7 (May 1992): 6–10.

Jost, Walter. "Rhetorical Investigations of Robert Frost." In *Roads Not Taken: Rereading Robert Frost*, edited by Earl J. Wilcox and Jonathan N. Barron, 179–197. Columbia: University of Missouri Press, 2000.

Monteiro, George. "Frost's Hired Hand," *College Literature* 14, no. 2 (Spring 1987): 128–135.

Richardson, Mark. *The Ordeal of Robert Frost: The Poet and His Poetics.* Chicago: University of Illinois Press, 1997.

"Come In" (1942)

The speaker feels called into the dark, into the woods, by the thrush, a bird known for its melodious song. He says that if it was "dusk outside, / Inside it was dark," and perhaps he is referring to "inner and outer weather" ("Tree at My Window"). He says that it is too dark for a "sleight" bird to be singing and that the bird should instead be seeking a "perch for the night."

In the bird's song, the speaker feels an invitation to "come in." The music entices him into the dark to "lament." But he is resistant; he says he was "out for stars" and "would not come in," "not even if asked"—he is asserting his will.

It seems that while the music appeals to him, it is "almost" a call to come in, but not quite. The speaker stands on the threshold of the woods, of darkness, and yet hesitates. He is separate from the darkness and wants to keep it at a distance. The "pillared dark" is the pillars of the trees but represents something more. This speaker seems to fear that the crossing of the pillars, into darkness, would be a yielding to death.

Almost like the sirens of Greek mythology, who lured sailors to their deaths with their beautiful singing, the thrush's music entices the speaker toward the dark. But just as Circe instructed sailors to put wax in their ears as guard against the sirens, the speaker holds strongly to the light, the "stars," for life. And he resolves, gratefully, that ultimately he "hadn't been" called. The phrase "come in" is commonplace and unthreatening in daily life, but here the luring phrase wears a malevolent shroud.

The poem was first published in the February 1941 issue of the *Atlantic Monthly* and was later included in *A Witness Tree*. See MYTHOLOGY AND FOLKLORE and STARS.

FURTHER READING

Pritchard, William H. *Frost: A Literary Life Reconsidered.* Amherst: University of Massachussets Press, 1993.

"A Concept Self-Conceived" (1962)

See CLUSTER OF FAITH.

"Considerable Speck, A" (1942)

The parenthetical subtitle, "Microscopic," points to Frost's sensitivity to the minutest manifestations of nature. Just as in "Departmental," about the death of the forager ant Jerry McCormic, where Frost finds significance and almost overwhelming sadness in the death of an otherwise insignificant insect, the poet relies on a playful use of rhyming couplets. In "A Considerable Speck" a microscopic mite crosses his path and teaches him something about himself.

The speaker, pen poised above the white page, considers obliterating the mite "with a period of ink" when "something strange" stays his hand. He realizes that this is a "living" being, not simply a "dust speck," and this forces him to consider the significance of life for life's sake before blotting it out so easily. He imagines the mite having "inclinations it could call its own" and then more closely observes the mite's behavior, ascribing to it a fanciful power of thought.

A mere "speck" on the white sheet, the mite "set[s] off across" the page, "racing wildly," running with "terror," creeping with "cunning." It even takes time to pause and either sip or smell the wet ink. The speaker imagines the mite turning away from the ink, his own writing, with "loathing," a suggestion perhaps of the author's feelings of insecurity about his work. Surely the mite is not judging his writing, he realizes, when he becomes aware that the intelligence he has ascribed to it is one he has "dealt."

The poem moves from the importance of life to meaning in life to the desire to continue living; from dust to mite to the manuscript and back to the mite again. The mite shares "inclinations" that we call our own: the desire to live, drink, smell, be free from terror, go on living, and "express how much" we do not want to die. We are as vulnerable to forces outside our control as is the mite on the page; we, too, may be seen as "cowering down" in the middle of what might be called an "open sheet," only we may be less apt to "accept" whatever "fate" brings.

In the case of the mite, it is the speaker who holds in his hand the power over life and death. He is like a god. It is not the same for us. Our lives, over which we seem to have so little control, make us akin to mites and cause us to wonder whether we will be wiped out as easily as a mite could be by some indifferent god or random event.

Frost cannot resist taking a swipe at modern liberalism: Unlike others of his time, he maintains he has no "tenderer-than-thou / Collectivistic regimenting love." That is, he is not altogether sympathetic to the fate of the many. Still, he is caught up in a concern for this mite at this particular moment, "now!" And since he imagines that there is nothing "evil" about the mite, he decides to let it be, let it "lie there," until, he hopes, it sleeps. It is unclear what sort of sleep the speaker wishes for the mite, whether a momentary rest or a perpetual sleep.

The speaker iterates that this gesture of kindness is due to a recognition of the "mind" of the mite. He prides himself on recognizing a mind "in any guise" and then cunningly adds that he is pleased when he can find demonstrated on "any sheet the least display of mind."

He and we are equated with the mite in our relative positions in the universe and in our ineluctable will to live. The speck is indeed "considerable." Perhaps the poet, too, would like to feel himself, if but a speck in the universe, at least a considerable one. First we try desperately to survive. The darkness enters when we give up and cower beneath the threat of a considerable circumstance or force.

Frost once said of the poem, "[it] has some of my animosities in it—buried, you know. Somebody said I didn't have to talk politics, they shone out of me" ("Frost,"). The poem was collected in *A Witness Tree* but was first published in the July 1939 issue of the *Atlantic Monthly* without its subtitle.

FURTHER READING

Faggen, Robert. *Robert Frost and the Challenge of Darwin.* Ann Arbor: University of Michigan Press, 1997, 261–263.

Parini, Jay. *Robert Frost: A Life.* New York: Holt, 1999.

"Constant Symbol, The" (1946)

One of Frost's best-known prose pieces, "The Constant Symbol" sets forth many of his theories about poetry. It was first published in the October 1946 issue of the *Atlantic Monthly* and was followed by his poem "To the Right Person," which had the subtitle "Fourteen Lines." The poem would later be collected in *Steeple Bush.*

Frost introduces the "folk saying . . . that easy to understand is contemptible, hard to understand irritating." The implication, he says, is "that just easy enough, just hard enough, right in the middle, is what literary criticism ought to foster." He draws on Homer's *Iliad* and *Odyssey* and Virgil's *Aeneid* to demonstrate that such an assessment is false. He also refers to works "lately to surpass all records for hardness," and presumably he is to some extent referring to T. S. Eliot's *The Waste Land* (1922). He resolves, however, that "hard or easy" is "of slight use as a test either way."

He moves on to "texture" as a necessary quality. He imagines that a "good piece of weaving takes rank" but also asserts that sometimes the texture can become "arty." Texture can be an achievement in itself, without the need for wholeness. There are many attributes in poetry, texture and difficulty among them, but "the chiefest" is metaphor, defined as "saying one thing and meaning another, saying one thing in terms of another, the pleasure of ulteriority." Poems are made of metaphor, but so, too, are philosophy and science. Frost's description of metaphor is meaningful not only to poetry generally but to his own poetry. He always says one thing in terms of another, and the pleasure he takes in ulteriority is undeniable. For him every poem has to be a new metaphor, has to reveal something all previous poems did not. At the same time, all poems share "the same old metaphor always," that is, have at their core essential metaphors about human experience.

The constant symbol is the poem itself made "small or great of the way the will has to pitch into commitments deeper and deeper to a rounded conclusion." The will works harder and harder to achieve as it makes itself known throughout a poem. With each line a greater commitment is made to the work, and with each finality the piece must be "judged for whether any original intention it had has been strongly spent or weakly lost." Frost compares the commitment to making poems to commitments made in other endeavors, such as politics, business, and marriage. In this way poetry making is not inaccessible but is like any other devotion, and "[s]trongly spent" becomes "synonymous with kept." The judgment becomes the "sentence" of the poem, a comparison to the sentencing of those who commit crimes. Poets "may speak after sentence, resenting judgment," but they are given no more license than others who have been victims of either praise or condemnation.

Frost speaks to the need for readers to "know anything so intimate as what [poets] were intending to do" and for poets to want their readers to be so able. "The answer is the world presumes to know," he says, a bit frustrated by the world's presumption in assuming such knowledge. The poet refers to the Austrian psychiatrist and founder of psychoanalysis Sigmund Freud (1856–1939) when he writes that the "ruling passion in man is not as Viennese as is claimed." The desire to know what the poet meant is described as a "gregarious instinct to keep together by minding each other's business." The English poet and critic Sir Herbert Read (1893–1968) wrote in his *Form in Modern Poetry* (1932) that "There are many instincts besides the sex instinct, and if any one instinct is more in question than another, I think it is probably the gregarious instinct." "Grex rather than sex," Frost emphasizes. *Grex*, "herd," is the Latin root of gregarious. To be egregious, therefore, is to be outside the herd.

"The beauty of socialism is that it will end the individuality that is always crying out mind your own business," Frost writes, offering one of the only instances where he seems to compliment socialism, albeit ironically. He says that Terence (185–159 B.C.), the Roman writer of comedies, would respond that "all human business is my business." Terence writes in his *Heauton Timoroumenos* ("The Self-Tormenter") that "I am a man: I hold that nothing human is alien to me" (l. 77). The implication for Frost is that not only are all metaphors in poems "the same old metaphor always" because they are human, but that all the poet intends becomes the business of his readers, because it is human and so are they. In this way the symbol becomes "[n]o more invisible means of support, no more invisible motives, no more invisible anything"; what is in the poem is seen there.

"The ultimate commitment is giving in to it that an outsider may see what we were up to sooner and better than we ourselves," Frost says, pivoting on the role of the poet. The poet is no longer the superior "seer"; what he sees must be grasped fully and permanently by someone else to reach its full potential. The poet, echoing Christ at the moment of his death, says, "Unto these forms did I commend the spirit," and in so saying he suggests that they are evident to all. But he will eventually confess that he only "betrayed the spirit with a rhymester's cleverness." It was not made as evident as he might have liked to believe.

Poetry has to be accessible, Frost holds. It cannot attempt to convey something that is known only to the poet. It has to convey universals, but universals that have as yet been unmarked. When they are recognized fully by the reader, the poet has succeeded. The questions the poet must ask himself are whether he had "anything to be true to," whether he was "true to it," and if so whether he "use[d] good words." He will not have achieved any of these goals if what he intended is not understood by his reader. If the reader cannot find the poem, then the author has failed, whether he thinks so or not.

"Every poem is an epitome of the great predicament; a figure of the will braving alien entanglements," Frost concedes. The great predicament is

conceiving of a metaphor and finding a way to convey it that makes the metaphor accessible but fresh. The "alien entanglements" are those known and unknown to the poet by way of his readers, who attempt to understand his meaning.

Frost shifts to the president in the White House for a "study of the success" of intention. He likens the effort to determine a poet's intention to the attempt to determine a politician's intention in becoming not only a politician but a politician for a particular party. He examines several possibilities as determining factors. Frost declares that in any case he will be hardly able to "remember how much credit he deserved personally for the decision it took." The politician becomes so "multifariously closed in on with obligations and answerabilities," Frost says, that he might as well have been a poet who got himself into "a sestina royal," a complicated and difficult verse form consisting of six six-line stanzas and a three-line envoy. The end words of the first stanza are repeated in varied order as end words in the other stanzas and recur in the envoy, which is dedicated to a patron or summarizes the poem's main ideas. Frost also compares the poet's intention, or lack thereof, to somebody of a "religious nature" who enters theological school by the same haphazard decision making. The original intention is again lost; the difference is that "at least he has had the advantage of having it more in his heart than in his head."

Frost refers to his own "recklessness" in "Stopping by Woods on a Snowy Evening," in which in the first line of the second stanza, "My little horse must think it queer," he made an unnecessary commitment to his rhyme scheme. He declares that he was "riding too high to care what trouble [he] incurred. And it was all right so long as [he] didn't suffer deflection." The choice did not make the poet suffer, as the poem is one of the best known and most beloved in the language.

"The poet goes in like a rope skipper," full of enthusiasm and rhythm. "If he trips himself he stops the rope," and he either tries a new skip or gives up the current game. For Frost the poet "has been brought up by ear," by what verse he has grown up on, which provides a choice of "two metres, strict iambic and loose iambic." An iamb is a metrical foot consisting of an unstressed syllable followed by a stressed syllable. The poet may have "any length of line up to six feet," up to hexameter. He uses English poet Robert Herrick's (1591–1674) "To Daffodils" as an example of "any line lengths for any shape of stanza." Within these limitations the poet is not "running wild" but is determining what will fit perfectly a "particular mood." The poet has gotten it right when the poem achieves "its own fulfillment." If it is told beforehand it is like telling love beforehand, he says, referring to the English romantic poet William Blake's (1757–1827) "Love's Secret," which begins, "Never seek to tell thy love." (Variant versions read, "Never pain to tell thy love.") Frost explains that if love is told beforehand, "it loses flow without filling the mould." In other words, the poem loses its momentum before it reaches its completion.

Poems must retain their freshness. The freshness the poet felt must be conveyed to the reader in its purest form: "A poem is the emotion of having a thought while the reader waits a little anxiously for the success of dawn." It needs to be just as fresh for the reader as it was for the poet. If it seems it has been entirely "thought out," its freshness will be lost. "The only discipline" a poet must begin with is an "inner mood." He begins with his mood and then attempts to find its shape. He may have a "false start or two," the way one does when one attempts to thread a needle. When the form is just right, the poet pierces his poem just as directly and perfectly as a thread passes through the eye of a needle. There is no "mystery" to that. It is exacting and can be likened to poet and reader as "familiar friends" who, when "approach[ing] each other in the street are apt to have this experience in feeling before knowing the pleasantry they will inflict on each other in passing." The poet has pierced his poem and his reader just the same. They are not separate.

Frost imagines that there is likely a connection between the mood and the form and meter chosen to express that mood. This time he uses William Shakespeare's Sonnet 29, "When in disgrace with Fortune and men's eyes," to illustrate. When the poet begins with such strength as Shakespeare did, he is committed to both the theme and the form. Frost jokes that it is "[o]dd how the two advance

into the open *pari passu*," Latin for "of equal step." Shakespeare has descended into Hades, in Greek and Roman mythology the underworld and land of the dead. He will descend into the abyss, and no one knows how far he can and will go before he makes his way back. He makes his way, committed to the sonnet, but not knowing if he will "outlast or last out the fourteen lines—have to cramp or stretch to come out even—have enough bread for the butter or butter for the bread." The sort of way he makes, "by what jutting points of rock," refers to the English poet Alfred, Lord Tennyson's (1809–92) "Morte d'Arthur": "He stepping down / By zigzag paths, and juts of pointed rock, / Came on the shining levels of the lake." As Frost sees it, Shakespeare did not quite know what to do with the last two lines. "Things like that and worse are the reason the sonnet is so suspect a form," he says coyly. Sonnets get poets into corners and therefore have "driven so many to free verse and even to the novel," he jokes, critically.

Frost continues to discuss the sonnet. The English poet and essayist Henry Austin Dobson (1840–1924) confessed in his poem "Urceus Exit," "I intended an Ode, And it turned into a Sonnet," and to Frost in this case it is "the usual order of being driven from the harder down to the easier." The reason for this, Frost claims is that Dobson "has a better excuse for weakness of will than most, namely, Rose," the woman who figures in "Urseus Exit."

The biblical prophet Jeremiah has even "had his sincerity questioned" as might a poet, "because the anguish of his lamentations was tamable to the form of twenty-two stanzas for the twenty-two letters of the [Hebrew] alphabet." Frost finds this foolish: "But there they go again with the old doubt about law and order." "To the right person," he allows, it is "naïve to distrust form as such." Form is meaningful and necessary. To distrust it is to distrust our very language. "Coining new words isn't encouraged"; we fashion our language from the words that are available to us, and in this sense every time we speak we embrace form and order. When spirit and form collide we have language. The "extravagance" can be likened to Walt Whitman's (1819–92) declaration in *Leaves of Grass* that the "body [i]s the soul."

And "here is where it all comes out." In closing, Frost declares that the "mind is a baby giant" with the playthings of "vocabulary, grammar, prosody, and diary" as stepping stones. The poet zigzags, but it is a "straight crookedness." Frost, the poet and teacher, asks for "pardon" from teacher, student, or investigator for pointing out "what ordinarily you would point me out." As he has said earlier, usually the reader reveals something to the poet that the latter has not yet seen; here the poet points it out to us. He teasingly explains that "To some it will seem strange" that he has been writing his "verse regular" all this time without knowing, hyperbolically, "till yesterday that it was from fascination with this constant symbol." But "To the right person it will seem lucky; since in finding out too much too soon there is a danger of arrest." He harkens that none should believe that he would commit himself as he has to certain rhymes, such as that in "Reluctance." If he had known that three words would have "exhausted the possibilities" when he set out, he might have made different choices. "No rhyming dictionary for [him]," or he would have had to "face the facts of rhyme." Instead it has left "something to learn still later."

"The Constant Symbol" closes with the sonnet "To the Right Person." The subtitle "Fourteen Lines" is its own metaphor. The poem and the entire piece have been written to the "right person" who will get out of it the metaphor, the symbol. The symbol is not constant, but what is constant is that it is a symbol. The poem has an unlikely rhyme scheme, aa/ba/bc/bd/bc/de/eb, and some unusual choices such as the following rhyming "phrase-ends": "situation," "estimation," "co-education," "fenestration," and "meditation." Showing off, he is. This poet, who believed free verse was like playing tennis without a net and was criticized by proponents of free verse for being shoved around by the rhymes, ends coyly, with yet another constant symbol.

"Conversations on the Craft of Poetry" (1959)

"Conversations on the Craft of Poetry" is a recorded and transcribed conversation among Frost; literary critic Cleanth Brooks; the novelist Robert Penn Warren; and the Holt, Rinehart and Winston editor Kenny Withers that took place in 1959. It is another source for Frost's theories about poetry.

Frost begins by explaining that a poem has to be "catchy." If it is not, "it will not stay in anybody's head." Frost's own ambition was to "lodge" a few poems where they would be hard to get rid of. When a poem is catchy it "stick[s] on you like burrs thrown on you in holiday foolery." Like burrs, but not painful burrs, burrs thrown in fun. What makes them catchy is "an archness or something," he explains. The basic meter of poetry is described as following in all languages the "beat of the heart." In this sense, iambic pentameter is instinctive in our nature and natural to our ears. Poetry, he says, makes its own "music," built on the beating of our own hearts. When verse needs to be set to music to achieve its ends, it does not have its own music and is "bad writing."

Meter is compared by the New England farmer to a donkey and a donkey cart: "for some of the time the cart is on the tugs and some of the time on the hold-backs." His metaphor comes from daily life, from the jog-trot of a cart. The poetry moves forward and back, back and forward; this is the rhythm. Frost criticizes the American poet Vachel Lindsay (1879–1931) for having to explain in what tone to read one of his poems. Brooks says the tone should be "built in," and Frost says that this is "why you have to have a meaning, 'cause you don't know what to do with anything if you don't have a meaning." If there is meaning, the readers can be carried by the cart. If the poet has to explain to others where the cart jerks and halts, the meaning is lost. Frost calls the built-in tone of the language its way of "acting up," using Geoffrey Chaucer's (1340–1400) "The Wife of Bath's Prologue" from *The Canterbury Tales* and "Merciles Beaute: A Tripel Roundel" as examples. He explains that he finds tone in the language of folks everywhere, that we all "act up" when we talk. This acting up is our "expressiveness," and to him expressiveness comes when "words aren't enough." It is particularly present in children.

Expressiveness comes before language, in the sounds that children make, and they "linger" after

Frost playing tennis at the Bread Loaf School of English in Vermont. "Conversations on the Craft of Poetry": "I'd as soon write free verse as play tennis with the net down." *(Courtesy Dartmouth College Library)*

language in our "um-hnm[s]" and "unh-unh[s]." Warren says in sincerity; "From a groan to a sonnet's a straight line" and Frost agrees. It is all about mood, Frost says, the mood "foretells the end product." Frost refers to the poets Robert Browning (1812–89), Walt Whitman (1819–92), Edgar Lee Masters (1869–1950), and Ezra Pound (1885–1972) as examples. Pound, he notes, wanted all meter "exirpate[d]." Frost was critical of free verse of the sort that Pound espoused. He admits to being "hard on free verse a little—too hard, I know." Free verse, Frost once said, and later in this conversation quotes himself as saying, "I'd as soon write free verse as play tennis with the net down." Free verse is too simple, too easy. Here he is a bit more sympathetic when Warren explains that "behind all good

free verse there's a shadow of formal verse." But still Frost wants the meter to be "something to hold and something . . . to put a strain on."

In this conversation Frost "guardedly" offers a definition of poetry: "It is that which is lost out of both prose and verse in translation." He also describes it as "dawn," as "something dawning on you while you're writing it." He often referred to his own education in poetry as coming by way of Mother Goose, and he says the same of his readers. He recalls explaining to the public how to read lines, until he realized that to some degree we have all been raised on Mother Goose and that the way to read lines is therefore instilled. He recalls the "pussy cat" rhyme and explains that it has "meant a lot to [him] . . . all [his] life" for what it says about "regionalists" and how they "could stay right at home and see it all," the way Emily Dickinson did.

Frost finds the conversation "fun," describing himself as not often having an opportunity to sit and talk about poetry in this way. He imagines that they have "come a good way" in their conversation about poetry. Like "The Constant Symbol," the conversation is a fine source not only for Frost's theories about poetry and an understanding of the breadth of his knowledge of other poets but also for what he reveals about his own process of writing. He does not appreciate a poem that he can "tell was written toward a good ending." That he calls "trickery." He wants to be the "happy discoverer of [his] ends." Poetry that is predetermined in prose and then set to verse is not poetry. This echoes his view, expressed in "The Figure a Poem Makes," that a poem "begins in delight and ends in wisdom." To find that Frost's experience with his own poems might be the same as his readers' is a delight indeed.

"Courage to Be New, The" (1947)

This satirical poem first appeared in a section titled "A Spire and Belfry" in *Steeple Bush*. In it the notion that anything is ever "new" is satirized as a desire to feel superior to one's predecessors. We may think we are above "brutality and fighting," but the truth is out. Those who believe they have somehow outgrown the inclinations of "ancient men" and therefore are above making the same mistakes are clearly putting on a face of courage in an attempt to conceal their own weakness.

The world is "heartbroken and disabled," and out of a desperation to set things right the courageous "renew talk" of the "fabled / Federation of Mankind," perhaps an analog for the United Nations, which had just been formed after the end of World War II. Its idealistic predecessor, the League of Nations, had failed.

The "courageous" are astute enough to at least suspect that they have gone poorly about the business of human relations. They imagine the possibility of the world uniting, despite differences of opinion and kind. They speculate whether there is a human trait more "base" than militating; a possibility that the basest human tendency is something positive that can unite rather than destroy. Frost plays on the various meanings of the term *base*: "contemptible" versus "basic."

But this is followed by a sardonic rejoinder: "They will tell you more as soon as / You tell them what to do." The suggestion is that no one is thinking, no one ever has, and a charter among nations, establishing new rules of conduct, is probably foredoomed. The masses await a leader, and leaders "militate"—bring about change. Everyone gropes toward an "ever breaking newness," but perceived newness is anything but new. The newness is just another form of the old, another exercise in self-righteousness that leads to the same outcome. Those who feel "blessed" will never be above brutality, because their feelings of superiority, of being blessed, are a kind of "courage," a courage that is but a mask for weakness and folly.

FURTHER READING

Marcus, Mordecai. *The Poems of Robert Frost: An Explication*. Boston: G. K. Hall, 1991.

"Cow in Apple Time, The" (1916)

During apple time a lone cow is so inspired that a wall no longer confines her; being fenced in is no different from being in an open pasture. And walls once again figure prominently in Frost's New England landscape. (*See* "MENDING WALL," "BOND AND FREE," and "ATMOSPHERE," among others.)

The cow has gotten off her feed, which is mainly grass, though this pasture does not have much to offer. Distracted by the sweet delights of the season, which are so much more appealing than the "pasture withering to the root," this free-spirited bovine drools cider syrup from the apples on which she has been feasting. She is drunk with cider and joy. She has moved from innocence to experience by "having tasted fruit."

Frost in Vermont. "The Cow in Apple Time": "Sometimes inspires the only cow of late / To make no more of a wall than an open gate, / And think no more of wall-builders than fools." *(Courtesy Lofman/Time Life Pictures/Getty Images)*

This giddy cow flies (as does the nursery rhyme cow that "jumps over the moon") from "tree to tree" consuming with gusto the fallen apples, until she makes herself sick. The poem ends with her "bellow[ing] ... against the sky, / Her udder shrivel[ing] and the milk [gone] dry."

The setting is Edenic: The apples represent a loss of innocence, and the cow's overindulgence is of an almost human kind. She is drunk on the fruits of knowledge. The danger in following one's bliss is possible loss not just of innocence but of purpose.

This poem was first published in ENGLAND in the December 1914 issue of *Poetry and Drama* and was later included in Frost's third collection, *Mountain Interval*. *See* WALLS.

FURTHER READING

Reed, Richard. "The Animal World in Frost's Poetry." In *Frost: Centennial Essays II*, edited by Jac Tharpe, 159–169. Jackson: University Press of Mississippi, 1976.

"Death of the Hired Man, The" (1914)

One of Frost's most compelling narrative poems, "The Death of the Hired Man" first appeared in *North of Boston*, a collection teeming with dramatic dialogues, including "Home Burial," "Blueberries," and "The Code," as well as the lesser-known "The Mountain," "A Hundred Collars," "The Fear," and others. As many of the poems in this collection do, "Death of the Hired Man," carefully constructs in everyday language a New England rural scene. In this instance the subtle unfolding explores one of Frost's most memorable lines: "Home is the place where, when you have to go there, / They have to take you in." The line appears roughly halfway through the poem, but it largely sums up the conflict on which the understated, unsentimental drama hinges.

In a preface to the poem written for the textbook *American Authors Today* (1947), edited by Whit Burnett and Charles Slatkin, Frost states facetiously that the "employee here depicted is no longer numerous enough to be dealt with statistically by the Department of Economics and Sociology. Nevertheless I should like to flatter myself that it is at least partly for his sake that the revolution [National Labor Relations] is being brought on." Frost says that he is glad to make the connection and "give [his] poems every extraneous help possible." He cautions his readers that it is "in blank verse, not free verse." The preface was not published during his lifetime, as the editors decided to write their own introduction.

The poem is concerned with the relationships among three characters: the wife Mary, her husband Warren, and Silas, a hired hand. The setting is a hay farm in winter. The poem, which has been performed as a one-act play, opens as a play might. Mary is introduced "musing on the lamp-flame at the table / Waiting for Warren." Warren has gone to the market in town, and while he is away, Silas, the former hired hand (who never appears "on stage"), has returned after what seems to have been an extended absence. Description soon gives way to dialogue, as more and more the conversation between husband and wife reveals what is and is not meant.

The terse opening phrases are Mary's: "Silas is back ... Be kind"—and the reader is abruptly alerted that there may be some reason not to be kind.

As is typical in other Frost narratives, such as "Home Burial," there is a conflict between two people. Warren's first lines are "When was I ever anything but kind to him?" and "But I'll not have the fellow back." Clearly the husband and wife have different approaches to the problem of Silas, though it will become clear by the end that they think somewhat similarly of him.

Silas apparently has had a habit of disappearing when he was needed most. His last disappearance came in response to his declined request for "a little pay, / Enough at least to buy tobacco with," as he did not want to have to "beg and be beholden." Warren simply could not pay, other than with room and board, though he wished he could, so Silas apparently moved on to someone who was able to "coax him off with pocket-money." Warren feels betrayed since Silas has a habit of leaving "[i]n haying time, when any help is scarce" and returning in winter, when Warren and Mary, and perhaps no one else, will have to take him in.

Mary throughout attempts to "Sh!" Warren, lest Silas overhear his grievances about him, while Warren expresses his objections to taking Silas in once again. Mary's descriptions of Silas reveal a broken and confused man who "jumble[s] everything" and is a "changed" and "miserable sight." Mary is sympathetic to Silas because she has seen him, though she has found him scarcely recognizable. At present Silas is "asleep beside the stove," having been unable to keep from "nodding off" despite Mary's efforts to keep him awake.

Silas has returned for another reason, but in an attempt to "save his self-respect" he has claimed to come to help "ditch the meadow" and "clear the upper pasture." His work is something he can be proud of, as opposed to his abandoning Warren at haying time, and it is a customary appreciation for work that makes him think that Warren and Mary might be sympathetic to him. (The New England appreciation for work is developed considerably in "After Apple-Picking.")

A boy named Harold Wilson, who has finished school and is now "teaching in his college," unexpectedly occupies Silas's thoughts. The boy is someone Silas had an ongoing quarrel with while working on the farm, and they are described as having "fought / All through July under the blazing sun." Mary says, hauntingly, "those days trouble

Silas like a dream." It turns out Silas was "piqued" by the boy's "assurance" and still spends time, according to Mary, trying to think of other points he might have made during their arguments. A clear distinction is drawn between the merely "school smart" Harold and the simpler but land-savvy Silas, who can "find water with a hazel prong." (Frost habitually favored life smarts over book smarts.) Mary, while reflecting on "[h]ow some things linger" says she knows "just how it feels / To think of the right thing to say too late," and this may constitute some oblique commentary on her years with Warren. Suddenly there is a bit of Silas in Mary, making the desires of the hired hand seem quite natural. Silas is described as wanting to go back and begin over with the boy, wanting another shot at teaching him "how to build a load of hay." This desire is reminiscent of the speaker in "Birches," whose own aging causes him to think he might like to "come back" to earth and "begin over."

Warren says Silas's "one accomplishment" was building a load of hay "every forkful in its place." Mary says that Silas "thinks if he could teach [Harold] that, he'd be / Some good perhaps to someone in the world," and with that Harold becomes a central figure in defining the worth of Silas's life. "Poor Silas," Mary continues, imagining that he has "nothing to look backward to with pride, / And nothing to look forward to with hope." Silas is a sad but prideful character who has spent his life working for others, if somewhat half-heartedly, and in the end finds that not only has he done little "good" in the world but tragically he has no place he can truly call home. His life has meaning, but it is the sort of meaning that is more easily found by readers of the poem than by Silas himself.

Here the narrative voice returns and provides a description of the moon "falling down the west, / Dragging the whole sky with it to the hills." The moon is clearly a highly significant metaphor, and before the final scene, the poem will return to it. In its earlier appearance, as the moon drags the sky with it, its light pours "softly" into Mary's lap. Mary is described in gentle terms as playing "Upon the harp-like morning-glory strings" some "unheard . . . tenderness." It is winter, and the stripped vines of the morning glory stretched on the trellis outside

the window might well resemble the strings of a harp. Mary appears to be deep in thought, quietly strumming the shadows cast by the "strings" onto her lap.

Now Mary calmly reveals to Warren what she and the reader have known all along: that Silas "has come home to die."

Warren "gently" mocks Mary's use of the word "home" in relation to Silas. But his wife responds that "it all depends on what you mean by home," and the reader is compelled to reflect on just what *home* means. At the same time Mary sadly opines that Silas is "nothing" to either her or Warren. Then she backs up a bit and reconsiders her choice of the word *home*. She says that instead she might have "called it / Something you somehow haven't to deserve," as if home were not a place but an action, something one does rather than has.

The conversation veers off to a discussion of Silas's brother, who apparently lives only 13 miles from Warren and Mary and is "rich." But they do not know this because Silas has told them; he has never revealed to them a kinship with anyone. Mary concludes that the reason Silas has no relationship with his family is that "Silas is what he is . . . just the kind that kinsfolk can't abide." Frost hints at the sort of disagreements that family members have as opposed to those that take place in the open with outsiders. There is a suggestion that family may accept fewer flaws in its members than will those who are not family. After all, Silas "never did a thing so very bad," never "hurt anyone," but he still will not be "ashamed to please his brother" by showing up on his doorstep and asking to be let in. There apparently is less shame associated with showing up on Warren and Mary's doorstep, as they are, importantly, not kin.

As the poem comes to a close, Mary sends Warren in to check on Silas with a warning not to "laugh at him." The notion of Silas being allowed to save face is paramount. In the meantime, Mary sits to "see if that small sailing cloud / Will hit or miss the moon." It "hit[s] the moon." The poet writes, "Then there were three there, making a dim row, / The moon, the little silver cloud, and she." A heavenly conjunction heralds Silas's end.

"'Warren?' she questioned."

　　　　"'Dead,' was all he answered."

Silas has come "home" to die.

The understated dialogue questions the relationships between the hired and the people who hire them, what a home really is, and what a person struggles with before dying. Its sadnesses are immense. A man may work his whole life for others, only to discover that a routine politeness is the extent of the bond shared, as ultimately a worker means "nothing" to his employer.

In his 1960 *Paris Review* interview with Richard Poirier, Frost used the poem to discuss Franklin Delano Roosevelt's New Deal. He distinguished between the masculine, Republican way of viewing home as "the place where, when you have to go there, They have to take you in" and the feminine, Democratic way as "I should have called it / Something you somehow haven't to deserve." He points out that "[v]ery few have noticed that second thing, they've always noticed the sarcasm, the hardness of the male one" (885).

Home is not a place where one chooses to go, nor is it a place where the inhabitants willingly take one in, deserving or not needing to be deserved. It is where, when one *has* to go there, "they *have* to take you in." When death is about, one might arrive on any doorstep, often the doorstep that allows death with the least remorse, as one's past and what one did or did not do with life will haunt enough.

While Warren and Mary are more gentle than "ungentle," there is something almost "departmental" about their relationship to Silas. *See* HOME, THEME OF.

FURTHER READING

Brooks, Cleanth, and Robert Penn Warren. *Understanding Poetry: An Anthology for College Students.* Rev. shorter ed. New York: Henry Holt, 1950, 388–397.

Charney, Maurice. "Robert Frost's Conversational Style," *Connotations: A Journal for Critical Debate* 10, nos. 2–3 (2000–2001): 147–159.

French, Warren. "'The Death of the Hired Man': Modernism and Transcendence." In *Frost: Centennial Essays III,* edited by Jac Tharpe, 382–401. Jackson: University Press of Mississippi, 1978.

Frost, Carol. "Frost's Way of Speaking," *New England Review: Middlebury Series* 23, no. 1 (Winter 2002): 119–133.

Frost, Robert. "*Paris Review* Interview with Richard Poirier," In *Robert Frost Collected Prose, Poems, and Plays.* Edited by Richard Poirier and Mark Richardson. New York: Holt, 1995.

Hoffman, Tyler. *Robert Frost and the Politics of Poetry.* Hanover, N.H.: Middlebury College Press, 2001, 103–106, 189–190.

Jost, Walter. "Lessons in the Conversation That We Are: Robert Frost's 'Death of the Hired Man,'" *College English* 58, no. 4 (April 1996): 397–422.

Monteiro, George. "Frost's Hired Hand," *College Literature* 14, no. 2 (Spring 1987): 128–135.

Pack, Robert. *Belief and Uncertainty in the Poetry of Robert Frost.* Hanover, N.H.: Middlebury College Press, 2003, 104–109.

Vogel, Nancy. "A Post Mortem on 'The Death of the Hired Man.'" In *Frost: Centennial Essays,* edited by Jac Tharpe, 201–206. Jackson: University Press of Mississippi, 1974.

"Demiurge's Laugh, The" (1913)

First appearing in *A Boy's Will* and originally subtitled "About Science," this poem has been characterized by Robert Faggen as one of Frost's "most terrifying versions of the flight into the wilderness from a fear of god."

Several critics have made much of the similarly "demoniac" and "unearthly" laughter of a loon on the pond as described in chapter 12 of Henry David Thoreau's *Walden,* a book with which Frost was thoroughly familiar.

The opening line is haunting: "It was far in the sameness of the wood." As a beginning, its matter-of-factness shares something with "Once upon a time." The setting for the poem has been pronounced, and the word "sameness" has eerily indicated that when one is in "far," all woods appear similar and finding one's way becomes difficult. There is in sameness something frightening and magical. The time has been set as well: "the light was beginning to fail," and the speaker will soon be engulfed in a wooded darkness. It is then that he "suddenly hear[s]—all [he] need[s] to hear" and that which haunts him still. The scene has something in common with a fairy tale or ghost story: It is deep in the dark woods where mystical creatures dwell.

The speaker is laughed at by the demiurge for trying to run "with joy on the Demon's trail." The demiurge is sometimes equated with a demon and with malevolence, but not always. There are various interpretations for Frost's selections of the word *demiurge* and the combination of the two terms in one creature. A demiurge is a Platonic deity who fashioned the world out of chaos. He is a lesser god, a demigod, and, more literally, a worker for the people. He did not create the world, but he did help build it. The demiurge may also be taken simply as the "genius," the informing spirit or character of a place. Demons are sometimes, but not always, characterized as evil. A demon may be a persistently tormenting force or passion. For Frost the demiurge and demon seem to be one and to represent a powerful creative force or personality. The range of interpretations for the term *demiurge* probably explains Frost's selection of it. In the poem the term is in some ways meant to hint at malevolence, but mostly it is meant as a strong force that may be interpreted as either internal or external.

At the outset the reader learns that the speaker feels foolish for being caught trying to hunt a "true god." The question of what it means to be true is raised. The speaker seems to have been seeking in nature something otherworldly, but in his joyous pursuit he is in turn pursued by a powerful creative force. The demiurge, as half-god, opposes the desire for God the creator.

The demon's laugh comes with the setting of the sun, when the speaker realizes that while he thought he was chasing something, it was really chasing him. As Faggen interprets it, the demiurge "goads us to chase our own tails and laughs at the comedy" (261–262). But if the force comes from within, Faggen's interpretation becomes more complex.

The sound of the laughter is "sleepy"; it is mocking and does not "care." The demon waking at night arises from his "wallow," his earthly dwelling, "brushing the dirt from his eye," and the poem asserts, "well I knew what the Demon meant." The reader is not aware of what precisely the demon meant, however, as Frost leaves it open to speculation, giving only the information he wishes to. (The phrase Frost wrote in his *Introduction to King Jasper* seems appropriate here: "If I wanted you to know, I should have told you in the poem.") Robert Hass maintains that while the speaker does not clearly reveal what is meant, the

> parable's lessons are clear: science can never lead to utopia nor satisfy humans' spiritual needs. The material world that science explores is not just indifferent to the human condition in a post-Darwinian universe; in Frost's early poetic imagination it is a malevolent force that mocks and abandons human beings in their most dire circumstances (3).

Here the demon has brushed the dirt from his eye; Frost uses similar imagery in his poem "Dust in the Eyes" from *West-Running Brook*, except that the speaker in that poem is the poet himself.

The speaker cannot forget the demon's laugh, as its mockery makes him foolish. Something haunts him. He tries to retain his pride by acting as though he is just looking in the leaves for something, but it is doubtful that he fools the demon. The speaker feels insignificant and imagines that he is not worth the demon's sticking around to see what he is up to. He at last resigns himself to his position, slumping against a tree.

While Faggen speaks of the poem as an expression of a fear of God, the other definitions of the words *demiurge* and *demon* would suggest that the poem is more internal than external. The creature, as a creative and not necessarily a demoniac force, could represent the place itself, the woods, or the poet's own personality. In any instance the laughter in the woods resounds only in the speaker's mind.

In these ways the poem may also be taken as a metaphor for the poetic process itself. The speaker thinks he is chasing after a "true god"—perhaps his "genius" in the modern sense—but feels insecure about it, worrying that when the "light . . . fail[s]" he will be mocked. That is, when his own light goes out, no one will care, and even if someone does, the response may be nothing but mocking laughter.

See PHILOSOPHY.

FURTHER READING

Coakley, John. "T. S. Elliot's 'Mr. Apollinax' and Frost's 'Demiurge's Laugh,'" *Explicator* 45, no. 1 (Fall 1986): 42–45.

Faggen, Robert. *Robert Frost and the Challenge of Darwin.* Ann Arbor: University of Michigan Press, 1997, 261–263.

Hass, Robert. *Going by Contraries: Robert Frost's Conflict with Science.* Charlottesville: University Press of Virginia, 2002.

Thoreau, Henry David. *Henry David Thoreau: Collected Essays and Poems.* Edited by Elizabeth Hall Witherell. New York: Library of America, 2001.

"Departmental" (1936)

Written one winter in Key West, the poem comprises a skillful selection of mostly rhyming couplets that Katherine Kearns picturesquely describes as antlike, "scurr[ying] down the page" (217n). During a reading, Frost once identified the ants as the Key West kind, not the New England kind, and called the poem a "funny one." The poem is comic in some ways, making it easy for readers to be swept up by the rhymes and the humor with little reflection. But further study makes evident typical Frostian political and social criticism, while revealing something characteristically human about his observations of nature at work, although Frost once claimed, "I wrote this in entire detachment. . . . And you can't go looking into it with a Freudian eye for anything that's eating me. It's about an ant, A-N-T, that I met in Florida" ("Speaking of Loyalty").

The winter during which "Departmental" was composed, Key West had become what Frost called "a safe place for slackers," thus displaying his unconcealed contempt for the policies of President Franklin Delano Roosevelt's New Deal. The year Frost made his statement, Key West had been identified as one of the prime targets for New Deal relief, and Frost, as always, turned his prodding on what he regarded as governmental charity. Some critics have dismissed the poem as somehow unworthy of serious study, but beyond the sometimes jogtrot rhymes (not that one necessarily wants to), there is both sadness and significance concentrated in the death of a mere ant.

The first part of the poem is commentary on the lives ants lead, suggesting how humans might reflect on themselves. The ants are described as a "curious race," and examples are provided as to why they are so curious. By curious Frost means not that they are inquisitive but that they are strange. This strangeness arises from each ant being severely limited in performing only its "duty." If an ant runs into a moth, he does not concern himself unless he is one of the departmentalized "hive's enquiry squad / Whose work is to find out God / And the nature of time and space." Otherwise, the ant will give it "scarcely a touch" before he is again "off on his duty run." And when an ant runs into one of its own dead, the response is the same: "he" is not given "a moment's arrest— / Seems not even impressed." Rather, as in the case of the moth, he simply reports the situation to some ant suitably designated, whose job is more closely related to orderly execution of necessary details. The similarity to military actions in the conduct of the ants is easily recognized and is highlighted in the choice of such words as "duty," "squad," and "reports." In many ways the scene resembles a battleground.

To further the significance of the description, the poem focuses on the death of the "selfless forager" ant, Jerry McCormic. McCormic (perhaps an Irish ant) is significant because, among myriad ants, he has a specific identity. The "Janizary / Whose office it is to bury" is ordered by the Queen of the ant colony to retrieve McCormic's remains. The Queen's regal speech is not just high-toned but humane and stirring. It is here that the poem transcends social criticism. The Queen's elegiac language and vivid imagery are intensely moving: "Go bring him home to his people. / Lay him in state on a sepal. / Wrap him for shroud in a petal. / Embalm him with ichor of nettle." The lyrical description may bring to mind the fanciful world of Puck and the other fairies in Shakespeare's *A Midsummer Night's Dream*.

Some of Frost's greatest rhymes appear in "Departmental," including the clever "any" with "antennae" (which Frost made a point of emphasizing at readings, invariably getting a laugh). Much of the humor lies in the selection of the rhymes throughout. Several come into play in the Queen's orders of what is to be done with McCormic, "Jerry" with "Janizary," "people" with "sepal," and "petal" with "nettle." Frost has fun not only with the rhymes but also in the selection of words such as "formic." Formic is a stinging acid that occurs naturally in ants, but in the poem it becomes the "language" of ants. The sepal is the green, leafy part of a flower, which becomes the pallet on which McCormic will be borne away for burial. Ichor is the ethereal fluid that flowed in the veins of the gods of the ancient Greeks. Being embalmed with ichor of nettle (a prickly, stinging plant) is royal treatment indeed. The regal sendoff for McCormic, as commanded by the Queen, is a highly elevated affair. Jerry must have been a very special ant. And the image of an ant laid out on a sepal and shrouded in a petal certainly suggests a funeral in fairyland.

The scene that is set later turns humorous when, following the Queen's declaration, the orders are carried out by an ant who in taking "formal position / With feelers calmly atwiddle, / Seizes the dead by the middle" and "Carries him out of there." "Atwiddle" absolutely got a giggle when Frost read the poem.

But the humor comes to an abrupt end. After 41 lines of playful rhyme without a stanza break, the final four lines are all seriousness:

No one stands round to stare.
It is nobody else's affair.

It couldn't be called ungentle.
But how thoroughly departmental.

A recurring theme in Frost, the same sentiment is expressed in "Home Burial": "Friends make pretense of following to the grave, / But before one is in it, their minds are turned / And making the best of their way back to life / And living people, and things they understand." Or in "Out, Out—," where the poet writes: "Little—less—nothing! And that ended it. No more to build on there. And they, since they / Were not the one dead, turned to their affairs."

Frost is troubled by the return to daily life after presiding over death that is inevitable for the living. Funerals among humans come and go as quickly as Jerry McCormic's, and the living go on living, for they must; there is nothing else to do except die, which would, in turn, lead to the same result, only for others. He is also troubled by the possibility that socialism will lead to everyone's assuming their own specified "duty run" and therefore not having time or even reason to "find out God / And the nature of time and space," unless it is involved in the task assigned. The criticism does not have to be limited to only military or socialist behavior, however. There is often in everyday matters a certain drudgery of living that can lead to a lack of reflection and inquiry and to an automatic, antlike, and duty-run state.

There is a departmental aspect to any death, as the living will ultimately return to their lives, but there is a particularly departmental quality to death in modern life, with its reliance on morticians rather than family internments in the side yard. Frost focuses on the experience of death from the view of one living, but of one living apart and untouched. Yet he manages to touch the alert and sensitive reader profoundly with the life of a forager ant so minuscule as not to be worthy of attention on any other occasion.

The poem can be enjoyed by children as well as adults, as its rhymes are every bit as engaging as those in any children's book, but what begins in fun does not always end that way, and with the conclusion of "Departmental" there comes a solemnity quite profound.

"Departmental" appeared in the "Taken Doubly" section of *A Further Range*, with the subtitle "or, the End of My Ant Jerry," after having been published earlier that year in the *Yale Review*. *See* HOME, THEME OF.

FURTHER READING

D'Avanzo, Mario L. "Frost's 'Departmental' and Emerson: A Further Range of Satire," *Concerning Poetry* 10, no. 2 (1977): 67–69.

Doyle, John Robert, Jr. *The Poetry of Robert Frost: An Analysis.* New York: Hafner Press, 1962, 92–99.

Faggen, Robert. *Robert Frost and the Challenge of Darwin.* Ann Arbor: University of Michigan Press, 1997, 91–93.

Kearns, Katherine. *Robert Frost and a Poetics of Appetite.* Cambridge: Cambridge University Press, 1994.

Monteiro, George. *Robert Frost and the New England Renaissance.* Lexington: University Press of Kentucky, 1988, 130–131.

Parini, Jay. *Robert Frost: A Life.* New York: Holt, 1999, 293–294.

"Desert Places" (1936)

"Desert Places," "Design," and "Departmental," three of Frost's most important poems, were all collected in *A Further Range,* and all of them use what seems a simple natural occurrence as material for philosophical reflection. In "Design" it is the spider and moth that are brought "thither in the night," in "Departmental" it is the death of the selfless forager ant Jerry, and in "Desert Places" it is the "snow falling and night falling fast, oh, fast" that halt the speaker and inspire contemplation. Also, both "Design," and "Desert Places" are collected in a section of the book titled "Taken Singly." Among the poems included in this section are "A Leaf-Treader" and "Afterflakes," which have much in common with the above-mentioned poems.

Frost once told his friend and fellow poet Robert Penn Warren that he wrote "Desert Places" straight through from beginning to end. Nature, death, the possibility of immortality, and, most of all, the inevitability of loss are what propel this poem. Perhaps the highly personal nature of these themes is what allowed Frost to create the poem almost without effort. Jay Parini asserts that "those deserts were there, in his life and mind, and every poem was an attempt to rescue some clarity, to find oases of language in deserts of thought and feeling" (444).

The first stanza presents an image of nature and of death: The snow is about to bury the remaining "weeds and stubble" in a field the speaker happens to be passing by. As in nearly all of Frost's poems, this observation of a natural occurrence is cause for reflection on the human condition. Frost once said in an interview, "I guess I'm not a nature poet, I have only written two poems without a human being in them," and as always, it is the human being in nature that makes this winter scene significant. In "Desert Places," as in "Stopping by Woods on a Snowy Evening," wherein the speaker has also stopped on a dark evening "[t]o watch the woods fill up with snow," the human being in nature is seeking a way of "going past" the winter of life that the snow symbolizes, perhaps because he too has "miles to go" before he sleeps. This desire to go past is also much like the desire of the "swinger of birches" to climb "*toward* heaven."

After the first stanza depicts the scene, the three remaining stanzas contemplate what this winter scene represents for the speaker: an immense loneliness. The loneliness the snow brings is all-embracing. It does not exempt the land, the animals "smothered in their lairs," or the "absent-spirited" speaker. The speaker is not immune because he is absent-spirited, and his lack of spirit causes him not to "count." He is lumped in with the rest of nature, rather than distinguished because of his humanity, because his "spirit" goes unnoticed. This echoes "Afterflakes," in which the speaker, while contemplating a "teeming snowfall," imagines that if he "shed[s] such darkness" then "the reason was in [him]."

It is the ultimate loneliness—the loneliness of a man that comes to the fore. And in particular, it is the loneliness of a man who has no spirit. The suggestion is that the man is faithless because he lacks faith in a superior being, though it could also be argued that it is because he lacks belief in himself. Because he is faithless, he is included "unawares," and the question becomes, Who is unaware, the speaker or the force that "includes"? The attribute that is to distinguish the speaker from the other animals is his faith and perhaps his soul. And if that is hard to make out, hard to find, either by him or by the force that brings on night and darkness, then he too will be "smothered" by the snow, just as other unaware animals are.

The speaker then informs his readers that the loneliness the snow brings is less lonely than the loneliness of death, as snow is only a temporary death. It is seasonal and will eventually pass, much as the speaker hoped to "pass" himself at the start of the poem, perhaps to move on to spring, again much like the speaker in "Birches," who wants to "begin over." But the speaker here knows that he cannot go past as he had hoped and that it "will be more lonely ere it will be less." To him the ultimate loneliness is death. This belief reinforces his lack of faith in the transcendent, since if one embraces Christian ideas of immortality, death should bring comfort and peace. But this speaker does not believe that death will eliminate his loneliness; rather, it will overwhelm.

The fear that nature brings with its weather is insignificant compared with the fear that the speaker feels is part of the human condition. The worst Frost can imagine is not death, but death in life—the triumph of the blank inexpressible "with no expression, nothing to express." Nothing outside him can evoke such strong emotions as the knowledge of his own absences. When he peers up at the stars, he becomes only more fully aware of his smallness—that "between stars" and "on stars" "no human race is."

The poem is a contemplation on the impersonal nature of the world, but in several ways it also displays a willfully malevolent natural force. If what includes the speaker "unawares" is a supernatural being, the presence of that being raises the question Frost raises in "Design": "What but design of darkness to appall?— / If design govern in a thing so small." Surely a creator who will "smother" unaware animals and human beings in their lairs for being "absent-spirited" is neither benign nor even involved. He is to be feared. There seem to be only two choices: a designer who appalls or no designer at all.

Many critics have imagined that the loneliness described is not simply a revelation about the human condition but rather a contemplation of what utter and absolute loneliness an absence of faith in a transcendent being can engender in

humans. But the loneliness that Frost describes in life and in death would be overwhelming not only for the faithless but also for those whose faith is in a being whose darkness appalls. And the human condition is a lonely one, with or without faith, as the speaker is fully aware, since he has it in him "so much nearer home / To scare [himself] with [his] own desert places." This is not the only night the poet "scares" himself. Night often brings on similar fears, as in "Acquainted with the Night" and "An Old Man's Winter Night."

Cleanth Brooks and Robert Penn Warren make a point of Frost's use of the colloquial, childlike, and somewhat understated "scare," noting that scaring is what the telling of ghost stories does to children. They hold that "by use of the word in the poem the man is made to imply that he is not a child to be so easily affected" (106). By not using a word such as *terrify* or *horrify*, Frost insinuates, according to Brooks and Warren, that the speaker has it within himself to overcome his fears, as "even in his loneliness of spirit he can still find strength enough in himself" (106). In Frost, human cunning is often pitted against nature's constant challenges and occasional malevolence, but human beings mostly overcome. However, in "Bonfire," another of the only 12 poems in which Frost uses a form of the word "scare," the speaker's ghost story frightens the narrator as much as it does the children. *See* NATURE and STARS.

FURTHER READING

Brooks, Cleanth, and Robert Penn Warren. *Understanding Poetry*. 3rd ed. New York: Holt, Rinehart and Winston, 1960, 104–107.

Brower, Reuben A. *The Poetry of Robert Frost: Constellations of Intention*. New York: Oxford University Press, 1963, 108–110.

Cook, Reginald. *The Dimensions of Robert Frost*. New York: Rinehart, 1958, 186–187.

———. *Robert Frost: A Living Voice*. Amherst: University of Massachusetts Press, 1974.

Doyle, John Robert, Jr. *The Poetry of Robert Frost: An Analysis*. New York: Hafner Press, 1962, 159–166.

Hass, Robert. *Going by Contraries: Robert Frost's Conflict with Science*. Charlottesville: University Press of Virginia, 2002. 98–100.

Heaney, Seamus. "Above the Brim." In *Robert Frost, Modern Critical Views*, edited by Harold Bloom, 201–218. Philadelphia: Chelsea House, 2003.

McInery, Stephen. "'Little Forms': Four Poems and a Developing Theme of Robert Frost," *Critical Review* 40 (2000): 59–74.

Monteiro, George. *Robert Frost and the New England Renaissance.* Lexington: University Press of Kentucky, 1988. 109–111.

Parini, Jay. *Robert Frost: A Life.* New York: Holt, 1999, 285–286.

Stone, Edward. "'Other 'Desert Places': Frost and Hawthorne." In *Frost Centennial Essays,* edited by Jac Tharpe, et al., 275–287. Jackson: University Press of Mississippi, 1974.

Von Frank, Albert J. "'Nothing That Is': A Study of Frost's 'Desert Places,'" In *Frost: Centennial Essays,* edited by Jac Tharpe, et al., 121–132. Jackson: University Press of Mississippi, 1974.

"Design" (1936)

One of Frost's most philosophical poems, "Design" appeared in its final form in the section titled "Taken Singly" in *A Further Range,* which includes other such well-known poems as "Desert Places," "Neither Out Far nor In Deep," and "Clear and Colder," the last of which employs imagery similar to that of "Design." Frost claimed that the poem was written as an answer to William Cullent Bryant's "To a Waterfowl," in which the speaker feels assured that his steps, as well as the waterfowl's, while taken alone, are overseen by God, a "Power whose care / Teaches thy way along that pathless coast." "Design" is a Petrarchan sonnet, with a variation in the final six lines. But while it may be a sonnet, it is an uncommon one.

It begins as many of Frost's poems do, with the narrator encountering something in nature that becomes a touchstone for philosophical inquiry. The speaker happens upon a spider atop a flower, holding aloft a dead moth. The descriptions of the spider, flower, and moth are intriguing. The spider is "dimpled," "fat," and "white"; it is a "snow-drop" spider. It is fat, one presumes, from having feasted on the liquid of the moth. Dimpled is a characteristic used to describe something appealing, cute, or attractive. The two adjectives dimpled and fat together are often associated with infants, not with predators. Roughly 90 percent of all spiders hunt rather than spinning webs to catch their prey, and while some critics have inferred that Frost's mention of a paper kite implies a web (since kites involve strings), that seems a forced inference. It is more likely that this spider is a hunter. Entomologist Allen Carson Cohen explains that "Many ambush spiders such as crab spiders sit cryptically in or on flowers awaiting prey," implying that the spider described here may indeed be a crab spider (70).

A heal-all is traditionally a blue, purple, or violet flower, but this one is white. Its habitat is generally along roadsides, in fields, and in waste places. The heal-all is so named because it once was assumed to have healing powers. But this heal-all is not at all healing; it is the background for "blight." The moth, also white and constituting the third of a trio of white objects, has wings "like a paper kite" and appears as a "rigid satin cloth." Readers have pointed out that the rigidity in such descriptions suggests rigor mortis. The word *white*, appearing five times in the poem—which was originally titled "In White"—draws a similarity among ordinarily disparate objects. White often represents innocence and purity but is also associated with fear, with which one may turn white, and, of course, with death. Here it seems to represent all of these conditions.

As in "Clear and Colder," which appears three poems later in *A Further Range,* where the recipe for a "Fall Elixir" creates a "witches' chowder," the recipe in "Design" is "like the ingredients of a witches' broth." The ingredients are the three objects, which are "ready to begin the morning right." Frost may have intended a pun on "rite" to suggest not only that this is a morning ritual, a common occurrence, but that there is something correct, or even inevitable, in what has happened. There is a Frostian tongue-in-cheek echo of the saying "Begin the morning right." The ingredients for this broth are "mixed" as are the ingredients in a cooking recipe. The final two lines of the first stanza read like instructions for their proper order: Add one snow-drop spider, whip the flower to a "froth," and garnish with dead wings "carried like a paper kite."

In keeping with the formal Petrarchan sonnet, the first stanza sets the scene and presents a "problem." The scene, though bleak, is framed by appealing imagery, however, while the rhyme scheme creates a harsher tone. Frost also relies on the rhyming of "cloth" and "moth," as he does in "Departmental," another poem in which witnessing an occurrence in nature becomes cause for reflection, but there the rhyming is more playful. The stark setting of "Design" subtly suggests the attitude of the speaker witnessing the unfolding of events. It presents its nature scene with bias partly concealed and holds off betraying any conclusions. The speaker cannot witness the scene, however, without being conscious of the destruction inherent in it; these are, after all, characters of "death and blight." It seems that design may dictate the recipe for this broth.

Whereas the first eight lines are largely descriptive, the last six seek to provide some resolution to the problem presented at the outset. But while the poem offers some element of resolution, its closing lines are made up largely of questions, either leaving what might be a resolution unresolved or suggesting that the conclusion is so obvious that it does not need to be stated.

The speaker wonders "what had that flower to do with being white," as though its whiteness was partly responsible for the death of the moth on its petals. He imagines the heal-all as "wayside blue and innocent." It seems its color has fallen by the wayside and that it has succumbed to the color of whiteness, the color of fear and death. (White heal-alls are uncommon in nature and generally cultivated.) The speaker came across something rare, a white heal-all. It is noteworthy, but he does not know why. The presence of death makes it hard for him to reflect on the rarity and beauty of the flower, causing him to consider instead its simple innocence in the morning begun right.

While Carson Cohen argues that "[w]ere the flower its ordinary color . . . the action of the poem probably would not have taken place," the speaker recognizes that the flower is not to be blamed for becoming the setting for this death drama (70).

The well-fed, dimpled spider also is white, as innocent of intention as its victim the moth. White makes all three—flower, moth, and spider—equally innocent. Both the "characters" and the setting are blameless.

The speaker continues to wonder "What brought that kindred spider to that height" raising the question of just what or whom the spider is kin to—the moth, the flower, or all living things. Height is generally associated with superiority, a higher position, but here the height is negative. The white moth is brought "thither in the night," so the poet has raised questions that have to do with purpose and design. He wonders if something "brought," "steered," and "govern[ed]" all this. The language is suggestive of control and of fate.

The poet theorizes on the notion of a carefully constructed design. He uses a typical scene in nature to contemplate what is horrifying in nature and in ourselves. Robert Pack writes that "Design" exemplifies the essence of the biblical Job, in whom terror and awe are mixed.

The philosopher William Paley, with whom Frost would have been familiar, argued that one can deduce not only the existence of god but all of his attributes simply by examining the design of the world. He used the analogy of a timepiece to confirm the intricate design of the universe and the necessity of a designer. Charles Darwin argued that the claim of being able to deduce the attributes of the designer was false through two examples: a cat playing with a mouse and a species of wasp that injects its eggs into the bodies of living caterpillars, which upon hatching eat the caterpillar from the inside for no other reason than to live.

The poem ends with the question "What but design of darkness to Appall?—/ If design govern in a thing so small." The choice of *Appall* is a careful one, since it also suggests *pall,* a cover for a coffin, as well as any covering which obscures or darkens. The speaker though concerned with something small, *is* appalled. It is often smallness that concerns Frost, as does the ant Jerry McCormic in "Departmental" or the mite in "A Considerable Speck."

Traditionally the second stanza of a sonnet provides some closure, but Frost's provides little. The "overwise" poet of "Dust in the Eyes" does not resolve his conflict. He provides three questions for the reader to consider, each one building on the previous and leading one to expect a harsh conclusion. This conclusion arrives in the form of a dilemma: One must either accept a designer who is malevolent and dark or conclude as Darwin did, that there is no designer and settle for the amoral character of nature.

See BELIEF and NIGHT.

FURTHER READING

Bagby, George F. *Frost and the Book of Nature.* Knoxville: University of Tennessee Press, 1993, 72–75.

Brower, Reuben A. *The Poetry of Robert Frost: Constellations of Intention.* New York: Oxford University Press, 1963, 104–108.

Calhoun, Richard J. "By Pretending They Are Not Sonnets: The Sonnets of Robert Frost at the Millennium." In *Roads Not Taken: Rereading Robert Frost,* edited by Earl J. Wilcox and Jonathan N. Barron, 217–235. Columbia: University of Missouri Press, 2000.

Carter, Everett. "Frost's 'Design,'" *Explicator* 47, no. 1 (Fall 1988): 23–26.

Cohen, Allen Carson. "Robert Frost's Anthropods," *American Entomologist* (Summer 1999): 70–72.

Cook, Reginald. *The Dimensions of Robert Frost.* New York: Rinehart, 1958, 106–107.

Hoffman, Tyler. *Robert Frost and the Politics of Poetry.* Hanover, N.H.: Middlebury College Press, 2001, 111–112.

Ingebretsen, Edward J. "'Design of Darkness to Appall': Religious Terror in the Poetry of Robert Frost," *Robert Frost Review* (Fall 1993): 50–57.

Jarrell, Randall. "To the Laodiceans." In *Poetry and the Age,* 88–91. New York: Vintage, 1955.

Kann, David. "Deadly Serious Play: Robert Frost's 'Design,'" *University of Hartford Studies in Literature: A Journal of Interdisciplinary Criticism* 14, no. 1 (1982): 23–32.

McClanahan, Thomas. "Frost's Theodicy: Word I Had No One Left But God." In *Frost: Centennial Essays II,* edited by Jac Tharpe, 112–126. Jackson: University Press of Mississippi, 1976.

Monteiro, George. *Robert Frost and the New England Renaissance.* Lexington: University Press of Kentucky, 1988, 34–43.

———. "Robert Frost's Metaphysical Sonnet." In *Frost Centennial Essays,* edited by Jac Tharpe, 333–339. Jackson: University Press of Mississippi, 1974.

Pack, Robert. *Belief and Uncertainty in the Poetry of Robert Frost.* Hanover, N.H.: Middlebury College Press, 2003, 56–60.

Parini, Jay. *Robert Frost: A Life.* New York: Holt, 1999, 111–112.

Perrine, Laurence. "Frost's 'Design,'" *Explicator* 42, no. 2 (Winter 1984): 16.

Timmerman, John H. *Robert Frost: The Ethics of Ambiguity.* Lewisburg, Pa.: Bucknell University Press, 2002, 30–33.

"Devotion" (1928)

This four-line poem from *West-Running Brook* provides a definition of its title word through analogy. It is meant as a brief but significant description of what it is to be devoted. The heart of the speaker "can think of no devotion / Greater than being shore to the ocean—." His description of the shores as "[h]olding the curve of one position, / Counting an endless repetition" is meant to be sufficient for understanding.

The sort of devotion described is the kind that asks for nothing in return except familiarity. The shore keeps the ocean buoyed, and the ocean's movement, the shifts of such a bewildering and magnificent force, are forever controlled. The shore knows what to expect and waits, never asking for anything different or more. And the ocean comes, rhythmically returning again and again.

The shore is solid, strong, and constant while the ocean is always in motion and changing. In this way, the shore acts as the stronger and more resilient of the two in the union and yet is receptive to the unpredictable and frequently dangerous and threatening ocean. The shore embraces the ocean and is a bulwark for it, despite the ocean's unpredictable nature. There remains a constant in the relationship that is predictable for both: The ocean will never leave the shore nor the shore the ocean.

The poem subtly suggests something sexual. The rhythmic movement and the "curve" of the shore suggest the pose of intercourse. Yet it remains hard to identify the gender one would associate with each, using traditional male and female stereotypes and gender roles. On the one hand, the shore seems more easily associated with woman, the curve of her body, her relationship to "home" as a place to return to. On the other hand, the shore represents strength and constancy, which is commonly associated with masculinity. Whether the shore or the ocean represents the male or the female is in the end, however, ultimately irrelevant to an understanding of the sexual aspects of the imagery.

While the kind of devotion described is steady and reliable, the poem may be read as suggesting a joylessness in devotion. The repetition is wrought with sadness. To count an endless repetition is to be completely without enjoyment or celebration; it is instead to remain at a constant hum, without peaks or valleys. The familiarity of this sort of union, the "holding" of "one position," can lead to stifling boredom.

If this poem is meant to be a description of devotion, then contrary to popular opinion, devotion is not a quality that is necessarily worthwhile for either party. Devotion becomes instead a characteristic that limits and restrains. While both the shore and the ocean need each other, it seems the shore, as steady and constant receiver, gains far less from the relationship. And devotion becomes something that, while reliable, is positively and utterly without enjoyment. The analogy ultimately leads to an understanding of the sort of devotion one finds between couples who no longer want to be together but can find no other way to be. And yet, what is a shore without an ocean, an ocean without a shore?

The view of repetition as leading to boredom contrasts starkly with Friedrich Nietzsche's notion of eternal recurrence, whereby all of one's experiences in life are repeated over and over again. In Nietzsche's view, repetition or eternal recurrence is an affirmation of all experiences, including those of the past and those that are not necessarily good. It is a way of embracing all in one's life. If "Devotion" is read from a Nietzschean perspective, the repetitive relation between shore and ocean can be an

affirmation for both shore and ocean, rather than cause for sorrow or despair.

FURTHER READING

Nietzsche, Friedrich. Aphorism 273. *The Gay Science.* Translated by Walter Kaufmann. New York: Vintage, 1974.

"Directive" (1947)

Described by Jay Parini as "both epitaph and poetic credo," providing "a map of [Frost's] inner landscape" (361), and by Thomas Dilworth as Frost's "most cryptic poem" (26), "Directive" was written fairly late in the poet's career. The setting, as Parini and others have pointed out, is inconsequential since "abandoned farms, even whole villages, are commonplace in northern New England." Frost himself described the poem in "On Taking Poetry" as "all full of dangers, sideways, off, and all that." It is a poem of pure descriptiveness that may be allegorical, but it can be read simply for its expression and the scene it so precisely lays out.

A directive is an order or instruction issued by a central authority, but as an adjective it means "serving to direct or guide." The poem begins by asking us to "back out of all this now" as it is "too much for us," and from the start the reader is made a part of the poem. The "us" seems to refer to both a listener within the poem and the reader without. As the reader backs up, away, or out, the poem goes on lyrically, drifting toward "a time made simple by the loss / Of detail, burned, dissolved, and broken off," and the images begin to echo the modernist idea of a world that has become a landscape of ruin, as somberly depicted in T. S. Eliot's post–World War I poem *The Waste Land* (1922). The poem's lack of stanza breaks and lengthy blank verse lines gives it a dreamy, almost otherworldly aspect. The repetition of certain words, particularly in the lines "There is a house that is no more a house / Upon a farm that is no more a farm / And in a town that is no more a town," creates an atmosphere somewhat similar to Eliot's "Love Song of J. Alfred Prufrock," which begins "Let us go then, you and I" and proceeds to take the reader on a similar sort of journey. (George Monteiro notes several other allusions to Eliot in "Directive.")

The tone and the scene are dreamy—not wistful but melancholic. Just as in old graveyards the inscriptions on headstones are so weathered as to be barely legible, the place the speaker describes is indistinct. There are remnants, dim outlines of house, farm, and town, but that is all. Parini reports that Frost once told an audience before a reading of this poem, "Go back to a favorite poet, or a place you almost forgot"; leading the reader further back in imagination, the unidentified "guide" travels down a road so rocky it "should have been a quarry." The images are not meant to be understood metaphorically. The rocky road is described as "monolithic knees the former town / Long since gave up pretense of keeping covered." The wear and tear of wagon wheels, over time, has created ledges that "show the lines" and "chisel work" of an "enormous Glacier" personified, bracing "his feet against the Arctic Pole." Roads are life's pathways in Frost, as in "The Road Not Taken," and this poem devotes many lines to making the image of the reader's guided path more vivid, following the road through changes in season and erosion of time.

As the poem continues to explore the ruins of a place that is no more, it becomes ever more haunted and haunting, and we must not mind being watched by 40 pairs of eyes peering out of forty cellar holes. A rustling in the trees suggests a shudder at the eeriness of it all. Halfway through the poem comes a question: "Where were they all not twenty years ago?" a reminder that this road leads further and further back in time. This is a place where woodpeckers "fretted apple trees" before those trees were "shaded out," and where there were two individual "village cultures" before something, whether too much change or just disuse, caused them to "fad[e] into each other."

In this time and place we can sing to ourselves "a cheering song" as we imagine someone traveling the road with us, just ahead, either on foot or "creaking with a buggy load of grain." The guide is reminiscing about a simpler, more bucolic time. By leading us back to this place, which can be found in either our mind or the guide's, we are given the key

to "finding" ourselves. Just as the two villages were lost when they came together as one, when united in the guide's vision we also are lost, so lost as perhaps to be able to find ourselves. It is by completely losing ourselves that we can be made whole again, as the very end of the poem advises.

But for now, we are lost enough to be found, we need to "pull in [our] ladder" and put up a "closed" sign, so that we will be the last to be guided down this road. We must secure the place before time and encroachment lead to further ruin. If we can do this, we not only will be found but will be able to make ourselves "at home."

The images that follow describe an overrun landscape. The only remaining field appears to be no bigger than the sore a harness makes. Of a children's playhouse all that remains are "shattered dishes" those "little things" that once made children glad. For this, we may weep. Of the house, all that is left is a "belilaced cellar hole" that is "slowly closing like a dent in dough." (The lilacs call to mind Walt Whitman's "When Lilacs Last in the Door-yard Bloom'd.") It is receding into the earth, being obscured by untamed foliage. The spring, the "brook that was the water of the house," is the only thing that is fresh and original because so near its source; it is "[t]oo lofty and original to rage," as does a swollen stream, and is the only thing remaining in this place that of itself can bring renewal.

In the now imaginary world of the past, the reader and guide unite, whether at the reader's or the guide's old, perhaps childhood, home. Just as Marianne Moore speaks of "imaginary gardens with real toads in them" in "Poetry," Frost has managed to steal an actual item from the distant past into this at least partly imagined world. The guide has hidden "in the instep arch / Of an old cedar . . . a broken drinking goblet like the Grail / Under a spell so the wrong ones can't find it." He remarks, teasingly, that he stole it from the children's playhouse. "Now, you must be thirsty, traveler: drink," he seems to say. The Grail is the chalice Christ is supposed to have used at the Last Supper.

Thomas Dilworth calls the poem a "guided tour through loss" (27), and the reader discovers that time is made simpler through loss, through going back. This is how we may find ourselves, but only the "right" ones, those able to yield to the imaginary force and travel the road the guide creates, can do so. The heightened rhetoric is almost biblical throughout, the Saint Mark reference being taken almost directly from Mark 4:11–12. While the poem seems to hint at Edwin Arlington Robinson's out-of-time "Miniver Cheevy," it also recalls a childhood place as far away as our own childhood and in its way as fantastical as Samuel Taylor Coleridge's Xanadu of "Kubla Khan." "Directive" first appeared in the *Virginia Quarterly Review* and later in *Steeple Bush*.

FURTHER READING

Bagby, George F. *Frost and the Book of Nature.* Knoxville: University of Tennessee Press, 1993, 30–31.

Berger, Charles. "Echoing Eden: Frost and Origins." In *Robert Frost,* Modern Critical Views, edited by Harold Bloom, 147–165. Philadelphia: Chelsea House, 2003.

Brower, Reuben A. *The Poetry of Robert Frost: Constellations of Intention.* New York: Oxford University Press, 1963, 232–242.

Charney, Maurice. "Robert Frost's Conversational Style," *Connotations: A Journal for Critical Debate* 10, no. 2–3 (2000–01): 147–159.

Cook, Reginald. *The Dimensions of Robert Frost.* New York: Rinehart, 1958, 138–142.

Dilworth, Thomas. "Frost's Directive," *Explicator* 58, no. 1 (Fall 1999): 26–29.

Doreski, William. "Meta-Meditation in Robert Frost's 'The Wood-Pile,' 'After Apple-Picking,' and 'Directive,'" *A Review of International English Literature* 23, no. 4 (October 1992): 35–49.

Doyle, John Robert, Jr. *The Poetry of Robert Frost: An Analysis.* New York: Hafner Press, 1962, 18–20.

Faggen, Robert. *Robert Frost and the Challenge of Darwin.* Ann Arbor: University of Michigan Press, 1997, 273–276.

Frattali, Steven V. "Frost's Critique of Humanism: A Rereading of 'Directive,'" *Robert Frost Review* (Fall 1994): 94–100.

Hass, Robert. *Going by Contraries: Robert Frost's Conflict with Science.* Charlottesville: University Press of Virginia, 2002, 84–86.

Levay, John. "Frost's 'Directive,'" *Explicator* 52, no. 1 (Fall 1993): 42–44.

Lynen, John. "Du Côté de Chez Frost." In *Frost: Centennial Essays,* edited by Jac Tharpe, 562–594. Jackson: University Press of Mississippi, 1974.

Marks, Herbert. "The Counter Intelligence of Robert Frost." In *Robert Frost,* Modern Critical Views, edited by Harold Bloom, 554–578. Philadelphia: Chelsea House, 2003.

Monteiro, George. "History, Legend, and Regional Verse in Frost's 'Directive,'" *New England Quarterly* 75, no. 2 (June 2002): 286–294.

O'Donnell, William G. "Talking about Poems with Robert Frost," *Massachusetts Review* 39, no. 2 (Summer 1998): 225–250.

Pack, Robert. *Belief and Uncertainty in the Poetry of Robert Frost.* Hanover, N.H.: Middlebury College Press, 2003.

Parini, Jay. *Robert Frost: A Life.* New York: Holt, 1999.

Richardson, Mark. *The Ordeal of Robert Frost: The Poet and His Poetics.* Chicago: University of Illinois Press, 1997.

Sanders, David Alan. "Revelation as Child's Play in Frost's 'Directive.'" In *Frost: Centennial Essays II,* edited by Jac Tharpe, 267–277. Jackson: University Press of Mississippi, 1976.

Watterson, William Collins. "Gerontion as Jokester: Humor and Anxiety in Robert Frost's 'Directive,'" *Robert Frost Review* (Fall 1992): 59–67.

"Discovery of the Madeiras, The" (1942)

First appearing in *A Witness Tree* as the last in the section titled "One or Two," "The Discovery of the Madeiras" is subtitled "A Rhyme of Hackluyt," referring to the 16th-century English writer, historian, and geographer, Richard Hackluyt (1552–1616). One of Hackluyt's chief works, *The Principal Navigations, Voyages, Traffiques and Discoveries of the English Nation,* contains the source for the tale. A basic retelling can be found in Jeffrey Cramer's *Robert Frost among His Poems.*

The poem uses the tale of two tragic romances that end in death as material for developing an explanation for how the Madeiras Islands, which make up an archipelago off Portugal in the northeast Atlantic Ocean west of Morocco, were discovered.

The poem opens by introducing us to a "stolen lady" boarding a ship. It is not clear whether the woman was "stolen from her wedded lord," a husband, "Or from her own self against her will." Frost selects his language carefully. The woman is described as cargo, as that which would be set forth in detail on a "lading bill," a slip indicating all the load for shipment. The woman is "weakly and blindly" led to the ship by her lover, who makes the "ordeal swift." The lover is described as kindly, even if the woman is described as stolen. As he lifts her onto the ship, she clings to him, demonstrating that "perhaps she went / Not entirely without consent." While the woman is uncertain about her departure, she does not seem uncertain about him. It is the act of boarding a ship as the only woman among "pirate sailors" and without the protection of English law that she finds deeply distressing. The opening stanza ends by noting that the two lovers are fleeing to some "vague Paphian" destination. Paphos was an ancient city of Cyprus that celebrated the temple of Venus, the Roman goddess of love and beauty.

After setting sail, the ship is tossed by a storm, causing it to do "more distance up and down, / . . . than on." The pirate sailors pray that if they survive and are left by God to die of old age, they will "go on pilgrimage" elsewhere. But as soon as the storm dies down without having harmed them in the least, they laugh off their prayers "as if they had turned a trick."

The third stanza returns to the stolen lady, explaining that this is "no lady's time of year." The woman is described as disappearing for long periods, apparently because of the seasickness brought on by the tossing of the vessel. When the sea calms, she is carried to the deck, where she lies in the sun and sleeps. When awake, she and her lover face each other, "darkly drink[ing] each other's eyes / With faint head shakings, no more wise," as if to suggest they are not sure what they have gotten themselves into. The man wants her eyes to tell him what "she does not want," but he also believes a " woman wants to be overruled." Frost asks know-

ingly, "Or was the instinct in him fooled?" Neither of them knows what they should think or feel and cannot read it well in the other. They are not unlike other couples in this; they can "only say like any two, 'You tell me and I'll tell you.'"

The lover, needing to "keep the captain's favor," "with her permissive smile," sometimes leaves the woman's side to "lean against the rail, And let the captain tell him a tale." On one occasion the lover learns that this very ship was once a slave ship that had "shipped a captive pair / Whose love was such they didn't care," presumably much like his own. When the male slave contracted "the fever," the "nigger-traders" decided to throw him overboard alive before the disease could spread to the others. His lover, a "savage jungle cat," created such a scene that the traders decide to make the ocean bed a "funeral-wedding" bed. The two were bound together naked at the waist. They threw their arms about each other's necks, "kiss[ed] and dr[a]nk each other's breath," and were hurled overboard, to "be their own marriage feast for the shark."

The opening line of the fifth stanza begins "When after talk with other men / A man comes back to a woman again / He tells her as much of blood and dirt / as he thinks will do her not too much hurt," creating a distinction between the behavior of men when alone, the blood and dirt they share, and what is acceptable in the company of women. Frost frequently draws distinctions in behavior between the sexes; a strong example can be found in "Home Burial."

When the lover returns to the woman after having the tale of the slave lovers, he intends not to share much "dirt," but she asks what was so amusing to the pirate captain, as the "jest seemed his and the plaudits his." The lover was not as amused by the tale as the captain: "He laughed but he did not make you laugh," she says. The woman seems to sense some ill intention in the captain's tale. After some prodding, the exasperated lover gives in with an "All right if you want the truth!" and retells the story. The woman retreats in horror: "I don't believe it! It isn't true!," her heart almost "ceas[ing] to beat." The woman is so pained by imagining such a horrific end to love that "[h]er spirit fade[s] as far away / As the living ever go yet stay." "Her thought" is that she has "had her pay," that she has been given her due. There is the implication of remorse for having stolen or been stolen away.

The stories of the two couples become intertwined. Herbert Marks writes that "the story of the fugitive lovers has the terrible rigor of a sphinx's riddle; for the interpolated tale of the slave couple sacrificed on the high seas is really a parable of the lovers' own fate." And as the poem continues, the woman is so tormented by the tale of the slaves lovers that her lover urges the captain to find the "nearest land"—an "untossed place" to "help her case," as though it is sea and not some other sickness that ails her. They land on some "nameless isle," but she does not heal, and the ship sails on without the woman or her lover. Her love grows dim, and eventually she is said to die of "thought."

Her lover carves her headstone, joining her name with his own, in what will be their only "marriage lines." They are joined in marriage only through an epitaph. He then makes a boat from a fallen tree and sets sail for the African shore.

When the lover arrives on the shore, he is taken prisoner by a Moor, but when he tells the tale of his voyage and of the land he discovered, he is sent to the king to be admired. The "nameless isle" of the Madeiras, where his stolen lady is buried, is verified, and the island is "named for him instead of her."

Frost sums up the scene with "But so is history like to err. / And soon it is neither here not there / Whether time's rewards are fair or unfair." With these lines, he seems to dismiss what he has made so significant: the loss of life, liberty, and love that comes with "discovery."

History books often obscure the truth in their retelling of events. In the same way, Frost's poem presents a different perspective from what might be expected from its title. His history is not sanitized, but his title is. He seems to be drawing a distinct analogy between what we learn in our history books and what really happens in his explanation of "The Discovery of the Madeiras."

FURTHER READING

Cramer, Jeffrey S. *Robert Frost among His Poems: A Literary Companion to the Poet's Own Biographical Contexts and Associations.* Jefferson, N.C., MacFarland, 1996.

Marks, Herbert. "The Counter-intelligence of Robert Frost." In *Robert Frost,* Modern Critical Views, edited by Harold Bloom. 554–578, Philadelphia: Chelsea House, 2003.

Meyers, Jeffrey. *Robert Frost: A Biography.* New York: Houghton Mifflin, 1996, 266–267.

Richardson, Mark. *The Ordeal of Robert Frost: The Poet and His Poetics.* Urbana, Ill.: University of Illinois Press, 1997.

"Doctrine of Excursions, The" (1939)

"The Doctrine of Excursions" was the preface to the *Bread Loaf Anthology* of 1939. In it Frost expresses his concern for the future of the BREAD LOAF SCHOOL OF ENGLISH in Vermont. He insists that it cannot become a "summer resort for routine education" and that no writer goes there "for correction or improvement" or to find a publisher. A writer can write to himself for years, but "[s]ooner or later to go on he must be read." "Bringing manuscript to Bread Loaf is in itself publication," he asserts. It is a place "where the writer can try his effect on readers."

The attitudes Frost expresses in this brief piece create a different impression not only of such gatherings of writers but of graduate programs in the fine arts. He argues that workshopping poetry is never about correction or improvement or even publication, as the brochures of many current graduate programs attest. It is simply about being "out in the world," where one can "brave the rigors of specific criticism." Such places are also where a poet "accrue[s] friends who will even cheat for him a little and refuse to see his faults if they are not so glaring as to show through eyelids." If a poet is worth his salt, he is so before he is ever read by anyone. Once he is heard or read, he either is "fitted into the nature of mankind" or not. Poets are born not made, and when they are born, "[f]or what have [they] wings if not to seek friends at an elevation?"

"Does No One at All Ever Feel This Way in the Least?" (1962)

Originally titled, "Does No One at All but Me Ever Feel This Way in the Least?," this was Frost's 1952 Christmas poem. It was later collected with the omitted "but me" in the poet's final volume, *In the Clearing*. What Tyler Hoffman calls a lament for the "erosion of nationality," the poem makes apparent the views that Frost expresses more delicately elsewhere. It also presents a particularly post–World War II attitude held by many humanists who began to criticize modern science for facilitating the atrocities of the early 20th century. Instead of embracing the nation with the hopeful passion of Walt Whitman nearly a century before, Frost, with hindsight, expresses disappointments over what America has become. While he had hoped that the "vast" ocean, which separates the Old world from New, would make America different, and perhaps better, by a "single trait," that is not what transpired. His disillusion seems to be almost the entire point of the poem.

Americans took the word *corn*, which is the Indian name for maize and the English name for wheat, and used that to comfort ourselves, but no matter what differences we sought to create, our English roots showed and we were unable to be "newly born." Here Frost seems to poke fun at Americans' constant striving for originality. He dismissively blames "homesickness" for creating the same result on our land as in the land of our forebears.

The third stanza depicts how changes in technology, from ship ("a bullet for a boat") to airplane, have made the distance between Old and New Worlds much shorter. No longer is the ocean a sort of moat that protects "castle," America, by making it difficult for others to gain access. Through technology, the previously protected continent is made easily accessible and therefore more vulnerable than it has ever been. Mark Richardson writes that the poem "speaks to the anxieties excited by military and political leaders who, throughout the post-

war years, warned that America was no longer invulnerable, that the blessing of geographical isolation we had long enjoyed . . . was extinct" (65). (Written more than a decade after the 1941 bombing of Pearl Harbor by the Japanese, the poem might also remind the 21st-century reader of the September 11, 2001, terrorist attacks.)

The speaker considers the sea useless and projects blame on it. In the fourth stanza he says he cannot hold it "innocent of fault." He addresses the sea accusingly, saying that it might as well spend its time grinding empty shells, so useless has it become. In the fifth stanza the speaker picks up a dead shell and tosses it back; again derisively, and with a bit of male chauvinism thrown in, he says, "Do work for women."

In the end the ocean is stripped of anything that made it important. It becomes a metaphor for America itself, which, according to the poem, no longer has any "salt." As a "pool," it becomes something common, familiar, in the backyard of every home, as opposed to something vast, exhilarating, and promising. The title, phrased as a question, expresses exasperation and despair over so far being unable to find others who feel the same.

This is not one of Frost's better poems, perhaps because, as in various other instances, he lets his politics get in the way of his inspiration. The poem lacks the ambiguities that underlie his better work, and the speaker is undoubtedly Frost himself.

Editors Richard Poirier and Mark Richardson point out that the line "the ocean had been spoken to before" is an allusion to King Canute and Lord Byron, among others. Sinbad is a sailor in the famous 10th century collection of folktales, *Arabian Nights' Entertainments* or *The Thousand and One Nights*.

See SCIENCE and TECHNOLOGY.

FURTHER READING

Hoffmann, Tyler. *Robert Frost and the Politics of Poetry.* Hanover, N.H.: Middlebury College Press, 2001, 197.

Richardson, Mark. "Frost and the Cold War: A Look at the Later Poetry." In *Roads Not Taken: Rereading Robert Frost*, edited by Earl J. Wilcox and Jonathan N. Barron, 55–77. Columbia: University of Missouri Press, 2000.

"Door in the Dark, The" (1928)

Included in a letter to Louis Untermeyer under the title "Speaking of Metaphor" shortly before its publication in *West-Running Brook,* "The Door in the Dark" lightly treats a serious subject and describes how one might lose one's ability to make valid comparisons. In an accompanying letter, Frost wrote, "The only thing that can disappoint me in the head is my own failure to learn to make metaphor. My ambition has been to have it said of me: He made a few connections" (Cramer, 99). The original version included a reference to Untermeyer's remarriage to his first wife after his divorce from his second. When Frost published the poem, he made the change to the title and removed the reference to his friend Untermeyer.

The speaker is walking in the dark and somehow manages to take a blow to the head that is so hard, he can no longer pair things and people through simile. As often happens in Frost, an inanimate object, in this case a door, seems to have a will of its own. But the narrator takes the blame for the accident, as, using a prize-fighter's lingo, he explains that he neglected to adequately protect himself. He could have, after all, made an arc with his arms and walked with them outstretched as protection against obstacles. Instead, he "reached out blindly to save [his] face, seemingly a reference to the idea of "saving face." Since he did not protect himself properly, either because he did not know to or because he knew better but forgot to, a "slim door" slips past his "guard" and hits his head so hard that his "native simile" is jarred. His native simile appears to be an instinctive desire to draw comparisons, or at least an instinctive talent for writing poetry. It suggests that when people are unable to draw such comparisons, they are somehow not quite right.

The poem presents a silly explanation for why "things don't pair any more / With what they used to pair with before," as great confusion (and a kind of divorce) comes from a blow to the head. But the poem has greater complexity. The speaker is going from "room to room in the dark," wandering without light or knowledge. And while wandering, he is making an effort to "save face," as often happens in a fractured relationship, when it later seems he should have been attempting to protect his head. The poem shows that the effort of trying to save face is futile and the notion of pride is insignificant. The speaker should have been concerned with things greater than pride. He also is presented as a having kept his arms too open at the start; because he did not close his arms "in an arc" to protect himself, he was injured. These lines suggest that basic things like self-protection, even in one's own home, are at times more important than the loftier abstract ideals with which we are often concerned.

But perhaps, while this can all be gleaned from the poem, it is really just a simple and humorous rhyme about a bump on the noggin that may make writing poetry a little more difficult, at least for a time. It certainly can be read and understood variously, without reference to the Untermeyer divorce and remarriage that seem to have been the original impetus of the poem.

See NIGHT.

FURTHER READING

Cramer, Jeffrey S. *Robert Frost among His Poems: A Literary Companion to the Poet's Own Biographical Contexts and Associations.* Jefferson, N.C.: McFarland, 1996.

Frost, Robert. *The Letters of Robert Frost to Louis Untermeyer.* New York: Holt, Rinehart and Winston, 1963.

"Draft Horse, The" (1962)

"The Draft Horse" is a bizarre tale about a "most unquestioning pair" who accept fate—no matter what. A couple is traveling down a road in a "frail" buggy, behind a horse that is "too heavy." They travel in total darkness because their lantern will not burn. There is no explanation for why the lantern does not burn, whether it is out of oil or wick, but Frost uses the word *wouldn't* to imply playfully that the *will* of the lantern explains why there is no light.

A freak and unexpected occurrence turns the horse into a "beast" slain by a nondescript man who suddenly comes out of the trees and stabs it dead. The lantern and the man's actions are made deliberate, but the horse is clearly a blameless victim. He was a draft horse who worked for the couple and was "too heavy," or as one might infer, too weary. He is described in broken terms, as would be expected of a very old and tired horse.

The horse is murdered callously by the man's "reaching back to his ribs" and stabbing him. When the horse falls, the night draws "through the trees / In one long invidious draft," as if to suggest some sort of cosmic antagonism. After the first three stanzas depict the strange and mysterious scene, the final two stanzas attempt to draw conclusions, as is characteristic in a parable.

The couple, that most "unquestioning pair," does not wonder why the horse was killed; rather, they accept its death as fate and ascribe a bizarre intention to the act. They assume that the horse died simply because someone wanted them to walk from there, drawing a startlingly solipsistic conclusion that suggests the notion that others die for the instruction and benefit of those of us still living. Such a view is dismissive of the person who dies, just as the view held by the couple here trivializes the horse's death. Frost seems to be questioning the order of such correlations and the motivation for such weird explanations of people's behavior. Instead of realizing that since the horse died they have to walk, they assume it was killed because someone wanted them to walk. This is similar to the notion that people die so that good can come of it, rather than that, when they do, good sometimes comes of it. The poet seems to be questioning humans' tendency to take random and senseless events and attribute logical and reasonable explanations to them, believing that "everything happens for a reason."

The couple's assumptions are so far off that the lantern must be seen to have a will as deliberate as the killer's. And they are so accepting of fate that instead of questioning the role of purpose in the world, they treat everything as part of a "master plan," because they do not wish "to ascribe" / Any more than [they have] to to hate." Their explanations are of the strangest kind because even though

they may satisfy, they do not at all explain why the violence was necessary, any more than we can explain unreasoning hatred.

The poem does not seek to explain why the man killed the horse; the explanation of the horrific and bewildering event comes solely from the couple in the buggy. No omniscient view is provided, no poet's voice. The poem presents the couple's foolishness without derision or correction. The conclusion is that the man, himself but an instrument and a victim of fate, merely had to "obey" someone, likely the "master" of the plan. This suggests that the man was not responsible for his own actions and may be justified in killing simply because he did it out of duty, as if that were sufficient justification.

First appearing in *In the Clearing,* the poem was written long before its publication, around 1920. An alternative manuscript title was "Percheron Horse," the name of a particular breed of gray or black horse originally used in France for drawing artillery and heavy coaches.

FURTHER READING

Cramer, Jeffrey S. *Robert Frost among His Poems: A Literary Companion to the Poet's Own Biographical Contexts and Associations.* Jefferson, N.C.: McFarland, 1996.

Gwynn, Frederick L. "Analysis and Synthesis of Frost's 'The Draft Horse,'" *College English* 26, no. 3 (December 1964): 223–225.

Kearns, Katherine. *Robert Frost and a Poetics of Appetite.* Cambridge: Cambridge University Press, 1994, 151.

Monteiro, George. *Robert Frost and the New England Renaissance.* Lexington: University Press of Kentucky, 1988, 51–53.

Pack, Robert. *Belief and Uncertainty in the Poetry of Robert Frost.* Hanover, N.H.: Middlebury College Press, 2003, 145–147.

Tomlinson, Sandra W. "Frost's 'Draft Horse,'" *Explicator* 42, no. 4 (Summer 1984): 28–29.

"Dream Pang, A" (1913)

In this sonnet, which appeared in Frost's first volume, *A Boy's Will,* the speaker withdraws into the forest, as he does in so many of Frost's other poems, including the opening poem of the book, "Into my Own." But only here is the speaker singing, apparently to lure someone into the woods with him, but the leaves swallow up his song. Although the other character in the poem is imagined as coming to the "forest edge" and considering going beyond the threshold, something causes hesitation. The "you" appears to be a lover, possibly even someone with whom the speaker has had a quarrel, as it was a "dream" of the speaker that she came.

The poem reads like a poetic rendering of the carefully orchestrated emotional dance of give and take that occurs between newly joined lovers or those who have had a disagreement. The listener comes close to entering the "forest" of the speaker but dares not "too far in his footsteps stray," and she expects that he must seek her if he is to "undo the wrong"—a wrong perhaps best imagined by the reader, as it is not revealed in the poem. He is closer to her than she realizes, however. He seems to duck down nearby, and the tension between who is willing to go further or give more is evident.

The speaker wants to be joined in the woods by his lover, but he does not force it. His withholding is described as a "sweet pang"—the oxymoron is bittersweet. He is not far, just far enough away to make coming together difficult and just near enough to make complete separation impossible. The same tensions are evident in "Meeting and Passing" in *Mountain Interval.* There is enormous withholding in the poem, which seems to suggest emotional withdrawal. The speaker is not able to express himself, but at the same time he says he is not aloof. The lover comes anyway; she is there "for proof." The lover shakes her pensive head, out of frustration perhaps, but certainly out of some knowledge. She seems quite familiar with the behavior, as if it is recurring. Also, she does not want to follow him too far inside his own thoughts, and she says that he must come to her if he is to undo the wrong.

As one of the early poems from his first volume, "A Dream Pang" seems to take for its subject Frost's tumultuous early relationship with his wife Elinor. It seems to be an example of what Jay Parini calls "a pattern in their relationship." Parini writes, "It was as if some invisible wall existed between them, and

neither could get through it to the other side; but neither could do without the other" (52).

Lawrance Thompson believes that this is a love poem, written to Elinor as a "gesture of courtship" (311). He believes that the forest is a metaphor for a "one-sided conversation" in a double bed where the speaker has awakened in the night, wishing to tell his beloved of the dream that has disturbed his sleep.

While the setting Thompson imagines may be a bit of a stretch, the word *dream* does complicate the poem. If it is meant to suggest a memory or an imagining, the metaphorical giving and taking in the poem is easily supported. If, however, it is meant to suggest an ideal situation, the description of the scene as far from ideal makes the relationship between the two all the more complex.

FURTHER READING

Kearns, Katherine. *Robert Frost and a Poetics of Appetite.* Cambridge: Cambridge University Press, 1994, 152.

Parini, Jay. *Robert Frost: A Life.* New York: Holt, 1999.

Poirier, Richard. "Choices." In *Robert Frost,* Modern Critical Views, edited by Harold Bloom, 43–61. New York: Chelsea House, 1986.

Thompson, Lawrance. *Robert Frost: The Early Years.* New York: Holt, Rinehart and Winston, 1966.

"Drumlin Woodchuck, A" (1936)

Written in Key West, far from the home of a New England woodchuck, and first appearing in the April 1936 issue of the *Atlantic Monthly,* "A Drumlin Woodchuck" was later collected in *A Further Range* with the subtitle "or, Be Sure to Locate." It should be noted that Mark Harris's biography of the distinctly urban novelist Saul Bellow, *Saul Bellow: Drumlin Woodchuck* (1980), takes its title from this Frost poem. Bellow's Chicago is in a sense even farther from Frost's woodchuck's native turf than are the FLORIDA Keys. So it is well to keep in mind that this poem is steeped in metaphor. While some have accepted it as simple and straightforward, it is remarkably complex given its simple but misleading title, though it has not attracted a great deal of critical attention.

When the poem opens, the speaker seems to be philosophizing on what sorts of refuge different creatures seek. He imagines that the sorts of shelter different "thing[s]" retreat to are based, in part, on the creatures' size and their need for comfort and security. "[C]ozier skies" will be found in ways that help "make up" for whatever inadequacies a creature lacking in "size" may have.

The speaker confides that his own "strategic retreat" is hidden and tucked away in the ground where "two rocks almost meet." A drumlin is an elongated hill left behind by a glacier, and this is Frost's descriptive for the home of the woodchuck. The speaker's sanctuary has two doors, like a woodchuck's burrow, allowing him to sit exposed to the outside world, even though, as he says, he only "pretends" that "he and the world are friends."

The title of the poem suggests that the speaker might be a woodchuck (a regional term, also known as a groundhog or whistle pig, which explains the "whistle" in l. 14), but it is unlikely that Frost was giving voice to such an animal. The speaker is in sympathy with the woodchuck, as his inclinations to snug dwelling and safety are similar to those of a burrowing rodent. And the poem soon becomes a meditation on those similarities.

Stanza four is marked by a shift in tone from speculation about unexpected similarities to a somber focus on survival. The speaker says that when alarmed, he gives a "little whistle" before diving "down under the farm." Frost the farmer strongly hints at his resemblance to the speaker here, suggesting to the reader familiar with his life that he may have used his various farms as a way of hiding from the rest of the world.

The hibernation of the woodchuck in winter is elaborated on in stanza five. In "After Apple-Picking," one of two other poems in which a woodchuck is prominent (the other being "The Self-Seeker"), Frost writes of the woodchuck's long, dreamless sleep, pointedly contrasting it with "just some human sleep." But in this poem the speaker supposes that the woodchuck's hibernation is to "allow

some time for guile" and an "occasion to think." Such activities certainly are not characteristic of an ordinary woodchuck. Frost's choice of "guile" renders the nature of the woodchuck all the more intriguing, as its sly character is described in terms strikingly similar to the sly poet. Frost, who often revels in deception, is purposefully assuming the guise of a woodchuck.

Much of the imagery in the poem is martial, such as the "double-barreled blast" in line 22. Elsewhere the imagery suggests battle. The speaker has his own "strategic retreat"; words like "at my back," "attack," and "alarm" all contribute to a battleground atmosphere and, presumably, a deeper understanding of the poem. In some ways, the poem itself seems almost a metaphor for war rather than for the poet's personality and challenges. In such a reading, the woodchuck's burrow is like a metaphorical foxhole, or redoubt. There are comrades behind. He has "those in mind" at his "back." They watch out for each other. They give a whistle when harm is near.

The double-barreled gun of hunters is introduced through a simile equated with "war and pestilence / And the loss of common sense." The point is tucked away within parentheses and thus is hidden as the woodchuck is in his burrow. This phrase therefore gains significance. The speaker imagines that if he can possibly outwit the hunters, disease, and other threats with his guile, he will be able not only to survive but to provide support and protection for someone else.

As the poem draws to a close, the speaker reflects on the meaning of his own survival. It is clear that this is no ordinary woodchuck, and the unexpected "I will be there for you, my dear" of the penultimate stanza brings human feeling to the fore in a gesture of guarded optimism (or muted hope). If he can just hang on "for another day, / . . . another year," he will be there for his love. If he makes it, it will be because he has been "so instinctively thorough" in the shelter he has sought refuge in as to outwit the threats arrayed against him.

Jay Parini holds that the "strategic retreat" of the speaker is evidence of "Frost's own . . . from national politics" (294), and the final stanza may bear this out. At the close he measures the small

against the "All," a cosmic comparison. His smallness is pitted against everything. Wistfully, he also
claims that the only reason he has survived thus far
is that he happened to dig the right hole, not
because of any extraordinary ability.

Other existentialist interpretations can also be
given. For example, the life of the woodchuck can
be viewed as one primarily of alienation. He is not
really "friends" with the world, so he deals with the
separation in the ways described. The battle imagery suggests the armor people develop to protect
themselves from other people and the world in general. This protection does not simply isolate the
speaker from the consequences of national politics,
as Parini has claimed, but can also be viewed as
providing the means necessary for him to successfully live in the world, whether living together or
apart. Survival depends on the quality of his
burrow.

Jeffrey Meyers finds the speaker very like the
narrator in Franz Kafka's "The Burrow," saying that
the poem, "like Kafka's story, describes how a writer
must protect himself by hiding from people who
make unwelcome demands and interfere with his
work" (216).

FURTHER READING

Edwards, Margaret. "Animal Anthropomorphism in
    the Poems of Robert Frost." In *Frost: Centennial
    Essays II,* edited by Jac Tharpe, 236–245. Jackson:
    University Press of Mississippi.
Meyers, Jeffrey. *Robert Frost: A Biography.* New York:
    Houghton Mifflin, 1996.
Oehlschlaeger, Fritz. "Two Woodchucks, or Frost and
    Thoreau on the Art of the Burrow," *Colby Literary
    Quarterly* 18, no. 4 (December 1982): 214–219.
Parini, Jay. *Robert Frost: A Life.* New York: Holt, 1999,
    293–295.

"Dust in the Eyes" (1928)

Included in *West-Running Brook* and used as an
advertisement for the same volume, "Dust in the
Eyes" focuses on a speaker who has apparently been
accused of "getting overwise," of being a know-it-

all. The prescribed folk "cure" is to throw a bit of
dust in the eyes. This is all, it seems, that is needed
to halt him in his tracks and keep his smartness
from getting out of hand. In just six lines with a
simple aa/bb/cc rhyme scheme, the speaker, tongue
firmly in cheek, toys with the idea others seem to
have that his eyes are the primary avenue for his
insights and knowledge. What he is able to "see" is,
after all, seen through his eyes. And surely the eyes
do not deceive. Yet while others think that their
wisdom comes from what they see, the speaker
knows better. He is not one for "putting off the
proof" and therefore will not keep anyone from
attempting to "blind" him by overwhelming him
with a blizzard's worth of snow in the eyes. He is
teasingly saying that he will not keep anyone from
making a point.

Frost referred to his poems as talk songs and
claimed that instead of reading them in public he
simply "said" them. When he refers to his talk getting overwise, he may be referring to his poetry, his
version of talk. And when he writes about letting
the dust be overwhelming, he goads others to try to
stop him. He cannot be blinded. The poet sees
what others cannot, and he does not do it with his
eyes. Nor can he be overwise; the exaggeration of
"overwise" is clearly a jab. Yet, while what he knows
may be more than others do, he is fully aware that
he still knows too little. He says it will blind him to
a "standstill" if it must, that he will not be able to
move forward, figuratively to walk while blinded.
But being stopped will come only if it "must."

This poem can also be interpreted as referring to
the comparison between the learned and the vulgar, the pedestrian knowledge of the masses versus
the trained and developed intelligence of a poet-
scholar. There is a degree of self-glorification in the
poem, as if Frost were daring someone to try to
make him stop thinking, stop writing, stop con-
densing (as his lesser-known contemporary Lorine
Niedecker characterizes the making of poetry in
"Poet's Work"), to cease using language in unusual
ways. In this sense, he is proud of his witty intelligence and twits those who would try to quash it.
This pride is made manifest in the suggestion that
it would take a blizzard of snow in the eyes to bring
his efforts to a halt.

FURTHER READING

Cramer, Jeffrey S. *Robert Frost among His Poems: A Literary Companion to the Poet's Own Biographical Contexts and Associations.* Jefferson, N.C.: McFarland, 1996.

Perrine, Laurence. "Frost's 'Dust of Snow,'" *Explicator* 29 (March 1971): 61.

Steward, Garrett. "Dust of Snow," *Robert Frost Review* (Fall 1993): 60–61.

"Dust of Snow" (1923)

This brief eight-line, single-sentence poem was collected in *New Hampshire* but had been published previously in the *London Mercury* as "A Favour" and in the *Yale Review* as "Snow Dust." It characteristically places a speaker in nature, where a simple occurrence becomes the catalyst for a change of heart.

A crow landing on a hemlock tree causes a bit of snow to fall on the speaker, and because of this the speaker's mood is significantly altered. Rather glum when starting out, he somehow has had his day turn about from being one he might have "rued" to one that is at least partly redeemed by a change of mood.

The poem eschews lyricism and striking images. It reads not as an important work but as something the poet might have dashed off, as in a diary. While it is presented mostly in monosyllables, with a simple abab cdcd rhyme scheme, beyond its rhyme it is stylistically simple. Its significance is that it is yet another example of how Frost uses nature as an avenue to meditation. It makes evident what is obscured in other more compelling and complex poems, such as "The Road Not Taken": that meaning is provided by humans. It is not in the crow or some natural occurrence to deliver meaning; meaning is found through the instrument of human consciousness.

FURTHER READING

Edwards, C. Hines, Jr. "Frost's 'Dust of Snow,'" *Notes on Contemporary Literature* 12, no. 2 (March 1982): 3–4.

Funkhouser, Linda Bradley. "Acoustic Rhythm in Frost's 'Dust of Snow,'" *Language and Style: An International Journal* 14, no. 4 (Fall 1981): 287–303.

Pearce, Donald. "The Secret Ministry of Frost," *Robert Frost Review* (Fall 1993): 59.

"Education by Poetry: A Meditative Monologue" (1930)

Frost delivered the lecture "Education by Poetry," which was based on one he had given at Bryn Mawr College a few years before, to the Alumni Council at Amherst College on November 15, 1930. It was recorded by stenograph and then revised for publication in the February 1931 issue of the *Amherst Graduates' Quarterly.*

"Education by Poetry" is one of Frost's longer prose pieces. He begins by declaring that he is "going to urge nothing in [his] talk" and that he is "not an advocate." He speaks about poetry in American colleges—how in some "poetry is barred" and in others, where they let some poetry in, "they manage to bar all that is poetical in it by treating it as something other than poetry." He has "hunted for" the reason professors do not teach poetry. First he considers satirically that it is due to a certain modesty, "Who are *they*" to teach poetry? He also considers, critically, that they are "markers" and "have the marking problem to consider." While he respects marking and as a teacher never complained of it, since in some sense we are all markers of each other, all judging one another, "the hard part," he explains, "is the part beyond that, the part where the adventure begins." He concludes that the removal of poetry from curriculums has partly occurred because no one is "willing to admit that his discipline is not partly in exactness" and "partly in taste and enthusiasm."

Frost inquires, "How shall a man go through college without having been marked for taste and judgment?" and the answer to this question is what he seeks. He pokes fun at night school as the place where college graduates return because they have discovered that they have not learned to judge any-

Frost gives a reading at Bryn Mawr College, Bryn Mawr, Pennsylvania. "Education by Poetry": "Let me ask you to watch a metaphor breaking down here before you." *(Courtesy Dartmouth College Library)*

thing. At this point the essay takes focus: "Education by poetry is education by metaphor." The lecture, like "The Constant Symbol," is chiefly concerned with metaphor and its role not only in poetry but in every aspect of a thinking life.

Poetry, "the only art in the college of arts," exists for "taste and judgment." In poetry there is "enthusiasm," the kind that is "taken through the prism of the intellect and spread on the screen in a color, all the way from hyperbole at one end—or overstatement, at one end—to understatement at the other end." Frost uses his own metaphor to describe enthusiasm. The enthusiasm becomes the "object of all teaching in poetry," but that enthusiasm must

be "tamed by metaphor." Everything must come down to metaphor, and not only in poetry: "Poetry begins in trivial metaphors, pretty metaphors, 'grace metaphors,' and goes on to the profoundest thinking we have."

Frost identifies all thinking except perhaps mathematical or scientific thinking, as metaphorical. He provides support for this belief, working through various metaphors and even groping his way toward the metaphor of EVOLUTION. All this serves his conclusion that "unless you have had your proper poetical education in the metaphor, you are not safe anywhere" because without education no one can be "at ease with figurative values."

None of the disciplines can afford us safety if we cannot press our thinking beyond the practical and into the abstract.

He wants to ride out metaphor. At the same time he acknowledges that we cannot ever quite know how far we can take the ride. He guides his listeners through the breakdown of a metaphor: "the universe is a machine." The metaphor is appealing, until Frost presses it further with questions like "Did you ever see a machine without a pedal for the foot, or a lever for the hand, or a button for the finger?" The metaphor falls away, but "[t]hat is the beauty of it. It is touch and go," he says.

The metaphor is "all there is of thinking," and it is best taught through poetry. All strong thinking is metaphorical, and while teachers ask students to think, Frost says, they seldom take the time to tell what it means or how to do it. In this sense, what professors attempt to teach in college is an utter failure if they cannot teach students how to think abstractly through metaphor and how to express their ideas through writing. Writing, after all, is about "having ideas" and learning to write about "learn[ing] to have ideas." Professors cannot teach anything if they do not begin with the genuine.

Students learn metaphor through writing or reading poetry. Frost says that he would never encourage someone to write it; that has to be "one's own funeral." While joking, he also offers insight here into his own poetic demise.

As a teacher, Frost explains, "one remark" by a student that is exacting and insightful, one "right" remark, was often all it took to know if a student came "close to Keats in reading Keats." The good marker becomes, then, a person who can judge how close others can come to understanding anything, anything at all.

As the piece closes, Frost turns to the question of belief, which he thinks can be learned better through from poetry than through religion. He speaks of "four beliefs that [he] know[s] more about from having lived with poetry." The first is the "personal belief, which is a knowledge that you don't want to tell other people about because you cannot prove that you know. You are saying nothing about it till you see." In this sense the farmer's belief would be a personal one. He knows that the

seeds are going to grow, but he cannot prove it until they actually do. This personal belief Frost also describes as the "love belief," which he says, "has that same shyness. It knows it cannot tell; only the outcome can tell." National belief is one "we enter into socially with each other, all together, party of the first part, party of the second part, we enter into that to bring the future of the country." A position on an afterlife applies directly to the last belief, which Frost identifies as the "relationship we enter into with God to believe the future in—to believe the hereafter in."

Frost also describes the literary belief, "believing the thing into existence, saying as you go more than you even hoped you were going to be able to say, and coming with surprise to an end that you foreknew only with some sort of emotion." This description is similar to his comparison of poetry to "dawn," to "something dawning on you while you're writing it," in his transcribed conversation with the literary critic Cleanth Brooks, the novelist Robert Penn Warren, and the Holt, Rinehart and Winston editor Kenny Withers in 1959.

The greatest metaphor is "the philosophical attempt to say matter in terms of spirit," and Frost calls this the "greatest attempt that ever failed." While it may have failed, "'twas the effort, the essay of love," and it is that sort of riding out that Frost's "Education by Poetry" entails. *See* BELIEF.

FURTHER READING

Peters, Joan D. "Education by Poetry: Robert Frost's Departure from the Modern Critical Edition," *South Carolina Review* 21, no. 1 (Fall 1988): 27–37.

Stanlis, Peter J. "Robert Frost's Philosophy of Education: The Poet as Teacher." In *Roads Not Taken: Rereading Robert Frost*, edited by Earl J. Wilcox and Jonathan N. Barron, 78–104. Columbia: University of Missouri Press, 2000.

"Egg and the Machine, The" (1928)

This poem became a part of *West-Running Brook* when the *Collected Poems* were published in 1930, but it had appeared in 1928 as "The Walker" in *The Second American Caravan: A Yearbook of American Literature.*

"The Egg and the Machine" begins angrily. The "traveler" rails, one might say, at a "rail." And the rail answers back in a pattern with which the speaker is all too familiar. He knows the code of the ticks on the tracks and falsely concludes that his hate has "roused an engine up the road," the type of inference that might be made by an adolescent. The traveler is rueful about the coming of yet another engine, and with hindsight he wishes that when he was alone, before he had to share the land, his land, with the engine and tracks, he had attacked the track "with a club or stone." It is significant that these primitive tools would have been his weapons of choice. This suggests that he represents the human condition, is himself a metaphor for all beings in a preindustrialized or pretechnological age.

The man's thoughts suggest that if he had destroyed the train track at the start, he might have been able to keep other engines, and perhaps people, from getting through. Then, rampant technology might have ended up derailed, in a ditch, and he might have held off technological growth altogether, instead of sharing the world with the track and the engine.

As the engine grows closer in line 10, the speaker stands aside for fear of being harmed. The engine represents the dangers that accompany technology; those who stand in its way will simply be run down. As the engine roars by, it drowns out the "cries he raise[s] against the gods in the machine." After the engine passes, all is quiet again. The "gods in the machine" are the new technologies. By referring to them in such a way, they become mysterious, uncontrollable, and uncaring, if not downright malevolent. (The phrase also alludes to the literary device of deus ex machina in Greek and Roman drama.)

After the engine passes, the sandbank "once gain lay serene." A sandbank is a precarious place for train tracks, so the laying of the tracks must have been fairly recent. There is a suggestion of the shifting sands of time. This shift in focus occurs precisely halfway through the poem.

The scene returns to a beginning and to the spawning of new life. The traveler unexpectedly notices a turtle's tracks in the sand, which he can make out by the "dotted feet" and "streak of tail." He follows the tracks, which lead him to a buried turtle's nest where he finds many "torpedo-like" eggs. Robert Faggen writes that the "eggs recall the aboriginal inhabitants of the Galapagos [Islands] in [Charles] Darwin's *The Voyage of the Beagle*" (155).

The traveler darkly imagines that if the engine should return to disturb his serenity again, he will be armed with the eggs "for war," and the next engine "will get th[e] plasm in its goggle glass." The traveler thoughtlessly plans to use the future, the young of the turtle, as ammunition against the "machine."

The traveler worries, in the first half of the poem, that he will be trampled, so to speak, by this iron "horse in skirts," but by the second half the tables are turned, and tellingly he uses the unhatched eggs of a primitive creature as armaments in his anticipated war against the intrusion of the machine. There are several implications here. First, once civilization makes a significant advance there is no turning back without destroying even more of the natural world. Second, those who resist will ultimately be overrun by technology. The multifarious connections to technology, therefore, are far-reaching. Third, and most starkly, once technology is unleashed, those out of sympathy with its purposes are rendered impotent against it and soon fall by the wayside or, rather, the tracks.

The poem presents the view that science simply leads to either finding better ways to destroy ourselves and others or separating from and excluding those who fail to fall in line. While the machine is well advanced in its power to destroy, the antitechnological, conservative man relies solely on archaic means of self-defense—exaggeratedly, in this case, clubs, stones, and "torpedo" eggs.

The poem's title juxtaposes the primitive birth, a turtle's eggs, with the modern world, the powerful machine. As an allegory for the march of history, it suggests that when we "had the track" alone, we should have kept it to ourselves.

It was the man's anger that roused the gods in the first place. We can either destroy our weapons before they destroy us or attempt to stop history in its tracks. Neither course seems likely, and the poem ends sadly and, as so often in Frost, resignedly. By standing far back perhaps we can keep from being scalded by the "squirts" of a headlong steam engine—technology—barreling through our midst.

Faggen calls the poem "an almost Aesopian fable" that offers "biting satire on the demonization of technology" (154). *See* TECHNOLOGY.

FURTHER READING

Faggen, Robert. *Robert Frost and the Challenge of Darwin.* Ann Arbor: University of Michigan Press, 1997, 154–155.

"Empty Threat, An" (1923)

Collected in *New Hampshire,* the poem opens with "I stay," and this statement is ultimately what the poem builds on. The threat of leaving is an empty one because from the start the speaker tells us he is not going anywhere. However, he imagines himself stealing away to be a part of the fur trade, far from men with "not a soul" but John-Joe, his French-Indian Esquimaux friend, between him and the North Pole. Henry Hudson, the failed captain, is referenced in stanza nine, where the speaker notes that "his crew left him where he failed, And nothing came of all he sailed." The speaker draws a parallel between himself and the old captain, opening the final stanza with "It's to say 'You and I' / To such a ghost, 'You and I / Off here."

The poem ends with the understanding that it is better to be almost defeated while seeing things clearly than to be filled with doubt. It is better to lose and gain understanding than to muddle through to some nagging ambiguity and have to go on and on just to make some sense of things. Robert Faggen takes this interpretation a step further when he writes that the poem is "about the fear of extinction" and that it "indicates that annihilation would be better than endless uncertainty" (100).

Frost was steeped in ambiguity; perhaps he longed for greater clarity. The typically Frostian

qualifier here is "almost." A complete defeat is not for him. He wants victory beyond doubt. Frost once complained that poetry wasn't more like a prize fight in which the referee raises the winner's arm to indicate his victory.

FURTHER READING

Faggen, Robert. *Robert Frost and the Challenge of Darwin.* Ann Arbor: University of Michigan Press, 1997.

Parker, Blanford. "Frost and the Meditative Lyric." In *The Cambridge Companion to Robert Frost,* edited by Robert Faggen, 179–196. Cambridge: Cambridge University Press, 2001.

Perrine, Laurence. "Frost's 'An Empty Threat,'" *Explicator* 30 (1972): 63.

"Encounter, An" (1916)

Like Wallace Stevens's "Anecdote of the Jar," here Frost criticizes technology's encroachment on nature. He describes what now happens when we leave the road and head into the woods. Unlike "On a Tree Fallen across the Road," where the fallen tree obstructs passage and causes the speaker to go around, here nature is so overgrown that the speaker must half bore through and half climb through. The line "Sorry I ever left the road I knew" is reminiscent of Frost's early forlorn (thinking that his then girlfriend Elinor was going to break off their engagement) journey into the Dismal Swamp, which runs along the Virginia-North Carolina border. Jay Parini, when writing of that early journey, notes that "so many of Frost's best later poems . . . return to the scene of a lone walker in a swamp or dense forest" (49). This scene, however, is not one of Frost's best.

As the speaker half rests, with his coat hooked upon a tree, he looks up toward heaven and finds standing over him a "resurrected tree." Once, when asked what he did on his walks in the woods, Frost said, "gnaw bark." Here we find a "barkless" tree that has been down and raised again, resurrected perhaps, as the speaker wishes to be. The poem at first seems to be a traditional "nature" poem in the spirit of "Into My Own" but soon reveals that this bark was not gnawed by Frost.

In the last six lines the poem takes a turn, perhaps not for the better. The description of the tree is keen, with its "strange position of hands" and "Up at his shoulders, dragging yellow strands," but the conversation that ensues seems to lack the impact of Frost's better work. The barkless tree has been interpreted as a telephone pole, the dragging yellow strands of wire as the telephone wire bringing messages from "men to men" of the "news" they "carry." The scene is strange: The speaker had to force his way into nature yet found something quite unnatural far from the road. The tree's wires also are reminiscent of a weeping willow's branches; perhaps the ever coy Frost intended such an allusion.

The conversation is limited, as though the speaker picked up a handset deep in the woods and only one side of the exchange is audible. The poem has little value, except in that it highlights the purpose of the speaker's journey: to look for and find the "orchid Calypso." The calypso, sometimes known as fairy slipper, is a wild orchid that grows sparingly in cedar swamps in the areas where Frost went wandering so frequently: Vermont, New Hampshire, Maine, and other such northern areas. Frost also makes reference to the *Odyssey* and perhaps Odysseus here, as Calypso was a beautiful nymph who welcomed Odysseus on his journeys.

The poem first appeared in the November 1916 issue of the *Atlantic Monthly* and was collected in *Mountain Interval*. See FUGITIVE and TECHNOLOGY.

FURTHER READING

Bieganmowski, Ronald. "Robert Frost's 'An Encounter,'" *Notes on Contemporary Literature* 10, no. 2 (1980): 4–5.

Kearns, Katherine. *Robert Frost and a Poetics of Appetite*. Cambridge: Cambridge University Press, 1994, 124–126.

Parini, Jay. *Robert Frost: A Life*. New York: Holt, 1999, 35.

"Ends" (1962)

In "Ends," which first appeared in *In the Clearing*, Frost depicts the end of a relationship in a kind of minidrama as overheard by passersby in the night. The trick is in taking a minor occurrence—minor to the passersby, major to the protagonists—the overhearing of an argument, and making a concise poem of it.

Just about every light in the house must be on, which adds to the starkness of what is unwittingly and perhaps unwillingly overheard. The "overlighted" house suggests that the couple are a long way from settling down for the night. The talk from within is so loud as to cause the passersby to "stumble." They may be stumbling from being startled, or from embarrassment at such a glaring display of, presumably, marital discord that they have stepped up their pace to get more quickly out of earshot. Given the tenor of the argument, they probably would not have had to strain to hear it, so it is unlikely that they wanted to eavesdrop.

The last two lines of the first three quatrains puts succinctly the end of this relationship, while suggesting that this is not an uncharacteristic end to many a relationship. The title, after all, is not "The End," or "Ending," but "Ends." As is often the case, the title is an important part of the poem and helps to guide a reading of it. Once there had been "night the first," but this was "night the last," suggesting a battle to end all battles. Unforgivable things are being said, and the differences are patently irreconcilable.

The second stanza highlights a couple of points in only one side of the argument: "He never said she wasn't young," and he never said she was not "his dear." But something "he might have said" was "insincere." This is, of course, filtered through the apprehension of the speaker, who may be betraying a slight bias in favor of the man. The narrator either "reports," what was heard or is leaving out what he heard and relating what he did not because of his identification with the man.

The final stanza makes the entire dispute seem foolish. The poet finds immaturity and rashness in the silly arguments that arise between lovers and those who are willing to "throw it all" away rather than just "a part"—the part that needs improving. Even more foolish are those who "say all sorts of things," even those who "mean what they say."

The wise poet advises that we should not say everything that occurs to us in the heat of a moment, nor should we be too quick to dissolve relationships. Certainly he intimates that throwing the handle after the hatchet is a rash and foolish trait among men, deserving of derision.

See NIGHT.

FURTHER READING

Reichert, Victor. "The Faith of Robert Frost." In *Frost: Centennial Essays,* edited by Jac Tharpe, et al., 415–426. Jackson: University Press of Mississippi, 1974.

"Equalizer, An" (1942)

This poem was collected in *A Witness Tree* in a grouping called "Quantula," along with other pithy poems, which suggests that Frost intended them to be together because of their small "quantity" and presumed force. (In Latin, *quantula* means "How little?" or "How small?") The reference to Kaiser, derived from Caesar, contains a sly suggestion that Franklin Delano Roosevelt, a democratically elected president, often behaved more like a modern Caesar. And it was the German Kaiser America had mobilized to defeat in World War I, so the comparison is unflattering. (When the poem was written, the nation had not yet entered World War II.)

Frost lampoons Roosevelt's New Deal, which sought to create jobs and lessen the disparity between rich and poor. Frost, often criticized by the American intelligentsia for his conservative bent, proposes that taking from the rich and giving to the poor reveals a disdain for robust capitalism. It is suggested that to "take an equalizer" as one might a pill, will not solve anything. The beneficiaries of Roosevelt's programs are seen to be in effect "stealing," presumably from the taxpayers, through government welfare rather than by stealth. Frost's disdain for Roosevelt's programs can be read as unsympathetic toward those the programs were intended to help.

FURTHER READING

Parini, Jay. *Robert Frost: A Life.* New York: Holt, 1999.

"Escapist—Never" (1962)

This poem, significantly written late in Frost's career, passionately depicts a character, a kind of everyman, who is not intent on "escape," who is "no fugitive" on the run, and who, while he "runs face forward," runs not out of fear or a desire to be free but because he must, as must we all.

The "pursuer" is a man who never looks back. He seems to be simultaneously in his future and in his past, as is time itself, which Leonardo DaVinci once compared to a moving stream in which one can touch the last of what has just been and the first of what is to come. The man in Frost's poem welcomes both, because he knows that they "creat[e] his present." The only fear he has is of what is on either side of him, for they are the here and now, the very present.

A similar attitude is expressed in "Carpe Diem," where the poet questions whether it is good to seize the day after all and whether life is more lived in the future or in the past than it can be in the present. In that poem the present is "too much for the senses, / Too crowding, too confusing— / Too present to imagine." That is, the present overwhelms, it is more than we can handle, so the poet proposes that it is not until we have some distance from experience that we can begin to "imagine" and make the most of our experiences.

In "Escapist—Never" the man lives willfully in the present but never stops striving, moving ceaselessly into the future. The "interminable chain of longing" suggests that while he may be in the present, he is always connected to and heading toward the future. That is, though the saying is "live for the moment," living in the moment means always to be longing for something hoped for in the future or something lost in the past. As such, this speaker is relentlessly in pursuit; he never looks back, so his past is not longed for, as it is in "Carpe Diem." With the absence of longing for the past comes the absence of regret.

The "interminable chain" does not only include the man, however; it is a chain of all those who pursue, linking their way from past to future selves and others throughout all human history. What they seek, of course, is both themselves and each other: "He seeks a seeker who in his turn seeks / Another still." This is notable, since Frost seems to be saying something not just about time but about our lives in general. Just as we have an unavoidable connection to the future, we seem to have the same infinite connections to other people. One life alone connects to so many others and should be viewed holistically.

The poem represents humanity at its best, where "life is a pursuit of a pursuit forever" and all days are seized. There is the vastness of time, and Frost claims that the desires and wills of humans are sufficient to keep up with it, to handle it. The vastness of time does not become an enemy; on the contrary, it seems to provide a playing field for the human spirit; in this sense the title of the poem can be seen as an anthem not only for humanity in general but also for Frost himself. "Escapist—Never" is a statement, not a question. As such, and with the dash separating the two words, it seems to be a personal statement that Frost couches in less-than-personal terms.

The poem expresses, as the best poetry can, the inexpressible—the inchoate loneliness of every human being, even while living among the many. The chain is, as is the pursuit, unending.

The poem was appropriately collected in Frost's final volume, *In the Clearing,* but was first published in a 1962 issue of the *Massachusetts Review. See* FUGITIVE.

FURTHER READING

Lynen, John F. *The Pastoral Art of Robert Frost.* New Haven, Conn.: Yale University Press, 1960, 174–182.

"Etherealizing" (1947)

One of Frost's typically uncharacteristic sonnets, "Etherealizing" begins with what the poet describes as the difference between a theory and a creed. The distinction he draws is between that which we imagine or would like to be true without questioning and that which we embrace after our inquiries are presumably done.

The "theory" that has been held "long enough" and "hard enough" to become a creed appears to be the philosophical theory of dualism, that mind and matter are two distinct things. Dualism usually entails two claims: First, that the world consists of only two properties, the material, in our case our corporeal selves, and the ethereal, in our case our souls. Second, the soul is more important than the corporeal self. The usual religious view that arises from dualism is that we can remove all our physical properties (our bodies) and still be ourselves—still be, in some way, human. We will somehow still have all the same qualities we had in our physical temporal lives: ideas, talents, values, desires, and so on.

The poem turns dualism on its head by questioning whether the mind can be at all "ethereal" and thereby "freed" after our deaths and whether when our "flesh has been slough[ed]" and our "arms and legs have atrophied," there will be anything remaining that matters. Given all the "mortal stuff" the poem graphically lays out, the poet seems to be sarcastically asking his readers, "Do you really think that 'we,' as we know ourselves, are going to be there when all that's left of our physical bodies is "'blobs of brain'"?

The imagery is appalling. Essentially the poet has accurately described what it is like for our physical bodies to rot, and he is forcing the reader to visualize the falling away of one's own flesh. Following these gruesome descriptions, Frost tauntingly suggests that we will still be able to lounge on the beach, only bodiless. He disturbs the positive associations with relaxing on the beach by recalling our evolution from "blobs of jellyfish" to corpses on the "opposite extreme" of evolution, considering the reversal of organization into more complex forms of matter.

The notion of dualism is pushed to its absurdity when Frost predicts that "as blobs of brain we'll lie and dream." Blobs of brain are equated to blobs of jellyfish, and thus, unless both extremes of the debate are accepted, this "creed" is clearly insufficient, has been held too long, and must therefore go.

Ironically, it is the blobs that theorize about "abstract verse." Perhaps the poet would like to "lie and dream" himself about continuing to write verse when he ceases to be made of "mortal stuff," but he knows that this is foolish. Frost is ever playful, wanting to keep his verse wetted by the sea, at least wet enough that it will not evaporate and disappear, as though the ebb and flow of the tide were somehow relevant to his not at all abstract verse. The only reason the tide becomes important is to sustain us, since we have become, or will become, blobs at the edge of the sea whence came the earliest forms of life in our world.

Frost sees grim humor in the idea that no matter how foolish the notion, if we embrace it long enough it becomes almost impossible to shed. While he challenges the idea of dualism, he also asserts a more general claim, taking aim at all unquestioned and unreasonably held traditional assumptions.

First published in the *Atlantic Monthly* in April 1947, the sonnet was later collected in *Steeple Bush* under the heading "Editorials." *See* BELIEF.

FURTHER READING

Calhoun, Richard J. "By Pretending They Are Not Sonnets: The Sonnets of Robert Frost at the Millennium." In *Roads Not Taken: Rereading Robert Frost,* edited by Earl J. Wilcox and Jonathan N. Barron, 217–235. Cambridge: University of Missouri Press, 2000.

the evening sky as the sparks that fly up the chimney contribute to the spectacle.

The description of the sparks floating upward among the still bare branches of the trees is the sugar coating on this evening, and an unobtrusive, almost background rhyme gently carries the poem along. Sparks tangling "[a]mong bare maple boughs" and making the hill glow, enhance the beauty of the new ("slight") moon. The scene is magical. The slender moon casts just enough light to reveal the sugar buckets hanging from every tree, and on the "black ground" of the hill, the "bearskin rug of snow."

The sparks do not compete with the moon. Soon they are figuratively conflated with the constellations Leo and Orion and the stars of the Pleiades. The poem at this point takes a sudden turn; the sparks mingle with the stars, "And that was what the boughs were full of soon," no longer earthly sparks but the stars themselves. The poem was collected in *New Hampshire* but first appeared in a University of Michigan publication, *Whimsies,* in November 1921. *See* FARMER, FROST AS and STARS.

FURTHER READING

Oster, Judith. *Toward Robert Frost: The Reader and the Poet.* Athens: University of Georgia Press, 1991.

"Evening in a Sugar Orchard" (1923)

As the title suggests, this classically lyrical poem obviously depicts an evening scene in a sugar orchard. It is March, a month on the cusp of changing seasons but not quite in the midst of spring, certainly not in Frost's New England. But the sap is running and farmers are stoking the fires that will convert the sap into maple syrup. In the sugarhouse the sugaring process is under way. The speaker wants to make sure the "fireman" keeps the fire going by giving it another stoke, not so much to speed up the process but because the speaker, not a participant, is enjoying the spectacle of lights across

"Evil Tendencies Cancel" (1936)

This sestet is the fourth in a group of poems titled "Ten Mills," most of which, including this one, were originally published in *Poetry* in April 1936 and later collected in *A Further Range*. It was published in *Poetry* under the title "Tendencies Cancel." The change in title is significant, because the omission of "evil" better expresses Frost's view of nature as neither sympathetic nor malevolent.

The poem begins with the question whether the blight will "end the chestnut" tree, and it is clear he is asking "for all time." Jeffrey Cramer explains that the blight to which Frost refers was a destructive fungal disease, referred to as "chestnut blight," which in 1930 was introduced from Europe, quickly killing all of the larger chestnut trees.

The poem reports that the farmers are hopeful and "guess not." The trees keep "sending up new shoots" in their natural urge to live. Frost slyly imagines that another "parasite," a "good" one, will eventually come "to end the blight." The poet again looks at a familiar theme that runs through much of his poetry: Nature's procreant cycle goes on, life feeding on life, giving life to life. Even death does not end the cycle.

FURTHER READING

Cramer, Jeffrey S. *Robert Frost among His Poems: A Literary Companion to the Poet's Own Biographical Contexts and Associations.* Jefferson, N.C.: McFarland, 1996.

"Exposed Nest, The" (1916)

The poem begins in fancy. The speaker is addressing someone, likely a child, since he or she is "forever finding some new play" and is down on "hands and knees in the meadow." The beginning is whimsical, and the use of the second person "you" is inviting to the reader.

At first the speaker thinks the child is attempting to set upright the new-mown hay. This image, while not as stark as what is to come, reveals a certain sadness. It points to a child's desire to make things right. She wants somehow to resurrect the hay that has been so violently cut down by the hayer.

Witnessing the scene while approaching, the speaker plans to go along with the "play," willing to "pretend" as he might at a child's tea party, but he soon learns that there is no such frivolous "make-believe" for today. The fanciful beginning of the poem comes to an abrupt end. The turnabout hinges on something quite common, something to which Frost and his children would have been frequently exposed in their farming lives: destruction in nature. But that destruction is not a natural one, for it is dealt by the haying machine that very nearly

brought death to a "nest full of young birds." The machine did not kill the birds but left the nest exposed, the birds vulnerable.

The child, hands full of "wilted fern, / Steel-bright June-grass, and blackening heads of clover," perhaps collected for a new nest, looks down hopefully on the young birds. The description of the machine is of one that "had just gone champing over"—the very word *champing* underscoring its cruel indifference and the destruction that not only nature but technology can sometimes bring. The child is soulful: She wants to make the birds right again, as one can in make-believe.

Frost's philosophical side interrupts the agrarian image, as his philosophy so often does when he describes natural scenes. He imagines that the child is attempting to "restore them to their right / Of something interposed between their sight / And too much world at once—could means be found." The birds' plight is considered "too much world at once," both for the young birds and for the child, and Frost's meaning stuns quickly but gently. The world is filled with hurt, and it must therefore be taken in slowly, a bit at a time. This echoes Emily Dickinson's lines in "Tell all the Truth but tell it slant—," where she writes, "The truth's superb surprise / As lightning to the Children eased / With explanation kind / The Truth must dazzle gradually / Or every man be blind—."

The speaker, or perhaps parent, and child imagine that aiding the baby birds may be too much of a "risk . . . in doing good." But the child, with hands full of clover and June-grass, continues to "buil[d] the screen / [She] had begun, and g[i]ve them back their shade" in an attempt to offer some protection to the birds. At that point, the responsibility of the speaker and child is lifted. They are done with this scene. "All this to prove we cared," the speaker says. The scene plays out as destruction often does: first shock and surprise, then memories, then an attempt to make things right, somehow, with a return to life for those, not directly harmed, who are left behind.

There are several haunting messages embedded in the poem. First, there is the notion of "too much world at once." Then comes the idea that all of the gestures of kindness are to "prove" that one cares—

as if it were something to be proved. The kindness is somehow lessened by such a judgment. Finally, after having demonstrated "care," even when there is nothing that can be done, the characters "tur[n] to other things." The poet wonders, half-heartedly, why there is "no more to tell" and why he does not have "any memory" of the scene after setting the birds to rest, or perhaps even to die, beneath the shade. As in "Out Out—," where the poet writes, "No more to build on there. And they, since they / were not the one dead, turned to their affairs," or in "Home Burial," where he writes, "Friends make pretense of following to the grave, / But before one is in it, their minds are turned / And making the best of their way back to life," once the desire to show care has passed, people turn back to life, as they must.

The closing three lines of the poem admit that speaker and child never returned to the meadow to check on the birds, to see if they made it through that night, or any other, or to see if they ever learned to use their wings and fly.

The poem is an account of a frequent occurrence in country life, but it is not just an account. Nature usually leads Frost to some other sort of meditation, causing him to reflect on the condition, or the plight, of many things. In "Nothing Gold Can Stay" he leaps from the turning of a leaf from green to gold to Eden sinking to grief. But while nature is beyond good and evil—in nature things simply happen, for good or ill—in this poem the nest is exposed not by nature itself but by the human beings who till its soil. Nature, if left alone, might have been able to bring the birds to flight, but our forcible intrusions are matters to be reckoned with.

Here that reckoning, that brush with death, leads to doubts about larger, human questions. It also leads to the need for humans, in the face of destruction, to offer some demonstration of sympathy, even if momentarily, before returning to their own affairs.

The poem was originally published in *Mountain Interval*.

FURTHER READING

Marcus, Mordecai. *The Poems of Robert Frost: An Explication*. Boston: G. K. Hall, 1991.

"Fear, The" (1914)

First published in the December 1913 issue of *Poetry and Drama* and later appearing in *North of Boston*, "The Fear" is a narrative poem written in blank verse and largely made up of dialogue. While different in most respects, it shares some resemblances to the relationships between husbands and wives as depicted in other Frost narratives, such as "Death of the Hired Man" and "Home Burial."

The fear that is described here at first seems to come largely from the unknown and the dark, but later it is revealed that there is something more specific to be feared. The poem at times has an omniscient narrator, as in the opening description of the scene. A man, Joel, and a woman, who remains unnamed, are seen in shadow outside a house. The woman is convinced she has seen a man's face in the bushes alongside the road and describes the vision as "just as plain as a white plate." The man and woman are presumably husband and wife. They soon enter into a disagreement about what she thinks she saw, and this becomes the central conflict of the poem.

The woman is unable to leave the vision alone— she cannot "leave a thing like that unsettled." The man, however, is doubtful and dismissive. These sorts of tensions are often evident in the conversations between characters in Frost poems, and it is this tension that drives the poem. The woman describes how returning to a dark house always makes her a bit uneasy and how it is easy to imagine someone "getting out / At one door" as they "ent[er]" another. The man, Joel, wants to hold her back from searching the bushes and grasps her arm to withhold her. He calmly says, "I say it's someone passing" in order to discourage her from further investigation.

The woman reminds Joel that where they live is isolated, and therefore there is more likely something to fear: "You speak as if this were a traveled road," she says. At this point, the fear is made more dramatic and personal when Joel reveals "There's more in it than you're inclined to say" and inquires, "Did he look like—," never finishing the phrase to reveal to the reader of whom they speak. While the poem never discloses whom they suspect it could have been, the reader is left knowing that it might have been someone to be feared.

As the tensions increase, the woman pushes herself past Joel to get a lantern and go looking, as she will not be able to rest until she quiets her fears. Now she dismisses him: "You're not to come . . . This is my business." She summons her strength to address the unknown man she fears lurks in the bushes: "If the time's come to face it," she says, "I'm the one / To put it the right way." The man might be an old lover of hers or a former husband, or something more sinister may be afoot.

As in "Death of the Hired Man" there is some debate and disagreement between husband and wife about how to deal with this unknown threat. She imagines that whether it is whoever they think it is or someone he has sent "to watch," it is time he is dealt with. Joel believes it is "nonsense to think he'd care enough," and the back and forth between them becomes a debate over how to deal with the possible intrusion of this outsider, whose history with the couple, as in "Death of the Hired Man," is unseemly. Again, it is the woman who warns the man about being too harsh: "We mustn't say hard things," she says. The dispute becomes a matter of who should be the one to go and address the unknown. In the end she forges ahead, but with Joel by her side.

"What do you want?" she cries to the dark, and an answer comes back: "Nothing." While she was so certain of his presence, the response still stuns her so much she almost faints, and she must hold onto Joel for support. She asks why he is there, and again, "Nothing," comes back to her. Then the stranger speaks. He is unthreatening and shares her trepidation. He offers to come into the light and let her see him. "You see" the voice says as he enters into the lantern light, revealing that he has a child by the hand, which immediately makes him an unthreatening figure, even in the near-dark.

The tension that has been building and the fear the poem instills—of the dark, of strangers, and of figures from the past that seem to threaten the present—is put to rest. The man and child were simply out for a night walk. The voice says: "Every child should have the memory / Of at least one long-after-bedtime walk." Frost might be the voice here, as he was known for taking nighttime walks alone and with his children and others. While it seems a more general association, Lawrance Thompson chronicles a specific incident in his biography of Frost. One might also note that Katherine Kearns comments on the significance of the stranger, as one who is "divested of mystery by his movement into the light, while he is also divested of his capacity to incite fear of sexual or physical violence by his paternal association with the child whose hand he holds." Kearns says that he is "the embodiment of the healthy-minded poet and of the paternalistic . . . force by which hysteria is abated" (149).

The closing stanza has much meaning that is only partly revealed, mostly hinted at. The woman says that if that is all there is to it, it is important that Joel does not "think anything." She says that they live in a "very, very lonely place" and therefore they "have to be careful." The poem leaves the reader to ponder what Joel would be expected to think: that she was just wrong, or that in her being wrong and yet imagining the man to be someone else, she has exposed something of her own feelings that she wished she had left hidden. Something in her regret and in her fear, now no longer of the dark or of the unknown voice but of what she might have revealed, causes her to lose hold of the lantern. Walter Jost writes that the poem "juxtaposes the fragility of human understanding against the frigidity of mere external codes or internal, emotional ellipses."

At the end the lantern goes out, and the fear that has been instilled throughout the poem returns, as the threatening dark engulfs all.

FURTHER READING

Jost, Walter. "Rhetorical Investigations of Robert Frost." In *Roads Not Taken: Rereading Robert Frost*, edited by Earl J. Wilcox and Jonathan N. Barron, 179–197. Columbia: University of Missouri Press, 2000.

Kearns, Katherine. *Robert Frost and a Poetics of Appetite*. Cambridge: Cambridge University Press, 1994. 149–150.

Perrine, Laurence. "Frost's 'The Fear': Unfinished Sentences, Unanswered Questions," *College Literature* 15, no. 3 (1988): 199–207.

Schiffbauer, Judith P. "Three Poems by Robert Frost: A Jamesian Reading," *Kentucky Philological Review* 8 (1993): 46–52.

Thompson, Lawrance. *Robert Frost: The Early Years.* New York: Holt, Rinehart and Winston, 1966, 344–345.

"Fear of God, The" (1947)

In his preface to Edwin Arlington Robinson's *King Jasper,* Frost wrote that "Two fears should follow us through life. There is the fear that we shan't prove worthy in the eyes of someone who knows us at least as well as we know ourselves. That is the fear of God. And there is the fear of Man—the fear that men won't understand us and we shall be cut off from them."

This poem first appeared in *Steeple Bush* in the section "A Spire and Belfry," followed by what might be considered a companion poem, "The Fear of Man." In *Steeple Bush* the note "The Fear of God—Acknowledgement to the Papyrus Prisse" appears. Jeffrey Cramer notes that after reading the poem during a 1961 interview, Frost said, "That's all I'm answerable to" (149).

The poem opens with an address to "you," the reader, as so many of Frost's poems do, and this makes the reader a significant character in the poem. While the title may suggest that the poem is about to define what the fear is, the address to the reader suggests that such an understanding must come from the reader himself. In a sense, the poem sets up from the very beginning a personal relationship to its reader.

The first two lines introduce the terms *Nowhere* and *Somewhere, No one* and *Someone,* capitalizing them as if they were proper nouns. This capitalization takes the idea of "being someone" to an extreme, suggesting that either people are important (rich, powerful, successful, famous) or they are nothing—Nowhere, No one. The opening words, "If you should rise," subtly suggest that any move from one extreme to the other is out of our control, thus subverting popular notions of "making something of yourself" and "going places." (Some critics

have argued, however, that Nowhere is meant to be the world and Somewhere a heaven or afterworld.)

The following two lines insinuate that the movement from Nowhere to Somewhere, from being No one to being Someone is made by being "chosen" by God. As the poem continues, there is a clear criticism of the process of being chosen. Frost writes in the third and fourth lines, "Be sure to keep repeating to yourself / You owe it to an arbitrary god." The criticism of God's mercy is a way for Frost to suggest that the way in which people become "chosen" appears to be random. But he also takes a jab at the reader when he says that when God shows mercy on us, it "[w]on't bear too critical examination." Why should you be accepted, rather than others?

Frost warns the reader that in such instances of God's mercy to "[s]tay unassuming." That is, if you are chosen, do not act superior to others. If you feel inadequate, as if you are not supposed to be there, do not overcompensate by acting "subordinating" (i.e., condescending) on the outside. As Cramer points out, do not show your pride, as it is the first of the seven deadly sins. God's mercy, or grace, is meant to be appreciated on a personal level, as a "curtain of the inmost soul," not to be flaunted to others, like "apparel."

Frost gives advice for intelligent people who are chosen but do not know why. For Frost and other reflective people, the greatest fear of God comes from one's own self-doubt. In Frost's view, this should take the form of a healthy, honest humility in the face of God's arbitrariness. *See* BELIEF.

FURTHER READING

Barry, Elaine. *Robert Frost on Writing.* New Brunswick, N.J.: Rutgers University Press, 1973, 118.

Cramer, Jeffrey S. *Robert Frost among His Poems: A Literary Companion to the Poet's Own Biographical Contexts and Associations.* Jefferson, N.C.: McFarland, 1996.

"Fear of Man, The" (1947)

"The Fear of Man" was first published in *Steeple Bush* as a part of "A Spire and Belfry." Its title was changed several times in the manuscripts and, significantly, was at one time "Her Fear." Jeffrey Cramer points out that in Frost's 1935 introduction to Edwin Arlington Robinson's *King Jasper,* Frost wrote, "the fear of Man—the fear that men won't understand us and we shall be cut off from them" (150).

Appearing in the same section of *Steeple Bush,* "The Fear of God" and "The Fear of Man" appear to be companion poems. Indeed, in the *King Jasper* introduction Frost also wrote, "Two fears should follow us through life. There is the fear . . . of God. And there is the fear of man." While the poems may have been intended as companions, they are quite different in both approach and message.

This poem opens very differently from "The Fear of God." Instead of addressing the reader, Frost takes as an analogy "a girl no one gallantly attends." The girl is clearly less than popular and in some way an outcast. She is someone no one wants, as she has no suitors. She is described as coming home late at night from a friend's and as hurrying to try to make it home as quickly as she can. Although she is trying to "make it in one catch of breath," it is not for a fear of death or injury. At first it appears she is not afraid, but then it becomes clear that she hurries out of fear of a different kind.

The city is somehow threatening, as it is described as "intoppling from a height," but the girl is not to be worried that it will "fall tonight," as it "will be taken down before it falls." The city is also depicted as dark, except for a single light in a bank, which Frost seems to use as a way of demonstrating greed, using the biblical term *Mammon* for those worldly riches. (Mammon is characterized as a false god in the Christian New Testament.)

The girl should feel safe under what little light there is, as the lights are so "jewel steady." But she is not safe, as it is likely that her "exposure" is going to be "misconstrued." It is not her life that is at risk in the night, but her reputation, and she is racing home for fear of being judged. She is outside and therefore may be considered exposed. She does not have a suitor now, and without her reputation, she will never have one.

In the last two lines, after the long description of the girl, the speaker reveals that he is just as fearful of being exposed. He hopes to be able to "bolt across the scene," through his short life, without being "misunderstood in what [he] mean[s]." It is too easy to fall out of favor with others inadvertently.

It is hard, other than the title, to see the poem as a companion piece to "The Fear of God." The fear in both is of something being exposed, but otherwise, the setting and message are quite unlike each other. However, "The Fear of God" points out the falsity in believing religion actually has clarity and that God has purpose in his selection of the chosen ones. In this poem the falsehood is what the people embrace as appearances. The appearances are the heart of each poem, and that is the basis of the poems' commonalities.

It should also be noted that money and reputation are highlighted as two primary ills with which people are afflicted. This may be indicative of what eventually will bring on the fall of the city and possibly of humankind.

FURTHER READING

Barry, Elaine. *Robert Frost on Writing.* New Brunswick, N.J.: Rutgers University Press, 1973, 118.

Cramer, Jeffrey S. *Robert Frost among His Poems: A Literary Companion to the Poet's Own Biographical Contexts and Associations.* Jefferson, N.C.: McFarland, 1996.

Kearns, Katherine. *Robert Frost and a Poetics of Appetite.* Cambridge: Cambridge University Press, 1994, 37–38.

"Figure a Poem Makes, The" (1939)

"The Figure a Poem Makes" served as the preface to *Collected Poems* (1939) as well as *Complete Poems* (1949). Many of the ideas presented here are either restated in or hinted at in other prose pieces, such as "The Constant Symbol" (1946) and "Education by Poetry" (1930).

Frost describes abstraction as "an old story with the philosophers" but a new one for the artists of his own day. He begins in a frustrated tone, examining why "we can't have any one quality in poetry we choose by itself." He suggests that for him there is such a quality, but for his colleagues there is not.

He first takes up the possibility of sound as the most significant quality. He states here as elsewhere that in the English language there are only two possibilities for meter: strict and loose iambic. He explains that the "possibilities for tune from the dramatic tones of meaning struck across the rigidity of a limited meter are endless."

Frost then takes up the possibility of "wildness." The problem with this, he elaborates, is the same as with the modern abstractionists; it is "be[ing] wild with nothing to be wild about." He explains that "Just as the first mystery was how a poem could have a tune in such a straightness as meter," the second is how it "can have a wildness and at the same time a subject that is fulfilled."

His theory comes in the third paragraph, where he describes the "figure a poem makes." His oft-quoted line is that "[i]t begins in delight and ends in wisdom" and that this figure is the "same as for love." His description here follows the same path as elsewhere. He describes poetry as beginning with an emotion or mood and then riding it out. The poem must end in "a clarification of life" both for the poet and the reader.

The experience of delight that the poet feels in creation is the same spirit that must be passed to the reader. And just as the reader will discover clarity at the end of a poem, so must the journey be the same for the poet. Frost warns that the clarity does not have to be "great"; that is, it does not have to be as significant as those that "sects and cults are found on." Instead it must be a "momentary stay against confusion." This stay, this pause, this moment of reflection, offers an insight, however brief, into our own existence, great or small. The confusion of living becomes for one moment clear, unblurred by our own visions. Poems should have "dénouement," or "an outcome that though unforeseen was predestined from the first image of the original mood—and indeed from the very mood." Once the poet begins, it is determined. As he says in "The Con-

stant Symbol," using a Shakespearean sonnet as his example, in the first line the poet makes "most of his commitments all in one plunge." The poet cannot know where he is headed; if he does he is performing a sort of trickery.

When the poem arrives where it should, there are "[n]o tears in the writer, no tears in the reader." The outcome is as it was meant to be: There has been no "surprise," and neither writer nor reader is left unsatisfied. Frost describes his own delight as "remembering something [he] didn't know he [knew]," and that is what the best poetry does. When Emily Dickinson describes good poetry as taking the top of her head off, she describes a certain recognition, the recognition of what truths can be found, as well as the unanticipated familiarity that comes upon seeing one's own image for the first time. As Frost says, "I am in a place, in a situation, as if I had materialized from cloud or risen out of the ground. There is a glad recognition of the long lost and the rest follows." Poets arrive at their conclusions indirectly, but when they arrive they are direct. It is their "straight crookedness."

When Frost concludes that there "may be a better wildness of logic than of inconsequence," it is his way of challenging the "abstractionists." The logic works backward in his game; it cannot be thought out and then put down on paper: "It must be a revelation, or a series of revelations."

Frost distinguishes between the scholar and the artist. Both work from knowledge, but the scholar, or "school boy" can "tell you what he knows in the order in which he learned it." The artist "snatches a thing from some previous order." He relies on a metaphor he will use again, the notion of "burrs" that stick.

Frost metaphorically describes the figure of the poem as "like a piece of ice on a hot stove" that "must ride on its own melting." A poem cannot be "worried into being." A great poem—that is, one that has "unfolded by surprise as it went"—can be read hundreds of times without it losing its "freshness." It is left to the reader to determine how often Frost, in writing his own poems, followed the guidelines he sets forth in this essay.

"Figure in the Doorway, The" (1936)

The poem opens with people "riding high" on a train in the mountains. The terrain is so full of scrub oaks that the oaks cannot grow any larger for lack of sufficient soil and space. As the train passes through, the passengers see from the dining car the "great gaunt figure" of the title, standing in his doorway. The figure appears so large that they imagine if he were to fall, he would reach the "further wall."

This figure is worth noting because he lives in an unexpected place, "miles and miles from anywhere," and his appearance is therefore unexpected. He is almost mythic, not only for his great size but for his ability to live in such a remote place, for his self-reliance, as he seems solitary. He lives minimally, and this is praiseworthy. He gets by with his hen, a pig, a well, and a garden. The passing train may be to him a "common entertainment," but to those in the dining car, he is not mere entertainment; he is an image of someone who is without "want," someone worthy of admiration. He is rooted; they are speeding past.

The poem offers to those who may be "riding high" on monotony an opportunity for meditation on accepting life as it is, knowing how to find it, and standing firm, "unshaken."

The poem was first published in the April 1936 issue of the *Virginia Quarterly Review* and was collected later that year in *A Further Range* with the subtitle "On Being Looked at in a Train." *See* WALLS.

FURTHER READING

Parini, Jay. *Robert Frost: A Life.* New York: Holt, 1999, 273–275.

"Fire and Ice" (1923)

One of Frost's most anthologized and aphoristic poems, "Fire and Ice" demonstrates much about his approach and style. It has an uncomplicated iambic rhyme scheme and presents easily accessible metaphors. But while on the surface it is an easy read, it says a great deal more than is at first apparent.

The title of the poem, "Fire and Ice," takes the focus off what is being described, the end of the world, and places it on the description itself. Tom Hansen reports that Harlow Shapley, an American astronomer who taught at Harvard for many years, claimed that he inspired the poem. Shapley felt that a conversation he had had with Frost about how the world might end, whether in fire or in ice, was behind Frost's poetic invention. Hansen goes on to point out that such an assumption on Shapley's part is a false one. He holds that the poem must be treated as "an astute diagnosis of the chronic malfunction of the human heart" rather than as "idle cosmic speculation" about a "catastrophe millions of years in the future" (29). In this way, Shapley's characterization is too limited in scope for Hansen's understanding of the poem's meaning.

While Frost takes up the subject of the end of the world, opening by addressing those who debate two "opposite" possibilities, the several layers of meaning embedded in the poem suggest much more than can be gleaned from a cursory reading. Frost notes that "Some say" the world will end coldly, in ice, and some say it will end hotly, in fire. "Some say" is wryly derisive of the sort of light conversation to be had on a topic of such magnitude. It is also clearly meant to posit the poet as one who filters the impressions of those around him and who arrives at deeper and more meaningful conclusions.

The knowledgeable poet writes that he "hold[s] with those who favor fire" because of what he has "tasted of desire." As Jay Parini notes, "the poet-narrator seems to have been through the torrid and frigid zones, to have loved and hated" (198). As in "Acquainted with the Night," the poet may be revealing that he speaks of experiences of a personal nature. The reference to the self indicates much about the source of the poem. Surely Frost is not just imaging an end to the world in general but rather seeing a broader scope of endings, not just through the extinction of the human race per se and all that is in nature, but through our own various endings on other levels—for example, in things closer to the human heart, such as relationships or love affairs. These too end either in fire (passion) or ice (cold detachment). This returns the reader to the choice of the title and the combustion or glacial passing of any relationship, whether between people and their hopes, dreams, and aspirations or between human beings and the world.

The suggestion that the world may end because of desire suggests much about the longings and loneliness of humanity and the constant striving after excess that can eclipse our awareness of the consequences of our actions, particularly those that affect the natural world. Fire is equated with desire; ice is equated with hate. The poem hearkens back to the Ice Age when he writes, "if it had to perish twice."

But to speak of the end of the world complacently, as "if it had to perish twice," and to say that "for destruction ice / Is also great" is to minimize the possible outcome to such a degree as to highlight the ending rather than the process of destruction. The closing line, "And would suffice," suggests a longing for an end, a desire that needs satisfying.

The poem reduces a fearsome topic to a sort of "Some say tomayto, some say tomahto" lightness. The images are not particularly disarming, as they are neither detailed nor gruesome, given the subject. The end is accepting but not embracing. Ultimately the poem is more or less an earlier exploration of the ideas in Frost's poem "Ends," making its message not so much about the end of the world as about the end of particular relationships. The later poem's lines "Oh, there had once been night the first, / But this was night the last" echo the finality and resignation of "Fire and Ice."

The poem first appeared in the December 1920 issue of *Harper's Magazine* and was later collected in *New Hampshire*. See SCIENCE.

FURTHER READING

Beacham, Walton. "Technique and the Sense of Play in the Poetry of Robert Frost." In *Frost: Centennial Essays II*, edited by Jac Tharpe, 246–261. Jackson: University Press of Mississippi, 1976.

Hansen, Tom. "Frost's Fire and Ice," *Explicator* 59, no. 1 (Fall 2000): 27–30.

Pack, Robert. *Belief and Uncertainty in the Poetry of Robert Frost.* Hanover, N.H.: Middlebury College Press, 2003.

Parini, Jay. *Robert Frost: A Life.* New York: Holt, 1999, 197–198.

"Fireflies in the Garden" (1928)

In this brief lyric, Frost compares fireflies to stars in the "upper skies." The poem employs a simple aaa/bbb rhyme scheme to consider what is a real star and what is not. The fireflies emulate the stars; they are our stars here on earth, and even though they are "never equal stars at heart," they achieve their own "starlike" status. The poem playfully concludes that the primary difference between fireflies and real stars is that fireflies "can't sustain the part."

The poem joyfully celebrates the fireflies while recognizing that their inadequacies are earthly. Their lives are as fleeting as ours. Human beings, in a way, are "emulating flies" since worldly things can never "equal . . . in size" what "fills the upper skies."

Notably, Frost said at a 1938 talk at Ohio Wesleyan University that poems "are fireflies. They represent lucid intervals and glow only for a moment" (Cramer, 88). Certainly Frost hoped that his poems would keep on glowing and someday become "real stars."

The poem was first collected in *West-Running Brook*. See STARS.

FURTHER READING

Cramer, Jeffrey S. *Robert Frost among His Poems: A Literary Companion to the Poet's Own Biographical Contexts and Associations.* Jefferson, N.C.: McFarland, 1996.

Fleissner, Robert F. "Frost's 'Fireflies in the Garden,'" *Explicator* 39, no. 4 (1981): 26–28.

"Five Nocturnes" (1947)

"Five Nocturnes" is the title of the second section of *Steeple Bush* and includes the numbered poems

"I. The Night Light," "II. Were I in Trouble,"' "III. Bravado," "IV. On Making Certain Anything Has Happened," and "V. In the Long Night." Though all of the poems had been published previously, *Steeple Bush* was the first book in which they were collected as a group. One of the poems, "On Making Certain Anything Has Happened," was Frost's 1945 Christmas poem, and two others were renamed: "Bravado," was originally "Bravery," and "Were I in Trouble" was originally "Were I in Trouble with the Night Tonight." The nocturnes vary in length and structure, but as the title and their grouping indicate, they share certain thematic similarities.

A nocturne is an instrumental composition, usually on piano, with a pensive and dreamy mood. It can also be a painting of a night scene. These five poems may be said to be both. Each paints a particular night scene and is composed in rhyme, though each rhyme is different. The structure is significant because the rhymes are altered but each poem follows a strict pattern. Frost experiments with the rhymes as a way of playing in the night with different moods and speakers.

"The Night Light" presents an interesting twist on the purpose night-lights generally serve, as a kind of protection against whatever may threaten in the dark. In this instance, however, the night-light is no protection against stubbing a toe or against other things that go bump in the night. An omniscient speaker observes a woman who always sleeps with a light burning by her bedside. The night-light does not protect; it brings "bad dreams and broken sleep," but the woman uses it because she nevertheless believes that it helps "the Lord her soul to keep." Why the Lord would need a light to guide him in the night is not clear, but she apparently feels that somehow the light aids his ability to protect, if not her mind and body, at least her soul. The "Good gloom on her was thrown away"—she is unable to embrace its healthy effects—though in what way the gloom, the darkness, is good, is not made explicit. The speaker claims that he has accepted this good gloom "by night or day," but the "darkest of it [is] still to dread": There will be no night-lights to guide the Lord to his soul for keeping.

"Were I in Trouble" presents a first-person narrator, apparently alone "on the mountain up far too high," who sees a headlight reflected on the natural granite steps of the mountain and is thereby made to feel less alone. The illustration of the headlight bouncing "down a granite stair / Like a star fresh fallen out of the sky" is striking, a turn on an image cast by a manmade light. The speaker, feels momentarily comforted by the knowledge that he is not entirely alone but becomes aware that were he in trouble, as the title indicates, the "traveler there could do [him] no good." In the end the light that is cast is "unintimate," and while there may be another presence on the mountain, the speaker is not at all comforted by the light or its relationship to another human being.

The four-line "Bravado" expresses a feeling of isolation. A solitary walker considers what would happen if a star were to fall from the night sky. Without its title, the four lines would have little resonance, but as a description of what it is to be brave, even brazenly brave, it is both humorous and haunting. The speaker's concern that he is somehow vulnerable to attacks from the stars is almost silly. To cast an "upward look / Of caution" seems a bit paranoid. But in another sense the "risk" that he takes makes the universe an unfriendly place, and if the speaker should be spared such an accident, it is only because the stars have "missed" him. The poem irrationally implies that he is more likely to be hit by a fallen star than not, since apparently when they are "shot" they are meant in some way to reach a target.

"On Making Certain Anything Has Happened" presents another first-person speaker. This time he imagines himself "employed" as a "watcher of the void." He is the gatekeeper, so to speak, of the stars that fall from the night sky. Similar to the ants in "Departmental," who have specific assignments, this figure "must report / Some cluster one star short," perhaps to someone "higher up at court." He must judge which fallen stars are worth reporting, in order to avoid "frighten[ing] church or state" unnecessarily. He checks his list for "every star in sight," a job that may "take ... all night," but his role is significant, as he must make certain whether "anything has happened." Without the reporter, there is nothing to report; without the observer, nothing has happened. This is a variation on the old philosophical question: When a tree falls in the forest, does it make a sound if no one is there to hear it?

"In the Long Night" also presents a first-person speaker. This setting is quite different from the others. The poem has moved from house to mountain to nature, and the speaker here imagines building a "house of crystal," in this case an igloo. This speaker would join a "solitary friend," and they would sit up all night reciting literature by the fireside and occasionally crawling out to "observe the Northern Light." Frost playfully creates Eskimos named "Etookashoo" and "Couldlooktoo" (the latter of which rhymes humorously with "and cooked too"). As the closing poem to the "Five Nocturnes," it seems to bring the light of stars to a safe place, where their falling is not a threat. Safe within the igloo the speaker is assured that "There will come another day."

The "Five Nocturnes" thematically center on one of Frost's most frequent and recognizable tropes: the night and all its implications. The poems express from various perspectives fears, hidden and not, and the desire for individuals to find safety, sometimes through manmade light and other times through one another, in a universe more vast than imaginable and darker than we would like to think.

See NIGHT and STARS.

FURTHER READING

Cramer, Jeffrey S. *Robert Frost among His Poems: A Literary Companion to the Poet's Own Biographical Contexts and Associations.* Jefferson, N.C.: McFarland, 1996.

"Flood, The" (1928)

The common distinction between blood versus water is a metaphor for family versus friends. The cliché is that blood is thicker than water, and therefore the ties that bind people to family are stronger than those that bind them to friends. On the negative side is the concept of "blood feuds." This son-

net opens with a similar comparison between blood and water, stating that "blood has been harder to dam back." Certainly Frost was aware of the familiar saying and seems to be playing on it from the start of the poem and throughout. He also manipulates the different connotations of the word *blood*. Along with the positive connotation of familial ties and the notion of the giving of ourselves, of our very blood for those we care about, blood also means other things negative: bleeding, exsanguination, and death. We also speak of "bad blood" between rivals, suggesting enmity. "The Flood" explores all these connotations.

Using gruesome imagery, the poem reports that just when we think we have managed to dam back blood, it manages to break "new barrier walls," like a hemorrhage or aneurysm, "in some new kind of slaughter." When blood is harmful "[W]e choose to say it is let loose by the devil," perhaps as a way of denying that we, as humans, could be so wicked to one another. But it is the power of blood in ourselves that releases blood, not some malevolent being from beyond. Bloodletting leads to more bloodletting. It is our power, through hate, love, jealousy, and other strong emotions, that can give rise to such release. It is not the devil or some outside force but the source of blood itself that leads to such destruction. Humans have it in themselves to be both wrathful and wistful. This point is important, since Frost is claiming that humans alone are responsible for their own undoing.

Blood is held too high: We can keep emotions bottled up too long, and the suggestion is that anything that is held at an "unnatural . . . level" will eventually find a way out, whether it be "brave" or "not so brave." Blood, a teeming force, is not particular about how its powers are loosed. In some instances it is for good, as a means to peace, and at other times for ill, as in war. In either case, it leaves "summits stained," as the memory of what has come and gone remains.

Frost extends the metaphor of blood from familial ties to national concerns when he introduces the examples of "weapons of war" and "implements of peace." Of note is the eventual choice of "The Flood" for the title. This places the emphasis on blood's inability to "be contained" rather than on blood itself. Robert Faggen also notes that the title "echoes the Biblical account of God's wrath" (133).

As a bond and as a metaphor, blood cannot be avoided and must be therefore reckoned with. That is, Frost's comments should be taken more generally, as dealing with the human condition. Humans are creatures of blood, and as such we will experience things that will make us angry, even sanguinary—bloodthirsty. Or we may be passionate (hot-blooded) or we may weep (tears of blood), and so on. The intensity of these emotions can change, but they cannot always be avoided. Knowing this, Frost seems to be holding up a mirror and issuing a warning. Knowing that blood "cannot be contained," we had better beware and know how to deal with it, before we leave more summits stained, familial and not.

"The Flood" was collected in *West-Running Brook* but was originally published as "Blood" in the February 8, 1928, issue of the *Nation*. *See* WALLS.

FURTHER READING

Faggen, Robert. *Robert Frost and the Challenge of Darwin.* Ann Arbor: University of Michigan Press, 1997.

"Flower Boat, The" (1928)

A yarn is a tall tale, and fishermen and hunters are often held to be the greatest tellers of yarns. In this poem a fisherman is at the village barber shop "swapping a yarn for a yarn." His audience is receptive, so his "deep-sea" boat has found a receptive "harbor."

The second stanza provides an image of the boat that is unexpected. It is riding the "sunny sod" full not of fish but of flowers. The water becomes sod, and the fish have become flowers. The image suggests that this dory is no longer in use and that the boat that was once "full to the gunnel" with cod has been retired. The reference to George's Bank is meaningful as the site has its own legend. George's Bank is at the southwestern end of a series of banks that stretches from Newfoundland to southern New England. It is known that vast numbers of fish exist at George's Bank, so legend has it that the cod there were once so abundant that the first European sailors were able to scoop them out of the water in baskets. The fisherman's days of grandeur were as great as these, the speaker implies, and even if not, his tale is as tall as the one about George's Bank.

The speaker says that he "judge[s] from that Elysian freight," referencing the Elysian Fields of ancient Greece, the resting place for the blessed after death. For a place of happiness, the fisherman's vision will bring him and his boat "by fate" to the "Happy Isles together." The fisherman has nothing but "yarn[s]" left of his days at sea and must await the day when he and his dory will ride "rougher weather" into a happier afterworld.

Collected in *West-Running Brook,* the poem was first published May 10, 1909, in the *Youth's Companion* and was printed in December 1909 in the *Pinkerton Critic*. It is a very early poem; Frost dated it as a part of a group of poems written in or before 1895.

FURTHER READING

Cramer, Jeffrey S. *Robert Frost among His Poems: A Literary Companion to the Poet's Own Biographical Contexts and Associations.* Jefferson, N.C.: McFarland, 1996.

"Flower-Gathering" (1913)

Included in Frost's first volume, *A Boy's Will,* "Flower-Gathering" is a cry of youthful love and longing. The first stanza presents a speaker who leaves his lover in the "morning glow" to take a walk. His lover walks partway with him, but cannot go on. Their parting makes him "sad to go" and leaves him wondering whether she will know him "in the gloaming" and in the "[g]aunt and dusty gray with roaming." He wonders why she is silent—whether it is because she knows him or does not know him; neither possibility is desirable. These images of detachment and separation are reminiscent of "A Dream Pang," in which the speaker is in a forest, waiting, and in the end remains unapproached and unapproachable.

In the second stanza the young lover returns from flower gathering to present his love with the "faded flowers gay" that took him from beside her for what seemed an inordinately long time, "the ages of a day." He holds that it is for her to "measure" their "worth" and to determine whether the flowers merit treasuring based on how she feels about his absence and whether she thinks it was long enough to warrant the gift of flowers. The closing two lines juxtapose the brief amount of time he has been gone with his feeling that he has been "long away."

This poem may seem overwrought. Frost was young and had not yet found his poetic voice. The descriptions are indeed flowery, the language uncharacteristically formal. Its conventional approach is unexpected from a poet well known for his ability to render so completely the New England figures that are characteristic of his mature work. The language here owes more to Frost's traditional training than to the techniques he had not yet perfected. His quaint use of such words as "dumb" for mute and "gay" to describe the flowers (perhaps from "nosegay," also an archaism), for example, are a far cry from the conversational and even colloquial expressions that came to characterize his later poems. While the poem expresses youthful longing, it also demonstrates the limitations of youth. It is more in the manner of the poet's predecessors than his own. It is a conventional love poem, with little of the complexity of Frost at his best. Perhaps worth further examination, however, are the references to knowing or not knowing and the heaviness of the silence the young love finds when he returns. The first instance calls to mind Troilus's doubt in Act 4, scene 2, of Shakespeare's *Troilus and Cressida*, where he says, "This is, and is not, Cressid."

Jay Parini says that after Frost and his wife Elinor were married, they took a long-postponed honeymoon to New Hampshire, where "Frost went for long walks in the woods and meadows around Allenstown, sometimes with Elinor for company but often not," because she was already pregnant with their first child. Parini maintains that "Frost's guilt over going on these walks without her was caught in 'Flower- Gathering'" (56).

FURTHER READING

Parini, Jay. *Robert Frost: A Life*. New York: Holt, 1999, 56–57.

"[Forgive, O Lord, my little jokes on Thee]" (1962)

See CLUSTER OF FAITH.

"For John F. Kennedy His Inauguration" (1962)

President John F. Kennedy and Frost had a friend in common, Congressman Steward L. Udall, whom Frost had gotten to know while poetry consultant for the Library of Congress. It was Udall who suggested to Kennedy that Frost read a poem at his inauguration. Kennedy liked poetry and in particular liked Frost's. During his campaign, he would often conclude a speech by quoting the final lines of "Stopping by Woods on a Snowy Evening" about having promises to keep: "And miles to go before I sleep." When Udall first suggested it, Kennedy is quoted as having said "Oh no! You know Frost always steals any show he is a part of." But the politician in him knew it was a good idea, and he had a telephone conversation with Frost to discuss the invitation. As poet William Meredith later recalled in an interview, "It was a novel idea, and one that focused attention on Kennedy as a man of culture, as a man interested in culture."

During their conversation about the inauguration, Kennedy, as Jay Parini puts it, "gingerly" suggested that Frost write a poem for the occasion. Frost did not particularly welcome the idea. Feeling obligated, however, Frost did write this poem specifically for the inauguration, but he began to draft it only days before the event. He worked on it until the night before, treating it as a "preamble to his reading of 'The Gift Outright,'" but the result, due partly to Frost's advanced age and partly to his limited enthusiasm for the task was a poem written more out of duty than inspiration (Parini, 414).

The poem, now treated as a sort of preface to "The Gift Outright," was in fact never read at the inauguration. On that day, January 20, 1961, the sun's reflection on the glaring white paper made it impossible for Frost to read the print. Recovering well, he recited "The Gift Outright" from memory, improvising on the last line: "Such as she was, such as she *would* become, *has* become, and I—and for this occasion let me change that to—what she *will* become" (Parini, 414). The poem was later collected in *In the Clearing*. Following the inauguration it also appeared in various newspapers and magazines. Another anecdote from Parini is that when the crowd stopped applauding Frost, the old man absent-mindedly thanked the "president-elect, Mr. John Finley" (a classicist whose name he knew from Harvard).

The poem's subtitle in *In the Clearing* is "Gift Outright of 'The Gift Outright': With Some Preliminary History in Rhyme." It begins, "Summoning artists to participate / in the august occasions of the state / Seems something artists ought to celebrate." Frost's choice of the word "seems" in the third line is easily glossed; it reveals a certain lack of celebration, not so much perhaps for being involved, as Frost always loved attention, but likely for being asked to write a poem for the occasion. In the poem Frost writes that "today is for my cause a day of days," the cause he refers to being poetry, because this was the first time a poet ever was invited to read at a presidential inauguration. He praised President Kennedy in line six for being the "first to think of such a thing."

After giving appropriate thanks and saying that he has brought his verse in "acknowledgment," Frost sets out to say something about the country and about poetry. As in "The Gift Outright," an outright love poem to his native land, Frost praises the United States by speaking of the "one to dominate / By character, by tongue, by native trait," summoning God as having "nodded his approval of as good." He harkens back to four great men who helped build the country: George Washington, John Adams, Thomas Jefferson, and James Madi-

Frost in 1961, the same year he would be the first poet to read at a presidential inauguration. *(Photo by Walter Albertin. Courtesy Library of Congress)*

son. He praises their ability to look forward and to "bring empires down about our ears."

The poem takes up the subject of the immigrants who come to our shores and become "our wards" to teach "how Democracy is meant." It raises the question of "confusion" and the need for a "New order of the ages." The poet returns to praises of Kennedy by referring to the close election, in which Kennedy's margin was a mere 113,000 votes out of 68.8 million cast, as "Come fresh from an election like the last, / The greatest vote a people ever cast." Certainly to call the vote the greatest ever is a bit sycophantic, but it is not surprising given that Frost had effectively been commissioned to write the poem. Frost even references Kennedy's own best-selling book, *Profiles in Courage*, which was awarded a Pulitzer Prize in 1956, in line 60 with "There was the book of profiles. . . ."

As the poem draws to its close, the poet leads his audience through various hopes for the new administration: "a little sterner, / And braver for the earner, learner, yearner"; "a next Augustan age"; "a power leading from its strength and pride, / Of young ambition eager to be tried." The last two lines, "A golden age of poetry and power / Of which this noonday's the beginning hour," express his hope that these political changes will bring a greater appreciation for poetry as well.

The praise Frost heaped on Kennedy may or may not have led to his trip to the Soviet Union in 1962, encouraged by Udall and endorsed by the President. Frost wrote a letter to Kennedy in which he said, "How grand for you to think of me this way and how like you to take the chance of sending anyone like me over there affinitizing with the Russians." In the end it seems Kennedy regretted his endorsement. When Frost returned, after having had a most enjoyable trip and having met the Soviet premier, Nikita Khrushchev (one of his stipulations in the agreement to go), he made some offhand remarks about being told in Russia that America was too liberal to fight. He later revised these remarks during a talk at the Library of Congress. Nonetheless, President Kennedy never contacted Frost after his return, making the hopes in this inaugural poem fall short of the poet's expressed desires.

Frost's good friend Louis Untermeyer once characterized the poem as the worst Frost had ever written.

FURTHER READING

Cramer, Jeffrey S. *Robert Frost among His Poems: A Literary Companion to the Poet's Own Biographical Contexts and Associations.* Jefferson, N.C.: McFarland, 1996.

Meyers, Jeffrey. *Robert Frost: A Biography.* New York: Houghton Mifflin, 1996, 322–323.

Parini, Jay. *Robert Frost: A Life.* New York: Holt, 1999.

"For Once, Then, Something" (1923)

In this highly visual poem, initially titled "Well" and then "Wrong to the Light," the poet questions what may or may not be seen by looking deeply.

Lore has it that by looking deeply into a water well, a person may be able to foretell the future or perhaps see into the unknown. Frost contrasts the earthly with the spiritual and the natural with the supernatural.

The poem opens with the speaker saying that "Others taunt" him for his inability to see in wells what they claim they are able to see. As Katherine Kearns puts it, "The 'others' are those who look out too far or in too deep"—drawing a connection to the poem "Neither Out Far Nor in Deep" (22). The suggestion is that the speaker does not share the same faith as those by whom he is surrounded and is therefore shunned by them.

When the speaker kneels at "well-curbs," or at the side of wells, the light is always "wrong" and does not allow him to see something that others assume is deeper than the water below. In this way the inadequacy is described as being in the light rather than in him, and the second title choice hints that this was important to Frost. The speaker does not see through the water to something assumed to be far greater, as others say they have, but rather his reflection is cast back at him in a "shining surface picture." And when he sees himself that way, with the blue sky behind him, he seems "in the summer heaven godlike." The image recalls the Greek myth of Narcissus, who gazed into a pool of water, saw his own reflection, and fell in love with it. It also suggests that this speaker, in not gazing into wells according to the customs of others, sets himself higher than the others. The answer in religion to those who deny the existence of God is that they in some way believe they are themselves godlike. Egotism is blamed for valuing the self and things earthly, rather than otherworldly. And reason or science is contrasted with faith and religion.

The speaker recalls that "Once," when he was straining hard to see something beyond his own image, he thought he saw "something white, uncertain, / Something more of the depths," but it was quickly lost. The speaker is unsure whether he had a moment of transcendence. But then one drop of water fell from a fern overhead, and that ripple "Shook whatever it was lay there at bottom." It took the image away and left him wondering what it was he had seen. He wonders whether it was "Truth? A pebble of quartz?" but arrives at no firm conclusion.

The title words close the final line: "For once, then, something." Frost's use of commas here, highlighting the pauses, dramatically slows the pace of the final line. The poem is mysterious, since the "something" is what was not seen and yet was, for once, *something,* though it is never identified by the speaker. His desire at the well-curb can be related to human passion for going beyond the current stage of knowing to understand fully once and for all the meaning of life. We strive to know, and at times we may believe we gain glimpses into this "something" more, but it is always uncertain. Another interpretation is that the speaker remains skeptical about the testimony of others and has simply used this experience, this something, as a means of becoming acceptable to those who taunt him. Now he is able to act as they do, given what he can say he has seen. But deep down he remains skeptical about their claims.

The poem also contrasts the abstract with the concrete, nothing with something. Truth represents the abstract, as does the "whiteness," whereas the pebble of quartz and the speaker's reflection represent the concrete. He is taunted, but it is unclear whether he believes that the others are missing something or that he is. Whiteness in Frost is often intriguing, as it is here. Does it represent death or innocence as it does in "Design"? Or does it represent the afterlife? Or was that whiteness merely his own reflection unrecognized?

The italicized *once* in the seventh line places the emphasis on that fleeting moment when the speaker came across something "uncertain," then "something." Perhaps the something lies in the return to his own image, since it is what he knows as "true." It also seems to connect to the speaker's honesty about his skepticism, suggesting that he will grant the one time that this experience happened to him. But he does not feel enough happened to warrant the same conclusions the others have made. The poem is ambiguous, relating the tension between those who believe and those who do not, no matter what they may believe in.

This poem was first published in the July 1920 issue of *Harper's Magazine* and was later collected in *New Hampshire.*

FURTHER READING

Brower, Reuben A. *The Poetry of Robert Frost: Constellations of Intention.* New York: Oxford University Press, 1963, 136–139.

Cappeluti, Jo-Anne. "For Once, Then, Something: The Sublime Reality of Fictions in Robert Frost," *Robert Frost Review* (Fall 1993): 86–92.

Cooper, David D. "Looking beyond the Picture: Robert Frost's 'For Once, Then Something,'" *Robert Frost Review* (Fall 1993): 47–49.

Frost, Carol. "Frost's Way of Speaking," *New England Review: Middlebury Series* 23, no. 1 (Winter 2002): 119–133.

Haddin, Theodore. "Surfaces and Depths: The Metonymic Wells of Thoreau and Frost," *Publications of the Mississippi Philological Association* (1985): 40–49.

Kearns, Katherine. *Robert Frost and a Poetics of Appetite.* Cambridge: Cambridge University Press, 1994, 21–23.

Meyers, Jeffrey. *Robert Frost: A Biography.* New York: Houghton Mifflin, 1996, 178–179.

Pack, Robert. *Belief and Uncertainty in the Poetry of Robert Frost.* Hanover, N.H.: Middlebury College Press, 2003.

Rogers, William E. "Mysteries in Frost," *Furman Studies* 32 (December 1986): 53–64.

"Fountain, a Bottle, a Donkey's Ears, and Some Books, A" (1923)

One of Frost's most alluring titles, given to one of his lesser-known narrative poems, this incongruous list sounds like the ingredients in a magic potion.

The poem begins with an introduction to Old Davis, who "owned a solid mica mountain / In Dalton." (Dalton is a town about 15 miles southeast of Concord, New Hampshire.) The story about Davis's mountain may or may not be true, since the poem makes it sound like a mere local legend passed on without confirmation. The speaker knows Davis and has been told that one day Davis, a guide, will take him to see the mica mountain. (Stones and rocks figure prominently in Frost's work.) The speaker decides that today is to be that day.

He asks Davis to take him, reminding him of a fountain there that Davis had once told him about. He describes a "stone baptismal font" that was built by Mormons, before their founder Joseph Smith called them "[t]o go West." While the mica mountain legend is not confirmed, Frost's friend Raymond Holden has noted that Frost, when he lived in Derry, New Hampshire, had often heard the legend that the Mormons once built a stone temple in the forest but only its corroded baptismal font remained. Davis, reluctant at first, deflects the speaker's wishes, saying, "Some day I will." The speaker persists, "Today." Davis minimizes the fountain's importance by saying, "old bathtub, what is that to see?" and suggests that they talk about it instead. Again the speaker asserts his will: "Let's go see the place." The tension between the two is somewhat relieved when Davis says he will "find that fountain" if only to shut the speaker up, even if it "takes all summer." It turns out that either Old Davis is not a very reliable guide or that the speaker is getting hints that the story is not true. Challengingly, the speaker says, "You've lost it, then?" and later, "I thought you were a guide." Old Davis dismisses the implied criticism of his abilities as a guide by saying that things can change with time and "bad masonry," and he claims that the mountain "may have shifted," which seems at best far-fetched. There is an almost childlike persistence in the speaker's prodding and a hidebound elder's resistance in Old Davis's redirection of the speaker to talking rather than seeing, relying on memory rather than presence. But Davis, a kind enough old man, reluctantly gives in, grumbling that he will let himself be dragged "all over everywhere" to find it. Thus the journey begins.

First they come to a cliff that has the likeness of a bottle painted on it. While it is not the fountain, Davis says it is the "famous Bottle." The reader is left to conclude that the bottle, "painted / or stained by vegetation from above" on the side of a cliff, if expected at all, was accidentally found, confirming

that Davis does not really know the location of the site. The speaker is not satisfied. He wants his fountain. Davis suggests instead that they head to the place where "two converging slides, the avalanches . . . look like donkey's ears." The speaker is again disappointed. This provokes from Davis a speech, the older and possibly wiser guide asserting, "You don't like nature. All you like is books," and a moral begins to seep into an otherwise straightforward poem. It also seems to get Davis off the hook, since he can now turn the speaker's attention to something other than the fountain. The reader gets the impression that Davis now knows where he is going.

"Be ready," thinks the speaker "for almost anything," his eager expectations now excited.

The two reach a road, which they follow to an abandoned house—there are quite a few deserted houses in Frost's poems. When they arrive, Old Davis, much like the minister in "The Black Cottage," figuratively introduces the speaker to the people "[w]ho used to live [t]here," the Robinsons, and especially to Clara Robinson, a "poetess." She was a woman who nurtured nature and wrote poetry. She "tended both" without ever tending to them herself, because her life was lived entirely in bed; she was "shut in," perhaps because of a debilitating illness or perhaps by choice—it is never specified.

"Our business first's up attic with her books," Old Davis says, and they make their way through an otherwise empty house to the attic, where they find books overflowing "like the poetess's heart of love." But though the books are abundant, they are "all of one kind"—all Robinson's poetry. Some are buried beneath window glass broken by "boys and bad hunters" who from time to time must have stumbled upon the abandoned home and wantonly stoned or shot out the windows. The boys and bad hunters had "known what to do with stone and lead to unprotected glass," the speaker observes sarcastically, and he wonders: "How had the tender verse escaped their outrage?" How might these vagrants have been able to "hurt a poem"? They could have thrown Clara Robinson's books out the window like tiles because of their "tempting flatness." What happens after a book is thrown this way is that it begins to fly just as the birds at Clara's windowsill had: "silent in flight, / But all the burden of [their] bod[ies] song." The lyrical poems are the books' songs, but they can lose their flight when struck: They will "tumble . . . stricken" and "lie in stones and bushes unretrieved." There is much sacrilege in the hurling of books, even when they become as airborne as birds. But there is no such glorious ending for these books; they lie "rejected," at least those that the poetess's life "Had been too short to sell or give away." It is possible that she never sold any at all.

Old Davis encourages the speaker to take a few of the books, perhaps encouraging him to give away some copies, to get them into the hands of other readers. The speaker makes off in the end with one "small book" in his pocket and imagines the poetess in heaven "having eased her heart of one more copy." The poem closes with the speaker imagining that the poetess had "felt the tug" and his "demand upon her" and that eventually, with time, she will manage to be rid of all her books, one by one, through other "legitimate" travelers.

The poem is in some ways about the journey and in others about the end result. The books, the vanguard of the title, become the focus in the end, making the journey almost incidental. At the same time, "discovering" the books, which Old Davis knew were there all along, is a part of the journey; the destination and the purpose have shifted. The references at the beginning, and the doubts the speaker had concerning Old Davis, become insignificant; they may simply have been ways for Old Davis to entice the young man, who had wanted to see a fountain, into finding a book.

Old Davis is presented as not really knowing where anything is and as a well-meaning but unreliable old man. After the rejection of the donkey's ears by the traveler, Davis says, "You don't like nature. All you like is books." Then he takes the speaker to the house. But this was his intention all along. He simply had to play things out, make sure the younger man took the journey. Telling him there would be a bunch of books, all but a few wet and swollen by rain, in an abandoned house was not going to be much of a lure compared with a mica mountain and the legend of a stone baptismal fountain, even for a young man who only likes books.

The books in the poem become the only presence, other than the characters themselves, that is real and interactive. Everything leads to the books. Everything else along the way is either fiction or a narrative device. The books are important, and have not been "thrown irreverently about."

The poem also dramatizes the fears of any poet that his work might one day be forgotten in a metaphorical abandoned house. The hope is that "people like the speaker, people who care," will somehow, "either looking for or finding something," discover the poems after the poet has gone. The role of the poet begins in life but clearly continues after death. This is in the nature of books and their legitimate perpetuators. Both the poets and the readers keep poetry alive. The journey of a poet does not end with death; it continues on in the words left behind—in books. Old Davis's role is vital, and one wonders just what his relationship to the living poetess might have been.

Jeffrey Cramer notes that Clara Weaver Robinson (1854–1905) "was indeed a poet who wrote about posies and birds, but that is about as far as she resembles the Clara Robinson of Frost's poem" (73). He goes on to say that Robinson did not have a book of poems published in her lifetime, nor did she live in New Hampshire. Frost and Robinson may have crossed paths a few times, however, as her father was the pastor of a church in Lawrence, Massachusetts, and she once taught at St. Lawrence University, which Frost's wife Elinor attended.

"A Fountain, a Bottle, a Donkey's Ears, and Some Books" was collected in *New Hampshire* but was first published in the October 1923 issue of the *Bookman*.

FURTHER READING

Cramer, Jeffrey S. *Robert Frost among His Poems: A Literary Companion to the Poet's Own Biographical Contexts and Associations.* Jefferson, N.C.: McFarland, 1996.

"[Four-Room Shack Aspiring High]" (1963)

In this late and slight untitled poem, a kind of riddle, in only seven lines the poet takes on television, a four-room shack that aspires to the heavens with its "scrawny mast," or antenna. Or the four-room shack might be a house furnished with a television, if not simply a wry description of the television set itself. The "visions in the sky," the programs, the commercials, which "go blindly pouring past" are not meant to be sympathetic images. They are indifferent to the viewer, who receives them passively. Frost uses the word "pouring" to suggest an enormous number of them and "blindly" to suggest that they are blind to us, as we may be to them.

Frost's mast, which may be either an indoor or an outdoor antenna, brings in visions that pale in comparison to those in the skies toward which the mast aspires. Think, for example, of the infinitely varied imagery in clouds above that also may be blindly pouring by. The speaker says facetiously, "What you get is what you buy," but those who live in a four-room shack have little means to buy much of anything. The purchase of a television set might well be seen as extravagant. The closing line, "Hope you're satisfied to last," suggests a speaker who believes that to waste time on such empty simulacra is to take time away from spiritual or aesthetic matters, which may, if aspired to, reveal immortality. The purpose of television is to bombard the viewer with products and programs that are spiritually empty.

If the antenna of the television were substituted for the steeple (note the "spire" in "aspire") of a church, the four-room shack would become the church itself, the televised images something worshipped, snatching visions from the sky. So, too, would the members of the church be looking for signals from on high. If taken this way, the rest of the poem seems to offer a perspective on religion in general, rather than a critical view of passive viewers fallen from grace.

Other than Frost's obvious irony, the poem's limited significance is that it reveals Frost's disdain for certain technological developments (as in "The Egg and the Machine" and elsewhere) and hints at more religious considerations than are customary in his work. However, if the four-room shack is meant to be a church, the presumably agnostic Frost of the other poems is more evident.

The poem was not collected in the first edition of *In the Clearing* but has been included in subsequent editions of the volume.

"Fragmentary Blue" (1923)

Frost once claimed that he wrote "Fragmentary Blue" to tease his friends who wanted him to stop writing lyrics (Cramer). The lyric consists of two complete sentences. The first stanza is the first sentence, a question. The speaker wonders why we "make so much of fragmentary blue" and provides a series of items in which blue can be found. He wants to know why we make so much of the color that we find "here and there" in fragments when "heaven presents in sheets the solid hue." A desire for blue seems equated with a desire for perfection, and he wonders why we look for blue in earthly things, when heaven presents whole sheets of it.

The second stanza is a statement that answers the question proposed in the first. The speaker says that since "earth is earth" and "not heaven," at least not yet, the blue on earth is but "a whet," an appetizer for the perfection we ultimately want. If earth is earth and not heaven, though the speaker seems confident that this world just might one day fill the role of heaven, then for now it will only partly assuage our appetite for blue, or ultimate perfection.

The first stanza evokes images but does not fully present them, because the poet sees their introduction as sufficient. The poem mentions butterfly, bird, flower, stone, and eye but provides no descriptive detail; instead, it allows each reader to evoke his or her own image from memory. The second stanza is imageless and presents a philosophical position.

The speaker distinguishes between the earth and sky, making the sky a part of heaven, not a part of earth. He speculates whether earth could be heaven after all, since the blue above is so far away and our wishes for blue can be granted so simply in the vision of stanza one.

In some ways the poem seems to contrast the Platonic with the Aristotelian view. Plato perceived all things in this world, such as truth and beauty, as having an ideal "form" in the transcendental realm. Aristotle, in contrast, believed that truth, beauty, and so on existed only in things themselves, in this world, and relied on no ideal form for their qualities. Plato assumes that these forms are the best examples of objects and that this world is a mere copy of the transcendent realm. The objects in this world may have value, but only because they are parasitic on the transcendental realm. The speaker seems to be resisting or even rejecting this view.

The images of blue on earth are graspable and clear, and heaven is nothing but blank sheets, without detail or form. In some sense, the poem seems to say, it is better to embrace this world with its fragmentary blues than to obsess over an abstraction in a transcendental world that only whets our appetites for more.

The poem first appeared in the July 1920 issue of *Harper's Magazine* and was later included as the first poem in the "Grace Notes" section of *New Hampshire. See* PHILOSOPHY.

FURTHER READING

Abel, Darrel. "Frost's 'Fragmentary Blue,'" *Explicator* 48, no. 4 (Summer 1990): 270–272.

Cramer, Jeffrey S. *Robert Frost among His Poems: A Literary Companion to the Poet's Own Biographical Contexts and Associations.* Jefferson, N.C.: McFarland, 1996.

"Freedom of the Moon, The" (1928)

This highly descriptive poem is almost an anthem for the artist. Frost celebrates creativity, the ability to manipulate surroundings and make whatever catches his fancy go "shining anywhere" he pleases. The poem also raises the question whether art imitates life or life imitates art since the reader is apt to become lost in the descriptions, blurring the perception of which is foremost.

The speaker intimately shares that he has "tried the new moon" everywhere. The freedom is not of the moon, but of the observer. Visual images abound for such a short poem: The moon is seen "above a hazy tree-and-farmhouse cluster"; it gets "pulled" from its "crate of crooked trees"; it has been tried on by the speaker "As you might try a jewel in your hair"; it can be combined with a star, the star itself being a gem of the first water—that is, of the highest level of excellence. The poem presents little in the way of ideas, relying heavily on the rendering of precise images to convey its point. It has something in common with the poetry of the imagists, who strove to render such particulars precisely and allow the images to carry the day.

The speaker's arrangement of the new moon is akin to the sampling of a new cuisine or wine. He tries it this way and that, with a "little" of this or a "combining" of that. He toys with the idea that nature is something to be arranged according to individual taste and preference and becomes the best plaything to those who can master it best. Nature's aesthetic arises from human intervention. A landscape is not fully a landscape until an artist has painted it, written of it, sung about it.

The artist, while nearly gloating over his powers, is also surprisingly unaware of their strengths and effects. He is amazed by the unexpected delights that his manipulations of nature can yield. The consequences of this manipulation are that, given the raw material of nature, the artist can see his arrangements multiply and becomes fascinated by his own designs. The colors in the last line run like the painter's palette, and "all sorts of wonder follow." The artist's power is also related to the power of thought, as in the second stanza, where he "pulled it" and "brought it." All, it seems, is within the artist's control.

The poem sings its own praises, but it does so in worthy images and language. In the end the speaker has managed to "put it shining" where he pleased. The world itself is the artist's canvas. And the poem tempts the creative reader to join in. More than one can play at this game.

The poem first appeared in *West-Running Brook.*

"From Iron" (1962)

This couplet has the subtitle "Tools and Weapons" and is dedicated to Ahmed S. Bokhari, an assistant secretary at the United Nations who, in 1956, invited Frost to write a poem for the Meditation Room at the United Nations Headquarters in New York City. The poem was to be inscribed on a piece of iron that had been sent to the United Nations by the king of Sweden.

Frost said he wrote the "little couplet ... from looking at a lump of iron that was supposed to be perfectly pure and meant to be the oneness that we could all attain—the purity" (Cramer, 179). As a skeptic about the efficacy of the United Nations, Frost wrote a couplet that seems to oppose unification and calls into question the presumption of a common interest among nations. It reads, "Nature within her inmost self divides / To trouble men with having to take sides." The couplet seems to contradict what the United Nations stands for, making Frost's intentions ambiguous. Given Frost's approach, it is no surprise that the couplet was not accepted by Bokhari and the iron went uninscribed. Still, its inclusion in *In the Clearing* is of note, since Frost could easily have done away with it altogether. While an earlier version titled "The Sage" was printed in *A Remembrance Collection of New Poems* in 1959, its inclusion in *In the Clearing* suggests that the couplet was inspired by Frost's political disposition.

The subtitle, Frost once explained, came from looking at the lump of iron. He said, "the purest iron ... is at once tools and weapons.... It's tools and weapons right while you're looking at it. Everything's like that." Frost knew that the lump, given human interests, could be used for good or ill, turned into something useful for peace or useful for war. As it was, it was only raw material; in human hands, it could be something much more or much less.

The couplet is surprisingly complex despite its brevity. It asserts that "Nature" or rather human nature, is always divided, and therefore taking sides is unavoidable. In many ways, the sentiment it expresses, while possibly realistic, is dispiriting, as it affords either no discernible hope for everlasting peace or a hope for peace that the United Nations is powerless to bring about.

FURTHER READING

Cook, Reginald. *Robert Frost: A Living Voice.* Amherst: University of Mass Press, 1974, 134–135.

Cramer, Jeffrey S. *Robert Frost among His Poems: A Literary Companion to the Poet's and Biographical Contexts and Associations.* Jefferson, N.C.: McFarland, 1996.

Seale, Lisa. "War and Peace: Robert Frost and the United Nations Meditation Room," *New England Quarterly* 77, no. 1 (March 2004): 108–114.

"From Plane to Plane" (1949)

The characters in this narrative (with, as is usual in Frost, plenty of dialogue) are Pike and Dick. Pike is also referred to as Bill, so the name Pike could be either a last name or a nickname. Either way, Dick's referring to Pike as Bill may be a further example of the social differences between them that are set down in the opening stanza.

The poem opens with the line, "Neither of them was better than the other," the colloquialism on which the entire poem is predicated. The second line, "They both were hired," sets the two men on equal footing, at least as far as their job is concerned. But the two men, according to their own accounts, do not seem to be. Pike's education comes from "having hoed and mowed for fifty years," while Dick's comes from "being fresh and full of college." The narrator makes it clear that "if they fought about equality / It was on an equality they fought," and thus begins their exchange.

Pike initially criticizes Dick for "not sticking to the subject," and Dick, as in other moments throughout, does not say what he "long[s]" to say in response to Pike's accusation: "Your trouble is bucolic lack of logic"; instead, he asks what the subject is. While this stanza seems to suggest simple confusion on Dick's part, it is actually meant to symbolize something deeper. The difference between Pike's straightforward assertion and Dick's philosophical response makes the subject of their conversation seem not nearly as simple and directed to Dick as it does to Pike. Dick's unstated response, with the use of the academic "bucolic," suggests not only a superior attitude but also his belief that there is something inherently flawed in Pike's navigation of ideas. After all, Dick's comment suggests that he sees country folk in general as illogical.

The subject, as it turns out, is "whether these professions really work." The definition of *work* is being called into question by Pike, who sees the sort of work he does as a laborer as real work and the sorts of work others do as something less. The profession he uses to make his point is that of a doctor. As Pike and Dick work, "giving corn / A final going over," and then turning to hay, they question "the subject."

The location of the field is made clear. It is somewhere along "the Bradford Interval / By the Connecticut" river, and from there they can easily see a doctor with "one foot on the dashboard of his buggy." The doctor becomes an example for their discussion and remains "in sight like someone to depend on." The time period is made evident by several references throughout to horses and buggies.

Pike is critical of the doctor. He sees him as staying in sight because he is "[t]aking his own sweet time as if to show / He don't mind having lost a case." The improper grammar reveals Pike's lack of formal education, while his opinion exposes a class prejudice. His criticism comes back to Dick in the end, making clear that the accusation has as much to do with Dick's formal education as with anything else. He believes that "Dick wishes he could swap jobs with the Doctor" because "[h]oeing's too much like work for Dick." Pike believes that those who work in white-collar jobs do so not because of their education or because of the advantages of their economic class but because they wish to avoid work. The doctor, even more distant than a bystander to this inquisition, becomes a third character and is set as a higher and more powerful figure, impossibly made able to "prescribe"—a word chosen with precision by Frost—"[f]or all humanity a complete rest / From all this wagery." Pike is quickly dismissive not of the doctor's position or abilities but of whether those abilities count as work. Pike claims that the doctor's "class of people don't know what work *is*." He goes on to draw a greater distinction between the haves and have-nots: that the haves believe they know what courage is but really do not. The haves believe the "moral kind's as brave as facing bullets," Pike says, reminding the reader that it is those of the poorer

classes who in times of war are usually on the front lines, whereas it is the haves who put them there, through their own "moral kind" of bravery.

Dick wants Pike to be "fairer to the Doctor." He sees the doctor not as going home "not mind[ing] having lost a case" but "going home successful." The doctor's foot on the dashboard is perceived by Dick not as a way of taking his time but instead as a way of "self-conferr[ing]" a "reward of virtue." The difference is in perception, for the doctor himself likely has his own view of his behavior, as may the reader.

Dick wants to demonstrate to Pike that the differences between the doctor and Pike are not all that great. He asks whether, when Pike "rewards" himself by shouldering his hoe and taking a walk of "recreation" after hoeing in one direction back in the other he is conferring on himself the same reward? "Isn't it pretty much the same idea?" he asks. Dick points out that rewarding oneself is not "avoiding work," as Pike suspects of the doctor. And Pike, again with his clear and matter-of-fact perspective, says he "wouldn't hoe both ways for anybody" as an explanation for why he would shoulder his hoe on his way "back," proving Dick's point that the doctor may be leisurely simply because he is on his way home from work.

To further the comparison, Dick goes on to draw an analogy to reading. Just as when Pike has hoed to the river, he will raise his hoe to his shoulder on his way back, and just as the doctor will, upon returning from a house call, place a foot upon the dashboard, when we read and get to the end of a line, we pick our eyes up and "carry them back idle / Across the page to where we started from." Dick's choice of analogy once again exhibits his schooling, as does his use of the word "boustrophedon," an ancient method of writing in which the lines were inscribed alternately from right to left and from left to right.

Pike "grunt[s] rather grimly with misgiving / At being thus expounded to himself / And made of by a boy." Certainly Dick's academic vocabulary and his lofty examples seem a bit patronizing to Pike. Pike, as the older of the two, wants to be the wiser and does not want a young and schooled whipper-snapper, as he might refer to Dick, getting a leg up on him in the discussion. When he reaches the riverbank this time, he says that the "important thing is not to get bogged down / In what he has to do to earn a living." Now the explanation for not hoeing both ways is that he wants to give his "enemies," the weeds, "a truce." There is some suggestion that he is also offering a truce to Dick. Dick, who is at the beginning of his life, and still does not know what he is to become, says that Pike should be careful how he uses his "influence." After all, Dick says that if he should become a doctor, Pike could be "to blame for furnishing the reasons"—a lack of work.

In the next stanza, Pike says he thought Dick wanted to be an Indian chief, but then he goes on to contrast two drastically different historical figures. It seems that either he misunderstood what Dick had said, or he is making a point of conflating the two names here. The Indian chief Tecumseh was a Shawnee leader who attempted to establish a confederacy to unify the Native Americans against white encroachment. General William Tecumseh Sherman was an American general who was appointed commander of all Union troops in the West and helped split the Confederacy through his campaign in Georgia. In this sense, Tecumseh seems to symbolize both unification of the classes, through the Shawnee leader, and division of the classes, through the general. In his comparison, Pike mockingly also tries to "imitate Dick's tone of voice."

Pike soon accuses Dick of having "no social conscience" and of not being any kind of "social visionary." Pike sees his views as more democratic and more informed than Dick's. But Dick says he merely wanted to point out that the doctor's idea of work is the same as Pike's, and that the "further up the scale of work you go," the more it may be so.

Pike disagrees. He says it is not at all the same, and then in his own patronizing manner, he calls Dick "schoolboy" and warns him that someday he will show him why it is not the same. But then he makes an abrupt shift to talking about the sun. Pike is attempting his own analogy now and relying on nature as his source. He uses the sun to make the point that everyone has to keep to his own particular task. Dick reads the analogy and says it is just the same for the doctor, only he accuses Pike of not

being able to see that—Dick says Pike can see it only in himself and in the sun.

Pike decides to go along with the boy and agrees that in some ways the doctor fits the example he has given. He notes that when people are sick, the doctor's "Morgan," his horse, "lights out," races to their aide. Humorously Dick gets lost in the analogy. When Pike says, "The sign of Sickness in winter," Dick hears "Cygnus" in place of sickness and grows confused. This confusion is partly due to his schooling and partly, perhaps, due to Pike's pronunciation of the word. It is at this point that Frost inserts a significant aside. The parenthetical line, "(He'd have to take / A half course in it next year)" narrowly confines Dick's knowledge to what he learns in his courses. Though he is educated, Dick is limited and is incapable of knowing more than others have taught him—incapable, perhaps, of learning on his own. Frost also demonstrates at this point that Dick and Pike have something in common: They both give a "superstitious cry for farmers' luck" when they run into some difficult hoeing, indicating that they may have had similar upbringings.

At the end the two reach some reconciliation, though their agreement comes in analogies that further the class distinction between them. Pike relies on references to Santa Claus and the sun, whereas Dick makes references to Milton and Shakespeare, though Pike is "innocent" of both.

The narrative offers Frost the opportunity to compare formal education to the education of experience, the difference "From Plane to Plane." Frost never much respected formal education. He once said, "I hate academic ways. I fight everything academic. The time we waste in trying to learn academically—the talent we starve with academic teaching!" (Parini, 173). It is clear here that when Dick says, "You've been a lesson in work wisdom / To work with, Bill. But you won't have my thanks," that Dick has somehow missed the point.

Dick so prizes his formal education and finds it so superior to Pike's knowledge gained from life and work experience, and Pike so prizes his 50 years of hard work, that neither seems to have gained any wisdom at all from the discussion. In the end the reader is left with the impression that neither one has understood the other, though both seem to have understood the "subject." Frost does not resolve the questions whether a judgment can be made in favor of either side and whether the distinctions in class between Dick and Pike are so deep as to exclude any reconciliation. The "planes" may run parallel, but they will never meet. In many ways the poem goes full circle to the early lines "So if they fought about equality / It was on an equality they fought."

This poem appeared as the closing poem of three in "An Afterword" to the 1949 *The Complete Poems of Robert Frost*. The other two poems included were "Choose Something like a Star" and "Closed for Good." *See* COUNTRY VERSUS CITY.

FURTHER READING

Parini, Jay. *Robert Frost: A Life.* New York: Holt, 1999, 173.

Further Range, A (1936)

A *Further Range* was Frost's sixth collection of poetry. It was first published with the dedication, "To E. F. / for what it may mean to her that beyond the White Mountains were the Green; beyond both were the Rockies, the Sierras, and, in thought, the Andes and the Himalayas—range beyond range even into the realm of government and religion."

The book is divided into several sections, beginning with "Taken Doubly," followed by "Taken Singly," "Ten Mills," "The Outlands," "Build Soil," and "Afterthought." The most notable poems in the first section are "Two Tramps in Mud Time" (subtitled "or, A Full-Time Interest") and "Departmental" (subtitled "or, the End of My Ant Jerry"). In the second section are "Desert Places," "A Leaf-Treader," "Neither Out Far nor In Deep," "Design," "Clear and Colder," and "Provide, Provide"; some of these are among Frost's finest poems.

The book was promoted by the Book-of-the-Month Club and immediately sold 50,000 copies, but it received harsh reviews. Jay Parini calls the poems in this book "if not conservative in tone . . . distinctly antiliberal" (274), and this antiliberalism provoked a great deal of criticism. Frost was often

out of favor with the intelligentsia because his politics were further to the right than seemed appropriate for so prominent a poet. He knew that his "conservative politics clashed with the prevailing interests in proletarian literature, in socialism, and all manner of expressive thinking" and so he did not expect to "have to wait long for the attacks to begin" (Parini, 306).

Despite Frost's expectation that the book would receive harsh criticism, when the reviews started coming in he fell into a deep depression. He was always sensitive about his work, and even this late in his career he was concerned about being widely accepted. No matter how fulsome the praise heaped upon him, he always wanted—indeed needed—more. He was and remained at once both confident and insecure.

Critics at the *Partisan Review*, the *New Republic*, the *Nation*, and *New Masses* had a field day with A *Further Range*. Newton Arvin, a well-known critic at the *Partisan Review*, castigated Frost for yet another collection presenting New England as a series of "unpainted farmhouses and so many frost-bitten villages and so many arid sitting-rooms."

In reaction against the criticisms of A *Further Range*, in 1937 Henry Holt and Company published a collection of essays titled *Recognition of Robert Frost: Twenty-Fifth Anniversary*. The collection included essays by Ezra Pound, William Dean Howells, Amy Lowell, Mark Van Doren, and others. Van Doren described Frost as "a poet of and for the world." Despite the reviews of A *Further Range*, Frost's position as a first-rate American poet had long been secured, as these essays affirmed. And A *Further Range* would receive a Pulitzer Prize that year, making Frost a three-time winner.

Despite the criticism the book received, A *Further Range*, if for nothing other than "Design," "Departmental," and "Desert Places," richly deserved the recognition it ultimately got. The three poems are among Frost's very best. The poet had without a doubt hit his stride.

FURTHER READING

Burnshaw, Stanley. *Robert Frost Himself.* New York: George Braziller, 1986.

Lehmberg, P. S. "Companion Poems in Frost's *A Further Range*," *Literary Criterion* 11, no. 4 (1975): 37–44.

Parini, Jay. *Robert Frost: A Life.* New York: Holt, 1999, 274, 305–308.

Poirier, Richard. *Robert Frost: The Work of Knowing.* New York: Oxford University Press, 1977.

"Future of Man, The" (1959)

This talk was a contribution to a symposium, also on the future of man, sponsored by Joseph E. Seagram and Sons, Inc., on the occasion of the dedication of the Seagram Building at 375 Park Avenue in New York City. The Seagram Building is considered one of modern architecture's grandest achievements. Other panelists at the symposium included the British philosopher and mathematician Bertrand Russell (1872–1970), the English biologist and writer Sir Julian Sorell Huxley (1887–1975), the British-American anthropologist Ashley Montagu (1905–99), and the American geneticist and educator Hermann Joseph Muller (1890–1967). There are a published version and a longer unpublished version of the talk. This entry discusses the published version.

Just as Frost begins "Education by Poetry: A Meditative Dialogue" with the declaration that he is "going to urge nothing in [his] talk" and that he is "not an advocate," he begins here by declaring himself a prophet intent on addressing the "challenge of the future" but not advocating it. The primary challenge, he says, is of "man's originality to his law and order, to his government." His originality will continually square off against his order. When Frost imagines the future, he sees "government paired with government for the championship of its era." Just as man squares off against his government, governments square off against one another. In Frost's time the great face-off was between America and Russia; it was the Cold War.

To this squaring off, Frost adds another dimension: God as the "Great Provider." "There will always be an issue for the two powers to pair off on," he says, and that issue, that "great" and "grave" issue, is God.

Frost also wonders whether man will become "another kind of people." Drawing on the evolutionary theories of Charles Darwin (1809–82) (*see* EVOLUTION) and of the anthropologists who had caused "young people" to find that there is "such an amusing distance between us and the monkeys," he asserts that the youth of his day will find that there "will only be another amusing distance from us to the superman." The concept of the superman comes from 19th-century German philosopher Friedrich Nietzsche's (1844–1900) term for the ideal superior man, in German the *Übermensch.* The term might also have been translated *Overman* or *Beyondman*, but George Bernard Shaw's *Man and Superman* (1903) helped establish the English term for Nietzsche's concept as *superman.* The superman is an ideal superior man who, according to Nietzsche, forgoes transient pleasure, exercises creative power, lives at a level of experience beyond standards of good and evil, and is the goal of human evolution. Frost says it "is a field day for all comic strip teasers," alluding to the popular, all-American 20th-century cartoon hero Superman, because "every man can make his own comic strip."

Frost's speech takes an abrupt turn when he declares that he "know[s] just what's going to happen or not happen." "Our self-consciousness is terminal," he says; "there's nothing beyond us. Life in us has reached a self-consciousness that terminates growth." By this he means that there will be no more EVOLUTION: Self-consciousness is the epitome, the pinnacle of evolution; there is nowhere to go up from there.

He turns to the "Chicago publication" of a "list of all the thoughts man has had." Frost likely was taking a jab at the University of Chicago's Great Books of the Western World program launched in the 1930s by the philosopher Mortimer Adler and the president of the university, Robert M. Hutchins. Frost facetiously states that there were only a few hundred of them, that evolution was included, but that the "plain word growth" was not. He jokes that Chicago must not think that growth is an idea, but he concludes that evolution would come under such a heading. All growth is limited, he says, and so, too, will be man's.

He speaks of the Yggdrasil, the great ash tree that holds together earth, heaven, and hell by its roots and branches in Norse mythology, as "our tree" and says that it has "reached its growth." But just because it has reached its growth does not mean that it has to "fall down because it's stopped growing." He sees our tree as continuing to blossom and have seasonal cycles for at least another 100–200 million years. And this tree, returning to Frost's earlier ideas, will still have "two parties always to it, some way." "It doesn't need another tree besides it," he says, suggesting that all humankind comes from the same tree, though we may live in different countries, and that within this tree is all the "doubleness" in the world: "good and evil, two sexes, one of *them* good and the other evil." This description also alludes to the tree of knowledge in the biblical Garden of Eden and to Adam and Eve. Frost deduces that we need to stop attending to our "height." Further growth is not of concern. In this same passage he says cheekily, "I hope that this tree is self-fertilizing—I guess I hadn't thought of that." His hope that humankind will last millions of years takes for granted that the Earth will make it too. (His poem "Why Wait for Science," provides another take on this idea.)

Concluding the piece, Frost returns to the idea of the "Lord [as the] Great Provider." He describes him as a "god of waste, magnificent waste" and describes waste as "another name for generosity of not always being intent on our own advantage, nor too importunate even for a better world." This suggests a view of God as one who set the universe in motion and then stepped away. He has little investment in us, and we share in this waste: "We pour out a libation to him as a symbol of the waste we share in—participate in. Pour it on the ground and you've wasted it; pour it on yourself and you've doubly wasted it."

Frost closes by saying that he has said enough, that there are "many details" he had in mind, details that are outlined in the unpublished version of the piece, but his aim is to keep it short. He reminds the reader that his original proposition was the challenge between man's originality and his law and order, and that is where we must remain focused. He ends as he so often does, with a remark that can be taken in various ways. Frost was often critical of science even while he stood in awe of it. In "Why Wait for Science" he refers to "Sarcastic Science"; in other poems he is likewise conflicted. (Robert Hass discusses the subject in his *Going by Contraries: Robert Frost's Conflict with Science*.) Frost ends with humor: "I sometimes think the scientists have got themselves scared; they're afraid they'll run away with themselves they are so original. They needn't worry; the executives will take care of them." Frost claims not to be an advocate of anything in his "Future of Man," but if nothing else, he is advocate of the idea that humankind has a future.

See SCIENCE and TECHNOLOGY.

"Gathering Leaves" (1923)

In "Gathering Leaves" Frost compares the "crop" of the fallen leaves of autumn to the usual crops of farms. In the opening stanza the speaker mentions what it would be like to use a spade to clear away the leaves, but their bulk does not permit that. He might as well be using a spoon, the process is so slow and fruitless. And one can gather leaves all day and still need to gather more. The image is Sisyphean.

The metaphors used to describe the leaves and this process of gathering them are both natural and synthetic. In the first stanza the lightness of the leaves in bags is compared to the lightness of balloons filled with air. This suggests that gathering leaves is like gathering almost nothing. In the second stanza the sound of rustling leaves reminds the speaker of the sound of a "rabbit and deer / Running away." And in the third stanza the piles of leaves become "mountains."

The imagery that runs throughout is of leaves that escape shoveling, grasping, and loading. The third stanza presents a childlike vision: The speaker is practically rolling in the leaves as he tries to embrace them and they flow over his arms and into his face. Gathering the dry leaves is like trying to collect smoke. The absence of their presence enthralls the speaker.

There is a shifting focus on weight throughout the poem, highlighting the analogy to a farmer's crop. "Cash crops" and "cash for crops" are phrases heard frequently in rural areas. Cash crops are crops that are grown for direct sale rather than for livestock feed, and they generally go by weight. If the leaves are a crop meant to be sold by weight, then they are a nearly worthless crop. While there is great effort and "great noise" in gathering the leaves, the effort leads to no monetary reward. The leaves are presented as antithetical to regular crops: They have bulk without weight. But there is something to be gained from harvesting the leaves. "Next to nothing for use / But a crop is a crop," the speaker says, suggesting that he must work at every crop just the same, regardless of the yield. There is the allusion to a certain work ethic, but there is also the impression that the effort is its own reward, not what it may or may not yield. Everything has some purpose. (Though not stated in the poem, leaves can be used as mulch, for example, for other, more productive crops.)

The transition from the opening images to the reflection on the process that occurs midway through the poem reveals the speaker's perspective and sensibility. He is dismayed when he realizes that while he may repeat his efforts "again and again," he has little to show for them according to the usual standards of money and barter. And in the second-to-last stanza there is an awareness of the life-and-death cycle that the leaves represent and the way this cycle relates to their value on the market. They grow "duller" after all, "from contact with earth." They have "[n]ext to nothing for color" compared with when they were at their colorful peak, which gives the reader the impression that they are less valuable. But unlike in "A Leaf-Treader," the speaker here does not continue in this vein. He returns to the harvest itself, and his analogue is the crop.

The poem ends with a question: "who's to say where / The harvest will stop?," and Frost seems to be talking about something more than leaves here. In some ways the speaker appears to be throwing his hands in the air, as if to say, "will it ever end?" But he also seems to be saying that the cycle is unending, and life goes on. While this harvest may

not yield much and may be symbolic of death, the next may yield something more and better. Even in death there is a kind of rebirth. There is a further analogy to how we construct our lives with the limited amount of time we have. We work, raise families, and sometimes wonder about the point of it all. Sometimes parts of our lives seem as though they are bulk without weight, fluff without substance, and somewhat duller than they used to be. And when we "fill" our sheds, we often wonder, "And what have I then?" Frost's answer seems to be that the value is in the gathering, even though much gathering may result in little gathered.

"Gathering Leaves" was collected in *New Hampshire* but was previously published in the *Measure* earlier that same year. *See* FARMER, FROST AS.

FURTHER READING

Dubinsky, James. "War and Rumors of War in Frost," *Robert Frost Review* (1995): 1–22.
Perrine, Laurence. "Frost's 'Gathering Leaves,'" *CEA Critic* 34 (1971): 29.

"Generations of Men, The" (1914)

One of Frost's longer narratives, this blank-verse tale concerns itself with a rainy day and a Stark family reunion in Bow, New Hampshire. Bow is a small town in Merrimack country with a current population of approximately 7,000. The members of the Stark family have come together in the hope that "[a]ncestral memories might come together."

The Stark family is described as having originated in the "rock-strewn" town of Bow, which used to be a farming town, before the "ax" was taken to it. The Stark family was once "so numerous a tribe" and such an important one that a governor proclaimed when the reunion would be held. When the members of the family arrive in town for the reunion, many people offer to shelter them, if not in a house then in a "tent in grove and orchard." While they are already gathered in Bow, they try to specify a good day for the reunion—a day for standing "together on the crater's verge / That turned them on the world, and try to fathom / The past and get some strangeness out of it." In this way the Starks quickly come to represent all families and individuals who explore their origins and what to make of them.

The weather interferes with the reunion. "No fête today," says one Stark to another, as a few of them "out of idleness" gather where the reunion was to take place. The two cousins who meet, man and woman, set about determining their relationship to each other. He shows her his "passport," and she explains how no matter whom her mother had married, they would have somehow been "Starks, and doubtless here today." "You riddle with your genealogy / Like a Viola," he says, a reference to the mistaken identity of Shakespeare's Viola from *Twelfth Night*. But they decide to sit on a cellar wall, beneath raspberry vines, "Under the shelter of the family tree," and work to determine their cousinship.

The woman carries three cards, one for each branch of the Stark family that she belongs to, and the man jokes that "a person so related to herself / Is supposed to be mad." He suggests that all "Yankees" who are concerned with genealogy are mad and that they are even madder for being so concerned with such things as to sit out in the rain to talk about them. Of course, there may be something more than genealogy at work that prolongs their conversation, but that never becomes clear.

An analogy is drawn between the crater that they stand on the verge of and the Indian myth of the "Chicamoztoc," which means "The Seven Caves that We Came out of." The idea is that all peoples come from a cave, or a "pit," perhaps an abyss, and for the Starks that pit is the town of Bow. The man wonders what can be gained from gazing into the pit, and the woman explains what she sees, not with her eyes but with her mind.

The woman imagines a boy "groping in the cellar after jam." The man breaks in, dismissing the boy and instead imagining a "Grandsir Stark" who soon becomes "Granny"—a granny with country character, who smokes a pipe and drinks cider from a jug. The two are having great fun imagining their Stark ancestors and wondering whether they them-

selves bear some resemblance to the ancestors they describe. They are so caught up in their imaginings that they become soaked with rain. They decide they "can't stay" forever, and the man suggests they head to the brook where they can "try something with the noise." They have "seen visions," and now it is time to "consult the voices." The man compares listening to the brook to the roar he used to hear while riding trains. He imagines that each is an "oracle."

Still, he listens for the voices, knowing that they provide what "you wish to hear," and wonders whether they can offer him his cousin's name. A name should not really matter, he says ironically, since the ostensible reason they have engaged in conversation is that they share a surname.

The oracle sends a message about the woman, saying call her "Nausicaä," the name of a maiden from Homer's *Odyssey* who befriended the wandering Odysseus. The reference suggests that the journey these two Starks have taken might in some sense be epic. The woman finds little truth in his oracle, however, since it does not "speak in dialect" as would their Grandsir or Granny. The man then takes up the dialect of a "nine times removed" Granny.

As the exchange draws to its close, Frost manages to squeeze a kind of axiom into an otherwise ordinary conversation: "But don't you think we sometimes make too much / Of the old stock? What counts is the ideals / And those will bear some keeping still about." This calls into question the value of the very study of genealogy. Is there really something of value in meeting one's kin? Frost asks the question and leaves it open, since an answer is not given and the conversation reverts to commonplaces.

The narrative ends as the two part with the hopes of meeting again, next time in "sunshine." Not one of Frost's better works, the poem seems to spill a lot of ink to make a few simple points. First it gauges the importance of reunions, reflecting on the "generations of men" and women that came before, and then it undoes itself by taking more than 200 lines to "make too much / Of the old stock." The man and woman finally reach a topic worth wondering about—whether ideals have been passed down through the generations and are valuable and worth keeping—and the poem comes to an end. There is a rather heavy-handed irony. The pair's genealogical relationship in the end seems irrelevant to their conversation or to the future of their friendship. Having kin and a common surname does not guarantee having other attributes in common enough to be friends or even to get along.

Beneath the lines there is a certain tension between the two, but the poet's reticence prevents him from getting any closer to the possible heart of the matter than a kind of enfeebled innuendo, which must be largely of the individual reader's own devising. Perhaps what is at work is the necessary reticence of kinship. The Starks go on; the two cousins will undoubtedly go their separate ways. They can share nothing more than genealogy and will meet again in no other setting than that of a family reunion.

The poem was collected in *North of Boston.*

FURTHER READING

Faggen, Robert. *Robert Frost and the Challenge of Darwin.* Ann Arbor: University of Michigan Press, 1997, 237–244.

Kearns, Katherine. *Robert Frost and a Poetics of Appetite.* Cambridge: Cambridge University Press, 1994, 91–93.

Westbrook, Perry. "Abandonment and Desertion in the Poetry of Robert Frost." In *Frost: Centennial Essays II,* edited by Jac Tharpe, 291–304. Jackson: University Press of Mississippi, 1976.

"Ghost House" (1913)

"Ghost House" is one of several Frost poems in which an abandoned house is employed as metaphor. In this case the speaker "dwell[s]" in the "lonely house" that "vanished many a summer ago." The poem has something in common with "Directive," which appeared in the later collection *Steeple Bush.* In that poem the reader is taken to "a house that is no more a house / Upon a farm that is no more a farm," and the house is described as having a "belilaced cellar hole," whereas in "Ghost House" the cellar is where the "purple-stemmed wild raspberries grow." Jay Parini reports that the poem was

written in 1901 and was inspired by "an old cellar hole with a broken chimney standing in it—what remained of a nearby farmhouse after a fire had destroyed it in 1867" (90–91). The remains were near one of Frost's farms in Derry, New Hampshire. When the poem appeared in *A Boy's Will,* it had the gloss, "He is happy in society of his choosing."

The opening stanza concerns itself with absence. The house is gone and there is little trace of it left behind except its cellar walls. In the second stanza the absence is extended to the grounds that once surrounded the place, and images of "ruined fences" and abundant nature are presented. Nature has overgrown everything: The once-mown field is now overtaken by woods; the footpath to the well that was once cleared and mowed is now "healed," as the grass has grown over what might have been described as a cut.

In the third stanza the descriptions extend beyond the grounds to the "disused and forgotten road." Night is falling, also a rich metaphor in Frost, and an array of images is presented, including the visual "black bats" that "tumble and dart" and the aural "hush and cluck" of the whippoorwill. The tone grows more melancholy as the poem continues, and the speaker confesses in the third stanza that he dwells not only in a lonely house but with a "strangely aching heart."

In the fourth stanza the lonely house begins to take shape. "It is under the small, dim summer star," and the "unlit place" is shared with "mute folk." The darkness of the daylight falling in the opening stanza and the image of cellar walls return, as it becomes clear that the ghost house is a burial place, perhaps the ruin of a crypt or mausoleum, in a cemetery. There are "stones out under the low-limbed tree," and they "[d]oubtless bear names that the mosses mar"—though the speaker is unsure, because he, apparently, has never seen the inscriptions.

The house is a "ghost house" not simply because it is abandoned but because it houses a ghost. The speaker is a ghost who is unable to read the names on the stones because he speaks from his cellar, from his plot in the ground. The cellar walls are like a tomb. He imagines they are covered with moss, but he cannot see them, since they are "out under" the tree and he is in the ground. An unexpected voice in Frost, the speaker in this second poem of Frost's first volume is dead and keeps company with a "lass and lad," perhaps lovers in life, who share the ground with him. The couple may have been the owners of a house that once stood there, and this may be a family plot.

They are all "tireless folk" because they dwell here beyond death. The word "they" in the first line of the last stanza appears to refer to all who dwell here. But the two who are "close-keeping" draw the speaker's interest, as if he in his lonely isolation envied their bond, their being buried side by side. He says that while neither of them sings, in view of many things they are "sweet companions as might be had" to each other and, it is implied, to him.

The poem grows more melancholy with each stanza and yet manages to end with a kind of contentment. In a way it becomes a love poem, not of the speaker's own love but of his fondness for the two who share his circumstance, if not his fate. The poem also in many ways embraces life, with the sounds of nature and humanity and with its eternally slumbering lovers. The satisfaction comes from the repeated references to nature, as if the speaker had not simply passed on. He either still can experience nature or still can recall the manifestations of nature he has experienced. There is comfort in knowing that life goes on after our individual deaths, and the speaker proclaims that message as having value in and of itself, despite the desperate longing that infuses the lines.

While the ghost house could be treated as a feeling rather than a place and the cellar as an image buried deep in the recesses of the speaker's mind where memories are interred, the descriptions near the end of the poem seem to resist such a reading. If the voice is treated as coming from the grave, then what the speaker longs for, aches for, is a return to life and to the house where the purple-stemmed raspberries grew.

The voice Frost adopts is unlike those in his later work. Voices from the dead might be expected in Emily Dickinson, but not in Frost. This poem, like others in Frost's first volume, emulates other poets to whom he felt indebted and for whom he had great respect. Dickinson was one of his favorites, and he had even presented his future wife Eli-

nor with the gift of a volume of Dickinson's poems when they were dating. The description of the moss marring the stones in "Ghost House" is similar to Dickinson's in "I died for Beauty—but was scarce," whose closing stanza reads, "And so, as Kinsmen, met a Night— / We talked between the Rooms— / Until the Moss had reached our lips— / And covered up—our names—." Dickinson's poem alludes to the English romantic poet John Keats's "Ode on a Grecian Urn."

"Ghost House" first appeared in the March 15, 1906, issue of the *Youth's Companion* before it became the second poem of Frost's first volume, *A Boy's Will. See* WALLS.

FURTHER READING

Cramer, Jeffrey S. *Robert Frost among His Poems: A Literary Companion to the Poet's Own Biographical Contexts and Associations.* Jefferson, N.C.: McFarland, 1996, 14.

Parini, Jay. *Robert Frost: A Life.* New York: Holt, 1999, 90–91.

Timmerman, John H. *Robert Frost: The Ethics of Ambiguity.* Lewisburg, Pa.: Bucknell University Press, 2002, 23–26.

Vail, Dennis. "Frost's 'Ghost House,'" *Explicator* 30 (1971): 11.

"Gift Outright, The" (1942)

"The Gift Outright" was first published in the *Virginia Quarterly Review* in the spring of 1942 and was collected in *A Witness Tree* later that year with the note, "Read before the Phi Beta Kappa Society at William and Mary College, December 5, 1941." The poem was written before the summer of 1936, however, because that year it was inscribed, untitled, in a copy of *West-Running Brook* for Frost's friend Lawrance Thompson. Jeffrey Cramer reports that this was one of the poems that Frost claimed to have "played . . . through without fumbling a sentence" (132).

On President John F. Kennedy's inauguration day, January 20, 1961, the sun's reflection on the glaring white paper made it impossible for Frost to read his poem "For John F. Kennedy His Inauguration." Recovering well, he recited "The Gift Outright" from memory, improvising on the last line: "Such as she was, such as she *would* become, *has* become, and I—and for this occasion let me change that to—what she *will* become" (Parini, 414). For this reason, "The Gift Outright" was later appended to "For John F. Kennedy His Inauguration" in *In the Clearing*. George Monteiro points out that "so clearly superior is 'The Gift Outright' to the poem he wrote for John Kennedy that some of Frost's readers wondered whether, not only welcoming the opportunity in that moment of confusion to skip his new poem, he had somehow engineered the whole thing (if only subconsciously)" (227).

On the surface the poem can be read simply as a love poem to his nation. Frost was nationalistic and patriotic, and certainly many poets before him mythologized their countries, going back to Homer. The poem begins "The land was ours before we were the land's. / She was our land more than a hundred years / Before we were her people." It moves from the claim "She was ours" in Massachusetts and Virginia, as if to say in all the original thirteen colonies, to saying "But we were England's." The poet gives his own version of history, of the developing nation's progress toward declaring its independence. Frost once called the poem "a history of the United States in a dozen [actually, 16] lines of blank verse" (Meyers, 324).

The poet asserts that even when the first Americans claimed this as their land and separated from Britain, they were still "possessed by" Britain and that in some way "we" (the nation in its beginnings) had withheld "ourselves" until declaring independence. What was withheld was nationality, because the nation was still a possession, a colony. The land was still possessed by Britain, even though its settlers were effectively unpossessed—that is, living on the opposite side of the Atlantic Ocean.

Frost hints at attributes that were retained from the mother country, saying that the new Americans were made "weak" by the connection to Britain, until they were able to discover in themselves what was being withheld "from our land of living, / And forthwith found salvation in surrender." Finding salvation also brings completeness, and such

completeness made possible for the colonists the giving of themselves "outright." Frost is putting a positive spin on something that many historians have come to consider negative: the theft of life and land from the Native Americans.

The poem can be seen to be celebrating love of war, love of ownership, and love of colonization. But the many battles are referred to only in passing, in parentheses, which are typically used to insert a digression or an explanatory or amplifying remark. In this case the parenthetical comes off casually, as a sort of aside. "The deed of gift was many deeds of war" understates those acts of war as merely a necessary means to a glorious end.

The final line was drawn out and elaborated on by Frost at the inauguration, but here it is succinct. The last two lines, in fact, can be perplexing, as in some ways they can be read as a hesitation, an undoing of what comes before: "But still unstoried, artless, unenhanced, / Such as she was, such as she would become." It suggests that despite all the losses, what was expected to be gained was at best slow in coming. Was the nation by 1942, when the poem was first published, still without stories, without art, and unenhanced? Frost does not say. After all, he does use his own art—which he certainly did not think was artless—to express all this. Perhaps he was to some extent seeing things from England's perspective. The viewpoint does not appear to be his own, unless the closing lines are simply one of Frost's characteristic twists, meant to leave the reader guessing.

Much of the poem suggests that the colonization of America was preordained, since gifts usually assume a giver and since it was "ours" before "we" knew it, more than 100 years before realization would come. John Robert Doyle, Jr., finds the point of view "central in Christian thought" and notes that "English poets for hundreds of years have not failed to make use of the idea up to the present, for the idea of the 'gift outright,' of finding 'salvation in surrender' is one of the three things said by the thunder at the end of [T. S.] Eliot's *The Waste Land*" (45). Certainly given the historical data, the reader is left with a feeling of ambivalence concerning its ordination.

"The Gift Outright" is structurally masterful. Doyle highlights the structure of the poem as it "runs from statement of historical fact, to a question for the existing situation, to an answer to the question, to the outcome after the answer" (45). While the poem takes as its subject the colonization of America and can be read, as it is above, as a patriotic love poem to the nation, in many ways it transcends that limited subject in its expression of love and even adoration.

The opening is highly romanticized, as is the start of any relationship. The speaker is consumed with his beloved, enraptured by her, feeling that their relationship must have been destined all along. Only fate could join two so inevitably meant for each other. It moves to a discussion of possession, of possessing the beloved, of ownership, and of submission. The two, not England and America, but person to person, are "possessed" by their feeling, so possessed that withholding such strong emotion makes each weak, even when their possession is still "unpossessed." When they "surrender" to such emotions and give themselves "outright" they take part in the process of becoming.

The poem is certainly not politically correct by current standards. And it is in its way, though about independence, Eurocentric, dismissing from the start any claim the Native Americans had to the land or any historical data concerning the first colonists' ignorance of the land. It glorifies the new occupants and ignores the native inhabitants who had roamed the land freely before the colonists' "discovery" of it, subsequent settling of it, and systematic extermination of those native inhabitants. But metaphorically it can be read as a love poem, a poem of immeasurable beauty in its passion and joy for the "gift" that comes in becoming possessed and unpossessed, and in finding salvation in the surrender to another, even when the result is "unstoried, artless, and unenhanced." The latter reading better expresses Frost's hopes. Frost leaves off his history at the time of the westward expansion. That is when he says the country was still unstoried, artless, unenhanced. Whether he thinks the process was well under way by his time cannot be determined. *See* BELIEF and POLITICS.

FURTHER READING

Bosmajian, Hamida. "Robert Frost's 'The Gift Outright': Wish and Reality in History and Poetry," *American Quarterly* 22 (1970): 95–105.

Burnshaw, Stanley. *Robert Frost Himself.* New York: George Braziller, 1986.

Challender, Craig. "Robert Frost's Strategies of Syntax in Selected Letters, 'The Silken Tent,' and 'The Gift Outright,'" *South Carolina Review* 19 (Summer 1987): 19–28.

Cramer, Jeffrey S. *Robert Frost among His Poems: A Literary Companion to the Poet's Own Biographical Contexts and Associations.* Jefferson, N.C.: McFarland, 1996, 132–133.

Doyle, John Robert, Jr. *The Poetry of Robert Frost: An Analysis.* New York: Hafner Press, 1962, 39–50.

Gozzi, Raymond D. "Frost's 'The Gift Outright,'" *Explicator* 41, no. 3 (Spring 1983): 44–45.

Meyers, Jeffrey. *Robert Frost: A Biography.* New York: Houghton Mifflin, 1996, 323–324.

Monteiro, George. "Frost's Politics and the Cold War." In *The Cambridge Companion to Robert Frost,* edited by Robert Faggen, 227–253. Cambridge: Cambridge University Press, 2001.

Parini, Jay. *Robert Frost: A Life.* New York: Holt, 1999.

Von Frank, Albert J. "Frost's 'The Gift Outright,'" *Explicator* 38, no. 1 (1979): 22–23.

"Girl's Garden, A" (1916)

"A Girl's Garden" was first collected in *Mountain Interval.* In a copy of the book Frost identified the neighbor as a friend in Raymond, New Hampshire. The poem speaks of a neighbor who, now a grown woman, likes to tell a story about how when she was a child she did a "childlike thing": tilled and nurtured her own garden. She asked her father for her own "garden plot / To plant and tend and reap herself," and he gave her a space "ideal" for a "one-girl farm."

She had no aid from modern equipment; her father said it was not large enough to plow, so she had to do all the work herself and by hand. While a girl-farmer she did childish things, such as leaving the dung fertilizer alongside the road, hiding, and begging the seed to grow, as if begging would make it happen. Her garden was a hodge-podge: "potatoes / Radishes, lettuce, peas, / Tomatoes, beets, beans, pumpkins, corn / And even fruit trees." She planted a "bit of everything," a "miscellany," and ended up with a "great deal of none." While the reminiscence is simple, filled with all the eagerness, awkwardness, and foolishness of a child, both the woman and Frost use it as a metaphor for something more.

The woman uses the story to say something about village life and her understanding of it. When she "sees in the village / How village things go" and they "come in right / She says, 'I know!'" When things turn out for the best, she is reminded of her garden and how when she was "a farmer" things came out right, despite her erratic efforts. The emphasis on the "I" dramatizes how much she thinks she knows or wants others to think she knows.

The poet uses the story differently. He knows that when things came in right in the girl's garden it was by accident, because she did not put forth the sort of effort that would bear fruit. She left by the roadside the dung that would have fertilized her crops and "hid from anyone passing." Her version of her own behavior does not quite agree what she tells the villagers.

Others in the village may do the same as she: wait until after things come in right to exclaim "I know!" The woman does not give advice from when she was a farmer because she never really was a farmer. She waits until after things come in right, since she cannot tell how they will turn out.

The story says something about the woman, about the villagers, and about people in general. People chime in after the fact to act as if they were always in the know. But Frost also is hinting at his own lack of sureness as a farmer. He once said, "I like farming, but I'm not much of a farmer. I always go to farming when I can. I always make a failure of it, and then I have to go to teaching" (Parini, 173). The woman pretends she was a farmer when she never was, and Frost may have thought the same thing about himself.

FURTHER READING

Janzen, J. Gerald. "Reassessing Frost's Fair Impression and His Mistrust," *Religion and Literature* 20, no. 3 (Autumn 1988): 71–87.

Parini, Jay. *Robert Frost: A Life.* New York: Holt, 1999.

"Going for Water" (1913)

In "Going for Water" two people go out for water because the well beside the house is dry. They take a pail and go behind the house into the fields to "seek the brook if still it ran." Jeffrey Cramer reports that the brook is Hyla Brook (see the poem of the same name) on Frost's Derry farm and that it dried up at the end of each summer. In the poem it is a "fair" and chilly autumn evening. *They* refers perhaps to a boy and girl, who may be adolescents but who are certainly young.

In the second stanza they make a game of their task. Like children, they run to "meet the moon," chasing and being chased by it as it "dawn[s]" behind the trees. They are moving through the woods playfully and without fear. Once they are in the wood, they pause "[l]ike gnomes that hid us from the moon, / Ready to run to hiding new / With laughter when she found us soon." They make a game of hide-and-seek with the moon, darting about, in and out. The gnomes are little woodland folk hiding the light from them and joining in the fun.

They are running and frolicking when they realize they need to be quiet to hear the brook. They lay on each other a "staying hand" to find each other in the dark and to keep themselves from making noise. They hear the "slender tinkling fall" of the brook and then the "silver blade" of water rushing full force. The two seem as smitten with each other as with the moon, the reaching for one another in the dark a hesitant but binding gesture.

The poem lacks complexity but is rich in imagery. A simple task is turned into a night of play, and the water of the brook becomes "drops that floated on the pool / Like pearls." John Robert Doyle, Jr., calls the poem a love poem. He writes that the "modern world may not see in [it] much of a love poem, but a love poem it is, a poem of almost inaudible young love" (138).

"Going for Water" appeared in Frost's first volume, *A Boy's Will.* Lewis H. Miller, Jr., "sets it apart from [the] group of love lyrics" in the collection because, he believes, the others present a "dreamy-eyed and sometimes tormented youth whose attraction to woods and flowers, ice and snow, has often dissociated him emotionally or physically . . . from his married lover." He writes that "Going for Water" is unique to the collection in "its unqualified compliment to both lovers for being what they are." And what they are is equal in their affection for each other and their love of and delight in nature.

FURTHER READING

Cramer, Jeffrey S. *Robert Frost among His Poems: A Literary Companion to the Poet's Own Biographical Contexts and Associations.* Jefferson, N.C.: MacFarland, 1996.

Doyle, John Robert, Jr. *The Poetry of Robert Frost: An Analysis.* New York: Hafner Press, 1962, 137–140.

Miller, David L. "Dominion of the Eye in Frost." In *Frost: Centennial Essays II,* edited by Jac Tharpe, 141–158. Jackson: University Press of Mississippi, 1976.

"Gold Hesperidee, The" (1936)

The poem was collected in *A Further Range* but first appeared in the September 1921 issue of *Farm and Fireside.* When it was collected, it was subtitled "How to Take a Loss," and the original gloss is helpful for an understanding of the poem. Jeffrey Cramer reports that the story came from an unidentified town history, but clearly Frost embellished quite a bit, given the biblical and mythological references in the poem.

This poem expresses longing and desire and then the disappointment that so often follows. The story is about "Square Matthew Hale," who grows an apple tree. The word square may be used to describe a person who is regarded as stodgy, or rigidly conventional. It may also describe someone who is honest and direct and who "goes by the rules." In this case it may signify a little of both.

When the apple tree is five years old it blossoms, sheds its flowers, and keeps three stems thriving. Matthew observes only two stems of apples, "one he missed," but he is encouraged by the two and brings his son, also Matthew and also five years old, to it. He warns him, "We mustn't touch them yet, but see and see!" In eagerness the two are to wait for the green apples to ripen to gold. Jeffrey Cramer sees an appealing reference to Frost's "Nothing Gold Can Stay" in the line, "what was green would by and by be gold."

In Greek mythology gold hesperidee are golden apples from the garden of the Hesperides, the daughters of the evening. (Their father, Hesperus, was changed into the evening star.) The tree on which they grew sometimes symbolized the tree of life, and Frost is aware that the image will lend itself to multiple interpretations.

Square Matthew checks the apples each time he passes by while tending to other chores, such as feeding the pig or milking the cow. As the apples grow they "sw[i]ng in danger" and seem like liquid "bubble[s] on a pipe-stem growing big." They are barely hanging on to life as they grow more full and heavy. Matthew feels "safe" with his three apples, rather than one or two, because they afford him better odds of reaching his goal of seeing them "picked unbruised and in a dish." He imagines that there is "nothing Fate could do" with a moth or a parasite to destroy his apples. He foresees nothing that could keep him "now from proving with a bite / That the name Gold Hesperidee was right."

With the first frost (an almost certainly deliberate pun on the poet's name), the apples are tossed to the ground. Matthew imagines that even so, he can still rescue them and "fulfill at last his summer wish." "But when he came to look, no apples there" the narrator reports. The apples have disappeared by the seventh stanza; it is not clear how or why, though it is likely that some animal feasted on them. Apparently, fate has had her way with the apples despite Matthew's earnest safe-keeping; he is unable to rescue them after all. While the reader expects a characteristic probing of Fate and her powers, the poem instead turns toward Matthew, quickly dismissing the sudden disappearance, as if that were not at all the focus of the poem. It is Matthew's reaction on which Frost chooses to dwell.

Dressed for church, Matthew takes off his "Sunday hat," throws it to the ground, and "[d]ance[s] slowly on it till he trod it flat." He is ashamed for having reacted this way and looks to see if anyone has seen him as this "was the sin that Ahaz forbid / (The meaning of the passage had been hid)." Ahaz, who also appears in Frost's "New Hampshire," was the 11th king of Judah who, in 2 Kings 16:2–4 of the Bible "did not that which was right in the sight of the Lord his God, like David his father. . . . And he sacrificed and burnt incense in the high places, and on the hills, and under every green tree." The sin of worshipping apples is a grave one, it seems, as it detracts from total adoration of God. When Matthew's temper tantrum, once spent, embarrasses him, he is in the position of Adam after the first sin in the Garden of Eden. But Matthew's God will prove more merciful than Adam and Eve's.

The final stanza reveals that God saw him dancing but kept the crowd from "witnessing the fault of one so proud." The story is not retold in Gath, one of the five royal cities of the Philistines. Biblically the city is associated with the story of David, in that Goliath came from Gath. God keeps Matthew's secret from being told, and for this reason Square Matthew vows to "walk a graver man restrained in wrath."

The title of the poem is misleading, as is the mention of fate and its possible hand in the disappearance of the apples. The focus is on the apples from the start and then on their safe-keeping, but the retelling of the entire tale seems predicated on demonstrating what it was Matthew had to learn. (Matthew is also the name of one of Jesus' disciples in the New Testament.) It seems a parable, meant to teach us not to be overly proud but to be restrained and modest in the face of setbacks. The allusion to the tree of knowledge suggests that we should not long for knowledge with such single-mindedness, as God's followers are best "restrained," like the worshipers in the crowd quietly passing by on the way to Sunday services. In the light of the apparent agnosticism in many of Frost's other poems, the "Gold Hesperidee" comes off as a wryly humorous rather than sermonizing parable. *See* MYTHOLOGY AND FOLKLORE.

FURTHER READING

Cramer, Jeffrey S. *Robert Frost among His Poems: A Literary Companion to the Poet's Own Biographical Contexts and Associations.* Jefferson, N.C.: MacFarland, 1996.

Fleissner, R. F. "Like 'Pythagoras' Comparison of the Universe with Number': A Frost-Tennyson Correlation." In *Frost: Centennial Essays,* edited by Jac Tharpe, 207–220. Jackson: University Press of Mississippi, 1974.

"Good-by and Keep Cold" (1923)

"Good-by and Keep Cold" apparently was written while Frost was in Derry, New Hampshire. Frost's friend Raymond Holden wrote that the poet presented this poem to him, having finished it the night before, when Holden arrived one morning to join Frost for a walk. Frost read the poem to him that morning, "while he explained to [Holden] how he had learned that apple trees are better off if they do not thaw out during the winter" (Cramer, 81). The poem was collected in *New Hampshire* but was previously published in the July 1920 issue of *Harper's Magazine.*

The poem opens with two "saying good-by on the edge of the dark." The speaker is reminded of what "can happen to harm / An orchard away at the end of the farm." His heart goes out to the orchard that is isolated, "cut off" in winter by winter. The speaker worries that rabbit, mouse, deer, and grouse will be nibbling away at the orchard. He imagines himself "warn[ing] them away with a stick for a gun," if only he could call them to him to make such a declaration.

The speaker wants assurance that the orchard will not be "stirred by the heat of the sun" and thinks he has eliminated that possibility by setting it "out on a northerly slope." He knows it cannot get warm, as a young orchard is better off at 50° below zero than 50° above. There is a transition near the end of the poem from speculation about what the speaker has done and may do to protect the orchard to his confession that he has to be "gone for a season or so." It seems the poem has been building, reluctantly, toward this admission and that the speaker feels guilty about his impending departure. He is going to be turning his attention to "different trees," the "[m]aples and birches and tamaracks" that will be used for firewood. The transition from "fruitful" trees that need protecting to those that will only serve to feed a fire to keep him warm is jarring. The empathy of the speaker for the orchard is heartfelt, yet he admits to taking an ax to other trees, demonstrating a variable relationship to nature. (Note that the speaker would not have pointed a real gun at those woodland browsers and foragers he wants to keep away from the orchard.)

In the closing five lines the speaker wishes that he "could promise to lie in the night / And think of an orchard's arboreal plight," but he knows that he will not. He has done what he can, and now he is saying "good-by and keep cold" as the wishful best that he can offer. His job is done, just as in "The Exposed Nest" the father and child "turned to other things." The speaker closes resignedly, as so often happens in Frost, with "something has to be left to God."

There is a recognition of the limitations of humans attempting to control nature, but there is also a recognition of how we make use of nature for our own, sometimes short-sighted ends. There is an almost rueful philosophical thrust at the end. The speaker does not really believe that God will be caring for his orchard anymore than he has. He knows that the fate of the orchard is just that, a matter of fate. It is out of his hands. It is time to say good-by.

As with the management and protection of nature, there is byplay between viewing nature as something human, with human characteristics, and viewing it as amoral and nonhuman. The metaphors can be easily applied to a couple having to separate for "a season or so." But hidden in the metaphors are strange twists that force the reader again to realize that nature is not after all human, as the title suggests, a turn on "Good-by and keep warm."

The use of parentheticals is intriguing, as they present not only asides in the traditional sense but second thoughts, doubts, and hopes. The reader may be left feeling that there is often a coldness at the heart of poetry as the heart of the orchard sinks slowly "under the sod."

FURTHER READING

Cramer, Jeffrey S. *Robert Frost among His Poems: A Literary Companion to the Poet's Own Biographical Contexts and Associations.* Jefferson, N.C.: MacFarland, 1996.

"Good Hours" (1915)

In this closing poem from the American edition of *North of Boston* (it did not appear in the 1914 English edition), the speaker takes a familiar evening walk. He is alone, and instead of heading into the woods, he passes by the cottages in his village. He is in town, as in "Acquainted with the Night."

In the first stanza the speaker passes by the cottages "[u]p to their shining eyes in snow." The shining eyes are the slits of light from the windows that can be seen above the snow drifts. Although he walks out alone, he has the townspeople within the cottages for company. They are with him without knowing it, just as the husband and wife are in "Ends," where their intimate quarrel is unknowingly overheard. The speaker is isolated but not completely alone.

He has the company "outward bound," but upon returning "there were no cottages found." Everyone has retired for the night when he returns home. The village is like clockwork. Everyone goes to bed at the same time, while he is up late. They all are on a similar schedule, perhaps a farmer's schedule, but he is on the outside of it, the lone walker in the night.

The speaker thinks that his creaking feet on the way home might disturb the peace and somehow trouble the serenity of the village. He considers such a disturbance a "profanation," presenting himself as someone "other." The creaking becomes "[l]ike profanation, by your leave," and it is the villagers' taking leave, by going to sleep, which makes his footsteps profanation at only 10 P.M.

Mark Richardson calls the pattern in the poem "one of wandering and return" (80). Tyler Hoffman says that in the poem "anaphora [the repetition of phrases at the beginning of lines] . . . appears to trope a night walker's effort to overcome social estrangement." Hoffman also calls the poem's "terminal position emphasized by being set in italics" at the end of *North of Boston* "a joke on Frost's part, since one of its dominant patterns—anaphora—constitutes a 'figure of repeated beginnings'" (79–80). ("The Pasture" was the original introductory poem to the volume and was also set in italics.)

The speaker wanders and returns, but without philosophical insight. He has journeyed, but it is unclear if anything has been gained. While the "glimpse through curtain laces" and "the sound of a violin" were his company from "the folk within," he is ultimately unaccompanied and isolated throughout. While he may return unchanged, as in "Into My Own," "more sure of all [he] thought was true," his physical and emotional isolation have grown all the more apparent as demonstrated by his creaking feet being the only sound heard, and heard only by him, in the stillness of the night.

See FUGITIVE.

FURTHER READING

Hoffman, Tyler. *Robert Frost and the Politics of Poetry.* Hanover, N.H.: Middlebury College Press, 2001, 79–80.

Richardson, Mark. *The Ordeal of Robert Frost: The Poet and His Poetics.* Chicago, Ill.: University of Illinois Press, 1997. 78–83.

"Grindstone, The" (1923)

Jeffrey Cramer reports that "The Grindstone" was inspired by Frost's experiences on Loren Bailey's farm in Salem, New Hampshire, in the summer of 1889. Bailey had a grindstone, and Frost was "taught how to turn the crank with one hand to give just the right speed to the stone, while the other hand, which held a tin can, poured a trickle of water to keep the stone moist under the pressure of the scythe-blade" (69). Cramer also notes that Frost once referred to the poem as a metaphor, and this is of significance for an understanding of the meaning of the poem.

In some ways the poem is reminiscent of William Carlos Williams's "The Red Wheelbarrow,"

though Williams's poem is brief and more in the style of the imagists. The similarities come from the speculation about the significance of the tool in human life and the imagery that carries the metaphor. In the Williams poem, "So much depends / upon / a red wheel / barrow / glazed with rain / water / beside the white / chickens." Frost, compares the grindstone to the wheelbarrow, but the wheelbarrow has the better position—as farm machinery that can "stand or go," it can get in out of the cold. Williams's wheelbarrow may be left in the rain, but Frost's grindstone is immovable. The empathy with the inanimate object is evident in each case. Frost says that "its standing in the yard" has "nothing any more to do with [him]," but the speaker feels some responsibility for the grindstone, as they had a relationship "one summer day" when they "ground a blade" together. Williams's empathy is more subtle, buried in the imagery.

As "The Grindstone" continues, the speaker reflects on his experience with it in more detail. Just as images in the first stanza, such as that of the grindstone "standing outdoors hungry, in the cold" make it almost anthropomorphic, in the second stanza the water on the grindstone jumps and flows "almost gaily." In this key stanza the speaker remembers being a boy and working at the grindstone, pouring on water that might have been "tears." While the boy worked at mastering the machine, he had a mentor, a "Father-Time-like man," complete with scythe, who slowed the boy to a halt with his criticisms. The boy was made to "chang[e] from hand to hand in desperation," trying to figure out how to master the machine. He grew angry with it, imagining that it had not been improved from the days when it "sharpened spears / And arrowheads itself."

The grindstone is worn and "struggl[ing] in its gait." The two, boy and grindstone, struggle together, the grindstone returning to the boy "hate for hate" in its kicks and struggles. Now a man, the speaker forgives the machine "as easily / As any other boyhood enemy / Whose pride has failed to get him anywhere." He wonders who his mentor thought did the grinding, the machine or himself, who "gave his life to keep it going round." He wonders if it is really up to the man to decide who gave more, the grindstone or himself, and these are the "bitter thoughts" to which he returns.

In the final stanza the speaker excuses himself and the man from his speculations, focusing solely on the grindstone, with which he is "so much concerned." He feels remorse for how he betrayed the grindstone, as once when it "almost jumped its bearing" he "laughed inside, and only cranked the faster." He rode the grindstone harder, taking advantage of its weakness and feeling glee in his supremacy. They grind together, sharpening, while the boy worries if they are "only wasting precious blade." When his mentor inspects the edge of the blade "over his glasses funny-eyed," he decides the blade needs a turn more. The boy "could have cried," as he was worried that he might go a "turn too much" and ruin the blade. The poem ends with a characteristically resigned "I'd / Be satisfied if he'd be satisfied." It is on this satisfaction that the poem rests.

The poem is fraught with childhood anguish. The grindstone begins as a tool for which the speaker has empathy. He recalls his childhood experience and is saddened to find the machine standing "beside the same old apple tree," all the more worn and weary. But soon the poem becomes about the boy, who, now a man, attempts to come to terms with his longing for recognition and acceptance by his mentor and his own sudden cruelty toward the tool he only wanted to master. He has regrets and feels somehow responsible for the isolated grindstone that he once rode hard. While his regrets about the grindstone are sincere, he has not quite resolved his feelings toward his mentor. In some way the poem expresses the desires of a boy to be embraced, as the closing lines suggest a lingering desperation. The use of "I'd" for "I would" indicates that the speaker still awaits acceptance. He is still unsatisfied and longs for a recognition that a "Father-Time-like man" likely no longer can give.

Reginald L. Cook calls the poem "a deceptively rambling blank verse narrative" (105), and in many ways it is. As with many of Frost's narratives, the poem's greater meanings are hidden beneath the surface. Cook writes that "Frost's wit, slow-breaking like a tricky curve ball, inobvious and idiosyncratic, pervades this rural parable" (106), and that wit is highlighted by Frost's calling the poem a metaphor.

As metaphor, the grindstone comes to represent the challenges, regrets, and unsatisfied desires of childhood.

"The Grindstone" was collected in *New Hampshire* but had been previously published in the June 1921 issue of *Farm and Fireside*.

FURTHER READING

Borroff, Marie. "Robert Frost: 'To Earthward.'" In *Frost: Centennial Essays II*, edited by Jac Tharpe, 21–39. Jackson: University Press of Mississippi, 1976.

Cook, Reginald. *The Dimensions of Robert Frost.* New York: Rinehart, 1958, 105–106.

Cramer, Jeffrey S. *Robert Frost among His Poems: A Literary Companion to the Poet's Own Biographical Contexts and Associations.* Jefferson, N.C.: MacFarland, 1996.

Faggen, Robert. *Robert Frost and the Challenge of Darwin.* Ann Arbor: University of Michigan Press, 1997, 177–184.

Guardeen, The

The Guardeen is a play of five scenes with seven primary characters described as the eloquent country man Henry Dow; the eloquent graduate student and "city boy" Richard Scott; Professor Titcombe, "Richard's debunking teacher, not many years older than Richard"; Lida Robie, daughter of the lumber camp; Charles Robie, Lida's brother; Socrates Robie, the father of Lida and Charles who remains offstage; and two lumberjacks, Tug and Guinea. There are also a few other lumbermen.

The Guardeen as well as *A Way Out* and "A Lockless Door," according to Donald Sheehy, "demonstrate the crucial tension in Frost between solitude and community as well as his shifting perspective on the role of the artist in society" (39). All three also have biographical connections to the summer of 1895, when Elinor was home from college and spent the summer near Ossipee Mountain and Lake Winnepesaukee in New Hampshire with her sister Leona. Frost took a nearby cottage in order to be near Elinor. Henry Horne, the owner of the cottage, kept cider in the cellar and saw in Frost a possible "guardeen" for his stash.

The play begins in late afternoon as Dow and Richard attempt to push a mattress through the door of a small room in the country cottage. Professor Titcombe soon enters with "blankets and a basket of provisions." They then set about establishing their relationships to one another. Richard is still somewhat Professor Titcombe's student, though Titcombe describes him as his "equalitarian equal in pursuit of happiness for all mankind." Shortly thereafter Richard shares his "new definition of Democracy: It's just one more form of government the upper class thought it could concede to the lower classes and still keep on top of them." Professor Titcombe describes Richard as "as radical as a bag of beets and carrots" and asserts that he is his "first choice for new youth leader of the permanently unemployed in the coming revolution."

Frost's biting sarcasm is evident in the early lines of the play and even in the descriptions in his list of characters. The boy is going to be left out here in the "[w]ild stretch of country" with these provisions, and Dow wants to assure him that nothing there is going to hurt him, though they do see a bear or a wild cat at least once a year. A constant theme in Frost is the disparity between city and country life. It is evident in a number of his poems, including "A Brook in the City," "Build Soil—A Political Pastoral," and "A Roadside Stand," among others. Richard asserts that he is unafraid, as Frost's speakers often do when faced with nature or the dark of the night.

We soon learn that Dow has invited Richard to stay in the country to keep an eye on his house, because he seems trustworthy and is not "much of a drinking man." Richard and Dow discuss the mattress, which is going to need some breaking in. It is stuffed full of hay, and Richard demonstrates his lack of country schooling when he suggests putting his trunk on it during the day to break it in. While the boy will be sleeping indoors, Dow calls this his "first experience camping out," further highlighting Richard's inexperience with country living and his naïveté about what he faces.

While Dow is putting the boy at ease, he also seems to be intentionally luring him toward dis-

comfort. He soon asserts that he hopes the boy did not come "without a weepon of some description." Richard assures him he has not and exposes a gun that Dow hardly calls a gun and instead more of a "bee sting affair." Richard, whom Dow seems to intend to make anxious, inquires, "What's all the anxiety?" Here the title of the play becomes clear when Dow declares that he wants the boy to be careful way out here, "out of the call of doctors and all," and to be "the guardeen" of himself "first and foremost."

Richard begins to wonder if he is being put on and whether Dow has been put up to something by Titcombe. He asks Dow, "What's the matter?" and Dow responds, getting a jab in, "Nothing's the matter. Only that revoliver is about as practical as you be." Soon Lida enters and is introduced to Richard. Lida leaves, and Richard is left wondering where she could possibly be going, as he thinks the house he is occupying is the farthest from everything and that there can be nothing farther. He has been led to believe that after him "the road turned into a squirrel track and ran up a tree."

Dow is revealed as a drinker, who drinks hard when he can get away from his "datters," who apparently keep a leash on him, and Lida has come to tell Dow one daughter is looking for him. Richard is not put off by the diversion; he persists in inquiring about Lida and discovers that her family is "a gang of left-overs from a lumber job." Dow warns that the boy should shoot his gun now and then to keep those "night prowelers," Lida's family, at bay. Lida is described as a girl who can "use the cant dogs like a man" and who chews tobacco. But again, Richard is not put off. As the scene closes, we learn what Richard is really guardeen of: the barrels of hard cider that Dow keeps in the basement.

In scene 2 night has fallen, and the lumberjacks Guinea and Tug are crawling toward the house on hands and knees with a galvanized iron bucket in search of cider. Richard is having target practice, firing off warnings as Dow suggested. Guinea and Tug suspect he is "practicing for something—a command in the army maybe." They try to figure out how they can get around Richard, knowing he is a city boy, as Leda described him, and probably does not know much about country living. Lida said she had "seen him first" and so "[h]e's hers," and they must leave him alone, at least to some degree. Charlie enters for the first time and tells Tug and Guinea to get their cider and go home, but they are having too much fun. Tug says, "Tain't a question of getting cider so much as it is of getting satisfaction." This is a game of country nagging the city boy, and they are not giving up without getting some good laughs out of it.

In scene 3 it is late in the forenoon of the following day, and Richard is exhausted by the antics of the night before. Lida enters, warning him that her brother Charles is on the way to speak to him, and Charles follows shortly thereafter. Richard nearly shoots them both by accident. Charles knows that Dow has put Richard up to firing and has warned him about their lumberjack family. He finds it all very humorous. A fire breaks out on the mountain, and Charles leaves to help put it out.

Lida and Richard are left talking, and she asks whether he knows that his purpose in being on the mountain is simply to guard the cider. Richard explains that he is there as a product of "two mistakes," the first being to guard the cider and the second to make a "social study" of Lida since she is "underprivileged" and "because it would be too hard to make it of the privileged." He is working on a thesis for Titcombe, who Lida says is a distant cousin of hers. While Lida is supposed to represent the lower class, it turns out that she substitute teaches, which makes Richard believe there has been a "complete misunderstanding."

As the two chat, Richard has an opportunity to express his ideas about politics and how the "Outs constitute the greatest of Have-Nots." They also have an opportunity to discuss poetry, which Lida thinks can be churned out once the writer has a topic, to which Richard condescendingly disagrees: "My dear child poems aren't written like that." Lida wants a poem written about her father who is "like Solomon only different. Solomon waited till he had got possession of everything before he turned against worldly goods and started to cry vanity of vanities. My father didn't wait to get property. He saw through it beforehand." Lida's father is allegorically Socrates.

Richard continues to disparage the girl, saying "Listen to her. The whole philosophy of riffraff rab-

bledom in one pretty little head." Richard concludes that he "used to think democracy meant giving everybody a college education free" and that he used to be "full of sympathetic ambition for everyone," but now after talking to Lida, he feels she has taken the "strength" out of him. He then calls her by the wrong name and, when corrected, pompously renames her. The romantic tensions that have been a subtext throughout their conversation come to a head when Richard asks for a kiss and for her to be his "guardeen." As Richard continues to talk about being "fond of criminals" and about how many "big ideas" he has for her to "come round and believe in when [she] can find time," Titcombe arrives.

Titcombe's arrival inspires further talk of sociology and the haves and have nots. Richard explains as he formally introduces Titcombe that Titcombe is "down on the country" and "hates all Jakes Rubes Hicks and Hayseeds, really because they don't vote with the city proletariat." The doctor's motto, he explains, is that "you've got to get down to the low down if you're going to get anywhere in sociology." Frost was antisocialist and anticommunist, and usually his poems reveal this indirectly more than directly, but here he is less metaphorical and makes his points satirically. Titcombe disagrees with Richard's depiction of himself, explaining, "No, my motto is you can't afford to be intolerant of any one you can put in a book."

The study of these country people reveals to Richard that folks out there "begin to think outrageous fiction" in order to "blackguard each other with." "Hate inspires them to imaginative slander," he says. Titcombe, ever the professor, corrects him by calling this "fiction" "a kind of poetry—what pastoral poetry has sunk to in New Hampshire." The play becomes farcical as Lida's father Socrates is described as a sage and Titcombe is revealed as being related not only to Lida and her family but to Dow as well. Titcombe says that he is "related to every single person in this town by breeding or inbreeding." Dow appears at the end of the scene, and the characters become self-conscious, revealing their awareness that they are characters. Titcombe says, "You can't keep an audience waiting forever for a climax. Let's have our catastrophe in the next scene."

When scene 4 opens, Richard is reading and Charles is in the doorway of the house with Tug and Guinea. They have all come for cider, and with their own cups to boot. Dow arrives as they are drinking his cider. His guardeen has not been much of a guardeen after all. Richard calls the men his friends, and Dow remarks that "[i]t beats the barnyard what a week's growth will do for a crittur like [him]." "You *have* come on," he says. Charles refers to Richard as Dick, suggesting he has in some sense become one of them.

Richard has switched sides, so to speak. He not only did not guard the cider but also helped drink all of it with his newfound "family." In scene five, the tables have completely turned. While Dow becomes desperate for the cider that has now disappeared, and just about chokes on water from the spring that they have spiked with a little pepper for fun, the lumberjacks and Charles turn on the professor, who has just arrived, accusing him of writing a book about them. They declare that it is their turn to have a little fun, and they decide to play a game with him called "Side O' Beef," which causes Titcombe to shout to Richard, "Traitor!" Professor Titcombe is soon tied up in country sport, and Frost writes tongue-in-cheek that Titcombe will mark Richard "off for this in college."

Although Frost was not much of a dramatist, the play is humorous and lively in its depiction of city dwellers' fears of the country, country bumpkins who can outsmart and outwit city folk, and the superiority of the educated becoming undone when faced with the realities of everyday living and a survival of the fittest—even when that survival is mostly about hard cider in the cellar. The play ends with Dow asking humorously, "Did it singe ye?" about a fire that has been put out by Titcombe that is described as just "one small fire," compared with those "he has kindled . . . in the breasts of his students." The play does singe in its way, but it is a very small kindling fire when compared with Frost's poetry.

In the holograph manuscript, an inscription under the cast of characters reads; "Second Version / for Earle Bernheimer / from his friend / Robert Frost / Cambridge Mass Jan 12 1942." Bernheimer was a wealthy collector who began collecting Frost's books and manuscripts in 1936.

FURTHER READING

Sell, Roger D. "Two Unpublished Plays: In an Art Factory, The Guardeen," *Massachusetts Review* 26, no. 2–3 (Summer–Autumn 1985): 265–340.

Sheehy, Donald G. "Robert Frost and the 'Lockless Door,'" *New England Quarterly* 56, no. 1 (March 1983): 39–59.

"Gum-Gatherer, The" (1916)

Frost once wrote in a letter that "The Gum-Gatherer" was a favorite poem of his because it "speak[s] poetically of chewing gum" (Cramer, 59). A remark like that might suggest a playful poem, like a fairy tale, in the way some other Frost poems are. But while the poem speaks of chewing gum and is not particularly complex, it has a distinct wryness.

The speaker is out for an early morning walk, but he is not alone, as is so often the case. He finds himself keeping company with a man who overtakes him on the road, as his downhill stride outpaces the speaker's slower gait. The two end up walking together, the man, with a bag "wound round his hand," talking loudly in an effort to "bar[k] above the din / Of water" from the stream they are walking beside. The speaker shares a bit about himself and where he lives, and the gum-gatherer does the same. He comes from "higher up" the mountain, where he lives in a "stolen shack / Because of the fears of fire and loss." There he gathers gum to sell in the town market. While other people from up high come to town with eggs or berries to sell, he brings the gum he gathers from the mountain spruce tree. The speaker describes the "scented stuff" as similar to "uncut jewels, dull and rough." The only image of chewing gum is the description of the resin turning "pink between the teeth."

One might expect the poem to end there, but if it did, it would lack the characteristic Frost twist. Although the poem appears to be a simple sketch of two men, strangers, sharing a morning walk, the closing stanza, set apart from the bulk of the poem, leaves the reader wondering. The speaker concludes that the gum-gatherer leads "a pleasant life." He imagines that putting his "breast to the bark of trees," and gathering resin with a little knife to "bring to market when you please" is a desirable way to live. But his presentation is romanticized. The description of gum-gathering is poetic and lacks the grit of hard work. The poem ends without the gum-gatherer's having had an opportunity to respond.

The speaker expresses a common view: that another person's life is more pleasant than his own, playing on the old adage that "the grass is always greener on the other side." It also suggests that our imaginations deceive us when we romanticize such things. Though nature does provide the uncut jewels for the market for the gum-gatherer as well as his "stolen shack," it has a darker side. It provides a constant source of fear and death through forest fires, "fire and loss," which is why "it had to be a stolen shack"—stolen from the forest and the fire, which can easily "steal" it away. Nature is dark when the smoke from burning is so thick that only a "sun shrunken yellow in smoke" is visible. Frost also points out another danger of living in the gum-gatherer's world: the constant blocking of the sun through those same trees, when "All your days are dim beneath."

But always Frost wants the reader to see both the good and the bad when in nature. Even if the speaker's romanticism is rejected, the poem still ends on a somewhat hopeful note. While some may live in sunlight, unconcerned with fire and loss, the gum-gatherer simply reaches up "with a little knife" to pick his living from the trees while others toil at the land. The reader is left with a question about the value of the trade-off.

"The Gum Gatherer" was collected in *Mountain Interval* but had been previously published in the October 9, 1916, issue of the *Independent*.

FURTHER READING

Cramer, Jeffrey S. *Robert Frost among His Poems: A Literary Companion to the Poet's Own Biographical Contexts and Associations.* Jefferson, N.C.: MacFarland, 1996.

"Haec Fabula Docet" (1947)

Haec fabula docet is Latin for "this story teaches." In this self-identified fable modeled after Aesop, the tale and its moral are separate, as Frost takes up the sort of pride that precedes a fall, a literal fall in this case. The poem teasingly introduces a "[b]lindman by the name of La Fontaine." (Jean de La Fontaine (1621–95) was a French fabulist, a sign that Frost is tongue-in-cheek from the start.)

The blind man is one who relies "on himself and on his cane." In the tale he is "tap-tap-tapping" down the street toward a trench in which a work crew is laying water pipes. Before having an opportunity to find the trench on his own with "his ferrule," the metal tip of his cane, and so avoid it, the blind man is warned "with a loud command" and run against "with a staying hand." The blind man is startled and then offended and "enraged" at this affront to, among other things, his dignity. He swings his cane at the person who attempted to rescue him and, missing, pitches himself forward into the trench. The workmen then proceed with "glee no less for being grim" to bury him in the trench.

The appended moral explains that those who try to go it alone out of pride are "sure to come to grief" at someone else's hands. Frost is wary of pride especially to the point of rejecting help. But not all who go it alone do so out of pride or choice. Frost's use of a fictive blind man as the chief character in his fable is perplexing, as a blind man relies on himself and his cane because he does not have many alternatives. The sighted person would be unlikely to wander into the situation in which the blind man finds himself to begin with. The blind man's lashing out against what he thinks an "officious" attempt to rescue him is an overcompensation for his lack of sight. It is his independence, his pride in self-reliance, that is at stake. But blindness in this poem can also stand for willful ignorance, an unwillingness to heed a well-meant warning. Self-reliance has gone too far, and probably out of pride. The advice that seems officious appears so only because there is urgency in the warning. The blind man in his pride fails to see that in more ways than one. And the workmen not only delight in his fall but bury him, thereby nullifying his very existence. A warning cry quickly turns to an extreme and dark schadenfreude. Such observations do not charitably characterize the cruel possibilities in human nature. To the workmen the blindman's pride is hubris, deserving of the brutal justice they exact. They too are blind, but in a moral, not a physical, sense.

"Haec Fabula Docet" was collected in *Steeple Bush* as an "editorial" but had been previously published in the December 1946 issue of the *Atlantic Monthly*.

FURTHER READING

Cramer, Jeffrey S. *Robert Frost among His Poems: A Literary Companion to the Poet's Own Biographical Contexts and Associations*. Jefferson, N.C.: MacFarland, 1996.

"Hannibal" (1928)

This four-line aphoristic poem collected in *West-Running Brook* is titled after the great Carthaginian general Hannibal Barca (247–182 B.C.), who skillfully waged war against superior Roman forces in battles known to history as the second two of three Punic Wars, which led to the complete destruction of the city and state of Carthage, in northern Africa. In the first Punic War, Hannibal's father, Hamilcar, fought Rome courageously but was defeated. Determined to have revenge, in the second Punic War Hannibal left New Carthage, defeated the Gauls, and crossed the Alps with elephants to invade Italy in just 15 days. This daring land approach was successful, but Hannibal found it difficult to maintain control of the situation and eventually had to withdraw. The general later took his own life by drinking poison in despair over the ultimate failure of his battles with Rome.

The poem poses a question broken into four lines with an ab/cb rhyme scheme. The poem asks, "Was there ever a cause too lost, / Ever a cause that was lost too long, / Or that showed with the lapse of time too vain / For the generous tears of youth and song?" While the brief poem is titled "Hannibal," its point is not limited to the great general. Frost uses his question to underscore an attribute of youth: that no cause is ever too great for the young. While celebrating the bold ardor of youthful adventure, he notes that with time, indi-

viduals often come to see their youthful actions as "vain." (Frost apparently assumes that the reader will be aware of Hannibal's tragic end.) By asking the question rather than making a statement, Frost leaves the idea open to interpretation. On the one hand, he asks whether the causes we take up in youth are ever as great as we believe them to be at the time, and on the other hand, he issues a challenge to youths in all times, who, with their great passion and "generous tears," must be the ones to take up the greatest of causes.

FURTHER READING

Dodge, Theodore Ayrault. *Hannibal*. Cambridge: Da Capo, 2004.

"Happiness Makes Up in Height for What It Lacks in Length" (1942)

This lyric consists of three sentences. In the first line the speaker declares, "Oh, stormy stormy world," and the poem goes on to describe stormy days as those "swirled" with "mist and cloud" or "wrapped as in a shroud." As part of the first sentence, the speaker explains that even though the days that were not stormy were "so very few," for some reason he has a "lasting sense / Of so much warmth and light."

In the second sentence, the speaker declares that if his "mistrust is right," that is, if he is right not to trust his feeling of lasting sense, then it is true that it was from "one day's perfect weather" that he gained such a romantic view.

The poem closes with his impression that it "may / Be all from that one day," but the closing four lines introduce another character, making what appears to be a simple poem—about the "happiness" of one day making up in "height," in its degree of happiness, for what it lacked in "length," or duration—a bit more complicated.

The four last lines, "No shadow crossed but ours / As through its blazing flowers / We went from house to wood / For change of solitude," introduce with the pronouns "our" and "we" what may be a friend, relative, or lover. While "[n]o shadow" crossed the sky in the form of clouds, their shadows did cross, and this is what really brought immense happiness. They walked through what appeared to be "blazing flowers," partly from the sun but partly too from their own feelings of joy, to the woods together, to seek a different form of solitude and privacy than they had at home.

The poem becomes a love poem. The lyricism and images build toward a romantic climax where two are joined, casting a new shadow on all that precedes their meeting. Suddenly the warmth and light and, in this case, happiness comes not just from the perfect weather of that one day but from the day their shadows crossed each other's paths. In the speaker's mind both sunny days and human life might be fleeting, but the happiness they can occasionally deliver makes up for this limitation.

The poem was collected in *A Witness Tree* but was previously published in the September 1938 issue of the *Atlantic Monthly*.

FURTHER READING

Doyle, John Robert, Jr. *The Poetry of Robert Frost: An Analysis*. New York: Hafner Press, 1962, 187–192.

Gozzi, Raymond. "Lowell's 'The Cathedral' and Frost's 'Happiness Makes Up in Height for What It Lacks in Length,'" *Explicator* 45, no. 3 (Summer 1987): 28–30.

Hays, Peter L. "Robert Frost 'Happiness' Line in FWBT?" *Hemingway Newsletter* 16 (June 1988): 2.

Janzen, J. Gerald. "Reassessing Frost's Fair Impression and His Mistrust," *Religion and Literature* 20, no. 3 (Autumn 1988): 71–87.

"Hardship of Accounting, The" (1936)

This brief aphoristic poem is the eighth in a group of poems titled "Ten Mills," most of which, including this one, were originally published in *Poetry* in April 1936 and later collected in *A Further Range*. When this was first published it was simply titled "Money."

The poem has its fun and makes its point. There is little to do in the way of unpacking; a biographical note from Jeffrey Cramer gives the poem some personal value to Frost, however. Frost once recalled that during his days as a university student at Dartmouth his grandfather, William Prescott Frost, Sr., paid him five dollars a week and for it wanted an accounting for "every penny spent, where it went, and what it was for." He added that he "rebelled and wanted to tell him to go to hell. But [he] didn't, [he] held" (118). The poem might be Frost's way of finally telling his grandfather what he wished to about such "accounting."

It should also be noted that this is the same grandfather who offered to help the young Frost try to become a successful poet by supporting him financially over a period of about a year. Frost is supposed to have replied, "Give me twenty! Give me twenty!," and it did in fact take him about 20 years to become successful. As Jay Parini says, Frost's estimation "proved uncannily accurate" (46); he was 39 when *A Boy's Will* came out.

FURTHER READING

Cramer, Jeffrey S. *Robert Frost among His Poems: A Literary Companion to the Poet's Own Biographical Contexts and Associations*. Jefferson, N.C.: MacFarland, 1996.

Parini, Jay. *Robert Frost: A Life*. New York: Holt, 1999, 46.

"Hear-Say Ballad, The" (1953)

In this brief preface written to *Ballads Migrant in New England* (1953), edited by Hartness Flanders, Frost describes the ballad form as belonging to the "none too literate." He describes the spirit of the ballad, and possibly of all poetry, as having its "safest keeping" with them. Those folks "know it by heart" and allow it to "weather and season properly." Ballads "lead their life in the mouths and ears of men by hear-say like bluebirds and flickers in the nest holes of hollow trees."

Frost reading, 1941. "The Hear-Say Ballad": "[B]rought to book now and then for sport and scholarship." *(Photo by Fred Palumbo. Courtesy Library of Congress)*

While he asserts that ballads belong to the none too literate, Frost also believes that they should be "brought to book now and then for sport and scholarship" because we have a "right to satisfy our curiosity as to what variants they may have been running wild into while our backs were turned."

Frost distinguishes the "true ballad," one that leaves the voice and ear at a loss for what to do until it is set to music, from the "true poem," which should not be set to music. Ballads "unsung" stay "half-lacking," whereas in "Conversations on the Craft of Poetry," Frost says that poetry makes its own "music," built on the beating of human hearts. When verse needs to be set to music to achieve, it does not have its own music and is "bad writing." But with ballads, this is not so.

Frost's own poetry is built on the stuff of the "none too literate," on their intonations, dialects, and subjects, but for "tune it depends on the music of music."

FURTHER READING

Ballads Migrant in New England. Edited by Helen Flanders. New York: Farrar, Straus and Young, 1953.

"Hillside Thaw, A" (1923)

Frost is at his playful best in "A Hillside Thaw," a poem Jay Parini calls a "vivid snapshot of rural New England life" (207). The poem, which Frost once referred to as "Silver Lizards," in a letter to Sidney Cox develops an extended metaphor from an image that Frost and his friend Raymond Holden once observed on his farm in Franconia, New Hampshire. Holden recalled, "We stood for awhile in the moonlight, watching the glitter of the frozen rivulets which, in the warm sun of the afternoon before, had been runnels of thaw-water, running down the sloping floor of the sugar orchard" (Cramer, 84).

The poem begins, "To think to know the country and not know / The hillside on the day the sun lets go," and this statement reveals the subject and attitude of the poem. The narrator chides those who think they know the country but have not witnessed a hillside thaw, because to him that is the country. The poem is filled with detailed imagery, beginning with the "ten million silver lizards out of the snow," the trails of water that trickle down from thawing snow on a hilltop. As the water slithers down the hillside, it looks as if silver lizards are coming out from under a rug. The narrator cannot imagine how "it's done," this illusion, except by "some magic of the sun."

Frost expands the image, describing it as a "wet stampede" and imagining catching a "lizard by the tail" or trying to stop one with his foot. He knows that even if he were to throw himself on the ground in "front of twenty others' wriggling speed," he would still "end by holding none," since lizards made of water cannot be grasped.

The closing stanza describes the sun as a wizard and the moon as a witch. The sun's wizardry has turned melting snow into lizards before the speaker's eyes, and the moon's witchcraft manages to turn them into "rock" when the sun sets and the temperature drops below freezing again.

This poem demonstrates how the human imagination works in the face of natural occurrences. Frost's poetic description of the hillside thaw skillfully extends one of his most unusual metaphors.

"The Hillside Thaw" was first published in the April 6, 1921, issue of the *New Republic* and was later collected in *New Hampshire*.

FURTHER READING

Cramer, Jeffrey S. *Robert Frost among His Poems: A Literary Companion to the Poet's Own Biographical Contexts and Associations*. Jefferson, N.C.: MacFarland, 1996.

Parini, Jay. *Robert Frost: A Life*. New York: Holt, 1999.

"Hill Wife, The" (1916)

"The Hill Wife" consists of five poems, "Loneliness: Her Word," "House Fear," "The Smile: Her Word," "The Oft-Repeated Dream," and "The Impulse." The two subtitled "Her Word" are dictated in the voice of the "hill wife." The others are presumably in the voice of a narrator, leaving the husband voiceless. The collection begins with the wife's voice and then dances between the two before ending with two poems crafted from the narrator's perspective.

"Loneliness: Her Word" begins with the wife recounting how much she and her husband care about the birds that "come round the house" seeming "to say good-by." The 12-line poem expresses the care they share for the birds and for their return. They are "too glad" for the birds' return and "too sad" for their departure. The birds "fill their breasts . . . with each other and themselves" and thereby become a symbol for their relationship and their affection toward each other. The birds gain their attention more than their own "built or driven nests" and demonstrate the loneliness they feel in each other's company, since they gain too much gladness from that "one thing." The loneliness the wife feels is expressed in her recounting the birds'

arrival in spring and departure in autumn. When they "come round the house," they bring the comfort and company that is lacking in the couple's own nest. And, in her word, this should not be the case.

The second poem, "House Fear," told from the narrator's perspective, is also concerned with departure and return. It opens as though it is in conversation with the first poem, "Always—I tell you this they learned— / Always at night when they returned," but this is an intentional deception meant for the reader to presume the narrator is talking about the return of the birds. It is the return of the couple that is being described. The title is highlighted in the third line, where the "lonely house" is described as being darkened with "fire gone gray." When the two return at night, they "rattle the lock and key" in an effort to scare away whatever might be lurking on the other side. They fear the lonely house, because it is their loneliness. Once inside they will be shrouded in gloom and the loneliness of their togetherness. They leave the door open until they can light a lamp indoors, hoping again to scare away whatever may lurk in the dark, but what lurks is nothing that can be affrighted by light—it is a personal fear within themselves that they cannot scare off. Bird imagery continues in this second poem with the line "[w]arning and time to be off in flight.

"The Smile" again returns to the wife's word, and this time the foreshadowing of leave-taking and return in the first two poems becomes more evident. "I didn't like the way he went away," she says. His smile, she imagines, did not come from happiness. The first impression is that the wife speaks of her husband's departure, but it is clear in the fourth line, when she says "we gave him only bread," that the smile she describes was not her husband's. The description is of a stranger, a beggar, and the images again lead back to the birds through the giving of bread. The wife imagines that they are "mocked . . . for being wed" or for "being very young" or even for being "poor," oddly, given that the man was a beggar. The parenthetical is disturbed and disturbing: "(and he was pleased / To have a vision of us old and dead)." She wonders how far he has gotten on the road, suggesting that perhaps it is not a man after all, but a bird. The closing line is haunting—"He's watching from the woods as like as not"—and suddenly the two are not alone but watched by someone unkind and possibly malevolent. The smile is interpreted not as friendly but instead as haunting. The insertion of a third character seems out of place. It also appears that the function of this addition is to demonstrate further the woman's unhappiness and her ability to ascribe to the most ordinary behavior some form of malice.

The remaining two poems take the narrator's perspective. "The Oft-Repeated Dream" opens by noting that the wife "had no saying dark enough" for the pine that attempted to open the "window-latch" in the bedroom at night. The image is reminiscent of "Tree at My Window." The tree's branches are like "ineffectual hands" attempting to break through the glass. It never is able to break through, but "one of the two / Was afraid in an oft-repeated dream / Of what the tree might do" upon breaking in. This poem makes the loneliness that is apparent in the preceding three suggestive of place as much as of relationship and returns to the theme of "House Fear." Suddenly the woman's isolation in the house and the house's vulnerability in nature become a cause for concern. And while it is not made clear that it is the wife "of the two" that has the dream, it seems likely.

The closing poem brings the theme of departure and return to a head. "The Impulse" explains from the viewpoint of the narrator that "[i]t was too lonely for her there, / And too wild," uniting the themes of physical and emotional isolation foreshadowed in the earlier poems. The couple is childless, and with little work to do in the house and no children to care for, the wife follows the husband during the day while he furrows a field or chops down a tree. She does not go along to help but follows out of boredom and loneliness, and yet she would rest, still alone, on a log and play at tossing fresh wood chips and singing a song "only to herself / On her lips"—another example of their detachment from each other. There is again bird symbolism here, when the woman is portrayed as a caged bird who exists only to accompany the man as if she were a domestic pet.

On one occasion when she goes with her husband to work the "impulse" strikes her, as suggested by the title, and she "stray[s] so far she scarcely hear[s] / When he call[s] her"; this is her departure from her husband. But she does not seem to have gotten lost, instead, she chooses to leave. She "didn't answer—didn't speak—" suggesting a willfulness in the matter, and she "stood" before she "ran and hid / In the fern." He looks for her, but she is nowhere to be found, not in the woods or at her mother's house. The closing lines make clear how "[s]udden and swift and light" departures can be, like the lift of a bird to flight, and highlights how easily the ties that at first may have seemed everlasting quickly fly away.

The poem ends with a kind of moral: "And he learned the finalities / Besides the grave." Suddenly the focus returns to the largely absent and voiceless husband as a primary figure, even though he has been secondary. He has discovered that while marriage is meant to last "until death do us part," endings often come sooner with the same resolve. In "Ends" Frost develops a similar theme only through a quarrel between husband and wife as heard by passersby. In that poem he poignantly states, "there had once been night the first, / But this was night the last."

The use of "her word" intertwined with a detached narrator's words is intriguing, as it indicates that certain lines are written from the wife's perspective. But this repeated subtitle may also be a warning to the reader that these sections are biased, since they are just "her word" (as in "her word against his"), and "his word" is never expressed. If this is the case, then the hill wife may be an unreliable narrator, building from her initial disappointment in "Loneliness" to her near-paranoia in "The Smile." And the narrator of the other three poems becomes the only one we can trust, providing more observation than interpretation of the couple's action. The narrator portrays the house as incomplete protection, but the wife sings like a bird in a cage.

Endings are of interest to Frost as is isolation, both physical and emotional. First-person speakers in his poems are often alone and in nature. Here we are given two characters bound by their commitment to each other but facing many of the same obstacles that are discussed in the other poems: loneliness, isolation, vulnerability to nature and to others.

"The Hill Wife" was collected in *Mountain Interval* but first appeared complete in the April 1916 issue of the *Yale Review*. "The Smile" had previously appeared in the December 1914 issue of *Poetry and Drama*.

FURTHER READING

Crannell, Kenneth C. "A Metrical Analysis of Robert Frost's 'The Hill Wife.'" In *Studies in Interpretation*, edited by Esther M. Doyle, et al., 99–114. Amsterdam: Rodopi, 1977.

Doyle, John Robert, Jr. *The Poetry of Robert Frost: An Analysis*. New York: Hafner Press, 1962, 54–59.

Gentry, Marshall Bruce. "Five Poems and One: Frost's 'The Hill Wife,'" *Conference of College Teachers of English Proceedings* 48 (September 1983): 110–115.

Kearns, Katherine. *Robert Frost and a Poetics of Appetite*. Cambridge: Cambridge University Press, 1994.

Perrine, Laurence. "Robert Frost's 'The Hill Wife': Evidence, Inference, and Speculation in the Interpretation of Poetry," *College Literature* 10, no. 1 (Winter 1983): 1–15.

Timmerman, John H. *Robert Frost: The Ethics of Ambiguity*. Lewisburg, Pa.: Bucknell University Press, 2002, 164–165.

Wallace, Patricia. "The 'Estranged Point of View': The Thematics of Imagination in Frost's Poetry." In *Frost: Centennial Essays II*, edited by Jac Tharpe, 180–182. Jackson: University Press of Mississippi, 1976.

"Home Burial" (1914)

One of Frost's most anthologized dramatic narratives, "Home Burial" was first published in *North of Boston*, a collection that included a number of narratives, among them the well-known "Death of the Hired Man" as well as "Blueberries" and "The Code."

The poem depicts the scene of a rural home burial, where husband and wife, in the burying of their only child, express their grief differently and cannot communicate their feelings of loss to each other. It develops themes commonly associated with loss, such as feelings of anger, denial, and blame. The poem has been described as "close to home" for Frost, since his first child Elliott died at age three. Friend Sidney Cox described Frost and his wife Elinor's response to the death as similar to that of the couple in the poem: "He covered his pain with talking, she with silence." It is also noteworthy that Frost said in an interview that he did not spend more than two hours composing the poem and that "it stands in print as it was in the first draft." Jay Parini imagines it as having come to him "in a blaze, having been smoldering for years" (68).

The poem, which John Robert Doyle, Jr., says "examines the relationship between the living and the dead," takes place in the house of the husband and wife, opening with his seeing her "from the bottom of the stairs." She is coming down the stairs but looking over her shoulder as she does so, as if experiencing "some fear." The husband asks her what she sees "From up there always." Frost, who was very alert to differences in tone and intrigued by them, implies an aggression in the husband's manner. Frost once said that he could not remain interested in sentences that did not convey tone of voice, and that interest in tone comes across strongly here.

The wife sinks down and is described as cowering, while the husband presses on with his inquiry. The wife remains silent, "refus[ing] him any help" in figuring out the matter. The narrator describes the man, from the wife's perspective, as a "[b]lind creature," blind to the thoughts and feelings that trouble her. He doesn't "see" at first, but then he does, and "at last he murmur[s], 'Oh,' and again, 'Oh.'" In a 1916 interview Frost elaborated on the expression "oh": "think of what 'oh' is really capable: the 'oh' of scorn, the 'oh' of amusement, the 'oh' of surprise, the 'oh' of doubt—and there are many more," he said (Cramer, 35). Here there is an "oh" of recognition.

"What is it—what?" the wife asks, as if she does not understand the tone of her husband's "oh." These subtleties in communication, and the lack thereof, create a feeling of discomfort for the reader of the scene. "Just that I see," he says. Somehow feeling rebuked, the wife insists that he does not know, insisting that he say what he sees for confirmation that he does know. He explains how he is surprised he "didn't see it at once," and he expresses that he must not have noticed it from there before because he must be "wonted to it"—so used to it that he does not notice it anymore. What he is describing is the home burial plot where his family and their child are buried. The use of the pronoun "it" is chilling, because while he is referring to the family graveyard plot, the focus of the conversation is on the child buried in it, so it seems that not only a distancing is at work in his use of the pronoun but also a kind of avoidance.

The "mound" of dirt on their son's grave is still fresh. The words the father uses to describe what the mother sees drives her pain deeper. The graveyard is described as "[s]o small" that its entirety can be framed by the window. The headstones of his ancestors are described but then dismissed in his "[w]e haven't to mind *those*"—the emphasis on *those* building to the final climax, where he utters, "it is not the stones, / But the child's mound—" and then breaks off, interrupted by his wife's interjection.

"Don't, don't, don't, don't," she cries. The repetition (reminiscent of Shakespeare's "Howl, howl, howl, howl" and "Never" repeated five times by the anguished king in the final act of *King Lear*) effectively expresses her grief. Frost believed that "the four don'ts are the supreme thing" in the poem. The woman's repetition conveys raw emotion by indicating a lack of clarity and control over her thoughts and feelings. The wife is described as withdrawing and sliding down the stairs with a "daunting look"—Frost's layering of such descriptions creates a vivid impression of the scene. Physical words like *cower, withdraw,* and *slide* constitute a withering description of the woman's behavior and emotional state.

The man asks, "Can't a man speak of his own child he's lost?" and he repeats it twice. Again, the use of repetition is compelling. The two repeat themselves in an attempt to make clear what they wish to communicate, but they are incapable of communicating what they feel, no matter how many times they repeat themselves. Just as some

approach foreign-speaking people by speaking louder, the couple approach each other through repetition. Neither approach works—the gap in communication and understanding is not bridgeable when two are not speaking each other's language. And the husband and wife do not speak the same language. The difference in their manner of grieving is evident: He is not to speak of it, but he does, and she cannot. The wife feels trapped by his forthrightness, almost disgusted by his ability to speak at all. Suffocating in his presence, she says that she has to "get out of here" and get some air. Both in defense and on the attack, she accusingly says she does not think any man can speak of the death of a child, as if such things were solely a woman's right.

Until this point both husband and wife have gone unnamed. Now he calls to her "Amy! Don't go to someone else this time. / Listen to me." Her response, "I won't come down the stairs," strikes an ominous note, suggesting that the wife has reason to feel physically threatened by her husband. It is clear that though the death is recent, enough time has passed for this gulf between them to grow and for her to seek solace in someone other than her husband. While attempting to draw her to him, he again fails: He somehow manages to focus on the stairs as the cause for her grief. Missing the point entirely, his words only push her farther and farther away. The idea that is developing but is not stated is what humans are compelled to tell to others when their pain is too great to be withstood: "You don't understand."

He wants to ask her something, but she says he does not know how. They lack the words to communicate their grief to each other. He cannot find the words, as his are "nearly always an offense," and she cannot find any words at all. The man is presented as attempting to right things. He is willing to "partly give up being a man" if it will somehow make things better. He does not like having such agreements between "those that love," as he clearly feels he should be able to express anything he feels forthrightly, but he is willing to make accommodations. While the husband expresses himself, the wife fiddles with the latch to the door. He is almost begging her to stay and tell him about her grief "if it's something human" and to let him in, but then he manages to say the wrong thing again: "I do think, though, you overdo it a little." Frost's representation of the masculine here is sympathetic, perhaps because he can identify with it, but it also relies on traditional conceptions of men and women. The notion that the father might become less of a man if he approaches his wife differently is old-fashioned. The woman's shrinking away presents her as fragile. The man's digging in the yard presents him as strong. The characters are clearly defined along the lines of traditional gender roles. In William Carlos Williams's "The Dead Baby," husband and wife grieve similarly.

The two begin to express themselves to each other more openly, but they still are unable to communicate. She thinks he does not know how to speak, because he speaks as though he does not have any feelings, and he thinks she asks too much of him. At this point part of what has been troubling Amy becomes clear: that he was able to dig the "little grave." She knows that she would have been unable to bury her son, and witnessing her husband do it makes her think him callous. The gravel is described as being made to "leap and leap in the air"—almost joyfully. Clearly her perception of the event is skewed. By witnessing her husband burying their child, she came to feel she did not know him. She saw him as detached and unfeeling. He was capable of something she was not, and this made him alien.

With this account the husband angrily says, "I'm cursed. God, if I don't believe I'm cursed." Certainly from his perspective the burial was out of love for his child, but his actions have been misconstrued. The husband took action, as men are expected to do, using physical labor to cope with his grief: He wanted to "do" something. The wife sank into her grief, attempting to halt time and avoid confronting the issue head on. If the wife had taken a shovel to the yard, her actions would have seemed inappropriate. The two are acting according to acceptable behavior for their sex, and the gap in their communication can be attributed to the different expectations for each.

Near the end of the poem the wife recalls a conversation with her husband shortly after digging the baby's grave. She remembers his saying, "Three foggy mornings and one rainy day / Will rot the best birch fence a man can build," and is appalled at his ability not only to talk about "everyday concerns" but to spout maxims about rain and rotting. The earthly images of decay resonate with her pain; the word "rot" tears at her, as she draws a parallel to the baby that once lay in "the darkened parlor."

At this point Frost expresses an attitude that is also suggested in "Departmental" and "Out, Out—": "The nearest friends can go / With anyone to death, comes so far short / They might as well not try to go at all. No, from the time when one is sick to death, / One is alone, and he dies more alone. Friends make pretense of following to the grave, / But before one is in it, their minds are turned / And making the best of their way back to life / And living people, and things they understand." Frost seemed to meditate on this concept. There is a line between the living and the dead that cannot be crossed. At some point in the grieving process loved ones must return to life, because they cannot follow to the grave without dying themselves and their desire to live is usually stronger. In "Home Burial" the mother wants to follow, wants to be swallowed up by her pain, and finds her husband's return to life an offense.

Amy says "the world's evil. I won't have grief so / If I can change it"; Frost once said that after the loss of Elliot, Elinor repeatedly said the same: "The world's evil." The wife in the poem does not want to be the way others have been. She does not want to return to life; she does not want to pretend to follow her son to the grave; she wants to follow him completely, though she knows she cannot. She again repeats herself: "Oh, I won't, I won't!" Again Frost has inserted the word "oh," this time with a different connotation, the "oh" of despair. And the repetition of "I won't" is similar to the repeated "don't" from earlier in the poem.

The poem closes with a masculine image of aggression. The husband insists that he will not let her leave him, which would represent a figurative death, causing him to lose both his son and his wife. Instead he will take her "back by force" if he has to. She sardonically tells him that he "think[s] the talk is all," but the talk has meant nothing.

Communication is not about talk. It takes place on many levels, and while this poem is composed almost entirely of dialogue, the only real communication is between poet and reader. Speaking and hearing are entirely different things.

The poem ends without conclusion. There is fear in the husband's observation that someone is coming down the road, but it is unclear what the fear is for. Is it because someone will witness their disagreement? Because his wife will leave with this someone? Or because there is a threat, perhaps a danger of her running into the road? He also threatens her: "Where do you mean to go?" he inquires, implying that she has nowhere to go and alluding to her physical dependence on him. While there is a climax, there is no resolution: His "I *will!*—" does not end the poem; there is the ambiguity of that dash. Frost uses the dash here as Emily Dickinson, whose signature mark is the dash, often does—to suggest no end to this end (the dash has been used similarly throughout). Robert Faggen rightly asserts that the "proliferation of dashes in the last two parts indicates a world of emotional reality beyond words, a world that is actively, physically threatening" (225), and the same can be said of Frost's use of the dash throughout.

Katherine Kearns writes that the poem "epitomizes Frost's intimate relationships between sex, death, and madness" (90). The madness comes from death and is expressed differently by the two sexes. Frost relies heavily on traditional gender roles in his interpretation of grief. He may also be relying on his own experiences with Elinor and the death of Elliot. The loss of a child, a reversal of nature, can provoke a sort of madness. Here the madness is present in the characters' inability to communicate their feelings to each other or even to themselves. They are consumed by grief. Their grieving is personal—too personal to share. And speaking about it might make it too real to bear.

Frost once commented at a reading, in relation to another poem, that to a physician the loss of patient life might approach 5 percent of his total patients, a statistic, but the loss of a spouse is 100 percent, not at all a statistic. The loss seems total. It is overwhelming, immobilizing to the wife, and mobilizing to the husband. In either case they are left speechless, for there are some feelings well beyond words.

The words of this poem, the words that convey the failure of words, are for Frost a major achievement. This home burial was so close to home for Frost that he could not utter his own words; he would not read the poem publicly. *See* HOME, THEME OF.

FURTHER READING

Bentley, Louise. "You Think the Talk Is All (Robert Frost's Poetic Conversational Power)," *Robert Frost Review* (Fall 1992): 52–57.

Carroll, Rebecca. "A Reader-Response Reading of Robert Frost's 'Home Burial,'" *Text and Performance Quarterly* 10, no. 2 (April 1990): 143–156.

Cramer, Jeffrey S. *Robert Frost among His Poems: A Literary Companion to the Poet's Own Biographical Contexts and Associations*. Jefferson, N.C.: MacFarland, 1996.

Doyle, John Robert, Jr. *The Poetry of Robert Frost: An Analysis*. New York: Hafner Press, 1962, 35–39.

Faggen, Robert. *Robert Frost and the Challenge of Darwin*. Ann Arbor: University of Michigan Press, 1997, 215–225.

Jost, Walter. "Ordinary Language Brought to Grief: Robert Frost's 'Home Burial.'" *Ordinary Language Criticism: Literary Thinking after Cavell after Wittgenstein*, edited by Kenneth Duaber and Walter Jost, 77–114. Evanston: Northwestern University Press, 2003.

Kearns, Katherine. *Robert Frost and a Poetics of Appetite*. Cambridge: Cambridge University Press, 1994.

McInery, Stephen. "'Little Forms': Four Poems and a Developing Theme of Robert Frost," *Critical Review* 40 (2000): 59–74.

Meyers, Jeffrey. *Robert Frost: A Biography*. New York: Houghton Mifflin, 1996, 49–50.

Norwood, Kyle. "The Work of Not Knowing," *Southwest Review*. 78, no. 1 (Winter 1993): 57–73.

Parini, Jay. *Robert Frost: A Life*. New York: Holt, 1999.

Schiffbauer, Judith P. "Three Poems by Robert Frost: A Jamesian Reading," *Kentucky Philological Review* 8 (1993): 46–52.

Summerlin, Charles Timothy. "The Romantic Absolute in Frost's 'Home Burial,'" *Robert Frost Review* (Fall 1994): 53–57.

Timmerman, John H. *Robert Frost: The Ethics of Ambiguity*. Lewisburg, Pa.: Bucknell University Press, 2002, 162–164.

Vanderburg, Peter. "Prosody as Meaning in 'To the Thawing Wind' and 'Home Burial,'" *Robert Frost Review* (Fall 1994): 17–22.

"Housekeeper, The" (1914)

This dramatic tale, which Frost in a letter once referred to as "a tragedy" is written almost exclusively in dialogue and begins with an intriguing "I let myself in at the kitchen door" (Barry, 83). While we do not know who the speaker is, we anticipate the reaction of the person inside, since he enters seemingly uninvited. The woman inside is someone, by reason of age and considerable bulk, who is unable to move to answer the door, but whereas this first seems to be exclusively a physical limitation, she extends it to "I can no more / Let people in than I can keep them out." There is an implication of an emotional as well as physical limitation.

While the woman sits beading a pair of shoes for someone's daughter, the speaker says that he has come looking for someone named John. Coincidentally, John was on his way to the speaker's house, but he may have gone to Garland's instead, as Estelle, John's housekeeper and the woman's daughter, has "run off." The two enter into a discussion about John and his Estelle, the housekeeper whom he should have married, in her mother's view.

It has been two weeks since Estelle left, making it seem to these two that "[s]he's in earnest" about leaving. As is often the case in Frost, the conversation takes place without the markers of "he said" and "she said" that are common in prose. So while the narrative unfolds as in a play, the reader must make an effort to keep in mind which character speaks.

Estelle's mother does not have the ability to bring her daughter back, although John would like her to. The conversation turns to what John will do now that Estelle is gone, not because of his emotional attachment but because he will not eat if she is not there to prepare meals and provide other things he will need to get by. The focus on their relationship is a practical one. A man and the woman he should have married are dependent on each other for practical needs, not emotional ones.

The house the speaker has let himself into is John's and, in a sense, Estelle's; the mother simply lives with them. She has apparently been left behind until Estelle finds a new home, at which time Estelle will presumably retrieve her mother and leave John altogether. The mother's situation is near-helpless: "they can't get me through the door, though: / I've been built in here like a big church organ."

It becomes clear that the poem is about the breakdown of relationships and the resulting difficulty of everyday arrangements such as living and eating. Mother and friend wonder how John will get by with "nothing but the furniture." The conversation is thus far only concerned with things. The mother criticizes John, saying that in his despair over Estelle's departure "[h]e's just dropped everything. He's like a child," and she blames his having been brought up by his mother for that. They are rural folk; John is letting the hay be rained on, and they imagine will let other things go too. The mother declares that she has never seen a "man let family troubles / Make so much difference in his man's affairs."

Frost often depicts men and women who fit traditional family roles. That is, he sometimes manipulates stereotypes of sexual behavior with his characters, as he does in "Home Burial," where he takes up the subject of a man's and woman's different ways of grieving. Here there is a suggestion on the part of the mother that John should not let "family troubles" interfere with any of his business, but that it would be more acceptable if a woman were to. Men should show their strength and persistence in times of difficulty, whereas it is more acceptable for a woman to suffer emotionally from such problems.

While John has been depicted as simply hurt, there is a turn in the poem when the speaker asks the mother if she is afraid of John, and "What's the gun for?" Suddenly John's behavior holds the possibility of violence, as he has already thrown a hoe in the air, lodging it in an apple tree. This leads to more generalizations about "menfolk" who are often "threatener[s]," but John is not. She is not afraid. But John has "made up his mind not to stand / What he has got to stand." Estelle has left because if it was "bad to live with him / It must be right to leave him." The poem is fraught with aphorisms suggestive of more than are made of them in the poem, as these last two quotations demonstrate. It is as if Frost had thought of them separately, and found a way to work them in.

It turns out the strain has not been so much on John and Estelle's relationship as on the fact that they have not been married. We learn that John is "kinder than the run of men" but that he always thought "Better than married ought to be as good / As married," and suddenly the poem falls into the cliché "why buy the cow if you can have the milk for free?" John is presumed to have made a mistake in allowing Estelle to "think of something else." Marriage is ownership, and he has given up his ownership by not binding her through the ties of marriage. John saw no reason why they would need to be married, since "[w]hat was his was always hers" and there was no property to fight over. Estelle was always in control of the finances—"always held the purse"—eliminating that as a threat to their relationship.

Mother and daughter came to John's home for Estelle to do the housework, and both board there. Estelle is the housekeeper of the title, but she was not only a housekeeper. She did housework and outdoor work and kept the purse, giving John money when he needed it. And while John is a bad farmer, they both like nice things and have always managed to have better hens and cows and pigs than they would be expected to afford. They also have treated the animals kindly and would rather keep an animal because "If they're worth / That much to sell, they're worth as much to keep." John even purchased and imported a "Langshang cock" for 50 dollars, simply to have it.

The poem moves from Estelle's leaving to why she left. This affords myriad possibilities: John's not marrying her, his not being good with finances, their not having friends, and possibly to their not having children. The poem is not complex, but it is compelling in its ability to mimic an insignificant conversation. The poem wanders as does a conversation, while the thread that holds the conversation together, however loosely, remains.

Although it seems the two are figuring out why Estelle had to go, the mother reveals she knows all along why. She reveals that Estelle "won't come back . . . she can't," because she has married someone else. The poem keeps the reader's attention by doling out information piecemeal. The poem does not provide startling images, fascinating inquiries, or compelling conclusions. Instead, it functions as any conversation, only in this case, one speaker has more information than the other, and she withholds it until the time when it will have the most dramatic effect.

The poem becomes a study of two figures by two others who know them well: Estelle's mother, who has lived with John, and John's close friend. John is depicted as typical, as the mother seizes every opportunity to comment on manly behavior, going so far as to say, "men will be ridiculous." Estelle is depicted as a woman who wants a legal commitment so much that when all else is right, she will still abandon a relationship for it.

The title is ironic, diminishing the relationship between John and Estelle to one between housekeeper and employer. The poem is essentially gossip, on which the reader eavesdrops. The relationship among all characters lacks authenticity. John and Estelle have "agreements" about cooking and finances, but no expressions of love are recalled. Their relationship might even be considered strictly an occupational one, except for the comment that John could have married her to keep her from marrying someone else. The mother and the friend talk of the two, but again on a superficial level.

John Robert Doyle, Jr., explains that "Their affair has nothing of the great passion that violation of the mores must have to develop the daring which will ignore all else." And without this daring their living together in "sin" as an unmarried couple becomes more important than anything else about John and Estelle. Doyle goes on to say, "Estelle has all that would make her happy—if she did not have to live constantly with the fact that John has not bestowed upon her what society has called that 'honorable estate' of 'holy matrimony'" (126).

All relationships become agreements. Wives may be housekeepers and husbands earners, but marriage constitutes an end, not a beginning, and the reader is left with the resonant: "I wonder why he doesn't marry her / And end it."

"The Housekeeper" first appeared in the January 15, 1914, issue of the *Egoist* and later was collected in *North of Boston*.

FURTHER READING

Barry, Elaine. *Robert Frost on Writing.* New Brunswick, N.J.: Rutgers University Press, 1973, 83.

Doyle, John Robert, Jr. *The Poetry of Robert Frost: An Analysis.* New York: Hafner Press, 1962, 121–126.

"How Hard It Is to Keep from Being King When It's in You and in the Situation" (1962)

This poem has as its source a story from the 10th-century collection of folktales *Arabian Nights' Entertainments* or *The Thousand and One Nights*, tale C, section 12, titled "Tale of the King Who Kenned the Quintessence of Things."

The poem opens with the king no longer wanting the responsibility of being king. He offers the crown to his son the prince, but his son is not sure he wants the crown either, so the two let the crown crash to the ground, scattering its jewels. The prince has been "looking on" at the kingdom, a figure from the sidelines, and he does not "like / The looks of empire" either, so the two flee the kingdom together.

The king (or ex-king) and prince take on the "guise of men" rather than royalty, highlighting the distinction between the two, in order to escape. They have not gone far when they rest, gazing up at the stars. The ex-king fears he will be returned to his "fate," to ruling his empire, since he views his kingly character as being in him and in the situation. When "it's in you," it is not something that can be gotten away from. He can run, but he cannot get away from what is inherent. The ex-king uses Julius Caesar as an example of how difficult it can be to escape fate: "[h]e couldn't keep himself from being King / He had to be stopped by the sword of Brutus," he says, and his lines suggest a foreshadowing.

The king and the prince soon realize they are penniless, and the ex-king suggests that his son sell him at the slave auction to remedy their financial situation. He imagines his sale will be enough for the Prince to begin a "business" or to make "verse if that is what you're bent on. / Don't let your father tell you what to be." This is ironic, and Frost is quite intentional. Few parents encourage their children to become poets, especially as a way of making a living. More likely is the advice to the speaker in Lorine Niedecker's poem "Poet's Work", "Grandfather / advised me: Learn a trade." In fact, Frost's grandfather, William Prescott Frost, Sr., offered to help the young Frost try to become a successful poet by supporting him financially over a period of about a year. Frost is supposed to have replied: "Give me twenty! Give me twenty!" And 20 years was just about how long it took him to become successful. As Jay Parini says, his estimation "proved uncannily accurate" (46): He was 39 when *A Boy's Will* came out.

The ex-king is sent to the market to be sold, but the first buyer cannot imagine what use he would be. Again, there is irony in Frost's words. The man who can run an empire seems at first glance to be of little practical use. The ex-king assures his prospective buyer that he knows "the *Quint*essence of many things," including food, jewels, horses, men, and women, and this is his royal selling point. While the meaning of "*quint*essence" is not entirely clear, it is impressive enough for him to be sold and sent "off to Xanadu to help the cook." Frost is having fun with the name, as Xanadu is the fictitious kingly palace in Samuel Taylor Coleridge's poem "Kubla Khan."

In Xanadu the ex-king begins work for another king and quickly impresses the latter not only with his cooking ability but with other abilities as well. The king needs help deciding between a large pearl and a smaller costly one, and someone thinks of the "kitchen slave" and seeks his guidance in putting an "end to the King's vacillation." The slave cook, the ex-king, is summoned since he claims to know the *quint*essence of things, and he once again proves himself worthy. He reveals great knowledge, aiding the king in making a clever decision on which pearl to purchase.

And "so it went with triumph after triumph" until one day the king summons the ex-king to ask him questions of a more thoughtful nature: "What ails me? Tell me. Why am I unhappy?" The ex-king arrives at his answer quickly. The King is not happy because he is "not where [he] belong[s]." The king is "not a King / Of royal blood"; his "father was a cook," and this is the simple explanation for his unhappiness. He is not doing what he was "fated" to do—he has somehow disrupted the natural order of things, and to this he owes his unhappiness. The king threatens the ex-king with death for the lie, until he seeks confirmation from his mother and learns that the preposterous assertion is actually true.

Until now the poem has required little explication, but at this point all of the subtleties in the text and the ironies of meaning begin to reveal themselves. Just as the king is exposed as the son of a cook, the ex-king, at present a cook, will soon be exposed as a king of true royal blood, and Frost's meaning and purpose for the poem will bubble to the surface.

At this point the poem begins to resemble a Socratic dialogue, in which the ex-king and king, and soon the prince as well, engage. The prince's role seems to be akin to the chorus of classical Greek literature: He provides commentary on the scene.

When the king returns from learning of his birth, he seeks an explanation for how the ex-king knew he was not of "royal blood." The ex-king declares that the king had only rewarded him for his food. The King's "one idea was food," and this was his giveaway. The ex-king knew that the King's father must have been a cook, because all he thinks about for his people is feeding them. That is, the ex-king judges the king's heritage by his habits. The king sees in his charity an act of giving, but the ex-king maintains that he has to give more than food to his subjects; he also has to give character.

The king calls himself "abject before" the ex-king and seeks instruction from him. He becomes the pupil in a Socratic fashion, admiring the ex-king and engaging in inquiry about grand ideas. From the discussion of character, the two quickly turn to the question of freedom; the king continues as pupil and the ex-king as a kind of Socratic

teacher. The prince, suddenly appearing "in rags" and with a "lyre," quickly enters the discussion.

The ex-king shares that his son was to make himself a poet on the money made from his own sale into slavery, "If such a thing is possible with money." But it seems money was not enough, which comes as no real surprise. His son has instead been begging "through the Seven Cities / Where Homer begged." (Homer was the Greek epic poet who wrote *The Odyssey* and *The Iliad*.) The ex-king refers to his son's situation several times in language suggestive of fate, claiming that "he may have to turn to something / to earn a living" and that he "want[s] him to be anything he has to."

Frost, who publicly criticized free verse on numerous occasions, has the ex-king explain that his son "writes free verse," or so he is told. One of Frost's best-known statements about free verse is that it is like "playing tennis with the net down." He disapproved of the lack of structure and formal rhyme. Here it may account for the prince's failure as a poet.

As the discussion of freedom continues, the ex-king states that some poets say that "Freedom is slavery," and it is clear that this is a reference to the lack of freedom in being vulnerable to fate, which has been an underlying theme throughout. The ex-king says that "The only certain freedom's in departure," implying that one has the freedom, if any, to make a choice about whether or not to refrain from being whatever it is that is "in you and in the situation." The ex-king resolves that "The problem for the King is just how strict / The lack of liberty, the squeeze of law / And discipline should be in school and state / To insure a jet departure of our going."

The king is further disheartened. He feels the "facility" at the ex-King's hands makes him more worthy of kingship than himself. The prince says not to "let him fool" him, as the ex-king is "a King already." Being a king is not something one can cease to do. But, as the son says, "he makes mistakes." One important mistake is that the prince is "not a free-verse singer": He "write[s] real verse in numbers," that is, blank verse in rhyme and meter. The son is kinder to free verse than Frost was known to have been, holding that it "has its beauty" even though he does not write it. He even admits that because he does not write it, that maybe he should not pass judgment on it.

The question of artistic freedom is the subject to which the prince has turned, and as he makes his way through his discussion of verse, he moves to "freedom" poets Walt Whitman and Carl Sandburg and to the Greeks. Whitman and Sandburg are criticized for their free-verse styles (Sandburg's has been described as Whitman-like), but Whitman is also criticized for his bohemianism and sexual proclivities, which represent another kind of freedom of which the prince could not approve.

The prince has a different take on things than might be expected. He claims that the freedom Whitman, Sandburg, and the Greeks seek is "by politics"; it is not real freedom, the freedom that artists need. In other words, free verse is really not free at all. Artists need a freedom that is not public but private, the "freedom of their own material," "never at a loss in simile" but always having the "exact affinity / Of anything they are confronted with." That precision, that moment of enlightenment comes "out of nowhere like a jinni." (In Muslim legend a jinni is a spirit often capable of assuming human or animal form and exercising supernatural influence over people.) This is his notion of departure, a leave-taking in the senses, something akin to the effect of "wine" or "love," a sort of "well-being in the body." It is the "Freedom to flash off into wild connections." This, the prince imagines, must be what his father meant by departure.

As the poem begins to draw to a close, the prince, having lost himself, having made his own wild connections, wonders where they are, and concludes it is "in transition / Changing an old King for another old one."

Ultimately, if the only freedom is in departure, then the ex-king is not free at all. The prince knows that his "father's in for what [they] ran away from." His father "blames the stars" or fate, referring to them for an explanation, but does not realize that his choices and habits have determined what has happened to him. It is all "[f]or looking on and not participating."

The prince concludes that the ex-king owes it to his own actions for the outcome, as it was "his display / Of more than royal attributes" that "betrayed

him." The poem closes with a return to the title, which has been stated previously in the poem: "How hard it is to keep from being king / When it's in you and in the situation."

The lengthy poem, very much a Socratic dialogue toward the end, shares something with the Greek myth of Oedipus. Oedipus fled home, attempting to avoid his fate as decreed by the oracle, and in doing so helped create his own fate. The ex-king flees his home to escape being king, but his kingly character leads him back to where he began.

Frost constructs a poem around the subject of free will, debating whether there is such a thing or whether when it's "in us" our fates are predetermined. He concludes glumly that this "is half the trouble with the world / (Or more than half I'm inclined to say)," as if the trouble is in its being in us, rather than in our betraying our attributes.

The piece seems to be largely about being a poet. It lapses into a discussion of poetry and free verse when the prince begins to speak about freedom, but even without that diversion, one of the poem's main concerns is whether poets are born or made and whether "it" is in the situations that poets take up or in the poets themselves. Frost has an opportunity to philosophize, speaking through the prince to express his ideas about poetry. There are also suggestions in the poem of the poet as ruler, the poet as king. After all, Frost, classically educated, knew that Plato banned poets from his utopian state for fear of their strange power.

The poem was written in 1950 and first published in the *Proceedings of the American Academy of Arts and Letters and the National Institute of Arts and Letters* (second series, number one, 1951). It was also published as "Hard Not to Be King" that year in a limited edition of 300 copies by House of Books, Ltd. It was later collected in *In the Clearing.* See MYTHOLOGY AND FOLKLORE and STARS.

FURTHER READING

Cramer, Jeffrey S. *Robert Frost among His Poems: A Literary Companion to the Poet's Own Biographical Contexts and Associations.* Jefferson, N.C.: MacFarland, 1996.

Finnegan, Sister Mary Jeremy. "Frost Remakes an Ancient Story." In *Frost: Centennial Essays,* edited by Jac L. Tharpe, et al. 389–397. Jackson: University Press of Mississippi, 1974.

Hoffman, Tyler. *Robert Frost and the Politics of Poetry.* Hanover, N.H.: Middlebury College Press, 2001, 201–204.

Parini, Jay. *Robert Frost: A Life.* New York: Holt, 1999.

"Hundred Collars, A" (1914)

"A Hundred Collars" was first published in the December 1913 issue of *Poetry and Drama* and later appeared in *North of Boston.* One of many narratives in that volume, the poem is made up largely of dialogue. It opens by focusing on a little town named Lancaster that "bore" a "great man."

The man is someone the town does not see much, as he has apparently moved away, but he keeps the old place and sends his children to Lancaster with his wife to "run wild in the summer—a little wild" and sometimes joins them for a few days to see old friends "he somehow can't get near." He is such a great man that those in Lancaster "seem afraid" of him, and this difference in kind is what keeps them estranged. But the man does not welcome this reaction. He is a "great scholar," but he is also a "democrat / If not at heart, at least on principle," so he wants to treat his peers and be treated by them democratically. This depiction creates class and education distinctions, distinctions familiar in Frost's poetry, between the man and the people of his upbringing. This characterization forms the man and can be relied on for information as the events unfold.

The opening stanza ends by placing the man in "Woodsville Junction," where the rest of the poem plays out, having been delayed by a train on his way to Lancaster and being left to take a room for the night. The dialogue begins when the night clerk at the hotel speaks: "No room . . . unless—." The dash forms a clear hesitation, carefully mimicking natural speech.

The description of Woodsville is brief but memorable: "a place of shrieks and wandering lamps / And cars that shock and rattle—and *one* hotel." The description is suggestive of a haunted town, a ghost town, and the poem takes on an eerie cast.

The man is offered a room to share with someone, and he inquires who it is. "A man's a man" the clerk explains, offering an evasive platitude in lieu of detail. There is a man sleeping in the lobby who was "afraid of being robbed or murdered" and refused the room, but the great man says he needs a bed and goes along with the clerk, following him up the stairs to the room. When the two accidental roommates are introduced, Lafe, the other man, says he is not afraid because he is not "so drunk" he cannot defend himself. Two men, neither trusting the other, are thrust into an unexpected situation of sharing. Frost highlights the natural tendency to mistrust strangers and the discomfort caused by unfamiliar surroundings.

The great man, Doctor Magoon, seems to be a professor, and after introductions the two enter into mundane conversation. Lafe talks about how he has gone up a shirt size and asks the Doctor what size he wears. The doctor is much smaller, and Lafe recalls that he must have a "hundred collars," shirt collars in size 14—hence the title to the poem. He wants to send the shirts to the doctor, and it seems the two have gotten off to an amicable start. But the mistrust is thick, and it soon reenters the conversation.

The doctor makes Lafe nervous by standing about and is urged to go to bed. Lafe offers to take his shoes off, and the doctor says "don't touch me, please," reminding the reader of the physical threat to privacy when sharing space with a stranger. The difference between the two men is noticeable in their language, and Lafe comments on it when he says the doctor "talk[s] like a professor." Lafe also articulates their fears: "Speaking of who's afraid of who," he says.

The tension builds as they reveal what they have worth stealing: Lafe has 90 dollars and the doctor has five; unexpectedly, the great man has less money. But Lafe says, "Who wants to cut your number fourteen throat," and the mention of such an act and the description, even if in the negative, is threatening. Lafe is the instigator of all such talk. He repeatedly points to their situation by speaking of their lack of trust for each other and offers up violent descriptions of the possibilities.

Lafe works as a collector for the *Weekly News* and says that if the doctor knows the paper, then he knows Lafe. Occupation equals the man, it seems. Lafe proceeds to speak of his job, how he is a democrat, and what he likes about his work: "the lay of different farms" in different seasons, as he describes it. The doctor says, "they might not be as glad / To see you as you are to see them" when Lafe talks about going house to house, and that is because he is looking for their money. But Lafe dismisses the doctor's comment, as he never wants what "they've not got"—a democratic sentiment.

The poem comes to an anticlimactic end, when Lafe takes a drink and heads out, and the Doctor slides "a little down the pillow." The narrative has followed a pattern of need, fear, trust, and resolve in the meeting of two strangers. The poem shows that differences become inconsequential in such a situation and that similarities, which are few, seem to have some significance in the end. Frost makes a point of mentioning that both men are democrats, and this sense of democracy, as mentioned in the opening stanza, ultimately explains how they get along.

Frost distinguishes between social democracy and political democracy, and the poem bears out that the doctor and Lafe are both democrats, "If not at heart, at least on principle"—on principle of pragmatism perhaps.

FURTHER READING

Doyle, John Robert, Jr. *The Poetry of Robert Frost: An Analysis.* New York: Hafner Press, 1962, 103–112.

Faggen, Robert. *Robert Frost and the Challenge of Darwin.* Ann Arbor: University of Michigan Press, 1997, 143–148.

Kearns, Katherine. *Robert Frost and a Poetics of Appetite.* Cambridge: Cambridge University Press, 1994, 27–28.

"Hyla Brook" (1916)

Hyla was the name of a brook on Frost's farm in Derry, New Hampshire. "Hyla Brook" was written there and published in *Mountain Interval.* Frost once wrote that the brook "always dried up in summer." The poet makes several references to this brook in his poetry, including one that may be found in "Going for Water."

Frost wrote that the "Hyla is a small frog that shouts like jingling bells in the marshes in the spring" (Cramer, 49) and he makes this same reference in the poem. The speaker explains that by June the brook slows, losing the rush and sound of spring. It either goes underground, taking with it the frogs that "shouted in the mist a month ago, / Like ghost of sleigh-bells in a ghost of snow," or it comes up elsewhere, in "jewel-weed." Jewelweed, also called balsam and touch-me-not (Frost knew his botany), is a plant that has yellowing spurred flowers and seedpods that dehisce into five valves when mature. The heat of the summer sun makes the bed of the brook so brittle and dry that the dead leaves stick together and it appears to be "a faded paper sheet."

The poem closes with a reminder that it is only the memories of those who witnessed its "song and speed" who can "love the things we love for what they are." Robert Hass writes that "Although the brook has literally disappeared, one can find it again if one is willing to accept the proposition that the brook survives in sustained moments of imaginative reverie, where all of the particulars of transience can be subordinated to an abstract permanence of continual change" (81). It is our remembering that allows us to overcome loss and allows things to go on eternally. We provide the vital links that allow those temporary things to continue to exist.

Hass also considers the poem a possible metaphor for the act of writing a poem. Or it might be considered not only a metaphor for the writing of a single poem but also a metaphor for creativity itself. Poetry can arise as swiftly as song comes to the songbird, but when it dries up, it goes underground, leaving a blank "faded paper sheet" and the remembrance of the things we love for what they are.

FURTHER READING

Bacon, Helen H. "'Getting among the Poems in Horace's Fons Bandusiae and Robert Frost's Hyla Brook," *Classical and Modern Literature: A Quarterly,* 14, no. 3 (Spring 1994): 259–267.

Borroff, Marie. "Robert Frost: 'To Earthward.'" *In Frost: Centennial Essays II*, edited by Jac Tharpe, 21–39. Jackson: University Press of Mississippi, 1976.

Brower, Reuben A. *The Poetry of Robert Frost: Constellations of Intention*. New York: Oxford University Press, 1963, 81–83.

Cramer, Jeffrey S. *Robert Frost among His Poems: A Literary Companion to the Poet's Own Biographical Contexts and Associations*. Jefferson, N.C.: MacFarland, 1996.

Hass, Robert. *Going by Contraries: Robert Frost's Conflict with Science*. Charlottesville: University Press of Virginia, 2002, 80–84.

Meyers, Jeffrey. *Robert Frost: A Biography*. New York: Houghton Mifflin, 1996, 137–138.

Pack, Robert. *Belief and Uncertainty in the Poetry of Robert Frost*. Hanover, N.H.: Middlebury College Press, 2003.

"I Could Give All to Time" (1942)

The speaker of this poem could give all to time, but it is clear that he never would. The opening stanza describes Time, personifying him as one who is modest. Time does not think he is brave when he pits himself against great natural occurrences, such as snow and water, which are juxtaposed as the temperate and extreme of the same element. Time is moderate and grave about the things he sets himself against, instead of gloating or being proud and exhilarated, as he might.

In the second stanza the speaker imagines the effect that time will have on the land. He says that what "now is inland shall be ocean isle," imagining a shift in land mass. The speaker aligns himself with Time, suspecting that such a shift would not bring him joy any more than it brings it to Time. He would be moderate and unresponsive as well; he would share a "lack of joy or grief."

In the final stanza the poem returns to the title, drawing more attention to the word *could*. The first line of the stanza is the poem's title, and then "except" is inserted and repeated. The speaker

clarifies that while he could, he will not give all to Time. He could give all, except what he has "held." It is unclear what has been held but the reader knows that while the speaker could share Time's lack of joy or grief for a "planetary change of style," he cannot share the same for his own change of "style."

The speaker wants to keep what he has and not be transformed by time. He implies that he has gotten around Time somehow. He draws an analogy to "Customs," capitalizing it and speaking of things to "declare." He has somehow, as a foreigner or a fugitive, gotten past the authorities and crossed to "Safety" with what he wants to keep, and so far he has kept it. He is "There," presumably on the other side, wherever that is, and this means that he will not give all to Time.

While Time never seems brave, the speaker is when he challenges Time. He is also skillful because he has managed to avoid Time in some important sense. Time is indifferent to the changes it brings; it has no real investment, it just is. But the speaker has an investment and will not give all except when forced, for he will not part with what he has "kept." What he holds is internal, private, everlasting. It will withstand Time.

The poem was collected in *A Witness Tree* but had previously appeared in a 1941 issue of the *Yale Review*.

FURTHER READING

Brogunier, Joseph. "Frost Homage to Melville at 'The Frontiers into Eternity,'" *Melville Society Extracts* 77 (May 1989): 14–15.

Poirier, Richard. *Robert Frost: The Work of Knowing*. New York: Oxford University Press, 1977.

"Imagining Ear, The" (1915)

"The Imagining Ear" was taken from notes that George H. Browne, headmaster of the Browne and Nichols School, took during a lecture Frost gave on May 10, 1915. Frost often spoke about tone in poetry and made a great effort to import the tones of natural speech into his poems, particularly his dramatic narratives. He begins by talking about the attention that is brought to the poet with "extraordinarily vivid sight" and wants to bring attention to the "equally valuable" ear. We all hear tones in speech, but Frost speaks of the problem or difficulty of "get[ting] them down in writing."

Frost attempts to move the schoolboys away from "simple, compound, and complex sentences" and toward the "*living* sounds of speech." He urges them to "note tones of irony, acquiescence, doubt etc. in the farmer's 'I guess so.'" He asks them how "can you get these down on paper? How *do* you tell the tone?"

Frost says, "I went to church, once." He uses his experience in church as a way of explaining that the tones he heard in the repetition of "Nows" were a predictable and "mechanical repetition." Church is, evidently, not the place to go for living speech. Instead he urges the students to "[g]et the *stuff* of life" into their writing, the "ACTION" of the voice.

He uses as an example the second stanza of his first professionally published poem, "My Butterfly: An Elegy." He can "recall distinctly the joy with which [he] had the first satisfaction of getting an expression adequate for [his] thought." He was so "delighted that [he] had to cry." He then quotes "The Pasture" as an example, providing in the margin descriptions of the tone, and gives a similar demonstration with "Mending Wall."

Frost closes with advice for the young schoolboys: "Gather your sentences by ear, and reimagine them in your writing." He followed his own advice. In the subtleties of tone in such poems as "Home Burial," his greatest contributions to American poetry are highlighted.

"Immigrants" (1928)

This iambic pentameter quatrain was collected in *West-Running Brook*, but it first appeared as the fourth stanza of "The Return of the Pilgrims," a poem included in George P. Baker's *The Pilgrim Spirit* (1921).

The poem asserts that no ship, whether by "sail or steam," has gathered more people to America's shores than the *Mayflower*, the ship on which the Pilgrims sailed to America in 1620. Frost uses it as a symbol of his optimism and hope for all immigrants who travel to the shores of his immigrant nation.

The *Mayflower* symbolically accompanies all immigrant ships to American shores "in a dream" that was also the dream of its original passengers. The *Mayflower* joins the ships to create a "convoy" of protection and aid. The dream of the *Mayflower*'s protection may exist in the minds of the immigrants at sea or in the mind of the poet, who wishes them well. In either case the journey to America is presented as a magical one that could lead to perhaps the most romantic of all immigrant dreams: the American Dream.

FURTHER READING

Cramer, Jeffrey S. *Robert Frost among His Poems: A Literary Companion to the Poet's Own Biographical Contexts and Associations.* Jefferson, N.C.: MacFarland, 1996.

"Importer, An" (1947)

First published with the title "The Importer" in the April 1947 issue of the *Atlantic Monthly* and later included in *Steeple Bush* as an "editorial," Frost is being satirical and more than a bit sarcastic, albeit as usual with a certain slyness, in this poem. America had quickly learned to mass-produce its inventions (Frost grew up in that period of invention and development) and was thought by many to have lost touch with old values and traditional craftsmanship.

Frost adopts his best down-home Yankee pose: "Mrs. Somebody," he almost snarls, meaning that she must really be somebody to have gone all the way to Asia (rhymes with "amaze ye") and brought back all those ancient artifacts that the Asians must be mass-producing by the carload to sell to the Mrs. Somebody's of the Western world. It seems that Yankee ingenuity, in discovering something more than widgets, has nothing to teach them. Might as well try to teach your grandmother how to suck eggs. According to Brewer's Dictionary of

Phrase and Fable, the phrase "tell your grandmother to suck eggs" was originally said derisively to someone who tried to teach his elders or those more experienced than himself, so it is an apt choice on Frost's part for the opinions set forth here.

"Sacred rigmaroles to mutter" pokes fun at mantras. "Subterfuge for saving faces" would be interpreted by the more race-sensitive academies of today as an unacceptable caricature of Asians as indirect and often downright "sneaky" (because of the attack on Pearl Harbor, the Japanese were frequently portrayed that way during World War II). Saving face is important in Asian societies, but Frost seems to treat the subject dismissively.

Frost betrays his chauvinism and his superior attitude toward Asia that borders on contemptuous. Whether he is tongue-in-cheek is questionable. Note that among the list of "imports" there is nothing so Yankee practical as the automobile or the safety razor. Frost is ever the pragmatist—and the patriot.

FURTHER READING

Evans, Ivor H. *Brewer's Dictionary of Phrase and Fable.* Centenary ed., revised. New York: Harper & Row, 1981.

"In a Disused Graveyard" (1923)

The poem takes place in an uncommon setting for Frost: a graveyard. This graveyard is no longer in use but is not abandoned. It is still kept up, since the living come with "grassy tread" to the gravestones that remain on the hill. The speaker remarks that the "graveyard draws the living still, / But never any more the dead." The living come to pay their respects to their ancestors, friends, and family. So while the dead are no longer buried here, the graveyard has not been in "disuse" for very long, as there are still living reminders of those who have passed.

In the second stanza the speaker turns to the "verses" inscribed on the stones that say, "The ones

who living come today / To read the stones and go away / Tomorrow dead will come to stay." The verses echo the voices of the dead who are buried there. The focus is the cyclical nature of life and the inevitability of death. The dead come, decompose, and leave behind only the stone's verses.

The third stanza comments on the rhyme of the verse: "So sure of death the marbles rhyme," as if rhyming indicated certainty. But it also indicates a sort of leisure, the time to rhyme and make play of what "men are shrinking from." The marble stones, being more informed about death by being constantly around it, are so certain that death will come that they are surprised that no dead have come recently; because the stones are trapped and immovable, they have no way of knowing or finding out why.

In the closing the speaker remarks that it would be "easy to be clever" and tell the gravestones simply that "[m]en hate to die" and therefore "have stopped dying now and forever." There is partial truth in what he says. Men do shrink from death, "hate" death, because they fear it. They hate to die but know they cannot stop it. The speaker knows that this truth about our fear of death would be hidden by his lie that people have stopped dying, and he thinks it would be fun to tease the stones. The stones, as symbols of those who were once so averse to dying, would willingly believe the lie, since the dead no longer come.

The irony comes in the question the stones ask. They do not understand why men are afraid; the poem is presenting a human view of death. The stones understand the living's attitude toward death, since they still draw the living, their sorrow and their pain. They know how much men hate to die, but they are indifferent to these feelings.

"In a Disused Graveyard" was collected in *New Hampshire* but had previously been published in the August 1923 issue of the *Measure*.

FURTHER READING

Beacham, Walton. "Technique and the Sense of Play in the Poetry of Robert Frost." In *Frost: Centennial Essays II,* edited by Jac Tharpe, 246–261. Jackson: University Press of Mississippi, 1976.

Jarrell, Randall. *Poetry and the Age.* New York: Vintage, 1955.

"In a Glass of Cider" (1962)

"In a Glass of Cider," one of the last poems in Frost's final volume, *In The Clearing,* shows the poet at his playful best. Frost once wrote a letter saying that a friend of his had told him he "was non-elatable." He went on to say that his wife Elinor balked at such a comment: "What a lie. You can't talk in public or private without getting elated. You never write but from elation" (Cramer, 178).

In this poem the speaker seems absolutely elated as he equates elation with bubbles in a glass of cider. When he is elated, he rides a bubble to the top of the glass by catching one in ascent. He posits himself as "a mite of sediment" that waits for the "bottom to ferment" before riding up astride a bubble. That is elation.

Optimistically, when the bubbles burst, the speaker does not have to be destroyed as he sinks back toward the bottom. He considers himself "no worse off than [he] was at first." After all, there is more elation to come, and he can "catch another bubble" if he just waits. The poem concludes resolutely: "The thing was to get now and then elated."

The poem is optimistic and humorous about the ups and downs of life. We may be mites at the bottom of a cider glass, scurrying around in sediment waiting for just one idea or passion to "ferment," but we also have bubbles in our lives that cause us to be elated, and when those bubbles burst we are not any worse off. The bubbles keep on coming.

FURTHER READING

Cramer, Jeffrey S. *Robert Frost among His Poems: A Literary Companion to the Poet's Own Biographical Contexts and Associations.* Jefferson, N.C.: MacFarland, 1996.

In an Art Factory

Frost's intentions are indicated by the title of this play. Certainly art is not produced in factories. The play opens by introducing Tony and Blanche, who are in a cold, badly lit "barn-like studio" at night.

Tony is finding his way toward the gas heat with a match. He finds it and lights it, but the cap on the chimney is gone so the heat does not work. He begins talking about Krail, who does not keep up the building; Blanche once posed for Krail as "Mary with the Body of Christ." "Old Peasley" played Christ and got to lie across her lap to make his ribs prominent. Blanche worked at getting into character so hard that she "went to mass every day to get into the spirit of it." She says she "hated" posing, and Tony chimes in, "And damn it, I hate it still." But Blanche believes he hates everything.

Tony is presented as a crotchety old man who is fed up and frustrated about something he is not ready to articulate. It seems the argument began when Blanche claimed that models deserve all the credit for artwork. Blanche urges Tony to share what is on his mind, but though he is tempted, he decides that he will let her "think it out" for herself.

There are three shrouded figures in the room, and Tony uncovers one, planning to tell Blanche what he thinks of it before a man named Campbell "comes to take her over." Campbell has a reputation, because once he touches the figure it will be "Campbellized," "nationalized," and "commercialized." For now, it is still Tony's, and Tony made her.

Tony's fondness for the figure incites Blanche's jealousy, and she flippantly says "[m]ake love to her. I don't care" and supposes that the figure is Evelyn Dace.

While the discussion begins in jealousy it is not long before Frost starts to make room for philosophizing. Tony argues that the artwork is "made truer" than the Evelyn who posed. It is not prettier than she is but more true. Blanche insists that she is more "beautiful" and insists that Tony say so, but he clarifies that she is only more beautiful "if [Blanche] understand[s] what [he] mean[s] by the word." "Beauty is truth," he suggests she might say, making a direct allusion to the final couplet of the romantic poet John Keats's "Ode on a Grecian Urn": "Beauty is truth, truth beauty,—that is all / Ye know on earth, and all ye need to know." But Tony continues to say "But beauty is just beauty too. There is the beauty of truth and the beauty of beauty." The continuation both simplifies Keats's lines and complicates them. The beauty of beauty, Tony explains, "is a kind of specialized beauty that we find isolated where any fool can see it in youth and health and models." He equates this beauty with Campbell's sculpture and later with craftsmen as differentiated from artists.

Campbell emerges as Tony's "business agent." His job has been to take Tony's "soul to market." This line is reminiscent of Emily Dickinson's poem that begins: "Publication—is the auction / Of the Mind of Man—." Tony creates and Campbell sells, and for this Tony "can't forgive him" because Campbell "alienate[s]" the work Tony creates. The studio in which Tony and Blanche stand is referred to as a "Genius Asylum or the Unknown Artists' Home." Tony is not an artist in his own right. He is, according to Blanche's description, a "fatted slave," but one who should be grateful to have the privilege "to go to Hell in his own way." At least he is making a living as an artist, even if it means surrendering his art to Campbell's hand.

Tony describes the Evelyn sculpture as "so good—that [he] shall never go as far again." He lights a torch and Blanche thinks he might destroy it. In the meantime, Blanche lifts another shroud and unveils a statue that Tony describes as "a dead thing." The Greek god Zeus was mad about mortal women, and Tony explains why: "Manhood reaches its height in immortal gods, womanhood reaches its depth in mortal maids. Gods are better than men but women are better than goddesses. That's why the gods couldn't let women alone."

"She's you," Tony says to Blanche, becoming unexpectedly affectionate. Blanche quickly dismisses the comment, saying "And a lot of other women." Frost seems to account for one of the difficulties of an artist's rendition here when he has Tony respond: "If women are mixed in our minds we're sorry. . . . [T]his is all you where it counts."

Talk turns to Campbell and how he will alter Tony's sculpture with a "correction" of the lip or an alteration in the eyelid to make it just right. The suggestion is that art that is mass-produced, or rather, produced for the masses, is brought to "perfection" by making it more realistic. Such art does not "deviat[e] the least bit for frailty." Tony concludes that Campbell will take Blanche "out of it," and since she is the piece, it will no longer be art. Blanche wants to plead with Campbell not to alter the sculpture, but Tony insists that he will be unable to "see what there would be to spare." Campbell does not have an artist's eye. Campbell can "only see the beautiful," but Tony sees "the defective, the tragic," which becomes the sole gift of the artist.

The conversation leads to a distinction between craftsmen and artists, and Tony clarifies that only an artist can tell the difference between the two. Blanche finds this funny, because she thinks it is about comparing two certainties. To her, comparing certainties is absurd because it is impossible to tell which certainty is more certain. Tony says you can tell the difference, and he refers to the biblical story of Solomon to make his point: "the same way Solomon found out who was the real parent—by threatening the child." Tony knows he is an artist and not a craftsman because he feels for his artwork as if it were his "own flesh and blood." The judgment between the two cannot be based on feelings, he says; it must be based on how the creator behaves. The conversation has become heated, and Tony believes that Blanche is accusing him now of being a craftsman. But she denies that, insisting, "I believed in you before you believed in yourself."

Tony persists in frustration, returning to the initial question of where art comes from. He says that "posies," those who pose for artists, think it comes from them and that Campbell thinks it comes from him, but that the real claim is that of the newspaper writers, who "make the artist and his art out of whole cloth." The suggestion, of course, is that an artist is not an artist until someone else identifies him as such, and this subtly reveals one of Frost's own insecurities about his poetry. Throughout his life he sought more and more recognition, never quite satisfied with what he had achieved. Indeed, a great disappointment came when he was near death and learned that once again the Nobel prize had escaped him. In 1963 John Steinbeck won, and Frost realized that "this, the ultimate accolade, would be denied him" (Parini, 440).

"With a gesture of concession," Tony says to Blanche, "You be my Beatrice—my Ann Rutledge." The first reference is to Dante Alighieri's (1265–1321) muse Beatrice, the second to the alleged fiancée of President Abraham Lincoln (1809–65). Blanche dismisses the romantic gesture saying, "You'll find me easier to kill than love." Playfully Tony responds with a French intonation, "sentimentahl," and the two begin speaking this way for a few beats.

As the play begins to draw to a close, Tony declares that Blanche has revealed herself as one of the public who does not know "the right thing to say to an artist." The only right things Tony has heard, he claims, he put in the mouths of the people who spoke them. They have spent the night trying to provide definitions, and Blanche says that "what's needed is a definition of [Tony]." She says that she knows what is the matter with him and it is two things: First, he is suffering from having loved his sculpture too much, and second he is breaking down his "feminine barriers . . . coarsening as a woman has to coarsen to stand a husband" and "being born some more," which is "supposed to hurt."

Blanche also asserts that Tony does not mind Campbell so much, which leads Tony to reveal that "an artist wants a public, the more public the better. But he lives in resentment toward their ways of mistaking him. He resists coarsening to them." This opinion is echoed in several of Frost's more directed statements about this poetry, such as when he said that "Stopping by Woods on a Snowy Evening" was overinterpreted and overread.

The drama reaches its climax when Tony announces that he is "undergoing [his] change . . . [l]ike a snake sloughing its skin." He returns to the ideas expressed at the beginning of the play, where he declared that he has done all he can do, there is nothing to take further in his art, when he asks, "What's there to do that I haven't done—except kill you or—make you watch me kill myself"? And then the play builds toward a blaze. Like the "Roman father that slew his daughter before he would see her violated by his prince," Tony destroys the sculpture, and the play ends in "Murder." The reference is to the story in book three of Titus Livius (59 B.C.–17 A.D.) of Vergineus and his daughter

Verginia. Tony has destroyed his beloved sculpture rather than allow her to be altered or taken from him.

Frost wrote in the holograph notebook in which this play appears that he had written the play years before and kept it for publication and presentation, planning to complete one or two more as companions. He further admits that it is "easy to see what I have been antagonized by all along. I moved the theme off into another art—for objectivity I suppose" (Poirier and Richardson, 995n). He also identifies Campbell as formed from conversations with sculptor Alfeo Faggi, sculptor and writer Lorado Taft, sculptor Aroldo du Chêne (who made a bust of Frost in 1920), and painter James Chapin (who made drawings of some of Frost's children).

Frost was antagonized by the public he sought because it took his art from him and made it its own. As he wrote in "The Lesson for Today" and as is written on his gravestone, he had a "lover's quarrel with the world." The love/hate relationship is revealed through the endless contradictions found throughout his work and through his continued attempt to clarify definitions and reconcile differing opinions, as evidenced here.

FURTHER READING

Parini, Jay. *Robert Frost: A Life.* New York: Holt, 1999.

Poirier, Richard, and Mark Richardson, eds. *Frost: Collected Poems, Prose and Plays.* New York: Library of America, 1995.

Sell, Roger D. "Two Unpublished Plays: In an Art Factory, The Guardeen," *Massachusetts Review* 26, no. 2–3 (Summer–Autumn 1985): 265–340.

"In a Poem" (1942)

This brief quatrain was collected in *A Witness Tree.* It appears in a grouping called "Quantula" along with other pithy poems, which suggests that Frost intended them to be together because of their small "quantity" and presumed force. (In Latin, *quantula* means "How little?" or "How small?") "In a Poem" presents Frost's view of the function of sentences, arguing what they must do when they appear in a poem and how they are made different in poems than they are in other writing.

Frost once wrote in a letter to John Freeman that "Sentences have the greatest monotony to the eye in length and structure and yet the greatest variety to the ear in the tones of the voice they carry" (Barry, 80). Frost was preoccupied with tone. Since many of his poems employ natural speech and everyday language to convey their meanings, they often appear to be made up of complete sentences rather than abridged ones or constricted ones. It is safe to assume that what he briefly lays out here is what he intended for the sentences in all of his poems.

In that same letter to Freeman, Frost went on to say, "The actor's gift is to execute the vocal image at the mouth. The writer's is to implicate the vocal image in a sentence and fasten it printed to the page" In "In a Poem" he states what "sentencing" (a curious double entendre, as if he were a judge sentencing the words to an ineluctable fate) must do when adapted from the spoken sentence to the printed page. Frost held that "[a] good sentence does double duty: it conveys one meaning by word and syntax another by the tone of voice it indicates" (Barry, 80). In this poem, the sentence keeps the "stroke and time" of the composition with the regularity and inevitability of a metronome.

Sentences lightheartedly make their way across the page. The sentences take the "playfully objected rhyme," and again, Frost is punning the grammatical use of "objected" as in the noun, pronoun, or noun phrase that is the object of the sentence. And just as "surely as [sentences] kee[p] the stroke and time" alludes to tone, it also alludes to rhythm and meter.

In the last line Frost plays with the word *undeviable*. He presents a double negative that essentially cancels itself out, suggesting that he is deceptively saying that sentences have their "viable" say. That is, sentences in poems say what they want to say by going "on [their] way," by being carried by tone and rhyme, but still speaking their meaning in what only appears to be, because they are fastened on the page, an undeviating and inevitable way.

FURTHER READING

Barry, Elaine. *Robert Frost on Writing.* New Brunswick, N.J.: Rutgers University Press, 1973, 80.

Marcus, Mordecai. *The Poems of Robert Frost: An Explication.* Boston: G. K. Hall, 1991.

"In a Vale" (1913)

One of Frost's earliest lyrics, "In a Vale" appeared in his first volume, *A Boy's Will,* with the gloss "Out of old longings he fashions a story." Lawrance Thompson wrote that the poem was begun while Frost was still in high school. While Frost dated the poem as between 1896 and 1901, he wrote in a letter to friend Sidney Cox in 1915 that "A place I passed at night alone something like twenty years ago made 'In a Vale' then and there in my head and I wrote it down with few changes the next morning" (Cramer, 20).

The poem begins with the speaker remembering that when he was "young" they "dwelt in a vale / By a misty fen that rang all night." A vale is a valley often coursed by a stream, and a fen is a marsh. It is not clear at first what "rang" there, whether birds or nocturnal creatures.

As maidens enter the poem in line three, it becomes apparent that this is no ordinary vale. The maidens are like fairies in the night whose "garments trail" behind them as they wander to the window of the speaker's home. Frost may have intended a pun on the word "vale" with "veil," as the image of the garments trailing behind the maidens suggests many brides in the night.

As the speaker goes on to detail the fen, he remembers that there was "every kind of bloom" and that "for every kind there was a face," as if the maidens had emerged from the flowers themselves. The voices he hears across the windowsill of his room came from these maidens, as each came "singly" to greet him out of the magical mist and talk until the "stars were almost faded away."

The maidens came to him speaking of "things of moment," throughout the night, before they returned "heavy with dew" to the place from which each came. That fen, that marsh, the speaker imagines, is where the "bird was before it flew" and "the flower was before it grew." They are one and the same there, as they, like the maidens, all grew from this vale of his childhood. All beauty comes from his youth. Even now the wonderful scent of flowers and the beauty of a bird's song come from this place in his memory.

As the poem comes to a close, the speaker says that he was not vain about what he listened to and witnessed. He appreciated it and knew well that he was privileged. Each night the maidens came until they all faded away—until, perhaps, he matured to a point where they could no longer visit him, as it is often children whose imaginations are fertile enough to be privileged with having such visions. But he knew, even in childhood, what he had gained. *Vale*, in Latin, means farewell, and it seems that this poem is a way of saying good-bye to the magical place from which all beautiful things come.

The poem is highly romanticized and full of archaisms, and it clearly was written by Frost in his youth. Frost said during a 1957 interview, "You can see in some poems some lingering words like 'fain' and 'list' that I was getting rid of, that I was ashamed of to begin with.... I don't remember thinking much about style except that I was ashamed at 'thee' and 'thou' and 'thine' and such things as that" (Cramer, 20). Frost could well have had "In a Vale" in mind here. By 1957 he had long cast off the youthful naiveté evident in this early but enchanting lyric.

As Katherine Kearns writes, "This speaker, young and receptive, predicts the duality of Frost's later speakers who can only hear human woe in birds' voices and who can use flowers only as metaphors for something else" (183).

FURTHER READING

Cramer, Jeffrey S. *Robert Frost among His Poems: A Literary Companion to the Poet's Own Biographical Contexts and Associations.* Jefferson, N.C.: MacFarland, 1996.

Kearns, Katherine. *Robert Frost and a Poetics of Appetite.* Cambridge: Cambridge University Press, 1994, 181–184.

Poirier, Richard. "Choices." In *Robert Frost,* Modern Critical Views, edited by Harold Bloom. 21–23. Philadelphia: Chelsea House, 2003.

Thompson, Lawrance. *Robert Frost: The Early Years.* New York: Holt, Rinehart and Winston, 1966, 303–304.

"In Divés' Dive" (1936)

This poem is the last in a group of poems titled "Ten Mills," most of which, including this one, were originally published in *Poetry* in April 1936 and later collected in *A Further Range.*

Jeffrey Cramer notes that Dives was the "name traditionally given to the rich man in Jesus's parable of the beggar Lazarus and the rich man (Luke 16:19–31) from a mistranslation of the phrase *"homo quidam erat dives"* ("there was a certain rich man")." In the parable, the rich man mistreated the poor when he was alive and is in the afterlife suffering for it. He then asks to be allowed to warn his family of what is to come if they follow in his footsteps. The title, therefore, is a pun, since the poem goes on to describe a speaker who is losing at cards.

It is late, and the speaker is losing the game but remains "steady and unaccusing." He holds, however, that as long as the Declaration of Independence guards his "right to be equal in number of cards," it will mean "nothing" to him "who runs the Dive." He is, of course, alluding to the statement in the U.S. Declaration of Independence that "all men are created equal."

The poem ends wittily with "Let's have a look at another five." Unlike the poor man in the parable, he is not about to repent or change his ways. Perhaps if somewhere beyond the poem his gambling leaves him poor, the speaker will have a change of heart.

If it were not for the Dives reference, the poem would simply be a playful rhyme. According to Cramer, it becomes a somewhat darker description. The card player may be steady and unassuming, but he is going down, taking a "dive," while also being the owner, the one who runs the "dive." Maybe, even, Divés' Dive is the rich man's place of business in hell. The numerous puns on the word "dive" are what make the brief poem carry a little more weight, though there is a limit to how far it can be stretched (and Cramer's note takes it about as far as it can go).

FURTHER READING

Cramer, Jeffrey S. *Robert Frost among His Poems: A Literary Companion to the Poet's Own Biographical Contexts and Associations.* Jefferson, N.C.: MacFarland, 1996.

"Ingenuities of Debt, The" (1947)

The speaker, musing on an inscription on a wall, assumes that the words were so deeply meant that they were carved by themselves in stone, just as our own worries carve "trouble in the brow above the eyes." The mostly aphoristic message carved is "Take Care to Sell your Horse before He Dies / The Art of Life is Passing Losses on." The message is itself as troubled as the furrowed forehead; it is one that seeks to sidestep tragedy simply by according it to others.

The speaker claims the city that said the message was Ctesiphon, an ancient city of central Iraq on the Tigris River southeast of Baghdad that was captured and plundered in 637. The message seems to be that war and trade are about making a decision to get out before it is too late.

The speaker observes what remains of the city and holds that "Not even the ingenuities of debt / Could save it from its losses being met," which denies the message. His observation instead suggests that there are times when there is no way to avoid tragedy; not even deftness in sidestepping misfortune or disaster will help. In the end, sand, a "serpent on its chin," is what will become of the wall, the hall, and all the rest: ashes to ashes and dust to dust.

The speaker comes off as a bystander, someone who happened upon an engraving and is simply passing it on. But in his very expression he submits to the stone's message: The loss he has passed on is the knowledge of the message itself. We may be clever sidesteppers if we follow the stone's advice, but the poem's message is that there are times when even the best sidestepping can only keep one "a little while" from being broken, whether city, hall, or person. Even the inscription itself will eventually fall prey to the eroding sand, which is waiting for an opportunity "To rear against" it.

The poem shares some of its historical imagery and message with the English romantic poet Percy Bysshe Shelley's "Ozymandias."

"Ingenuities of Debt" was first published in the December 1946 issue of the *Atlantic Monthly* and was later collected in *Steeple Bush* in a grouping titled "Editorials."

"In Hardwood Groves" (1913)

"In Hardwood Groves" shares a scene with "A Leaf-Treader" but not a common attitude. The speaker in this poem begins by remarking, "The same leaves over and over again!" His exclamation expresses not surprise but frustration. He is commenting on the fallen leaves of autumn, which when they meet the ground begin to fit the "earth like a leather glove." He notes how they create shade when they are above, but when they have fallen they become nothing but "one texture of faded brown." Instead of being filled with grief, he focuses on the leaves having two different purposes, depending on their position.

The speaker embraces the cyclical nature of life. He is content that the leaves will become fertilizer for the earth, by going "down past things coming up," decaying, and feeding the trees in a different way. They must undergo this process before they can "mount again" and be on top for another season.

The speaker acknowledges that they "*must* be pierced," and the language he chooses is graphic and violent, though he does not continue in this vein. George F. Bagby sees "explicitly Christian hints about the way in which death may lead to further life" in the poet's emphasizing "the suffering and difficulty involved in that process" (56). Bagby also maintains that words like "pierced," and "mount" have "Christological as well as dendrological implications" (57).

But while the speaker recognizes that all living things must die and must be "put / Beneath the feet of dancing flowers," he does not despair. Certainly there is bite to the dance of the flowers, but the speaker ends not just resigned but somewhat satisfied. While it may be different "in some other world," he knows for certain that "this is the way in ours," and that, since it cannot be changed, he will accept.

"In Hardwood Groves" was first published as "The Same Leaves" in the December 18, 1926, issue of the *Dearborn Independent*.

FURTHER READING

Bagby, George F. *Frost and the Book of Nature*. Knoxville: University of Tennessee Press, 1993, 56–57.

Gowler, Steve. "Frost's 'In Hardwood Groves,'" *Explicator* 40, no. 3 (Spring 1982): 48.

"Innate Helium" (1947)

Frost begins by calling religious faith "a most filling vapor." The description of faith as something as vague and airy as vapor underscores the traditional immaterial attributes associated with such concepts as spirit and soul. The line can easily be taken two ways. On the one hand, while he calls faith a vapor, he also refers to its having a "filling" quality, which suggests a positive effect. On the other hand, by calling it a vapor at all, he suggests that while those with faith may feel "full," they are full of nothing but vapor—something illusory.

Frost speaks of the vapor swirling "occluded in us," and his use of a plural pronoun demonstrates that he, too, is inclined to such faith. In meteorology, *occlude* refers to the act of forcing air upward from the earth's surface, as when a cold front overtakes a warm front, and it seems that the lift of such activity is in keeping with what the poet describes in the third line: "Compression to uplift us out of weight—," to make us feel good even when things are bad. The uplifting quality of faith is described as something similar to the buoyancy of "bird bones": It allows human beings to take flight. Frost concludes that such a propensity "must be innate," as that "filling vapor" of religious faith has the effect of helium: It lifts us to otherwise unattainable heights.

Given Frost's generally agnostic bent, it seems that if he is putting a positive spin on religious faith it is only for its psychological effect, as his word choice indicates that he still pokes and prods at faith's lack of fixed physical qualities. He describes faith in physical terms, using words like "weight," "buoyant," and "compression." But as soon as he begins to express faith in material terms, he seems to reduce faith to merely its psychological effects and to the properties of this world rather than the transcendent. In this sense, there is no divine inspiration or divine connection to the source of faith. The source is within the individual experiencing it.

In calling faith innate, Frost suggests two things: first, that we come by such inclinations naturally, and second that it is something produced by the mind rather than learned about or acquired through experience. The double meaning of the word *innate* seems to hold the key to the double meaning of Frost's poem.

"Innate Helium" was first collected in *Steeple Bush*.

"In Neglect" (1913)

"In Neglect" was written on the Derry farm in 1905 and first published in Frost's initial volume, *A Boy's Will*. While the book was being printed, Frost described the biographical situation of the poem to Ezra Pound, who later stated in a review: "There is perhaps as much of Frost's personal tone as in anything else." He wrote, "It is to his wife, written when his grandfather and uncle had disinherited him of a comfortable fortune and left him in poverty because he was a useless poet instead of a money-getter" (Richardson, 69).

In a letter to friend Sidney Cox, Frost included Ezra Pound's review of the book, which contained Pound's inaccurate story as the supposed inspiration for the poem. Frost crossed out certain lines and wrote, "I have scraped out some personalities (very private) which are not only in bad taste but also inaccurate" (Cramer, 20) Frost later told his version of the story to his biographer Robert Newdick, who noted that "Robert showed his mettle and Elinor's by turning the intended rebuke into a poem!" (Cramer, 21).

Jeffrey Cramer notes, however, that the poem does not deal directly with Frost's grandfather and uncle; rather, it "deals with the years of neglect on the Derry farm when both Frost and Elinor felt Frost's poems were very good but not the fashion of the moment" (21). Cramer also believes it is more Elinor's attitude than Frost's that is expressed in the poem.

The poem can be read without any of this biographical information as simply an expression of "neglect" by those who "feel forsaken." It begins "They leave us so to the way we took," introducing a relationship between those who make their own way and those who wish they would take a different road. In this line there is some foreshadowing of the later "The Road Not Taken" in the implication that there are two roads and that this speaker feels he has made the better choice. This time, however, he is not alone.

The poem continues as the two prove the others "mistaken." They sit contented in their little "wayside nook," having a "mischievous, vagrant, and seraphic look." The description is a jest: They are mischievous wanderers who maintain an angelic look, since they have pursued a path criticized by others and have excelled. The "neglect" here is almost preferred by the two people, since they are exactly where they want to be and do not need to align themselves with those who are more ordinary.

In the final line Frost emphasizes that they "*try*" to feel forsaken. The poem is playful but caustic. Whether or not the biographical information is accurate, after publishing his first volume of poetry Frost might have been pridefully celebrating his success and thumbing his nose at those who doubted him.

FURTHER READING

Cramer, Jeffrey S. *Robert Frost among His Poems: A Literary Companion to the Poet's Own Biographical Contexts and Associations.* Jefferson, N.C.: MacFarland, 1996.

Richardson, Mark. *The Ordeal of Robert Frost: The Poet and His Poetics.* Chicago, Ill.: University of Illinois Press, 1997.

In the Clearing (1962)

In the Clearing was Frost's final volume of poetry. Its working title had been "The Great Misgiving," from

line 229 of "Kitty Hawk," a poem that appeared in the volume. Frost may certainly have had some misgivings about the poems in *In the Clearing,* as the book was postponed many times before finally reaching publication on Frost's 88th birthday. It had also been 15 years since his last volume, *Steeple Bush,* was published in 1947.

The book's final title was derived from its third poem, "A Cabin in the Clearing," which had also been Frost's Christmas poem in 1951. When the volume first appeared, a signed limited edition of 1,500 copies also was published. The volume had a sly epigraph, "And wait to watch the water clear, I may," and was dedicated, "Letters in prose to Louis Untermeyer, Sidney Cox, and John Bartlett for them to dispose of as they please; these to you in verse for keeps." All three of the men named were longtime friends of Frost; the "you" of the dedication was another dear friend, Kay Morrison.

Despite Frost's initial reservations, the volume was an immediate best-seller, which eventually reached 60,000 copies. The reviews of the book were also fair, though written largely by friends and admirers. John Ciardi wrote in the *Saturday Review of Literature* that there were "two main stages" in Frost's verse: "The poet of passion and the poet of wit and whimsy" (Parini, 424). Since the book was his final volume, it was likely not held to the same standards as his earlier work but was instead viewed as another step in the poet's lifelong journey in verse.

Stephen D. Warner writes that "The real value of the volume is in the new confidence reflected through the tone and statement of the poems. They affirm the truths of earlier poems through a broadened application and an elevated perspective" (411). Referencing Frost's pun in "The Milky Way is a Cowpath," he adds: "Frost's career became the 'parabolic curve' that didn't overshoot the moon but plunged back into matter to complete the cycle explicit in his early orthodoxy" (411).

The contents of the book were preceded by an excerpt from "Kitty Hawk" titled "But God's Own Descent," which begins with that title line and ends with the line "Into the material." The excerpt can be read as a kind of self-proclamation of the poet's life's achievement of "risking spirit in substantiation" and of "charg[ing] into earth / In birth after birth" in his poems.

The volume does not hold the great gems of Frost's career, such as "Birches," "Death of the Hired Man," "Design," "Home Burial," "Departmental," "Neither Out Far nor In Deep," "The Road Not Taken," or "Stopping by Woods on a Snowy Evening." It does not reveal Frost at his creative best. It does, however, include some good poems.

There are playful pieces that have some merit, such as "In a Glass of Cider" and "The Objection to Being Stepped On." In the first the poet equates elation with bubbles in a glass of cider; when he is elated, he rides a bubble to the top of the glass by catching one in ascent. The second has a speaker who is struck in his "sense" by "an unemployed hoe." These two poems are reminiscent of the poet of "Departmental" in their playfulness.

Some poems reveal an aging, thoughtful poet who can write skillfully even when he is not masterly. Frost still had much to say about the nature of things, and the volume includes not only poems of the playful sort but a number of poems that reflect earlier propensities, as well as quite a few of what might be called philosophical poems. In some ways the poet's work had become more philosophical and scientific though less inspired in his later years, as if he were working on getting his ideas out.

The more philosophical poems, include "Accidentally on Purpose," in which the poet postulates existence as a purposeful accident, and "A Never Naught Song," which, in keeping with the theme that there has always been a "purpose," proposes that there was never "naught," nothing, "[t]here was always thought." This poem imagines the Big Bang as a "burst" of matter and the bursting forth of the universe as an "atomic One." Both of these are included in the Cluster of Faith.

In still other poems in the Cluster of Faith, there are meditations on the nature of religion, a subject that interested Frost throughout his career. He remained, it seems, agnostic until the end, asking for "forgiveness" in his usual tongue-and-cheek fashion when he writes to God, "Forgive, O Lord, my little jokes on Thee / And I'll forgive Thy great big one on me."

Some of the poems express Frost's wish that art continue long after he has ceased, such as "Escapist-Never" and "Closed for Good." In the first Frost represents humanity and himself at their best, where "life is a pursuit of a pursuit forever." In the second the poet knows that eventually he will cease his role as a "foot printer," and "some slight beast / So mousy or so foxy" will take his place. By paying homage to those who came before him, he indicates that those who follow him should not forget him either but should instead "print there" as his "proxy."

Frost also chose to include some occasion poems, such as "For John F. Kennedy His Inauguration" and "On Being Chosen Poet of Vermont." He seemed to be thinking about the future of his country, revealing his nationalistic and patriotic side in "Does No One at All Ever Feel This Way in the Least?" and "America Is Hard to See." Indeed, the many facets of Frost that were evident in the earlier poems find their way, at least to some extent, into the poems in this valedictory volume.

The closing poem, "[In winter in the woods alone]," Jay Parini maintains, could have easily been included in *A Boy's Will*. The poet returns to a similar theme, himself alone in nature. And as in so many of his earlier poems, he sees in "Nature no defeat." He overcomes. Frost once said at a reading that the last line of the poem "Or for myself in my retreat / For yet another blow" was a "threat to write another book" (Parini, 421). Parini says that "Many poems in this book fall into the category of light verse, though there is often a darker side to the joke" (421), and this darker side is characteristic Frost, right until the end.

Some poems seem to look back to old insecurities and childhood wishes. In "Auspex" Frost writes, "I have remained resentful to this day / When any but myself presume to say / That there was anything I couldn't be." Even after accumulating numerous honorary doctorates and awards, the old poet seemed to feel he still had something to prove, and even on the "Eve of a Great Success" those lines could be, borrowing from one of Samuel Taylor Coleridge's titles, "Written in Dejection." But Frost had made his point long before: "How Hard It Is to Keep from Being King When It's in You and in the Situation."

Frost puns on his own name a number of times in his works. In this volume he does so pointedly in "Peril of Hope." He begins "It is right in there," without specifying what "it" is. He continues, "Betwixt and between / The orchard bare and the orchard green," depicting the orchard as the fertile ground for his life's work. "When the orchard's right," he says, "[i]n a flowery burst / Of all that's white, / That we fear the worst." What is "in there" is the fear that all will be undone, that all will be forgotten. The poem closes, "For there's not a clime / But at any cost / Will take that time / For a night of frost." Any who have spent a night with the poetry of Frost know that there was no peril to his hope. As his last formal gesture to the world, the ever-insecure Frost still hid in a familiar landscape, fearful and hopeful at once.

FURTHER READING

Brown, Terrence. "Robert Frost's *In the Clearing*: An Attempt to Reestablish the Persona of 'The Kindly Grey Poet,'" *Papers on Language and Literature* 5 (1969): 110–118.

Cramer, Jeffrey S. *Robert Frost among His Poems: A Literary Companion to the Poet's Own Biographical Contexts and Associations.* Jefferson, N.C.: MacFarland, 1996.

Parini, Jay. *Robert Frost: A Life.* New York: Holt, 1999, 421–424.

Richardson, Mark. "Frost and the Cold War: A Look at the Later Poetry." In *Roads Not Taken: Rereading Robert Frost,* edited by Earl J. Wilcox and Jonathan N. Barron, 55–77. Columbia: University of Missouri Press, 2000.

Warner, Stephen D. "Robert Frost in the Clearing: The Risk of Spirit in Substantiation." In *Frost Centennial Essays,* edited by Jac Tharpe, 398–411. Jackson: University Press of Mississippi, 1974.

"In the Home Stretch" (1916)

"In the Home Stretch" was first collected in *Mountain Interval* but had been previously published in the July 1916 issue of *Century Magazine.* The title is a pun on the situation in which the couple finds themselves. They are in the home stretch, so to speak, of their lives. At the same time, the poem centers on the notion of home and the upheaval that moving inevitably causes. Predictably, the transition becomes a source for reflection on what the past has brought and what the future might bring.

The poem opens with the image of one not at home in her home: a woman dressed for the outdoors rather than the indoors, standing in the kitchen of her new home and looking out the window at what she describes as a dilapidated view. The confusion in her home is caused by the movers who stack furniture haphazardly atop other furniture but also by the confusion she feels is caused by a change in surroundings. This new home is isolated; the city folk have, as is typical, retired to the country, to a home some 15 miles outside of town that was a "bargain." The movers address the woman formally, and she makes fun of being called "lady" so many times, as she was never so "beladied" before. There is a certain formality in the address that is unfamiliar to her. She humorously wonders if so many "ladies" will make her a true lady by "common law." The discomfort of her situation causes her to make light of it and be playful.

The woman is not happy with the move, though she is unwilling to admit to as much, and this is a slight source of tension for the couple. Like many of Frost's other dialogues, such as "Home Burial," this poem is primarily concerned with tone and what is expressed through language but without words.

The woman views the weeds in the yard as happy; they seem to flourish on dishpan water. She, however, imagines her life passing before her as she washes dish after dish, and the weeds inevitably growing far more happily than she. In conversation with her husband Joe, she reflects on her own mortality as the years will come and go in this house. Joe persists in asking if she likes the house, but she manages to avoid a response. Instead she talks about how they will treat the house, which is better than the movers have; they agree that they are past slamming doors and that at the very least they will tread more softly.

The couple has physically moved from the city to the country but has also moved in age from the early to the latter years, and they avoid counting how many years they have left. The country is not idyllic, they have not retained the optimism of youth; instead it represents "darkness." The window acts as a looking glass into the future and the unknown, so Joe encourages his wife to move from the window where she "see[s] too much." He wants her to look at the "livelier view"—the men leaving. But this view is not the more lively; instead, it inspires panic. They are unprepared for the darkness, and no romanticism about telling the time by the moon will abate it. While the new moon will see them through their first weeks in their new home, without comforts such as the stove or a mere match and a candle they will be somehow unprotected and all the more vulnerable in their new surroundings. The country life is contrasted significantly with city life, and while country folk may be able to tell time by the moon, this city couple wonders if they will be able to do the same. Fear causes them to engage hurriedly the movers in uprighting the stove and getting it fired up before their departure. Again the couple's apprehension causes them to seek comfort in strange ways; they say it is good luck that the stove fits snugly into the wall on the first try. Joe tells the movers to leave the city work for people who can do nothing else, since he believes they look like they could be good farmers. There is a suggestion that Joe has somehow been forced into farming, perhaps a subtle allusion to Frost's own experiences. The French boy says the movers are giving their chances at farming to Joe and his wife.

Joe fears what he has been "left to" on the farm. There is a description of the game "ten step" that children play, which is suggestive of "green light, red light," in which the players take steps forward and backward in the attempt to reach some goal. The farm is something to be feared, something that can "steal a step" on them when they avert their eyes even for a moment. The vulnerability the couple feels lies not only in their arrival in a new home but in their seeming apprehension at trying a whole new way of making a living. Frost takes up the subject of the city versus the country in other poems as well, such as "The Code," "Christmas Trees," and "An Unstamped Letter in our Rural Letter Box."

The husband and wife feel left to their "fate," somehow abandoned in the wilderness. They are shaken by the sudden reality of their situation. They feel lonesome, even as two. "It's all so much," she expresses; it is an overwhelming feeling. Bad for a moment seems worse than ever, and isolation leads to discomfort and fear. They begin to speak of things taken away, of what cannot be taken, of what security comes from, such as the meals they have already eaten in their lives. There is a return to the basics such as food and light. And "dumped down in paradise we are and happy," one says. Soon the simplicity of the situation is equated with biblical beginnings. Nature is a paradise, yet, just as in Adam and Eve's Garden of Eden, danger lies within it. And soon begins the debate over whose idea it was to move.

There is a play on language here when the wife begins to point out that there are no such things as endings and beginnings; instead, "There are only middles." It seems that they are not in the home stretch after all; they are just somewhere in the journey. They begin to wonder if anything is ever new, if even they were ever new to each other. "End is a gloomy word," so they relive what it is to find a home. The home is filled with all that is not new: their relationship to each other, their belongings. All that is new are the walls that protect them, and this offers the comfort that until this moment was elusive. There is a pleasant view of the farm at the end, causing the poem to end on a positive note. The couple will sleep in their own beds tonight, albeit in a different place, and they will be themselves, will be "as much at home as if they'd always danced there"—just like the light from the stove that dances in "yellow wrigglers on the ceiling." There is a precious chance to reestablish and create a new life.

There is an analogy between the house and the life they find themselves in, an analogy between the house and starting over. It is about re-creating meaning and value, about beginning all over again without there ever having really been an end. They can create order out of chaos, out of the furniture that is haphazardly stacked. The analogy lies in our relation to this planet and the value we must create from scratch out of the chaos of our universe.

The poem raises questions of what it means to be home and what it means to be uprooted and replanted. The weeds will thrive on dishpan water, and so will the couple if that is what farming brings. All life is transitory and temporary in some sense, but there is that which can remain, such as our ideas and our relationships. Although transplanted, the couple will continue on, the jarring transition but a blip on the screen. Frost's famous line from "Death of the Hired Man," "Home is the place where, when you have to go there, / They have to take you in" also raises questions of what is home. Home is something much more intangible than the arrangement of a table and chairs.

This narrative does not focus on the conflict between a couple as in Frost's best-known narratives, such as the previously mentioned "Home Burial" and "Death of the Hired Man," but instead on an outer conflict that the couple must and can satisfactorily face together. *See* HOME, THEME OF.

FURTHER READING

Abel, Darrel. "Frost's 'In the Home Stretch,'" *Explicator* 45, no. 2 (Winter 1987): 37–39.

Wakefield, Richard. "Robert Frost's 'In the Home Stretch': The Renewal of New England," *Robert Frost Review* (Fall 1999): 45–61.

"In the Long Night" (1947)

See "FIVE NOCTURNES."

"In Time of Cloudburst" (1936)

The speaker begins by exclaiming "Let the downpour roil and toil!" He is not fearful of the rain, he proclaims, putting his bravest self forward. After all, "the worst it can do," he imagines, is to the soil, which will simply be moved a little nearer to the sea. But it becomes clear as he continues that this is not the worst it can do, as there is a "little of future harm" in the bursting of clouds, and as always in nature, a reminder of the transience of man. The poem becomes a speculation about present gain versus future harm, but the sort of harm that can be caused is not entirely specified.

The speaker reflects on the huge continental and climatic shifts that take place over thousands of years. Certain areas will be "scoured poor" over time, he knows, but other areas will be made better and more fertile as the "slope of the earth is reversed." The farmer at different times and in different places can begin again, "all over to hope." The speaker fantastically envisions digging up his old tools on the other side of the earth and finding them being as "ready to wield as now." As is common in Frost, observations of nature, in this instance simply of a downpour, lead to a reflection on man's place in nature. The speaker has moved from reflection to an understanding and agreement with nature. He hopes his knowledge of the potentially destructive power of nature and the repetitive cyclical dynamic between this power and man's constant recovery from it does not make him "tired and morose and resentful of man's condition."

While the rain is not so powerful a force as to eliminate the "farmer"—not this specific farmer, but a supposed farmer—for all time, it can do him present harm for some other farmer's future gain. Frost is, as so often, speaking out of the side of his mouth about resentment. The fact is, this particular farmer knows he cannot simply "run / To the other end of the slope." He does not have time to wait for his tool of "wood" to be "changed to stone." The worst the cloudburst can do to him is far greater than the opening lines of the poem suggest, but in times of bursting clouds one must retain hope, even in the face of possible harm.

Robert Faggen writes that the "social and political underpinnings of the poem are unmistakable," pointing out that the "farmer remains a farmer" (164). But this suggests a narrower interpretation of the farmer's experience than is presented here.

The poem first appeared in the April 1936 issue of the *Virginia Quarterly* and was later collected in *A Further Range*.

FURTHER READING

Brower, Reuben A. *The Poetry of Robert Frost: Constellations of Intention*. New York: Oxford University Press, 1963, 114–117.

Faggen, Robert. *Robert Frost and the Challenge of Darwin*. Ann Arbor: University of Michigan Press, 1997, 164.

"Into My Own" (1913)

In "Into My Own," the prophetic first poem of Frost's first book, *A Boy's Will*, Frost goes deep into nature. The poem appeared with the gloss, "The youth is persuaded that he will be rather more than less himself for having forsworn the world." Frost wrote in a letter to F. S. Flint on January 21, 1913, that "When the life of the streets perplexed me a long time ago I attempted to find an answer to it for myself by going literally into the wilderness," (Barry, 86), and that is precisely what he does here. As George F. Bagby writes, "the self is lost or overwhelmed in order to be clarified" (30).

Growth and understanding are discovered by a journey into dark trees, "So old and firm they scarcely show the breeze." Frost largely wrote in traditional verse form and had an affinity for the sonnet, which he once described as "eight lines, then six lines more," and after the first eight lines, a turn "for the better or the worse." Here we are presented with a series of dark images early on: "the merest mask of gloom" in line three and "stretched away unto the edge of doom" in line four. The "mask" alerts us that something is unrevealed, and it seems that it is nature that is deceptive. The poem begins, "One of my wishes is that . . ." and we later learn that the speaker seeks the truth, and perhaps wants it to "br[eak] in," as it does in "Birches." He wants nature to reveal itself and its "doom," rather than hide itself behind an agreeable mask.

As in "The Road Not Taken," here the speaker avoids the road and seeks instead the darkness of the forest. His goal is to "steal away" into it, "fearless of ever finding open land, / Or highway where the slow wheel pours the sand," and with purpose. While he wants nature to reveal itself, he wants to conceal himself. The slow wheel here refers to the wheel of time, the image of pouring sand to an hourglass. He wants to be fearless of nature and time, which are frequently linked.

The speaker seeks to discover what nature means for him. The third stanza presents a turn for better or worse when, upon entering the darkness, he says, "I do not see why I should e'er turn back, Or those should not set forth upon my track / To overtake me, who should miss me here / And long to know if still I held them dear." The will carries the speaker into nature because it holds answers, but it is only through entering it wholly that he can find them. Indeed, there he becomes, as the final line states, "more sure of all [he] thought was true." The ending demonstrates a shift in that the speaker is surprisingly unchanged; his friends "would not find me changed from him they knew," but at the same time he is "more sure." The final couplet, generally meant to make all come clear, is somewhat ambiguous. He both is and is not himself, just as in Shakespeare's "Troilus and Cressida," Troilus finds that Cressida "both is and is not my Cressid."

Knowledge and understanding are acquired by the end of the poem. The early intuition of things as they are becomes, at journey's end, an affirmation grounded in experience.

Frost frequently makes an effort to set aside his fears and to forge ahead. In this sonnet, instead of resisting the "edge of doom," he wants to hover at the edge, freeing himself to delve deeply into nature and absorb all that it holds. We may sometimes struggle to break free from nature and to deny our susceptibility to its forces, but Frost often struggles to separate himself from mankind and go into nature. It is not that he sees them as distinct; he seems to feel that living in the world of people rather than the darkness of the little-known trees inhibits understanding of life in its fullness, and in this respect he is similar to the British romantic poets and the American transcendentalists. Avoiding the darkness keeps us in the dark. For Frost, we must head into nature in order to head into ourselves. The answers are to be found in the darkness, and the darkness is internal, not external, and therefore is not to be avoided. *See* "The VANTAGE POINT" for an example of the poet considering retreating from nature and "seek[ing] again mankind."

"Into My Own" was first published in the May 1909 issue of *New England Magazine*. *See* NATURE and FUGITIVE.

FURTHER READING

Bagby, George F. *Frost and the Book of Nature.* Knoxville: University of Tennessee Press, 1993, 30.

Barry, Elaine. *Robert Frost on Writing.* New Brunswick, N.J.: Rutgers University Press, 1973, 86.

Calhoun, Richard J. "By Pretending They Are Not Sonnets: The Sonnets of Robert Frost at the Millennium." In *Roads Not Taken: Rereading Robert Frost,* edited by Earl J. Wilcox and Jonathan N. Barron, 217–235. Cambridge: University of Missouri Press, 2000.

Parker, Blanford. "Frost and the Meditative Lyric." In *The Cambridge Companion to Robert Frost,* edited by Robert Faggen, 179–196. Cambridge: Cambridge University Press, 2001.

Richardson, Mark. *The Ordeal of Robert Frost: The Poet and His Poetics.* Chicago, Ill.: University of Illinois Press, 1997, 213.

"Introduction to E. A. Robinson's King Jasper" (1935)

Shortly after the American poet Edwin Arlington Robinson's death in 1935, Frost was contracted to write the introduction to his lengthy poem *King Jasper,* which Robinson had finished just before dying. Frost wrote a short piece but was asked by the publisher, The Macmillan Company, to write even more and to include some Robinson quotations, an early indication that the piece was as much about Frost's views on poetry as it was about his views of Robinson's poetry. The final version picked up where the first had left off and was quite a bit longer than the first. The two parts smoothly fit together, making it hard to discern without manuscript copy where it had originally ended, which was with the line; "The utmost of ambition

is to lodge a few poems where they will be hard to get rid of, to lodge a few irreducible bits where Robinson lodged more than his share."

Frost had known Robinson since 1915 and felt a great kinship with him. Frost admired Robinson the most of his contemporaries and at times this even led to a feeling of rivalry that strained their friendship, which Frost's official biographer Lawrance Thompson and Hermann Hagedorn, in *Edwin Arlington Robinson: A Biography* (1938), address. The introduction to *King Jasper* not only is a tribute to Robinson but reveals distinctly Frost's own views about poetry in general.

He opens by stating that "It may come to the notice of posterity (and then again it may not) that this, our age, ran wild in the quest of new ways to be new." He suggests that this desire to be new partly came from science but that it found its way into all disciplines, including poetry. He identifies ways that poetry tried to be new, such as with little punctuation or no capital letters, without a strict meter or any images other than visual, and so on. Readers would be able to associate such stylistic innovations with poets such as e.e. cummings (1894–1962), Ezra Pound (1885–1972), and the imagists, among others. Frost's descriptions of the ways to be "new" are not favorably spun: "It was tried without phrase, epigram, coherence, logic, and consistency." He is in many senses taking aim at just the sort of poetry that gave him pause. He closes his first paragraph by stating that "The limits of poetry had been sorely strained, but the hope was that the idea had been somewhat brought out." While the opening has much to do with Frost's own attitudes toward the poetry of the period, he makes his way to Robinson by explaining that "Robinson stayed content with the old-fashioned way to be new." By this Frost implies subject, language, metaphor and imagery, not all the "flash" that he was criticizing.

Frost inquires, "How does a man come on his difference, and how does he feel about it when he finds it out?" He later asks, "What assurance have they that their difference is not insane, eccentric, abortive, unintelligible?" The difference that Robinson had and that Frost likely presumed he himself had was one he had to find a way to embrace.

"There is such a thing as being too willing to be different," he says, and presumably he is referring to that party of poets who would fall into his first description of ways to be new. The embracing of difference is an ultimately dangerous action that can leave a person dangling from a precipice. Frost says that there is always "the fear that we shan't prove worthy in the eyes of someone who knows us at least as we know ourselves," and that that is "the fear of God." He explains that "[i]t has been said that recognition in art is all" and that is the great effort to convince another mind that "it can uncurl and wave the same filaments of subtlety, soul convince soul that it can give off the same shimmers of eternity." Frost was convinced that this was true of Robinson.

Frost takes on the "experimentalist" poets in their desire to "use poetry as a vehicle of grievances against the un-Utopian state." There was in Frost's time, and still is, a debate over whether literature ought to be political or should transcend politics. Frost cites a young person to demonstrate the turn for the worse: "Whereas we once thought literature should be without content, we now know it should be charged full of propaganda." "Wrong twice," Frost told him.

Frost says, "I don't like grievances. . . . What I like is griefs and I like them Robinsonianly profound." Frost wanted "grievances" to stay in prose; if you have a bone to pick, do it there, he seems to say. Poetry is for heartache, and it should be left "free to go its ways in tears." Further distinguishing between grievances and griefs, he writes that grievances are a form of impatience, griefs a form of patience. Robinson gave us griefs. Frost criticizes Robinson only slightly, allowing that he did give a "few superficial irritable grievances" but that those "are forgotten in the depths of grief" to which we were plunged.

Frost recalls his first meeting with Robinson and how their minds were joined. Neither cared "how arrant a reformer or experimentalist a man was if he gave [them] real poems." They were agreed that they would "hate to be read for any theory upon which [they] might be supposed to write," and further "doubted any poem could persist for any theory upon which it might have been written." That

would be reductionist. They wanted full recognition of a poem and honesty in the writing of one. Frost suggests, as he does in "The Constant Symbol" and other prose pieces, that poems must retain their freshness. The freshness the poet felt must be conveyed to the reader in its purest form: "A poem is the emotion of having a thought while the reader waits a little anxiously for the success of dawn." If it seems a poem has been entirely "thought out," its freshness will be lost. "The only discipline" a poet must begin with is an "inner mood." He begins with his mood and then attempts to find its shape. If he begins with an agenda, a grievance, then he is in some sense dishonest. To begin with a grief is quite different.

"[T]o lodge a few poems where they will be hard to get rid of" was one of Frost's own ambitions, and he found that "Robinson lodged more than his share." To lodge a poem in a fellow poet's mind is one of the greatest accomplishments, and this is in some sense Frost's greatest compliment to Robinson. He also praises Robinson for his "grazing closeness to the spiritual realities."

Frost says that the first poet he ever discussed poetry with was Ezra Pound, and the first poet they ever discussed was Robinson. He refers to the closing lines of the second-to-last stanza of Robinson's "Miniver Cheevy" and the delight he and Pound shared in the fourth "thought": "Miniver thought and thought and thought / And thought about it." The delight is that three would have been "adequate." The fourth makes "the intolerable touch of poetry"; that is where the "fun" begins. The "last one turns up by surprise round the corner," and this is poetry.

Later Frost defines taste as "set[ting] the limit" in poetry. In "Education by Poetry" he describes poetry as "the only art in the college of arts" that exists for "taste and judgment." Taste and judgment are how a reader finds the "mischief" and humor in poetry. Frost was quite mischievous himself. He once said in a letter that "Ever since infancy I have had the habit of leaving my blocks carts chairs and such like ordinaries where people would be pretty sure to fall forward over them in the dark. Forward, you understand, and in the dark. I may leave my toys in the wrong place and so in vain. It is my intention we are speaking of—my innate mischievousness." That is the figure of his poems and what he much admired in Robinson's (Frost, 344).

Frost speaks of the reader who wants "the heart out of . . . mystery." He despised a poem's being overinterpreted, overread, as he felt "Stopping by Woods on a Snowy Evening" was. Here he explains that for readers who "stan[d] at the end of a poem ready in waiting to catch you by both hands" in a desire to know what is "behind it" the answer must be "If I had wanted you to know, I should have told you in the poem," and such a response is one of Frost's most profound statements about poetry. Poetry must stand on its own, must be tripped over in the dark, and cannot become prose.

Robinson's "theme was unhappiness" but his skill was a "happy" and "playful" one. "The style is the man," Frost intones. Frost further clarifies: "If it is with outer seriousness, it must be with inner humor. If it is with outer humor, it must be with inner seriousness." Frost makes further example of some of Robinson's best-known poems, not only "Miniver Cheevy" but also "The Mill" and "Mr. Flood's Party." "Poetry transcends itself in the playfulness of the toast," he remarks.

Frost describes Robinson's death as "sad to those who knew him, but nowhere near as sad as the lifetime of poetry to which he attuned our ears." He describes the man as having "gone to his place in American literature and left his human place among us vacant." The introduction serves as a description of Robinson the poet that transcends his death. He becomes, through Frost's words, a character of the likes of "Miniver Cheevy" a man out of his time, and at the same time one who surpasses it. Frost pinpoints the sadness in Robinson's poems when he says "Give us immediable woes—woes that nothing can be done for—woes flat and final." These are not the woes of "grievances"; they are honest woes, heartfelt aches. They come to us with a sense of immediacy, not through an intellectualized redundancy. To Frost, "[t]he play's the thing."

Frost admired Robinson because they were fashioned of the same cloth. Their newness was in tone, in language, in character, in the immediacy of the human experience that can be found in "Miniver

Cheevy" and in "Death of the Hired Man." He described Robinson as a pessimist and himself as neither pessimist nor optimist, and that difference can be fairly arrived at by reading the poems. But the mark each made on American poetry and their shared difference account for both Frost's admiration for and jealousy of Robinson. They arrived by two different courses at some of the same conclusions, only Robinson had beaten Frost there, having published several books of poetry and gained renown before Frost was out of the gate. Frost's introduction betrays him momentarily when one senses the rivalry beneath the lines, but for the most part his admiration for Robinson shines because it is also thinly veiled admiration for himself. The essay reveals his own conflicts with the moves poetry was making in his time and his desire to put down in prose what can be found in poetry—to use the American poet Marianne Moore's phrase, "a place for the genuine."

FURTHER READING

Frost, Robert. *Selected Letters of Robert Frost.* Edited by Lawrance Thompson. New York: Holt, Rinehart and Winston, 1964.

Hagedorn, Hermann. *Edwin Arlington Robinson: A Biography.* New York: Macmillan, 1938.

Robinson, Edwin Arlington. *King Jasper.* Introduction by Robert Frost. New York: Macmillan, 1935.

Thompson, Lawrance. *Robert Frost: The Years of Triumph, 1915–1938.* New York: Holt, Rinehart and Winston, 1970.

"Introduction to *The Arts Anthology: Dartmouth Verse*" (1925)

Five hundred copies of the *Arts Anthology: Dartmouth Verse* was published by Mosher Press of Portland, Maine, in 1925. Frost was the editor and wrote a short introduction. He opens by saying that "No one given to looking under-ground in spring can have failed to notice how a bean starts its growth from the seed." Then he discusses a poet's "germination" as being less like a "bean in the ground" and more like "a waterspout at sea." The poet "has to begin as a cloud of all the other poets he ever read. That can't be helped," he says, a reminder that each poet has to make his own mark, but he also comes out of a tradition. When Ezra Pound writes in "A Pact," "I make a pact with you, Walt Whitman— / I have detested you long enough," he is both recognizing his forebear and breaking away from him. He closes that same poem, "We have one sap and one root— / Let there be commerce between us," and that sap and root are what Frost is referring to here. Frost's own first book of verse, *A Boy's Will*, demonstrates that he was at that time still in the "cloud" of other poets and had not yet entirely found his own way.

Frost describes the process of becoming a poet: The "first cloud reaches down toward the water from above and then the water reaches up toward the cloud from below and finally cloud and water join together to roll as one pillar between heaven and earth." The poet is a pillar of the elements. He joins the earth with the transcendent; he transcends the earth and brings his readers with him. And "the base of water he picks up from below is of course all the life he ever lived outside of books."

Frost explains that these are the "three figures of the waterspout and the first is about as far as the poet doomed to die young in everyone of us usually gets." Frost recognizes that the young poet "brings something down" from those who came before, listing four of them: Ernest Christopher Dowson (1867–1900), William Butler Yeats (1865–1939), William Morris (1834–96), and John Masefield (1878–1967) as well as a school of poets, the imagists, led by Ezra Pound (1885–1972). While he says the young poet "lifts little or nothing up," he cautions that "you can't be too careful about whom you will ignore in this world" and advises us not to set aside these youthful poets quickly, as some poets have been known to refuse "at the last minute to abdicate the breast in favor of the practical" and to live and write verse until old age, like the English poet Walter Savage Landor (1775–1864). Frost himself did not publish a book until he was 39, so he spoke from experience. He may have "hardly be[en] worth getting excited over in college or else-

where" if he had not lived long enough to establish himself and be published and recognized.

Frost distinguishes the verse in the book in several ways. There are those who are "accomplished and all that—are of the first figure and frankly derivative," those who "survive into the second figure of the waterspout," some who make it to the "salt water," and some who even make it to the third figure. He describes those who make it to the salt water as having "realism" that "represents an advance" and as "show[ing] acceptance of the fact that the way to better is often through worse." This description easily characterizes some of Frost's own writing, such as his desire to get down on the page authentically tones of the human voice.

He also reveals his bias against formal schooling, at least for poets, when he describes the book as "getting a long way with poetry, considering all there is against it in school and college." The piece may seem insignificant given the statements about poetry in other prose, such as "The Figure a Poem Makes" or "The Constant Symbol," but Frost addresses important elements in the making of a poet. He reminds his readers that a poet "must strike his individual note sometime between the ages of fifteen and twenty-five." He "may hold it a long time," as did he, "or a short time, but it is then he must strike it or never." It is in the "freshness" and passion and spirit of youth that a poet must begin, and formal education can only interfere. He urges that we set the "expectation of poetry forward a few years" the way we set the clocks forward for daylight savings. Colleges keep the poet busy "till the danger of his ever creating anything is past. Their motto has been, the muses find some mischief still for idle hands to do."

Frost could not find his way in college. He attended Dartmouth and Harvard, but college was never to his liking and he did not graduate. He could not be cultivated there and even when he became a teacher himself, largely on the merits of his poetry, his attitude toward formal schooling would remain.

This introduction reveals Frost's ideas not only about the germination of poets and about the role of education, or lack thereof, in such a germination but also about his own growth as a poet, about the shared sap and root of all poets, and about the need to convince others not to judge a young poet too quickly. When young Frost's grandfather offered to fund him a year while he tried his hand at poetry, Frost asked for 20 years, and that is precisely what it took.

"Investment, The" (1928)

A sonnet expressing a mixture of optimism and despair, "The Investment" paints two perspectives of life that hint at the old saying about a glass being half empty or half full. This circumstance is not about optimism or pessimism, however, but about seeing life as simply a form of "staying," of lasting, of survival, or as something more. The view is presented as one held "[o]ver back" in some unidentified but familiar place where getting by has become, if not acceptable, at least accepted. In this same place there is a solitary house, however, that has renewed paint and a piano playing as signs that those within are demanding more. An old farmer digging potatoes is listening to the piano as he looks at the practical side of life: a winter's worth of potatoes to sustain them. The signs of life from the solitary house lead to questioning, as they do not speak of food, shelter, or other basic necessities. The piano and paint are so unlikely in this region that the narrator of the poem wonders where the vigor came from. Surely it must be due to new money, a new love, or "an impulse not to care" of an elderly couple. The piano and new paint end up bringing new life to the whole area, as even the practical digger has "half an ear" to the sound of the piano.

The poem concerns the haves and the have nots, but the difference seems to be less about economics than about perspectives. It is in some senses a tale about those who see life as something to survive versus those who see it as something to embrace, a life of drudgery versus one of music.

Further consideration can be given to the last two lines in relation to the title. The ending suggests that the old farmer and his wife might "sink under" their relationship, but the newly painted piano house and its investing owners are getting "color and music out of life." What seemed simply a financial investment in a new coat of paint and a piano becomes a more categorical investment, an investment in bringing a marriage out from under itself.

Frost once said, "There are two types of realists: the one who offers a good deal of dirt with his potato to show that it is a real one, and the one who is satisfied with the potato brushed clean." He defined himself as "inclined to be the second kind. To me, the thing that art does for life is to clean it, to strip it to form" (701).

"The Investment" first appeared in *West-Running Brook.*

FURTHER READING

Frost, Robert. *Frost: Collected Poems, Prose, and Plays.* Edited by Richard Poirier and Mark Richardson. New York: Library of America, 1995.

Rood, Karen Lane. "Robert Frost's Sentence Sounds: Wildness Opposing the Sonnet Form." In *Frost: Centennial Essays II*, edited by Jac Tharpe, 196–210. Jackson: University Press of Mississippi, 1976.

"[In Winter in the Woods Alone]" (1962)

This untitled final poem of Frost's final collection, *In the Clearing*, returns Frost to familiar territory. Readers begin the journey into Frost by reading "Into My Own," the first poem of his first book, *A Boy's Will.* There he hopes to "steal away" into the "vastness" of old and firm trees. But in this poem he goes instead "against the trees." In many respects the poems appear as bookends, intentional companion expressions of the poet's life and career. The reader is kept wondering, however, if Frost has "changed from him [we] knew" or if he is "only more sure of all [he] thought was true."

In this final poem the speaker fells a tree in late afternoon in winter, "mark[ing] a maple for [his] own." It is an apparent seasonal metaphor marking where he finds himself on his life's journey, and instead of disappearing into the dark trees, he makes a satisfactory single selection.

The speaker ends triumphant, even if having felled only one tree. The sometimes ambivalent, always insecure Frost who has given us nature sometimes in its darkest, sometimes in its most spectacular moments resounds, "I see for Nature no defeat / In one tree's overthrow / Or for myself in my retreat / For yet another blow." George F. Bagby writes that the poem is "about the opposition between human effort and natural fact" (67). Frost has not defeated nature, nor has it defeated him; there is simply a recognition of the limits of each force's powers. But there is also another aspect to this "standoff"—that humans can and do persevere in spite of nature. In this sense, we often overcome. It is as definitive a closing to a poetic career as might be hoped for from Frost. There is no defeat in his metaphorical retreat; he is retreating, giving up his pen, but not from defeat. Instead it is in preparation for Nature's final blow: the ending of his life, his death, and a way of going out with as much determination as he came into his own. *See* NATURE.

FURTHER READING

Bagby, George F. *Frost and the Book of Nature.* Knoxville: University of Tennessee Press, 1993, 66–67.
Monteiro, George. *Robert Frost and the New England Renaissance.* Lexington: University Press of Kentucky, 1988, 86–87.

"Iota Subscript" (1947)

Iota is the ninth letter of the Greek alphabet, the letter I. In this playful poem about inversion, Frost writes, "Seek not in me the big I capital," instead of "capital I." He also cautions not to seek the lowercase "i" either. Instead he holds that the only "I" he has in him is the iota subscript, which is written beneath a preceding vowel, when iota is silent. He paints himself as so small, the lowercase "i" being the smallest letter of the Greek alphabet, that he is an attention beggar instead of an attention getter. He ends up a subscript not for "a," "e," or "o," but for "u." The speaker presents himself in complete submission to the other; he becomes no individual except in his partner, he is a mere subscript of

"you." Ward Allen also extends the metaphor by noting that the vowel sound is lengthened when subscripted by iota, suggesting that the speaker's existence is also extended because of the coupling.

Frost adopts an unexpected diminutive stance here, and the poem becomes an expression of love, a great and unexpected love poem. The read, then, is whether it is a personal love or directed at the reader.

The poem was first collected in *Steeple Bush*.

FURTHER READING

Allen, Ward. "Frost's 'Iota Subscript,'" *English Language Notes* 6 (1969): 285–287.

"Iris by Night" (1936)

George F. Bagby describes "Iris by Night" as a "quasi-autobiographical account" and explains that the companion is unmistakably modeled after Frost's good but short-lived friend Edward Thomas, who was a Welsh poet and critic killed in World War I, only a few years after the two had met. He goes on to explain that the "Malvern side" line positions the two on the border between Herefordshire and Gloucestershire, where Thomas and Frost frequently walked in the summer and fall of 1914 (166).

In Greek mythology Iris is the personification of the rainbow that unites Heaven and Earth and is man's messenger to the gods. "Iris by Night" then refers to witnessing a rainbow at night, a strange and miraculous perception of "confusing lights," which Frost makes somewhat analogous to the legend of the Roman army's encircling and subsequent conquering of Memphis, an ancient Egyptian city, under Alexander the Great.

In the poem the pair are united by the circumstance that Frost, having outlived his dear friend, is the one who has "lived to tell." At the end of the poem something even more startling happens; the rainbow bends around the two, encircling them in a ring. The vision Frost presents is filled with love for his dear friend, as the ring protects them meaningfully "[f]rom all division time or foe can bring."

Bagby describes the rainbow as the "central Wordsworthian image of 'natural piety,' of the covenant between man and nature" (169). And "Here the arc of concord between man and nature is transformed into a circle enclosing and binding two extraordinary friends, a ring attesting to the marriage of true minds" (169).

Thomas wrote a piece, "This England," that appeared in the *Nation* the following autumn, on November 7, 1914, and contains an allusion to the same scene Frost describes here. Thomas expresses that bearing witness to something extraordinary brings about a sort of epiphany. He recounts the long walks he would take with his friend and then writes about "one evening the new moon made a difference." He describes the evening as the end of a wet, warm, and muggy day when the "moon, a stout orange crescent, hung free of cloud near the horizon," and he realized that either he "had never loved England" or he "had loved it foolishly, aesthetically, like a slave, not having realized that it was not mine until I were willing and prepared to die rather than leave it" (*Elected Friends*, 35). And die for it he did.

The term "elected friends" became the title of a book of Thomas's and Frost's correspondence published in 2003. The poem was collected in *A Further Range* but had previously appeared in the April 1936 issue of the *Virginia Quarterly Review*. See MYTHOLOGY AND FOLKLORE.

FURTHER READING

Bagby, George F. *Frost and the Book of Nature.* Knoxville: University of Tennessee Press, 1993, 166–169.

Elected Friends: Robert Frost and Edward Thomas to One Another. Edited by Matthew Spencer. New York: Handsel Books, 2003.

Perrine, Laurence. "Frost's 'Iris by Night,'" *Concerning Poetry* 12, no. 1 (1979): 35–43.

Thompson, Lawrance. *Robert Frost: The Early Years.* New York: Holt, Rinehart and Winston, 1966, 455–456.

"It Bids Pretty Fair" (1947)

Frost provides his own twist on an old analogy. As Shakespeare has Jacques say in act 2, scene 7, of *As You Like It*, "All the world's a stage, / And all the men and women merely players." On the surface Frost's brief poem seems to be a simple commentary about a stage, actors, and a play, but as always, it is more than that. Frost notes that while we may believe life is "out for an almost infinite run," that is not the case, for us individually or for humanity as a whole. The speaker imagines humanity holding up its end if nothing goes wrong with the sun—if our resources do not give out. In this way he reminds us that we rely not only on ourselves to keep going but also on powers beyond our control. And the speaker seems to be worried only about these powers, not about the conflicts and scuffles of the players. In this sense, the true act of our demise will not come from us but from nature. The "lighting" can also be read as the light of life, as when the lights go out, one is no longer "home."

"It Bids Pretty Fair" was first collected in *Steeple Bush*.

FURTHER READING

Richardson, Mark. "Frost and the Cold War." In *Roads Not Taken: Rereading Robert Frost*, edited by Earl J. Wilcox and Jonathan N. Barron. Columbia: University of Missouri Press, 2000, 72–73.

Rosenblatt, Louise M. "The Poem as Event," *College English* 26, no. 2 (November 1964): 123–128.

"It Is Almost the Year Two Thousand" (1942)

In this poem, written more than half a century before the millennium, Frost toys with the attitudes of apocalyptic millenarians, including the parenthetical aside that "science ought to know." The grandeur of the year 2000, when some say the end of the world will occur, is hardly anticipated as humanity busies itself with simple tasks like weeding gardens as well as such preparations as annotating texts. The ending has a bite: Humanity "well may raise" its head to "watch this end de luxe." The millennium would end our luxury here on earth, and we would watch from an emotional distance such disruption to our world. (But, Frost suggests, what a spectacle it would be!)

The separation of "de" and "luxe" in the Library of America version of the *Collected Poems* signals a pun, though even if it is not separated in a particular edition, it could be. Frost plays on both deluxe and luxury. It is an amusing usage: The ending would be sumptuous, an extravagant cosmic fireworks holiday, with all the frills. Also, *lux* is the Latin for "light." The end of "de luxe," of light, has a double meaning: the light-filled ending Frost describes versus the end of light, of life as we know it.

The best puns of the best poets are not often obvious; they are implicit or subsumed. Perhaps Frost never intended a pun at "deluxe," and we have, by his leave, provided it for him. However, he chose an extraordinary setting for the word "deluxe" and found a place for it nobody else would have thought of, taking the reader by surprise. He hid its variety and implications where they were bound to be found.

The poem first appeared in *A Witness Tree*.

"[It takes all sorts of in and outdoor schooling]" (1962)

One of the short poems etched in wood along the Frost Trail in Ripton, Vermont, this aphoristic couplet acts as a quick guide to reading Frost. In the first line he suggests that his poetry is not only for those who are "book smart" (or paper-trained, like a domestic pet) but for farmers, laborers, and laymen of poetry. Then he reveals a secret he has not kept well: that his is a "kind of fooling." The inside joke is that his poetry is a sort of trickery, and it is not only the masters of literature who can get it.

The poem was meaningfully first published as "The Poet" in *A Remembrance Collection of New Poems* (1959), but later became one of the closing poems of Frost's last collection, *In the Clearing*.

"I Will Sing You One-O" (1923)

As are many of Frost's speakers, this one is up late at night, alone. He lies awake, probably suffering from insomnia, though it later seems he has been awakened, "[w]ishing" the clock tower would "name the hour" by ringing its bells to tell him whether "[to] call it a day / (Though not yet light) / And give up sleep." He knows he can rely either on daylight to tell him the night is done or on the bell's ringing a morning hour.

It is snowing. The snow is described as "deep / With the hiss of spray." It may be a blizzard, with the wind whipping the snow up and down the streets. The descriptions of snow contain some of Frost's best imagery. The speaker imagines that it is so cold that the tower clock has frozen and its "hands of gold" are tied together in front of its "face," as if in self-protection against the storm's buffetings. The clock's time may be off; the cold may have "checked the pace," altering it.

The second, lengthy, section begins with an exclamatory "Then came one knock!"—the "knock" of the clock is its chime. The tower rings one o'clock in the morning, and "then a steeple." The steeple suggests that a church also rang one, though the hands on the one and the 12 of the tower may also suggest a steeple. The steeple and the clock tower speak to themselves, perhaps one and the same, hearing each other's bells. The scene is deserted. The bells ring for the "few people" who have been roused by the wind, as the speaker has. The bells strike the speaker's frosted window, described as like "a beaded fur."

In one ring they seem to speak of all the moon and stars and even the constellations. The bell's peals speak for the clock. The clocks fill their "throats" and speak to "the furthest bodies / To which man sends his / Speculation"—those cosmic bodies, the constellations and stars that are "[b]eyond" where God is. The furthest stars are cosmic specks of "yawning lenses."

The bells' ringing is "not their own." Instead they speak for the clock. The word *one* is described as a "grave word," the word *grave* appearing twice in the poem. The word *one* is grave because it is singular and solitary, utterly alone. But that singular word, not even a word but a chime, makes a single star, unable to ring, instead tremble and stir. The vibrations of a knock somehow affect a star millions of miles away. Robert Hass writes that "The word 'one' . . . not only refers to the sound of the clock tower as it strikes one o'clock but also to the poet's imagined cosmic unity, 'beyond which god is'" (155).

The star is so far beyond that its "whirling frenzies" appear to stand still. It is as alone as the speaker: Only the two are awake to hear the knocking of the clocks. The star's isolation is underscored by its having become a nova, a very bright star, but with no one on Earth knowing it because of the star's distance from the planet, making it all the more isolated. The star exists alone, as the man is alone in the night.

The poem then turns to the process of human history, observing both the origin of man in relation to the distant star going nova and man's relationship to man since his origin.

The poem ends on a stark note, with man dragging down "man / And nation nation." The poem is not about man dragging down man, though the result of this would lead to the utter loneliness, the single and solitary "One" of the meditation.

The poet sings with the chimes, perhaps seeking refuge from his isolation in the frenzies of a star beyond God, rather than in Him.

"I Will Sing You One-O" was collected in *New Hampshire* but had been previously published in the October 1923 issue of the *Yale Review. See* STARS.

FURTHER READING

Bagby, George F. *Frost and the Book of Nature.* Knoxville: University of Tennessee Press, 1993, 154–157.

Hass, Robert. *Going by Contraries: Robert Frost's Conflict with Science.* Charlottesville: University Press of Virginia, 2002, 153.

Perrine, Laurence. "Frost's 'I Will Sing You One-O,'" *Explicator* 34 (1976): 48.

Timmerman, John H. *Robert Frost: The Ethics of Ambiguity.* Lewisburg, Pa.: Bucknell University Press, 2002, 140–141.

"Kitchen Chimney, The" (1923)

The poem presents itself as a formal request to the builder of a home, but by the end becomes something more like sage advice. The speaker makes only one request, that the kitchen chimney not be built on a shelf. He is unconcerned with cost or labor in the building of the chimney, as long as it is full-length and built "clear from the ground." He has learned a lesson from the past, as he knows of houses that "didn't thrive" when their chimneys were not built properly. He wants his to be built thoroughly from the bottom up, and he falls back on the cliché about not building castles out of air. He wants a chimney that is firmly anchored on terra firma so that it will have permanence and stability. Methods of knowing are not successful when they are used incompletely and haphazardly. They are the cause of houses not thriving, of having tar stains, and of having the smell of fire drowned in rain (ironically, chimneys are often the only structures still standing after a house fire). This last metaphor clearly uses fire as the light of reason and knowledge and claims that only strong structures will help nourish such flames.

The final two stanzas draw an important analogy to knowledge, the ways we go about building our knowledge and having integrity about what we know. There are those who believe without asking why. But the final two stanzas are about the consequences of being wrong, citing the "ominous stain of tar." Those who simply believe without offering substantial reasons for their belief build castles in air—airy nothings. This is just the sort of foolishness of which, when younger, he himself was guilty.

The poem was first published in the August 1923 issue of the *Measure* and was later collected in *New Hampshire.*

FURTHER READING

D'Avanzo, Mario L. "How to Build a Chimney: Frost Gleans Thoreau," *Thoreau Journal Quarterly* 9 (October 1977): 24–26.

Marcus, Mordecai. *The Poems of Robert Frost: An Explication.* Boston: G. K. Hall, 1991.

"Kitty Hawk" (1962)

The poem is subtitled "Back there in 1953 with the Huntington Cairnses (A Skylark for Them in Three-

Beat Phrases)." Frost began the poem in the summer of 1953 after visiting Cairns, a lawyer and author, and his wife, Florence, in Kitty Hawk in 1953. While there he had the opportunity to stand where Orville and Wilbur Wright made their first successful flight at Kill Devil Hills near Kitty Hawk, North Carolina, in 1903. While Frost regarded the poem as "the most important poem that he wrote in his last decade" and as one that had "immense personal meaning," the poem is not at all among his best (Parini, 388). Written late in his career, the poem places much emphasis on allusions and shows a seeming desire on Frost's part to write an epic poem.

Frost called it "a longish poem in two parts." He described the first part as being personal and a description of an "adventure" from his boyhood. Here he refers to the real journey that the youthful Frost took in November 1894 when he set off in a bleak mood, stimulated by his fear of losing his then girlfriend Elinor, for the Dismal Swamp, which runs along the Virginia and North Carolina border. His "symbolic journey" through this "frightening place, full of bogs and quicksand" came to an end "rather flatly" when, exhausted, he hitched a ride out of the bog with duck hunters (Parini, 49–50). He drew on this experience in a number of ways as a poet; "Reluctance" provides another example. Having returned to the same area 60 years later to visit the Cairnses, Frost must have imagined his life coming full circle in some way. He once explained that he used his own story of the place to "take off into the story of the airplane" and noted how he might have used his early experience to write an "immortal poem but how, instead, the Wright brothers took off from there to commit an immortality." The second part of the poem he described as the "philosophical part" (Parini, 388).

The poem is riddled with allusions, among them: "Alastor, or the Spring of Solitude," written in 1816 by Percy Bysshe Shelley; the "tower shaft" that Herbert Hoover "[r]aised . . . / To Undo the wrong," a 60-foot granite shaft with a beacon that was erected during President Hoover's administration in 1932 at Kill Devil Hills; Cape Hatteras, off the North Carolina coast, a dangerous navigational point in the Atlantic and the site of a 193-foot lighthouse that had to be abandoned in 1936 when the ocean came

too close; Theodosia Burr Alston (1783–1813), the only child of Aaron Burr who attended her father's trial for treason in 1807 and whose charm was said to have helped sway the court; "And the moon was full," a line from Alfred, Lord Tennyson's "The Passing of Arthur"; the Moabite stone, discovered in 1868 at Dhiban, a ruined city of Palestine, a block of black basalt with a 34-line inscription in the Moabite alphabet dating from the ninth century B.C. that is the oldest extant Semitic inscription and an account of the wars of Mesha, king of Moab, including those against kings of Israel; "Darius Green and His Flying-Machine," by John Townsend Trowbridge (1827–1916); and so on.

The poem's simple rhyme moves from the individual to humanity and expresses a reaching forward. The poem establishes, with the plane as its metaphor, that humanity has not gotten far off earth, that we could have gotten just as far walking. It references the beginning, with Adam's naming of things, the apple, knowledge, and Satan. The poem concludes that while we do not have the sun's rays, we have our own rays of reflection—our minds. The poem is celebratory and powerful in its message, and Frost ends by thanking "you," perhaps the reader, for "this token flight," his life's experience, as he moves from himself to the universe in 60 years. As Mark Richardson explains; "Here, Frost is addressing not only the 'pilots' of that first feeble aircraft at Kitty Hawk, whose efforts he takes as the *type* of man's effort to slip the bonds of Earth. He is also addressing 'pilots' more generally, a category that extends to include such pioneers and farmers as 'The Birthplace' concerns, and also . . . the figure of the poet himself" (229).

Robert Faggen notes that "its emphasis on the spirit's descent in the material world echoes a chord struck in 'The Trial by Existence' from [Frost's] first book *A Boy's Will*" (255). He describes the poem as "clarify[ing] the continuity between Christianity and modern science and technology," and finds that "The Fall for Frost is a story of freedom and departure that represents the first act of science, the pursuit of knowledge, which in its attempt to ascend only leads deeper into matter. All human history is a recapitulation of the myth" (253).

The poem began as "The Wrights' Biplane" in *A Further Range*. A later version was Frost's 1956 Christmas poem, and yet a later version was published in the November 1957 issue of the *Atlantic Monthly*. A version was also published in W. S. Braithwaite and Margaret Carpenter's *Anthology of Magazine Verse for 1958* and the *Saturday Review*. The final version was collected in *In the Clearing*. The contents of the book were preceded by an excerpt from "Kitty Hawk" titled "But God's Own Descent," which begins with that title line and ends with the line "Into the material." The excerpt can be read as a kind of self-proclamation of the poet's life's achievement of "risking spirit in substantiation" and of "charg[ing] into earth / In birth after birth" in his poems.

See FUGITIVE and TECHNOLOGY.

FURTHER READING

Abshear-Seale, Lisa. "What Catallus Means by Mens Animi: Robert Frost's 'Kitty Hawk,'" *Robert Frost Review* (Fall 1993): 37–46.

Bagby, George F. *Frost and the Book of Nature.* Knoxville: University of Tennessee Press, 1993, 98–102.

Crane, Joan. "Robert Frost's 'Kitty Hawk,'" *Studies in Bibliography: Papers of the Bibliographical Society of the University of Virginia* 30 (1977): 241–249.

Faggen, Robert. *Robert Frost and the Challenge of Darwin.* Ann Arbor: University of Michigan Press, 1997, 253–255.

Hass, Robert. *Going by Contraries: Robert Frost's Conflict with Science.* Charlottesville: University Press of Virginia, 2002, 175–180.

Kau, Joseph. "'Trust . . . to go by Contraries': Incarnation and the Paradox of Belief." In *Frost: Centennial Essays II*, edited by Jac Tharpe, 99–111. Jackson: University Press of Mississippi, 1976.

Meyers, Jeffrey. *Robert Frost: A Biography.* New York: Houghton Mifflin, 1996.

Parini, Jay. *Robert Frost: A Life.* New York: Holt, 1999.

Perrine, Laurence. "Robert Frost and the Idea of Immortality." In *Frost: Centennial Essays II*, edited by Jac Tharpe, 87–89. Jackson: University Press of Mississippi, 1976.

Richardson, Mark. *The Ordeal of Robert Frost: The Poet and His Poetics.* Chicago, Ill.: University of Illinois Press, 1997.

Stott, William. "'Living Deeper into Matter': Robert Frost's 'Kitty Hawk' and the Creation of Nature," *North Carolina Literary Review* 12 (2003): 46–56.

"Last Mowing, The" (1928)

This poem is like another of Frost's, "The Demiurge's Laugh," which also begins like a fairy tale with "It was far in the sameness of the wood." "The Last Mowing" opens with "There's a place called Far-away Meadow," immediately drawing the reader to expect a Neverland of imaginary creatures, fairies, and ghouls.

But there is a quick shift in line two to something far more practical: the regular mowing that is required of a meadow. The men of the farmhouse have decided that there is a meadow that should be left to overgrow itself, as it is apparently no longer ripe for farming; it is "finished with men." Instead, at least initially, flowers will flourish; they will overtake the meadow for as long as there is no threat of trees.

Trees are damnable, it appears, as their shade can be ruinous to the blossoms. Trees eventually will encroach given enough time. As Mark Richardson observes "these men, these Frostian mowers and plowers, contend for dominion over the flowering field, as in a battle, with trees that are themselves proprietary martial figures who 'march into a shadowy claim'" (*Ordeal*, 62).

The flower's life is short, and so is its opportunity in the meadow. It must seize the day, since the "moment is ours." The meadow has lost its farming purpose, has perhaps been overcultivated, overmowed, and now it is the flower's limited time to shine.

Richardson also remarks that "[i]n his subtlest vocational poems Frost arrives at a kind of androgyny: his mower-poets are always also ever so slightly feminine, as much on the side of the flowers of the field as on the side of the order that would 'subdue' or harvest them" (*Ordeal*, 63). This speaker is so intimately acquainted with the flowers that he "needn't call [them] by name."

The last mowing has come, and it is time for celebration. But there is also a clear acknowledgment of a pattern and system that exists outside of human control. There seems to be a time when we should let nature "take its course" and simply follow along. We may not like the long-term result, but there is a clear deference to the authority of nature when its processes have overcome the jurisdictions of human control.

"The Last Mowing" first appeared in *West-Running Brook*.

FURTHER READING

Richardson, Mark. "Frost's Poetics of Control." In *The Cambridge Companion to Robert Frost*, edited by Robert Faggen, 203–210. Cambridge: Cambridge University Press, 2001.

———. *The Ordeal of Robert Frost: The Poet and His Poetics*. Chicago, Ill.: University of Illinois Press, 1997, 61–63.

"Last Word of a Bluebird, The" (1930)

The poem is subtitled "As Told to a Child" and mentions by name Frost's second child and first daughter, Lesley. Frost also mentions Lesley in "Maple."

"The Last Word of a Bluebird" is the closest Frost comes to being a children's poet. The tone is tender, playful, and sweet, adjectives that hardly come to mind in regard to the publicly portrayed Frost, but these characteristics are sometimes subtly revealed in various sections of Jay Parini's biography, *Robert Frost: A Life*.

The crow's ability to survive the winter is contrasted with the bluebird's fragility. The bluebird, who has had its first indication of winter with the ice on the trough, has "just had to fly!" but has thoughtfully sent the stronger and more able crow with a message of "Good-by, / . . . And do everything!" to his child friend. The poem sends a brief moral message to the child to experience all there is to experience, all she is capable of, though the weaker bluebird cannot because he must flee to survive. Lesley also is asked to behave herself and be "good," which sounds like something the second messenger, in this case the girl's father, has apparently thrown in.

The poem is filled with hope for the return of the spring, when the bluebird might again come back and sing, but it is also a somewhat obscure (for the ears of a child) reminder of the threats of winter against which nature's creatures must protect themselves. It can also easily be viewed as a poem of optimism, of an attitude that speaks of some creature's ability to overcome in the face of challenges.

The poem was not included in the first edition of *Mountain Interval* but was added to *Mountain Interval* in the *Collected Poems* of 1930; it shares its subtitle with "Locked Out."

FURTHER READING

Dell, Roger D. "Three Separate Leaves from Robert Frost's Derry Years: A Note and Transcriptions," *Studies in Bibliography: Papers of the Bibliographical Society of the University of Virginia* 36 (1983): 229–232.

"Late Walk, A" (1913)

It is late in the season, and the speaker, as in "A Leaf-Treader," is out for a walk. He is again solemn about the change in season that in this instance is evidenced by the bare tree. In "The Last Mowing" the speaker is filled with wary exuberance in expectation of the blossoms that will overtake the field the longer it remains unmowed. Here the mowing field is nearly "headless" in the "aftermath" of autumn mowing. Frost's use of "aftermath" partially suggests seasonal change and partially suggests an unnatural disaster. The word evokes humans' responsibility, if not for the turned leaves, then for the headless flowers, for humans have mowed them down in the field.

The birds are "sober," the whir of their wings "sadder than any words." And the speaker's thoughts are so stark that they rattle one of the last leaves from the tree's limb. The speaker's walk is brief. He finds in the now barren landscape a "last remaining" unmowed aster, which he harkens to bring "again" to his beloved—apparently a ritualistic gesture—before its blueness has completely faded or humanity snatches its head with the mower. The speaker, while melancholy about the loss of wild flowers, does not hesitate to pick the last surviving flower for his love, making this decapitation nearly as ruthless as those that disturb him. Ironically, this gesture is suddenly presented not as melancholy but as romantic. The poet's choice of the aster, a flower native to New England, is significant, as the aster is robust and hearty, tending to outlast other flowers.

It is easy to imagine the young Frost bringing such a flower to his future wife Elinor, since the poem was collected in Frost's first volume, *A Boy's Will*. It had been previously published in the October 1910 issue of the *Pinkerton Critic*.

"Leaf-Treader, A" (1936)

Frost is sensitive to even the minutest manifestations of nature. Just as in his poem "Departmental," about the death of the forager ant Jerry McCormic, where he finds significance and sadness in the death of a tiny insect, in "A Leaf-Treader" he improbably but persuasively associates himself with fallen leaves that he finds "threatening." The poem has been described by Katherine Kearns as "about being mired down, being dragged toward death" (76), yet in the end the speaker survives and persists past the death of leaves and the cycles of nature.

During his autumn walk, the speaker feels that he might have with too heavy a tread crushed the leaves under his weight. But if he has done so, he has not intended to; he has been "too fierce from fear." It is not so much nature he is fearful of as what nature reveals about his own uncertain hold on life. Our attachment to the tree of life is just as fragile as that of the leaves to their trees, and we are as vulnerable to nature's buffets as they are.

The speaker identifies with the leaves and finds in their falling a reminder that all things must "go."

Admiring the leaves in their heyday brings the realization that this time of elation soon will pass. Frost said that a poem "begins in delight and ends in wisdom." Delighting in nature's beauty is inseparable from the sense of impending loss. What is particularly haunting is that the leaves were "more lifted up than I" and still they withered and fell. In a sense, the speaker suggests he should have expected that the leaves were less vulnerable to nature's ways than he, because of their "higher" station, but they have not been. And their vulnerability is undeniable, unlike ours, which we can, however futilely, deny.

The speaker realizes how much a part of nature he is. Nature is not something distinct and distant; it is a constant reminder of all of which we are a part. To be in nature and not to see this is to be culpably ignorant. We cannot behold the cyclical passage of seasons or the perpetual life-and-death struggles in nature and not see that we struggle with the same forces. In the poem "Design" the speaker cannot witness the spider's capture of the moth without seeing the arachnid and the insect as "assorted characters of death and blight" and without wondering at the "design" that governs "in a thing so small." The poet tries to come to terms with this same realization in "A Leaf-Treader."

The consciousness of nature and the speaker's empathy with the leaves cannot be shaken off. The leaves "tapped" at the speaker's eyelids and "touched" his lips with "an invitation to grief" because his mind can recognize and acknowledge the similarities between them. When he says he has "safely" trodden, he knows that his safety is not something that can be taken for granted. Now he must raise high his knee to be "on top" of the coming snow and to go on. But just as the leaves were above him once, he, now on top, will one day fall. It is knowing this that makes him apprehensive. Indeed, he considers himself a "fugitive." But, oddly, the overall tone of the poem is not so much fearful as it is candid. The speaker seems resigned to this revelation. Instead of continuing to grieve, with strength he lifts up his knee and continues on his way—his life's path. This determination is consistent and habitual in Frost. Even though we humans are cyclical and die, we also persist and continue into the next generation. The species endures as nature does.

The long lines and end rhymes in this poem contribute to a trodding sound that has been described by Kearns as the lines dragging themselves "like wounded snakes across the page" (76). Tyler Hoffman writes that the poem's lines "which swell to iambic heptameter proportion, indicate the long, unbroken stretch of his life's journey and his determined resistance to the transcendent experience of death" (156). Richard Poirier writes that Frost is "in danger of succumbing to the call of nature, of losing himself, of having his sound in words absorbed into the sounds made by the natural elements," but Frost's leaves do not *crunch* underfoot (57).

Ironically, the title could indicate a certain intentionality, but the speaker's reflection exempts him from such a criticism, as his "success is marred by [his] consciousness of cruelty" (Faggen, 273). Robert Faggen takes a somewhat darker approach, writing that "survival values and toughness are regarded above pity for those who do not succeed" (273).

"A Leaf-Treader" was collected in *A Further Range* but had first been published in the October 1935 issue of the *American Mercury. See* NATURE.

FURTHER READING

Bagby, George F. *Frost and the Book of Nature.* Knoxville: University of Tennessee Press, 1993, 2–3.

Borroff, Marie. "Robert Frost: To Earthward." In *Frost: Centennial Essays II,* edited by Jac Tharpe, 21–39. Jackson: University Press of Mississippi, 1976.

Doyle, John Robert, Jr. *The Poetry of Robert Frost.* New York: Hafner Press, 1962, 235–236.

Faggen, Robert. *Robert Frost and the Challenge of Darwin.* Ann Arbor: University of Michigan Press, 1997, 273.

Hoffman, Tyler. *Robert Frost and the Politics of Poetry.* Hanover, N.H.: Middlebury College Press, 2001, 156–157.

Kearns, Katherine. *Robert Frost and a Poetics of Appetite.* Cambridge: Cambridge University Press, 1994, 76–77.

Miller, David L. "Dominion of the Eye in Frost." In *Frost: Centennial Essays II,* edited by Jac Tharpe, 141–158. Jackson: University Press of Mississippi, 1976.

Poirier, Richard. "Choices," *Robert Frost Modern Critical Views,* edited by Harold Bloom. N.Y.: Chelsea, 1986.

"Leaves Compared with Flowers" (1936)

What begins as a simple exercise in comparison leads to the observation that comparing leaves with flowers is like comparing night and day. Leaves can be admired in the dark, as their rustling can still be heard, but flowers need the light of day to shine fair and be appreciated. The speaker acknowledges that trees do not always bear "flower or fruit" and that even some "giant trees have blossom so small" that they might as well have none, but he soon dismisses the assumption that having blossoms is of any real value. Smoothness and roughness become satisfactory enough.

The use of dark and light and night and day as metaphors is a bit timeworn. But in its reliance on several associations with these terms to send its deeper message the poem says as much about people as about trees. Leaves and flowers are both fragile, seasonally dependent, and not as everlasting as trees and bark, which remain throughout the changing seasons, and the poem suggests that it is what lasts that eventually appeals. The transition between night and day represents emotional shifts, as leaves are all the speaker's "darker mood" but also represent shifts in time, not only in the course of a day but over the course of a life. Petals represent youthful pursuits, and while the speaker may have "once pursued" them, there is a sense that he has outgrown such foolishness and has gained the wisdom to embrace the leaves, the darker side, and the bark, the stronger side, which resists temporal shifts.

Blossoms become a metaphor for what beauty can come of putting the "right thing" at a growing source's root, but beauty in the end takes a back seat to resistance, strength, and endurance.

The poem was first published in *The Saturday Review of Literature* on February 2, 1935. It was later collected in *A Further Range. See* NIGHT.

FURTHER READING

Jost, Walter. "Rhetorical Investigations of Robert Frost." In *Roads Not Taken: Rereading Robert Frost*, edited by Earl J. Wilcox and Jonathan N. Barron, 179–197. Columbia: University of Missouri Press, 2000.

"Lesson for Today, The"
(1942)

"The Lesson for Today" was first published in *A Witness Tree* but previously read at a June 20, 1941, anniversary celebration of Harvard University's Phi Beta Kappa Society. The occasion for which it was written accounts for the poem's teacherly tone and title.

Frost is setting out to instruct, as the learned do on particular subjects, and to counter the "sages" he takes issue with. He begins by ridiculing the notion that we live in a more uncertain age than anyone else who has ever lived, and this becomes the crux of the piece.

Halfway through the first stanza, Frost refers to Edwin Arlington Robinson's "Miniver Cheevy" by writing that he would "Seek converse common cause and brotherhood / . . . With poets who could calmly take the fate / Of being born at once too early and late." Robinson, who thought of himself in just such a way, was a significant predecessor of Frost's; some have even gone so far as to claim that there would have been never a Frost without a Robinson. Robinson's eponymous Miniver Cheevy dreams of "the days of old / When swords were bright and steeds were prancing" and "of Thebes and Camelot." He is a man who imagines himself "born too late" and romanticizes medieval times, failing to acknowledge the difficulties of life at that time.

On being asked in a 1955 interview whether or not the 20th century was the worst time for poetry,

Frost responded "I wrote a poem about that, 'The Lesson for Today.' I don't know how to measure. In our time, anyway, you are a rank insider. You can't tell" (Cramer, 135). Apparently, even if Frost believed that times were bad, he would refer to an earlier time and set about comparing the conditions for poetry then and in his own time. People tend to feel, like Hamlet, that "the time is out of joint" (Timmerman), but Frost is quick to step forward to denounce such a claim.

Frost imagines engaging in discussion with the "Master of the Palace School," Alcuin (735?–804), the ecclesiastic teacher and scholar of York, and asks "Tell me as pedagogue to pedagogue." He later acknowledges that Alcuin has not said a thing, unless Frost put it in his mouth to say. He sets out in a conversation with the dead to make his point, alerting us that he "never take[s] [his] own side in a quarrel," making his position, as always, a bit obscure.

Frost points out that it would have been easy for Alcuin to blame his age for not having "won Virgil's fame" but reminds his readers that Alcuin never made such a claim. He hooks arms with Alcuin against the poets of his own day who use "excuses lame" to explain their not being famous. He argues that the poets troubled today have too much "social fact" on their minds; they are not focused on the creation of poetry as they should be. They need to narrow their subjects lest they become "mentally agape," or, he teases, "die of philosophical distention."

Earlier poets paved the way for the poets of today, but the "groundwork of all faith is human woe." Times stay the same as much as they change. Frost's lesson is to remind the sages what it would have been like for the poets of earlier times and explain through example the obstacles they faced and how similar they are to those of "today."

Frost suggests to his interlocutor a comparison of the ages to see which is "darker." He lists the usual problems—war, sordid peacetimes, corruption—counting them alike for both time periods. He raises the awareness of space in modern times as a way of recognizing how tiny and insignificant humanity is, but he also notes that the Golden Age created insignificance from under the heel of God;

both are "belittlements," simply different in kind. Both science and religion belittle humans, making them feel microscopic. As Robert Faggen writes, "Frost linked science and religion in the way they both serve to humiliate man" (250). Frost wonders "how to take the curse, tragic or comic." Faggen says he took it both ways: "neither purely tragic nor purely comical but a blend of both, a happy-sad humility without resolution" (250).

Each age ends up being just like the others "for the soul," and the joke is on all of us. The poet, like Hamlet, ends in a graveyard, reflecting on death, our short lives, and the frustration of trying to compare present day to the ages and ages hence. We all seem to be destined to grapple with the same problems, no matter when we live or who we are; it is the human condition. Frost shows this through the reference to memento mori. Alcuin, wrote his own epitaph, which became a model for others. Its full translation can be found in the notes of the Library of America's edition of Frost's *Collected Poems*. In brief it reads, "What you are now ... I have been ... what I am now, so you will be.... Now I am ashes and dust, and food for worms."

Frost closes, "And were an epitaph to be my story / I'd have a short one ready for my own. / I would have written of me on my stone: / I had a lover's quarrel with the world." And so he did, as can be seen on his gravestone in a little churchyard in Bennington, Vermont.

FURTHER READING

Cramer, Jeffrey S. *Robert Frost among His Poems: A Literary Companion to the Poet's Own Biographical Contexts and Associations*. Jefferson, N.C.: MacFarland, 1996.

Faggen, Robert. *Robert Frost and the Challenge of Darwin*. Ann Arbor: University of Michigan Press, 1997, 250.

Kearns, Katherine. *Robert Frost and a Poetics of Appetite*. Cambridge: Cambridge University Press, 1994, 24–25.

Sutton, Betty S. "Form as Argument: Frost's 'Lesson for Today,'" *Fu Jen Studies: Literature and Linguistics* 18 (1985): 81–96.

Timmerman, John H. *Robert Frost: The Ethics of Ambiguity*. Lewisburg, Pa.: Bucknell University Press, 2002, 101–104.

"Letter to *The Amherst Student*" (1935)

"Letter to *The Amherst Student*" was published in *The Amherst Student* on March 25, 1935. Frost was born on March 26, 1874, and the opening refers to birthday greetings from Amherst students.

Some have held that the age in which they live is "particularly bad," worse than any that preceded it. Frost challenges such attitudes, writing that "[w]e have no way of knowing that this [our] age is one of the worst in the world's history." He targets Matthew Arnold (1822–88) and William Wordsworth (1770–1850), saying that they each claimed the same, and on it goes "back through literature." He writes that "they claimed the honor for their ages" or "rather for themselves," describing such an attitude as "immodest." We narrow our view of the ages when we place ourselves at the center, and we disregard all human experience when we give our own the greatest significance.

"All ages of the world are bad—a great deal worse anyway than Heaven," Frost proceeds, demonstrating that compared with an ideal, all ages are likely to come out poorly. He also implies that a religious view of this life is secondary, since one that serves as a stepping stone to the good life, or afterlife, is certain to make this one seem inadequate. If all ages did not face struggles, "the world might just as well be Heaven at once and have it over with," Frost teases, suggesting that there would be no need for this life if it did not involve struggle. Progress does not necessarily make life easier. Besides, our view of progress is always informed and constrained by our perspective: "it is not possible to get outside the age you are in to judge it exactly." Frost uses a number of examples to describe just how "dangerous" it would be to try to "get outside of anything as large as an age," and compares it to trying to "engorge a donkey."

We do not need to know how good or bad an age is, as there "is always so much good in the world that it admits of form and the making of form." "In us nature reaches its height of form and through us exceeds itself," and this is even more true for the artist, the poet. In this sense, the human being is of utmost importance. In some ways this attitude contradicts his earlier, more religious view, as it implies that human beings have it in them to reach the pinnacle of their potential and to be the source of meaning and virtue, even in this life. This is in some ways similar to philosopher Friedrich Nietzsche's notion of the *Übermensch* or Superman: "Anyone who has achieved the least form to be sure of it, is lost to the larger excruciations." Each person reaches his or her own pinnacle, and "it must stroke faith the right way." That is, it must come close to faith in what it gives us. We do not need "to get a team together before we can play," as the gratification is highly individual and given from within rather than "from above."

We do not have to hover over an abyss; the "background is hugeness and confusion shading away from where we stand into black and utter chaos," but "against the background any small man-made figure of order and concentration" can stand. The confusion that we face, that comes from our place in the world, can be pleasant, and we can "look out on it with an instrument,"—literally, a telescope or, figuratively, our imagination—and "tackle it to reduce it" to human terms, as Emily Dickinson and so many others did before Frost and as Frost does himself. Our place in existence as we face off against chaos is assured: "we like it, we were born to it, born used to it, and have practical reasons for wanting it there," because it challenges us to exceed ourselves. Like Nietzsche, Frost believes that this "yes" to existence, this antinihilistic attitude, is the attitude that should be adopted.

To Frost "any little form [he] asserts upon" this chaos this confusion "is velvet." That is, it provides the greatest satisfaction, comfort, and status to the senses. It is the supreme satisfaction of being. If he were a Platonist, he would have to consider this "for how much less it is than everything." Plato is known for claiming that the transcendent is the only place where we can find the realm of Being, which contains unchanging ideas and the real and true "Forms" of Beauty, Truth, and so forth as opposed to those existing in less-than-real form in this world. Aristotle, Plato's pupil, in contrast, argued that "forms" only exist in the things themselves, as they are perceived in this world, and Frost reveals himself as an Aristotelian, as he does elsewhere.

This letter provides insights into Frost's philosophies not only about our position in the universe and in the history of human existence but also about his own attitudes toward art and its ability to provide us with the transcendent in this world. He is realistic and it is romantic. His realism and directness are the source of his romanticism. He works with the stuff of human experience and celebrates nature through our experience with it, without placing us any more at the center of the universe than any other human being who came before or who is to come. And he remains deceptive about his religious beliefs, as always.

See PHILOSOPHY.

FURTHER READING

Richardson, Mark. *The Ordeal of Robert Frost: The Poet and His Poetics*. Chicago, Ill.: University of Illinois Press, 1997.

Thompson, Lawrance. *Robert Frost: The Years of Triumph, 1915–1938*. New York: Holt, Rinehart and Winston, 1970.

"Line-Gang, The" (1916)

The line-gang are the workers who, "pioneering by," are responsible for putting in the latest progressive technology of Frost's time: the telephone line. The speaker observes that their mistreatment of the forest breaks it, manipulating the emotional association of what it means to be "broken." The telephone poles become dead trees that are planted in place of living trees, the "living thread" the telephone line that strings them together.

The speaker bemoans the new technology as something that not only has tarnished the landscape but has done so by setting the "wild at naught." He is highly critical of the new technology, and the poem's temporality places Frost as a stodgy and change-resistant fellow to its intrusion. It is not one of his works worthy of great attention, but if his views toward technology are of interest, other poems concerned with the telephone, such as "An Encounter," might be of value, as well as "The Egg and the Machine," where the view of technology is that it simply leads either to finding better ways to destroy ourselves and others or to separating from and excluding those who fail to fall in line.

The poem was first published in *Mountain Interval*. See TECHNOLOGY.

"Line-Storm Song, A" (1913)

A line storm is a violent rainstorm near the time of an equinox. Here the poet pays tribute to a line storm's power, marveling at how the hoof-prints "vanish away" and the flowers along the road "bloom in vain," since they are too wet for a bee to make use of. Romantically the speaker embraces the storm and invites a lover to "[c]ome over the hills and far" with him and "be [his] love in the rain."

Katherine Kearns finds that the poem "reiterates the seemingly inextricable bond in Frost's poetry between sexuality and danger or violence . . ." (173), but this seems to be a bit of a stretch. The poem, appearing in Frost's first volume, *A Boy's Will*, demonstrates competence but shows little evidence of what would later come to be recognized as signature Frost. It more closely resembles one of his predecessor's works than it does his own better recognized poems. It is in a sense a skewed version of Christopher Marlowe's "The Passionate Shepherd to his Love" (1599), which begins "Come live with me and be my love, / And we will all the pleasures prove / That valleys, groves, hills, and fields, / Woods, or steepy mountain yields."

In many ways the poem is strikingly identifiable as one from *A Boy's Will*, since those often demonstrate some strain to pay homage to poets of the past and frequently lack the ingenuity and originality of his later work. The poem is full of effort, aiming at being poetic, but it does have an undeveloped irony that can be appreciated as characteristic of Frost, even if a bit too tame.

The poem was first published in *New England Magazine* in October, 1907.

FURTHER READING

Kearns, Katherine. *Robert Frost and a Poetics of Appetite*. Cambridge: Cambridge University Press, 1994.

"Lines Written in Dejection on the Eve of Great Success" (1962)

The Soviet Union's *Luna 2* space probe was the first to impact Earth's moon in 1959, just before this poem was written and in the midst of the Cold War. This is a poem not about personal success but about the success of a nation, one that was at the time in fierce competition with the United States to be first in space.

Many poem titles have begun "Lines written . . ." This title also suggests William Butler Yeats's "Lines Written in Dejection," which speaks of "the dark leopards of the moon," and Samuel Taylor Coleridge's "Dejection: An Ode." Frost may have been playing on either or both. The cows in Frost's poem jump over the moon, as in the Mother Goose rhyme; they do not land on it.

Jeffrey Cramer reports that Frost once joked, during a reading at BREAD LOAF SCHOOL OF ENGLISH, that this poem was a "joke about science . . . a comic strip teasing . . ." (176). Certainly the old farmer has a bit of fun with this one. He harkens back to the beginning of his poetic life with the imagination of "godmother Goose" but offers a sardonic twist, making the poem a nursery rhyme for grown-ups. The implication is that although as a society we have gotten more involved in the concrete, all this dazzling science has yet to match the beauty of the imagination. Frost's cow, the imagination, jumps over moons, not onto them as spacecraft would.

The postscript, far longer than the rest of the poem, seems to be an account of the ordinary, a shift in setting and purpose. The transition between the poem and the postscript is rough, almost as if to jar the reader out of a reverie, an immersion in the dreams of science. It becomes an account of something quite ordinary as if to supplant the initial appeal of thinking that science and the concrete ever replace (or compete with) the stuff of imagination.

The poem talks about people's tendency to think that science can catch up with human dreams. The moon used to be the stuff of imagination, of nursery rhymes and high-flown poetry, connected to the strenuosities of imagination and the magic of stories. But now the moon is realized in a scientific and concrete way—it is old, cold rock in the vastness of space. It is a target for rockets and space vehicles, a place to land rather than something fantastically elated cows might jump over. The poem suggests that all this scientific mumbo-jumbo should not be seen as a substitute for time-honored imagination. We are goosier now—more foolish, though more scientific—but we have not caught up with the cow, might be his claim.

The postscript ends by hinting at more realistic and immediate concerns to focus the reader back to the concrete, to the questions that might be asked about a space program—not about its overall goals but about those who promote such programs simply to make the papers and to compete with other nations, to outrace them. He is clearly not in favor of this "Great Success."

The poem was first published in Frost's *A Remembrance Collection of New Poems* (New York, 1959) without the "Postscript" stanzas and was later collected in *In the Clearing. See* SCIENCE and TECHNOLOGY.

FURTHER READING

Cramer, Jeffrey S. *Robert Frost among His Poems: A Literary Companion to the Poet's Own Biographical Contexts and Associations.* Jefferson, N.C.: MacFarland, 1996.

"Literate Farmer and the Planet Venus, The" (1942)

The poem's subtitle is "A Dated Popular-Science Medley on a Mysterious Light Recently Observed

in the Western Sky at Evening." In this lengthy conversational poem, which Robert Faggen finds "gives considerable insight into the interplay of scientific ideas and human drama" (102), the speaker, a stranger, knocks unexpectedly on a door, throwing those inside into a tizzy. A large farmer comes to the door, and a number of children come outside with him. The speaker and the "literate farmer" begin their conversation on "an equality."

After the introduction of the scene in the first stanza, the poem is made up entirely of dialogue. The speaker explains that the reason for his stopping was to compliment these folks on their sky view. There is a particular star in the sky that, from this location, is so beautiful and bright that it appears to be the sun. This compliment seems to just be a ploy on the part of the stranger, however, because no sooner does he compliment the view than he asks for a place to stay for the night, or at the very least a drink of milk.

The mighty and also apparently learned or insightful farmer, perhaps surprisingly to the stranger, responds that those dining happened to be discussing the star as well, and it is not the one that is "Serious by name," a pun on Sirius the Dog Star, brightest in the evening sky. Its strong light has been "going on" for several years. He believes it is not a star at all but a "patented electric light" put up by some "Jerseyite" inventor (Thomas Edison was from New Jersey) who is trying to promote and bring about further EVOLUTION. The farmer is sure this is the case, unless the "monkey jokes" of the last 50 years and Darwin himself are "proved mistaken, not the Bible."

Frost provides an unlikely characterization for a farmer, who is stereotypically often depicted as illiterate, and the stranger assumes that this literate one is also a liberal who is all for a "better race." Soon the discussion oddly leads to Native Americans and the return of European immigrants on the *Mayflower*. In this way, the "star" becomes a subject of inquiry for various political questions about equality and evolution and whether the white race should be commended and glorified for the invention of electricity or whether it should be viewed as one further injury against the Native Americans.

In Frost unlikely candidates often end up debating subjects that seem far beyond their usual circumstance: a farmer and a stranger on a doorstep here, two fellows working a field in "From Plane to Plane," or two strangers sharing a room in "A Hundred Collars."

As the dialogue continues, the stranger is uncertain that the bright light is a star. The farmer uses as evidence the fact that it only goes so high in the sky and then slowly seems to come back down, asserting that it is all "one big blob / of electricity." There is, as elsewhere in Frost, the implication that country folk are generally more instinctively knowledgeable than city folk, as the farmer points out that the stranger "might not notice if [he's] lived in town."

The discussion then turns philosophical. The stars, not the artificial lights, are a way of keeping us from being too "overtight." They are a way of interrupting the night, but they are still more divine. The farmer is disagreeable, feeling that it is all "sick talk" and that the slave, in this case the stranger ("I see what *you* are"), never thanks his emancipator.

The stranger realizes that the farmer thinks that artificial lights are "a patent medicine / Put up to cure the world by Mr. Edison," and the farmer agrees. The reference here and earlier in the poem is to Thomas Alva Edison (1847–1931), the American inventor who patented more than 1,000 inventions, among them the microphone (1877), the phonograph (1878), and the incandescent lamp (1879). In New York City he installed the world's first central electric power plant (1881–82). The farmer says that Edison "argues science cheapened speed."

Frost's familiar criticism of technology becomes apparent when the farmer ironically identifies the "good cheap twenty-four-hour day" as the goal of Edison. He positions unnatural light as an acknowledgment that "sleep or slowness is the deadly crime." Further, the farmer begins to see the invention of the lightbulb as associated with "human hate" and war. This clearly hyperbolic comment contains some technological truths.

In the end evolution is about needing no sleep at all. This is the connection to Darwin that was being made earlier. The farmer is dismissive of himself (he does not really mean it): We "haven't got the mind," he says, that the great Edison and others like him have, so what we know of nature, of rising and set-ting with the sun, of hard work, and of leisure when the day is done is something to be set aside (following the stereotype of country folk). The farmer is really on the attack when he cautions that Edison and others "have no other object than our good."

Certainly human beings did not live among dinosaurs, but Frost uses the point of the discovery of rubbing sticks together to make fire "to scare away the pterodix" as an example of the beginning of the lightbulb. The poem ends with the question whether there should be any limits to technology.

While the poem is mostly concerned with how new technologies irreversibly alter our lives, it is also concerned with how they can ultimately lead to further destruction, as evidenced by Frost's comment that mankind has "one loving and one hating hand." Certainly further technological developments have influenced our lives, taking away more of our valuable time while being promoted as time savers, but they have also aided in, on the one hand, great improvements such as the speed and amount of information that can be disseminated and, on the other hand, the ability to destroy, as in war. The planet Venus in the end seems to be a simple street light, the "Evening Star" an unnatural baseball in the sky lit up by Mr. Edison.

The poem was first published in the March 1941 issue of the *Atlantic Monthly* and was later collected in *A Witness Tree. See* STARS.

FURTHER READING

Faggen, Robert. *Robert Frost and the Challenge of Darwin.* Ann Arbor: University of Michigan Press, 1997, 102–104.

Perrine, Laurence. "The Tone of Frost's 'The Literate Farmer and the Planet Venus,'" *Notes on Contemporary Literature* 5, no. 2 (1975): 10–13.

Schutz, Fred. C. "Frost's 'The Literature Farmer and the Planet Venus': Why 1926?" *Notes on Contemporary Literature* 4, no. 5 (1974): 8–11.

"Locked Out" (1930)

Subtitled "As Told to a Child," Frost here offers a different notion of what it means to be locked out of the house. In this instance it is the flowers that are left outside, not children. And they fare well: Only one flower is found the following morning with "bitten stem." Even so, the speaker imagines it was himself, as a child, who was responsible.

We fear being locked out in nature and the dark, but there is little to be afraid of. Or, rather, there is much for adults to be afraid of, but when they tell children what it is to be in the outdoors, they must understate the possibilities. What causes the most damage, it seems, is inside the house, where one should least expect it.

"Locked Out" shares its "As Told to a Child" subtitle with "The Last Word of a Bluebird." It was first published in the *Bouquet*, a magazine compiled by the Frost children, in September 1914. It was later reprinted in February 1917, in the *Forge*. The poem was not included in the first edition of *Mountain Interval* but was added to it in the 1930 *Collected Poems*.

FURTHER READING

Kearns, Katherine. *Robert Frost and a Poetics of Appetite*. Cambridge: Cambridge University Press, 1994.

"Lockless Door, The" (1923)

Lawrence Thompson discusses important biographical connections to the poem but reiterating them would limit what is a simply stated but surprisingly complex poem. Putting aside whatever actual experiences Frost had allows for better scrutiny of what was metaphorically built of his experience. The various meanings are particularly layered in this verse, where Frost slips "over the sill" not only literally but figuratively.

The poem manipulates concepts of inside and outside, protection and vulnerability, and home and the self. The speaker exists on the other side of a door, separated from the world for some time. When someone at last wants to come in, he fearfully prays and then sneaks out a window before inviting the stranger in. He admits in the end that he "emptied" his cage quickly and easily when first noticed, but also that he continues to hide on the outside, in the

world, and "alter with age." The alteration does not come from being inside or out—it comes from time. But because the door is lockless anyone could have gotten in at any time. And while he refers to his home as a cage, he also was not trapped, since he, likewise, could have gotten out at any time. The implication is that people can neither be kept out nor in, but a knock coming from the outside can be what it takes in order for one to stir—especially when it happens to be a persistent knock, not just a casual knock. There is an important difference highlighted here between physical and social hiding.

It is ironic that the speaker still puts forth the effort to invite the stranger in. He could have just as easily slipped over the sill and stolen away, without any backward gesture. His invitation is perplexing but could have been made out of habit, or, what is more compelling, simple longing for another.

The lockless door could easily explain us, our personalities, our hidden selves that we allow only a few people to see (if at all), the knock at the door being that of someone who wants to come inside and get to know us, to know the self that we normally hide from others. The speaker thinks of the door to which he had previously paid little attention, implying that most of us are not aware of our vulnerability until someone knocks. We can sometimes be elusive. We tiptoe about and hide in the dark, praying that if and when we let others in we can continue to hide. In the world one uses a mask, sometimes the mask of poetry, to hide behind.

The poem was first published in *A Miscellany of American Poetry* (1920) and was later collected in *New Hampshire*. *See* HOME, THEME OF.

FURTHER READING

Sheehy, Donald G. "Robert Frost and 'The Lockless Door,'" *New England Quarterly* 56, no. 1 (March 1983): 39–59.

Thompson, Lawrance. *Robert Frost: The Early Years*. New York: Holt, Rinehart and Winston, 1966.

"Lodged" (1928)

Frost once said that his utmost ambition in writing poetry was to lodge a few poems where they would be hard to get rid of. In "Lodged" he explains what it is to be lodged. The word has the positive definition that Frost uses in relation to poetry but also a far more negative one. To lodge can also be to hide and protect oneself. In the case of poetry it is to keep a few best efforts from being forgotten; in the case of flowers in the wind and the rain it is to keep from being so beaten down as to be destroyed. As humans it means to get in a position to be able to withstand the beatings that nature can and does administer.

George F. Bagby calls the poem "as basic an emblem poem as one could imagine," adding that while "it does not deal with natural process, it is typical of those fablelike poems which see nature as massive and inimical to individual concerns" (55). Bagby calls emblem poems those that begin with the "observation or description of a natural emblem (object, scene, or incident) and then 'translates' the emblem's significance or lesson, 'reads,' the natural text" (ix).

In many ways the brief six lines are characteristic of Frost's nature poems. As in so many of his others on the same subject, nature pushes and pelts, and we are affected, afflicted, altered, and often worn, but rarely, if ever, broken. When we do not die from the forces of nature, we survive scathed and often all the more lodged. But while lodging is a form of hiding, it is also a form of endurance. The poem is confessional and is reminiscent of the tragedies in Frost's life and everyone's, as it seems we all know "how the flowers felt."

The poem was first published in the *New Republic* on February 6, 1924, and was later collected in *West-Running Brook*.

FURTHER READING

Bagby, George F. *Frost and the Book of Nature*. Knoxville: University of Tennessee Press, 1993.

"Lone Striker, A" (1936)

The opening is ominous, with a mill bell changing its toll to one that is "like the count of fate." It sends everyone running late, and one mill worker is unable to make it to the gate before it closes. The punishment for being late is that for half an hour the gate is locked and those on the outside have their pay docked. The "lone striker" who does not make it to the gate wonders if there is an unmanned machine inside and imagines one that is.

He goes on to envision someone spinning yarn with a great deal of help from a machine. Still, she is valuable as the "spinner still was there to spin. / That's where the human still came in." While the factory is made up largely of machines, they are still manned, as "Man's ingenuity [is] good." Robert Faggen writes that "the spinner is a metaphor for the inextricable presence of the human in any machinery including nature's harmonious 'harplike' oversight of all its individuals. Without any specific mention of what it produces, this machine becomes a thing of beauty in its cooperative power, bringing single strands together not artificially 'tied' but fluidly 'blend[ed]'" (153).

The poem essentially deals with the difference between those who work in a mechanized factory and those who are reminded of nature. The lone striker is one who sets out for the wilderness, goes "on strike" from the factory, has a desire to return to nature, but is willing to return to the factory if needed, the way he might avoid going to war until he is drafted.

The poem appeared with the subtitle "Without Prejudice to Industry" in *A Further Range* in a section titled "Taken Doubly." The subtitle is telling. The prejudice toward industry is individual rather than overarching. As Tyler Hoffman writes, the lone striker is "not a fellow clamoring for general work-stoppage or seeking to throw a wrench in the machine" (160). After all, the "factory was very fine; / He wished it all the modern speed," but it just was not the natural choice for him, and the poem suggests that he participates in the mechanized work reluctantly.

Faggen argues, "If on the surface 'A Lone Striker' appears to be political, deeper down it verges on satire of the humanistic rebellion against technology" (154). The lone man is going on strike, but he is also striking out against technology and for the wilderness.

The poem was first published in booklet form as number 8 of Borzoi Chap Books in 1933.

FURTHER READING

Faggen, Robert. *Robert Frost and the Challenge of Darwin.* Ann Arbor: University of Michigan Press, 1997, 153–154.

Hoffman, Tyler. *Robert Frost and the Politics of Poetry.* Hanover, N.H.: Middlebury College Press, 2001.

"Looking for a Sunset Bird in Winter" (1923)

"Looking for a Sunset Bird in Winter" is one of a handful of poems in which the poet puns on his own name. He laments the cycles of nature. Frost cannot quite be read the same in less seasonal climates as there is so much of New England in his poetry, so much of northeastern weather.

The poem opens with the West running out of gold, that is, with the sun almost fully set. The air is brutally cold, and the speaker is "shoeing home across the white." The speaker remembers how in summer, in the very same place, a bird's sweet swinging could be heard. But now all birdsong has ceased. There is the stillness and silence of winter. "[G]oing twice or more around a tree" would offer no advantages, as there is nothing thriving in the tree, except a single desperately clinging leaf. Likewise, all it takes is walking twice around a tree for seasons to change—that is how quickly they seem to come and go.

The speaker is reminded that the "crystal chill" adds nothing to the beauty of the snow; it simply adds "frost to snow" like "gilt to gold that wouldn't show"—a humorous play on the poet's name and his perception of the scene.

The image then becomes like a painting with its brush strokes; the "crooked stroke" of "either cloud or smoke" across the blue sky is symbolic of isolation, with only one star piercing through when the sun falls this winter evening. The speaker initially thinks he sees a sunset bird but is left with one piercing little star. He does not seem at all disappointed.

George F. Bagby holds that the poet "learns a lesson akin to [English romantic poet William] Wordsworth's faith that nature did betray the heart that loved her" (142). Even so, the star seems to represent hope and the recognition that life goes on, that the next season the bird and leaves will return. For all its vagaries, this poem expresses a certain predictability of seasonal nature and a trust in what nature can bring, even though it can be haunting. The speaker retains hope, as the title indicates, continuing to look for a sunset bird in winter.

The poem was first published in *New Hampshire.*

FURTHER READING

Bagby, George F. *Frost and the Book of Nature.* Knoxville: University of Tennessee Press, 1993.

"Loose Mountain, A" (1942)

The poem bears the subtitle "(Telescopic)." Appearing three poems earlier in *A Witness Tree* is "A Considerable Speck," which has the subtitle "(Microscopic)," suggesting that Frost intended the two to be companion poems.

The subtitle here suggests that a telescope is needed to see what the speaker sees, that what is seen is barely or not at all visible to the naked eye. The speaker opens by asking if we stayed up to watch the star shower known as Leonid that is "mysteriously pelted at us" once a year. He announces that the Magi did. Leonid is one of the falling stars of the meteor shower that recurs annually in mid-November. And in the New Testament the Magi are the three wise men who traveled to Bethlehem to pay homage to the infant Jesus. A magus is also a sorcerer or magician.

The meteor shower is one of nature's seeming threats that amounts to little more than "fiery puffs of dust and pebbles." The onslaught is apparently retribution for our foolishness in embracing electricity, "artificial light," over the "sovereignty of night." "The Literate Farmer and the Planet Venus" makes similar accusations about natural versus unnatural light.

Electricity is so overwhelming that we do not even notice the meteor shower anymore; besides, it "never reaches earth except as ashes." There is a complete deflation of the natural by the artificial. What once guided the three wise men to Bethlehem now goes with barely a notice. The "loose mountain" is the breaking up of the mountain into meteor parts and coming at us as ashes. George F. Bagby writes that perhaps in no other Frost poem "does his astronomical perspective lead to a grimmer view of natural hostility" than in this one (70).

Frost ends the poem on a direr note, suggesting that the meteor shower is a hint of something much more dark, "outer black," and that the personified vastness of space is using the impotent showers because of its present indecision. It is holding back its true power to destroy us, simply deciding when would be the best time to do it.

The poem was first published in *A Witness Tree.* The manuscript title for the poem was "Telescopic—A Loose Mountain." *See* STARS.

FURTHER READING

Bagby, George F. *Frost and the Book of Nature.* Knoxville: University of Tennessee Press, 1993, 70–72.

"Lost Follower, The" (1942)

Those who leave poetry, the "golden line / Of lyric" never do it for "darkness" but instead for "golden light divine." Our spirit is often swayed by "religious pranks," but those who fail at being poets never do it in favor of "money-metal banks." Instead, the danger to poetry is always in a different direction, toward what individuals believe are greater callings, such as music, politics, and so forth.

Jeffrey Cramer reports that Frost said the poem was about Jean Flexner and Carter Goodrich, who he felt "forsook poetry to do something for the next election." Frost went on to say, "I ought to say this of them: that they were two whom I had set my heart on for the poetry they were going to write, and both of them left the poetry to do social work. Both of them" (138).

It is clear that it would be difficult to measure up to the Golden Age, but to live "ungolden with the poor" is satisfactory. Frost writes tongue-in-cheek that this has always been "poetry's great anti-lure."

Frost urges the lost follower not to stray but, when he does, knows that he will forsake poetry for "Something about a kingdom in the sky"—something he imagines to be a greater good but is an illusion. In this sense, poetry seems to be the only reality, the only thing above such interests as music and political progress.

Mark Richardson describes the poem as one that "considers the case of a young poet who left the pure calling of lyric for the impure poetry of grievance and social struggle" (157). Frost hopes to lure the lost back with his own golden lines, but he puts forth little effort in his argument. The poem is matter of fact, a general description of the state of affairs: Poetry is not meant to be written by everybody. He might also have added that it is not meant to be read by everybody.

The poem was first published in the *Boston Herald* on September 13, 1936. It was later collected in *A Witness Tree.*

FURTHER READING

Cramer, Jeffrey S. *Robert Frost among His Poems: A Literary Companion to the Poet's Own Biographical Contexts and Associations.* Jefferson, N.C.: MacFarland, 1996.

Richardson, Mark. *The Ordeal of Robert Frost: The Poet and His Poetics.* Chicago, Ill.: University of Illinois Press, 1997, 157–159.

"Lost in Heaven" (1936)

The speaker is lost on a stark night and looks to the sky as a guide, but storm clouds cover the stars either completely or at least enough to make distinguishing among them impossible. No individual star is bright enough to help him identify one constellation from another, making his usual guiding "skymarks" unavailable. He realizes he is lost but finds he is happy not knowing where he is. He embraces his "lostness" because as long as he is on earth he does not need to know where he is. His is a heaven on earth.

The poem supplants the idea that this world is merely a vestibule to the next. It dismisses heaven as some otherworldly place and affirms this place as one of great value. A similar sentiment is expressed in "Birches," where Frost writes: "Earth's the right place for love / I don't know where it's likely to go better."

"Lost in Heaven" was first published on November 30, 1935, in the *Saturday Review of Literature*. It was later collected in *A Further Range. See* STARS.

"Love and a Question" (1913)

Lawrence Thompson writes that "Love and a Question" was inspired by an experience Frost had on the Derry farm. A tramp had stopped one evening asking to spend the night, and Frost reluctantly allowed him to do so. But the poem, appearing in Frost's first book, *A Boy's Will*, seems also to express something of Frost's youthful fears that his future wife Elinor might be lost to him while she was away at college. While she was studying at St. Lawrence, Frost arrived with a copy of his book of poems *Twilight*, which he had printed—a copy for himself and one for Elinor—and when she received him coolly he became convinced that she would break off their secret engagement and that, even more, she had an allegiance to another. Frost was a fiery-tempered and imaginative adolescent.

While it is rarely necessary that a good poem be read autobiographically, this, like several others in Frost's first volume, is not particularly inspired in other ways. Instead, it asks to be read autobiographically, as it comes off as almost confessional. The poem simply concerns a young husband who is uncertain about his relationship with his new bride and wonders whether the stranger seeking shelter is a threat. The bridegroom wants his bride encased in gold and pinned—captured and protected like a wild butterfly. The protection is as much his own as it is hers, as a bride trapped in a box will be unable to be untrue.

The bridegroom wants to do the right thing and offer the stranger a place to sleep, but he is not sure if it will jeopardize his own happiness. The poem is a parable that John H. Timmerman compares to Jesus' parable of the wedding feast, in which those who arrive late will be cast out (115). But more importantly, it is about where to draw the line between one's own and another's happiness. As Timmerman explains, the poem raises the ethical question, "Do I have obligations to others, even if they should interfere with my own happiness and freedom?" (115).

In the last stanza the bridegroom is portrayed as being willing and eager to aid the poor through food, money, or prayer, but he remains worried whether it is his religious duty to aid a man when the risk could "mar the love of two." Katherine Kearns writes that the poem "creates a stranger whose presence is most specifically felt to threaten man and wife but who also clearly sounds the integrity of the individual soul by urging it away from domestic community and toward isolation" (152).

The poem raises important questions about what individuals can and should risk to help someone else. *See* NIGHT.

FURTHER READING

Collins, Michael. "A Note on Frost's 'Love and a Question,'" *Concerning Poetry* 8, no. 1 (1975): 57–58.

Kearns, Katherine. *Robert Frost and a Poetics of Appetite*. Cambridge: Cambridge University Press, 1994.

Perrine, Laurence. "The Dilemma in Frost's 'Love and a Question,'" *Concerning Poetry* 5, no. 2 (1972): 5–8.

Thompson, Lawrance. *Robert Frost: The Early Years*. New York: Holt, Rinehart and Winston, 1966.

Timmerman, John H. *Robert Frost: The Ethics of Ambiguity*. Lewisburg, Pa.: Bucknell University Press, 2002, 114–116.

"Lovely Shall Be Choosers, The" (1930)

"The Lovely Shall Be Choosers" is a poem that might, oddly for Frost, be called feminist. It may also be thought of as something of a mini–verse play for voices. The setting of the piece is hard to pin down but seems to be a not-so-heavenly heaven. The opening voice bellows, "Hurl her down!," suggesting an angel being cast from heaven. Hurling is a brutal act, and when the unknown "she" is cast down through "Seven levels of the world" it is hard not to imagine the action taking place in some other, albeit skewed, transcendent place. One voice asks how much time they have to hurl her, and the answer is 20 years, in which time the woman also will make many of the major choices of her life.

The voices allow for the unidentified woman, the "lovely" (which seems to be categorical for woman), to "choose," but they assume from the outset that "She *would* refuse love safe with wealth and honor!" They seem to know what she would choose if she were given choices, because her choices are so limited. But the voices do not say clearly what she would refuse love safe with wealth and honor for. However, the insinuation seems to be that she would choose anything else save a life with wealth and honor.

"Invisible hands" crowd around the woman, prepared to press on her shoulders and weigh her down. She remains proudly erect, but the force of the unknown weighs heavily on her. Haughtily one voice asserts that they can let her choose and "still triumph." The scene is set; she will do as expected, even if they let her believe she is choosing, because, ultimately, she does not really have any choices. She is somehow fated (since she is always left "blameless"), apparently not because of the pressing hands of these many strangers but because of the options that will present themselves.

All of her so-called choices are in some sense burdens but are presented ironically as "joys." They follow the various milestones of the average woman's (and one might add, man's) life: getting married, having children, and so on. Her role at all times is to remain humble, grieving secretly, and above all to remain ever silent. Hers is not among the voices heard in the poem.

Near the end of her life, the voices declare, send "some *one*" (Frost's emphasis) to hear her, but not her entire story. But even in the end, she is unable to speak. Her heart goes out to this one who cares to listen, but she seems to die before she can "almost spea[k]." The poem ends with the ominous phrase "Trust us."

The woman is to hide her grief and her pain, to withstand and survive, not to be joyful. Her role is to keep things secret so as not to be shameful and to take her joy in this humility. She is downtrodden, and she ends up becoming aware of her predicament: "Give her the comfort . . . of knowing / She fails from strangeness to a way of life / She came to from too high too late to learn."

Everything is out of the woman's control, and the poem seems to highlight the limited options a woman in Frost's time was faced with, as well as how little support she had for how she conducted her life. It is important to note, however, that everything is also out of a man's control, beyond the control of human beings. Their lives in the seven levels of the world are predetermined.

"How Hard It Is to Keep from Being King When It's in You and in the Situation" is also constructed around the subject of free will. It consists of a debate over whether there is such a thing as a free will, or whether when "it's in [us]" our fates are predetermined. There the speaker concludes glumly that this "is half the trouble with the world / (Or more than half I'm inclined to say)," as if the trouble is in its being in us, rather than in our betraying our attributes. In several ways the two poems are similar in what they suggest about human circumstance.

The poem is pained and painful. Lawrance Thompson reads it biographically. He writes that years after Frost's mother died of cancer Frost "paid poetic tribute to [her] by dramatizing poetically what he sometimes viewed as the unmerited injustices that had ruined her noble life." He further adds that the poem "ironically and sarcastically represented all her freely willed choices as illusions, arranged by higher powers (either angelic or Satanic, or perhaps both working in collusion) to mete out retribution or punishment for her refusal to accept the proper kind of marital love" (291–292).

Robert Faggen takes a different approach. He writes that in the poem, "we have a demonic expression of the fear of woman's power to reject male authority, to refuse 'love safe with wealth and honor'" (194). He concludes that the "sadness in Frost's domestic dramas can be seen in the terrible isolation of women and men stemming from ancient fears of their wills and desires" (195).

The poem is among Frost's strangest, but it navigates themes that are common to his work. The voices in the last utterance claim, frightfully, "Trust us," a poignant reminder that in Frost little trust is placed in anything transcendent.

The poem was first published in booklet form in The Poetry Quarto series (1929). It was not initially collected in *West-Running Brook* but was added to it in the 1930 *Collected Poems. See* POLITICS.

FURTHER READING

Faggen, Robert. *Robert Frost and the Challenge of Darwin*. Ann Arbor: University of Michigan Press, 1997, 194–195.

Thompson, Lawrance. *Robert Frost: The Early Years*. New York: Holt, Rinehart and Winston, 1966.

"Lucretius versus the Lake Poets" (1947)

In this poem Frost turns to the philosophy of Titus Lucretius Carus (96?–55? B.C.), while satirizing the view of nature espoused by the English Lake Poets. The Lake Poets were the English romantic poets, such as William Wordsworth and Samuel Taylor Coleridge, who were associated with the Lake District of northwest ENGLAND and derived inspiration from the surrounding natural environment. Frost plays with the rhyme here, as he does in "Departmental." The poem is facetious and lighthearted, but it honestly portrays Frost's ideas of nature and academia.

Frost begins with an epigraph from Walter Savage Landor's "I Strove with None": "Nature I loved; and next to Nature, Art." The poem closes "But you say in college nomenclature / The only meaning possible for Nature / In Landor's quatrain would be Pretty Scenery." Frost knows better than that. He may love the pretty scenery of nature, but he knows not only what it represents but what it conceals.

Lucretius, like Epicurus (341?–217 B.C.), before him, believed that two fears caused human unhappiness: fear of divine intervention and fear of death. He was therefore interested in earthly and natural, rather than divine, explanations for creation. He did not believe that the gods interfered with or determined human affairs, and he thought that death was not an experience like other experiences. He saw it as the absence of all experience; when death comes, we are not really there.

Frost suggests that while human beings are susceptible to nature's forces, they do not have to attribute them to otherworldly phenomena in order to explain them or come to terms with their existence. The words *Goddam* and *Machinery* reveal these attitudes. While the Lake Poets viewed nature romantically, in Frost's view nature is devoid of purpose and can be explained by physical law. Like the birds in "Acceptance," Frost suggests that he is willing to let what will be simply be.

The acceptance of what will be for Frost is not to be found in reasoning that explains all through supernatural forces; he does not ignore the human connection to nature. Instead, acceptance is to be found in the recognition that, as part of nature, we have a history and a knowledge of nature that is internal and inherent. We are in some way linked to the "vapor" from which we came. The agnosticism of this poem reveals why Frost is able to seek resolutions when faced with conflict. Rather than lash out at some god or controller of the universe, he recognizes the inevitability of nature's effects, knows that he can hold no one accountable for them, and instead of succumbing to them finds there is no other recourse than to persist. This same ability to accept this world as an unexpected happenstance is expressed in other poems such as "Acceptance" and "A Leaf-Treader." And it is with a certain contentment that Frost says "'twas the effort, the essay of love."

Frost seems also to be mocking the administrative notion of academia. He is taking Epicurus and Lucretius as having important worldviews, but after those views are filtered through administration they become simply "pretty scenery." By doing so he completely negates these ancient philosophers' importance and their relationship to art. He also facetiously portrays academia's authoritative nature in discussion, ending with a facetious wish that all the dean's offices be complete and unlimited.

Like Lucretius, Frost takes on the "Whole Goddamn Machinery." *See* NATURE.

FURTHER READING

Fleissner, Robert F. "Frost's Ancient Music," *Paideuma: A Journal Devoted to Ezra Pound Scholarship* 13, no. 3 (Winter 1984): 415–417.

"Maple" (1923)

"Maple" reads like a children's tale. It is about a little girl named Maple who spends her life trying to follow the course her name's meaning has set for her, yet the meaning of her name remains a mystery throughout, making her life's course seem less fated after the fact than it at first appears.

The opening of the poem calls attention to the innocence of children and their failure to recognize difference until another child or an adult points it out. In this case the child is not aware that the name Maple is uncommon until a teacher decides to call her Mabel, assuming there has been a misprint. When she asks her father, he dismisses the teacher's comment and goes into an important discussion about how the child got her name. Her mother, who died while giving birth to her, named her. It is for them, he says, to guess why she named her Maple. The child, as children will do, nearly forgets the meaningful conversation until years later, when she begins to question her name again, concluding that "Its strangeness lay / In having too much meaning."

Maple considers names that have a meaning, such as Rose, and considers how, in growing up in the same house that was her mother's as a child, she might glean something of her name's meaning. She looks everywhere for any hint of an explanation, including a page of the family Bible marked by a maple leaf.

The girl continues to look for "herself, as everyone / Looks for himself, more or less outwardly," the poem hinting at where the fault in her examination lies. Her looking sends her in various directions, including to the "highest city built with hands," where she holds an office job and people continue to get her name wrong. Succumbing, she lets them call her "what they like." While she works

in the city, a man says she reminds him of a maple tree, and that is all it takes for them to marry. She now has a partner to seek the answers with, and they, married, return to her father's home looking for answers. It is in vain, however, as nothing more is discovered. This leads to a series of speculations as to why she believes her father put her off, when in actuality he had just "put himself off."

The moral comes at the end: "A name with meaning could bring up a child, / Taking the child out of the parents' hands." Instead, Frost concludes, it is better to have a meaningless name and leave the rest to "nature and happy chance." Another moral seems to be connected to the way in which Maple's search for meaning "made" her marriage and "ruled her life." The search for meaning can be what is important, not the finding of it. This attitude also seems to be manifest in "Escapist—Never."

This is the only poem where Frost names several of his children, including Lesley, Carol, Irma, and Marjorie. Another poem in which he names one of his children is "The Last Word of the Bluebird," where he mentions Lesley. Here, when he names his children, he mentions that those names "signified nothing."

Robert Pack calls the poem "replete with subtle laughter" (223). Robert Faggen writes, "Though the narrator may hope that single metaphors do not govern people's lives, he expresses a tacit recognition that a certain reality does indeed govern them and that we might be happier if our consciousness did not deceive us into pursuing deeper meanings" (208). It seems that there is no deeper meaning for Maple, or the poem.

"Maple" was first published in *The Yale Review* in October 1921 and was later collected in *New Hampshire*.

FURTHER READING

Cook, Marjorie E. "The Serious Play of Interpretation," *South Carolina Review* 15, no. 2 (Spring 1983): 77–87.

Faggen, Robert. *Robert Frost and the Challenge of Darwin.* Ann Arbor: University of Michigan Press, 1997, 203–208.

Kearns, Katherine. *Robert Frost and a Poetics of Appetite.* Cambridge: Cambridge University Press, 1994.

Pack, Robert. *Belief and Uncertainty in the Poetry of Robert Frost.* Hanover, N.H.: Middlebury College Press, 2003.

Masque of Mercy, A (1947)

Masques were popular in ENGLAND during the 16th and early 17th centuries. They were dramatic plays usually performed by masked players who represented mythological or allegorical figures. Frost wrote two masques in dramatic verse, *A Masque of Mercy* and *A Masque of Reason.* Each masque satirically addresses modern skeptical concerns with Christian theology. Sidney Cox describes the piece: "[Frost] teases fellow-writers, comments on recent politics, offers a new—and convincing—explanation of how scientific method led, through the discovery of fire insurance, to the concept of compulsory 'mass mercy,' all in the same blank verse dialogue which illuminates the profoundest mysteries."

The setting of the poem is a bookstore late at night. The characters are the owner of the bookstore, whose full name is My Brother's Keeper (but is referred to as Keeper), a revolutionist, [Genesis 4:9 "And the Lord said unto Cain, Where is Abel thy brother? And he said, I know not: Am I my brother's keeper?"]; the storekeeper's wife, Jesse Bel, a pun on Jezebel, the wife of Ahab who in the Old Testament was a cruel and immoral queen (the name has become colloquial for a shameless and scheming woman); Paul, the doctor, "analyst" of Jesse Bel [The Jewish Apostle Paul whose given name was Saul and whose life is mostly described in the book of Acts]; and a Fugitive (Jonah).

Introductions reveal that the name My Brother's Keeper was a political choice "left over from the Brook Farm venture," a reference to the Brook Farm Experiment in communal living established by early American transcendentalists. The form was situated on 200 acres of land in West Roxbury, Massachusetts, and was in operation from 1841 to 1847. Ralph Waldo Emerson was among those associated with the experiment. The reference is tongue-in-cheek, of course, suggesting that the same reference in the Bible suggests similar earthly political concerns as those of the Brook Farm transcendentalists.

While Jesse Bel is closing up shop for the night, a Fugitive appears, demanding to be let in. He claims that "God is after [him]!" and he is therefore seeking protection. Keeper asserts "This is a bookstore—not a sanctuary!" But the Fugitive is in search of a Bible. Keeper teasingly inquires whether the book will be used to "get away from God" and goes on to explain that is what "people use it for too often," indicating the direction the masque will take.

Unlike *A Masque of Reason,* this masque is more concerned with the relationship of man to God than God to man. As in *A Masque of Reason,* a character, in this case the Fugitive, undergoes a name change only a few pages into the play. Again, Frost's choice of names intentionally draws allegorical parallels. Here the fugitive turns out to be Jonas Dove, alias Jonah. In the Bible, Jonah was a prophet swallowed by a whale and disgorged three days later unharmed.

The Fugitive is on the run because he believes God is planning to make him prophesy, and he refuses to do it. The Fugitive points out his role in the Bible in the "story you may have forgotten / About a whale." Keeper satirically points to Herman Melville's *Moby Dick* but claims it was written by Rockwell Kent, an illustrator and political activist for the left (1882–1971). The conversation returns to Jonah's claim of prophesy as he asserts that this is the "seventh time [he has] been sent / To prophesy against the city of evil." The conversation then turns toward cities more generally and the distinction between agrarian and urban cultures. Here we learn that Jesse Bel is a tippler who took to drink because she and her husband are poor: "My man can't earn a living," she says.

Keeper inquires what city Jonah is against, and Jonah uses New York as the inclusive example. He claims he was hired to speak, to prophesy, that very evening at an engagement. Jesse Bel insists that Jonah's "courage failed," and Frost draws a reference to Edwin Arlington Robinson's "Mr. Flood's Party" with the lines, "Them is my sentiments, and, Mr. Flood, / Since you propose it, I believe I will."

What the Mr. Flood of Robinson's poem will do is have another drink.

The reason that Jonah refuses to prophesy is finally revealed: "I've lost my faith in God to carry out / The threats He makes against the city evil. / I can't trust God to be unmerciful," Jonah says. His lack of faith prompts jeers from Keeper and Jesse Bel. "How wicked of / you," Keeper says; Jesse Bel quotes the nursery rhyme "The Three Little Kittens": "You naughty kitten, you shall have no pie."

Frost gets his own political jabs in, suggesting that there is a kind of Unitarian who has gotten by the process of elimination from "many gods to Three and Three to One" to practically none at all. Paul sets things straight with Jonah. He clarifies what Jonah is really running from: not God but God's "mercy-justice contradiction." Paul sets out to prove to Jonah "[h]ow relatively little justice matters." Paul is a doctor who believes that Jesse Bel's cure lies in "getting her idea / Of the word love corrected."

Jonah is soon trapped in the bookstore, where he will be "treated" by Paul. Jonah insists he will break the door down and claims that his struggles are Sisyphean in that the results are "[a]lways the same": They result in the biblical story of the whale each time. The difference here is that they are "modern," so Jonah claims that the whale he will be thrown to now will be some "soulless lunatic asylum." Frost's attitudes toward city life, politics, modernity, and science are made more and more evident throughout the masque and echo many of the comments made in other poems, as well as lectures and prose pieces. On the whole he found much of contemporary life disagreeable, and this masque bears that out.

One of the more humorous lines is Jesse Bel's "You poor, poor swallowable little man." Jesse Bel grows more and more intoxicated as her shamelessness is further revealed. Frost makes a reference here to his and his wife Elinor's own child Elliott's death at age three (reflected upon in "Home Burial") when Jonah describes Jesse Bel as having "some loss she can't accept from God" (Parini, 69).

Paul in many ways becomes a modification of the prophet that Jonah was to be. His consolation of Jonah leads him to profess that Jonah "can't trust God to be unmerciful. / There you have the beginning of all wisdom." The tables have turned. Paul is taking the wind out of Jonah's sails. Keeper steps in, commenting that before the conversation leaves religion altogether, they should find out exactly what form of ruin the prophet Jonah had in store for this city. His gloomy request is accompanied by the thoughtful insight that "the right style of coat for prophecy" is philosophy, not religion. And it is precisely philosophy and not religion that Frost is sporting here, though later Paul will say that he "won't have Keeper calling [Jonah's prophecy] religion" either.

The doom and gloom Jonah had planned was an earthquake that "only needs a finger touch from God"—a palpable threat—to "fracture in the rocks beneath New York." Jonah is so "lost in the virtuosity / Of getting up good ruins" that he has, according to Paul, "forgotten / What the sins are men ought to perish for." Jonah claims that he is hearing from God as they speak, but he is the only one. He claims God is jealous and has a great disregard for Keeper's books—all but his own, the Bible.

The masque later returns to the question of mercy, and Paul asserts that Jonah's book in the Old Testament is the first place in literature where "Mercy is explicitly the subject." The question remains on the table: Can God be trusted to be merciful? And should we ever expect Him to be unmerciful out of an appetite for justice?

A distinction is drawn between politics and Christianity; Paul "almost had poor Keeper in a corner" where he would have to choose between them. Frost takes a familiar aim at communism or socialism through Paul when he addresses the "outbreak of mass mercy" and the homogenization of mankind through a "holy impulse towards redistribution." The politics of the play are not unlike the politics of "Build Soil—A Political Pastoral." As Robert Faggen asserts, "Paul . . . advocates the 'discrimination' of the selective process, conveying his distrust of the motives of socialism and Christianity to limit the 'cream from rising,' parodying the supernatural idea of the resurrection" (106).

Paul ultimately poses a question: "if you've got to see your justice crossed," which is preferred, "evil-crossed or mercy-crossed?" Keeper, the revolutionist, not surprisingly speaking as the poet, offers a third option: "star-crossed as a star-crossed lover," once again jabbing a facetious pinprick into the dialogue. The distinction between evil-crossed and mercy-crossed is similar to a distinction between a glass being half empty and a glass being half full. Keeper's addition takes away the intentionality, whether evil or merciful, and suggests instead a fate that is unbiased and indifferent.

Mercy comes into play with Paul's reference to Christ's Sermon on the Mount. He then quotes Christina Rossetti's "Mother Country" (1898) to further his point that "we all fail together": "Oh, what is a king here, / And what is a boor? / Here all starve together. / All dwarfed and poor." According to Paul, the Nazarene in the Bible, Jesus talks about placing mercy at the core of what God is supposed to be. Keeper characterizes this by saying that the Sermon is "Just a frame-up to insure"—a return to his earlier claim of the "modern lenience . . . of fire insurance"—"the failure / Of all of us will be / Thrown prostrate at the Mercy Seat for Mercy." Keeper also characterizes it as a "lofty beauty no one can live up to / Yet no one turn from trying to live up to." For some reason, Paul finds this beautiful and calls it a mystery one must accept; Keeper finds it foolish and says, "I would rather be lost in the woods / Than found in church." To Paul, mercy is at the core of God's relationship to man because Paul accepts the claim from the Sermon on the Mount, which is that anything short of perfection (i.e., humans) is sinful and deserving of mercy by design.

Keeper responds to Paul's positive characterization of this design by challenging Paul in the form of a dilemma; one either accepts the irrational mystery and the preestablished sinful design, the "irresistible impossibility," or turns away from it and ignores it. After Keeper chooses the latter option, Paul's response is name-calling: "You Pagan!" he exclaims. Then Paul turns to Jonah for his response to the dilemma and the challenge. Paul is originally characterized as an analyst, but in the end he seems to be trying to convert the Keeper to Christianity, and later Jonah will announce, "I am your convert. Tell me what I think." Paul posits Jonah now as, instead

of a runaway or fugitive, a pilgrim on a quest. Jonah admits to being "all turned round," and the admission is not merely physical. He seems to side with Paul on Keeper's challenge even after all of Keeper's warnings. Jonah instead wants to "run / Toward what [he is made to] see beyond the / world."

Frost's New England landscape then comes into play with the cellar in the bookstore (there are a number of cellars in Frost's work, one of the more ominous being in "The Vanishing Red"), which represents to Jesse Bel a place to "bring faith back" and is presented to Jonah as an "exit door." Keeper does not resist his chance to make more biting comments about religion and its history, referring to faith as something "to be fanatical about / So as to justify the orthodox / In saving heretics by slaying them, / Not on the battlefield, but down in cellars."

Keeper seems to reflect most directly Frost's own agnostic voice, particularly at the end, when he asserts that "We have all the belief that's good for us. / Too much all fired belief" is not good for us. Belief needs to be tempered by reason because once belief turns irrational, "we'd be back / Down burning skeptics in the cellar furnace."

When Jonah asks Paul to tell him what he thinks, Paul reveals the curious "truth" about religiosity. He wants his disciples to "Contemplate Truth until it burns [their] eyes out," but at the same time he wants to be able to tell them what to think. Keeper and Jesse Bel, two resistant to conversion, have not been sent to the cellar to "lie in self-forgetfulness." Jonah seems caught in the middle because before he goes down into the cellar he is drawn by Keeper's doubts about Paul's claims. Paul says that "[s]ome lingering objection holds [him] back." Jonah's response is "If winning ranks / The same with God as losing, how explain / Our making all this effort mortals make?" Keeper says, "Good for you, Jonah. That's what I've been saying," and it seems that is what Frost has been saying all throughout the masque, since the first proposition of the mercy/justice contradiction, and it will be reiterated in his powerful final line: "Nothing can make injustice just but mercy."

Jonah still attempts entry to the cellar, but just as he steps on the threshold, the door, seemingly attended to by God himself, slams in his face.

Jonah's response is "I think I may have got God wrong entirely," and it suddenly seems that the cellar, that place described as "[j]ust an oubliette," is a modernized version of heaven or at least a place of connection to the salvation of those believers who enter it. From this view, it seems evident that Jonah's response is supported by the theme of the play: that there is not only no justice, no "just deserts," but, it seems, no mercy as well. If Jonah has gotten God wrong, then everybody has. Keeper dismisses Jonah's disappointment by reassuring him that "[a]ll of us get each other pretty wrong" but this is not much consolation for a prophet.

Jonah falls to his knees. He admits that justice was "all there ever was to [him]" and that without justice, by the doors slamming him in the face, he will "fade," which here is a euphemism for dying. Paul remarks, "Mercy on him for having asked for justice," making that request Jonah's primary fault, which apparently killed him. Keeper toughly says, "Die saying that," and Jonah apparently does, as there is no evidence that he has heard him. Jesse Bel insists that there be "a funeral oration." God has made the last decision about Jonah, which provokes some final philosophical statements from Keeper.

Keeper admits that Jesse Bel was right about the glorification of courage, because courage is the only attribute that can overcome the fear of the soul, a fear that all humans have, Keeper included. Paul, however, assigns a specific source to the fear and to all fear, which is the fear of God's ultimate judgment: "the fear / Of God's decision lastly on your deeds." Keeper denies this, despite Jonah's experiences, claiming that he is simply too much afraid of God in general and cannot judge himself, as that "would be irreligious." His admission that "fear is of the soul" provokes a response: The cellar door swings wide and slams again, apparently as evidence of God's presence and power. He resignedly denies the basic and ultimate human capacity for moral judgment. Keeper resolutely acknowledges the deep nature of fear and its pervasive hold and is somewhat tolerant of the prayers of millions, even though they are made in darkness, without the bright light of truth. Keeper is revealed as a reluctant and frustrated agnostic about the role of God

and His relationship to fear. He remains hopeful, however. The closing line suggests that all is worthwhile in the end, even the injustice that Jonah has been dealt, if God's ultimate judgment is merciful: "Nothing can make injustice just but mercy."

Timmerman quotes Heyward Brook's "Robert Frost's Masques Reconsidered" and Paola Loreto's "A Man in Front of His God" in looking at the masque/antimasque configuration. Loreto observes that

> The two masques can be taken together as one dramatic piece. *A Masque of Reason* can be interpreted as an antimasque representing the disquieting doubt that there is no motivation for the heap of misfortunes God sent to Job, a man who had always been exemplary for his integrity. *A Masque of Mercy*, then, should be seen as the masque proper, whose function is to dispel the impression that the world is dominated by chaos and to restore man's faith in divine justice. In the masque, though, man's idea of God's justice is corrected. Man's merchant mentality is done away with and replaced with God's freely given mercy. (quoted in Timmerman, 29)

The masque is complex, and Frost struggles with his own ideas in a way that he does not in his first masque, *A Masque of Reason*, where he begins with the well-known book of Job. *A Masque of Mercy* gives a foretaste of Frost's later work, as it invokes not only Frost's usual skepticism about religion but also much of his criticism of the modern world that he articulated more as he aged. *A Masque of Mercy* was less celebrated than *A Masque of Reason*, which received largely favorable reviews.

A Masque of Mercy was first published in a signed, limited edition of 751 copies. *See* BELIEF and PHILOSOPHY.

FURTHER READING

Cox, Sidney. "Mr. Frost's Blank Verse Dialogue." *New York Times Book Review*. November 9, 1947. Available online. URL: http://www.nytimes.com/books/99/04/25/specials/frost-masque.html. Accessed January 5, 2006.

Doyle, John Robert, Jr. *The Poetry of Robert Frost: An Analysis*. New York: Hafner Press, 1962.

Faggen, Robert. *Robert Frost and the Challenge of Darwin.* Ann Arbor: University of Michigan Press, 1997, 106.

Irwin, W. R. "The Unity of Frost's Masques," *American Literature: A Journal of Literary History, Criticism, and Bibliography* 32, no. 3 (November 1960): 302–312.

Loreto, Paola. "A Man in Front of His God, A Man in Front of Himself: The (Post) Modernity of Frost's *A Masque of Reason,*" *Robert Frost Review* (Fall 1999): 29.

Pack, Robert. *Belief and Uncertainty in the Poetry of Robert Frost.* Hanover, N.H.: Middlebury College Press, 2003.

Parini, Jay. *Robert Frost: A Life.* New York: Holt, 1999.

Sullivan, D. Bradley. "'Education by Poetry' in Robert Frost's Masques," *Papers on Language and Literature: A Journal for Scholars and Critics of Language and Literature* 22, no. 3 (Summer 1986): 312–321.

Timmerman, John H. *Robert Frost: The Ethics of Ambiguity.* Lewisburg, Pa.: Bucknell University Press, 2002, 85–92.

Masque of Reason, A (1945)

Masques were popular in England during the 16th and early 17th centuries. They were dramatic plays usually performed by masked players who represented mythological or allegorical figures. Frost wrote two masques in dramatic verse, *A Masque of Mercy* and *A Masque of Reason.* Both satirically address modern skeptical concerns with Christian theology. In *A Masque of Reason* the poet addresses the book of Job and the problem of evil.

The setting of the poem is a "fair oasis in the purest desert," and the characters are Man (Job), Wife (Job's Wife), God, and, toward the end, Satan. Frost presents the modern scene of Man and Wife (not husband and wife) lying together and addressing each other in modern conversational diction. The conversation between Man and Wife begins with numerous religious references; to the burning bush of Exodus 3:2: "Behold the bush burned with fire and was not consumed. . . ."; the Christmas tree; myrrh, the aromatic resin that is the principal

ingredient in holy anointing oil (Exodus 30:23); and the star of Bethlehem over the traditional birthplace of Jesus Christ. God enters the poem quickly and is initially presented comically, getting stuck in the burning bush. The Wife claims she would know "Him by Blake's picture anywhere"; Frost's allusion is to the romantic poet William Blake's (1757–1827) illustrations for his own works and for the book of Job. The conversation quickly turns to Judgment Day and how we "lay aside / [our] varying opinion[s] of [ourselves] / and come to rest in an official verdict" come from on high. The Wife plays a traditional role. Here she acts as the sometimes nagging, mostly prodding housewife, urging Man to speak to God. The Wife says "Tell Him He may remember you: you're Job." The suggestion that God may merely remember Job is sarcastic, considering the afflictions God visited upon Job in the Bible. Hereafter Man and Wife are referred to as Job and Job's Wife, making the allegorical relationship between Man and Job explicit. God remembers Job well and calls him "my Patient"—the one who bears or endures pain and suffering. God is quickly dismissive of the suffering he inflicted, casually saying "I trust you're quite / recovered, / And feel no ill effects from what I gave you." Job likes the "frank admission" that God gives him about what he gave; in Frost's version God ends up admitting that he was responsible, not the devil, as many suppose.

Job's name has become "a name for being put upon," generically referring to one who bears excessive and seemingly unnecessary suffering without questioning. Job urges God to explain whether Heaven is nothing more than a calculated letup from suffering on Earth—his boldness suggesting that he feels justified in taking jabs at God for what happened to him and that he still harbors hard feelings. God admits that there is no logical connection between what a person deserves and how much that person suffers, essentially dismantling what most would find morally just. God is made weak not only in his admission that there is no connection but in his admission that he waits for words like anyone else. He is made human, as Frost provides a satirical twist on omnipotence. While God admits that he owes Job an apology, implying a moral obligation, Frost then undoes the logic, having had God already say in the previous lines that such moral obligations do not exist and are not to be found or asked for. Frost's twist on the story of Job becomes more twisted as the logical and illogical expand and contract.

As the masque continues, God asserts to Job that the "demonstration we put on . . . came out all right," and God tries to explain how important Job's role was in the whole masquerade, how Job released God from the "moral bondage to the human race." This statement implies that in using Job as a means, something that would ordinarily be judged morally wrong by human standards, God has successfully shown humans that we simply cannot judge him.

While God originally says that he had to allow good to prosper and had to punish evil unless he would suffer loss of worship—the phrasing here makes it sound like God wants or needs worship in some vain way—thanks to Job, he was no longer bound by that. Evil can prosper and good can now be punished, because there is now no logical connection between what people deserve and what they receive on earth. For that favor, God promotes Job and his wife (since she was also involved) to sainthood.

Job's wife is not impressed by God's explanation of the new title, "Saint," and she proceeds to lodge a complaint with God concerning the sexism involved in prophecy; that is, that women are burned as witches for their prophecy while men are honored. God asks whether Job's wife is a witch—which seems to be a way for Frost to mock the sexism easily found in the Bible. Job's wife asks God why a friend of hers, the Witch of Endor, was burned, and God, surprisingly, says (another jab at the limitations of God's omnipotence) that he did not have the burning of the witch in His "Note Book" that way. (The Witch of Endor in 1 Samuel 28 is said to have called up the ghost of the prophet Samuel at the request of King Saul; the ghost then predicted Saul's downfall.) "Well, she was," Job's wife replies, "and I should like to know the reason why." God replies that he does not need to give an answer to that question, that Job's situation has relieved him of that obligation.

In fact, God seems to go on the offensive against Job's wife and reminds her that she tried to make Job turn against God. She replies forcefully, "I stood by Job. I may have turned on You," and makes a claim that the poor should be treated by the state, and that God should put the care of the poor on his agenda. She essentially tells God how to do his job and then accuses God by saying, "All You can seem to do is lose Your temper / When reason-hungry mortals ask for reasons." It is clear that Job's wife still harbors hard feelings against God for what he did to Job, also evident in the line, "You don't catch women trying to be Plato"—that is, transcendentalists. Job tries to calm his wife by telling her that "God needs time just as much as you or I"—again implying that God is indeed not omnipotent as is assumed.

It is notable that in this section Job's wife's name is revealed as Thyatira, which in Revelation 2:18–29 is the ancient city of Lydia. It is one of the seven churches of Asia that receive messages prophesying the final judgment in Revelation 1–3, God's victory through Christ over evil in the world.

God is then asked by Job's wife, "who invented earth?" The reply is that God and the Devil "groped that out together," much like Job and God interacted to show that man needed to submit to unreason. This submission is important, according to God, "So he wouldn't find it hard to take his orders / From his inferiors . . . especially in war." God suggests here that faith is mostly important in war as a tool to make people fight one another, an insulting characterization.

God criticizes science as "self-superseding on" Genesis and leaving it behind. Here Frost's comments on "Sarcastic Science" from "Why Wait for Science" are reiterated through God's claims.

Job and God proceed to reminisce, and Job asks why everything had to happen at his expense. Curiously, God replies, "It had to be at somebody's expense"; again, there is a jab at God's omnipotence. Human societies, to God, cannot think things through, and they need devoted actors to play things out in order to get the point, an idea that seems to be a plug for the masque form on Frost's part. Just as God claims, Frost is relying on the masque and its devoted actors to force the audience to think things through.

But Job, in his reminiscing, has a lot to say to God, perhaps because he has kept it inside all this time. Job first finds it odd that we are supposed to belittle reason (and embrace faith) when we are concerned with reason for every other important aspect of our lives. Job then tells God that even though he "let God off" from giving him a reason for making him suffer (a curious phrase, implying that God was obligated to provide one), Job never thought that God never had one. "I knew You had one," he says. Job does not accept God's teamwork argument, and he claims that, on the contrary, God knew all along what he wanted before Job was even involved. Job says that he would give more for this "beforehand reason" that God had than all the reasons given by theologians after the fact. Job says that he is willing to keep up appearances so that others will believe that God does not need to give a reason, but now that it is just the two of them, Job wants to know why. This is reminiscent of Frost's couplet from *In the Clearing*—"Forgive, O Lord, my little jokes on Thee / And I'll forgive Thy great big one on me"—and furthers the connection between Man and God.

Job continues forthrightly: "I fail to see what fun, what satisfaction / A God can find in laughing at how badly / Men fumble at the possibilities / When left to guess forever for themselves." He then doubts if all the transcendental longing is for anything, whether we really do not know the important things: "Who says we don't? Who got up these misgivings? / Oh, we know well enough to go ahead with." This seems to imply that this world is the only one we will ever know, and that that fact itself is just fine, because it is all that knowledge ever was or ever implied.

This view is similar to that in "Fragmentary Blue" where Frost seems to contrast Platonic with Aristotelian views. Plato perceived all things in this world, such as truth, beauty, and so on, to have an ideal "form" in the transcendental realm. Aristotle, on the other hand, believed that truth, beauty, and the rest existed only in things themselves, in this world, and relied on no other realm for their existence. Plato assumed that the forms were the best examples of objects, and that this world was a mere copy of the transcendent realm. The objects in this world may have value, but only because they are parasitic on the transcendental realm. Frost seems

to be resisting or even rejecting this view both in "Fragmentary Blue" and here, as elsewhere throughout his work.

Robert Faggen asserts that in the masque "Frost's Job uses the emblem ouroboros [a circular symbol of a snake or dragon devouring its tail, standing for infinity or wholeness] as 'the symbol of eternity' or 'the form of forms,' only to say that in modernity it stands for the circularity of our thought—from matter to form and back again—not mysteriously more but 'less than I can understand'" (29). This circuitous logic is present throughout.

As the masque proceeds, Job curiously tells God that all of his questions could be answered if God simply just came out and told him if humans survive death. Job's wife agrees: "One simple little statement from the throne / Would put an end to such fantastic nonsense. . . ." But then God answers Job first and tells him that all the suffering he endured was simply so that God could "show off" to the devil, that he was provoked almost as if by a dare—a surprisingly narrow and immature response. Job tries to ascribe such a confusing response to the traditional notion that what seems confusing to us is just eternity presenting itself to finite minds. But in the end, Job remains skeptical, as did Frost.

God continues in vain, asserting that he wanted to show the devil that he could count on Job, that he was better than the devil in that sense. Job facetiously suggests that all three of them should get together, and God suddenly summons Satan. For a moment all three are present, a reunion of sorts, and at the end of the masque Job's wife is talking, humorously arranging the devil alongside Job and God as if she plans to take a photograph of the three of them: "Now if you three have settled anything / You'd as well smile as frown on the occasion." This will be the second image of God in the poem, the first, Blake's, being the "best" God had ever had taken. Job's Wife is particularly biting in her coy remark to the devil: "Oh, by the way," she teases, "you haven't / By any chance a Lady Apple on you?" referring to the forbidden fruit in the Garden of Eden: "I saw a boxful in the Christmas market. / How I should prize one personally from you. . . . !"

The poem ends with typical Frostian boldness, as the poet notes that he has in this poem added the last, necessary chapter to the book of Job. Frost's version is meant to have an epic quality not unlike John Milton's *Paradise Lost* or Ralph Waldo Emerson's "Uriel," both of which he refers to in the poem.

In his 1960 *Paris Review* interview with Richard Poirier, Frost writes that the masque turns on one association: "God says, 'I was just showing off to the Devil, Job.' Job looks puzzled about it, distressed a little. God says, 'Do you mind?' and 'No, no,' he says. 'No,' in that tone, you know, 'No,' and so on. That tone is everything, the way you say that 'no.' I noticed that—that's what made me write that. Just that one thing made that." John Robert Doyle, Jr., compares the masque to "Neither Out Far nor In Deep" in that it shows "that man's inability to see far or deeply did not discourage his continued search" (242). He claims that together the masques "give an answer to a way of accepting life on earth, though, as always in Frost, never a final and absolute answer, but an answer which offers a solid 'stay against confusion'" (250). They offer an answer to not merely accepting but embracing life on earth and a fair dismissal of what lies beyond, echoing Frost's phrase from "Birches": "Earth's the right place for love: / I don't know where it's likely to go better."

Jay Parini notes that "The question of why God would permit human suffering engaged [Frost] passionately" (350), and it is no surprise given the great amount of personal suffering Frost experienced in having outlived his parents, sister, wife, and most of his children. But it is also evident that Frost had great compassion for humankind that extended beyond his own personal experiences to a value for humanity and a desire to understand why there is no logic to the amount and random distribution of suffering.

A Masque of Reason was first published in a limited, signed edition of 800 copies to favorable reviews. According to Parini, however, Frost believed Lawrance Thompson's review demonstrated "his total misunderstanding of the essential point of the satire by claiming it was an ironical 'unholy play' which satirized Christianity." Frost held instead that the play embodied his "stance as an Old Testament Christian" and "underline[d] his

philosophical dualism of spirit and matter . . . underscor[ing] the conflict between justice and mercy" (357). Frost even said in the *Paris Review* interview that neither of the masques are "rebellious," that they were rather "very doctrinal, very orthodox, both of them." While this may be an accurate portrayal of Frost's beliefs about the masque, the author's own views are hardly evident in the text itself. If Frost disagreed with Thompson, he would likely disagree with the reading of *A Masque of Reason* above as well. Then again, there was much to disagree about with Thompson regarding his work on Frost's biography, and perhaps Frost was simply feeling disagreeable. In any case, Frost's presentation of God in *A Masque of Reason*, while it may be true to an Old Testament Christian's views in some respects, certainly contrasts the traditional and deferential view that would be held by a devout worshipper. Everything else (of which there is ample evidence to the contrary, since the Book of Job ends at Chapter 42) aside, Frost brazenly pronounced his play the final chapter in the book of Job. *See* BELIEF and PHILOSOPHY.

FURTHER READING

Doyle, John Robert, Jr. *The Poetry of Robert Frost: An Analysis.* New York: Hafner Press, 1962.

Faggen, Robert. *Robert Frost and the Challenge of Darwin.* Ann Arbor: University of Michigan Press, 1997, 29.

Gage, John T. "Rhetoric and Dialectic in Robert Frost's a Masque of Reason," *Pacific Coast Philology* 17, no. 1–2 (November 1982): 82–91.

Irwin, W. R. "The Unity of Frost's Masques," *American Literature: A Journal of Literary History, Criticism, and Bibliography* 32, no. 3 (November 1960): 302–312.

Loreto, Paola. "A Man in Front of his God, a Man in Front of Himself: The (Post)Modernity of Robert Frost's A Masque of Reason," *Robert Frost Review* (Fall 1999): 27–39.

Nathan, Rhoda. "'Perfect and Upright?' Frost's Fidelity to Hebrew Scripture in *A Masque of Reason,*" *Studies in the Humanities* 19, no. 1 (June 1992): 58–67.

Pack, Robert. *Belief and Uncertainty in the Poetry of Robert Frost.* Hanover, N.H.: Middlebury College Press, 2003.

Parini, Jay. *Robert Frost: A Life.* New York: Holt, 1999.

Perrine, Laurence. "Robert Frost and the Idea of Immortality." In *Frost Centennial Essays II,* edited by Jac Tharpe, 85–87. Jackson: University Press of Mississippi, 1976.

Sullivan, D. Bradley. "'Education by Poetry' in Robert Frost's Masques," *Papers on Language and Literature: A Journal for Scholars and Critics of Language and Literature* 22, no. 3 (Summer 1986): 312–321.

Timmerman, John H. *Robert Frost: The Ethics of Ambiguity.* Lewisburg, Pa.: Bucknell University Press, 2002, 77–84.

Todasco, Ruth. "Dramatic Characterization in Frost: A Masque of Reason," *University of Kansas City Review* 29 (1963): 227–230.

"Master Speed, The" (1936)

This sonnet was written as a wedding present for Frost's daughter Irma and her bridegroom, John Cone, for their marriage in Franconia, New Hampshire, on October 15, 1926. Frost is not at all remembered as a relationship idealist, but his practical and sophisticated presentation of relationships can at times be most romantic, as his "In the Home Stretch" and this sonnet demonstrate.

Frost contrasts various types of speed, beginning with the speed of water and wind and moving on to the speed of man. People can swim upstream, he notes, not just directionally follow the whims of nature. They also can metaphorically climb "a stream of radiance" in sometimes unbridled optimism. Frost remarks on humanity's ability to go back through history, relying on its memory and its mind's eye. He imagines that such gifts were bestowed on humanity, "given" as reminders that minds have the power to move beyond the physical limitations of movement. Frost's stance is somewhat dualistic, contrasting with the poet of "Etherealizing." In any case, the master speed can be seen as referring to the love and strength that can come from human relationships. Once a relationship is good and solid, the bond can withstand just about anything.

Given the context of its composition, it is clear who the "two" who cannot be parted and will be

"Together wing to wing and oar to oar" are. But given Frost's own relationship to his wife Elinor, the poem is also partly autobiographical. In fact, the shared gravestone of Frost and his wife reads, "Together wing to wing and oar to oar" beneath Elinor's name.

The sonnet was first published as "Master Speed" in the winter 1936 issue of the *Yale Review* and was later collected in *A Further Range.*

FURTHER READING

Jackson, Sarah R. "Frost's 'The Master Speed,'" *Explicator* 51, no. 1 (Fall 1992): 33–35.

"Maturity No Object" (1957)

"Maturity No Object" was the introduction to *New Poets of England and America* (1957), edited by Donald Hall, Robert Pack, and Louis Simpson. Frost opens: "Maturity is no object except perhaps in education where you might think from all the talk the aim and end of everything was to get sophisticated before educated." The piece reflects several of Frost's attitudes that can be found in other prose pieces, such as those on education and on the way poets are cultivated.

After this opening, Frost soon offers a corrective: "My theme is not education, but poetry and how young one has to be or stay to make it." Just as in "Education by Poetry," Frost argues for metaphor: "it is but an extension from the metaphors of poetry out into all thinking, scientific and philosophic." He holds that the poet and scholar have much in common, their material is the same, and they differ only a "little in being differently come by and differently held in play"; this echoes his line in "The Figure a Poem Makes" that scholars and artists "[b]oth work from knowledge, but I suspect they differ most importantly in the way their knowledge is come by." The scholar absorbs as much knowledge as he can, "dredging to the dregs," whereas the poet's "instinct is to shun or shed more knowledge than he can swing or sing." He gains his knowledge "unconsciously," as "dogged determination . . . can only result in doggerel," a concern expressed in his "Conversations on the Craft of Poetry." The poet's "danger is in rhyming trivia," and his depth is in the "light-some blue depth of the air."

As in his "Introduction to 'The Arts Anthology: Dartmouth Verse,'" Frost addresses the notion that the poet "must strike his individual note" early. In that piece he says it must happen between ages 15 and 25; here he notes that some poets have done it "long before forty." Poets find their notes young; the "statistics are all in favor of their being as good and lyric as they will ever be" then. That is why the contributors to *New Poets of England and America* are all younger than 40. Just as in the introduction to Dartmouth verse, Frost recalls Walter Savage Landor, who prolonged the "lyric out of all bounds," writing until age 90. In each piece he says that though poets must strike their notes young—"[y]oung poetry is the breath of parted lips"—they can "go phasing on into being good poets in their later mental ages." Some poets "need live to write no better, need only wait to be better known for what they have written," as Frost himself had to.

This turns Frost to the necessary reader, who is actually "more on trial" than the poets he reads. The reader must tell the difference, "all by himself," without schooling, "between the poets who wrote because they thought it would be a good idea to write and those who couldn't help writing out of a strong weakness for the Muse, as for an elopement with her." This idea arises in other Frost pieces, such as "The Figure a Poem Makes," where he writes, "A poem may be worked over once it is in being, but may not be worried into being." He explains that "[t]here should be some way to tell just as there is to tell the excitement of the morning from the autointoxication of midnight"; Frost himself claimed that "Stopping by Woods on a Snowy Evening" came to him when he went outside to look at the sun after he had been working all night on "New Hampshire." He said, "I always thought it [the poem] was a product of autointoxication coming from tiredness" (Cook, 66).

Frost closes by criticizing the time spent in school as deleterious to the cultivation of the poet as he does in the Dartmouth verse piece, suggesting that we might "at least play hooky a good deal to season slowly out of doors rather than in an oven or in a tanning vat." He closes with a reminder that readers are of the utmost importance and that he is "in on the ambition that this book will get to them—heart and mind."

"Maturity No Object" largely restates comments Frost had made in the other prose pieces referred to here, but it offers further reinforcement for those ideas and some new turns of phrase in expressing them.

FURTHER READING

Cook, Reginald. "Frost on Frost: The Making of Poems," *American Literature* 27 (March 1956): 66.

"Meeting and Passing" (1916)

One of Frost's often-anthologized sonnets, "Meeting and Passing" is a sophisticated love poem. Two characters, a man and a woman, are out walking when they unexpectedly encounter each other. The speaker, the man, meets someone who, it seems, eventually becomes his lover, and he is enthralled with the accidental nature of what appears to be their first meeting.

He is leaning at a gate for the "view" when he turns and sees an even more compelling one: She is there, coming up the hill. They meet. And for only a moment they "mingle great and small / Footprints in the summer dust." They mingle their footprints in something transitory, both seasonally and materially, but the poem recounts how everlasting the meeting was. They were probably together for only a few moments, the meeting lasting mere seconds, but the impression lasted.

"[B]eing less than two / But more than one" is an expressive description of what it is at first to be romantically inclined toward each other. They are only a decimal off becoming more than one but less than two. The woman's eyes are averted; she smiles at the dust demurely. The exclamatory "without prejudice to me!" is exuberant. The young speaker is euphoric that he has had such an effect on the young woman.

They continue on in opposite directions, but there is a clear acknowledgment (or hope) that this will not be their only meeting. The last two lines are indicative of the staying power of the first impression. They have each other on their minds as they pass what the other had passed before. They are united by traveling the same path. They have left an imprint on each other, and now all they experience will be more valuable.

In spirit, this poem is connected to many of Frost's other poems where the connections humans make with one another are extremely valuable and important. People can bring meaning to one another's experiences. Their lives can be enriched simply because time spent with others can heighten their own perceptions of the world.

"Meeting and Passing" was first published in *Mountain Interval*.

"Mending Wall" (1914)

The opening poem of Frost's hailed second collection, *North of Boston*, "Mending Wall" is one of his most popular and celebrated poems. Much anthologized, the poem has almost come to symbolize Frost, for good or ill. On a visit to Moscow in 1962, nearly 50 years after the poem's first publication, Frost said, "People are frequently misunderstanding [the poem] or misinterpreting it. The secret of what it means I keep." Providing a bit of a hint, he also once explained that the poem contrasted two types of people: "I've got a man there; he's both a wall builder and a wall toppler. He makes boundaries and he breaks boundaries. That's man" ("On Taking Poetry").

The poem opens with the statement, "Something there is that doesn't love a wall," and Frost's readers are left to speculate for the remainder of the poem precisely what that something is. Winter does not love a wall, we learn in the second line; it creates gaps in the wall. The ground swells and the less securely placed boulders tumble off. The speaker explains that hunters are also sometimes responsible for the gaps. When they are chasing a rabbit to "please the yelping dogs," but mostly themselves, they too have been known to send boulders tumbling.

The gaps are mysterious, however. The winter and the hunter are suggestions: No one ever actually hears them or sees the gaps made. It is not until spring, when the speaker and his neighbor ritualistically meet at the wall for mending, that they discover the gaps and set about filling them. The two walk together, the wall between them, replacing the boulders that have been left behind during the winter when there has been no cause to venture out to the wall.

Mending a wall takes work, but there is also a sort of sorcery to it. Sometimes one even needs to cast a spell to make the boulders balance just so: "Stay where you are until our backs are turned!"

A game is made of mending the wall; it becomes almost a country version of bowls. The speaker remarks that mending the wall essentially "comes to little more" than a game, since the wall itself is unnecessary. Neither neighbor has on his property anything that would disturb the other's. One has pine trees and one has apple, but neither has livestock. As the speaker teasingly tells his neighbor: "My apple trees will never get across / And eat the cones under his pines." The wall mending is not about keeping things out, the speaker explains, raising the question whether it is about keeping things in.

The other neighbor is cryptic when the speaker, the forthright one, questions him about the purpose of the wall. He simply responds with his father's old saying: "Good fences make good neighbors." This becomes his mantra, the only words we hear from him. The speaker acts as though his own questions are about making mischief more than anything else, which suggests he already knows the answers to them. They are questions anyone might be expected to ask about such a wall, and not just in the mischief of spring; there is something more to it than that. The speaker wants to know why good fences make good neighbors. He is curious, inquiring, and reflective. The neighbor is cast as his opposite: someone who does not ask questions and is content to accept what has always been. He is unreflective, simply parroting back the phrase he learned from his father, carrying out his generation's duty without question.

The speaker continues to question, despite his neighbor's lack of interest. Frost teases as the speaker wonders, "to whom I was like to give offense." He puns on the word offense, another part of the game in and of the poem. The speaker continues to want to know what the "Something there is" is, and he is not content to let it be. The most telling and coy lines are "I could say 'Elves' to him, / But it's not elves exactly, and I'd rather he said it himself." The suggestion is subtle, but the speaker clearly knows who undoes the wall. The lines suggest that the "elf" who leaves gaps in the wall is the neighbor himself, as if the speaker knows something about the neighbor he is unwilling to admit. At the least, it suggests that the speaker wants the neighbor to admit that deep down he also does not love the wall. The speaker suggests that the thing that does not love a wall is actually the very thing that does. It seems that the neighbor may take down the wall just so they can engage in the game of putting it back together again. A visual is presented for the reader: "I see him there / Bringing a stone grasped firmly by the top," and the speaker remarks, "He moves in darkness it seems to me, / Not of woods only and the shade of trees." The sort of darkness his neighbor moves in is metaphorical. He may remove boulders in the dark, but he also moves in another kind of darkness. The neighbor moves not only in nature's darkness but in the darkness that keeps him from more meaningful human connections. It is his lack of reflection, his lonely isolation of the sort encouraged by his father's saying. Yet each spring he needs to meet with his neighbor once again to enact this ritual of building up together the wall that separates them.

Walls are not nature's things; they are human things, created to keep neighbors apart, but in this case the wall also brings them together. There is a division here between what is civilized and what is natural, just as in Frost's "The Middleness of the Road." The neighbor personifies this division.

The two types of people are highlighted throughout but even more so in the irony of the second-to-last line: "he likes having thought of it so well." It seems that those who move in darkness believe that their thoughts are original when they really are not. The individual is simply following what came before, seeing neither "out far or in deep," being narrowed by custom, embracing it without question. The speaker is presented, in contrast, as the reflective and questioning freethinker.

The wall is being mended throughout the poem, but it is also a mending wall, doing its own mending. It is providing both characters with human contact as they wear their fingers rough by handling the stones. It takes a lot of effort to keep the wall there, but it seems to fulfill its complex function.

Frost wrote in a May 1932 letter to his friend Louis Untermeyer that he was "in favor of a skin and fences and tariff walls" (Cramer, 133).

Mark Richardson holds that the speaker is "obviously of two minds: at once wall-builder and wall-destroyer, at once abettor and antagonist of seasonal entropies" (142). Richardson describes the line "Something there is that doesn't love a wall" as having a tone that "*almost* acquires an air of finger-wagging, country pedantry" (142). "Mending Wall" "at once acknowledges the limitations of walls (and aphorisms) and also their seductions and value," he says (142).

"Mending Wall" was first published in *North of Boston*. Jeffrey Cramer reports that Frost once referred to the poem as "Building Wall" in a letter to Sydney Cox in 1915 (30). In Frost's "On Taking Poetry," his 1955 address to the BREAD LOAF SCHOOL OF ENGLISH, he said that the poem is "about a spring occupation in my day. When I was farming seriously we had to set the wall up every year. You don't do that any more. You run a strand of barbed wire along it and let it go at that. We used to set the wall up. If you see a wall well set up you know it's owned by a lawyer in New York—not a real farmer."

See WALLS.

FURTHER READING

Attebery, Louie W. "Fences, Folklore, and Robert Frost," *Northwest Folklore* 6, no. 2 (Spring 1988): 53–57.

Clarke, Peter B. "Frost's 'Mending Wall,'" *Explicator* 43, no. 1 (Fall 1984): 48–50.

Coulthard, A. R. "Frost's 'Mending Wall,'" *Explicator* 45, no. 2 (Winter 1987): 40–42.

Cramer, Jeffrey S. *Robert Frost among His Poems: A Literary Companion to the Poet's Own Biographical*

Contexts and Associations. Jefferson, N.C.: MacFarland, 1996.

Morrissey, L. J. "'Mending Wall': The Structure of Gossip," *English Language Notes* 25, no. 3 (March 1988): 58–63.

Richardson, Mark. *The Ordeal of Robert Frost: The Poet and His Poetics.* Chicago, Ill.: University of Illinois Press, 1997, 141–144.

Timmerman, John H. *Robert Frost: The Ethics of Ambiguity.* Lewisburg, Pa.: Bucknell University Press, 2002, 116–118.

Trachtenberg, Zev. "Good Fences Make Good Neighbors: Frost's 'Mending Wall,'" *Philosophy and Literature* 21, no. 1 (April 1997): 114–122.

"Middleness of the Road, The" (1947)

"The Middleness of the Road," plays at an illusion, opening with the image of a road that "take[s] off into the skies." It is primarily concerned with the contrast between civilization and nature. The road ends metaphorically, leaving behind only woods and sky and suggesting that practical limitations are set on the expansion of civilization. People cannot develop beyond nature and into the skies because there is a point at which civilization is no longer useful.

The third stanza contrasts the rest. The "mineral drops that explode / To drive [the] ton of car" refer to gasoline. Everything in a car is essentially an explosion for the engine. Frost emphasizes that the car may be useful for the road, but it has no purpose when the road ends, and even roads themselves are limited in their function. The line "almost nothing to do" in the fourth stanza is intriguing because it suggests that something civilized is capable of transcending the limitations of the road. Gasoline also is a natural product. It is not purely synthetic but is made from natural ingredients and derived from oil. This is a reminder that while most of our technologies cannot exceed the boundaries civilization has set, there is a common source for all we have developed, and that source is nature.

George F. Bagby writes that the "natural world may seem to offer rest in the green of the woods or perfect freedom in the blue of the sky, but the wayfaring human mind can attain neither certainty; it is condemned to middling alternatives . . ." (63). The middleness of the road becomes where we stand at the end of the road, because the end of the road becomes the dividing line between civilization and nature, where what is familiar to us is almost impotent in the face of nature. Yet human beings are participants in both worlds: We create civilization and are creatures of nature. We are at the end of the road, stuck between two things. How far can civilization expand and still have "absolute flight and rest?"

The poem was first published in the winter 1946 issue of the *Virginia Quarterly Review* and was later collected in *Steeple Bush.* The manuscript title was "The Middleness of the Road/Blue and Green."

FURTHER READING

Bagby, George F. *Frost and the Book of Nature.* Knoxville: University of Tennessee Press, 1993, 62–63.

"Milky Way Is a Cowpath, The" (1962)

In this poem, first published in Frost's final collection, *In the Clearing,* Frost expresses the growing concerns for the future of mankind that he feels as he nears the end of his life. Frost manipulates the nursery rhyme about the cow that jumped over the moon as he does in "Lines Written in Dejection on the Eve of Great Success." In both poems he is concerned with the space race of the cold war following World War II.

The poem begins with humanity traveling on "wings too stiff to flap," and the image of a rocket with its stabilizing fins comes to mind. "We star[t] to exult" having left the earth, the "map," on the penultimate journey into space. But the speaker remarks that when our rockets "got nowhere / Like small boys we got mad / And let go at the air / With everything we had," making a clear allusion to war.

We sent our rockets into the sky, but when they did not land on the moon, we got angry. At the time of the poem's publication, the United States had not yet landed on the moon. The poem is a reminder that while rockets may travel in search of the moon, they can also be used to deliver warheads. All such efforts are seen as juvenile—both trying to go to the moon and building nuclear weapons.

The United States is described as "incorrigible Quid-nuncs," busy-bodies, and the knowing speaker asserts that "We *would* see what would come" of nuclear weapons. They will lead to self destruction. He sets about downplaying going to the moon by putting woman in the position of thinking that a cow has again simply "overshot the moon." She is in the knowing position, contrasted with the juvenile "boys" who should be men. The woman views what the men are doing as trivial. She has a more sensible attitude and is cast as the wiser sex. Here the poet who has been described as a male chauvinist is anything but.

The parabolic curves of the cow and the rocket work with a double meaning. A parabola describes either the cow jumping over the moon or the curve of a spaceship's trajectory. *Parabolic* is also describes something that is a parable, making the word function doubly.

The rocket and the cow go on feasting on stars, foraging across the universe by accident, but the universe has a "razor edge." Because humanity has been starved for space travel, it has gone off the path it is supposed to be on, and that will not lead to good. If humanity does not take care, it will get its "gullet cut."

The fourth line of the poem speaks of the space race as "journey the penult," and the message is clear and haunting: This mission is the second-to-last step. The last step will undoubtedly be total destruction. The author-farmer who has been "unconcerned" with whether flocks and herds can earn money is now the only person in the know. He knows something of cows and seems to know something of those who have gotten off their usual feed, their "natural" graze.

See STARS.

"Minor Bird, A" (1928)

A "minor bird" is one that sings in a minor key, often described as more solemn or sad than a major key, but this bird is minor in another sense. The experience described is trivial—simply a bird's song the speaker wishes would cease, perhaps because it strikes him as too melancholy. The first few lines of the poem are not intuitive—usually a bird's song is welcomed and embraced. As is common in Frost, the poet puts his reader off balance right from the start.

The experience may be minor, but the speaker is affected by it greatly. The bird's song becomes noise that the speaker wants quieted, but he soon realizes the bird is just doing what birds do. The bird sings because singing is in its nature. The speaker realizes that there may be something wrong with wanting to silence any song. His annoyance at the bird is partly his fault, so the poem becomes a mode of self-reflection, suggesting that people can use nature to understand themselves better. The job, in that sense, is not simply to clap hands and try to drive nature away when we can "bear no more," but to stop and hear what nature has to tell.

Jeffrey Cramer reads the poem as reflective of Frost's experiences as a teacher, about "Frost's annoyance as a teacher with having to read and correct the writings of his students." He also notes that at about the time of its composition Frost would have been teaching in either Methuen or Salem, Massachusetts (91). In contrast, Katherine Kearns writes, "In short, the speaker reveals himself as the minor bird, and the poet by his precisely appropriate form confirms him as the minor bird while confirming his own transcendent song. Plagued by what he senses to be his own serious limitation—there is 'something wrong' with him for wanting to silence any song—he sings the very monotonal, abbreviated song that most aptly declares his own depressed state. By the logic of this poem, to silence the bird's song would be to silence himself" (172). That is something no poet would set out to do, even if he thought of himself as a minor bird, as the much celebrated Frost often did.

The poem was first published in the January 1926 issue of the University of Michigan's *Inlander*.

FURTHER READING

Cramer, Jeffrey S. *Robert Frost among His Poems: A Literary Companion to the Poet's Own Biographical Contexts and Associations.* Jefferson, N.C.: MacFarland, 1996.

Kearns, Katherine. *Robert Frost and a Poetics of Appetite.* Cambridge: Cambridge University Press, 1994, 171–172.

"Misgiving" (1923)

In "Misgiving" the poet is again sympathetic to the plight of leaves, as in "A Leaf-Treader." Katherine Kearns refers to the poem as a "consciously parodic version of [Percy Bysshe] Shelley's 'Ode to the West Wind,' where the wintry West Wind drives the sickened and pestilential leaves before it along with the winged seeds that will give birth to spring" (165).

The poem begins in tears. The personified leaves cry, "We will go with you, O Wind!" attempting to fulfill the flight they had "promised" themselves in the spring, when they had yearned to fly off the trees. They had wanted to follow the wind and were welcoming the expected journey. But in autumn, when the time comes for flight, they are described as falling asleep on the way and ending up wishing the wind would leave them behind. They are enthusiastic as they rustle in the wind in spring, but in the fall they would instead be glad to shelter themselves up against a wall, in a thicket, or in a hollow place.

Now when the wind sends a "summoning blast," they stir more reluctantly, "vaguer and vaguer." They are on the ground where "a little reluctant whirl" drops them "no further than where they were" before, where they will be wasted.

The natural process becomes a reflection of human ambition as the final stanza brings the speaker's disposition into play. The death of the leaves becomes an inquiry into human attitudes toward death and into the possibilities of an afterlife. When it comes time for the speaker's flight, he hopes that he will be encouraged to go with the "wind." He can only hope that at the moment of death he can go onward in quest of knowledge beyond the bounds of life. He says he hopes it "may not seem better to [him] to rest," to have sleep "oppress" him the way it does the leaves. The choice of "may" is noteworthy because it reflects his uncertainty. The speaker is not sure if an afterlife is the right thing. He wonders if he will be more content to succumb to the deep sleep of death or to keep going. His hope is based on his expectations for an afterlife, his misgivings about his choice to go on.

"Misgiving" was first published in a January 1921 issue of the *Yale Review* and was later collected in *New Hampshire.* See WALLS.

FURTHER READING

Kearns, Katherine. *Robert Frost and a Poetics of Appetite.* Cambridge: Cambridge University Press, 1994.

"Missive Missile, A" (1936)

"A Missive Missile" was first published in the autumn 1934 issue of the *Yale Review* and later collected as the closing poem in *A Further Range*, under the heading "Afterthought." Its manuscript title was "A Stone Missive." The poem is compelling as an afterthought, as in it the speaker is concerned with "missive[s]," letters or messages whose purpose and meanings are lost to time. It is the sort of afterthought that might occur to any artist, but it bears an original cloak.

The speaker is distraught in trying to comprehend a message intended by the pattern on a pebble wheel created by an individual from Mas D'Azil. Le Mas D'Azil, a commune of southern France, is the site of a cave that was discovered in 1887. In that cave cultural artifacts were found, including those described here: pebbles with painted lines, dots, and geometric figures, from the early Mesolithic Period at the end of the last glacial age. The artifacts are described precisely, and the speaker coming into contact with them strains to discern their message and meaning.

The speaker wants to get the message right and wonders if the individual artist's ghost is standing by and watching him in his frustration. He feels inadequate to the task, referring to himself as "slow uncomprehending me." He says the meaning is unknown, but he fears that he is entirely responsible for the failure. The intention of the ancient caveman should be clear, he expects, and he feels he has somehow failed the artist by not being able to ascertain it. It is unsatisfying to them both: The speaker wants to know the message; the original messenger wanted to send one. The resolution is that there is "an aeon-limit" to messages, so that they simply cannot travel such an expanse with accuracy. Robert Faggen finds that the "great anxiety here . . . is about what message can be preserved or recovered from the ruins of a civilization" (119).

The poem is one of Frost's own now-historical messages, a series of black dots, so to speak, created in his time and sent forward for all time. The speaker of the poem is aware that his failure to read the ancient man's message will turn into some other man's failure to read his. All communication breaks down with the great distance of time. There is a point "[b]eyond which they are doomed to miss." George F. Bagby calls the poem a "more pessimistic consideration of the relationship between perception and meaning" that is found in "Design" (133).

FURTHER READING

Bagby, George F. *Frost and the Book of Nature*. Knoxville: University of Tennessee Press, 1993, 133–136.

Cook, Marjorie E. "Dilemmas of Interpretation: Ambiguities and Practicalities." In *Robert Frost the Man and the Poet*, edited by Earl J. Wilcox. Rock Hill, S.C.: Winthrop College, 1990, 125–141.

Faggen, Robert. *Robert Frost and the Challenge of Darwin*. Ann Arbor: University of Michigan Press, 1997.

Hancher, Michael. "'Sermons in Stone': An Explication of Robert Frost's Poem 'A Missive Missile,'" *Centrum* 2, no. 1 (1974): 79–86.

"Monument to After-Thought Unveiled, A" (1892)

Frost and his future wife Elinor graduated from Lawrence High School, in Lawrence, Massachu-

setts, sharing valedictorian honors in 1892. "A Monument to After-Thought Unveiled" was Frost's valedictory speech and was published in the *High School Bulletin*. It reflects a fresh, young Frost, full of passion and hope for himself and the world. It opens romantically in nature. He acknowledges men who came before, the "poet who has left us uniting the battered harp the sea storm cast for him upon the shore." He optimistically intones that "nobility distinguishes personality only in the degree of its development, and the broader future, will give to every soul the opportunity to come into the possession of this, his divine right." He speaks of living an "[a]ggresive life" and of the leader who is formed not in action or crisis but in the "after-thought." The "supreme rise of the individual" and the inspiration he provides to his fellow classmates are the aims. "The poet's insight is his after-thought," and life itself is an after-thought. Frost urges classmates to have unbounded aspirations as the "[s]trength and all the personality that [they] can crowd upon the world are [theirs] to give in obligations." It is the youthful Frost of *A Boy's Will*, and in its subject and erudition the speech offers small insights into the man and poet he would succeed in becoming by afterthought.

"Mood Apart, A" (1947)

The first authorized publication of "A Mood Apart" appeared in 1944 in *Fifty Years of Robert Frost*, a Dartmouth College exhibition catalog edited by Ray Nash. "A Mood Apart" is the first of seven poems in the section "A Spire and a Belfry" of *Steeple Bush*.

The poem begins with a man, or possibly a boy, down on his knees in a garden, working with plants and singing a "medley of sotto chants." *Sotto*, meaning *under* in Italian, is most often heard in English in the phrase *sotto voce*, in a soft tone (so as not to be overheard). Despite the speaker's cautious singing, some boys, from school and perhaps his own school, hear him and stop by the fence "to spy." For the speaker, "any eye is an evil eye," and their watching nearly stops his heart.

The poem is about being found out. What we do privately, even when in public, is meant to be kept private. When we feel we are violated and exposed, even if we have done little to protect ourselves, we recoil as the speaker does here. Being found out causes an automatic assumption of malevolent intent. The speaker is so fearful of being "caught" that his heart almost stops when he sees the boys looking on. They have intruded upon his privacy. The poem evokes a recognition of feeling. It also, as a part of the "A Spire and a Belfry" section, has religious undertones, suggesting that God may intrude upon our privacy as well. The reference to "the evil eye" is also significant.

FURTHER READING

Cramer, Jeffrey S. *Robert Frost among His Poems: A Literary Companion to the Poet's Own Biographical Contexts and Associations.* Jefferson, N.C.: MacFarland, 1996.

"Moon Compasses" (1936)

"Moon Compasses" expresses a visual experience but also metaphorically describes sexual love. Late at night, between two downpours, there is a "dripping pause." The speaker takes a moment to look up into the sky, where he sees rays of moonlight surrounding a mountain in the midnight haze. The rays from the "masked moon," so masked by the haze and the clouds, seem to measure or constrain the width of the mountain as would a compass. The mountain is measured by the "calipers" of the moon's rays.

The image seems to the speaker the same, only inverted, as the hands that cup on either side of a lover's face. Words like *measure, estimate, caliper,* and *compass* treat the experience of love and beauty as somehow mathematical, something of which one takes the measure. There seems to also be a play on the word *compass* to suggest *encompass*. Perhaps Frost is cautioning us on the distinction between judgments of beauty and love and the assured function of scientific tools and precise measurement.

The feminine moon has the power to make the "final estimate." The mountain is male and is sub-

ject to the judgments of the moon. The width or breadth of a male thereby becomes measured by the hands and love of a female, her calipers. Whether or not a man is exalted depends on the hands of a woman, just as the mountain without the moon's rays would not be exalted, but the exaltation is only momentary. Relationships have their downpours. The moment here is brief; it exists in a dripping pause, the eye of a storm, the calm between two tumultuous events.

Some of the images lend themselves to an overtly sexual reading that is uncommon in Frost. It is possible to read this poem as an expression of the aftermath of a climactic experience. The images of nature can easily be transposed into images of a couple physically joined in an embrace, the downpour following their expressions of sexual love, the calipers the encompassing thighs, and so on. Given Frost's usual subject matter and general avoidance of such graphic material it is perhaps unlikely, but it functions as an easily supportable reading given the sensuality of his descriptions.

The poem ends with an ellipsis, which is also uncommon in Frost. He is not a poet who tends to leave his readers trailing off, but instead tends to end with punctual thrust. In this instance the ellipsis seem to demonstrate that the final estimate remains unknown. Love is, after all, only an estimate.

The poem was first published in the autumn 1934 issue of the *Yale Review* and was later collected in *A Further Range.*

FURTHER READING

Bagby, George F. *Frost and the Book of Nature.* Knoxville: University of Tennessee Press, 1993, 92–93.
Fleissner, Robert F. "Frost's 'Moon Compasses,'" *Explicator* 32 (1974): 66.
Slakey, Roger L. "Frost's 'Moon Compasses,'" *Explicator* 37, no. 1 (1978): 22–23.

"Most of It, The" (1942)

The speaker is in the woods alone, standing opposite a cliff on the other side of a lake. All he can hear when he calls is his own voice returning to him as an echo. He says that all that people want from life is the companionship of another. When they shout out to the world, they wait for someone else to respond. They do not want a copy of themselves, their own voices returning to them; they want "original response." They want to be loved, but in another person's way, not in their own way. The "counter-love" that the poem discusses is not necessarily romantic love but the deepest kind of caring one person can have for another, whatever the relationship.

On this morning the speaker hears stirring and is hopeful that another person will emerge from the lake or wood. The response he gets is another life, but it is not human. He holds that "nothing ever came of what he cried" unless it is the embodiment of his cries that splash in the water and appear as a great buck, "pushing the crumpled water" ahead of him and "pouring like a waterfall." But this falls short of what he desires. He all but dismisses this other life, with the poem ending "and that was all." It is a downcast statement. The speaker has not found the human contact he longs for, the original response he has craved, and he is clearly disappointed.

The poem's title, "The Most of It," suggests that the most of what people want from life is the companionship of another human being. Most of existence is trying to find the original response and the counter-love desired but coming up short. There is utter loneliness in the absence of "someone else additional to him," and it is the deepest kind of loneliness—the loneliness that is the human condition. While the speaker simply seeks another, in fact people seek to join with another completely, in a way that is beyond possibility and leaves them lonely even when in the company of those they care about most. In the end we still keep "the universe alone."

"The Most of It" was first published in *A Witness Tree*.

FURTHER READING

Bagby, George F. *Frost and the Book of Nature.* Knoxville: University of Tennessee Press, 1993, 34–36.

Borroff, Marie. "Robert Frost's 'The Most of It,'" *Ventures: Magazine of the Yale Graduate School* 9 (1969): 76–82.

Cook, Marjorie E. "The Serious Play of Interpretation," *South Carolina Review* 15, no. 2 (Spring 1983): 77–87.

Pack, Robert. *Belief and Uncertainty in the Poetry of Robert Frost.* Hanover, N.H.: Middlebury College Press, 2003.

"Mountain, The" (1914)

"The Mountain," one of several poems that Frost claimed to have written in a single sitting (Cramer, 33), opens with a speaker who has journeyed into nature to explore the mountain. He sleeps for the night, and when he awakes he heads further on "at dawn to see new things." He seems to be lost, a wanderer who, when he first crosses a river and swings around the mountain, must ask, "What town is this?" He is unconcerned with his predicament, however, simply curious about where he finds himself. The man he asks is moving so slowly that "it seem[s] no harm to stop him altogether." From here the poem becomes a slowly spun yarn of a tale that moves from one absurdity to the next in the style of Mark Twain's "The Jumping Frog of Calaveras County."

The man the speaker encounters answers directly the speaker's question about what town he finds himself in, "Lunenberg," but from there provides only a few direct answers to the speaker's questions. There are things the man has heard and things he has actually experienced about the mountain, but much of what he recounts is hearsay that he later undoes with further hearsay. It turns out that he is not sure about much of what he says. And near the poem's close is the most telling line of all: "But all the fun's in how you say a thing." The yarn he has spun should itself be satisfactory. He has no need for actual facts or understanding that would get in the way of telling a good story.

The poem is at times humorous. As the poem progresses, the man's tale meanders more and the absurdity of the speaker's experience deepens. The ending is perhaps the most comical as the man simply decides to pull out with his oxen, mid-sentence. The speaker is willing to hear even more misinformation, but he is simply left in the lurch.

For all the talk and conversation just about the only thing the man knows for sure is what the speaker already knew at the outset: that there is a mountain. The mountain, as the only certain statement, becomes the poem's title. The speaker does not even find himself in the right town. He goes looking for guidance, and the person who lives there is of no help. He is out of place and out of house, and the only thing he knows for sure is that the "mountain held the town as in a shadow"—the first line of the poem.

Robert Faggen describes the poem as "Frost's postromantic ethnographic response to Wordsworth's 'Resolution and Independence,' in which the leech-gatherer saves the romantic, self-obsessed, and tortured wanderer by becoming an icon of moral strength and humility" (136). He also notes that the "brother who understands the importance of work and the survival value of play may have greater integrity than the wandering 'brother' seeking miraculous springs" (139).

"The Mountain" was first published in *North of Boston*. See STARS.

FURTHER READING

Cramer, Jeffrey S. *Robert Frost among His Poems: A Literary Companion to the Poet's Own Biographical Contexts and Associations*. Jefferson, N.C.: MacFarland, 1996.

Faggen, Robert. *Robert Frost and the Challenge of Darwin*. Ann Arbor: University of Michigan Press, 1997, 135–139.

Heath, W. G. "The Scholar and the Poet in Robert Frost's 'The Mountain,'" *Gombak Review* 2, no. 2 (December 1997): 97–107.

Muldoon, Paul. "The End of the Poem: 'The Mountain' by Robert Frost," *American Poetry Review* 30, no. 1 (January–February 2001): 41–46.

Perrine, Laurence. "Frost's 'The Mountain': Concerning Poetry," *Concerning Poetry* 4, no. 1 (1971): 5–11.

Mountain Interval (1916)

The first edition of Frost's third collection was published in 1916 by Henry Holt and Company, and was dedicated "To you who least need reminding that before this interval of the South Branch under black mountains, there was another interval, the upper at Plymouth, where we walked in spring beyond the covered bridge; but that the first interval of all was the old farm, our brook interval, so called by the man we had it from in sale." Jeffrey Cramer explains that the "you" to whom Frost refers is his wife, Elinor, to whom most of his works were dedicated; the "South Branch," the Frost's farm in Franconia, New Hampshire; "Upper at Plymouth," their time spent in Plymouth, New Hampshire; and "first interval" their time in Derry, New Hampshire (44). The brook is Hyla Brook, a brook by Frost's old farm in Derry, which provides the title for another of his poems. Jay Parini explains that "interval" is a "New England dialect term for land in a valley" and that therefore "mountain interval" carries a double meaning, as it suggests a "pause in a journey as well as a dip in the landscape" (278).

The collection, though it did not sell as well as *North of Boston*, perhaps because it was rushed into print by Frost's publisher, included some of Frost's best-known and most celebrated poems, such as "The Road Not Taken," "An Old Man's Winter Night," "Meeting and Passing," "Hyla Brook," "Birches," and "Out, Out—." Many of the poems included in the volume had been written during his time in ENGLAND; others were written before and were simply reworked for publication, such as "Birches" and "Putting in the Seed." "The Road Not Taken" opened the volume, perhaps signaling a reference to the "mountain interval."

Frost was disappointed by the lack of attention the collection received, but it was perhaps to be expected of a third book following so quickly his first two, *A Boy's Will* and *North of Boston*. *Mountain Interval*, despite the lack of attention, was one of his epoch-making collections, simply on the basis of "The Road Not Taken" and "Birches."

FURTHER READING

Bieganowski, Ronald. "Robert Frost's Sense of Choice in *Mountain Interval*," *College Literature* 11, no. 3 (Fall 1984): 258–268.

Cramer, Jeffrey S. *Robert Frost among His Poems: A Literary Companion to the Poet's Own Biographical*

Contexts and Associations. Jefferson, N.C.: MacFarland, 1996.

McPhillips, Robert T. "Diverging and Converging Paths: Horizontal and Vertical Movement in Robert Frost's *Mountain Interval*,'" *American Literature* 58, no. 1 (March 1986): 82–98.

Parini, Jay. *Robert Frost: A Life.* New York: Holt, 1999.

"Mowing" (1913)

In this irregular sonnet, the characteristically New England Frost presents an image of hard farm labor, as in his "After Apple-Picking." Robert Faggen writes that "Frost's allegiance to the pursuit and love of fact is apparent" in this poem, noting that it was Frost's "favorite poem of his first book (*A Boy's Will*)" (45). One of his most quoted lines, "The fact is the sweetest dream that labor knows," appears as part of the memorable closing couplet.

The poem opens with the sound of a "scythe whispering to the ground" as a fellow does a hard day's work while speculating about the sound his scythe makes beside the wood. He wonders what his scythe whispers and why it whispers instead of speaking. His labor is a sweet dream and an "earnest love," something he does with great passion but also something he does not know well himself. He knows that it is not the "dream of the gift of idle hours" and that the golden hay that he mows is not caused by a fairy or elf. Instead, it is his love that lays the "swale in rows," the rhythmic motion keeping him from fully absorbing the act himself. As Faggen asserts, the poem "reflects a desire to unify work and play . . . but also expresses the frustration of limited revelation" (45).

The second half of the poem is somewhat elusive. The speaker tells the truth about the love he has for his labor, as "[a]nything more than the truth would seem too weak" but it is unclear what would be more than the truth. The whispering of his scythe is the same action of which the scythe cannot speak. It is the whispering that scares the snake, the truth of its purpose that lays the land in rows. It whispers something about the truth to the land, something about a farmer's encroachment, something about what he mows down. It is the technology of the scythe, the force of it. It is the laying of the land that spares some "feeble-pointed spikes of flowers." Faggen writes that "the persistence of flowers reminds the mower of his weakness, his inability to control completely the environment and his unwitting participation in the creation of stronger forms" (48). But the flowers are feeble in relation to the scythe, as are the snakes. The fact of what the speaker can do with his labor—the immediate effects of his labor—is what he hopes for as a reward. There is no long-term guessing about his actions. There is an immediacy in mowing something down, as there is in making something, that is "the sweetest dream that labor knows." The next task is in the distance, and this scythe will leave the "hay to make," will leave disorder behind for the tossing of a pitchfork.

Cleanth Brooks and Robert Penn Warren comment that ". . . Man is set off from nature because he is capable of the 'dream,' because he is an ideal-creating being. . . . But man is also of nature, he fulfills himself in the world of labor and his ideals develop from the real world; he does not get his ideals from some Platonic realm of perfect 'Ideas,' but must create them from his experience and imagination" (371). Neither the speaker nor the reader is told what is whispered; both are left only to theorize. It seems, however, that the scythe and the ground have a special relationship, one that is just beyond human perception. Perhaps an understanding of nature will always be just beyond our grasp.

Two further considerations might lend some insight. John H. Timmerman writes that "Frost supplies a metacommentary on poetics in the poem" (44) and that "[i]f the poem is successful, the reader stores the hay the poet has cut" (45). Jay Parini observes that mowing is also a traditional euphemism for lovemaking.

Despite the cruelty and brutality of the scythe, there is a rhythmic and lulling beauty to its whisper. *See* TECHNOLOGY.

FURTHER READING

Beach-Viti, Ethel. "Frost's 'Mowing,'" *Explicator* 40, no. 4 (Summer 1982): 45–46.

Brooks, Cleanth, and Robert Penn Warren. *Understanding Poetry*. 3rd ed. New York: Holt, Rinehart and Winston, 1960, 371.

Elder, John. "The Poetry of Experience," *New Literary History* 30, no. 3 (Summer 1999): 649–659.

Faggen, Robert. *Robert Frost and the Challenge of Darwin*. Ann Arbor: University of Michigan Press, 1997, 45–48.

Lentricchia, Frank. "The Resentments of Robert Frost." In *Out of Bounds: Male Writers and Gender(ed) Criticism*, edited by Laura Claridge and Elizabeth Lanland, 268–289. Amherst: University of Mass Press, 1990.

McInery, Stephen. "'Little Forms': Four Poems and a Developing Theme of Robert Frost," *Critical Review* 40 (2000): 59–74.

Parini, Jay. *Robert Frost: A Life*. New York: Holt, 1999.

Paton, Priscilla M. "Robert Frost: 'The fact is the sweetest dream that labor knows,'" *American Literature* 53, no. 1 (March 1981): 43–55.

Scott, Mark. "Andrew Lang's 'Scythe Song' Becomes Robert Frost's 'Mowing': Frost's Practice of Poetry," *Robert Frost Review* (Fall 1991): 30–38.

Timmerman, John H. *Robert Frost: The Ethics of Ambiguity*. Lewisburg, Pa.: Bucknell University Press, 2002, 40–45.

Vail, Dennis. "Frost's 'Mowing': Work and Poetry," *Notes on Contemporary Literature* 4, no. 1 (1974): 4–8.

"My Butterfly" (1913)

"My Butterfly: An Elegy" was Frost's first professionally published poem. It was self-published privately in 1894 in *Twilight*, appeared in the November 1894 issue of the *Independent*, and was then collected in Frost's first collection, *A Boy's Will*. Frost claimed it as his "first real poem," having recounted to Louis Untermeyer that he had read his first poem at 15, written his first at 16, and written his first published poem at 18 (Cramer, 26).

The poem is reminiscent of the English romantic poet William Wordsworth's "To a Butterfly!" and is in many ways sentimentally written in the style of the romantics. It is one of several poems in Frost's first volume where it is difficult to identify the Frost the young poet would later become. Frost is trying to find his own identity as a poet, but he appears unsure of himself, relying on the poetic language and style of his predecessors. The poem is overwrought with *thee*'s and *thou*'s and uses the awkward "I wist." While Frost recalled in "The Imagining Ear," his lecture at the Browne and Nichols School on May 10, 1915, "distinctly the joy with which [he] had the first satisfaction of getting an expression adequate for [his] thought" as being in the second stanza of this poem, and that he was "so delighted that [he] had to cry," the natural speech rhythms and colloquial language that make his later poems so authentic are largely absent in this poem. Perhaps the public was not yet ready for the later Frost.

Some Frostian themes are present, however, even if the style is nearly unrecognizable. He is concerned with nature and transience as he is in so many of his best-known poems. The opening image is stark and arresting—"Thine emulous fond flowers are dead, too"—and the poem continues in this vein until at last it closes with the broken wings of the butterfly being found "with the withered leaves / Under the eaves." Nature gives beauty and life but just as dependably and predictably gives death and destruction. Two ideas follow from Frost's depiction of these natural processes. First, they seem to be cyclical, amoral, and apathetic; second, people are the reason for value judgments about nature. They are the ones who give beauty to nature, and they are the ones who recoil from its seemingly malevolent processes and cycles.

Frost would continue to struggle with the forces of nature and what God let "flutter from his gentle grasp" throughout his career.

FURTHER READING

Bagby, George F. *Frost and the Book of Nature*. Knoxville: University of Tennessee Press, 1993, 139–141.

Cramer, Jeffrey S. *Robert Frost among His Poems: A Literary Companion to the Poet's Own Biographical Contexts and Associations*. Jefferson, N.C.: MacFarland, 1996.

"My November Guest" (1913)

Mark Richardson explains that in this lyric

> we hear Frost's own distinctive voice blending with the voice of the Tennysonian-Swinburnian [Alfred, Lord Tennyson (1809–92) and Algernon Charles Swinburne (1837–1909)] strain he was even then setting himself against; here, the 'pillar' revolves pretty much unbroken, as Frost carries something down from the cloud of all those other poets while drawing up something of his life lived outside of books. (109)

Appearing with the gloss "He is in love with being misunderstood," in Frost's first collection, *A Boy's Will*, this third poem of the collection owes much to Frost's predecessors, as Richardson notes. It is concerned with themes that are found elsewhere in Frost, however. John H. Timmerman, for example, calls the poem a companion to "Ghost House" in both form and content, since both are written in iambic tetrameter and five-line stanzas and address feelings of separation and loneliness (25).

The speaker's feminine "November guest" is his sorrow. Some critics have taken this sorrow to be a lover, but there seems apt room for speculation about a reading of this as a courtship poem. Sorrow here is arguably a personification of a mood and an emblem. As nature moves from autumn into winter, the trees become barren, the singing birds fly south, and the sky is overcome with gray. Sorrow finds beauty in November, but the speaker initially focuses on the negative aspects of autumn. The poem seems also to be a complex interior monologue wherein the speaker does not want to admit that there is beauty in the barren landscape, as he would do so in vain. He loves it despite the desolate imagery, but he refrains from focusing on the positive aspects in order to hear sorrow sing its praises. There is a part of him that cannot help but recognize his own sorrow and mourning at the passing seasons; this is the Sorrow with which he finds himself in conflict.

The poem was first published in the November 1912 issue of the *Forum*.

FURTHER READING

Richardson, Mark. *The Ordeal of Robert Frost: The Poet and His Poetics.* Chicago, Ill.: University of Illinois Press, 1997, 106–108.

Timmerman, John H. *Robert Frost: The Ethics of Ambiguity.* Lewisburg, Pa.: Bucknell University Press, 2002, 23–26.

"Nature Note, A" (1942)

Frost once said that a poet never takes notes, as one does not take notes in a love affair. But in this simple nature poem the poet keeps track of the seasons and the last calls of certain birds before they head south for the winter. Here he observes that September 23 is the latest he remembers the birds ever staying, though some leave earlier and some later. It is remarkable that the whippoorwills have stayed late to comically "give us a piece of their bills" because it seems to the poet "out of time." According to his calendar, something is not quite right, and he is not "in on the joke."

The poet's note about nature, perhaps scribbled down in a calendar, becomes "A Nature Note." The word *note* is also a pun on the musical notes of the birds' songs. *The poem* is a playful tribute to nature and the passing of a season. Note too the mimicry of the whippoorwill's call in the "twenty-third of September . . . September the twenty-third" of the concluding stanza.

"A Nature Note" was first published as "A Nature Note on Whippoorwills" in the December 1938 issue of the *Coolidge Hill Gazette* and was later collected in *A Witness Tree*.

"Need of Being Versed in Country Things, The" (1923)

House and home figure prominently in Frost, as do chimneys. Here the house is on fire when it brings "[t]o the midnight sky a sunset glow." And the chimney is all that remains after the fire, similar to the chimney in "Ghost House." "Ghost House" was written in 1901 and was inspired by "an old cellar hole with a broken chimney standing in it—what remained of a nearby farmhouse after a fire had destroyed it in 1867" (Parini, 91). The remains were near one of Frost's farms in Derry, New Hampshire. The image here might have been inspired by the same experience, except it is cast as a reminder of a flower stem that has lost all its petals; the chimney is the remaining pistil.

The wind went in the opposite direction of the barn, saving it from the fire. But the barn has been abandoned since the house burned down. There are no longer teams of livestock kept there. The birds still come through broken windows, but they sigh about what is gone and their chirping is not cheerful, "[t]heir murmur more like the sigh we sigh / From too much dwelling on what has been," the speaker says. For the birds there is still something of home, however. The lilacs are still there, the elm scarred by its touch of fire, the dry water pump, the fence post. These objects all remain for a bird to alight upon. But the speaker muses, "One had to be versed in country things / Not to believe the phoebes wept." An outsider would believe the birds are weeping, but a country person knows better. Robert Faggen finds that "education or uneducation of human emotions is the focus" of the poem (69).

To be versed in country things is to, if not anticipate, at least expect happenstance. Those not versed in country things think that nature cares about human beings and other living things. Those who are versed know about the indifference of nature, that it does not respond to human affairs. To be versed in country things is not to know how to mow a field or lead a team of cattle, as city folk might suppose. It is deeper than that. Those who think nature is concerned with human affairs are not at all versed in country things.

The expression sounds like a shallow country saying, but it is more serious than that. It appears to be playful, but it is too dark. Faggen describes the title as sounding "like a prelude to a piece of moral wisdom, but its folksy sound belies the cruelty of what is to come. 'Country Things' echoes Hamlet's question to Ophelia about indecent 'country matters'; Frost lures his readers to consider nature's

wisdom only to find that the joke is on them" (69). The poem is not about milking a cow but about knowing that for nature "there was really nothing sad" in the burning down of a house. Faggen further notes that "[s]adness is our emotion, and the true need of being versed in country things is to recognize the uselessness of that emotion and to avoid attributing it to other creatures" (70).

Demonstrating the pun on the word "verse" as well as Frost's own knowledge of country things, Robert Pack writes, "One must understand the indifference of nature and country things, and be versed in nature's separateness to write (in verse) a believable nature poem" (157).

The poem was first published in the December 1920 issue of *Harper's Magazine* and was later collected in *West-Running Brook. See* COUNTRY VERSUS CITY and HOME, THEME OF.

FURTHER READING

Bagby, George F. *Frost and the Book of Nature.* Knoxville: University of Tennessee Press, 1993, 132–133.

Elder, John. "The Poetry of Experience," *New Literary History* 30, no. 3 (Summer 1999): 649–659.

Faggen, Robert. *Robert Frost and the Challenge of Darwin.* Ann Arbor: University of Michigan Press, 1997, 69–70.

Pack, Robert. *Belief and Uncertainty in the Poetry of Robert Frost.* Hanover, N.H.: Middlebury College Press, 2003.

Parini, Jay. *Robert Frost: A Life.* New York: Holt, 1999.

Wolosky, Shira. "The Need of Being Versed: Robert Frost and the Limits of Rhetoric," *Essays in Literature* 18, no. 1 (Spring 1991): 76–92.

"Neither Out Far nor In Deep" (1936)

A often-anthologized poem, "Neither Out Far nor In Deep" criticizes "The people along the sand" who "All turn and look one way." The people described are those who all look only in one direction and therefore wear blinders to keep from seeing anything else. They look out at the sea, turning their backs on the land, and in doing so they turn their backs on something meaningful. But the condition described is not a general human condition. Frost is not criticizing all people. He singles out a particular type of person, a specific group of people for criticism.

The people along the sand are like those in Plato's (427?–347? B.C.) Allegory of the Cave, where the people chained inside the cave are unable to turn their heads and are therefore unable to see anything but the shadows cast on the wall of the cave. These they take to be reality. The people in Frost's poem also mistake shadows for reality; the reflection of the standing gull on the "wetter ground like glass" may be an allusion to Plato's allegory. The reflection may also be the people's own reflections. What they are seeing could be themselves, only they are unaware.

The people along the sand are fixated on a particular perspective from which they cannot break free. They are narrowly focused. There is variety on the land, but there is safety in looking at the sea, which is strangely constant. It provides security and predictability in a way that the land cannot.

Frost suggests that what we should all be looking for is the truth, wherever that may be. But for these people looking "out far" or "in deep" is not a goal. It never was "a bar / To any watch they [have] ke[pt]." The truth could be anywhere, but they have only been willing to look for it in one direction because of the assumptions of their particular kind of watch. It is comparable to looking toward the sky in the hopes of finding answers when in truth the answers could be right here on Earth.

Robert Pack writes that "On the one hand, the lines can be read in tones of astonishment implying wonder at how dumb the people can be; on the other hand, the lines can be heard to suggest heroic perseverance and determination; the people will not be discouraged from believing in some kind of transcendent truth, like God, even though neither Truth nor God can be known" (186). But implying that Frost presents the two positions equally seems false. Certainly the closing question comes in the form of ridicule. The critique is that the perspective of the people on the sand is narrow and shallow and that they should strive to look far and deep in

all directions. They must learn instead to measure what they do according to where the truth lies. It should be noted that Frost avoids capitalizing the word *truth*, allowing it to be varied and inclusive. He is driving at what is ultimately accurate in any case, however.

Reginald Cook writes, "Just as this is not a cozy poem softening the blow of human inadequacy, neither is it a shrill one exhibiting the plight of man in a scornful way" (289). But there is clear criticism in Frost's lines. Cook also holds that ". . . this is not a pessimistic poem. It faces the dual facts of human limitations and destiny unblinkingly. No matter how formidable the situation, the poet withholds judgment as to the ultimate outcome. Men may yet make the best of a difficult situation" (287). Cook is hopeful, and perhaps Frost was too. If he had any hope, it was that he would one day have no one to ridicule.

One necessary point is that the people "cannot" look out far nor in deep, it is not simply that they "do not." There is a limitation, possibly self-imposed, placed on these people along the sand, and Frost never explains what holds them back.

The poem was first published in the spring 1934 issue of the *Yale Review* and was later collected in *A Further Range*. *See* PHILOSOPHY.

FURTHER READING

Cook, Reginald. *Robert Frost: A Living Voice*. Amherst: University of Mass Press, 1974, 286–290.

Hines, Edward C., Jr. "'Neither Out Far nor in Deep': Frost's Use of a Traditional Metaphor," *West Georgia College Review* 21 (May 1991): 7–10.

Hoffman, Tyler. *Robert Frost and the Politics of Poetry*. Hanover, N.H.: Middlebury College Press, 2001.

Monteiro, George. "Robert Frost's Liberal Imagination." In *Roads Not Taken: Rereading Robert Frost*, edited by Earl J. Wilcox and Jonathan N. Barron, 153–175. Columbia: University of Missouri Press, 2000.

Pack, Robert. *Belief and Uncertainty in the Poetry of Robert Frost*. Hanover, N.H.: Middlebury College Press, 2003.

Pearlman, Daniel. "A Political Satire Unveiled: Frost's 'Neither Out Far nor in Deep,'" *Agenda* 17, no. 2 (1979): 41–63.

Poland, Peter. D. "Frost's 'Neither Out Far nor in Deep,'" *Explicator* 52, no. 2 (Winter 1994): 95–96.

Seib, Kenneth. "Robert Frost's 'Neither Out Far nor in Deep,'" *Contemporary Poetry* 1, no. 2 (1973): 28–29.

Timmerman, John H. *Robert Frost: The Ethics of Ambiguity.* Lewisburg, Pa.: Bucknell University Press, 2002, 75–76.

"Never Again Would Birds' Song Be the Same" (1942)

This sonnet was written for Frost's close friend and devoted secretary Kay Morrison. At his 88th birthday party, held on the same day he received the Congressional Gold Medal from President John F. Kennedy, he said the poem slowly and gestured with his hand toward Morrison when he spoke the last two lines (Parini, 425).

This is another of Frost's creation stories such as those found in "The Aim Was Song" or "Too Anxious for Rivers." Here he speculates that the birds' song was altered in the Garden of Eden by the presence of Eve. Their singing sounded different before she came, and her coming was to aid them in their song. Her "eloquence so soft" influenced them and added to their own an "oversound," causing birds' song to "never again" be the same. Now Eve's voice has been a part of the birds' so long that the speaker cannot imagine that it will ever be lost.

Robert Pack writes,

> What Eve has brought into the world, according to this speaker in his own fictional act of believing, is the human capacity for art. Eve in Frost's upbeat representation here did not come into the world to bring death and grief to all creatures, including Adam, but rather to bring art and the capacity for celebration, though the phrase "probably it never would be lost" sounds the one tentative and perhaps ominous note in the poem. (152)

But the ending, despite Frost's intention, can also be read as pessimistic. Eve can also be read as merely being used as a means to an end. If Eve's presence was meant to alter and influence the birds' song, it may be in some ways positive, as it was not meant solely to bring death and grief to all creatures. However, she came to aid in the beauty of nature, and while this is a romantic and praiseworthy ideal it is still a way of reducing woman to no more than a pleasing aesthetic.

Robert Faggen writes that in the poem "Frost uses the organic metaphor of the tree to describe an evolution based on material causes" (126). He also notes that "Frost added later that he 'would go on from there to say that people think that life is a *result* of certain atoms coming together, instead of being the *cause* that brings the atoms together,' and felt that his own toying with the concept of life as a final cause was an 'extravagance'" (127).

Given Frost's intentions for the poem with regard to Morrison, it might be regarded as a personal expression of gratitude. Frost's "song," perhaps, was never the same, and in a rather self-absorbed way he might have believed that this was why Morrison came to him.

The poem was first published in *A Witness Tree*.

FURTHER READING

Cramer, Jeffrey S. *Robert Frost among His Poems: A Literary Companion to the Poet's Own Biographical Contexts and Associations.* Jefferson, N.C.: MacFarland, 1996.

Faggen, Robert. *Robert Frost and the Challenge of Darwin.* Ann Arbor: University of Michigan Press, 1997.

Pack, Robert. *Belief and Uncertainty in the Poetry of Robert Frost.* Hanover, N.H.: Middlebury College Press, 2003.

Parini, Jay. *Robert Frost: A Life.* New York: Holt, 1999.

Smith, Evans Lansing. "Frost's 'On a Bird Singing in Its Sleep,' 'Never Again Would Birds' Song Be the Same,' and 'The Silken Tent,'" *Explicator* 50, no. 1 (Fall 1991): 35–37.

"Never Naught Song, A" (1962)

See CLUSTER OF FAITH.

"New England Tribute, A" (1961)

"A New England Tribute" is taken from the official program of the inaugural ceremonies for President John F. Kennedy and Vice President Lyndon B. Johnson on January 20, 1961. President Kennedy and Frost had a friend in common, Congressman Steward L. Udall, whom Frost had gotten to know while poetry consultant for the Library of Congress. Udall suggested to Kennedy that Frost read a poem at his inauguration. Kennedy liked poetry and in particular liked Frost. During his campaign, he would often conclude a speech by quoting the final lines of "Stopping by Woods on a Snowy Evening" about having promises to keep: "And miles to go before I sleep." When Udall first suggested it, Kennedy is quoted as having said, "Oh no! You know Frost always steals any show he is a part of." But the politician in him knew it was a good idea, and he had a telephone conversation with Frost to discuss the invitation. As poet William Meredith later recalled in an interview, "It was a novel idea, and one that focused attention on Kennedy as a man of culture, as a man interested in culture."

During their conversation about the inauguration, Kennedy, as Jay Parini puts it, "gingerly" suggested that Frost write a poem for the occasion. Frost did not particularly welcome the idea. Feeling obligated, however, he did write a poem specifically for the inauguration, but he began to draft it only days before the event. He worked on it until the night before, treating it as a "preamble to his reading of 'The Gift Outright,'" but the result, partly because of Frost's advanced age and partly because of his limited enthusiasm for the task, was a poem written more out of duty than inspiration (Parini).

The poem, "For John F. Kennedy His Inauguration," now treated as a preface to "The Gift Outright," was in fact never read at the inauguration. On that cold, windy day the sun's reflection on the glaring white paper made it impossible for Frost to read the print. Recovering well, he recited "The Gift Outright" from memory, improvising on the last line: "Such as she was, such as she *would* become, *has* become, and I—and for this occasion let me change that to—what she *will* become" (Parini).

In the prose piece "A New England Tribute," Frost, the New Englander, refers to the inauguration as a "turning point in the history of our country, even perhaps in the history of Christendom." He describes the turning point as one when the "old agonies and antagonisms were over." He sees the inauguration as "another gift," one "to make sure of the more than social security of us all in a greater strength, a greater formidability," and he "look[s] forward with confidence to the young leadership." It is a solid endorsement of the president and speaks of the need of giving ourselves again in the revolution. It closes with "The Gift Outright," reprinted with the title "Our Gift Outright."

FURTHER READING

Parini, Jay. *Robert Frost: A Life*. New York: Holt, 1999.

New Hampshire (1923)

The first trade edition of Frost's fourth volume, *New Hampshire*, was published in New York in November 1923 by Frost's only American publisher, Henry Holt and Company. Originally 5,350 copies were released, along with a limited edition of 350 numbered and signed copies. The book, dedicated "To Vermont and Michigan," had the subtitle *A Poem with Notes and Grace Notes* and included woodcuts by J. J. Lankes. The book met with rave reviews and earned Frost his first of four Pulitzer Prizes the following year.

The book is divided into three sections: the title poem, "New Hampshire"; the "Notes," which included 14 poems; and the "Grace Notes," which included 30 shorter poems. This format was meant as a parody of T. S. Eliot's heavily footnoted and celebrated *The Waste Land*. Notably, Frost's footnotes, offering a further criticism of Eliot's work, refer readers to other poems in his own volume instead of to other works of literature.

It is interesting that the volume received such rave reviews after the disappointments of *Mountain*

Interval, since it includes fewer of Frost's best-known poems. Among those included and much celebrated are "Fire and Ice," "Nothing Gold Can Stay," and "Stopping by Woods on a Snowy Evening." Given the number of poems in *Mountain Interval* that have been so widely taught and anthologized, such as "The Road Not Taken" and "Birches," it is a wonder that Frost's first Pulitzer did not come sooner.

New Hampshire is a varied collection, including playful poems like "Maple," the anthologized ones such as "Stopping by Woods on a Snowy Evening," darker, autumnal meditations such as "Nothing Gold Can Stay," those with a scientific angle such as "Fire and Ice," and a little-known gem, "Blue-Butterfly Day." The title poem, "New Hampshire," is an introduction to the many dramatic narratives of the collection. The book was hailed partly because Frost's "overall use of colloquial, regional language reached new heights in this collection. In a poet of lesser talents, this language might well have seemed no more than a turn on the idea of regionalism," but in Frost it was a tour de force (Parini, 226).

As John Farrar wrote of the volume, "Some of the best pictures are of grim and terrible events, and the whole body of his writing indubitably shows a decaying and degenerating New England. That he fails to see the other side of life is untrue. Passages of great beauty shine from drabness" (Parini, 227). Frost had finally, at age 49, fully arrived.

FURTHER READING

Cramer, Jeffrey S. *Robert Frost among His Poems: A Literary Companion to the Poet's Own Biographical Contexts and Associations.* Jefferson, N.C.: MacFarland, 1996.

Parini, Jay. *Robert Frost: A Life.* New York: Holt, 1999.

Uirak, Kim. "The Seasonal Cycle in Robert Frost's Poetry," *Arkansas Review* 5, no. 1–2 (August 1996): 81–87.

"New Hampshire" (1916)

"New Hampshire" is one of Frost's longest poems and is the title poem of his fourth collection, which won him his first of four Pulitzer prizes. It is said to have been written in one night during either June or July 1922. Jay Parini calls the poem an important one in the Frost canon, "not so much for its effectiveness as poetry but for its sly cogence in putting forward a theory of poetry" (209).

The poem begins with the speaker meeting a woman from the "South" whose family never "worked or had a thing to sell." The move from this to the final lines of the first stanza, "The having anything to sell is what / Is the disgrace in man or state or nation," is an indication of what will be significant in the poem. It moves forward satirically, switching back and forth between people the speaker has met and the conclusions he has drawn about them.

In the second stanza he recounts having met "a traveler from Arkansas" who is boastful about his state. Then he moves to a Californian who speaks of his state as "blessed," and so on, until he arrives at New Hampshire, where the only person "really soiled with trade" was someone who had just come back from selling things in California. New Hampshire, after all, just has "specimens" and she "doesn't care to sell" them.

Then comes a discussion of what else New Hampshire has, which continues to be "[o]ne each of everything as in a show-case." In New Hampshire, after all, "quality makes up for quantity." At last Frost gets to poets and how poems are produced more than any other thing. The speaker concludes: "No wonder poets sometimes have to *seem* / So much more business-like than business men. / Their wares are so much harder to get rid of."

Soon the speaker is comparing Vermont and New Hampshire as the "two best states in the Union." In this section he reveals himself, calling himself "a sensibilitist" and an "environmentalist" and explaining that he can "make a virtue of [his] sufferin'" and that as a "creature of literature" he "shall not lack for pain to keep [himself] awake." But New Hampshire, it turns out, is a good place, a better place. Its only real problem is how a writer can set about writing a "Russian novel in America / As long as life goes so unterribly."

The poem continues to discuss New Hampshire and to consider what has raised the speaker to his "throne / Of intellectual dissatisfaction." He knows that the more of a sensibilist he is the more he wants what is wild, though by claiming "[n]othing not built with hands of course is sacred," he still recognizes the importance and overriding value of things that are crafted. He finds the people of New Hampshire "not quite short enough for Art" but "She's still New Hampshire, a most restful state." He does not want to be a "runaway from nature," he would not mind "being a good Greek" but jokingly says he has been told that course "isn't offered this year."

The poem closes with the speaker avoiding, in a very New England way, the choice between being a "prude or a puke" and instead choosing to be a plain New Hampshire farmer. This farmer, however, unlike the "plain" farmer, has money coming in from a publisher in New York. In this way he can find it "restful just to think about New Hampshire," though he is "at present" living in Vermont.

After singing New Hampshire's praises, and nature's as well, the speaker reveals that he does not even live in New Hampshire, and he earns his living not as a farmer but as a poet. The poem is a tribute to New Hampshire, the collection *New Hampshire* a tribute to New Hampshire and New England, but the speaker makes his long and meandering way to conclusions that have little to do with the reverence he expresses.

Frost once wrote to Louis Untermeyer, "I satisfied my conscience with hints at the truth, as in the last part of the poem 'New Hampshire'" (Cramer, 61). Clearly the truth is that Frost wants to adopt the "plain New Hampshire farmer" persona, though he is actually a New York City writer.

FURTHER READING

Cramer, Jeffrey S. *Robert Frost among His Poems: A Literary Companion to the Poet's Own Biographical Contexts and Associations.* Jefferson, N.C.: MacFarland, 1996.

Kearns, Katherine. *Robert Frost and a Poetics of Appetite.* Cambridge: Cambridge University Press, 1994.

Linneman, William R. "Robert Frost's 'New Hampshire': A Most Jestful State," *Studies in American Humor* 6 (1988): 52–60.

Parini, Jay. *Robert Frost: A Life.* New York: Holt, 1999.

Perrine, Laurence. "Frost's 'New Hampshire' 1–60," *Explicator* 29, no. 3 (Spring 1981): 38–39.

"Night Light, The" (1947)

See "FIVE NOCTURNES."

"No Holy Wars for Them" (1947)

This sonnet was published shortly after the end of World War II, when readers would certainly have been fully aware of the atrocities of war. Tyler Hoffman writes that the speaker "measures the political climate, spoofing the disparities between countries, some of which have attained superpower status and others of which are wholly inconsequential on the international scene" (168).

There is certainly sarcasm in the first line, because it is clear that those with power rarely, if ever, do good. The states "strong enough" to which the poem refers at the start would be the United States, Great Britain, and the Soviet Union. The poem moves from questions of power and goodness in relation to states to power and goodness in relation to God, signaling that God might be included in this discussion of powerful "states."

The speaker then calls God's attention to the behavior of man. He wonders whether God knows what is going on on Earth and, if so, what his position on man's behavior is. By raising the question of the divine position on "war in nominal alliance," he points out that God either has a hand in what happens or does not seem to care much about what happens. He also asks, if God has the power to intercede, why he does not, just as he asks the same question of the great states. If God does nothing, then the speaker implies that God should be perceived as and grouped instead with the powerless "puny little states." The fact that the wars described are "holy wars" and not just wars calls attention to why people are fighting and why God should be involved. Either they are fighting for religious reasons or they are at least making it seem as though they are by taking self-righteous stances that God could easily mediate.

The speaker, probably equating himself with the "puny little states" that "can only be" seems to wish that he could "wage a Global Mission" but feels in many ways powerless. All he can do is ask questions of God and hope that God intervenes before "the world's supply / Get[s] parceled out among the winning giants."

The poem was first published in the April 1947 issue of the *Atlantic Monthly*. The manuscript title was "No Holy Wars." *See* POLITICS.

FURTHER READING

Hoffman, Tyler. *Robert Frost and the Politics of Poetry.* Hanover, N.H.: Middlebury College Press, 2001.

North of Boston (1914)

The working title for this, Frost's second collection, was *Farm Servants and Other People*. Frost reported in his preface to an expanded *North of Boston* that the book "found a name for itself in the real estate advertising of the *Boston Globe*." The newspaper advertisement mentioned properties for sale in the area "north of Boston." Frost explained that the volume "was not written as a book nor towards a book." Instead it "was written as scattered poems in a form suggested by the eclogues of Virgil." The Latin poet Virgil's (70–19 B.C.) eclogues consist of 10 poems with rural settings. Frost described the poems in *North of Boston* as some being "a little nearer one act plays than eclogues but they seem to have something in common that I don't want to seek a better name for. It's like its being locative." He also explained in his "Preface to Poems in *This Is My Best*" that in *North of Boston* he "took group enough to show the people and to show that I had forgiven them for being people." The inscription to the book reads, "To E. M. F.: This Book of People," the initials referring to Frost's wife, Elinor Miriam Frost, to whom so many of his books were dedicated (Cramer, 28).

North of Boston was originally published in London on May 15, 1914, by David Nutt, during Frost's brief sojourn in ENGLAND. Two weeks of silence followed before there was a mention of the book in the *Times Literary Supplement*. While Frost himself believed the book was "epoch-making," awaiting reviews filled him with anxiety and caused his usual self-doubt to surface (Parini, 157).

The first developed and positive review came on June 13 in the *Nation* and was written by Lascelles Abercrombie. Abercrombie wrote, "We find very little of the traditional manner of poetry in Mr. Frost's work"; he found that Frost's poetry got "back again into touch with the living vigours of speech" (Parini, 147). The "traditional manner of poetry" of which Abercrombie speaks abounds in several of Frost's poems from his first volume. Frost's friend Edward Thomas wrote in an unsigned review in the *English Review* that the "language ranges from a never vulgar colloquialism to brief moments of heightened and intense simplicity" and that some of the poems were "masterpieces of deep and mysterious tenderness" (Thornton, 30). Another review came from Ezra Pound and was printed in Harriet Monro's *Poetry*. Pound wrote, "Frost has been honestly fond of the New England people, I dare say with spells of irritation. He has given their life honestly and seriously. He has never turned aside to make fun of it. He has taken their tragedy as tragedy, their stubbornness as stubbornness. I know more of farm life than I did before I had read his poems. That means I know more of 'Life.'" Pound further explained that "Mr. Frost's people are distinctly real. Their speech is real; he has known them" (Cramer, 28). Yet another critic commented that by the end of the book "you realize that in a simple, unaffected sort of way he has put before you the whole life of the people of *North of Boston*" (Parini, 149). Frost might have believed the book to be epoch-making, but he had not expected anyone to say so. He had written to his friend Sydney Cox upon the book's publication, "All I ask now is to be allowed to live" (Parini, 157). And let him live they would.

Pound's review of the book put Frost off a bit however. In addition to singing Frost's praises, Pound had taken aim at poets in America, making

Frost worry that Pound's criticisms would count against him when he returned. He joked that "Another such review" and he "shan't be admitted at Ellis Island" (Parini, 157).

Henry Holt published its own edition of the volume in New York in 1915. Mrs. Holt, a Vermonter, persuaded her husband to offer Frost a contract for the American rights. Elinor felt that Holt's adoption meant they could now return home to America, and so they did, but Frost did so with some trepidation. He had concerns about finding work upon his return from England (Parini, 156–157).

North of Boston is a shorter collection but is brimming with great dramatic narratives, such as "Home Burial," "Death of the Hired Man," and "Blueberries." It also includes such critically acclaimed poems as "Mending Wall," "After Apple-Picking," and "The Black Cottage." Although it would not be until *New Hampshire* that Frost would receive his first Pulitzer Prize, *North of Boston*, more than *A Boy's Will*, firmly established the poet's unique voice. Frost had gone to England to devote himself fully to writing and to become a recognized poet, and that he did. He would return to America with his credentials securely in hand.

FURTHER READING

Calder, Alex. "Robert Frost: North of Boston." In *A Companion to Twentieth Century Poetry,* edited by Neil Roberts, 369–380. Oxford: Blackwell, 2001.

Chavkin, Allan. "The Ordering of the Sequence of Meditative Lyrics in Frost's *North of Boston,*" *Markham Review* 10 (Summer 1981): 67–68.

Cramer, Jeffrey S. *Robert Frost among His Poems: A Literary Companion to the Poet's Own Biographical Contexts and Associations.* Jefferson, N.C.: MacFarland, 1996.

Matterson, Stephen. "'To Make It Mean Me': Narrative Design in *North of Boston.*" In *Rebound: The American Poetry Book,* edited by Michael Hinds and Stephen Matterson, 45–55. New York: Rodopi, 2004.

Parini, Jay. *Robert Frost: A Life.* New York: Holt, 1999.

Sanders, David. "Frost's *North of Boston*: Its Language, Its People, and Its Poet," *Journal of Modern Literature* 24, no. 1–2 (Fall 2003): 70–78.

Thornton, Richard, ed. *Recognition of Robert Frost: Twenty-fifth Anniversary.* New York: Holt, 1937.

"Not All There" (1936)

This eight-line poem is next to last in a group of poems titled "Ten Mills," most of which, including this one, were originally published in *Poetry* in April 1936 and were later collected in *A Further Range.* Its manuscript title was "Don't Anybody Laugh," which is the sixth line of the poem.

The first stanza of "Not All There" focuses on the speaker's turning to God for answers to the "world's despair." He is disappointed, as the world's despair becomes his own despair when he finds that God is not there. In the second stanza, the speaker says God turned to him and found he was not there, "At least not over half."

The poem is facetious, manipulating the question of what it means to be "there," and can be read as a play on the dualism of body and soul. When the speaker turned to God, he turned as he would to another person and found God to be unknowable and intangible; since he could not see him, he could not find him. When God turned to the speaker, he turned to the intangible and the non-physical, the soul, and found he was not there, "[a]t least not over half." The only half of him that was there was his physical body. If God is to speak to man, the poem suggests, he needs to have a receptive listener, in effect, one with a soul. The speaker's faith is "not all there" because God, to him, is less than half. There is always a conceptual gap between God and humanity, which is why the audience would be apt to "laugh" if the speaker were to claim he was addressed by God. A person can only pray to what he or she thinks exists, but anyone who thinks God talks to him or her is presumed to be "not all there," that is, mad.

"Nothing Gold Can Stay" (1923)

One of Frost's most anthologized lyrics, this eight-line poem is composed of four rhyming couplets. Despite its brevity, the poem underwent many alterations (Cramer, 76). The result was a great success. The poem compacts observations about nature and human nature into a tightly sewn, seamless, and breathtaking package.

Nothing gold can stay in nature, not sun, not flower, not leaf, not human being. The gold represents what is most prized, spring's first green and first flower. But all beauty is brief. There can be no permanence to nature and living things as the seasons illustrate. As autumn nears and "leaf subsides to leaf" the brief golden hour disappears, just as the Garden of Eden could not remain a paradise and so "sank to grief." Nature once again provides us with gold and beauty, but only temporarily. As with Frost's other poems about nature, there is a constant struggle between transience and the longing for the everlasting.

George F. Bagby explains that "Frost moves from a detail of vegetable growth to the history of human failure and suffering" and adds that "[w]e need to remind ourselves how remarkable it is to see so slight a vehicle expanded into such a weighty tenor," citing Emerson and Thoreau to demonstrate how thoroughly "rooted in a tradition of American nature writing" Frost's ways of "perceiving reality" were (48).

Richard D. Cureton maintains that the meter of the poem is very important to its overall effect as it is "very strong, regular, internally complex [. . .] and independent of the language that elicits it" (10). He holds that to read the poem purely for its meaning "says nothing about the precise ordering and proportioning of the meanings in the text and our developing response" to it (2). This is one of several reasons why one might identify "Nothing Gold Can Stay" as one of Frost's quintessential nature poems uniting pure rhyme and imagery with the tragic. The only permanence that can be found is, perhaps, in such things as poetry.

"Nothing Gold Can Stay" was first published in an October 1923 issue of *The Yale Review*, but was later collected in *New Hampshire*.

FURTHER READING

Anderson, Charles R. "Frost's 'Nothing Gold Can Stay,'" *Explicator* 32 (1964): 63.

Bagby, George F. *Frost and the Book of Nature*. Knoxville: University of Tennessee Press, 1993, 47–49.

Cramer, Jeffrey. *Robert Frost among His Poems: A Literary Companion to the Poet's Own Biographical Contexts and Associations*. Jefferson, N.C.: MacFarland, 1996.

Cureton, Richard D. "Temporality and Poetic Form," *Journal of Literary Semantics* 31, no. 2 (2002): 37–59.

Hoffman, Tyler. *Robert Frost and the Politics of Poetry*. Hanover, N.H.: Middlebury College Press, 2001.

Perrine, Laurence. "Frost's 'Nothing Gold Can Stay,'" *Explicator* 42, no. 1 (Fall 1983): 38–39.

Quinn, Sister M. Bernetta. "Symbolic Landscape in Frost's 'Nothing Gold Can Stay,'" *English Journal* 55 (1966): 621–624.

Rea, John A. "Language and Form in 'Nothing Gold Can Stay,'" In *Robert Frost: Studies of the Poetry*, edited by Kathryn Gibbs Harris, 17–25. Boston: Hall, 1979.

"Not of School Age" (1913)

The speaker of this poem might be seen as another boy but is more likely an adult who, the child assumes, is able to go where he cannot yet go. Frost does not often, if ever, take on another identity, but in this case the arguments for a lone adult traveler or a boy of school age may be almost equally supportable. The poem conjures up all the anxiety and confusion of a first day of school: the journey, the making of friends, and so on. At the same time, the speaker's voice is mature and some of the language is difficult to attribute even to an older boy.

One might still imagine the speaker as a boy on his way to school, perhaps his first day, and making his way "around bend after bend" on what seems to be a great and challenging journey. It is a brisk and windy day, and the scene presents the traveler alone as a little boy lost, whether literally or figuratively. He eventually comes to "one house" and makes "but the one friend." The friend he makes is a boy of about four, one too young for school.

The four-year-old is out in the yard, his "cheek smeared with apple sand," and in the "gale" he shouts to the speaker about the "big flag, the red— / white— / And blue flag, the great sight" that the older of the two would be fortunate to observe and perhaps pledge allegiance to should he find his way to the school. The young boy is appropriately eating the traditional gift for a teacher, an apple, and points up the road, directing the lost speaker "[a]s one having war-command." The speaker's walk to the school would seem to be against all odds, the wind, the confusion of the woods, culminating with the gesture of war. The young boy's mother, his "gentler" parent, looks on, wondering about her son's encounter with the unknown and lost traveler. The speaker jocularly calls the boy's way of speaking an "accent" that is "not good." All of the images of what seems to be a first day's walk to school are somehow equated with a soldier lost on foreign soil and on orders from his commander to keep moving onward.

The poem ends with the young child, who is apparently eager to go to school (or perhaps even into battle) himself, sending the speaker off like a soldier with a gesture, in some respects, as a canary might be sent into a coal mine. In this case his elder will be checking to see if the great American flag is "out today." The flag that stands as a symbol of patriotism, freedom, and hope can also serve as a symbol for the fallen in war, by waving at half-mast. In this case the flag becomes a goal for the speaker and a desired goal for the boy he leaves behind. The answer to the young boy's inquiry whether the flag is out today, if answered, will signal the "soldier's" completion of his journey and his survival.

It has also been suggested that the voice of the poem is that of a new schoolmaster, as anxious as any schoolboy for the first time wending his way to school and adventures unforeseen.

First published in *A Witness Tree*, the manuscript was titled "An Admirer of the Flag."

"Not Quite Social" (1936)

We never learn what the speaker "did" in this poem, and that is how the poet forces reflection on the part of the reader. The speaker speculates about his punishment for being "Not Quite Social" in his actions and explains that the "thing" he did was

not really forbidden, nor was it imposed or expected. He explains away, seeming to ask forgiveness, but his request is not entirely genuine.

In the second stanza "the city's hold on a man is no more tight / Than when its walls rose higher than any roof," and the allusion to fortress walls is evident. There is a sudden recognition that men who are free are little less controlled than those who are confined. The reader is forced to look at society in terms of what is deemed appropriate and acceptable behavior and to reflect on his or her attitude toward antisocial behavior.

By not revealing his crime, the speaker focuses not on his behavior but on our behavior as a society, in terms of our attitudes and the subsequent penalties on those who do not adhere to social norms and the mores of our time. The poem is laden with images of trial and condemnation.

The speaker is trapped on earth, unable to flee, but he has opportunity in other ways. He is able to will his air to nature, after all. And if anyone who is "free to condemn [him] to death" should "leav[e] it to nature to carry out the sentence," nature will allow him to grow old and die of natural causes as opposed to artificial ones, with this action on his conscience.

The poem is largely polite, though tongue-in-cheek, but in the end some of the politeness is set aside. The plea for forgiveness is not authentic; the speaker does not take himself seriously, nor are we to take him that way. He withholds. He will adhere only to minimum standards of politeness, as in death, when he will pay a "death-tax of fairly polite repentance." The walls that we build around acceptable behavior are particularly confining, even after death.

To be social is to behave in acceptable ways. Those who do not we imprison. The idea that impolite behavior is criminal is compelling as it requires a different way of looking at what is considered transgressive behavior.

Frost once noted during a reading that this poem "goes with" another of his poems, "The Lost Follower," where those who leave poetry, the "golden line / Of lyric" never do it for "darkness" but instead for "golden light divine" (Cramer, 114). Our spirit is often swayed by "religious pranks," but those who fail at being poets never do it in favor of "money-metal banks." Instead, the danger to poetry is always in a different direction, toward what people believe are greater callings: music, politics, and so forth.

While the poem can be read as a discussion of the social consequences of transgression, it is clear that, given Frost's connection between "The Lost Follower" and "Not Quite Social," the speaker in this poem is a poet. The poet has never really been and never really will be social, in the usual sense of the word. Here Frost wills to us "common stock" the "air of his breath," his words, his poetry, and only subtly offers what might be described as a "fairly polite repentance." It was never in him to be too polite.

The poem was first published on March 30, 1935, in the *Saturday Review of Literature*. It was later collected in *A Further Range. See* WALLS.

FURTHER READING

Broderick, John C. "Not Quite Poetry: Analysis of a Robert Frost Manuscript," *Manuscripts* 20, no. 2 (1968): 28–31.

Cramer, Jeffrey S. *Robert Frost among His Poems: A Literary Companion to the Poet's Own Biographical Contexts and Associations.* Jefferson, N.C.: MacFarland, 1996.

"Not to Keep" (1923)

"Not to Keep" is a touching and sensitive blank-verse poem about wartime. Letters come home during war, usually to deliver the painful news of a loved one's death. Here the letter comes, saying in effect that "she could have him," and the soldier, in a strange twist of fate, is sent home to his bride "[l]iving." He is injured but not "disfigured visibly"—the disfiguration is deeper than the skin. But, most important, he is back.

At first the bride feels privileged, one of the lucky few to have her spouse survive and return to her alive. "Everything seem[s] won"—the war, her spouse—but he withholds. Not everything is won. She asks, "What is it, dear?" the question seeming to

be both about his injury and about his frame of mind. He explains that he was shot "high in the breast" but that it was nothing that spending a week with her, with medicine and rest, cannot cure. The shock of his statement brings the sudden realization that their reunion will be only temporary.

They can no longer speak of "it"; instead, they communicate without words, through looking. In Frost especially "Home Burial," communication about the most painful things is often oblique or unspoken. Frost re-creates speechless moments with accuracy. As Tyler Hoffman notes, "caesurae represent agonizing twists and turns of mind—the psychic derangement imputed to the wife who is forced to piece together news of her husband's fate" (165). He has been given back to her, but not to keep, and that is all there is to know, leaving nothing to say.

The poem is fully expressive of the pains of war. What is said is said with brevity, but there is depth of emotion. To have but not to keep, rather than to have and to hold, is not only something recognized at wartime but is ultimately one of the conditions of love. The play on wedding vows is evident, and the poem makes it painfully clear that one's time with a beloved is always limited, whether because of circumstance or nature. What we cannot keep, we dare not ask.

"Not to Keep" was first published in the January 1917 issue of the *Yale Review*. It was later collected in *New Hampshire*.

FURTHER READING

Hoffman, Tyler. *Robert Frost and the Politics of Poetry.* Hanover, N.H.: Middlebury College Press, 2001.

"November" (1942)

"November" was first published in *The Old Farmer's Almanac 1939* as "October" and was later published as "November" in *A Witness Tree,* after it was realized that *A Boy's Will* included a poem titled "October." The manuscript title was "In Praise of Waste," but it also held several other titles, including "For the Fall of Nineteen Thirty Eight" and "Lines Written Last Autumn" (Cramer, 139).

Autumn is a season Frost wrote about frequently. October and November are transitional months, and since Frost was very much concerned with the transition from fall to winter, the two months tend to figure prominently in several of his poems about nature.

In this poem he follows the leaves from "glory" to being "beaten down and pasted" by the rain. Almost like migratory birds, the leaves drift partway "down the lane" before the rain roars "'Tis over" and it is ended. Another year of leaves "wasted." Despite our efforts at "storing," "saving," and "keeping," the moment leaves us, just as do the moments of "sleeping" and "weeping."

The poem has a subtext of war. The leaves become a metaphor for the soldiers who, too, initially leave on what seems to be the way "to glory" but often make it only partway down the lane to war, before being brought down in a rain of bullets. "'Tis over" can refer to a season, but it is also what is said when a war or battle has ended. We save and keep leaves in books, as we save and keep mementos of loved ones. We boast of what we can save and keep safe, but we neglect to pay due attention to what we waste and what is lost through our wasting. We lose pleasure in weeping. We also, on a far more cataclysmic level, waste human life and nations entire, by "denying and ignoring" their warring.

Frost moves from something as ordinary and easily accepted as the leaves falling from the trees in autumn to what we have come to treat as inevitable—war. But war is something brought about by people, not by seasons, and it is a waste that we could avoid. We cannot keep the seasons from destroying the leaves. Pleasure weeping is an oxymoron that ruefully describes humankind's inclination to war.

Mark Richardson finds that "November" and "The Lost Follower" illustrate Frost's point in the introduction to *King Jasper* that poetry should confine itself to "melancholy" (159). He also interprets the last seven lines of the poem to suggest that "nothing we 'keep' is ever really preserved, no matter what our efforts, from the inexorable tendency toward decay symbolized by the season of fall" (159). Tyler Hoffman writes that the "accretion of syntactic parallels symbolizes the fact that every new day will bring with it mounting destruction" (81).

November symbolizes not only the end of a season but a "denying and ignoring" of what is to come, even when its coming is within the sphere of human control.

FURTHER READING

Cramer, Jeffrey S. *Robert Frost among His Poems: A Literary Companion to the Poet's Own Biographical Contexts and Associations.* Jefferson, N.C.: MacFarland, 1996.

Hoffman, Tyler. *Robert Frost and the Politics of Poetry.* Hanover, N.H.: Middlebury College Press, 2001.

Monteiro, George. "A Pre-publication Version of Robert Frost's 'November,'" *Robert Frost Review* (Fall 1991): 5–6.

Richardson, Mark. *The Ordeal of Robert Frost: The Poet and His Poetics.* Chicago, Ill.: University of Illinois Press, 1997, 159–160.

"Now Close the Windows" (1913)

As one of the poems from Frost's first book, *A Boy's Will*, that more resembles his later work, this lyric concerns itself with various of the poet's prominent themes. Here the closing up of windows in preparation for and protection from winter means keeping nature safely on the other side of the windowpane. But nature is in many ways out of our control, even though, somewhat contrarily, people have some control over what happens to them in nature. Many references are made to nature's loveliness in relation to our senses, such as seeing and hearing. So even when nature's sounds are not so pleasing and we do not have control over nature, we can still "hush all the fields" and watch with the sound off.

The birds are no longer heard singing, nor are the leaves heard rustling in the trees. Nature can be seen "wind-stirred" through the glass, but the sounds are lost once we have closed ourselves indoors. There is protection from the cold, but there is also a loss. It will be a "long" wait before the earliest bird of spring returns. In the meantime, the trees will "silently toss," and we will have an overwhelming feeling of absence.

"Objection to Being Stepped On, The" (1962)

Frost's wife Elinor once stepped on a rake and broke her nose, and that experience is said to be the inspiration for this poem. One of Frost's particularly humorous ones, the skillful and playful rhyme has something in common with his "Departmental." Robert Faggen also finds that the "futility of social progress and the cultural wavering between invention or discovery and destruction is summarized comically" in this poem (165).

The speaker accidentally steps on a hoe that has been left in the field, and it rises up to meet him. It hits him in the "seat of his sense" rather than the seat of his pants. The speaker says that the hoe is not to blame, but he curses it just the same. He also imagines that the blow the hoe dealt was premeditated. He then alludes to the book of the prophet Isaiah, where it is written that swords will be beaten into ploughshares and spears into pruning hooks. This hoe has reversed the biblical prophesy and become a weapon. He reminds himself and us that it is only because of our position that it is viewed as a tool. We are also reminded how quickly our perceptions can change, since the moment the speaker steps on the hoe, it quickly turns on him, as friend becomes foe, by turning into a weapon.

The personification of the hoe coupled with the feeling of malice indicates important distinctions among tools, weapons, nature, and people. Weapons are human inventions associated with intention and malice, whereas tools are associated with nature and assistance. Tools can be found among numerous species, but weapons appear to be distinctly human. The fact that the speaker curses the hoe and attributes intentions to it also fits the Frostian theme of attributing intentions to nature when there are none. What happened with the hoe was accidental, but the speaker still feels compelled to attribute to it some malice. We know that he should not, and so does he, and the same would apply for other situations where we attach human intention to natural processes such as disease and disaster.

To the fields a hoe is a weapon, to us a tool. It is all a matter of perspective. The poem becomes another instance where Frost teaches his readers what it means to be "versed in country things." As Reginald Cook writes, "The poem eases, it does not torment. It is not obscure, only playfully simple. When the poet refines the problem of encumbrances, as he has in this poem, his materials suggest a perfectly fathomable profundity—a verifiable truth (good from evil) that does not exclude its opposite (evil from good)" (260).

Stanley Burnshaw retells an amusing story of Frost's experience reciting the poem at a United Nations (at whose New York headquarters the lines from Isaiah are prominently displayed) luncheon on March 17, 1960, with a group of Soviet writers. Frost introduced the poem by calling it "an innocent pastoral poem, which should be familiar to Russians, who have always been a great agricultural people." The interpreter present "threw up his hands." "Hoe? hoe? Did he say 'hoe'?" he said. Frost said to Burnshaw, "Is there *no* word in Russian for hoe? I thought you told me the Soviets have millions of farmers!" A drawing depicting the farm tool clarified things enough for the interpreter to continue, but Burnshaw was not sure what he said. In any case Frost graciously said his good-byes and congratulated the interpreter on enlarging his command of English by learning one of Frost's "favorite non-intellectual words" (125–127).

The title itself is particularly amusing since the objection to being stepped on is the hoe's but in the poem the speaker is objecting to having been struck by the hoe.

The poem was first published in booklet form as "My Object to Being Stepped on." It was Frost's 1957 Christmas poem and was later collected in *In the Clearing.*

FURTHER READING

Burnshaw, Stanley. *Robert Frost Himself.* New York: George Braziller, 1986.

Cook, Reginald. *Robert Frost: A Living Voice.* Amherst: University of Massachusetts Press, 1974, 259–260.

Faggen, Robert. *Robert Frost and the Challenge of Darwin.* Ann Arbor: University of Michigan Press, 1997, 165.

Fleissner, Robert F. "Markin' the Frost Line: On Robert Frost and Edwin Markham," *South Carolina Review* 16, no. 2 (Spring 1984): 120–124.

"October" (1913)

"October" is quite similar to Frost's "November" in *A Witness Tree.* In fact, "November" was first also titled "October" before it was realized that this poem of the same name had already been collected in *A Boy's Will.*

The speaker asks October to begin the day slowly. He knows that the leaves have already "ripened," or turned, and a rough and "wild" wind will cast them from the trees, will "waste" them all. *Waste* is the same term Frost uses in "November."

The speaker also knows that the days have shortened and asks that October make the day seem less brief, beguiling "us in the way you know." The speaker wants to be deceived by October because if everything can simply be slowed, the loss of the beauty of nature into the death of winter may not be such a blow. October could "[r]elease one leaf at break of day; / At noon release another leaf; / One from our trees, one far away." The speaker hopes to deceive October as well, claiming it is for the "grapes' sake" rather than his own. But in the end, the speaker knows the futility of such a request. Nature has its cycles, and our pleading with it only results in the absence of response or caring.

According to Jeffrey Cramer, Frost referred to the poem in 1962 as "innocent of everything I know of" (25). Yet this is another of the few poems where the poet puns on his own name. Here the grapes' leaves "already are burnt with frost," suggesting that it is fitting for the poet to be so concerned with the transition from autumn to winter and the prospect of frost.

The poem was first published on October 3, 1912, in the *Youth's Companion.*

FURTHER READING

Cramer, Jeffrey S. *Robert Frost among His Poems: A Literary Companion to the Poet's Own Biographical Contexts and Associations.* Jefferson, N.C.: MacFarland, 1996.

Richardson, Mark. *The Ordeal of Robert Frost: The Poet and His Poetics.* Chicago, Ill.: University of Illinois Press, 1997, 141–142.

Scheick, William J. "Frost's 'October,'" *Explicator* 62, no. 2 (Winter 2004): 96–98.

"Of the Stones of the Place" (1942)

There is a strong connection between individuals and where they reside. The speaker, possibly Gransir Ira, farms a pasture where the boulders lie as close together "as a basket full of eggs." While the claim is that he farms the pasture, the description of the pasture is of one that cannot easily be farmed. It is filled with boulders, obstacles to farming.

The speaker likely addresses a grandchild who lives in "wind-soil to a depth of thirty feet, / And every acre good enough to eat, / As fine flour put through a baker's sieve." The description is of a highly farm-worthy pasture, unlike Gransir Ira's own. The speaker wishes to send one of his boulders to his grandchild, one that he could set up like an "eolith palladium," a crude stone safeguard to help preserve the "West" and "keep the old tradition safe." The description is of a midwestern farm where the traditions of New England could be carried on. The crude boulder would be a representation of the old tradition and ancestry, and the connection between people and place would be solidified and preserved.

"Carve nothing on it," the speaker announces. He suggests that the boulder be claimed as a "portrait of the soul," since where one lives is a representation of who one is, and the land is a part of the one who cultivates it. The boulder would be a tribute to the older generation of farmers simply by having come from where Gransir Ira came from.

The poem was first published in *The Old Farmer's Almanac* in 1942 as "Rich in Stones" and was later collected in *A Witness Tree*.

"Old Barn at the Bottom of the Fogs, The" (1936)

The poem begins jokingly by asking, "Where's this barn's house?" The question suggests that barns have houses as children have parents. But the barn at the bottom of the fogs has "never had a house, / Or joined with sheds in ring-around a dooryard" the way children play ring-around-the-rosy. This barn has been houseless and largely abandoned.

The hunter uses the barn during hunting season, but when the season is "close[d]" the barn is also closed. The prop-locks that are generally used for propping the doors open become props for "propping shut," and the doors come to have an "advantage-disadvantage" of locking someone in just as easily as keeping them out. A tramp who takes "sanctuary" in the abandoned barn must leave the doors unlocked, but in doing so he also "betray[s] his presence" and runs the risk of being locked in, since the doors lock "from the outside only."

The speaker encounters one of the tramps who slept in the barn for the night. The two realize that their "details agre[e]" about the barn at the bottom of the fogs. The tramp now works at sea, in a mill, or in a mine—he is no longer a tramp. He is made wiser by his experiences, however, and is in a position to criticize the rich and elaborate on what foolish people cherish.

The rich are apt to ignore a perfectly good barn in favor of a house they cannot fully own, one that they must mortgage to be able to afford. The rich are also equated with conservativism and not "know[ing] what to save" since they "leave such lovely shafts outdoor to perish." The wood of which the barn is made may eventually become a "relic of a vanished race of trees" because of the wastefulness and weak values of the rich.

The "tramp" had almost had "troubled dreams" because of his lack of control over his own destiny.

Since he could not lock himself in, he had to worry about being locked in by the "cheapest tramp that came along that way," and in this way the "cage of silver bars" that is created by the crevices letting the moonlight in "[a]ll up and down it" suggest how much power the wealthy have over the poor and how much the destiny of the poor seems fixed. A similar perspective is expressed in "How Hard It Is to Keep from Being King When It's in You and in the Situation."

"Old Barn at the Bottom of the Fogs" was first published in *A Further Range* and was subtitled "Class Prejudice Afoot."

"Old Man's Winter Night, An" (1916)

One of the great poems in *A Mountain Interval* and one of the few in which Frost puns his own name, "An Old Man's Winter Night," provides a NEW ENGLAND scene made quite familiar by the old country poet. The poem describes the "inner and outer" weather on a winter night, as in "Tree at My Window." Here, also, the curtain on the window is not drawn as if to separate man from nature, and that exposure allows "All out-of-doors" to look "darkly in."

The descriptions of winter are faithful. The thin frost on the windowpane, when reflected by the light of an oil lamp, is described as "almost in separate stars." And that reflection on the windowpane also keeps the man from being able to see out or to give "back the gaze" to the outdoors looking in. The creak of a cold and silent house is familiar to any who have spent a winter night alone; the "clomping" of a solitary man in an empty house of many rooms is also heard clearly. "[T]he roar / Of trees and crack of branches" are winter sounds in the night that here musically seem to accompany the man's breathing as he sleeps. The poem gives a vivid depiction of the cold loneliness that winter in the country brings, but the poem consists of more than truthful visions.

Somewhat similar to the old man who went to bed, bumped his head, and did not wake up until morning, this old man finds himself in a room try-ing to remember what it was that brought him there, as though he has bumped his head and tem-porarily lost his memory. The experience of walk-ing from one room to another in search of something and then wondering why he is there is familiar. But in this instance the impression is that this is a more common occurrence for an old man who lives iso-lated and alone.

The "in clomping here" and "in clomping off" is "nothing so like beating on a box" but re-creates the image of the "treading—treading" of Emily Dickin-son's "I felt a Funeral, in my Brain." In Frost it also seems that "sense" is "breaking through." But, as in Dickinson, "then a Plank in Reason" breaks, and Frost states that "[o]ne aged man—one man—can't keep a house, / A farm, a countryside."

In "Desert Places" Frost writes, "They cannot scare me with their empty spaces / Between stars—on stars where no human race is. / I have it in me so much nearer home / To scare myself with my own desert places." In "Old Man's Winter Night" the old man "scared it once again . . . scared the outer night." The creaking in the night seems to be what brings this man from one room to the next, checking up on things. But he also finds that the empty house reminds him that he is a "light to no one but himself" and a "quiet light, and then not even that." His isolation causes him to be "con-cerned with he knew what."

Resignation comes later in the poem, when the man consigns himself to the "broken" moon. And with nature bearing down, the "snow upon the roof" and the "icicles along the wall to keep," he falls into a deep sleep, in preparation for the long day of work waiting for him on the other side. Even a log that "shifted with a jolt / Once in the stove" disturbs only briefly the deep sleep that night brings for the man who must keep a house, a farm, and a countryside tomorrow. The country tiredness is reminiscent of the dreamy imagery and the distant, repetitive "rumbling sound / Of load on load of apples coming in" in "After Apple-Picking."

John Cunningham holds that "his burning lamp, and his concerns, and his fire to which he responds even in his sleep all represent the presence of his humanity" (272). Laurence Buell points out the similarities to Edwin Arlington Robinson's "Mr. Flood's Party," of which Frost was fond. *See* NATURE, NIGHT, and WALLS.

FURTHER READING

Buell, Laurence. "Frost as a New England Poet." In *The Cambridge Companion to Robert Frost,* edited by Robert Faggen, 101–122. Cambridge: Cambridge University Press, 2001.

Cunningham, John. "Human Presence in Frost's Uni-verse." In *The Cambridge Companion to Robert Frost,* edited by Robert Faggen, 261–272. Cam-bridge: Cambridge University Press, 2001.

Davis, Charles G. "Frost's 'An Old Man's Winter Night,'" *Explicator* 27 (1968).

Hoffman, Tyler. *Robert Frost and the Politics of Poetry.* Hanover, N.H.: Middlebury College Press, 2001, 165.

"On a Bird Singing in Its Sleep" (1936)

This piece considers the purpose and value of evo-lutionary traits. A "half wakened" bird sings "half-way through its little inborn tune," and the speaker questions whether by singing in its sleep it "ven-tured less in peril than appears." After all, if singing half asleep were a threat to the bird's survival, how would the species have survived? It might be partly because it sings "ventriloquist" and partly because it sings only "once all night" that it has survived. In any case "singing out of sleep and dream" that way has clearly not "made it much more easily prey."

Frost makes a connection between the bird and "men on earth." As Robert Faggen writes, "Frost shows how we take the traits and survival of certain creatures as evidence of a providential plan that includes ourselves." Faggen adds that "Seeing the activity of a bird singing in its sleep would, of course, appeal to humans (and poets) because it reflects the value we place on our minds, our dreams, and our singing" (88).

Faggen hauntingly concludes that the bird "may have survived thus far singing as it does, but there is no guarantee about the future," a reminder that human beings are as susceptible to the negative consequences of their habits in relation to the environment as is the bird and that there are no assurances about their ability to survive either (89).

The poem was first published in December 1934 in *Scribner's Magazine* and was later collected in *A Further Range. See* NIGHT.

FURTHER READING

Bagby, George F. *Frost and the Book of Nature.* Knoxville: University of Tennessee Press, 1993, 85–86.

Faggen, Robert. *Robert Frost and the Challenge of Darwin.* Ann Arbor: University of Michigan Press, 1997, 88–89.

Smith, Evans Lansing. "Frost's 'On a Bird Singing in Its Sleep,' 'Never Again Would Birds' Song Be the Same,' and 'The Silken Tent,'" *Explicator* 50, no. 1 (Fall 1991): 35–37.

"On a Tree Fallen across the Road" (1923)

The powers that nature has over humanity and that humanity has over itself were of great concern to Frost. He once claimed that he had written only two poems without a person in them and therefore he could not be considered a nature poet. People often find themselves in confrontation with nature in his poems, and these confrontations are usually a cause for reflection and an opportunity for learning.

Instead of depicting the effects of nature on human beings after a confrontation, in this sonnet Frost describes the process of working through a conflict with nature and resolving it somewhat satisfactorily. In the opening stanza a conflict is depicted: A party, which we later learn is traveling by sleigh, has had its journey obstructed by a fallen tree: "the tree the tempest with a crash of wood / Throws down in front of us." The choice of the word *tempest* reveals the violence in the action.

This tree, having fallen on this particular road at this particular time, does not have great meaning, but still there is the sense that what "happened"

had not only cause but purpose. Indeed, the tree has fallen to "ask us who we think we are." This random event has a significance that transcends the mere falling of a tree. Nature is questioning human beings—a strange twist. It is usually the other way around, as in Frost's poem "Design." Nature wants to know who we think we are trying to make our way in it, who we think we are even being a part of it. We are intruders. We are, ironically, out of our element.

The second stanza reveals what nature finds so disagreeable in us: "Insisting always on our own way so." Nature does not obstruct us so much as we interfere with it. We insist on making our way, even when that means cutting a swathe through a forest or taking an ax to a fallen tree. Our intrusion on nature here is reminiscent of Wallace Stevens's "Anecdote of the Jar," in which the human will is judged by nature, the desire to shape things and to control what is beyond controlling. In Frost, nature likes to stop us in our tracks, to slow our progress and make us consider what we are doing. Usually we are in such a race with life that we do not take the time to slow down and contemplate it, so, on occasion, nature reminds us that we exist both inside and outside of it.

The poem goes on to suggest that nature need not control us: "And yet she knows obstruction is in vain: / We will not be put off the final goal / We have it hidden in us to attain." We will go on, and this gives us a certain independence from nature. We will not be hindered by its whims. Our willing and our determination are both criticized and admired. But even more than that, there is a shared goal among us that is not totally revealed in the poem; we only know that it is "hidden in us to attain."

There is a power struggle going on in which the prevailing force is human will. Frost asserts that we do not "have to seize earth by the pole." While we may be striving to master nature, we do not have to seize and restrain it in order to do so. Our ability lies in mastering nature with our attitudes, a philosophical approach quite usual with Frost. It is not necessary to cut a swathe through a forest or to take an ax to a fallen tree in order to resume our path after nature's intrusion. It is in our power to overcome the impediment with mind and will, as Frost does in the writing of this poem.

The poem is a reminder that we will not be restricted by nature's force. Nature is met, contended with, and circumvented. The larger meaning is that whatever causes havoc in our lives, we must go on, one knee up after another (as in the poem "A Leaf-Treader") until we have made our way. The thirst for greater knowledge sends us off in search of even greater challenges. We become bored with circling; eventually we will steer off into space for "something."

Significantly, Frost is not uncritical of the very human desire to veer off after something. While the poem discusses the natural landscape, it has more to do with inner landscapes. (In the poem "Tree at My Window" Frost is similarly concerned with both "inner" and "outer" weather.) Veering off into space describes the human appeal to the universe for meaning and explanation. While Frost encourages us to not let nature impede us, he also warns us to keep our demand for answers in check. While the poem places man in nature contending with an obstacle, the obstacle in the end becomes himself—ourselves.

Jeffrey Cramer reports that Frost wrote to his good friend Louis Untermeyer in 1949, "Most accidents are just to ask us who we think we are. And after all who in Hell are we?" (85).

"On a Tree Fallen across the Road" was first published in October 1921 in *Farm and Fireside* and was later collected in *New Hampshire* with the subtitle "(To hear us talk)." *See* NATURE.

FURTHER READING

Bagby, George F. *Frost and the Book of Nature*. Knoxville: University of Tennessee Press, 1993, 112–114.

Cramer, Jeffrey S. *Robert Frost among His Poems: A Literary Companion to the Poet's Own Biographical Contexts and Associations*. Jefferson, N.C.: MacFarland, 1996.

"On Being Chosen Poet of Vermont" (1962)

Frost parodies the well-known lines from Sir Walter Scott's "The Lay of the Last Minstrel": "Breathes there the man, with soul so dead, / Who never to himself hath said, / This is my own, my native land!"

This quatrain was first published untitled in newspapers following Frost's installation as poet laureate of Vermont on July 22, 1961, and was later collected as one of the last poems of *In the Clearing*. It is a brief expression of appreciation consisting essentially of a single-sentence question. In it the poet speculates that there must not be a bard who has ever not been moved by being embraced by his country and his neighborhood but, more important, has been "understood / And not entirely disapproved." The poem, and probably the occasion too, was a rare moment for Frost in which he has no need for metaphor, though he does mischievously fall back on Scott's lines.

"On Being Idolized" (1947)

Idolization always involves illusion. Frost provides compelling imagery for what it means to have the feeling of a firm footing but the knowledge that all can be taken away with "the swift rush" of "sandy dregs."

Being idolized places a person in a precarious position. Just as the character standing seaside can easily and quickly be made to "totter" by the rush of a wave, the idolized can be made to totter and even "be tipped over." Idolization pits an individual against an ocean. It is good neither for those being idolized nor for those doing the idolizing; expectation is not always a good thing. We run too great a risk in mistaking a lover.

The poem also suggests people's idealization of themselves and how quickly and easily nature can put them in their place. Charles Darwin once asked why thought being a secretion of the brain was more wonderful than gravity as a property of matter; he concluded that it is only in our arrogance and our admiration of ourselves.

The imagery in "On Being Idolized" is similar to that in "Etherealizing," where water is also used as an analogy for the affirmation of the physical over the soul. Frost, who was idolized by many as a poet, must have fully understood or at least been sensitive to what it means to be idolized and how quickly he might fall out of favor with the public. Presumably he took his steps cautiously in order to keep from tipping over.

"On Being Idolized" was first published in *Steeple Bush.*

"Once by the Pacific" (1928)

The power of the sea is depicted ominously in this sonnet. Frost had harrowing memories of the sea from his boyhood in SAN FRANCISCO. On many occasions his father swam in the San Francisco Bay while leaving the young Frost alone on the beach "in a terrible state of agitation until his father returned" (Parini, 14). Frost also had a fearful memory of an occasion when the family dined at the Cliff House, a restaurant with a view of the Pacific, and went for a stroll along the beach after dinner. Frost became "absorbed in a solitary game of lashing stone targets with a seaweed whip" and was inadvertently left behind on the beach (Thompson, 35). A storm was brewing, and as the dark clouds came into view he raced terrified to catch up to his parents.

In the poem the powerful waves threaten the land in a way they never have before. The clouds are "low and hairy in the skies / Like locks blown forward in the gleam of eyes." The sea is portrayed as feminine and capable of great destruction. It has greater power than ever, and the land is fortunate to be backed by "cliff" and "continent." The ocean is depicted as malevolent and filled with "rage." It is expected to release its power either in a "night of dark intent" or, if not in a night, then in an "age." While the power is the sea's, it intends to supersede God and do its harm before the end of the all, before "God's last *Put out the Light* [is] spoken."

Frost's poems about nature most often depict man's cunning pitted against nature's constant challenges. Frost generally portrays humans as having skills to contend with nature and the strength to overcome its indifferent forces. Nature is not only nor always seen as simply picturesque in Frost, but it is also not often seen as purely malevolent. Here,

however, nature is filled with a rage it waits to unleash on humanity. It seems clear that this is one instance where the poet's experiences shaped his perceptions. The poem's title, after all, is not "The Pacific" but "Once by the Pacific." The depiction is of a singular experience and is not intended to provide a comprehensive understanding of the sea. It comes as no surprise that the poet lived largely landlocked in NEW ENGLAND throughout his adult life.

The poem was first published on December 19, 1926, in the *New Republic* and was later collected in *West-Running Brook. See also* NIGHT.

FURTHER READING

Fleissner, Robert F. "Frost's 'Once by the Pacific,'" *Explicator* 40, no. 4 (Summer 1982): 46–47.

Hines, Edward C., Jr. "Frost's 'Once by the Pacific,'" *Explicator* 39, no. 4. (Summer 1981): 28–29.

Holland, Norman N. *The Brain of Robert Frost.* New York: Routledge, 1988, 16–23.

Parini, Jay. *Robert Frost: A Life.* New York: Holt, 1999.

Perrine, Laurence. "Frost's 'Once by the Pacific,'" *Explicator* 41, no. 3 (Spring 1983): 44.

Saunders, Judith P. "Frost's 'Once by the Pacific,'" *Explicator* 39, no. 4 (Summer 1981): 29–31.

Thompson, Lawrance. *Robert Frost: The Early Years.* New York: Holt, Rinehart and Winston, 1966.

"On Emerson" (1958)

On October 8, 1958, Frost received the Emerson-Thoreau Medal from the American Academy of Arts and Sciences. The Emerson-Thoreau Medal was established the same year, Frost being its first recipient, to give recognition for distinguished achievement in literature. It is named in honor of the American writer and philosopher Ralph Waldo Emerson (1803–82) and the American writer and naturalist Henry David Thoreau (1817–62). Frost's talk of the evening was "On Emerson," and as George Monteiro describes, the essay is "a storehouse of self-revealing perceptions and teasing observations" (138).

Frost begins appreciatively: "All that admiration for me I am glad of." But he quickly reminds the audience, "I am here out of admiration for Emerson and Thoreau." Frost describes Emerson as his favorite kind of both "poetic philosopher" and "philosophical poet." He soon turns to the question of Emerson's monistic philosophy. "A melancholy dualism is the only soundness," he says, and he begins to describe his "own unsoundness" as coming from his family history and teachings. His mother was a Presbyterian turned Unitarian but also a Swedenborgian. Frost is not sure if he was "baptized in them all," but he says he was largely "under the auspices of Emerson."

Emerson affected Frost early; Frost's first thoughts about his own language came from Emerson. He quotes Emerson as writing, "Cut these sentences and they bleed." The line is from "Montaigne; or the Skeptic" in Emerson's *Representative Men* and continues "they are vascular and alive." Frost reports with admiration his own reaction to the words: ". . . he had me there. I never got over that." Emerson's influence is evident as Frost strove to re-create in poetry the tones and sounds of vernacular speech. Frost traces Emerson, explaining that he "blended praise and dispraise of the country people of New Hampshire." Frost did the same with his New England characters.

"I took Emerson's prose and verse as my illustration," Frost confesses, saying that "[w]riting is unboring to the extent that it is dramatic." In *Preface to A Way Out* (1929) Frost wrote that "Everything written is as good as it is dramatic. It need not declare itself in form, but it is drama or nothing." He emphasized "the speaking tone of voice somehow entangled in the words and fastened to the page for the ear of the imagination." In this way, his comments do not illustrate new conclusions drawn but those drawn over a long period and reiterated.

Frost explains, "I owe more to Emerson than anyone else for troubled thoughts about freedom." He continues: "Never mind how and where Emerson disabused me of my notion I may have been brought up to that the truth would make me free. My truth will bind you slave to me." Emerson's influence is evident not only in the poet's style and verse subjects but in some of his views on politics and life. Frost describes his own view of freedom as "nothing but departure—setting forth—leaving

things behind, brave origination of the courage to be new." This view to a large degree reflects the form his poetry takes.

Frost is romantic in this piece, but he is not a romantic. He is directed and thoughtful, articulating where he began and where he finds himself at age 84. "What's worth living for is worth dying for. What's worth succeeding in is worth failing in," he says. And while that reads as a bit of a cliché, his tone suggests a seriousness, a commitment that cannot be reduced so easily.

"No subversive myself I think very Emersonian of me that I am so sympathetic with subversives, rebels, runners out, runners out ahead, eccentrics, and radicals. I don't care how extreme their enthusiasm so long as it doesn't land them in the Russian camp," Frost says. There was a limit to Frost's sympathies, as his politics were largely conservative. He was antisocialist and anti–New Deal. The sort of rebel he sympathized with was not political but individual, the sort of rebel he himself was.

As Frost begins to close he admits, "I am disposed to cheat myself and others in favor of any poet I am in love with. I hear people say the more they love anyone the more they see his faults. Nonsense. Love is blind and should be left so." He reminds his audience that he is "not quite satisfied with the easy way Emerson takes disloyalty," but for the most part his speech has been full of praise.

Near the end Frost returns to the question of religion and its role in his own life and in Emerson's. He describes Emerson as Unitarian for the reason that "he was too rational to be superstitious and too little a story teller and lover of stories to like gossip and pretty scandal." We know that Frost fits this description of Emerson as well. He seems to tip his own hand when he then says, tongue firmly in cheek, "Nothing very religious can be done for people lacking in superstition. They usually end up abominable agnostics." Frost has a great fondness for Emerson and was influenced by him greatly, but there is also a departure to some degree in politics and in Emerson's monism versus Frost's dualism, though Frost characteristically alludes to the distinctions more than arguing them.

The piece ends in admiration of the beauty of Emerson's words in the "Hymn Sung at the Completion of the Concord Monument, April 19, 1836" and in United States nationalism. Frost quotes Emerson's lines that surpass "any other ever written about soldiers" and closes by saying, "I am not a shriner but two things I never happen on unmoved: one, this poem on stone, and the other, the tall shaft seen from the Lafayette Park across the White House in Washington."

Although the piece was begun in praise of Emerson on a day when Frost was receiving praise himself, it is largely about what the two poets have in common; Frost's praise for Emerson is at times veiled praise for himself, and this may be only partly unintentional. Frost also pointedly distinguishes himself from Emerson, lest anyone relate them too closely.

FURTHER READING

Emerson, Ralph Waldo. *Collected Poems and Translations.* Edited by Harold Bloom and Paul Kane. New York: Library of America, 1994.
———. *Ralph Waldo Emerson Essays and Lectures.* New York: Library of America, 1983.
Monteiro, George. *Robert Frost and The New England Renaissance.* Lexington: University Press of Kentucky, 1988.
Thoreau, Henry David. *Henry David Thoreau: Collected Essays and Poems.* Edited by Elizabeth Hall Witherell. New York: Library of America, 2001.

"One More Brevity" (1962)

"One more brevity" is not at all brief, though Frost once called it a "little lyric . . . about a dog" ("On Taking Poetry"). The speaker, before retiring for the night, opens the door to be sure his "last look" of the day is "outside a house and book" and into nature instead. He hopes to take a quick look up at Sirius, otherwise known as the dog star, the one that keeps a "watch-dog eye." But when he has scarcely opened his door, a Dalmatian unexpectedly enters, slipping past his leg and settling himself on the floor. The poem plays on earthly versus heavenly dogs.

The dog seeks asylum in the speaker's home, and the speaker offers the dog food and water, without gaining much of a response from the animal. Soon the speaker begins to adapt his life and his mind to this unexpected pet. He imagines that the dog "failed of the modern speed" and that he may have some sorrow either from being left behind or having run away. This dog has seen his day. The speaker projects onto the dog his full imagination, giving him his own name and imagining this night's situation, the dog's situation, and the way their lives might be from this night on, together. He is ready to adopt the pet, ready to welcome him for always.

The next morning brings disappointment. The dog was merely passing through. The minute the speaker awakes the dog asks to be let out, and as soon as the speaker opens the door, the dog is gone and off to other things. The speaker allows that this is because the dog's life is so brief—"a fraction of ours at most." He thinks he might even have dreamt the encounter. He says things have been going strangely since the dog's departure and moves from earthly dogs back to heavenly ones.

The speaker would not be "too hard to convince" that the dog was in fact Sirius, the "star itself, Heaven's greatest star." Perhaps the star had dropped in to assure him that it did not resent the poet's not having written in "song" about him before. (*See also* "BOND AND FREE," "CANIS MAJOR," and "The LITERATE FARMER AND THE PLANET VENUS," among others, for references to Sirius.)

It is significant that Dalmatian Gus, the Sirius of the imagination, is the mirror, or reverse image, of the constellation. If Sirius chose to come to Earth, he would likely present himself as one of the "carriage breed." As a star Sirius is a white spot on a black sky; the Dalmatian is the reverse: black spots on a white coat.

The poem ends somewhat cryptically. The dog that slipped indoors the previous night might have simply been an "intimation, a shot of ray." And perhaps its presence was to provide, the speaker speculates, "A meaning I was supposed to seek, / And finding, wasn't disposed to speak." He does not specify what the meaning was that he found but cannot say.

The "brevity" of the title refers to the brief life span of and visit from the dog, but it may also refer to the brief experiences we have relative to heavenly things. Our lifespans are extremely short compared with the lives of stars or planets, and our experiences with others can be just as fleeting. Lives intermingle for a moment, and we may never see one another again. Though we often have some friends for the long-run, so many more of our everyday experiences involve anonymous people we do not even fully notice or acknowledge. If the dog was the embodiment of the dog-star Sirius, then perhaps this cosmic messenger brought the following message. Always be aware of how fleeting your existence is and savor your relationships, for you never know how long they may last. In this sense, the switch between an earthly and a heavenly dog is telling: People might comment on how brief an ordinary dog's life is, but if the dog is Sirius, then the tables are turned and people are the ones with the brief lifespan.

The poem was first published in booklet form as Frost's 1953 Christmas poem with the original manuscript title "Down to Earth." The occasion of the poem might signal that Frost intended to share, however cryptically, something of his experience with heavenly and earthly things in an effort to bring the transcendent down to earth.

"One More Brevity" was later collected in *In the Clearing.*

"One Step Backward Taken" (1947)

This is another poem where Frost presents a speaker who feels his hold on life is precarious. It is in certain ways reminiscent of the poet's "On Being Idolized" or his poems that reflect on autumn, such as "A Leaf-Treader." In many poems the speaker is presented as consistently aware that he is on the brink or one step away from some sort of decline. In this poem everything is thrown off balance. The world is torn loose by an apparently torrential downpour; it is only "one step backward taken" that saves the speaker from "going" with the "muddy gallons" of "[g]reat boulders." There is a

"universal crisis," and the speaker's "standpoint" is shaken, but he manages to keep from losing his balance and the sun in the end comes to dry him. He has survived the great downpour this time, but it was through such a chance event that his endurance is not to be trusted or relied on for an explanation of what happened. In fact, there seems to be no reason for his survival. He might be vulnerable again, he well knows, and if he should survive again, it might only be because of a fluke.

First published in January 1946 in *The Book Collector's Packet* as part of Ray Nash's "Robert Frost and His Printers," the poem was later collected in *Steeple Bush.*

"On Extravagance: A Talk" (1962)

"On Extravagance: A Talk" was an address at Dartmouth College on November 27, 1962, on the occasion of the school's newly built Hopkins Center. Frost begins by speaking about the extravagance of his audience, the "easy chairs and a beautiful hall," but respectfully admires the contributors: "a penny saved is a mean thing, and a penny spent, you know, is a generous thing and a big thing—like this, you see." Although he begins concerned with financial extravagance, he quickly turns to "what an extravagant universe it is" and to the most extravagant thing in that universe: man. Man is the "most wasteful, spending thing" in it. In his usual roundabout way he finds the true purpose of his talk: poetry as a sort of extravagance. "What's the need of it?" he asks. The answer is "no need—not particularly. That is, that's the first one," he says coyly.

Frost shares an anecdote about catching a man "red-handed" reading his poetry. He explains that "there's an indulgence of poetry, a manly indulgence" and likens it to "the manly indulgence of women." He quotes Arthur Edgar William O'Shaughnessy's "Ode" and then concludes that "all poetry asks is to be accorded the same indulgence that women are accorded."

Frost also observes that women are the "go-betweens," the "ambassadors to the men," and that they "break the poetry to the men." Women are the source of poetry—"[i]t's to and for them"—but "it's a strange thing that men write poetry more than the women; that is the world's history is full of men poets and very few women." Here Frost gives his age away.

The speech is all about extravagance, the extravagance poetry affords, and what Frost wants afforded the poet in the writing of it. He explains that "people hold you" or at least try to hold a poet to his poetry. "You say something sad or something pessimistic and something cynical, and they forget to allow for the extravagance of poetry—that you're not saying that all the time," he says. He wants to be allowed the metaphor. He does not want to be read as a preacher. He says a poet "loathe[s] anybody that wants you to be either pessimist or optimist," and it is clear that late in life Frost was still struggling against the labels that crowded him. He creates an imaginary dialogue. The reader asks, "Are you happy or are you unhappy?" "Why are you?" he shoots back, "you have no right to ask," a response similar to his line from the "Introduction to E. A. Robinson's *King Jasper*" where he explains that for readers who "stan[d] at the end of a poem ready in waiting to catch you by both hands" in a desire to know what is "behind it" the answer must be, "If I had wanted you to know, I should have told you in the poem." Frost explains that the "extravagance lies in 'it sometimes seems as if.'" He says, "If only I could tell you." "Beyond participation lie my sorrows and beyond relief," he says profoundly, stressing that there is no more to be said than is already said in a poem, no more to be done.

In his *King Jasper* introduction Frost writes, "I don't like grievances . . . What I like is griefs and I like them Robinsonianly profound." Here, too, he distinguishes between griefs and grievances. He describes politics as an extravagance about grievances and poetry as one about griefs. "And grievances are something that can be remedied, and griefs are irremediable." From this point on he spends more time quoting "extravagances," poems, than he does talking.

Frost recites several poems as an illustration of extravagance. He begins with "The Most of It" and moves on to "Never Again Would Birds' Song Be the Same." After the second he refers to the expressions in the audience: "And now I can see some people are incapable of taking it, that's all. And I'm not picking you out. I do this on a percentage basis. And I can tell by expression of faces how troubled they are, just about that." Frost could be fierce and corrective of an audience, as he once was when folks chuckled at his introduction to "Provide, Provide," a serious poem.

Frost turns to a Mother Goose nursery rhyme, "another kind of extravagance," maybe for release or to go temporarily easier on the audience. He describes extravagance as something one either can keep up with or cannot. He describes the experience metaphorically: "It's like snapping the whip, you know. Are you there? Are you still on?—you know. Are you with it? Or has it snapped you off?"

Frost then turns to "A Never Naught Song" as one that is "one in thought." He recites it and upon concluding says that his extravagance "would go on from there to say that people think that life is a *result* of certain atoms coming together, see, instead of being the *cause* that brings the atoms together," actually telling his audience more than he told in the poem (which is what he despises being asked to do).

Frost recites "Once by the Pacific," a poem begun while he was himself at Dartmouth, then "Lines Written in Dejection on the Eve of Great Success," and then an excerpt from "Kitty Hawk." Following these, he further explains the game of poetry. "Some people can't go with you," he says; it is "[t]horoughly undemocratic, very superior" because the thing, the extravagance, is said in parable, in metaphor. Frost takes up metaphor more fully in "The Constant Symbol."

Frost says to his audience, "I like to see you. I like to bother some of you." He twits them, returning to his earlier questions about what the need for poetry is: "What do we go round with poetry for?" He explains that it is not just for "kindred spirits" or for "criticism" or "appreciation" but for "nothing but just awareness of each other about it all."

Frost shares some other "extravagances," Arthur Christopher Benson's (1862–1925) "The Phoenix" and the anonymous "Preparations." Then he reads with less commentary "The Road Not Taken," "Stopping by Woods on a Snowy Evening," "Away!" "Escapist—Never," "Closed for Good," "Peril of Hope," "The Draft Horse," and "One More Brevity." He identifies his only free-verse poem as written spontaneously in response to an inquiry about his being conservative or radical. The poem is two lines: "I never dared be radical when young / For fear it would make me conservative when old."

He reads a long portion of an even longer poem, "How Hard It Is to Keep from Being King When It's in You and in the Situation." As he draws to a close, he admits, while saying that he would never admit it, that "So many of [the poems] have literary criticism in them—*in* them. . . . I try to hide it. So many of them have politics in them, like that— that's just *loaded* with politics. . . . I'm guilty, and all that."

Frost closes the talk fairly abruptly and without returning to the question of extravagance. It seems he tired, reading as he was at age 88. He takes a quick jab at contemporary poets, whom he says to let "be mystery." He says, "If I was sure they meant anything to themselves it would be all right." Then he recites "The Night Light," which he calls ending on a "dark note." He has made his point about the extravagance of poetry and that is that.

"On Going Unnoticed" (1928)

People are "vain to raise a voice as a sigh / In the tumult of free leaves on high" and to consider their own importance in relation to nature's. Even the coral root has no leaves and is still more important. We "linger" for an hour, grasping, perhaps in desperation, "the bark" a "rugged pleat" of the tree for the goal of grabbing leaves, but then we are content and leave, while the woods continue to undergo their tumult, not even noticing the coral root taken instead of a leaf. Nature, in a sense, goes unnoticed

by us, and we largely go unnoticed by nature. Though we think we leave our mark on nature by taking life from it, in this case through a "trophy" of one coral-root flower, "the woods sweep leafily on," uncaringly. Humans may contribute to the process of decay by taking the life of the flower, but the point seems to be that in the end people will always go unnoticed as nature simply goes on.

When a leaf drops from "forest's feet" and our name is "not written on either side," we are forced to recognize that nature is indifferent to our interests. It is simply not about us. We do, however, have the capacity to destroy nature, sometimes slowly, by taking a "trophy" one at a time. This seems to be the only vanity worth mentioning in the poem, that we believe nature is ours to do with as we wish.

First published on March 18, 1925, in the *Saturday Review of Literature* as "Unnoticed," "On Going Unnoticed" was later collected in *West-Running Brook*.

on his own poetry: Preface to Poems in *This Is My Best* (1942) and *The World's Best* (1950)

Frost was asked to write prefaces to his poems for two anthologies of poetry edited by Whit Burnett: *The World's Best* and *This Is My Best*. In the first he included "The Need of Being Versed in Country Things," "The Mountain," "The Road Not Taken," "The Grindstone," "The Gift Outright," and "One Step Backward Taken." In the second he included: "The Need of Being Versed in Country Things," "Come In," "The Onset," "Stopping by Woods on a Snowy Evening," "On a Tree Fallen across the Road," "The Wood-Pile," "Willful Homing," "A Blue Ribbon at Amesbury," "Two Tramps in Mud Time," "A Prayer in Spring," "Mowing," "A Drumlin Woodchuck," "Sitting by a Bush in Broad Sunlight," "Sand Dunes," "A Soldier," and "The Gift Outright."

In the longer preface to *This Is My Best,* Frost begins by explaining that it would be "hard to gather biography" from his poems. Other than being written by the same poet, one who is learned in written English, out of the same general region north of Boston, he says that little else would be revealed. Looking back over his work for "one meaning it might seem absurd to have had in advance," he says it would be "all right to accept from fate after the fact" any continuity he could find there. He wonders if he could "learn if there had been any divinity shaping" the poetry, "anything of larger design, even the roughest, any broken or dotted continuity, or any fragment of a figure." He imagines that if they could not be determined by conviction, perhaps they could by "native prejudices and inclinations." He describes how he chose the poems for *A Boy's Will* (1913) "to plot a curved line of flight away from people and so back to people" and, for *North of Boston* (1914), how he "took group enough to show the people and to show that I had forgiven them for being people." He closes by speaking of the group he has chosen for inclusion in *This Is My Best* as bringing out his "inclination to country occupations" and his "favorite implements (after the pen)": the ax and the scythe. Mark Richardson notes that "With characteristic ambivalence he [Frost] wavers between ascribing the integrity and design in his work—signal attributes of 'authorship'—to three agencies: to fate, to his own retrospective interpretive gestures, or to his 'convictions,' 'native prejudices,' and 'inclinations,'" nailing Frost's ambivalence, or even his sarcasm, on the head (216).

In the preface to *The World's Best,* Frost says, "It would be a very false pose for me to pretend to know what I have done best," explaining that any choice he made would be undone shortly thereafter and that what he had published in his own books "represents a pretty strict essential selection." Instead, he chooses to include those that he has "been looking fondly back over as deserving more attention than they get."

In the two pieces Frost is coy as always, but they are still useful criticism for understanding a poet's resistance to order, plan, and labels.

FURTHER READING

Richardson, Mark. *The Ordeal of Robert Frost: The Poet and His Poetics.* Chicago, Ill.: University of Illinois Press, 1997, 215–217.

"On Looking Up by Chance at Constellations" (1928)

The speaker looks up "by chance" at the constellations and, commenting on himself and others, acknowledges that people will "wait a long, long time, for anything much / To happen in heaven." Looking at the universe, we wait for something to happen at the speed at which things happen here on Earth. But the sun and moon cross without collision, "nothing ever happens," and "no harm is done." Universal and cosmic time is not human time, and collisions and harm happen more frequently here on Earth.

The suggestion is that rather than looking skyward for something to happen, we should "go patiently on with our li[ves] / And look elsewhere than to the stars and moon and sun / For the shocks and changes we need to keep sane." Shocks and changes come in more terrestrial and immediate forms, such as the drought that ends in rain and the peace that "will end in strife" in China. In other words, there are shocks and changes aplenty on Earth to keep our attention. It does not take long for something to happen to us. Our sense of time is very different, yet we tend to expect the same from nature that we do from our constructed world. There is an acknowledgment of the differences between nature and people, but there is also a suggestion that we can and ought to emulate nature in its calmness and patience.

The comment that no harm is done in the universe, "no crash out loud," is an interesting one. The comment also suggests that we should not look to the heavens or past the terrestrial in order to keep our sanity. Rather, we should concern ourselves with this world and our own behavior and what is within our control. We look skyward because we want something beyond ourselves to hold onto, but it is not going to come, at least not in our sense of time. Instead, we need to ask, With what do we provide ourselves and where should we look instead? Inward seems to be a beginning.

Looking up by chance also suggests the randomness that governs natural processes. There is no reason for what happens in the universe. All the metaphors of the poem become human metaphors. The "sun and moon get crossed," a playful hint that the two bodies may at times be at odds with each other. They might be expected to "strike out fire from each other," as people do, but they never do because their crossing is nothing like ours. They do not touch; they do not contend as we do. We must not consider the moon and sun from a human, and therefore skewed, perspective.

The poem leaves two questions unanswered: Why do we need shocks and changes to stay sane? and Why must we look skyward at all? The answer to both seems to be that we do not.

"On Looking Up by Chance at Constellations" was first published in *West-Running Brook.*

"On Making Certain Anything Has Happened" (1947)

See "FIVE NOCTURNES."

"On Our Sympathy with the Under Dog" (1942)

This poem is the sort of thing with which poets amuse themselves in spare time. The punchy quatrain appears in a grouping called "Quantula" along with other pithy poems, which suggests that Frost intended them to be together because of their small "quantity" and presumed force. (In Latin, *quantula* means "How little?" or "How small?") In this poem the poet manipulates the concepts of "under dog" and "top dog." The top dog one day is the under-

dog the next, because the ground he stands on is ever-changing. Similar to "On Being Idolized," where the surf knocking the speaker off his feet is used as a metaphor for how quickly an idol's feet are shown to be clay, here the main idea is how quickly a person can go "First under up and then again down under."

It is all a circus, the poem declares. We watch "revolving dogs" that transition as quickly as revolving doors. Politics and politicians are volatile. "No senator dares in to kick asunder," because he might be bitten by that same dog when the dogs revolve again. Better to stay silent and in between dogs, "Lest both should bite him in the toga-tags."

The quickness with which dogs move up from being under and then back under again shows how nearly interchangeable they are. They are in the end essentially the same dogs, though of different breeds.

"On Our Sympathy with the Under Dog" was first published in *A Witness Tree.* The manuscript title was "On the Difficulty of Keeping Up in Sympathy." *See* POLITICS.

"Onset, The" (1923)

The poem begins with the declaration that the onset of winter is "always the same." There comes a "fated night" when the snow first begins to fall, "hissing on the yet uncovered ground." The hissing is caused by snowflakes meeting with a still warmer ground, as the ground is not yet covered with snow. The speaker watches the "death descend" while stumbling and "looking up and round" as though taken by surprise, stunned, and vulnerable. He has a sense of "giv[ing] up his errand," willing to succumb to the powerful snowfall and the death it could bring. He knows that he has not achieved his goals. With "nothing done / To evil, no important triumph won," his life is incomplete. It is as if his "life had never been begun." The poem begins with the speaker conceding to the powerful onset of winter, but the second stanza takes a turn.

The speaker knows that spring will come, burgeoning life will return, and nothing will be left white except the birch trees, a handful of houses, and a church. So while the feeling overwhelms him each year with the onset of winter, and he starts thinking death is coming, he knows ultimately that the spring peepers will return and April will melt what remains of the winter's snow. "[W]inter death" repeatedly fails at overtaking the earth; he knows this with certainty since "all the precedent is on [his] side."

George F. Bagby writes that "Synecdochic expansion seeps into the description of the arrival of winter, which soon becomes emblematic not only of death but of a failure of moral will (always a deep fear in Frost), and so a waste of life itself" (83). The speaker's feelings reflect nature's seasons; the rejuvenation of spring is his own rejuvenation and overcoming. The poem begins despondent but ends triumphant. The onset of winter may be like death, but the speaker needs to remind himself that it is not death and that life will go on.

The poem was first published in January 1921 in the *Yale Review* and was later collected in *New Hampshire*. *See* NIGHT.

FURTHER READING

Bagby, George F. *Frost and the Book of Nature.* Knoxville: University of Tennessee Press, 1993, 83–84.

"On Taking from the Top to Broaden the Base" (1936)

The speaker exclaims, "Roll stones down on our head!" chiding the old mountain as a "squat old pyramid" that has had its "last good avalanche." Again Frost is using nature as a metaphor for human experience. The speaker underestimates the power of nature. Even old mountains can still bring down an avalanche. Here the speaker seems to incite the old mountain, and coinciding with his exclamation, a "pebble hit[s] the roof." It takes only a pebble to start an avalanche, and soon "panic hands" are "fighting for the latch."

The old mountain perhaps represents an old man. As we age our "bases" broaden, and what we

can bring about in terms of avalanches generally subsides. The exclamation then would express the boldness of youth. But the old mountain still has it. Provoking the old man starts an undesired "avalanche" so that soon none is "left to prate / Of an old mountain's case." Mocking the mountain can create a mudslide.

The poem can be read as a metaphor for many experiences. In any case, its focus is the underestimation of a person's or a thing's nature and the downfalls that can come from taking such a haughty position. We had best be careful what challenges we issue lest we find ourselves buried in mud that comes in "one cold / Unleavened batch."

"On Taking from the Top to Broaden the Base" was first published in *A Further Range.*

"On Taking Poetry" (1955)

"On Taking Poetry" is an address Frost gave at the BREAD LOAF SCHOOL OF ENGLISH in Vermont on June 30, 1955. The school is located near Frost's Homer Noble Farm, and the poet returned to the school each summer for all but three of 42 years. He is concerned with "how people take a poem" and begins, "I suppose a poem is a kind of fooling." He would write near the end of *In the Clearing* the aphoristic poem, "It takes all sorts of in and outdoor schooling / To get adapted to my kind of fooling," which is inscribed on a piece of wood on the Robert Frost Trail, also near Bread Loaf.

Frost says that "if the height of everything is fooling—God's foolishness—then poetry mounts somewhere into a kind of fooling"; he also explains that poetry is "something hard to get." He insists that we spend a lot of education "just getting [poetry] right." In his "Education by Poetry" he argues that "[e]ducation by poetry is education by metaphor" and that it is a necessary education.

Frost delivers a brief tangential discourse about Puritanism before returning to the question of poetry. He says that the New Testament says something "very harsh and undemocratic"—that "these things are said in parable so the wrong people can't understand them and so get saved." Frost articu-

Robert Frost Trail, Ripton, Vermont. "It takes all sorts of in and outdoor schooling / To get adapted to my kind of fooling." *(Photo by Deirdre Fagan)*

lated quite the same pronouncement elsewhere, including "On Extravagance: A Talk." What he is getting at is that poetry is said in parable as well as metaphor.

Frost was often reminding audiences that we get our literary beginnings from Mother Goose, and he does that again here. If we take "God's foolishness as the question," we discover that it is the "thing [we] acquire through years of poetry." What we take from poetry we can take "a good deal [our] own way" and leave the rest for conversation. We "don't have to contradict it," to undo what is said. We can let folks "have their say" and then take it our own way. This leads Frost to ask what sort of people can take his poetry their own way and get away with it. He says, "the right kind of people that

can take it their way." Poetry is undemocratic because not everyone will "get it," and not everyone should. The right people will; it is for them, and that is enough. Frost describes his own poetry as having "a good deal of sway in it." It "sways at its anchor," and "that's the fun of it."

A reader may be able to have his way with Frost's poetry but may also "be utterly wrong." He brings up the "common laugh" students share over a teacher who takes a poem too far, but he notes that in growing up with Mother Goose we learn about "getting it right and wrong, in and out, trial and error with it—in this spirit of the thing." There are poets who write "just throwing dust in the eyes," but he calls that an insult. He calls that "going a little over the edge about this play, this fooling." He insists that "[t]o tease people is all right but to insult them is going too far."

Frost says he is going to begin to recite some of his own poems, but he continues to talk philosophically about poetry instead. He says that he would have preferred to talk someone else's poetry but that audiences always want to hear him recite his own poems. He grew up reading aloud and confides that the difficulty of reading aloud for him is having "almost too hard a time with [his] emotions." "Where do I let on?" he asks. "I never let on; I try to hide it." He does not lose control of his emotions over something sad but over something magnanimous: "It's always something about the largeness, something about the greatness of spirit." This emotion "is more than compassion—this magnanimity."

Frost discusses whether life is a "pursuit of a pursuit of a pursuit of a pursuit" or an "escape from an escape from an escape from an escape," repetitions that are reminiscent of his delight and shared laughter with Ezra Pound over the fourth "thought" in Edwin Arlington Robinson's "Miniver Cheevy."

Frost reads "The Gift Outright" and then "Stopping by Woods on a Snowy Evening," and he says of the latter that "the first thing about that is to take it right between the eyes just as it is. . . . And then, you know, the next thing is your inclinations with it." He has returned, however subtly, to his earlier concern with how to take a poem. He speaks poetically about what it is to absorb and understand a poem: "[Y]ou can almost say in a poem that you see in it the place where it begins to be ulterior . . . where it goes a little with you, carries you on somewhere." It may even take several days for the reader to follow, but he says of himself that he will "resume [his] thread," and no matter what he will want to be sure that if he differs with someone else's understanding that he knows "what it is that [he is] differing with." In this way he illustrates to his audience what it is to take a poem and how much work it is to get it right.

Frost speaks about the inquiries he has received about "Stopping by Woods on a Snowy Evening"; inquiries about how high the snow was, readings that asserted it was the coldest or darkest evening of the year, and questions about what sorts of promises he had to keep. His response is, "What does it say there?" He reminds his readers that what must be found in a poem can be found in the poem. There is no need to go outside of it with inquiries; if the poet wanted his readers to know, he would have told them in the poem (as he says in so many words on many occasions). Frost says that the "aesthetic moral" of all this is "to go any poem one better, not one worse, and you just don't chew it, take it all to pieces; just get another poetic something going—one step more poetic anywhere."

Frost reads "Mending Wall," explaining that it is "about a spring occupation in [his] day." A man once told him he had written a "true international poem," and he wondered how he arrived at that. It is another example of a person taking the poem the way he wanted to. "That's where the great fooling comes in," Frost says. His explanation of the poem is that "I've got a man there; he's both a wall builder and a wall toppler. He makes boundaries and he breaks boundaries. That's man."

Although Frost has been talking about carrying a poem a certain distance, he also is quick to offer a corrective: "I'm always distressed when I find somebody being ugly about it, outraging the poem, going some way, especially if it's on some theory I can see their applying to everything." This is similar to the distinction he makes between grievances and griefs in poetry in his "Introduction to E. A. Robinson's *King Jasper*." He wants to allow readers to take a poem a distance, but he still wants to remind them that they need to correct themselves: "If you are going to think of something, study them out, grind them, nothing much to it." He provides the example of EVOLUTION and his mother's religious distress over it: "Your idea was that God made man out of mud; the new idea is that God made man out of prepared mud. You've still got God you see—nothing very disturbing about it."

Frost reads "Directive," which he describes as "all full of dangers, sideways, off, and all that"; "To an Ancient," which he describes as a "little curious one . . . an archaeological one"; "Desert Places"; "Reluctance"; "The Tuft of Flowers"; "Paul's Wife"; "Acquainted with the Night"; "Choose Something like a Star"; "One More Brevity"; and "Come In" before ending the evening.

Frost has had his say about how to take a poem, and it has been instructive and corrective. While he says that he is not esoteric in his thinking, only the "right person" will get it.

"On the Heart's Beginning to Cloud the Mind" (1936)

Frost once said, in reference to this poem during a reading, "I was looking out of a train window away out in Utah and way in the night, and I saw one lonely light way off, you know, far from any other all around. I made a whole poem out of that" (Cramer, 107). In "The Figure in the Doorway" the speaker also makes an observation while riding a train.

In this instance, riding in the lower berth of a train through Utah and observing only a few stars in the sky and a single lit house dotting the Earth, the speaker concludes that the only light on earth at that moment is a "flickering, human pathetic light." He sees in that light the likelihood that it will "flutter and fall in half an hour," and in this he finds despair. That light's going out will be like the "last petal off a flower."

His heart clouds his mind as he begins to imagine what he perceives, putting a better spin on the image he has of "God-forsaken brute despair." He tries to imagine instead a "tale of a better kind." He adds more to his visual field by contributing attributes of his imagination. He knows the "light flickers because of trees" passing between the speeding train and the source of the light. He is hopeful that people can burn their lights as long as there are trees, and when "their interests in it end" they can leave it to someone else. He imagines that when one person leaves through abandonment or death, another takes his or her place, and that traveling by train through this same terrain some other summer, he would find the same light shining "no less intense."

The wife sees in the landscape "spots of gloom" that are cedar trees, not people, and therefore have "no purpose, have no leader." There is no threat in this isolation. Commenting further on this couple, the speaker speculates on their attitudes. Life for them is not so "sinister-grave," so "Matter of fact has made them brave." Husband and wife have no fear of each other or life. They know there are other lights in the world but because of where they live they are the only light in proximity. The only disagreement in putting out the lights would come from each other. There are no threats for the couple, and they have nothing to contend with but each other. This is what the speaker observes when he looks "Far into the lives of other folk." How far he looks is facetious; after all, his is a "surface flight."

There is speculation about the different lives people lead and what does or does not threaten them. The poem is clouded by the speaker's imagination and by his need to empathize with those he observes. There is also in the supposed "brute despair" a better attitude that focuses on some hope in the metaphorical light that will continue to shine, whether it be through this couple's lives or the lives of the couple who take their place. The light of the spirit of life is one that does not go out. The poem presents a romantic idea of humanity keeping its light going.

The poem was first published in April 1934 in *Scribner's Magazine* and was later collected in *A Further Range* with the subtitle "From Sight to Insight." *See* STARS.

FURTHER READING

Bagby, George F. *Frost and the Book of Nature*. Knoxville: University of Tennessee Press, 1993, 123–126.

Cook, Marjorie E. "The Serious Play of Interpretation," *South Carolina Review* 15, no. 2 (Spring 1983): 77–87.

Cramer, Jeffrey S. *Robert Frost among His Poems: A Literary Companion to the Poet's Own Biographical Contexts and Associations*. Jefferson, N.C.: MacFarland, 1996.

Hoffman, Tyler. *Robert Frost and the Politics of Poetry*. Hanover, N.H.: Middlebury College Press, 2001.

"On the Poems of Hervey Allen" (1951?)

This piece is an unfinished preface to an unfinished collection of Hervey Allen's verse (1889–1949). It is relevant to Frost only in that the first paragraph provides additional insights into his theories about poetry, as when he describes the course of "true poetry" as being "from more ethereal than substantial to more substantial than ethereal." "Nothing can be done with nothingness," he says; "[n]othing but weight can put on weightiness." His assertion that the "most diaphanous wings carry a burden of pollen from flower to flower" and that there is "no song without a burden" calls to mind the weight of his own poetry.

"One Guess" (1936)

"One Guess" first appeared in A *Further Range* as the fourth in a group of poems titled "Ten Mills." Most of the poems were originally published in *Poetry* in April 1936, but this was not one of them. Its title prior to publication was "A Riddle.—Who Is Intended." And a lively riddle it is.

Similar to Emily Dickinson's "I like to see it lap the Miles—," where the poet writes cryptically about the steam engine, Frost here makes a game of his poesy. He gives his readers "One Guess," as in a guessing game. The game of his three-line poem is the play of his description.

Although the poem initially seems to be about a grasshopper, it is also possible that it is metaphorically about a manual typewriter. As Richard Polt writes in his piece "How to Collect Antique Typewriters," the thrust mechanisms of old mechanical typewriters were also called "grasshopper" mechanisms. "On thrust-action machines, the typebars slide forward horizontally to the front of the platen, instead of swinging through an arc. The 'grasshopper' arrangement, used on the American Williams and the British Maskelyne [typewriters], uses horizontal typebars which 'hop' up, forward, and down onto the top of the platen," Polt explains.

"He has dust in his eyes and a fan for a wing, / A leg akimbo with which he can sing, / And a mouthful of dye stuff instead of a sting." Frost gives his readers one guess, knowing there is little room for error. Perhaps the ever-mischievous Frost was metaphorically describing a typewriter, but with only one guess, it is a far safer bet to go with a grasshopper.

FURTHER READING

Cramer, Jeffrey S. *Robert Frost among His Poems: A Literary Companion to the Poet's Own Biographical Contexts and Associations.* Jefferson, N.C.: MacFarland, 1996.

Polt, Richard. "How to Collect Antique Typewriters." www.Brighton-U.K.com. 1997. Available online. URL: http://www.etedeschi.ndirect.co.uk/howto4.htm. Accessed June 30, 2006.

"Our Doom to Bloom" (1962)

"Our Doom to Bloom" was first published in booklet form as Frost's 1950 Christmas poem. It was later collected in *In the Clearing* with an epigraph from Robinson Jeffers: "Shine, perishing republic." William Wordsworth's description of pre-Revolutionary France being a "budding rose above the rose full blown" (*The Prelude,* book XI) becomes in Frost the postrevolutionary "The bud must bloom till blowsy blown."

Frost does not often mention his contemporaries. It is therefore interesting to note that when, in a 1928 interview, he was asked if he would be willing to predict which of the younger poets might achieve prominence, Jeffers was among the five he named. The others were Raymond Holden, Archibald MacLeish, Joseph Moncure March, and Stephen Vincent Benét (Thompson, 353).

This political poem opens with the speaker addressing "Cumaen Sibyl," the female prophet who guided Aeneas through the underworld in Book VI of Virgil's (70–19 B.C.) *Aeneid*. The speaker wants to know what the simple facts of progress are that he "may trade on with reliance / In consultation with [his] clients." The prophetess responds that he must go back to his clients in Rome and tell them, "if it's not a mere illusion / All there is to it is diffusion— / Of coats, oats, votes, to all mankind." The conclusion is that the "state's one function is to give" as the "Surviving Book," most likely the Bible, says. Progress is about giving shelter, food, and votes to all mankind. Liberal or conservative, the goal of the state is the same. If it does not give it will wilt rather than fade naturally, as all states do that are "doom[ed] to bloom." But whether it perish by wilting or fading, all states are only for a time.

FURTHER READING

Brophy, Robert. "A Frost Poem on Jeffers," *Jeffers Studies* 3, no. 1 (Winter 1999): 14–15.

Rosen, Kenneth. "Visions and Revisions: An Early Version of Robert Frost's 'Our Doom to Bloom,'" In *Frost Centennial Essays,* edited by Jac L. Tharpe, et al. 369–372. Jackson: University Press of Mississippi, 1974.

Thompson, Lawrance. *Robert Frost: The Years of Triumph, 1915–1938.* New York: Holt, Rinehart and Winston, 1970.

"Our Hold on the Planet" (1942)

Taking into account the entire history of nature and human nature, the speaker resolves that nature "must be a little more in favor of man." He imagines that if we added up all the times that nature brought us something that did not kill us but brought some good, such as sun and rain for good crops (or brains complex enough to understand agriculture), then overall there has been slightly more in favor of man than disaster. The proof, of course, is that we are still standing. Not just that, but we have increased in number steadily, so "our hold on the planet" cannot be half bad. But the poem cautions against arrogance, since our "advantage" over nature is but "a fraction of one percent at the very least."

Tyler Hoffman writes that Frost "links this contest to world war . . . asserting his belief that as horrible as that event may be, we will survive yet another round of mass killings." He also asserts that the "sharp halts at line ends" in the last seven lines of the poem "also lend force to Frost's charge, as clauses and phrases hold themselves much as we have through great struggle managed to hold onto the planet" (168).

The poem was first published in booklet form as Frost's 1940 Christmas poem and was later pub-

lished in the spring 1942 edition of the *Virginia Quarterly Review.* It was later collected in *A Witness Tree.* The poem's manuscript title was "A Fraction of One Percent."

FURTHER READING

Hoffman, Tyler. *Robert Frost and the Politics of Poetry.* Hanover, N.H.: Middlebury College Press, 2001.

"Our Singing Strength" (1923)

"Our Singing Strength" is written in iambic pentameter and made up primarily of couplets, though the scheme varies. The entire opening stanza of this lyric is a description of a late-season snowfall in early spring when the earth is so warm and dry that the flakes can find no "landing place to form" and therefore melt quickly, unable to make a "white impression on the black."

It is not until the snow comes down in "strips and tapes of ragged white" overnight that the grass and garden "confess it snowed" by the accumulation of some snow. All of the landscape is "flattened" the following morning by the heavy snowfall except the road, which had gotten so warm from either "inward fires or brush of passing feet" that even the heavy overnight snow would not stick. One of Frost's most compelling images is of the bough that "anticipated fruit" with "snowballs cupped in every opening bud."

In spring the "mortal singers" are the various birds that come north, some to stay and build nests, most to go farther on or head back south. These have already arrived in NEW ENGLAND and therefore must now withstand the late snowfall. They gather on the road, its warmth providing safe haven. The image is breathtaking: nearly a thousand birds made kin and creating "a channel running flocks / Of glossy birds like ripples over rocks." The speaker walks through them, causing them "in bits of flight" to "almost disput[e] right / Of way with [him] from apathy of wing."

The speaker explains that the birds cannot learn from one late snowfall that the road is not a smart place to gather. As his walking forces them to disperse, they continue to return in front of him to "suffer the same driven nightmare over." Not learning quickly, "none flew behind [him] to be left alone." One late "storm in a lifetime couldn't teach them / That back behind pursuit" from the snowfall, and the speaker "couldn't reach them."

The poem ends optimistically, expressing contentment with the snowstorm's bringing together the "country's singing strength" that "though repressed and moody with the weather / Was none the less there ready to be freed." "[R]epressed and moody" probably refers to the speaker as well. The strength of the bird's singing brings the "wildflowers up from root to seed" and, despite the late winter, heralds the beginning of spring.

The poem was first published May 2, 1923, in the *New Republic* and was later collected in *New Hampshire*.

FURTHER READING

Bagby, George F. *Frost and the Book of Nature*. Knoxville: University of Tennessee Press, 1993, 88–90.

Garrison, Joseph M., Jr. "'Our Singing Strength': The Texture of Voice in the Poetry of Robert Frost." In *Frost Centennial Essays*, edited by Jac L. Tharpe, et al. 340–350. Jackson: University Press of Mississippi, 1974.

"'Out, Out—'" (1916)

"'Out, Out—'" is one of Frost's most dramatic and celebrated poems. It was written in memorial to a neighborhood boy Frost knew when he was living in Franconia, New Hampshire. Raymond Tracy Fitzgerald, a 16-year-old twin, lived on the South Road outside of Bethlehem. An article about his

Frost with chainsaw. "Out, Out—": "The buzz saw snarled and rattled in the yard." *(Photo by Hanson Carroll. Courtesy Dartmouth College Library)*

sudden death appeared in the *Littleton Courier* on March 31, 1910. Frost knew the boy well; Frost's children and Fitzgerald had played together. Fitzgerald lost his life from shock and heart failure on March 24, 1910, within moments of having his hand lacerated by a buzz saw (Thompson, 566–567).

The "'Out, Out—'" of the title is a reference to Act 5, scene 5, of Shakespeare's *Macbeth*: "Out, out, brief candle! / Life's but a walking shadow, a poor player / That struts and frets his hour upon the stage / And then is heard no more: it is a tale / Told by an idiot, full of sound and fury, / Signifying nothing." Robert Pack holds that Frost's "'Out, Out—'" "is a confrontation with such nothingness" and that the "meaninglessness of death is anticipated early in the poem with the image of dust" (158).

The young boy is assisting in the sawing of wood in his backyard. He is a "big boy / Doing a man's work, though a child at heart." The buzz saw is depicted as animate and malevolent from the start. It is described as snarling and rattling in the yard, seemingly out of control, as if on the lookout for something to tear into. The wood the boy is cutting, in contrast, is referred to as "[s]weet scented stuff," calling to mind the child's youth and innocence in contrast to the work he is doing. The brutality of the saw and how quickly it can cut through wood or flesh also is acknowledged. The scene is seductively picturesque. It is dusk, and five Vermont mountain ranges are visible "[u]nder the sunset." The scene has a rustic serenity that the saw's buzzing, snarling, and rattling interrupt.

The speaker explains how the saw snarled and rattled, yet "nothing happened: day was all but done." In other words, the saw had been doing its job without causing any harm until now. He wishes they had simply "call[ed] it a day," because by doing so the incident might have been avoided. It was all in the timing. There is a sense that the slightest change in the day's events would have changed everything. If only the boy had been given a half an hour at rest or at play instead, Frost speculates in hindsight.

The boy's sister comes to call the workers for supper and "At the word, the saw, / As if to prove saws knew what supper meant, / Leaped out at the boy's hand, or seemed to leap— / He must have

given the hand." The description of the accident is startling. It is presented as a chain effect. The girl announces "Supper," and her simple utterance begins the chain reaction. The poem treats her as the beginning, if not the cause. She has called the boy for dinner and has somehow met the time frame of the saw, perhaps by drawing the boy's attention away. The responsibility is not hers, but her role makes clear the pain she would feel about her involvement. The animated saw is seen to respond to her utterance, rather than, as might be supposed, her call causing the boy to avert his eyes from his task to look up, thereby losing control of the saw. It is suggested that the saw actually leapt, as though it was waiting, anticipating the moment when it could do so. Its actions appear premeditated. But then Frost writes that the boy must have "given" the hand, returning to reality, to the sudden recognition that the chain of events he has described is inaccurate. His conclusion is an acceptance that neither hand nor saw "refused the meeting." There is a macabre element to this insight, as though hand and saw somehow sought each other out.

"The boy's first outcry [is] a rueful laugh," as though he recognizes the severity of what has happened and can somehow anticipate his death. The boy laughs because he is caught by surprise—what has happened is not yet real. He is in shock, thinking his hand remains intact when it has already been terribly lacerated. He holds it up to keep the "life" and blood "from spilling" but also in "appeal," in the hope that something can be done, that something can be undone. The boy "saw all spoiled," as if he saw his brief life passing by in an instant. Robert Faggen notes that the "boy loses his hand, one crucial part of human anatomy that distinguishes this species from all others and represents the variant that enabled the creation, production, and use of tools. Ironically, it is cut off by the form, the tool that it created. The tool that it created becomes, ironically, a weapon against its creator" (153).

The doctor comes and places the boy "in the dark of ether." But he is only with the boy a moment before the boy is gone as quickly as his hand. "No one believed" that he had died any more than the boy had believed his hand was lost. They listen, the snarling and rattling of the buzz saw silenced; the scene is without sound, except for the boy's faint pulse. "Little—less—nothing!" is the pronouncement, and "that end[s] it."

The scene, the boy's life, are ended. "No more to build on there," the speaker, detached, resolves coolly; "And they, since they / Were not the one dead, turned to their affairs." The ending phrase echoes sentiments about death from the wife at the end of "Home Burial":

> One is alone, and he dies more alone.
> Friends make pretense of following to the
>   grave,
> But before one is in it, their minds are turned
> And making the best of their way back to life
> And living people, and things they understand.

Both poems concern the death of boys, though of different ages and by different means. Jay Parini writes that "However heartless these lines have sounded to some ears, Frost is making a point about a way of dealing with grief; by plunging back into the affairs of life, which demand attention (especially in the context of a poor farm at the turn of the century), the grieving family is able to work through their grief." Parini also notes that when Frost and his wife Elinor lost their young son Elliott to cholera, they "could not simply stop in their tracks." They had a 14-month-old daughter, Lesley, and chickens that needed tending, among other demands (70).

Still, the phrasing comes off as cold and factual, like a newspaper report. But when faced with such loss of a person, with such brutality in nature, how can people be expected to respond? Robert Pack holds that the speaker is "outside the story he is telling" but "wishes to enter into the scene as one of the characters as if he might be of some help" (158). This is clear from the speaker's efforts in the beginning of the poem to turn back time, to call it a day, to undo before it is done. Faggen also finds that "the poem is rather stoic in its ultimate tone of acceptance of the way individual lives become sacrificed unexpectedly in a general machinery. Here the machinery, a buzz saw, takes on a life of its own and destroys the hand that created it" (152). The recognition of the randomness of life, of vulnerability in the face of meaningless acts, ends the poem

abruptly. But the poem also might be said to end in bitterness and frustration rather than cool detachment. After all, the speaker is not among those who have "turned to their affairs" but is still trying to build on what is "no more."

The poem was first published in July 1916 in *McClure's*; it was later collected in *Mountain Interval*.

FURTHER READING

Bruels, Marcia F. "Frost's 'Out, Out—,'" *Explicator* 55, no. 2 (Winter 1997): 85–88.

Cramer, Jeffrey S. *Robert Frost among His Poems: A Literary Companion to the Poet's Own Biographical Contexts and Associations.* Jefferson, N.C.: MacFarland, 1996.

Faggen, Robert. *Robert Frost and the Challenge of Darwin.* Ann Arbor: University of Michigan Press, 1997, 152–153.

Hoffman, Tyler. *Robert Frost and the Politics of Poetry.* Hanover, N.H.: Middlebury College Press, 2001.

Locklear, Gloriana. "Frost's 'Out, Out—,'" *Explicator* 49, no. 3 (Spring 1991): 167–169.

Pack, Robert. *Belief and Uncertainty in the Poetry of Robert Frost.* Hanover, N.H.: Middlebury College Press, 2003.

Parini, Jay. *Robert Frost: A Life.* New York: Holt, 1999.

Sears, John F. "The Subversive Performer in Frost's 'Snow' and 'Out, Out—,'" In *The Motive for Metaphor: Essays on Modern Poetry,* edited by Francis C. Blessington and Guy L. Rotella, 82–92. Boston: Northeastern University Press, 1983.

Thompson, Lawrance. *Robert Frost: The Early Years.* New York: Holt, Rinehart and Winston, 1966.

"Oven Bird, The" (1916)

An oven bird is a thrushlike North American warbler with a shrill call, sometimes referred to as the teacher bird. In this sonnet, first published in *Mountain Interval*, the bird is described as a "midsummer and a mid-wood bird" that "everyone has heard." His song attunes us to the quickly passing summer and alerts us that soon autumn will arrive. He warns that "leaves are old and that for flowers / Mid-summer is to spring as one to ten," in effect, that the leaves have had their heyday and that the time between midsummer and spring is as brief as a count to 100.

The "early petal-fall is past" when the blossoms of the pear and cherry trees fell "in showers." This is one of the first signals, the first "falls," that indicates that soon will come that "other fall we name the fall." Everything is on its way to the next seasonal phase, including the highway dust. Things are moving along in temporal ways as time that passes "over all" living things.

The poem closes by raising the question, "what to make of a diminished thing?" The bird is unsatisfied, unlike the bird of "Acceptance" that, when the night comes, "thinks or twitters softly, 'Safe! / Now let the night be dark for all of me. / Let the night be too dark for me to see / Into the future. Let what will be, be."

How does one accept the passing of life, the diminishing spring? The oven bird is made to ask such questions, the speaker projecting onto it the human emotion and suffering he feels he hears in the bird's song. The oven bird sings, much as we do, to ask for everlasting summer. He purposely sings in the context of knowing he is not supposed to; he is singing to fight against the transition.

George F. Bagby writes that the closing line of the poem "may be read . . . as a description of the situation of the modern poet." Robert Pack writes, "Frost is playing a game with the reader's credulity, for the question of what we can believe on the basis of the little that we know is precisely the problem Frost is exploring. What he is leading the reader toward is the contemplation of the design of the poem itself" (138). Pack continues, "What the poem believes, beyond what he hears and sees, is necessarily of his own invention" (138). The oven bird, in a sense, is the poet, warbling in order not to "cease and be as other birds."

FURTHER READING

Bagby, George F. *Frost and the Book of Nature.* Knoxville: University of Tennessee Press, 1993.

Bock, Martin. "Frost's 'The Oven Bird' and the Modern Poetic Idiom," *Texas Review* 7, no. 1–2 (Spring–Summer 1986): 28–31.

Hollander, John. "Robert Frost's Oven Bird." In *Sewanee Writers on Writing,* edited by Wyatt Prunty, 80–91. Baton Rouge: Louisiana State University Press, 2000.

Monteiro, George. "Robert Frost's Solitary Singer," *New England Quarterly* 44, no. 1 (March 1971): 134–140.

Pack, Robert. *Belief and Uncertainty in the Poetry of Robert Frost.* Hanover, N.H.: Middlebury College Press, 2003.

Rotella, Guy L. "Metaphor in Frost's 'Oven Bird,'" In *Robert Frost the Man and the Poet,* edited by Earl J. Wilcox, 19–30. Rock Hill, S.C.: Winthrop College.

Timmerman, John H. *Robert Frost: The Ethics of Ambiguity.* Lewisburg, Pa.: Bucknell University Press, 2002, 46–48.

"Pan with Us" (1913)

In Greek mythology Pan is the god of shepherds and hunters, woods, fields, and flocks. He has a human torso and head with a goat's legs, horns, and ears. He is associated with the worship of Dionysus and was known for singing and playing his pipes, as described in this poem. Wine is the symbol of Dionysus, so he represents freedom as well as ruin.

In Frost's version, Pan has become old and his hair and eyes are gray. He stands in the zephyr, the gentle breeze of the west wind, and is content. He lives peacefully alone and protected from any tales that could be told, because the only people he sees are children who are "so little they tell no tales." He seems satisfied that his job is done. He does not command the land anymore as "all the country he did command." He has "tossed his pipes, too hard to teach." He is not passing the torch to someone younger; rather, he has determined that it is too hard to teach, so he decides to give up altogether. Tyler Hoffman writes, "Pan's surrender of his pipes leads to his speculative frame of mind, his creative freedom registered through freedom of the sentence to range across these lines" (140).

Frost's depiction suggests that times have changed irrevocably since the world of Pan. Pan is no longer with us; he has become internalized, a distant memory. Pan is no longer clear about his purpose. What should he play? Is there to be no song from the pipes anymore? The poem suggests a change in attitude toward nature and the rapidly changing landscape. All is urbanized and modernized, and nature is no longer magical, no longer the home of gods. Nature has become barren, devoid of any kind of intention or personification, and we have lost touch with our pagan natures. We no longer believe, as the Greeks did, in a god who would live in nature.

"Play? Play?—What should he play?" The repetition suggests there is no tune for nature to play. The question is already answered. Nature does not play a tune that is intentional as one would play a flute or pipes—nature just is. Robert Faggen writes,

> Ending with an unanswerable question, as do many of Frost's best lyrics, the poem's final dissolution stems from doubts about the "new terms of worth." Those new terms could be the Christian world of sin and redemption, which contradicts the world of "pagan mirth." Play, of any kind, is not as important as the work of purification in a Protestant work ethic (evoking a muted pun of "panning for gold"). (49)

Faggen also points out that "*Pan* is no longer a god but an indeterminate creature" (49).

The poem was first published in *A Boy's Will* and is followed by "The Demiurge's Laugh," a poem that also presents mythical creatures of the wood, but from a darker perspective. *See* MYTHOLOGY AND FOLKLORE.

FURTHER READING

Faggen, Robert. *Robert Frost and the Challenge of Darwin.* Ann Arbor: University of Michigan Press, 1997, 49–50.

Hoffman, Tyler. *Robert Frost and the Politics of Poetry.* Hanover, N.H.: Middlebury College Press, 2001.

"Paris Review Interview, with Richard Poirier" (1960)

This interview was conducted for the summer-fall 1960 issue of the *Paris Review.* It is considered one of the more important interviews with Frost, as it covers not only his views on poetry and other poets but also subjects such as his family history, science, politics, and other areas of interest.

Early in the piece there is a fairly lengthy discussion of Frost's association with Ezra Pound. Frost relates their first meeting at Harold Monro's Poetry Book Shop in London and offers insights into his own views on Pound and Pound's assistance in the reception of Frost's first book, when he wrote a favorable review of *A Boy's Will.* Frost is critical of Pound, though sometimes indirectly, throughout, but he also says that one of the best things about Pound is that "he wanted to be the first to jump," that is, the first one to be in on something, as he was with *A Boy's Will.* Frost makes fun of the weekly gatherings Pound had with fellow poets, where they rewrote each other's poems "[t]o squeeze the water out of them." Frost says, "That sounds like a parlor game to me, and I'm a serious artist." Later he mocks Pound's view that anyone could be a poet and speaks of "Pound's gentle art of making enemies." He also, however, when talking about politics, speaks of his efforts to release Pound from jail and his treason indictments, not wanting to "highhat him" or make him feel beholden. He says of Pound's politics, "He was very foolish in what he bet on and whenever anybody really loses that way, I don't want to rub it into him."

Richard Poirier, the interviewer, attempts to move Frost in certain directions, but Frost is mostly resistant. Poirier asks whether Frost made a "choice against the kind of literary society" he found in London. Frost says, "I didn't know whether I had any position in the world at all, and I wasn't choosing positions," reminding his interviewer that his first book was not published until he was in his late 30s. Poirier pushes again, inquiring about "a gang feeling among the literary people" in London. Frost resists inclusion, saying he did not "belong" in England or in America.

Poirier inquires about Frost's style, wondering if Pound and others in England, such as his friend Edward Thomas, influenced Frost. Frost finds it difficult to identify influences for his work, except what he has read, such as Latin and Greek poetry. Poirier wants to know who he admired, and Frost says he "was the enemy of that theory." Poirier wants to know for whom Frost might have felt an affinity, say, Edwin Arlington Robinson or Wallace Stevens, both acquaintances of Frost's. "I don't know who you'd connect me with," Frost says, dodging the inquiries again. What is revealed throughout the interview is never revealed by intention. It is subtle, always indirect. Frost explains that he appreciates certain poems rather than the entire work of individual poets. He finds a poem he likes in an anthology and goes looking for more and finds "[n]othing. Just a couple like that and that's all." He resists influence and comparison. He has fondness for some, but that is where he wants to leave it.

On modern poetry Poirier points out that Karl Shapiro in the *New York Times Book Review* praised Frost for being "not guilty of 'Modernism' as Pound and [T. S.] Eliot are." Frost admits that he dodges this category as well. Then he offers a definition of the modern poet that resembles Wallace Stevens's views as expressed in his poem "Of Modern Poetry": "A modern poet," Frost says, "must be one that speaks to modern people no matter when he lived in the world. That would be one way of describing it. And it would make him more modern, perhaps, if he were *alive* and speaking to modern people."

On science Frost reflects that "the greatest adventure of man is science, the adventure of penetrating into matter, into the material universe." He admits having been influenced by the science of his time, and it is notable that many of his later poems take for their subjects questions about the limits of science. He describes himself as an unhappy Democrat, unhappy since 1896.

On politics Frost says, "They think I'm no New Dealer. But really and truly I'm not, you know, all that clear on it." He uses for an example "The Death of the Hired Man" and speaks of the Republican and Democrat, fatherly and motherly, ways of things.

The conversation turns to Frost's poetry and the poems that are anthologized. The interview also takes up the question of Frost's "darker mood" and of critics who have had "preconceptions" about his work and seemed to anthologize only those poems that fit those preconceptions. Lionel Trilling, at

Frost's 85th birthday celebration, spoke of the "darkness" or "terror" in Robert Frost, and it caused quite a stir. Frost himself was jarred, not so much by what Trilling said but by his not having anticipated it and his having to read after Trilling's introduction. Some folks even came to Frost's defense, such as J. Donald Adams in the *New York Times*. But as Poirier points out, those who defend Frost against such claims do not understand him very well. Frost's own response is, "I might run my eye over my book after Trilling, and wonder why he hadn't see it sooner: that there's plenty to be dark about, you know. It's full of darkness."

Frost speaks of not wanting to be difficult but wanting to be mischievous. He says that one "[c]ould unsay everything" he has said "nearly." "Talking contraries," he says, is about "hinting" and *"double entendre,"* about a "feat of association." He speaks about tones of voice and "[f]amilies that break up when people take hints you don't intend and miss hints you do intend." He speaks of the risk of being a poet and says that there is less risk in a climate where every poet finds himself supported by prizes and academies. If we take the risk out if it, we will "lose a lot of the pious spirits." He calls poets beggars, and scholars, too, though they let the presidents of colleges do their begging for them. Poirier has a political agenda of his own, arguing that such support might lead to "mediocrity," being "exalted." He asks, "And won't this make it more rather than less difficult for people to recognize really good achievement when it does occur?" Frost, ever sly, dodges again: "I never knew how many disadvantages anyone needed to get anywhere in the world." Frost's aim in writing poetry is to communicate "what a *hell* of a good time I had writing it." To him the whole thing is prowess and performance.

Near the end the "San Franciscans" are brought up by Poirier, again trying to get Frost's take on other poets. He is referring to the beat poets, Allen Ginsberg and Jack Kerouac, among others. He again does not get much out of Frost, who is elusive about specific poets and indicates what he looks for in a poem: the rhymes first, "the realm of performance." He wants to be unable to tell which rhymes the poet thought of first and which ones he had to "makeshift." He wants poems that are "thinking forward," that come mostly from "animus," as he always insisted his did.

The interview shows Frost at his most elusive, but his elusiveness is sometimes as revealing as what he tells straight.

"Passing Glimpse, A" (1928)

"A Passing Glimpse" was first published on April 21, 1926, in the *New Republic* as "The Passing Glimpse." It was then collected in *West-Running Brook* with a dedication to the midwestern poet Ridgely Torrence. The phrase "on last looking into his 'Hesperides'" was later added to the dedication. This is another poem whose speaker is on a train, as in "The Figure in the Doorway" and "On the Heart's Beginning to Cloud the Mind."

Here Frost is concerned with the possibility of having direct knowledge of what is real. From the speaker's train car, passing glimpses are all that are presented to him. The flowers he can view from his window "are gone before [he] can tell what they are." Indirect perceptions become all he has to work with. Reality becomes an ideal that is not quite clear: "I name all the flowers I am sure they weren't." The speaker finds that he is gaining glimpses of heaven. Heaven as an ideal is just as elusive to his perceptions, just as much of a blur, as these flowers viewed from the train car. Ultimately, passing glimpses are all that this world gives us. A passing glimpse does not necessarily imply a direct perception of some Platonic ideal, of which there is no mention in this poem. Instead, the poem is more constructively viewed as Aristotelian: The speaker comes to understand what is real through his somewhat blurry perceptions of this world, not through the ideal perceptions of the forms of bluebells or fireweed. (*See* "The BEAR," also published in WEST-RUNNING BROOK.)

The second-to-last stanza is facetious: "Was something brushed across my mind / That no one on earth will ever find?" Just because the speaker has a passing glimpse does not mean that that is all there is to be found in this world. People who get to see more do not always see closely, and those who see a blur can still find reality within it: "Heaven gives glimpses only to those / Not in position to look too close." The speaker looks so closely that he can be given only glimpses; otherwise, he would see it all.

See PHILOSOPHY.

"Pasture, The" (1914)

In this pastoral lyric, first published as the opening poem of *North of Boston* and later introducing Frost's *Collected Poems* (1930), the speaker invites the reader to come along on his pastoral duties. He is going to clean the pasture spring and fetch the calf, and the reader is invited to "come too." It seems someone else is always present for country duties. As an opening poem, it functions not only as an invitation within the poem but as an invitation to the work for Frost's readers. The poet is going to be traveling into nature, working in it, grappling with it, and wants others to come along. It is a Frostian version of the line in T. S. Eliot's "The Love Song of J. Alfred Prufrock" "Let us go then, you and I."

The journey highlights the intermingling of nature with human nature, of living off the land. Our lives are intertwined with those of the young calf and its mother, and we are dependent on one another. These are the lives of those north of Boston. The examples provided are essential, highlighting the basic nature of farm life and making it positive, human, and inviting. The speaker will "wait to watch the water clear," wait for all to become evident. There is patience in his voice, an acceptance of his duty and an embracing of his place in the natural cycles of the world.

"The Pasture" was used in Frost's May 10, 1915, lecture at the Browne and Nichols School as an example of "the appreciative tones . . . of live speech." He provided descriptions of the tone in various lines, indicating them with such words as "light, informing tone," "reservation," "possibility," "after-thought, inviting," for each, in order, of the four lines of the first stanza, and "similar, free, persuasive, assuring, and inviting tones" in the second stanza.

FURTHER READING

Freedman, William. "Frost's 'The Pasture,'" *Explicator* 29 (1971): 80.

Ingebretsen, Edward. "Robert Frost's 'The Pasture' and Wendell Berry's 'Stay Home': Figures of Love and the Figure a Poem Makes." In *His Incalculable Influence on Others: Essays on Robert Frost in Our Time*, edited by Earl J. Wilcox, 81–88. Victoria, British Columbia: University of Victoria Press, 1994.

Moore, M. Shawn. "Robert Frost's 'The Pasture': Poem and Metapoem," *Virginia English Bulletin* 36, no. 2 (Winter 1986): 49–51.

Oehlschlaeger, Fritz. "Robert Frost's 'The Pasture': A Reconsideration," *CP* 16, no. 2 (Fall 1983): 1–9.

"Patch of Old Snow, A" (1916)

The poet presents an image, playing the same trick on his readers that his eyes play on him. A patch of snow in a corner resembles a sheet of paper. The patch is "speckled with grime" and appears to be a sheet of paper with writing on it, a newspaper. Both images are "news of a day" the speaker has forgotten, if he ever "read it" in the first place.

The image is everlasting, but neither the snow nor the "news" it depicts is. And both, even when present, are not so often regarded. Snow melts away, and comparing the two suggests that so does the news of the day. Only freshly fallen snow and new news are worthy of note, and both are easily forgotten when the "weather" changes.

The poem was first published in *Mountain Interval*.

"Paul's Wife" (1923)

This lengthy poem tells a yarn about Paul, a logger at a lumber camp who exceeds every other logger in his "feats of logging." The poem presents a Frostian version of the folk tale of the legendary Paul Bunyan. Here Paul's Achilles heel is his wife. Whenever he is asked "How is the wife, Paul?" he disappears and moves to another logging camp. This is the one question his fellow, weaker loggers can use to twit him.

Several rumors are presented as to why Paul is sensitive about the subject. Some say he was left at the altar, others say his wife left him for another man, still others say he married someone not his equal, and some say he has a wife who, he worries, will get "into mischief." But, the speaker concludes, "if the story Murphy told was true, / She wasn't anything to be ashamed of," and it is Murphy's mystical tale that spins the greatest yarn of the poem. In Murphy's version, Paul literally "sawed his wife / Out of a white-pine log."

The loggers are hard at work when they discover a pine log that appears to have a "black streak of grease" down the center of it, but it is not grease; it is an illusion. The darkness is the hollowness of the inside. Paul returns to the tree later that evening to see if it is empty. Looking inside, he makes "out in there / A slender length of pith, or was it pith?" (Pith is the soft, spongy center of the stems of most flower plants.) He takes the tree to a nearby pond to see how it will respond to water, and it seems at first to melt and disappear. Then a girl emerges, the pith having described her softness, and there was "a moment of suspense in birth" just as a newborn makes its transition from swimming in amniotic fluid to breathing air, and the girl catches her breath "with a gasp / And laugh[s]." The two then walk together, "falling in across the twilight mill-pond," a modern folk version of husband and wife (Adam and his rib) as they make their way "[a]cross the logs like backs of alligators."

The next night Murphy and some other boys sneak out drunk to find "Paul and his creature keeping house." From where they observe the two, the girl is like a bright star and Paul is her shadow. In "brute tribute of respect to beauty" or sheer savage jealousy, the "ruffians put their throats together, / And let out a loud yell," hurling a bottle at the house. While the bottle falls "short by a mile," the shouts reach the house and have a tremendous effect: They put out the girl's "light" or lights: "[s]he went out like a firefly, and that was all."

The poem ends with the recognition that "[e]veryone had been wrong in judging Paul." Paul was a "terrible possessor" because he believed "[o]wning a wife . . . meant owning her." The speaker concludes that "Murphy's idea was that a man like Paul / Wouldn't be spoken to about a wife / In any way the world knew how to speak," suggesting that Paul's larger-than-life status meant that his wife would be held to a similar standard.

Robert Faggen writes that "Rather than stressing his image as the intrepid individualist whose power as logger underscores the human dominion and control of nature, Frost undermines the legend by exposing Paul's susceptibility to fear of sexual competition and humiliation" (208).

Frost's tale of love selects an unlikely Romeo and Juliet, but its effect is powerful. The love between Paul and his "wife" and the brevity of both is as fleeting as the life of a firefly. It is achieved only in an otherwordly realm beyond the limited comprehension of men.

The speaker also seems to suggest that the relationship between men and their wives is not something that can be expressed in language to others. Among other men, a man's love for his wife can only be characterized by possession and protection from outsiders. The love between men and women and the communication between them surpasses the understanding of others. Only larger-than-life Paul can transcend such mediocrity.

The poem was first published in November 1921 in the *Century Magazine* and was later published in *New Hampshire. See* MYTHOLOGY AND FOLKLORE.

FURTHER READING

Benoit, Raymond. "Folklore by Frost: 'Paul's Wife,'" *Notes on Modern American Literature* 5, no. 4 (Fall 1981): 22.

DeFalco, Joseph M. "Frost's 'Paul's Wife': The Death of an Ideal," *Southern Folklore Quarterly* 29 (1965): 259–265.

Faggen, Robert. *Robert Frost and the Challenge of Darwin.* Ann Arbor: University of Michigan Press, 1997, 208–211.

Wallace, Patricia. "The Estranged Point of View: The Thematics of Imagination in Frost's Poetry." In *Frost Centennial Essays II,* edited by Jac Tharpe, 190–194. Jackson: University Press of Mississippi, 1976.

"Pea Brush" (1916)

John, the speaker's neighbor, is chopping down birch trees and has told the speaker he is welcome to come gather some for the care of his pea plants. The once-wild birch trees will be used in a more disciplined way for human needs. The twigs will be "for garden things / To curl a little finger round," for the pea brush plants to curl themselves around as they grow. "Sunday after church" the speaker makes his way to the "new-cut narrow gap," the clearing made by the taking down of trees. The poem reflects on the apparent strangeness of taking something wild and taming it for a human purpose, in this case as protection for another natural thing growing under cultivation, the peas.

Once we have killed a natural thing, it does "[s]mall good to anything growing wild." It must then be used to protect another wild thing, but one that is under control. Control and use of nature are opposed to letting nature run wild, like the flowers and trillium of the poem, which are now being put upon by the birch trees that crush them by being on the "flowers' backs."

The "stumps" that are "bleeding their li[ves] away" are presented in a sacrificial way to emphasize their new function. The speaker's senses are heightened, the "odor of sap" being the odor of decay. Man is once again portrayed as alien to nature. Even the spring peepers react to the speaker's presence and stop peeping when he comes near.

Chopped birches are not good for anything but "garden things." They have little use now that they are dead. The image of the curling of the finger of the pea plant around the birches, "same as you seize cat's-cradle strings," introduces human complexity. The birches will be used as a tool. They will have a new purpose but are no longer any good for their old one. The work of humans has altered the natural landscape. (*See* "An ENCOUNTER.")

Nature has its own instructions and its own functions. The final line, "And since it was coming up had to come," indicates that our presence is always the difference in the context. The trillium were already on their way and so had to come, even though the birch boughs were in their way. Nature is in some respects unstoppable; in others, we halt it in its tracks and make it bend to our will.

In the end there is a return to the stability that the boughs now represent as the peas "lift themselves up off the ground," a new type of stability particular to the human lifestyle. We project human characteristics onto the dying tree and its purpose and meaning. It now exists only in relation to us and our needs, whereas its previous existence had nothing to do with us. Frost again plays on the irony between two seemingly extreme characterizations about the relationship between humans and nature: Nature is in one sense innocent of and indifferent to the presence of humans, but at the same time it is dominated and controlled by humans.

The poem was first titled "Pea-Sticks" and appeared in July 1914 in "The Bouquet" a typewritten magazine compiled by the Frost children. It later was collected in *Mountain Interval*.

See FUGITIVE.

"Peaceful Shepherd, The" (1928)

The poet criticizes royalty, economics, and religion by presenting a peaceful shepherd who, if given the opportunity to remake the world, would do it his way. Looking up at the constellations, he imagines them as his "pasture bars," where he would connect the dots, the stars, fashioning a new and improved world. If heaven "were to do it again," build the world over, and he were the designer, he would be "tempted to forget" those three aspects of the world that have been "hardly worth renewal." He narrows the ills of the world to three primary forces—the "Crown of Rule," "Scales of Trade," and "Cross of Faith"—and concludes that these are primarily

what govern and disrupt our lives, so well, in fact, that they might as well be swords.

In the background of the poem there is a clear acknowledgment that these three forces will be present for a long time. For now, at least, we are bound by them. They govern our lives, and that is unfortunate. But the phrase that undoes the poem is "I fear," which suggests that while the peaceful shepherd may long to redesign the world neglecting these three realities, it would be a peacemaker's foolish mistake. These forces remain with us because they are inevitable and essential aspects of a functioning world. Connected to this suggestion is the further claim that the speaker is mildly concerned with the subtle social blasphemy in even thinking about such radical concepts as abandoning these constants.

The poem is at once both romantic and disillusioned, two qualities that might be said to characterize Frost the man as well. It was first published on March 22, 1925, in the *New York Herald Tribune* books section and later collected in *West-Running Brook*. In the *Herald* it was grouped with "On a Star-Bright Night" under the title "A Sky Pair." *See* STARS.

FURTHER READING

Vail, Dennis. "Point of View in Frost's 'The Peaceful Shepherd,'" *Notes on Contemporary Literature* 4, no. 5 (1974): 2–4.

"Peck of Gold, A" (1928)

Representing a time when the West was still wild, this poem plays on the old NEW ENGLAND adage that we all must "eat a peck of dirt before [we] die," offering a new twist from a man who was born and grew up partly in SAN FRANCISCO and then in the Northeast. For him, the saying was "all must eat our peck of gold." The image is of the old West and the Gold Rush.

The town is dusty, existing as it does in the hills, except when the bay's "sea-fog la[ys] it down." The hope for gold is all the boy remembers of "life in the Golden Gate" for it was all they "drank and ate."

The poem skillfully contrasts the images of the San Francisco Bay with the fog that lays down the dust and the dry coast of the west. There is significance to the speaker's being "one of the children told"—a recognition that it was a false hope. Not that no one reaped great rewards during the gold rush, but clearly all did not have the same opportunities. And finding gold took great sacrifices; one eats false gold—or perhaps fool's gold—as if it were the dirt of the adage. As the novel *Treasure of the Sierra Madre* (1935), by B. Traven, demonstrates, the Gold Rush was not all glamour.

Aside from the placating function of trying to distract a child's mind from life's obvious hardships, the closing "We all must eat our peck of gold" suggests two additional interpretations in an approach to life. First, we all must eat that original peck of dirt because life is not always sunshine and flowers, and second, among those pecks of dirt lies something golden.

The poem was first published in the July 1927 edition of the *Yale Review* as "The Common Fate" and was later collected in *West-Running Brook*.

"Perfect Day—A Day of Prowess, A" (1956)

"Perfect Day—A Day of Prowess" was published in the July 23, 1956, issue of *Sports Illustrated*. It praises baseball and is reminiscent of the boy in "Birches" who is "too far from town to learn baseball." Frost was himself a good ball player; his first career goal was to pitch in the major leagues. As a boy he was known for his fastball, which he called a "jump ball." He was very knowledgeable about the game and could name major and minor players going back a half century with ease. He played until late middle age, "often dazzling his colleagues and students at the Bread Loaf Writers' Conference with his pitching ability and determination" (Parini, 22).

It is the boyish Frost in a different hat expressing poetically his passion for something other than poetry: "I never felt more at home in America than at a ball game be it in a park or in sandlot. Beyond this I know not. And dare not."

FURTHER READING

Parini, Jay. *Robert Frost: A Life.* New York: Holt, 1999.

"Peril of Hope" (1962)

The title prepares the reader for what is to come. For a farmer, a bare orchard represents peril and a green one represents hope. The orchard bare means after the crop, the orchard green before. It is when the orchard is at its prime that fear sets in. Will it make it through? Will it avoid a frost? The poet almost surely puns on his own name here, as he does in "The Gold Hesperidee." There is also a suggestion of what the poet's observations might do to influence his reader's hopes. He might get "right in there / Betwixt and between."

We fear the worst when things are at their best because that is when we have the most to lose. But the loss described is clearly human, not really a loss from nature, since frost or growth either happens or does not happen, and both are part of the same indifferent processes. Again, nature seems to "loom" over the horizon to "ruin" what we see as an amazing possibility—but, again, from the perspective of nature, a night of frost killing orchards in the "flowery burst" is not evil; it just is. Orchards may go through bursts, but that they are the cause of peril or hope is clearly a human designation. Night frosts happen sometimes; they are just part of the cycle of nature. The value judgment of what happens when the night frost ruins a flowery orchard comes from us, not from nature. Peril, hope, fear, excitement, enjoyment—all of these are human emotions about nature, not nature itself. And it is the human presence in the poem that is responsible for its title and emotional pull.

Frost again reminds us that we find not only our greatest hopes in nature but also our greatest fears—and, more important, these value judgments have little connection to nature itself. These are games that are only about us, and also only from us. We are the source, the players, and in the end the only ones truly affected by the consequences of such games.

The poem was collected in *In the Clearing*.

"Pertinax" (1936)

"Pertinax" was first published in April 1936 in *Poetry* and was later collected in *A Further Range* in a group of poems titled "Ten Mills." Its three short lines deal with the fashioning of form from chaos. The first two lines end with exclamation points, addressing the urgency and power of the chaos. The final line contrasts the first two; it is patient, as the speaker, when faced with the swarming cloud shapes of a storm, simply "wait[s] for form."

The poem alludes to at least two examples where form is built on chaos. The first is the creation of the world as described in the book of Genesis, the second a personal commentary on the craft of poetry. In crafting poetry, the poet creates form through both his language and the shape his poem takes. In either case, form is not something that can be forced but something that must be waited for. This notion of creation in some ways lessens the role of the poet and of God. Each becomes a conduit, waiting for inspiration, waiting for something beyond himself to determine the shape ideas will take. If the reasoning is sound, then neither god nor poet retains supreme rank as creator.

Pertinax is a Latin term meaning persistent, firm, mean, stubborn, or obstinate. There was also a Roman emperor named Publius Helvius Pertinax (126–193 A.D.) who rose from humble origins to sit on the throne of the Caesars, but his three-month reign (192–193 A.D.) marked merely the beginning of years of civil war after the murder of his predecessor, Marcus Aurelius Commodus Antoninus (161 A.D.–192 A.D.). A pertinacious poet, like Frost himself, will wait obstinately for form to develop out of chaos.

"Place for a Third" (1923)

The poem begins, "Nothing to say to all those marriages!" and the meaning of the title, "Place for a Third," becomes evident; third place also comes to mind. The man, Laban, and the woman, Eliza, have each been married twice before, and therefore the

"score was even for them, three to three." In the opening stanza the wife imagines a burial row where she will be forced to lie by the two previous wives. "Laban," she says, "You have done a good deal right; don't do the last thing wrong." It is clear that she is ill and nearing death and that "[t]ime would press / Between the death day and the funeral day."

Eliza imagines three children in a burial row and finds this "sad." When she imagines three wives in a burial row, she has a different reaction. To this she becomes "impatient with the man," and suddenly the even score of three to three is somehow uneven. The man is quickly responsible for a row of women in a way that apparently changes the meaning of the "score."

The name Laban is taken from the Old Testament. Laban was the son of Bethuel, who was the son of Nahor, Abraham's brother in the book of Genesis. Laban's sister Rebekah was Isaac's wife. Jacob, one of the sons of this marriage, fled to the house of Laban, whose daughters Leah and Rachel he eventually married (Genesis 29). The allusion might be intentional, but the biblical tale seems to bear little relevance to the poem.

In the second stanza Laban concerns himself with determining an appropriate burial plot for Eliza. He does not want to "make her lie / With anyone but that she had a mind to." He imagines how he might please her and "exceed his promise, / And give good measure to the dead, though thankless." He imagines first that perhaps she would like a fresh new grave of her own. He could buy her the greatest headstone and plant flowers for her that would allow that "once grief sets to growing, grief may rest," the sort of flowers that will not make the grave "seem neglecting or neglected." Laban's thoughts then turn to the young boy who married Eliza "for playmate more than helpmate." He wonders, "How would she like to sleep her last with him?"

In the third stanza Laban goes in search of the young boy's grave a few towns away. The stone is engraved, "John, Beloved Husband." There is also a place reserved beside John for Eliza, a place his sister had reserved. Laban imagines how John would feel about being buried beside Eliza but is reminded that the "dead [are] bound to silence" and that he would have to ask the sister. Not thinking of what Eliza would want but knowing what she does not, he begs the sister for the grave. The sister needs time to think about "how much she cared— / And how much Laban cared—and why he cared."

The sister and Eliza had been friends as Eliza moved from her first husband's to her second husband's grave to going "the poor man's widow's way." The sister wonders who she is to judge Eliza's three marriages or her housekeeping for "the next man out of wedlock" or "to judge marriage in a world / Whose Bible's so confused in marriage counsel." But the sister eventually does judge. In the end she determines that "Eliza's had too many other men" and must not lie with John. Laban then purchases a plot for Eliza to lie in alone.

The poem ends on an ironic and poignant note as Laban realizes that this purchase "gives him for himself a choice of lots / When his time comes to die and settle down." The settling down is clearly facetious. Settling down comes only in death for these two since there seems to be no acknowledgment of "settling down" to marriage in life.

Frost, a man married to his high school sweetheart, Elinor, until death, offers commentary on those whose fickle love leaves off after death. While the sister expresses that she is not one to judge in a world so confused about marriage, in the end she does, and apparently so does Frost.

The poem was first published in the July 1920 edition of *Harper's Magazine* and was later collected in *New Hampshire*. The poem was at one time titled "Eliza."

"Planners, The" (1947)

Frost considers the possibility of the end of the world by means of a nuclear disaster. He argues that those never born would be untouched by "[w]hat they never had of vital bliss" but he is critical of the living. The majority, wherever and whenever they might live, would have little to say. Only a handful would seem to know what they really

have. It is not living that is bliss but having the opportunity to live. The phrase "vital bliss" is reminiscent of vital signs—a medical term suggesting that just being alive is blissful. It has nothing to do with anything beyond a pulse; a pulse is enough. And being alive is blissful even when living is not.

The minority who know this are the only ones who would be bothered by what happened, would have some understanding of why it happened. And he imagines who this select few might be: "The guild of social planners / With the intention blazoned on their banners / Of getting one more chance to change our manners." Ironically, there is praise in this jab at "social planners." On the one hand, they are the only ones who would care enough to try to change human history, which sets them above the unquestioning majority; on the other hand, they are ridiculed banner-carriers, card-holding members of some group who are intent on changing manners. By diminishing concern over nuclear destruction to a preoccupation with politeness, the poet facetiously makes the select few seem petty. Bad manners might be considered the cause of the world's problems, but Frost knows that the problem is far deeper. It is certainly "important / That human history should not be shortened," and it is tragic that only "the planners" seem to know this.

The recognition that it is only the radical, the minority, the questioning few that would challenge what is going wrong and has gone wrong is important. The title is, after all, "The Planners." And while Frost suggests that some would be critical of the planners and the poem even seems to criticize that minority, it is all satire. The poem also asserts that they are the ones who should be listened to the most.

The poem was first published in the December 1946 issue of the *Atlantic Monthly* and was later collected in *Steeple Bush*, where Frost has his say on the politics of his day. "The Planners" is a part of a section titled "Editorials"; "An Importer" precedes the poem, and "No Holy Wars for Them" follows it. There are a number of other political poems in the volume, both in the "Editorials" section and elsewhere.

"Plowmen" (1923)

In this quatrain the natural agricultural practice of plowing is contrasted with the modernized mechanical practice of snowplowing. The poet is manipulating the dual meaning of *plow*: "A plow, they say." Frost's use of the word *snowplow* suggests a tool that cultivates the earth as an ordinary plow does in preparation for planting. He presents a trick on the eyes as he does in "A Patch of Old Snow," where the patch "speckled with grime" appears to be a scrap of newspaper. Here the trick is that the movement of a snowplow imitates that of a common plow with soil, only when an ordinary plow has done its work, it has cultivated soil, whereas when snow is plowed all that is revealed is the rock beneath, the road beneath the snow.

Snowplowing is a metaphor; it is not like real plowing, which has a substantial purpose in a more natural and traditional sense. The difference between plowing a furrow and plowing snow is that one is for food and life and the other is simply for convenience. We cannot plant snow; its value is not in planting. Plowing is an act deserving of the name, whereas snowplowing is derided. This comparison is accented by the last two lines, in which the snowplowers are described as mocking real plowers by having "cultivated rock." The word *mock* suggests two meanings, the first to ridicule, the second to imitate, leaving the intention, as so often in Frost, elusive.

The poem was first published in *A Miscellany of American Poetry 1920* and was later collected in *New Hampshire*.

"Pod of the Milkweed" (1962)

The milkweed is a plant having milky juice, variously colored flowers grouped in umbels, and pods that split open to release seeds with downy tufts. Robert Faggen notes that "In [Henry David] Thoreau's later notebooks milkweed served as an important example of the power of regeneration in nature through the dispersal of seeds over great distances" (74). He also observes that "While Frost

may not have read or known of this late manuscript [Thoreau's "The Dispersion of Seeds"], he seems to rebut Thoreau's faith in seeds" (74).

Frost pays tribute to the pod of the milkweed by suddenly realizing "the theme of wanton waste in peace and war" that the milkweed brings up to his door. The poem opens by calling "all butterflies of every race" to the pod, which serves their "countless wings" with bountiful milk and honey. Butterflies, unlike bees, have no hives and instead flit from source to source "unknown but from no special place they ever will return to all their lives." A significant element in the poem is the brevity and necessary selfishness of a butterfly's life.

The speaker admits that the milkweed is drab but wonders at its stunning ability to captivate butterflies so that they become "intemperate." He discloses that anyone who has ever broken the stem of one and sucked a bit from the "wound" created would know that its "bitter milk" is so powerful it "might be opiate." The butterflies lustfully feast on what is to them the sweetest honey, knocking one another off the desired plants so hungrily that their rivalry is likened to a sexual feast. They raise a cloud of "flower dust" as they struggle to satisfy their appetites.

The speaker recognizes that the "sober weed has managed to contrive" this as the one day of all the year that is "too sweet for beings to survive." Many butterflies will be as "spent" when the day is done as one who has spent the day beating himself in "vain / Against the wrong side of a window pane."

Returning to the theme of "wanton waste in peace and war," the closing stanza concludes that the "waste was the essence of the scheme." The waste is what made the frenzy so beautiful, so desired. That which is fleeting holds our attention the most. And it is no matter what good the union of the pod and butterflies has done for "man or god" because in the end all that is left is "an inheritance of restless dream" to one pod that "hangs on upside down with talon feet . . . [a]s any Guatemalan parakeet." The blissful union, the consummated passion, was nothing but a dream for one pod. For this reason alone it seems that the "reason why so much / Should come to nothing must be fairly faced." In this sense, Frost seems to be hinting at some positive view of nature's wastefulness, and perhaps at waste in general.

The poem is one of the most erotic in the Frost canon, wrought as it is with sexual imagery. The bitter milk, the juice of passion, the sweet honey, and the struggle for gratification are explicit. The spent pod hanging upside down by its talon feet with the dream just out of reach of his "talon clutch" suggests a satiated lover. Science has "staked the future" not only on the coupling of butterflies and pods but also on many a species, including, as is made obvious by the poem, humanity. The reason that so much should depend on such a fit of passion sprung from opiate shall be discovered in "due course," the poet teases in an added line.

The poem was first published as Frost's 1954 Christmas poem in booklet form as "From a Milkweed Pod" and was later published as "Pod of the Milkweed" in *In the Clearing. See* NATURE.

FURTHER READING

Bagby, George F. *Frost and the Book of Nature.* Knoxville: University of Tennessee Press, 1993, 79–82.

Faggen, Robert. *Robert Frost and the Challenge of Darwin.* Ann Arbor: University of Michigan Press, 1997, 73–74.

Perrine, Laurence. "Frost's 'Pod of the Milkweed,'" *Notes on Modern American Literature* 5 (1980): 5.

"Poetry and School" (1951)

Frost did not think poetry and school were a good combination. In his "Introduction to the Arts Anthology: DartmouthVerse" (1925) he reveals his bias against formal schooling, at least for poets, when he describes the anthology of student verse as "getting a long way with poetry, considering all there is against it in school and college." He also argues that poets are made when young. It is in the "freshness" and passion and spirit of youth that a poet must begin, and formal education can only interfere. He urges that we set the "expectation of poetry forward a few years," the way we set the clocks forward for daylight savings. Colleges keep the poet busy "till the danger of his ever creating

anything is past. Their motto has been, the muses find some mischief still for idle hands to do."

In "Poetry and School," published in the *Atlantic Monthly* in June 1951, Frost begins by wondering why "poetry is in school more than it seems to be outside in the world," and he imagines the children must wonder, too, as they certainly "haven't been told." He divides the "authorities" who keep poetry in school into two kinds: "those with a conscientious concern for it and those with a weakness for it." The piece functions as a series of aphorisms in which Frost makes his points about what we go to college for and what reasons there are for poetry not to be "read in course" or "made a study of." "Practice of an art is more salutary than talk about it," he says.

Early on, Frost says that "School is founded on the invention of letters and numbers. The inscription over every school door should be the rhyme ABC and One Two Three. The rest of education is apprenticeship and for me doesn't belong in school." Near the closing he returns to this idea and says, "What marks verse off from prose is that it talks letters in numbers. Numbers is a nickname for poetry." By "numbers" he means not only metrics but poetry itself.

Frost resisted formal education as a boy, though he made his living at it once he was a grown poet. He often made arguments about the poet not belonging in school. Here he provides an argument for the claim that poetry does not belong there either.

"Poetry of Amy Lowell, The" (1925)

Frost's fellow poet Amy Lowell (1874–1925) died on May 12, 1925; these comments appeared in the *Christian Science Monitor* on May 16. They are a glowing tribute to Lowell's poetry. Frost identifies her work as central to the period, calling it "distinguished" at a time when "in the effort to include a larger material," poetry "stretched itself almost to the breaking of the verse." Frost speaks of the "exciting movement in nature," saying that "throw[ing] our arms wide with a gesture of religion to the universe; we close them around a person," Lowell. These remarks are reminiscent of Frost's "Any Size We Please," in which "He stretched his arms out to the dark of space / And held them absolutely parallel / In infinite appeal. Then saying 'Hell' / He drew them in for warmth of self-embrace."

Frost begins with more general points. He argues that it is "absurd" to think that we need to wait and see if a poem "lasts" before determining its merit because the "right reader of a good poem can tell the moment it strikes him that he has taken an immortal wound—that he will never get over it." Frost often spoke of the "right" person or reader. His language is unforgettable. He speaks of "permanence in poetry as in love" as being "perceived instantly," of the immortal wound and of a "barb" and a "toxin" that are "owned to at once." While he is admiring Lowell, he is appreciating all poetry that wounds.

Frost wrote in his "Introduction to E. A. Robinson's *King Jasper*" that "[t]he utmost of ambition [of a poet] is to lodge a few poems where they will be hard to get rid of," and here he echoes the sentiment, saying that "Lowell had lodged poetry . . . to stay." His closing comments have a particular beauty. He speaks of the "water" in the eyes of those mourning as being "not warm with any suspicion of tears" but "water flung cold, bright and many colored from flowers gathered in [Lowell's] formal garden in the morning."

FURTHER READING

Lowell, Amy. *The Complete Poetical Works of Amy Lowell.* Edited by Louis Untermeyer. Boston: Houghton Mifflin, 1955.

"Poet's Boyhood, A" (1960)

"A Poet's Boyhood" appeared in a brochure announcing a Frost reading to be held at the Berkeley Community Theater on November 6, 1960, in Berkeley, California. At age 86, Frost was returning to the region of his birth as an esteemed poet. He opens the piece by recalling one of his earliest SAN FRANCISCO memories.

Frost speaks of politics, of his father's role in nominating the popular Democratic candidate for the presidency in 1880, Winfield Scott Hancock, and of his father's disappointment when Hancock was narrowly beaten by James Garfield and "even greater disappointment when Hancock as an old friend and fellow soldier of Garfield's went to Garfield's inauguration and shook hands with him in public right on the platform." Frost himself was a fierce competitor, and it seems he at least partly inherited his nature from his father.

The family were "Democrats and very intense ones." Frost recalls accompanying his father to work when his father was chairman of the Democratic City Committee since Frost was "kept out of school" when young because of his poor health. Each year through the third grade, Frost attempted to attend school, but each time he suffered from nervous stomach cramping and returned home, where he and his sister Jeanie were homeschooled by their mother. Later Frost would tell his good friend Louis Untermeyer that when he was a child he "played sick to get out of going to school" (Parini, 16).

Frost knows his audience, reminiscing about the region of his birth and appealing to its liberal stronghold and then to his recollection of "a few preliminary earthquakes." He also recalls Woodward's Gardens and the Cliff House restaurant. Woodward's Gardens was in operation from 1854 to 1927 and occupied six acres in San Francisco's Mission District. The admission fee was 25 cents, and the gardens housed the largest aquarium in the country at the time, zoological gardens, greenhouses, and a restaurant. Frost writes about it in "At Woodward's Gardens." The Cliff House was a restaurant with a view of the Pacific where the family dined; Frost referred to the restaurant in "Once by the Pacific." Here he says, "Have I not written poems about both these places?" And "I wish I could get you to read 'Once by the Pacific' to yourself before I have to read it to you. It took me a long, long time to get over the idea that the Pacific Ocean was going to be more important in our history than the Atlantic. If I ever got over it." He may be territorially referring to World War II the bombing of Pearl Harbor, and the threat of Japan, but he is primarily referring to the westward expansion, as the lines from an unpublished poem he includes indicate: "Our future is in the West on the other sea." He also uses the occasion to remind his audience that his father was a newspaperman at San Francisco Bay area papers long defunct: the *Post* and the *Bulletin.*

Frost closes wryly: "Nothing but idyllic politics." That is his game, and he plays it well with his audience.

FURTHER READING

Parini, Jay. *Robert Frost: A Life.* New York: Holt, 1999.

"Poet's Next of Kin in a College, The" (1937)

"The Poet's Next of Kin in a College" was a Princeton University address on October 26, 1937. Both this piece and "Poverty and Poetry" were prepared by Lawrance Thompson from stenographic records. Thompson edited heavily, taking some liberties with the transcription.

Frost does not think "it matters much" whether a poet has any kin or friends in a college. He says that "a poet should lead a dog's life for a long, long time" and that he "should be late in knowing too well that he is a poet," as, presumably, Frost himself was. He knew no other way, of course. He does, however, find that English departments are the kindest to the poet, and sometimes the teachers in those departments are even overly kind, since they "love" their students and therefore do not often prepare them for the "hate" of editors. They are friends to the poet. But there are also folks in these departments who can be distinguished in the following ways: those who are "the keeper[s] of texts," those "interested in poetry as it represents its age," and those of the "general critical approach," which is "very dangerous" as it "puts too many words around poetry" and is "not the spirit, quite, of the young poet." All three, however, are disagreeable to the poet.

Frost considers the possibility of other departments being good places for poets to look for kinship.

Socioeconomic departments are not good, as a "poet's main interest is in doing something well" and the people in those departments are interested in "doing people good, doing the world good." A poet must prefer doing something well to doing something good. Science is "nearer" to kin, because "it is nothing if it is not achievement, if it is not creative," but the scientific can intrude on the artistic as well. The philosophy department is one of Frost's "prejudices," as he has a great admiration for it, and that admiration grew after he was 40. This leads him to a discussion of the "flashes" of insight that come to young poets, which are "like the stars coming out in the sky in the early evening." When poets are older they will only be able to "see forms, constellations."

Frost argues that poets grow through flashes, making an argument similar to the one he made in "Introduction to the Arts Anthology: Dartmouth of Verse" and elsewhere that poets have to begin when they are young. "Sight and insight makes poetry," and that is for the young poets; older poets "die into philosophy . . . into wisdom." Frost compares the prowess of the poet to that of the athlete, arguing that the two are very similar. Form comes later, but the "spirit" comes first in both and must be struck while hot. He argues that one can "go back over a poem and touch it up" but that the spirit has to be there; "the great pleasure in writing poetry is in having been carried off." Frost draws an analogy to riding a horse. Mark Richardson describes his metaphor as "The rodeo artist giv[ing] form to the unpredictable and forceful motions of the horse; he expresses them and in a sense is also expressed by them" (198). Frost compares "[K]eeping the thing [the poem] in motion" to walking on a rolling barrel.

Frost has gotten away from the poet's next of kin in college, meandering in this address, but he closes with one request: "all I ask is to be smitten." He says he has "boasted" that he could tell whether a poem was composed in "morning calmness or midnight intoxication," but what it comes down to is whether or not he will be smitten.

FURTHER READING

Richardson, Mark. *The Ordeal of Robert Frost: The Poet and His Poetics.* Chicago, Ill.: University of Illinois Press, 1997.

poultry stories: a sampling

Between 1903 and 1905 Frost wrote a number of poultry stories and articles for the New England magazine *Farm-Poultry*. In *Robert Frost: Farm-Poultryman* Edward Connery Lathem and Lawrance Thompson write that Frost was "fascinated by the fluffy creatures" (9) and that when he purchased the Derry farm in New Hampshire, the *Derry News* reported on October 5, 1900, that "R. Frost has moved upon the Magoon place which he recently bought. He has a

flock of nearly 300 Wyandotte fowls" (9). Further, the two editors write that the lines of the stories "may also serve to heighten any reader's awareness that Robert Frost's years as a farm-poultryman left their indelible mark on his literary career, as a prose-writer and as a poet" (11). Two stories in particular are of interest: "The Cockerel Buying Habit" and "Dalkin's Little Indulgence: A Christmas Story."

"The Cockerel Buying Habit" was printed in the February 1, 1904, issue of *Farm-Poultry*. It concerns a conversation between two gentlemen

Frost with chickens in Ripton, Vermont. "The Cockerel Buying Habit": "At the age of sixty the indications are that I'm about ready to begin over again—dress the lot and begin over again. And I call myself a breeder? So much for the cockerel buying habit." *(Courtesy Dartmouth College Library)*

about "in-breeding." They stand among the hens, and the narrator says that he is a "safe man to talk [in-breeding] over with." The gentleman is afraid of in-breeding because of the "[l]aw of nature" and because "[i]t's attended to with awful consequences in the human family." The narrator is less concerned and would "risk it." A man named George Hill bred Cochins until "he got them squat and fluffy," but they "come to set their eggs one year there wasn't a single one fertile." The gentleman then sets about describing each of his hens and explaining what is the matter with it. The piece closes with the man wondering if he should at "another time . . . breed in," but he is 60 now and wonders if he can "begin over" and, if so, what would come of it. He wants to know if he should "chance it" and whether he would "come out any worse" than he already has. The suggestion is that it is too late to begin over and that the hen farmer will be left wondering if he could have come out better if he had made a different choice. The piece is simple but resembles Frost's narrative poems in which the NEW ENGLAND dialect is evident and the meaning conveyed in the tone of the language. The ending also resembles "The Road Not Taken," where the speaker is left to question his life choices.

"Dalkin's Little Indulgence," reminiscent of Mark Twain's stories, was printed in the December 15, 1905, issue of *Farm-Poultry.* The story begins in Peacham, Vermont, and concerns Dalkin, ·who purchased a bird for $1.50 from a man who later, upon learning that the "bird was framed by nature" and "better than any score reputable judges are willing to sign," regretted having sold the bird for such a measly sum. He made out that he had been "badly cheated" by Dalkin and set about talking "early and late to all comers about his misfortune that was another man's fault." He "showed himself a poor loser." Among poultry farmers the story was not unfamiliar. Everyone at one time or another sells a bird that later seems to have more value than they thought. Bird buying and selling comes to resemble the stock market in terms of wagering and risk taking.

Dalkin receives a letter by a mischief-maker, and this sets him to his own mischief-making. He decides to bring the letter writer, Durgin, and the original owner to a show in New York. The two men are led along on what seems to be a practical joke. In the end Dalkin surprises them both. The bird has been sold, and on the last day of the show, it is discovered that the price was $200. Dalkin holds the owner's hand out "as in a vice" as the $200 worth of bills are heaped into his hand. He tells the original owner to do right with the money and put it "where it belongs." The original owner, the poor loser, leaves as if in "a dream amid the uproar of roosters." He hears in his dream Dalkin saying, "Go tell that up in the hills, and make them stop breeding mongrel stock." The owner gets his comeuppance in an unusual way, by having all his ruffled feathers unruffled.

Lathem and Thompson include a humorous letter Frost wrote to friend John Bartlett, who had "got[ten] himself into journalist difficulties by giving too much play to his own fancy in describing a picturesque character known as 'Biblical Smith.'" As part of Frost's "gentl[e] repriman[d]," he admitted, "I wrote up one or two poultrymen as you did Biblical Smith filling in the gaps in my knowledge with dream material." Frost told Bartlett he "mustn't fake articles any more" because "[i]t is taking an unfair advantage of the gentlemen who profess fiction" (Frost, 23).

FURTHER READING

Frost, Robert. *Robert Frost: Farm-Poultry Man.* Edited by Edward Connery Lathem and Lawrance Thompson. Hanover, N.H.: Dartmouth, 1963.

"Poverty and Poetry" (1937)

"Poverty and Poetry" was a Haverford College address on October 25, 1937. Both this piece and "The Poet's Next of Kin in a College" were prepared by Lawrance Thompson from stenographic records. Thompson edited heavily, taking some liberties with the transcription.

Frost "gave out a subject," but since it did not reach the audience and since he was "free to talk about what [he] please[d]" he spoke about "a little matter that ha[d] been on [his] mind": the question of "class" or "the ordinary folks" he felt he belonged to. He speaks of *North of Boston* as *A Book of People,* and he is chiefly concerned with those people in this piece. He speaks about those who have been critical of his uncultivated and uneducated country neighbors. "Let the rich keep away from the poor for all of me," he says. He never intended to write about the poor and never wanted anything to be "made of it." These were just the people he knew, for "no matter how educated or poor a man is, a certain level up there in Vermont and New Hampshire stays about the same."

Frost wonders about the general relation of poetry to the poor and finds that "maybe falsely, hypocritically—poetry has praised poverty." This address seems dictated by an emotional whim, a grievance, something that Frost criticized in poetry. Although the lecture might not have been off the cuff—it was surely prepared—it reflects where he found himself at the moment. This was what was on his mind and this was the course the reading took. The occasion also led him to take up the question of mercy and justice. He cautions that "we're in danger, in our way of thinking that mercy comes first in the world. It comes in, but it comes in second." For Frost's thinking on mercy, his *Masque of Mercy* offers insight. Fairness should be our chief concern, he says, not mercy.

Frost recites several poems for the audience, including "The Lone Striker," "The Death of the Hired Man," "A Drumlin Woodchuck," and "Two Tramps in Mud Time," all of which reveal something about class. He is crotchety and frustrated throughout, but in the end he takes an upward turn. Following "Two Tramps in Mud Time," he urges that the poem "has nothing to do with the times" and is "a very general thing: getting your need and your love together in everything."

"Prayer in Spring, A" (1913)

"A Prayer in Spring" is literally a farmer's prayer. The deferential tone identifies the poem as among Frost's early work, appearing in his first book, *A*

Boy's Will. As Robert Faggen points out, "Being one of Frost's most beautiful and gentle poems, it trusts a God above, not immanent, 'who sanctif[ies]' love in nature 'to what far ends He will'" (249). Such a presentation of God is more reverent than those in Frost's later work.

The speaker prays for pleasure today in the flowers, the white orchard, the happy bees, the darting hummingbird, "the meteor that thrusts in with needle and bill," and asks not to "think so far away / As the uncertain harvest" that has been planted. We are to seize the day, whatever is immediate and direct. The harvest cannot be sanctified because, in spring, it is always uncertain. The presence of doubt is precisely what raises the need for prayer.

The whole process of nature is in this prayer. Doubt exists only in relation to the harvest we have planted. All the bees, orchids, and so forth are fine until the harvest. The harvest is uncertain because it is only partly natural; it depends on the seeds that we have planted. It may become part of the natural landscape and flourish, that is our hope, but it is not of nature in the same way as the birds and the bees are.

The speaker leaves the harvest up to God in the last stanza, but he does not completely trust that God will come through. If God's ends are uncertain when it comes to our harvest, our bread and butter, then we are reminded of our dependence on God's good graces. The uncertainty is in the poet's use of *which*: "which it is reserved for God above," "which it only needs that we fulfill." Even if we do our part, it does not guarantee what is going to happen. We could do our entire part, we can do everything we are supposed to do with the harvest, and still not get a good harvest. It is not entirely up to us, and neither the harvest nor God can be trusted.

Everything is beautiful about this prayer except the one thing that is connected to us: That is the only glitch in a perfectly serene setting. Perhaps all prayers are about uncertainty. In prayer, a person submissively grants God's will but is quickly reminded that his will may not be the will of humans and that we will have to accommodate, accept, and maybe even survive that possibility. Mark Richardson reads the final four lines of the poem differently: "The idea is that the affections that draw and bind us together—those we express sexually, for example, are in fact continuous with the larger forces even of magnetism and gravity" (171).

FURTHER READING

Faggen, Robert. *Robert Frost and the Challenge of Darwin.* Ann Arbor: University of Michigan Press, 1997, 249.

Richardson, Mark. *The Ordeal of Robert Frost: The Poet and His Poetics.* Chicago, Ill.: University of Illinois Press, 1997, 171–172.

"Precaution" (1936)

This well-known couplet is first in a group of short verses titled "Ten Mills," most of which, including this one, were originally published in *Poetry* in April 1936 and were later collected in *A Further Range.* In "On Extravagance: A Talk" Frost refers to it as his only free-verse poem.

The couplet "I never dared be radical when young / For fear it would make me conservative when old," is in the spirit of Winston Churchill's dictum that any man who is not a liberal when young has no heart, and any man who is not a conservative when old has no brain.

Frost often quoted the couplet in response to queries about his politics.

"Prerequisites, The" (1954)

"The Prerequisites" is the preface to a selection of Frost's poems, *Aforesaid,* published by Henry Holt in a limited edition in 1954. The piece is worth mention for certain morsels it contains, but they are only morsels. Frost quotes and discusses Ralph Waldo Emerson's "Brahma" as a way of providing a general declaration of the "prerequisites" of reading poetry. He makes an example of a young reader of "[s]ome sixty years ago," presumably Frost as a boy, who encountered the Emerson poem with some difficulty. He uses this example as a way of explaining that poems can be had by their readers only when their readers are ready for them. And that "[a]ny immediate preface is like cramming the night before an examination. Too late, too late! Any footnote while the poem is going too late." Poems must be understood in the going, not after the fact. Frost insists that "Any subsequent explanation is as dispiriting as the explanation of a joke. Being taught poems reduces them to the rank of mere information." Frost argues that we learn to read poems by reading poems. We read each poem we encounter a bit better "in the light of all the other poems ever written" and read. The approach a reader takes to a poem "must be from afar off, even generations off," and it was so for the boy of his example. Fifty years later the boy was better able to handle the "Brahma" poem because by then he was a "confirmed symbolist," though Frost was a symbolist only in the general sense, an employer of imagery, tone, and rhythm, never a member of the symbolist school of modern verse, as were T. S. Eliot and Wallace Stevens.

"Provide, Provide" (1936)

This poem is based on a students' strike in support of the cleaning women at Harvard. It has been described by Jay Parini as "a wry commentary on [President Franklin Delano] Roosevelt's New Deal (and its bureaucracy) and a paean to self sufficiency" (286) and by Lawrance Thompson as "bitterly sarcastic" and as an expression of Frost's "*laissez-faire* attitudes," "a taun[t] against the providers-for-others" (438–439). "Provide, Provide" is among Frost's most discussed and anthologized poems.

The women who come to wash the steps are described as having become "witch[es]" and "withered hag[s]." They were once great beauties, like the "beauty Abishag," a biblical reference. Abishag, a young woman of Shunam, distinguished for her beauty, was chosen to minister to King David in his old age (Kings 1:3, 15). After King David's death, Adonijah persuaded Bathsheba, Solomon's mother, to entreat the king to permit him to marry Abishag. Solomon suspected in this request an aspiration to the throne, and therefore Adonijah was put to death (1 Kings 2:17–22).

The cleaning women, described as having been the "picture pride of Hollywood," have fallen from "great and good" as all eventually do. The poem recognizes growing old and falling from greatness as an inevitability. There is no "doubt[ing] the likelihood" that it will happen to us all as well. Frost argues that we could die early to avoid the fate, or "if predestined to die late," we can make up our minds to "die in state," die while still holding a high social position, rank, or status. He urges us to decide early on to have a certain rank economically or as royalty, even to "[m]ake the whole stock exchange [o]ur own" so that we are above criticism. With such success nobody can call us "crone."

The poem recalls that some have relied on "what they knew; / Others on simply being true" to keep from becoming crones. We can try what has worked in the past. We can achieve rank and status with ideas and knowledge or with truth.

The poem's closing stanzas assert that death will be difficult no matter what position we hold when the time comes, and when we fall from that great height, the memory of having once been popular or beautiful will not be enough to "kee[p] the end from being hard." But Frost concludes that it is "[b]etter to go down dignified," even if the friendship at your side has been bought (which suggests that all friends at the top have been purchased), than to go down undignified or with no friends at all.

A cynical approach to life is presented. "Provide, provide!" Frost exclaims at the end, "Prepare, prepare!" or, as he occasionally added to the end of the poem when reading, "or someone will provide for ya, and how would ya like that!"

The whole game of rising high and falling low, going down dignified, is all human convention and custom. These judgments we place on people are not to be found in nature. We have artificial means of status and degradation in the end. What one prepares for is a social cycle. While aging is natural, the downfall is social. It has nothing to do with real values.

Frost is being tongue-in-cheek about what people value. He does not actually say that these are the values; rather, the poem is a comment on what people assume about certain values, namely, that they are valuable, which, Frost demonstrates, they

are not. Frost is the adviser with the inside information, which is that all this is not permanent, neither the preparation nor the result, no matter how secure we might feel with this superficiality.

Robert Pack calls the poem one that "raises the question of what one can believe in old age to bring solace for one's decline and social abandonment" (186). Pack asserts that the "irony of the final words 'Provide, provide!' denies the possibility that any true provision in the face of endings is possible," and "[t]his is as dark a truth as one will find throughout Frost's poetry" (188).

Frost's reminder that going down is hard, no matter who we might think we are when we go down, is honesty that is hard to take. It is the truth that most attempt to avoid in their struggle to gain and hold onto status. Just as the sun rises and sets and the seasons come and go with dependability and predictability, so do we. And no "memory for having starred, / Atones for later disregard": The same attitudes that apply to human status dissipate as surely and quickly as we do.

The poem was first published in September 1934 in the *New Frontier* and was later collected in *A Further Range*.

FURTHER READING

Abel, Darrel. "Frost's 'Provide, Provide,'" *Explicator* 46, no. 3 (Spring 1988): 24–26.

Pack, Robert. *Belief and Uncertainty in the Poetry of Robert Frost*. Hanover, N.H.: Middlebury College Press, 2003.

Parini, Jay. *Robert Frost: A Life*. New York: Holt, 1999.

Perrine, Laurence. "Provide, Provide," *Robert Frost Review* (Fall 1992): 33–39.

———. "Robert Frost's 'Provide, Provide,'" *Notes on Modern American Literature* 8, no. 1 (Spring–Summer 1984): 5.

Thompson, Lawrance. *Robert Frost: The Years of Triumph, 1915–1938*. New York: Holt, 1970.

"Putting in the Seed" (1916)

"Putting in the Seed" is an expression of "a springtime passion for the earth." The speaker invites the reader, or a listener, to come fetch him from his work, to try to get him to come to supper, to see if he can leave off doing his spring ritual. He is going to bury the "[s]oft petals" from the apple tree. The petals are soft "but not so barren quite" because they will act as sustenance for the "smooth bean and wrinkled pea."

The speaker wants to know if he will accompany the listener or if the listener will also lose sight of supper and become a slave to the same passion. The speaker is a slave to watching for the "early birth" that is depicted like a mammal's birth: the "arched body" of a seedling "shouldering" its way and "shedding the earth crumbs" as it breaks through the ground's surface with its vitality. The speaker is a slave to putting in the seed and waiting for it to grow because he takes great pleasure in embracing the seasonal predictability of the bursting forth of new life.

The metaphor of making love is intentional. Spring is the time for lovers. It is the time when women, like the earth, become "not so barren." The poet equates love and making love with planting. Sexual love is about procreation. Nature and people's natural urges take over in rhythm with the season. "Love burns" through the whole act of procreation from sexual intercourse to the birth of a baby, from the planting of a seedling to the bursting forth of new life. Farming is eroticized. It is not merely work; it is an act of love. The ground is submissive and passive during the planting of the seed, and the female seems to be viewed in the same way.

The poem was first published in December 1914 in *Poetry and Drama* and was later collected in *Mountain Interval. See* NATURE.

FURTHER READING

Barnes, Daniel R. "Frost's 'Putting in the Seed,'" *Explicator* 31 (1973): 59.

"Quandary" (1962)

The speaker works from the false premise that there must be bad for there to be good. He acts as though the contrast is a logical necessity, a popularly cited fallacy about the evil in the world. He applies it humorously to a contrast between "brains" and "sweetbreads" and then launches into a sophisticated discussion about discrimination. As John H. Timmerman describes, "Frost neatly bysteps the similar New Testament to love one's neighbor as one's self to include the Delphic injunction to hate one's neighbor as one hates oneself" and asks "Is one simply the dualistic converse of the other, like good and evil?" (100).

The poem begins with the speaker explaining his acceptance of badness as necessary in the world for there to be good and then concluding simply, "That's why discrimination reigns." The word *discriminate* suggests two entirely different meanings; to be discriminating versus discriminating against someone. And that is "why we need a lot of brains," not only to determine goodness and badness but to choose between being discriminating and discriminating against someone or something.

The poem turns everything on its head. Good and bad become translated as "what to love and what to hate." Discrimination is diminished to "I like this" or "I hate that," to simple human desires or aversions, instead of representing thoughtful, reasoned, and logical conclusions. The poem also significantly deflates the idea of an absolute morality.

The poem works partly by building on identifiable tensions between religion and science. The speaker says we learn from the Bible that our soul is the reason for our thinking; we "learned from the forbidden fruit" of Genesis that badness is an aspect of will. When the listener within the poem suggests that "sweetbreads" (organ meats used for food) might be the substitute for brains with an "innuendo [the speaker] detest[s]" (an innuendo also present in the speaker's own words), discrimination becomes a natural behavior instead of one based on will. This clearly undermines the explanation of will as found in the Bible.

"Drive[n] to confess in ink" in this poem that brains and sweetbreads are the same thing (another example of an inability to discriminate), the speaker ultimately confesses he was a fool to think biology and brains were equivalent. He sarcastically admits that he was "put to shame," first by a butcher, then by a cook who no doubt knew what sweetbreads were, and then by a "scientific book," presumably on anatomy. In the end the speaker resolves facetiously that he is short on brains himself and has passed with a high I.Q. on sweetbreads alone.

The relationship between the good and the bad is like the relationship between brains and sweetbreads. In order to discriminate, a person needs a lot of brains—and guts, too. The good and the bad in the world are co-dependent with our needing brains in order to discriminate. The brains might not have come first, but the good and bad have lasted simply because of our ability to distinguish between them. As is much of Frost's poetry, the poem is concerned with our presence in and contributions to the world, not the world devoid of humanity. Good and bad exist because we do, not the other way around, hinting at the line from Shakespeare's *Hamlet*: "There is nothing either good or bad, but thinking makes it so" (II.ii.232).

The poem was first published in the *Massachusetts* Review in fall 1959 as "Somewhat Dietary" and was later collected in *In the Clearing*. It is one of the most heavily revised of Frost's poems, having nine lines cut from the initial version (Timmerman, 100). *See* SCIENCE.

FURTHER READING

Timmerman, John H. *Robert Frost: The Ethics of Ambiguity.* Lewisburg, Pa.: Bucknell University Press, 2002, 99–101.

"Question, A" (1942)

This quatrain was collected in *A Witness Tree*. It appears in a grouping called "Quantula" along with other pithy poems, which suggests that Frost intended them to be together because of their small "quantity" and presumed force. (In Latin, *quantula* means "How little?" or "How small?")

The poem is straightforward. A voice says, "Look me in the stars, / And tell me truly, men of earth, / If all the soul-and-body scars / Were not too much to pay for birth." It addresses the basic questions we have about why we must endure such great suffer-

ing and whether being born is worth it. Being born becomes in the poem a kind of transaction. The question is whether the transaction is a fair one given all the scars we sustain.

In another pithy poem, an untitled couplet in "A Cluster of Faith," the poet writes, "Forgive, O Lord, my little jokes on Thee / And I'll forgive Thy great big one on me." In the context of "A Question," the great big joke might be that our world was born at all.

Robert Faggen observes that "The 'voice' here is only 'a' voice, not unlike that from the whirlwind but less of a God than of a riddling sphinx represented in the material fire of the stars" (259). It seems, however, that it could be God who asks the question. After all, he says, "Look me in the stars," rather than in the eyes.

The only aspect of the poem that is not straightforward is the voice. While the brevity and directness of the poem give it an appearance of simplicity, its complexities run deep. In only four lines, the poem calls into question the very concept of being, and if it is God's voice, then the poem also paints a picture of God not only as unknowing but also as neither powerful nor good, or perhaps as ironic to the point of cruelty. God is unknowing because he does not know what we find worthy of great pain; he does not know what it is to be men of earth and what it is to survive in spite of such pain. He also loses his power and perhaps, too, his goodness, as he is fully aware that we sustain scars but does not take any responsibility for protecting us, when, if he were good and all-powerful, he would.

If it is not God's voice, then another more existential and optimistic interpretation can be gleaned. Since the poem concerns existence, and since it is a question, it seems to prompt the reader to look into himself or herself to answer it. At this point, there is a dilemma. Either we answer "yes" to life and all its pain, or we answer "no" and reject life. The existential aspect of the poem surfaces when we determine that we are the source, the only source, able to provide an answer to the question.

The poem seems simple enough, but it is not merely "A Question"; it is *the* question.

FURTHER READING

Faggen, Robert. *Robert Frost and the Challenge of Darwin.* Ann Arbor: University of Michigan Press, 1997, 259.

"Questioning Faces" (1962)

The questioning faces of this lyric belong to the "glassed-in children" who stand at the windowsill and gaze out at nature. They see a winter owl turn just in time to miss the windowpane. The owl puts on a beautiful display of "underdown and quill" in the last of the "evening red" sunset. The children are protected from winter by being on the other side of the glass. But the same window that protects them from nature is dangerous to the owl, who does not expect to have to veer to avoid a collision with a mere reflection.

The poem was inspired by an experience Frost once had from his own kitchen window. Frost recalled, "The sight of that bird right close to you is just like a favor, something you did not expect—as if someone were on your side" (Parini, 406).

Jay Parini describes the poem as beckoning to Wallace Stevens and more specifically to the ending of his poem "Sunday Morning." The lines to which Parini refers are "At evening, casual flocks of pigeons make / Ambiguous undulations as they sink, / Downward to darkness, on extended wings." Parini also concludes that "Frost was himself the winter owl, banking repeatedly to avoid smashing into the glass wall of death. Again and again, he rose to triumph—in readings, in lectures, in flights of fancy—in a kind of private war on dissolution" (406).

The poem was first published as "Of a Winter Evening" in the April 12, 1958, issue of the *Saturday Review* and was later collected as "Questioning Faces" in *In the Clearing.*

FURTHER READING

Parini, Jay. *Robert Frost: A Life.* New York: Holt, 1999.

"Quest of the Purple-Fringed, The" (1942)

The speaker goes on a quest for the purple-fringed orchid. He knows that the "day [i]s the day by every flower that blooms," because he "fe[els] the chill of the meadow underfoot, / But the sun overhead," but he needs confirmation that summer is done and that "fall might come and whirl of leaves." The state he finds the purple-fringed orchid in will tell him whether it is time for a season change.

The speaker goes for "miles and miles" in search of the orchid and eventually follows the path a fox has created to where he finds the "far-sought" flower beneath the alder tree. It is late in summer, so there is no bee to "disturb their perfect poise." The speaker kneels and gingerly puts the pale "boughs aside" to reveal what he has sought. He goes home having completed his quest and satisfied his curiosity, knowing with certainty that summer has come to its end.

The quest is a question about a season, and the speaker needs nature's response. The inquiry is not answered by the chill in the air alone. The orchid holds the only trustworthy answer. Frost, a great botanist, turns to nature, not an almanac, for his knowledge. The relation that is portrayed between the speaker and nature is one of dependability and of comfortable certainty. While nature is indifferent, its cycles are still regular and can be predicted.

George F. Bagby notes that the poem spans the poet's career; although it was first collected in *A Witness Tree,* it had been published in essentially its final form nearly 41 years earlier in the *Independent* and may have been composed as early as 1896. He also notes echoes of William Cullen Bryant's "To the Fringed Gentian" (1832) and Ralph Waldo Emerson's "Woodnotes" (1840) (148–149).

First published as "The Quest of the Orchis" in the June 27, 1901, issue of the *Independent,* the poem was later included in *A Witness Tree.*

FURTHER READING

Bagby, George F. *Frost and the Book of Nature.* Knoxville: University of Tennessee Press, 1993, 185–189.

Monteiro, George. "Frost's 'Quest of the Purple-Fringed,'" *English Language Notes* 13 (1976): 204–206.

Thomas, Ron. "Thoreau, William James, and Frost's 'Quest of the Purple-Fringed': A Contextual Reading," *American Literature* 60, no. 3 (October 1988): 433–450.

West, Michael. "Versifying Thoreau: Frost's 'The Quest of the Purple-Fringed' and 'Fire and Ice,'" *English Language Notes* 16 (1978): 40–47.

"Rabbit Hunter, The" (1942)

The rabbit hunter is depicted as not having a care in the world, of being detached from his actions and the harm he is about to bring. He is ready to bring bloodshed, lurking as he does through the "[g]hastly snow-white" alder swamps. His hound is filled with delight, his yelping, singing, and romping appearing demonic given the circumstances and the description of him as "one possessed." The hunter and hound are interesting death dealers; both are unable to comprehend the responsibility of killing, apparently by nature. The hunter does not reflect on his actions, and the speaker at the end reflects but is unable to understand.

Mark Richardson concludes, "This hunter merely executes some larger, more 'comprehensive' will that things should die; and like his hound, he is agency, not agent. This makes it seem as if even *human* violence were beyond our management, as if our destructions were subsidiary functions of some larger natural force" (161). There seems to be, however, some understanding on the speaker's part that while we have little control over death, we should have at least slightly more control over the death blows that are delivered by our own hands, if only we would exercise it.

The poem was first published in *A Witness Tree.*

FURTHER READING

Richardson, Mark. *The Ordeal of Robert Frost: The Poet and His Poetics.* Chicago, Ill.: University of Illinois Press, 1997, 160–161.

"Range-Finding" (1916)

The bullet, on its way to killing a human, disturbs nature in various ways. It rips through a "cobweb diamond-strung" and cuts a flower, causing it to "ben[d] double and h[a]ng." The spider has lost the butterfly it caught and was going to eat and sullenly "withdr[a]w[s]"; when the bullet ripped through the cobweb it took the butterfly with it. There is a connection between the flower beside the bird's nest, the flower and the butterfly, and the butterfly and the spider. Indeed, all of nature is connected, and everything we do, as we are a part of that natural world, affects nature.

The bullet might have met its target and killed a human being, but the central focus of this poem is not that, but the minutiae that has been affected by the malevolence. Taking one life always means affecting all those in the vicinity of that life, like ripples in a pond, whether on the human, animal, or insect level.

In human terms, the impact of death is far-reaching, far beyond the death of an individual to the recognition that the individual was someone's spouse, parent, sibling, friend, coworker, and so on. The emphasis is on the connections. Frost once said that statistics are curious things. A five percent loss for a doctor seems small, and the doctor can sleep at night. But in that five percent is someone's beloved, and to him or her that five percent can be 100 percent. The poem suggests such a recognition.

Snipers find range. "Range me," one sniper says to another, and the sniper is supposed to be able to use that range in order to kill the target with just one bullet. Here the word is used in two ways, to mean the range needed to meet a target and the far-reaching range of a particular event—that is, how far the ripple effect will go.

Robert Faggen notes that "The human world becomes peripheral to a drama of smaller scale observed by the naturalist's eye of the narrator, who leads the reader to see 'the battle' not only as human combat but also a pervasive struggle for survival that includes in its machinery flowers, flies, and spiders" (71). Faggen adds that "the poem in its own machinery of surprise leads the reader to sympathetic appeal to nature as innocent and suffering from the ramifications of human warfare" (71).

In various poems Frost makes use of the insect world as a way of demonstrating something about human affairs, such as in "Design," "A Considerable Speck," and "Departmental." The descriptions here, as always, are compassionate and moving and demonstrate Frost's keen eye for nature. But it is also important that notions of death are asymmetrical. That is, the spider ordinarily would have met its prey in its web and would have killed it, but clearly not in the same way that snipers kill. Nature's creatures, in the words of George Bernard Shaw, have "[n]o reason for destroying anything that [they do] not want to eat."

The poem was first published in *Mountain Interval.*

FURTHER READING

Abel, Darrel. "Robert Frost's 'Range Finding,'" *Colby Library Quarterly* 22, no. 4 (December 1986): 225–237.

Faggen, Robert. *Robert Frost and the Challenge of Darwin.* Ann Arbor: University of Michigan Press, 1997, 70–71.

Mansell, Darrel, Jr. "Frost's Range-Finding," *Explicator* 24 (1966): 63.

Rood, Karen Lane. "Robert Frost's Sentence Sounds: Wildness Opposing the Sonnet Form." In *Frost Centennial Essays II,* edited by Jac Tharpe, 196–210. Jackson: University Press of Mississippi, 1976.

"Record Stride, A" (1936)

The stride that breaks the record is the straddling of the country with one foot in either ocean. The poem is a meditation on two old shoes that now stand in the bedroom closet. They are "Old rivals of sagging leather." One stepped in the Atlantic at Montauk on Long Island while the owner retrieved his hat; the other was wetted in the Pacific at the Cliff House, a restaurant with a view of the ocean by an "extra-vagrant wave." The salt of each ocean can still be tasted on the leather, but the shoes are "past-active" like their owner. They ask him "a

thing or two / About who is too old to go walking, / With too much stress on the who," and it is clear the narrator has hung up his shoes as one does a hat. The speaker exalts in his memory of the "double adventure" he took with his grandchildren and holds that all, including his grandchildren, will forgive him for being "over-elated" about his shoes and the adventures he had in them. His shoes may have been retired, but not before he "measured the country / And got the United States stated."

The connections between human beings and the objects in our lives are examined. The shoes become a symbol for how much someone can accomplish in one lifetime. Lives can be lived in record strides. The poem is ironic when read biographically, as Frost, despite his many awards and honorary degrees, perpetually desired assurances that his life's work had been a record stride.

The poem was first published in the *Atlantic Monthly* in May 1936 and was later collected in *A Further Range* with the subtitle "The United States Stated."

"Reflex, A" (1962)

Frost pinpoints distinctions between intentional behavior, unintentional or reflexive behavior, and the general role of science. The reflex is supposed to refer both to natural processes that do not involve the presence or existence of "It[s]" and to the whole of thought coming back on itself through reflection.

Two "experiments" are juxtaposed. In the first, science sticks a pole down a "likely" or predictable hole, and it is bitten. In the second, science stabs and what it stabs grabs back. Then science concludes, "Qui vive" and wonders what should be believed about the experiments. *Qui vive* is a sentinel's challenge, meaning "long live who?", meant to determine a person's political sympathies. It also means alert or vigilant—on the lookout.

Science is intrusive with its sticking and stabbing, and the conclusions science draws can be vapid. Frost was enthralled by science, but he was also a skeptic and felt he knew science's limitations, that it could only go so far in its understanding of abstract ideals such as love, friendship, and so on. In a public reading, Frost once sarcastically pointed out that science cannot determine or measure how far one will go in friendship, what one is willing to put up with from a friend, or what one hopes to get out of a friendship.

The scientist is expected to draw grand conclusions from empty data, but the only thing the scientist can conclude here is that there is an "It." The kind of god that science wants to provide is nothing like a personable god or a monotheistic conception. It seems more like an impersonal force, and we cannot say anything more about it from a scientific perspective.

Who lives? Who goes there? and What are we to believe? are the questions asked. It is almost as if the scientists are speaking among themselves. They gain hints about nature, but if they wish to draw cosmic conclusions from those hints, they are going to be left with incomplete and flawed conclusions.

Science sticks its pole down a "likely hole," a hole we would ordinarily stick a pole in anyway, diminishing the role of science in our lives. There is also a lack of certainty in science. A likely hole is not necessarily the right one. Science works with assumptions and hypotheses that are uncertain to begin with. Frost's "rigmarole" is a sort of diatribe, his reflexive response to his reflection on science and its "reflexes."

The poem was first published in *In the Clearing*.

"Reluctance" (1913)

On a journey "out through the fields and the woods," in this last poem of *A Boy's Will*, the speaker finds knowledge and understanding but no comfort, as "[t]here are things that can never be the same" (as the initial gloss on the poem stated). Instead, this journey is a reminder of death and passing. The speaker observes the "dead leaves" lying "huddled and still," but he finds that an acceptance of such things is "a treason" to "the heart of man." Rather than going "with the drift of things," he points out that to "yield with a grace to

reason / And bow and accept the end" is not really in man's nature, whether it is the end of a "love or a season." The speaker is tortured by what he has learned "by the highway home," and he is not able to reach a contented resolution to the life-and-death conflicts he finds himself witnessing with this change of season. Still, while he may not reach a resolution that comforts him, he does come up with a question that satisfies. The poem ends rhetorically and on a somewhat positive note. The refusal to accept and go with the drift of things means not that the speaker surrenders or gives up but that he moves ahead, unwilling to just sit back and wait to "accept the end." But despite the upbeat note at the end of the poem, there is a reluctance, as the title indicates, to accept either the end or the journey. While the speaker may not give up, he is certainly troubled by all that he sees.

Jay Parini notes that this poem stemmed from a real journey that the youthful Frost took in November 1894 when he set off in a bleak mood, stimulated by his fear of losing his then girlfriend Elinor, for the Dismal Swamp, which runs along the Virginia and North Carolina border. His "symbolic journey" through this "frightening place, full of bogs and quicksand" came to an end "rather flatly" when, exhausted, he hitched a ride out of the bog with duck hunters (Parini, 49–50). Perhaps this accounts for the lack of acceptance in "Reluctance."

The poem was first published on November 7, 1912, in the *Youth's Companion* and was collected the following year in *A Boy's Will*.

FURTHER READING

Parini, Jay. *Robert Frost: A Life.* New York: Holt, 1999.

"Remarks on Receiving the Gold Medal" (1939)

On January 18, 1939, Frost received the gold medal from the National Institute of Arts and Letters in recognition of his poetry. In his address he speaks about the greatest reward of all: self-esteem. "The sensible and healthy live somewhere between self-approval and the approval of society," he finds. He criticizes what he calls the "stuffed shirt" but what might be called the sellout: "He cares not what he thinks of himself so long as the world continues to think well of him." An artist must often "rely too heavily on self-appraisal for comfort," he says, as it is not often accorded him by society. And if, like Frost, "[f]or twenty years the world neglected him; then for twenty years it entreated him kindly," then he "has to take the responsibility of deciding when the world was wrong." He quotes Thomas William Parsons's (1819–92) "On a Bust of Dante": "O Time whose verdicts mock our own / The only righteous judge art thou" to demonstrate that the artist "can't help wishing there was some third more disinterested party such as God or Time to give absolute judgment."

Frost contrasts the artist with the scientist and the engineer, both of whom have concrete ways of identifying whether they are "good without being told." The artist has "no such recourse of certainty at all." Instead, he must hope that he has somehow "fitted into the nature of people." Frost hopes that by receiving the medal he has "in some small way [fitted] at least into the nature of Americans—into their affections," as he surely had.

"Revelation" (1913)

"Revelation" shares similarities to "The Lockless Door" and "A Mood Apart," where the poet is also concerned with boundaries and protection, and with notions of "inside" and "outside." In this poem "[w]e make ourselves a place apart" and hide "[b]ehind light words" until someone can really understand us and "find us out." But while we are playing the game, our heart is "agitated," as we are withholding somewhat reluctantly and unhappily. The words we use "tease" and "flout" the other; they are not only indirect but also seem to mock. In the third stanza, the poem goes on to say that we only speak "literal[ly]" when we want to gain the understanding of a friend; otherwise, we remain coy and seductive through subtleties.

Frost suggests that it is a pity that we should have to speak literally in order to be found out; he believes we should be able to speak metaphorically, as he so often does. Even though we can hide ourselves from other people through metaphor, we must eventually provide some more direct clues or answers about ourselves if we are to be "found." The poem also meditates on the difference between hiding ourselves from people generally and revealing ourselves to a particular someone. It is when we reveal ourselves to a particular someone that revelation can come for the other person and for us and can also act as a conduit for understanding through the use of future metaphors.

The poem expands the childhood game of hide-and-seek to a game played by adults not with their bodies but with their emotions, minds, and language. The poem is not about playing hide-and-seek with "God afar" but about playing it with oneself or with a friend. In the end the poem cautions not to hide too well, lest no one finds and no one seeks. Those who hide "too well away / Must speak and tell us where they are" or they will be forgotten.

The poem was first published in *A Boy's Will*. *See also* "ALL REVELATION."

FURTHER READING

Perrine, Laurence. "Frost's 'Revelation,'" *Explicator* 42, no. 1 (Fall 1983): 36–38.

"Riders" (1928)

"The surest thing" is that "we are riders, / And though none too successful at it, guiders." We ride the land and the tide and the air of this earth, but we are not particularly good at guiding others or ourselves. Frost provides an analogy between human existence and being mounted on a horse. What sort of riders we are becomes clearer as the poem unfolds.

Our "mystery of birth" is described as being "mounted bareback on the earth." We are infants with our "small fist[s] buried in the bushy hide" of the earth, the dirt and grass clumped between our fingers. Our "wildest mount" is the headless horse we ride. There are other mounts, not all headless, but those will never be as wild as the first mount of existence. That one is a headless horse, metaphorically, because we cannot see where we are going. The horse is untamed and unbridled; our existence is the wildest ride. And though we are sometimes run off, and coaxing and flattery has not made the horse tame, there are other ideas that we can try for steering our course. We are not good guiders because we cannot know where we are going, but we are fierce riders holding on with a fist buried in the hide from the moment of birth. And we persist, careening through space, despite the inevitability that we will eventually be bucked off. Katherine Kearns writes, "The acknowledged truth is simple—just as a good poet knows how far to ride and how to control his metaphors, so are men born to ride the maverick earth and little by little to tame it" (121).

The poem represents one of Frost's most optimistic attitudes toward humanity. Our ability to ride is certain and our guiding abilities can be improved. Our heads and our ideas are the focus of the optimism, even though we are forever riding a headless horse, for two reasons: First, there are always new ideas to discover and new things to explore, and second, we are the ones who will do the discovering. We become responsible for our own knowledge, as well as our ignorance.

In a sense, the horse does not need a head, as we provide the course anyway; we guide the unbridled with our intellect.

The poem was first published in *West-Running Brook*.

FURTHER READING

Kearns, Katherine. *Robert Frost and a Poetics of Appetite*. Cambridge: Cambridge University Press, 1994, 121–123.

"Road Not Taken, The"
(1916)

After being named poet laureate in 1997, Robert Pinsky took a year-long poll to determine who was America's favorite poet. With more than 18,000 votes cast, from participants aged five to 97, Frost came out on top. When participants were asked which poems they most liked to read, they most often cited "The Road Not Taken" and "Stopping by Woods on a Snowy Evening."

One of Frost's best-known poems, opening his third book, *Mountain Interval*, "The Road Not Taken" was first published in the August 1915 issue of the *Atlantic Monthly*. While Pinsky's poll demonstrates the poem's broad appeal, that appeal is at least partly due to its being most often read by people who do not read it closely enough to discover its complexities or who quickly dismiss those complexities in favor of the trite paraphrases that come to mind when people are asked what the poem might be "about." Many attempt answers such as "taking a different road from that of the masses" or "being an individual" or "finding one's own road in life." And while none of these answers would be altogether incorrect, they all reduce the subtle complexities of the poem to platitudes.

Part of what accounts for the popularity of "The Road Not Taken" is that Frost, until the latter half of the twentieth century, was viewed as a nature poet, in the purest NEW ENGLAND sense. But beginning with Randall Jarrell and continuing through Lionel Trilling, Roberts W. French, and others, the dark side of Frost or the "other" Frost, as Jarrell phrased it, has been given much attention. It has become clear that to know Frost is to apprehend the darkness in his poems as well as the light, and this darkness is evident in "The Road Not Taken" when it is read closely.

There is some biographical support for a cursory reading of the poem. Frost wrote a portion of the poem while in Gloucestershire, ENGLAND. Lawrance Thompson writes that Frost had said to his friend Edward Thomas after "one of their best flower-gathering walks" that "No matter which road you take, you'll always sigh, and wish you'd taken another" (88). When Frost completed the poem, he sent a copy to Thomas as a letter, without comment. Thomas called the poem "staggering" in his response, explaining that "the word 'staggering' . . . did no more than express (or conceal) the fact that the simple words and unemphatic rhythms were not such as [he] was accustomed to expect great things, things [he] like[d], from." Thomas said it "staggered [him] to think that perhaps [he] had always missed what made poetry poetry if it was here. [He] wanted to think it was here" (Spencer, 62).

The poem begins, "Two roads diverged in a yellow wood." The speaker is out for an autumn walk and is confronted with two paths. He cannot take both, so he looks down one as far as he can to where it "ben[ds] in the undergrowth," hoping to determine which road might be better to take. He decides on "the other," which is described as just as "fair" and as "grassy and wanting wear." The speaker imagines the other road might have the "better claim" on him, as it has not been often traveled.

The first contradiction of this seemingly simple poem occurs in the latter half of stanza two, when the speaker reveals that "Though as for that the passing there / Had worn them really about the same." The roads, then, are not worn differently, as the speaker first suggests; rather, they have both been traveled (or not), and the grass of both has either been beaten down or untouched. Just how "worn" they are is unclear. In fact, stanza three reveals that "both that morning equally lay / In leaves no step had trodden black." At this point, the first image of a grassy path is juxtaposed with a path of fresh leaves that has not yet been blackened by steps. That each path earlier that day "equally lay" suggests that the paths themselves have always been "equal," with neither more worn than the other. That morning neither path had been traveled, making the chronology of the poem somehow miss a step. If they were both untouched that morning, then there is a hint that at least one is no longer untouched. Frost will confirm this at the end of the poem.

The traveler decides that he will keep one road for another day, but "knowing how way leads on to way" is aware that one decision leads to another and another and that he will never be faced with this same decision again. Because of this awareness, he doubts that he will "ever come back." He imagines that some day he will tell this story with a "sigh," whether of regret or satisfaction is unclear.

The choice of "sigh" establishes the uncertainty of interpretations. Will he be disappointed that he could not take both roads, disappointed in the road he took, or altogether satisfied?

Although the traveler took the road "less traveled by," it remains unclear at the end of the poem which one that was. He claims it "has made all the difference," but it is clear that either road would have made all the difference. In the end the difference appears to have nothing to do with which road is chosen, as each would have had an impact on the traveler's life. Also, the question of equality has little to do with the roads themselves. The speaker knows he will sigh, perhaps because he cannot make all decisions or do all things, and that there are limitations to his choices, but he will not know what sort of sigh he will emit until he reaches the end of this road, his road.

The poem is not just about individuality, as one might suppose; instead it is about an individual's choices and experiences. While the road is often read as the focus of the poem, it is the speaker's perspective that is at its center. The complexities lie in how he views the roads. At first one seems grassy and lacking wear, but then the speaker catches himself and says that in actuality they were worn essentially the same. He could not see past the undergrowth of one, "Though as for that the passing there / Had worn them really about the same." Whether fresh or trodden, the roads are now equal. Either they are equally configured or it is not they that are equal but the possibility that they hold for travel that is equal. After all, any value placed on one road over the other has only to do with the speaker's recollection and interpretation.

The road is valuable because the traveler took it; it has no value in and of itself. And yet the title is about a road that was not taken. It could be about the road that, prior to his taking it, had not been taken. But if the sigh at the end of the poem is one of regret, or simply weariness, then perhaps the title is about the road the speaker did not choose, rather than about the one he took. The question remains whether it is a sigh over the road that had not been taken before he took it or over the road he did not take. This, like all else in the poem, is intentionally ambiguous.

The poem is celebrated at least partly because it can be easily reduced to an adage, but it is among Frost's best, most riveting, and most complex. It is an epic work in its ambiguity and seeming simplicity. The roads do not intertwine, but the language does until the reader is lost in that autumn yellow wood, wondering if neither road was traveled or if both were. The "I" of "I took the one less traveled by" makes all the difference, as the repetition of the first person throughout emphasizes.

The poem moves from a story about a walk in autumn to a story about the traveler himself. Soon it is not about the season or the road. Frost once denied being a nature poet, saying that he must not be one since he had written only two poems without a human being in them, and this is a particularly important point to keep in mind in the reading of this poem.

The human condition is that we can travel only one road at a time. What makes all the difference in the end, we are left to ponder. And what difference it makes (to us, to nature, to the universe), we are also left to wonder. Frost purposely leaves many of the questions raised by the poem unanswered. Perhaps the sigh most of all indicates that it is not about taking both roads or about which road was taken but about having to choose only one. We will always sigh that we cannot take both roads, but the fact that we make the choice to do something at all is of ultimate importance. The repetition of "Two roads diverged" is the reminder of the opportunity to decide and to make a choice. As Mark Richardson writes, "Our paths unfold themselves to us as we go. We realize our destination only when we arrive at it, though all along we were driven toward it by purposes we may rightly claim, in retrospect, as our own" (182).

A final consideration is the choice of the word "road." Certainly a road might be defined as a course or a path, but it is also most often thought of as a public thoroughfare. That Frost selected "road" over "path" seems to complicate even further the reading of the poem. One imagines a road well traveled, and a path seldom traveled. Perhaps this is further support for reading the roads as having been equally worn to all but the speaker. It is "ages and ages hence," and we can never know what made all the difference.

FURTHER READING

Faggen, Robert. *Robert Frost and the Challenge of Darwin.* Ann Arbor: University of Michigan Press, 1997, 269–273.

Finger, Larry. "Frost's Reading of 'The Road Not Taken,'" *Robert Frost Review* (Fall 1997): 73–76.

Fleissner, R. F. "Whose 'Road Less Traveled By'? Frost's Intent Once Again," *Robert Frost Review* (Fall 1999): 22–26.

Fowler, James. "Frost: The Poem Mistaken," *Publications of the Arkansas Philological Association* 23, no. 1 (Spring 1997): 41–47.

French, Roberts W. "Robert Frost and the Darkness of Nature." In *Critical Essays on Robert Frost*, edited by Philip L. Gerber, 155–162. Boston: G. K. Hall, 1982.

George, William. "Frost's 'The Road Not Taken,'" *Explicator* 49, no. 4 (Summer 1991): 230–232.

Hornedo, Florentino H. "All the Difference: Frost's 'The Road Not Taken,'" *Unitas: A Quarterly for the Arts and Sciences* 75, no. 3 (September 2002): 490–495.

Jarrell, Randall. "The 'Other' Frost." In *Poetry and the Age*, 28. New York: Vintage, 1955.

Ketterer, David. "The Letter 'Y' in The Road Not Taken,'" *Robert Frost Review* (Fall 1997): 77–78.

Micelli, Pauline. "Frost Misread: The Road Not Taken," *Occident* 103, no. 1 (1990): 275–278.

Richardson, Mark. *The Ordeal of Robert Frost: The Poet and His Poetics.* Chicago, Ill.: University of Illinois Press, 1997, 181–183.

Savoie, John. "A Poet's Quarrel: Jamesian Pragmatism and Frost's 'Road not Taken,'" *New England Quarterly* 77, no. 1 (March 2004): 5–24.

Spencer, Matthew. *Elected Friends: Robert Frost and Edward Thomas to One Another.* New York: Handsel, 2003.

Timmerman, John H. *Robert Frost: The Ethics of Ambiguity.* Lewisburg, Pa.: Bucknell University Press, 2002, 69–73.

Thompson, Lawrance. *Robert Frost: The Years of Triumph, 1915–1938.* New York: Holt, Rinehart and Winston, 1970.

Trilling, Lionel. "A Speech on Robert Frost: A Cultural Episode," *Partisan Review* 26 (1959): 445–452.

"Roadside Stand, A" (1936)

"A Roadside Stand" was first published in the June 1936 issue of the *Atlantic Monthly* before being collected in *A Further Range* with the subtitle "On Being Put out of Our Misery." Frost at one time considered the title "Euthanasia" for the poem (Thompson, 439).

"A Roadside Stand" is another quarrel over modernization. Frost resists contemporary encroachment here as he does in other poems, such as "Lines Written in Dejection on the Eve of Great Success" (1962) about the United States space program or "The Line-Gang" about the telephone.

The roadside stand is a sad symbol of a past that is fading rapidly. As it is depicted, it is also evidence of a decline in agricultural prosperity. The roadside farm stand is characterized as a person selling berries, almost pleading with the people who drive by to make a purchase. The poem begins with the "little new shed" and traffic speeding by. The folks at the stand are hopeful that some "of the cash, whose flow supports / The flower of cities from sinking and withering faint" will be spent on the goods at the stand. The comparison of fueling the growth of a city to keeping a flower from withering is apt, as it demonstrates that the speaker, a farmer, draws analogies to nature, not industry, to make his points.

The speaker goes on to describe the "false alarms," when people simply use the pullout to turn their car around, ask for directions, or ask to buy a gallon of gas, even though there is no gas for sale. The "wooden quarts" contain only wild berries and "crook-necked golden squash with silver warts."

The "polished traffic" of nonresidents only minimally and rather dismissively notices the unrefined stand signs, "with N turned wrong and S turned wrong," and views them as marring the otherwise pastoral landscape. The "squeal of brakes" and the "plow[ed] up grass" from city folk who have taken a wrong turn and who use the yard "to back and turn around" also cause the people at the stand to be annoyed by the disruptions and "marring" of their landscape that does not bring sales. The loss of sales, despite how insignificant the purchases may be to city folk, has a significant impact on a farmer's way of life. And the question whether it is the stand or the traffic that mars the landscape highlights the difference in perspective between the city and the country people.

The folks "far from the city" are forced to become beggars in this contrast between city and rural life, because they are made to "ask for some city money to feel in hand." Those responsible for this decline in a farmer's lifestyle are identified as the "party in power," which "is said to be keeping from [them]" the "moving pictures' promise," the promise of affluence and glamour as portrayed by Hollywood. (*See also* "PROVIDE, PROVIDE.")

In the second stanza the speaker bemoans that people are going to live in larger and larger places, places that are "in villages next to theater and store." He imagines the consequences of corralling people in such a way, arguing that it will make everyone lazy because people will not have to think for themselves. Again, the responsible party is identified satirically: the "good-doers" (not do-gooders) and "beneficent beasts of prey."

The city is the source of financial stability, and the country is largely dependent on the city folk to survive. This dependence causes, in the last stanza, significant misery and disappointment. The speaker can "hardly bear / The thought of so much childish longing in vain" for a car to stop. He concludes that in "the country scale of gain, / The requisite lift of spirit has never been found" and resolves that he would be relieved to "put these people at one stroke out of their pain," hence the consideration of "Euthanasia" as a title. Then the speaker catches himself and wonders what it would be like if someone should choose to do the same to him and "offer to put [him] gently out of [his] pain."

Several interpretations of these last lines present themselves. One is that the speaker is imagining the opposite possibility of putting city folk out of their pain. Another reading might be that the speaker, in his empathy with the country folk and their hardships, identifies with these people, seeing himself as the old world that will long be passed by and forgotten after the changing of the guard. The speaker might realize that the world sees him as behind the times, living out the rest of his days in simply trying to achieve the most basic type of functioning in an increasingly complex world. Preceding "Departmental" in *A Further Range*, the poem could also be read as a criticism of socialism, given its description of apartment houses and political promises that are not kept.

For other contrasts between city and country life, *see* COUNTRY VERSUS CITY, as well as "BUILD SOIL—A POLITICAL PASTORAL," "The Code," and "An UNSTAMPED LETTER IN OUR RURAL LETTER BOX."

FURTHER READING

Faggen, Robert. *Robert Frost and the Challenge of Darwin.* Ann Arbor: University of Michigan Press, 1997, 106.

Thompson, Lawrance. *Robert Frost: The Years of Triumph: 1915–1938.* New York: Holt, 1970.

"Rogers Group, A" (1947)

American sculptor John Rogers (1829–1904) was known for his mass-produced small sculptures such as *Checkers Up at the Farm* and *The Slave Auction,* both created in 1859. In this poem the "young and unassuming" family is so poignantly positioned that they appear to the speaker to be a Rogers sculpture.

A family is waiting for a trolley, probably in a city such as SAN FRANCISCO, where Frost was born. They are weighed down by armfuls of babies and baggage and are clearly out-of-towners. Their youth and innocence and the burdens of their lives, as indicated by their worn appearance and their encumbrances, make them seem vulnerable when contrasted with a bustling city of "clanging" trolleys. A further indication of just how far out of their element they are is that they are waiting for their ride on the wrong corner. They are in need of guidance and assistance, yet no one has bothered to point out to them their error or to aid them in making what would be a laborious move of the luggage from one side of the street to the other. There

is no aid to the travelers, as no one is "touched" besides the speaker, despite the "Rogers Group they ma[k]e."

The poem is simple, but the observation has great implications. There is clearly a mistrust of city dwellers who distance themselves from one another so much that there is no communal concern for the well-being of others, just as people have ignored the lost travelers in this poem as they might pass by a sculpture. The argument is that the distancing has implications for the future of humanity. But there is also the insinuation that either art has limitations in its ability to affect human behavior or it is egregiously ignored, which in some ways, given the poetic form of such reflection, has even greater implications. Indifference to art is not only a dismissal of individual human beings but a dismissal of the greatness to which humanity can aspire.

The poem was first published in the *Atlantic Monthly* in December 1946 and was later collected in *Steeple Bush.*

"Romantic Chasm, A" (1948)

"A Romantic Chasm" was the preface to a British edition of *A Masque of Reason* (1948). The romantic chasm is a metaphor for the sea that separates the United States from its mother country, though Frost wonders if it is "anything more than a 'romantic chasm' of poetry and slang." He begins by reminding his readers that having a book published in London in 1948 is not quite the same as having his first book of poetry ever, *A Boy's Will,* published in 1913. He was received by the British before he was received by his native United States. In this preface, however, his chief concern is with the "national differences" of the American and English languages.

Frost writes that he "would go to any length short of idolatry to keep Great Britain within speaking, or at least shouting, distance of America in the trying times seen ahead." He would like for there to be a "limited few" words in both languages that could be agreed on as sharing the same meaning. "It is beyond idealism of mine to think of closing the gulf so tight," he says. At the same time, he "should hate to miss the chance for exotic charm [his] distance overseas might lend [him]."

Frost speculates as to what would happen should the American language get as far away from his American vernacular poetry as current English has from the language of the 14th-century poet Geoffrey Chaucer. He muses that he would "be raised to the rank of having to be annotated," needing a "glossary" and to be "studied."

Frost concludes by speaking of metaphor, which was central to any discussion he had of poetry. He tells of the "estrangement in language" being "due to the very word-shift by metaphor." A "word-drift" is a "chain of word-shifts all in one direction," he says humorously, and while he is speaking, and even questioning, the accessibility of his American vernacular to foreign ears, he encourages the "risk," saying it is "in the play" and that the "pride" of his readers will be "in what [they] dare to take liberties with."

Frost is grandiose in his closing, suggesting that the "future of the world may depend on [Britain and America] keeping in practice with each other's quips and figures." The preface is bold and at times even cocksure. Frost attempts to close the gulf, because if his work is to be received well he must, but his plea seems overstated.

"Rose Family, The" (1928)

The opening lines to "The Rose Family" are reminiscent of Gertrude Stein's "Rose is a rose is a rose" from the 1913 poem "Sacred Emily." Frost writes that a "rose is a rose, / And was always a rose." He then goes on to explain that the "theory now" is that it is not only the rose that is a rose, but the apple and pear and plum, too. He cannot imagine what else will be "prove[n] a rose." The poem concludes that "You, of course, are a rose—But were always a rose."

Given the title, the poem seems to be a comment on the attempt of science to deduce and, in this instance, to group things in a way that is unfamiliar and foreign and then to assume a broad application of those deductions. A "family" is one

of the scientific classifications for a category of related organisms, ranking below an order and above a genus, so the title indicates such a classification. But the poet is also demonstrating that the classification of a rose into a family is irrelevant to what poets and other authors do with it. Even if science does tell us that, according to a particular theory, the rose should be grouped with apples and pears, it does not say anything about the significance of the rose as a symbol in art. The rose can be a signifier, a symbol for something more, regardless of its scientific classification, and it is foolish to think that poetry and literature could be affected by or reduced to scientific classifications. In the closing lines the speaker takes back the literary metaphor, and as Robert Faggen writes, "evokes the poetic family lines in Shakespeare, Stein, and [Edna St. Vincent] Millay that attempt to assert the eternal essence of the rose as a sign of love" (204). In the end, Frost essentially reaffirms and restates Shakespeare's lines from *Romeo and Juliet,* "That which we call a rose / By any other name would smell as sweet" (II.ii.1–2). These are also echoes of William Blake's "The Sick Rose."

"The Rose Family" was first published in July 1927 in both the *Yale Review* and the *London Mercury* and was later collected in *West-Running Brook.*

FURTHER READING

Collins, Michael J. "Poetry and Empiricism: The Example of Three Poems," *Crux: A Journal on the Teaching of English* 16, no. 1 (January 1982): 21–27.

Faggen, Robert. *Robert Frost and the Challenge of Darwin.* Ann Arbor: University of Michigan Press, 1997, 204.

Fleissner, R. F. "Sub Rosa: Frost's 'Five-Petaled' Flower," *Colby Literary Quarterly* 20, no. 4 (December 1984): 206–224.

Perrine, Laurence. "Frost's 'The Rose Family,'" *Explicator* 26 (1968): 43.

"Rose Pogonias" (1913)

The speaker and his companion happen upon a small "saturated meadow" that sparkles like a jewel in the sun. The air is "stifling sweet," smelling of many flowers. In the ring of the meadow there appear to be a thousand orchises, so many that every other spear of grass seems to be an orchid. The image is magical, a description of a fairyland. The two bow down in the summer's heat to pick a few of the flowers "where none could miss them." The flowers are described as being "tipped with wings of color," an image suggestive of Emily Dickinson.

The experience is almost religious. The speaker and his companion are worshipful and "rais[e] a simple prayer" that the meadow will be forgotten and therefore the grass and, more important, the orchises will not be mowed down. Their hope is that the mower will miss the spot "[w]hile so confused with flowers," mistaking it for a garden rather than a meadow, and forget it at least until the flowers have faded on their own. As in "An Exposed Nest," the hope is never shown to be answered, since we all inevitably "[turn] to other things."

The poem is one of Frost's most engaging in his first book, *A Boy's Will*, because of the sheer rapture of its language and tone. Other poems in which Frost is concerned with mowing are "The Last Mowing," "A Late Walk," and "Mowing."

FURTHER READING

Richardson, Mark. *The Ordeal of Robert Frost: The Poet and His Poetics*. Chicago, Ill.: University of Illinois Press, 1997, 141–142.

"Runaway, The" (1923)

"The Runaway" is about a young Morgan colt who is startled and fearful of the falling snow. It attempts to run away from the snow, making "miniature thunder" as it goes. It does not yet know that the snow will follow wherever it goes. The speaker attributes the colt's innocence to its not being "winter-broken." It is not able to have fun with the snow because it does not realize that it will survive the snow and that the snow will not last.

"The Runaway" has something in common with the "The Onset." Without the ability to reflect and communicate, the colt's mother is unable to prepare the colt for the snow and to tell it "Sakes, / It's only weather" to ease its fears. The poem closes with a criticism of "[w]hoever it is that leaves him out so late," suggesting that humans have a responsibility toward animals who are not able to care for their young. The speaker does not take on the responsibility himself, however. He says that someone "[o]ught to be told to come and take him in," but it is clear that no one will be told. The responsibility toward animals is a boundary an outsider cannot overstep.

Runaway is a term generally reserved for children who, through some sort of rift with their parents or caretakers, attempt to make it on their own. Children want to run away when they do not understand certain things or do not receive what they want. It is usually based on a misunderstanding about what is really going on, as it is here. Applying such a human term to the colt is a way of projecting the speaker's own understanding of the snow. His first reaction is also likely to be his hair standing up and his shuddering in an effort "to throw off" the snow, but his knowledge that spring will come keeps him from despair.

The poem was first published in the *Amherst Monthly* in June 1918 and was later collected in *New Hampshire*.

FURTHER READING

Charney, Maurice. "Robert Frost's Conversational Style," *Connotations: A Journal for Critical Debate* 10, no. 2–3 (2000–2001): 147–159.

"Sand Dunes" (1928)

"Sand Dunes" reflects some of the attitudes of the sonnet "Once by the Pacific," where the power of the sea is depicted as an ominous force. Here, following the sea waves, "[r]ise others vaster yet," the waves of land, sand dunes that are "brown and dry." The sea comes to the "fisher town" to "bury in solid sand" the men that "she could not drown" at sea, suggesting that the ocean's destiny is to destroy man any way it can. The sea is depicted as not only powerful but malevolent.

Despite the sea's "intention," its designs can be botched. There is a limitation to its power because it has limited "knowledge." It may know "cove and cape," but the speaker argues that "she does not know mankind" if she hopes by any means to "cut off mind," that is, if she thinks she can ignore or destroy people's intellectual attributes. The poem closes with the speaker resolving that the sea can sink ships and can even "sink" huts on land, but it will not sink humankind. Instead, we will be made "more free to think / For the one more cast-off shell."

This freeing of the human mind is reminiscent of Frost's "Etherealizing," in which we "take our daily tide baths" from the sea "smooth and rough." Rather than viewing this "freeing" as positive, in "Etherealizing" Frost turns dualism on its head by questioning whether the mind can be at all "ethereal" and thereby "freed" after our deaths or whether when our "flesh has been slough[ed]" and our limbs "atrophied," there will be anything remaining that matters. Given all the "mortal stuff" "Etherealizing" graphically lays out, the poem seems to be asking, "Do you really think that 'we,' as we know ourselves, are going to be there when all that's left of our physical bodies is 'blobs of brain'"?

While "Sand Dunes" is another example of Frost's awe at the power and threat of the ocean, it ends with man overcoming. The threat is not all-encompassing; humanity will prevail. The sea can send its waves, but she can take only so much of the land. And when she hurls her sand dunes at us in an attempt to bury "in solid sand" those she was unable to drown, we will simply retreat further. We leave empty shells for her, "a ship to sink" or a "hut."

George F. Bagby calls this a poem where the "unnatural impulse to resist nature is not only asserted but acted out" (106). He goes on to say that "the assault of the fact clearly does not oppress the human mind or spirit but strikes a Promethean spark of self-assertiveness from it" (107). When Frost writes of the sea's hoping to "cut off mind" and how men will be "free to think," the focus on mind and thinking is a way of expressing how the ability to reason is what enables us to prevail even against so powerful a force as the sea. We can out-

wit her. She has might but we have mind. She can take our "shells," but she cannot take us. The sand dunes are simply the beginning of land's protection from the sea.

The poem was first published in the December 15, 1926, issue of the *New Republic* and was later collected in *West-Running Brook*.

FURTHER READING

Bagby, George F. *Frost and the Book of Nature.* Knoxville: University of Tennessee Press, 1993.

Brogunier, Joseph. "Walking My Dog in 'Sand Dunes,'" *Journal of Modern Literature* 16, no. 4 (Spring 1990): 648–650.

D'Avanzo, Mario L. "Frost's 'Sand Dunes' and Thoreau's Cape Code," *Notes on Contemporary Literature* 10, no. 5 (1980): 2–4.

"Secret Sits, The" (1942)

This couplet is one of the poems encountered on the Robert Frost Trail in Ripton, Vermont. It is on a signpost near a pond, and the setting supports both a tranquil and a haunting interpretation. The allusion is to the children's game of ring-around-the-rosy, from the nursery rhyme. The couplet was first published as "Ring Around" in the April 1936 issue of *Poetry* as part of "Ten Mills" and was later collected in the section "Quantula" in *A Witness Tree*. Consisting of pithy poems, the "Quantula" grouping suggests that Frost intended them to be together because of their small "quantity" and presumed force. (In Latin, *quantula* means "How little?" or "How small?") The poem may refer to a children's game, but the game being played is very much adult.

"We dance round in a ring and suppose," as children do, but we do not know much more than they, despite our greater intellectual capacity. The secret at the center of things is not only unknown to us but apparently unknowable. We know little despite our "dancing." We live our lives and theorize as we go round and round, but the full understanding seems always to be just beyond us. We are holding hands in a circle, but the secret lies in the center, unreachable to hands that are held out to one another rather than toward the secret.

The secret is presented as powerful and all-knowing. The emphasis placed on it also implies that it is the greatest of all: perhaps the meaning or source of life. And the capitalization of the word makes the secret a proper noun, but it is not quite personified. Is the secret ultimate truth? Meaning? Science (or its limitations)? An Almighty?

While the poem argues that we will in our ignorance continue to dance round in a circle, unable to go directly to the source to seek answers, it also advances the notion that there is an answer to be found. That makes this one of the few poems in which Frost took something of a believer's stance rather than an agnostic one. People are cast as children who know little when in the presence of this secret, and their relationship to the secret resembles the traditional one between human beings and the Christian God. In this way the poem seems to echo the proverb that "We are all God's children."

Other more indirect interpretations also present themselves. Legend has it that the game of ring-around-the-rosy has a connection to the Black Plague (1347–50), which killed roughly one-third of Europe's population. While this connection is folklore, it offers a horrifying twist on what seems to children like a harmless game and suggests a much darker interpretation of the poem. The secret in this sense would be viewed as demonic in its withholding of information. It does not tell even though it can. In this case, we are not really players after all, since we cannot play a game when we do not know the rules. *See* NATURE.

"Self-Seeker, The" (1914)

"The Self-Seeker" is largely a dialogue between the "The Broken One," who remains unnamed, and his friend Willis. It opens with The Broken One saying that he did not want Willis to visit today because there is a lawyer coming and he is going to "sell [his] soul, or, rather, feet." The description is an attempt at humor in the face of misery. The Broken One jokingly says that he is selling his feet as a pair

for $500. He has injured his legs in a mill accident, and he will sign paperwork this day to settle the case. Willis responds that his feet nearly are his soul, and we learn later what he means. His feet are not his soul, but they can take him to what is: "[Y]ours are no common feet," he says. Willis insists that if The Broken One is going to sell his soul to the "devil," he is going to stick around and see it happen.

The speaker thinks that Willis is going to help The Broken One "drive a better bargain," but Willis is unconvinced about the deal. He is not certain that The Broken One will ever walk again, nor is he convinced that the settlement is adequate compensation for the loss. The Broken One says the doctor thinks he will "hobble." Willis argues that there are "[s]o many miles you might have walked you won't walk" and that he has not yet "run [his] forty orchids down." There is disappointment and empathy in his tone. The Broken One is a great lover of orchids and apparently spends his leisure time trying to find, identify, and catalog them. The loss of his legs is not only a loss of what he can do with them to make a living; the even greater loss is that it will interfere with the fulfillment of his orchid aspirations.

The Broken One likens himself to a "starfish laid out with rigid points." He is afraid even to look at his legs. Throughout the conversation, Willis remains unconvinced that the settlement is necessary. He wonders if it is all in The Broken One's head and if it is not that he cannot walk but that he will not. It is here that we learn a bit more about how The Broken One lost the use of his legs.

As always in Frost the damage was done through work, not play, similar to the poor boy in "Out, Out—," who not only loses his hand to the saw but his life. Here the "shaft had [the speaker] by the coat" in the wheel-pit, and his "legs got their knocks against the ceiling." The leather belt of the machine is personified in their discussion, as is the buzz saw in "Out, Out—"; the machine had it in for The Broken One. Malicious intent on the part of an object is not unfamiliar in Frost. The Broken One says that the belt did not "love [him] much" because of the work he made it do, likening his own work to Ben Franklin's with electricity and a "kite-string." He says, "[t]hat day a woman couldn't coax him [the belt] off." The speaker becomes romantic about his mill work, calling the sounds of the buzz saws music and the work his life. Willis says with despondent practicality, "[w]hen it's not our death." The comment is dismissed: "What we live by we die by," The Broken One says. Here it is also mentioned that The Broken One boards with a Mrs. Corbin. He is a blue-collar worker with little goods or money to show for the work he has done. He is selling his feet because he must, because he has to "take what [he] can get."

Willis remains unconvinced about the speaker's decision. "But your flowers, man, you're selling out your flowers," he says desperately; "What about your flora of the valley?" But The Broken One is not shaken; he does not want to fight. Instead he wants to be "settled" in his life, to "know the worst, / Or best" and get on with it.

Willis is concerned The Broken One will be giving up his soul, his love of nature. In his inability to walk, he will be unable to gain pleasure from all the flowers for the "next forty summers" by continuing his orchid quest. The Broken One is consistent in his decision, showing no vulnerability. He insists that even his passion for flowers has its price—that is, no price, since "they never earned [him] so much as one cent."

Their conversation is interrupted by the lawyer ringing the doorbell. The big-city Boston lawyer soon appears, accompanied by a shy young girl named Anne whose hands are held behind her back. Soon Anne and The Broken One engage in a discussion about flowers. The girl has hidden in her hands two ram's horns orchids. The Broken One is pleased that she did not pick all of those she saw and left the "rest for seed." He is her teacher, she his study.

Anne will, if the Broken One does not regain the use of his legs, do his "scouting in the field" for flowers. He has trained her not to gather bouquets, but always to leave some flowers for reproduction. The lawyer is in a hurry and urges The Broken One to sign the documents he has brought without reading them. He explains that he stopped by the mill on the way and feels that it would be "ill-advised" to push for more than the $500, but Willis thinks it

is a swindle, saying that a "thousand wouldn't be a cent too much" and continuing to advise The Broken One against the signing of the papers.

The poem ends in heartbreak. The Broken One believes that Willis wants him to be paid for the flowers, but he knows that the lawyer does not know what that means. Willis wanted him to be compensated for all of his losses, not only the loss of his legs, but the loss of where those legs could have taken him. His love of botany makes the flowers his greatest loss. The Broken One finally reveals his emotions truthfully in the final line, when he is at last alone, by flinging his arms around his face. He is truly broken now, though throughout he resisted such a description.

"The Self-Seeker" is not one of Frost's finer narrative poems, but it does highlight many of the concerns found in some of his other, better poems. Frost the botanist is revealed here in his discussion of the ram's horn, the yellow lady's slipper, the purple lady's slipper, and the *Cyprepedium regina.*

Frost's love of nature and human sympathy is revealed through the value Willis places on the loss of The Broken One's legs; first and foremost it will be a loss of the enjoyment of flowers for him. The poem also highlights Frost's concern with class issues and the contrast between city and country life so often found in his work. The Boston lawyer is contrasted with the poor mill worker and is not cast in a positive light. He is not to be trusted and is described as the devil. The mill worker is reduced to "selling" his legs because as a laborer, his body is his work and is all that he can sell. The dialogue of the poem is not particularly engaging, and the imagery, other than the description of The Broken One as a starfish, is limited. The poem is not highly metaphorical, nor does it demonstrate a skillful use of particulars. But it does paint a vivid picture of the utter vulnerability of the working class when an accident can destroy not only one's livelihood but one's life. The poem pales in comparison to the many other narrative poems in *North of Boston* such as "Death of the Hired Man," "Mending Wall," and "Home Burial," but is not out of place in the volume.

The title is a bit vague as well, referring perhaps to The Broken One, who, with the loss of his feet, has lost his essential self, his "soul." But it might just as well be applied to the lawyer, who, by signing people's lives away in hasty settlements, is a "Self-Seeker" of the worst kind.

FURTHER READING

Faggen, Robert. *Robert Frost and the Challenge of Darwin.* Ann Arbor: University of Michigan Press, 1997, 155–160.

Perrine, Laurence. "The Sense of Frost's 'The Self-Seeker,'" *Concerning Poetry* 7, no. 1 (1974): 5–8.

"Semi-Revolution, A" (1942)

The speaker here "advocate[s] a semi-revolution," arguing that a total revolution only "brings the same class up on top." The tone is clearly ironic, but the poet makes his point. In a total revolution there can be a 360-degree turn, which simply returns us to where we began, instead of a 180-degree turn. It is a geometric reference. Frost plays on the word *revolution,* which not only means the overthrow of one government and its replacement with another or a sudden or momentous change in a situation, but also the orbital motion around a point. This is the same notion that Frost puts forth in another politically critical poem, "On Our Sympathy with the Under Dog," where the quickness with which "dogs" move up from being under and then back under again shows how nearly interchangeable they are. They are in the end essentially the same dogs, though of different breeds.

There is a certain ridicule for political revolutions in general. The poem is satirical because we cannot plan to go "halfway and stop" once a revolution has begun. At the same time that Frost advocates a semi-revolution, he admits that they are, in a sense, impossible. But the poem still endorses them as the only "salves" to political inequality and despair.

A Rosicrucian is a member of an international organization, especially the Ancient Mystic Order Rosae Crucis and the Rosicrucian Order, devoted to the study of ancient mystical, philosophical, and religious doctrines and concerned with the application of these doctrines to modern life. There were a number of Rosicrucian secret organizations or orders during the 17th and 18th centuries that were concerned with the study of religious mysticism and professed esoteric religious beliefs. The comment that we should ask any "reputable Rosicrucian" about the "trouble with a total revolution" refers to a Rosicrucian espousal—shared by some historians, such as Arnold Toynbee (1889–1975)—of a cyclical view of history in which the growth and decline of civilizations tend to manifest recurring patterns.

The poem was first published in *A Witness Tree.* It appears in a grouping called "Quantula," along with other pithy poems, which suggests that Frost intended them to be together because of their small "quantity" and presumed force. (In Latin, *quantula* means "How little?" or "How small?")

"Serious Step Lightly Taken, A" (1942)

"A Serious Step Lightly Taken" provides an aerial view of a lake, a town, and a people. The view provided by a map diminishes hills to two burrs, a stream to a snake, and a lake to the snake's head. A town becomes a dot; the homes within that town imperceptible.

The serious step lightly taken was to put down roots where the family did, but it occurred by happenstance. They simply broke down on the road, the car having overheated, and ended up purchasing a house. They "knocked at the door of a house [they] found, / And there today [they] are."

There is a shift between stanzas three and four from a focus on a particular family putting down roots to a country doing so. The speaker recollects that it is "turning three hundred years / On our cis-atlantic shore," referring to the "discovery" of the United States of America. This "discovery" was just as accidental as the family's discovery of the house.

The poem is concerned with endurance and staying power, with adding "family after family name" for "three hundred more" years. The poem pays homage to the country's and possibly the speaker's (and

Frost's own) forefathers. Through all the wars, the "front-page paper events," and 45 presidents, the country and we survived.

Where a person lives is connected to who he or she is, and the land is a part of the person who cultivates it, just as in "Of the Stones of the Place." The speaker believes it is important to recognize the efforts of those in the past since we are connected to them. That is why we can move in time so easily to 300 years before and after.

The poem shifts in its technological references from an overheated car to the beginning of the country and the docking of the Mayflower. There is an appeal to the present at the end but also to the past with the "[e]nriching soil and increasing stock." We must simply repair the fences and roofs and keep going. In this way, time becomes collective and fluid. The people of the past who sacrificed themselves and those of today are all lumped together as one. The poem also emphasizes the role of the agricultural lifestyle in how we started. We are living off the land, "For our name farming here." We are "aloof" from Europe, from our mother countries, and from our forefathers, yet not aloof. We are physically but not emotionally distant.

The poem ends optimistic about our endurance, but with a caution to not be too haughty despite our front-page events, wars, and presidents.

The poem was first published in *A Witness Tree*. *See* "Our Hold on the Planet," where Frost takes into account the entire history of nature and human nature and resolves that nature "must be a little more in favor of man." *See also* TECHNOLOGY.

"Servant to Servants, A" (1914)

In this dramatic monologue, a woman "servant" addresses a man who camps on the land she and her husband, Len, own. Several commentators have noted the similarity of the title to "and thou shalt be a servant of servants," Noah's curse on Ham, the father of Canaan from the Old Testament (Genesis 9:25). The listener is without a

voice, leaving the reader with no other perspective on the information the woman provides about her life other than her own. The poem reads stream-of-consciousness: The monologue rattles on as the talkative woman veers from subject to subject.

When the poem opens, the woman is expressing gratitude for the man having camped on the land. She seems to be making excuses for being distant or unfriendly, saying that she wanted to come down to the man's camp and visit him, to see how he lives, but that she has been busy with "a houseful of hungry men to feed." She is a self-described servant, seeing herself as put upon by those who camp and work on the land. The man she addresses is one of these men, and while in some sense her monologue may be seen to address all of them with her concerns and complaints, she is only directly addressing one.

The woman reveals that she cannot express her emotions any longer. She cannot even raise her voice in anger, nor does she "want" to lift her hand to strike someone. She is listless. She says she can raise her hand if she has to, a sort of implicit self-protective warning, but she is uninspired. She implicitly describes herself as without expressible emotion and without a voice, despite hers being the only voice of the poem. She is broken; she has lost her spirit and is full of uncertainty.

The relationship between the speaker and the listener is unclear throughout, though there are subtle indications of what it might be. Her apology near the opening insinuates that she had planned to come visit, perhaps even that she was invited to but never responded to the invitation. The real reason for why she did not respond is unknown, but she claims it is because she has been too busy. There is a slight suggestion here and near the end that theirs is a relationship that could become intimate, though either it is not yet or, if it was briefly, it no longer is. Indeed, near the end she confesses: "I've lain awake thinking of you, I'll warrant, / More than you have of yourself, some of these nights."

In the fourth line the woman exclaims, "I don't know!" and this phrase is repeated several times. She is so uncertain that she can no longer "know for sure" whether she is "glad, sorry, or anything." In this way her lack of knowledge can be an indication of two types of not knowing: (1) not knowing how to respond to the man's interest in her should there be a romantic undertone to the poem, and (2) not knowing how she feels about not only her life or this man but her husband as well. She further explains that there is nothing but a "voice-like left inside" to tell her how she ought to feel. The choice of "voice-like" is complicated, because it is not exactly an inner voice; it is like a voice, but not quite. She says she would feel and would trust her feelings whatever they are, another hint at the possibility of a romantic relationship, if she "wasn't all gone wrong." We are left to wonder what has gone wrong as she moves from a discussion about her feelings to one about her surroundings.

The woman talks about the lake that she envies for its "advantages" of being "[c]ut short off at both ends" and being "so long and narrow" as it is. She appears so trapped by her own life that she measures not the distance between herself and the nearby Lake Willoughby but the distance between the lake and where she washes dishes. This is reminiscent of the woman in Frost's "In the Home Stretch," who stands at the kitchen sink imagining her future in her new home as she looks "out through a dusty window / At weeds the water from the sink made tall."

Lake Willoughby is in northern Vermont. Frost stayed at the Conley Farm on the lake in 1909, which is now the Willough Vale Inn. The woman in this piece was said by Frost to be partly based on Mrs. Conley, the hardworking woman he got to know during his stay. Some critics have suggested that the woman is more of a composite of similar women Frost knew throughout his life.

Shortly thereafter it is revealed that the listener has chosen to camp here because of a "book about ferns." The woman is incredulous that a person would "let things more like feathers regulate" his "coming and going." The listener may represent a romantic ideal, a person whose life is the opposite of the speaker's: impractical. It seems to the woman that ferns, like feathers, are a flimsy reason to make life decisions. But she is envious, too, and later discloses that she thinks she could almost "Drop everything and live out on the ground" as well—and, she seems to imply, maybe even with him. She is some-

one who runs, who seeks change as a medicine, but somehow the changes always "w[ear] out like a prescription." The change in moving to her current location with her husband certainly has worn out, despite their having moved there precisely because her husband, Len, wanted the best for her. The move took some sacrifice, and Len is overworking "to make up the loss." His absence may also make her more vulnerable to another's advances.

The woman wonders if the man likes the place, saying, "I can see how you might" and implying that she does not, that they are different in meaningful ways. But she again repeats, "I don't know!," leaving it unclear what exactly she does not know. Is it everything or something specific? It seems it is everything and that in "serving" others she has lost any sense of self. While the repetition of "I don't know" reveals that she does not know how she feels, it also betrays great anxiety. She is compelled to keep chatting, not letting the man get a word in. The talking is nervous chatter but apparently also self-protection.

The woman continues to disclose while concealing. The monologue is masterful in its withheld information. While the poem fills several pages, the information that seems most pertinent in the piece is revealed only through subtleties.

The woman soon moves from a discussion of the place and the investment she and her husband have in it to saying that Len thinks she will be "all right / With doctoring." This sudden revelation is startling and unsettling. It suggests that there is something quite wrong with her, perhaps something terminal. It is clear that what is the matter is not physical but is instead this lack of connection to herself, this loss of self that she has experienced. She does not want medicine; she wants rest, and that is something that no one is likely to understand. Her life is Sisyphean; it is about doing "[t]hings over and over that just won't stay done." Here she is momentarily hopeful, saying that her husband's advice is that the "best way out is always through." This aphorism is instructive; she seems to be trying to make her way through her life, despite her lack of desire and her discontent.

The monologue eventually finds its way to mental illness and an uncle of the woman who "wasn't right." We know, too, that she was not always right (nor is she now) and that she has "once been away" to the state asylum. She did not think she belonged there; she was "prejudiced" because her uncle was kept at home, albeit in a cage, so she thought that was how things should be. She says that though her uncle is gone, the cage is still there, and she had "half fooling" said on occasion, "It's time I took my turn upstairs in jail." It seems the move to this location was an effort on Len's part to remove her from the scene, to take her away from the memory of that crate. She "waited till Len said the word," and when they moved she "looked to be happy . . . for a while." However, she says again, "but I don't know!"

As the poem draws to a close, the woman declares: "I s'pose I've got to go the road I'm going." She is aware that she is trapped in her situation and sees no way out of it. She says that she "almost think[s] if [she] could do like" the camper and be free on the land, she would be better, but she also imagines that she will quickly become dissatisfied despite whatever changes take place: "come night, I shouldn't like it, / Or a long rain." She lies awake thinking about how these campers in their tents live and imagining what it might be like for her to live this way as well. But she does not have the "courage for a risk like that." She sees the campers as vulnerable to nature, knowing that their tents could be "snatched away" by the wind, or something more malevolent, while they sleep.

The woman is deeply lonely and longs for more comfort and security than life provides. People come and go for her, and there are few to connect with. She knows there is "more to it than just window-views / And living by a lake," but she "need[s] to *be* kept." And she is kept in the deepest sense. The two primary themes of her monologue are her being kept and how it relates to her current surroundings, and her family illnesses and how it relates to her current state. If she left, she would have to be kept by someone else, and her unhappiness would return after the newness of the situation wore off. This she seems to know well.

Frost is surprisingly sensitive to the plight of women and wrote about their struggles on several occasions. One of his more sensitive poems on the subject is "The Lovely Shall Be Choosers."

The monologue is not one of Frost's best poems, but it is intricate and subtle, offering complexity of the strangest sort. In a sense it is gothic, the crazed uncle an oddity in Frost's work. That the woman's mother as a young bride "had to lie and hear love things made dreadful" by the uncle's "shouts in the night" also indicates the extent to which we become ourselves in some sense, in ways that we just "don't know."

"A Servant to Servants" was first published in *North of Boston*.

FURTHER READING

Cawthon, W. U., and Tom Fitzpatrick. "Frost's 'A Servant to Servants,'" *Explicator* 53, no. 3 (Spring 1995): 163–166.

Faggen, Robert. *Robert Frost and the Challenge of Darwin*. Ann Arbor: University of Michigan Press, 1997, 225–233.

Kearns, Katherine. *Robert Frost and a Poetics of Appetite*. Cambridge: Cambridge University Press, 1994, 86–89.

Michaels, Walter Benn. "Getting Physical," *Raritan* 2, no. 2 (Fall 1982): 103–113.

Rooke, Constance. "The Elusive/Allusive Voice: An Interpretation of Frost's 'A Servant to Servants,'" *Cimarron Review* 38 (1976): 13–23.

"Silken Tent, The" (1942)

One of Frost's most frequently anthologized sonnets, "The Silken Tent" is also one of the poet's most skillful and elegant. Mark Richardson writes, "Frost's sonnet is itself loosely bound to Petrarchan and Shakespearean traditions, owing its rhyme scheme to the latter, its logical structure to the former, and its theme—praise of a woman's loveliness—to both" (184).

The poem was presented to Frost's dear friend and secretary, Kay Morrison, after Frost's wife Elinor's death, but Jeffrey Cramer writes that though Kay was presented with the poem, it is likely that Elinor was its original inspiration. Jay Parini also notes that Frost's daughter Lesley claimed to have typed a version of the poem before her mother's death.

The sonnet is a single descriptive sentence that eulogizes a woman's strength to support her countless "ties of love and thought" to family and friends. She is compared to a silken tent that "sways at ease" in the wind but never gives. The ties grow taut when strained, but these are the only times the woman is even "of the slightest bondage made aware" of her responsibilities. The poem praises the woman who is gentle while strong, stable while flexible, and at all times has a "sureness of soul" that points heavenward. The woman is in some respects the "supporting central cedar pole" for all her relations; in other respects it is her countless ties that keep her centered and bound. Her ties bind her, but it is not bondage. Her stability comes from within but also from her kin.

Robert Pack writes that "The recurring (four times) crucial verb of the poem, 'is,' which introduces the poem's first and last lines, insists that this is a moment of physically existential being that, nevertheless, is infused with a sense of the immanence of the immortal soul contained within a mortal body" (133). The sonnet is almost religious in its glorification of woman. Frost may have been old-fashioned in some respects, but his appreciation for women was anything but—presumably because of his deep and lengthy relationship with Elinor. Similar representations of the plights of women appear in "Servant to Servants" and "The Lovely Shall Be Choosers."

The poem was first published in winter 1939 in the *Virginia Quarterly Review* and was later collected in *A Witness Tree*. According to Cramer, it was originally titled "In Praise of Your Poise" when presented to Kay Morrison in 1938 (124).

FURTHER READING

Cramer, Jeffrey S. *Robert Frost among His Poems: A Literary Companion to the Poet's Own Biographical Contexts and Associations.* Jefferson, N.C.: MacFarland, 1996.

Muldoon, Paul. "Getting Round: Notes towards an Ars Poetica," *Essays in Criticism* 48, no. 2 (April 1998): 107–128.

Pack, Robert. *Belief and Uncertainty in the Poetry of Robert Frost.* Hanover, N.H.: Middlebury College Press, 2003.

Parini, Jay. *Robert Frost: A Life.* New York: Holt, 1999.

Perrine, Laurence. "Misreadings of Frost's 'Silken Tent,'" *Notes on Modern American Literature* 9, no. 1 (Spring–Summer 1985): 3.

Richardson, Mark. *The Ordeal of Robert Frost: The Poet and His Poetics.* Chicago: University of Illinois Press, 1997, 183–185.

Smith, Evans Lansing. "Frost's 'On a Bird Singing in Its Sleep,' 'Never Again Would Birds' Song Be the Same,' and 'The Silken Tent,'" *Explicator* 50, no. 1 (Fall 1991): 35–37.

"Sitting by a Bush in Broad Sunlight" (1928)

At the beginning of the poem the speaker is like a child; sitting in the sunlight he attempts to catch a ray of sun between his fingers as a child might attempt to grasp the motes dancing in the sun's rays, but "[n]o lasting effect of it lingers." The speaker then recalls that there was only one time when the "dust really took in the sun," and that was when life was created: "from that one intake of fire / All creatures still warmly suspire."

The speaker asserts that if we have been watching for a long time and have never seen "sun-smitten slime / Again come to life and crawl off"—a direct reference to Darwin's theory of EVOLUTION—"We must not be too ready to scoff" at the notion. The poem continues with a reference to the burning bush in the Old Testament, the bush that burned without being consumed, from which God spoke to Moses (Exodus 3:2–4).

The poem reflects on the beginning of all life and the beginning of faith in the transcendent. Frost is satirical in the third stanza with his "sun-smitten slime," criticizing both religion and science as explanations for our beginning. We can never again see the beginning of life on this planet, but we cannot scoff at that. God used to speak to people "by name," but he does not do that any longer and we cannot scoff at that either. The evidence we have for our being we can try to trace back because we have our breath, but our only other option is faith.

Sun provides energy for the Earth; without it, life could not have evolved. And while we do not feel as though we came from sun-smitten slime, our feelings do not make it untrue. That we no longer speak to God does not make it untrue that we once did. In this sense there are parallels between evolution and religion, belief and faith. The sun may now be an intangible ray with no lasting effect on us, but its importance to us is still evident.

Robert Faggen describes the poem as "explicit about the way evolution and materialism have threatened faith" (280). He argues, however, that Frost's "answer . . . asserts that religion has always demanded building a tentative bridge across the vast gulf separating man, the world, and God" (280). He also writes that the "evocation of Moses questioning God in the burning bush becomes a parable of the modern scientific attempt to establish religious belief through knowledge, an attempt that must be rebuked by the 'veil'" (281). Faggen concludes that "'Faith' becomes a fire more physical and literal than figurative. That we 'persist' through our impulse to faith is the most we can be sure of" (282).

The poem was first published in *West-Running Brook*.

FURTHER READING

Faggen, Robert. *Robert Frost and the Challenge of Darwin*. Ann Arbor: University of Michigan Press, 1997, 280–282.

"Skeptic" (1947)

The speaker moves between two positions: belief and disbelief. He addresses the "Far star" that "tickles" his "sensitive plate" and whose heat is so intense that it can fry black atoms white. He refers to his body as his armor from the star, his "plate," like a reptile's.

"I don't believe I believe," the speaker says to the star; he "put[s] no faith in the seeming facts of light." Light is visible but not graspable; it seems to be but cannot be held. The grammar of "I don't believe I believe" is essential to the poem, as is the

repetition of the phrase. It is its own contradiction. The speaker cannot believe that he believes is one way to read the line, but another is to read it as a considered contradiction: He at once believes and does not believe.

The speaker addresses the star, asserting that he is not certain it is the "last in space" or that what makes it "red in the face," makes it shine so brightly, is "after explosion going away so fast." The philosopher-poet is referring to the Big Bang theory. Stars shift to the red portion, or lower frequencies, of the visual spectrum as they move away from us. The faster a star moves away from us, or the farther it is from us when it moves, affects how its light reaches us and how it appears to us. So, too, if it moves in the opposite direction; if it moves toward us or is closer to us, its appearance is supposed to shift to the higher frequencies and therefore to the violet area of the visual spectrum. Also, in cosmic time, stars eventually die, extinguishing all life that relies on those stars as a source of energy. A dying star is indeed "red in the face."

The closing stanza speculates as to whether the universe is as immense as we believe. The speaker is confronted with facts that make it seem cold and distant, but there are occasions when the universe feels like home and like protection despite those cosmic facts. At times it is as if he is in the womb; he feels as securely wrapped as a baby in a caul, or fetal membrane. The universe feels like his; he is not as inconsiderable as science would make him seem.

The poem is ultimately about how we should view the universe. Should we see it as an antihuman void or as the foundation of our existence and, somehow, a comfort? The poem is titled "Skeptic," but it seems simply indecisive. The speaker is uncertain which view of the universe he should adopt. He goes back and forth on the discoveries of astronomy and in the end concludes, unscientifically, that "[t]he universe may or may not be very immense," pointing out that both scientific data and a human factor are necessary for a full grasp of the nature of the universe with all its cold emptiness. The universe still has qualities that can make humans feel comfortable, and these should not be discounted.

Frost here, as in "Lines Written in Dejection on the Eve of Great Success," tries to limit the reach of scientific conclusions compared with human experiences. Depending on the context, he suggests that human "common sense" can be just as informative as, or even more so than, scientific observations. Frost does not seem to be critical so much of science per se as of the overarching conclusions of some scientists. In relation to these people, Frost sees himself as a skeptic.

The poem, first published in *Steeple Bush*, can be compared to "Any Size We Please," in which the speaker tries to embrace the universe. *See* HOME, THEME OF and STARS.

FURTHER READING

Sanders, Charles. "Frost's 'Skeptic,'" *Explicator* 40, no. 3 (Spring 1982): 47–48.

"Snow" (1916)

A narrative in the manner of Frost's better-known "The Death of the Hired Man," this poem also presents a couple, Fred and Helen Cole, discussing the plight of a man, Meserve, who at the opening has disrupted their sleep in the middle of the night. Meserve, making his way in a blizzard, has stopped to rest at what appears to be the midpoint of his journey. In the second stanza, he phones his wife to tell her that he will be making his way home from the Coles' now and to say goodnight before it gets too late. It is clear that his wife is displeased. Only one side of the conversation is recorded, but when Meserve says, "I didn't / Call you to ask you to invite me home—" it is clear what his wife thinks of his journeying out so late in such dangerous weather. She is silent in response to his tough comment.

Following the phone conversation, Meserve goes out to check his horses and make a better judgment about continuing based on the condition in which he finds them. Mrs. Cole insists that Meserve head to the barn himself, so that she can talk to her husband without Meserve present. The dialogue that follows shows that Helen is not fond of Meserve and that she actually "detest[s] the thought of him

/ With his ten children under ten years old." He is a preacher who "seems to have lost off his Christian name," but he is clearly not of the same faith as Fred and Helen, and this seems to contribute to her disdain.

The ensuing conversation is similar to the one in "The Death of the Hired Man," where Warren and Mary debate the fate of Silas. Here Fred and Helen consider their responsibility toward Meserve and the possibility of keeping him from a foolish journey. He is out in this weather because he "had to preach," and Fred believes "[h]e'll pull through" if he continues, a sort of self-convincing on his part, but he also seems to think that Helen has a chance to make Meserve hear her. Helen decides she should call Meserve's wife again, as though the two women could somehow unite in the decision that he shouldn't travel anymore this night and convince the stubborn man to stay at the Coles'.

The tension of the differences between Meserve and the Coles is highlighted by the statement, "One thing: he didn't drag God into it." It is clear that Meserve's company is not wanted and that their differences run deep. Still, there is a country politeness of appearances. In contemplating his death under a pile of snow, Fred declares that he has no reason to care what happens to Meserve if it "takes / Some of the sanctimonious conceit / Out of one of those pious scalawags." Helen and Fred are ultimately caught between the desire to protect anyone from harm and the desire to let foolishness run its course. Helen is worried and knows that Fred "want[s] to see him safe," but Fred brings gender into it, arguing that women simply put on airs to impress men and to shame them into behaving with one another.

When Meserve returns from the barn, Helen begs him to reconsider his journey and Meserve rests a bit, beginning to preach about a leaf in a book that cannot determine whether to go backward or forward. Meserve's monologue seems to have a subtext that acts as a metaphor for his own situation. If the leaf moves forward, "then it's with a friend's impatience," and if it moves backward, "it's from regret for something you have passed and failed to see the good of." Meserve's philosophizing about the leaf is reminiscent of Frost's "The Road

Not Taken"; Meserve concludes that "nothing / Ever presents itself before us twice," suggesting that all decisions lead to other decisions, just as choosing the road "less traveled by . . . made all the difference."

Meserve tells several stories before taking leave. The next is about the snow and about a boy and about not being able to "get too much winter in winter." The Coles let Meserve ramble on, thinking it means he has decided to stay, but he says his piece and takes his leave. The stories do not shed much light on the situation and seem designed simply to create pause.

Helen puts forth one last effort before Meserve leaves, reminding him of the risk he takes traveling in such weather. In Meserve's response, Frost's own attitude toward nature is evident: "Our snow storms as a rule / Aren't looked on as man-killers," he says. While Frost often saw nature as wreaking havoc in people's lives, he rarely attributed actual malevolence to it. Such things simply happened.

While Meserve's departure is welcome, the Coles will not sleep until he is safely home. The poem takes a gothic turn with phone calls in the night that reach Meserve's wife but create suspense over Meserve's not yet having made it home. In the end there is a dangling phone, Helen and Fred straining to hear on the other line, and the threat from the snow, which makes the journey a matter of life or death. At the close Meserve has safely returned and takes the phone, thanking the Coles. The Coles offer a polite response again, and Helen, upon hanging up the phone, adds that the "whole to-do seems to have been for nothing. / What spoiled our night was to him just his fun." Fred is less critical and claims that they have learned more about him than they had hoped to learn; they have "had a share in one night of his life." And even though both of them probably feel put out, Fred accuses Helen of having been "too much concerned."

"Snow" is not about snow, but about the evasive politenesses and tensions of casual neighborly conversation, about what goes on behind closed doors, and about how far we will or will not go to protect others who are not kin, whether it be from nature or from themselves. Frost once said that science cannot tell us how far we will or will not go in

friendship for what we can get out of it, and there is a measure of that here. Frost creates tension in the dialogue by revealing just how selfishly we can behave when no one is listening, how intolerant we can be of others who are not within earshot. Meserve's philosophizing and his role as a preacher are highlighted by the Coles as further reasons to find him disagreeable, but what is most disagreeable is that they have been awakened in the night not only by Meserve's stay but by their forced concern. They did not ask to be involved in his journey or his subsequent choice of risk. They would have been content to let the snow rage outside, not knowing who was traveling in it or what dangers others might be facing. And yet, Frost's depiction of the Coles does not cast them as villains. They are just people—people whose private conversations have been revealed for us to identify ourselves in them. Frost has again captured, through careful selection and arrangement of dialogue in everyday language, human vulnerability, peril, weakness, and strength.

The poem was first published in the November 1916 issue of *Poetry* and later collected in *New Hampshire. See* NIGHT.

FURTHER READING

Iadonisi, Richard A. "(In)Felicitous Space: The Interior Landscape of 'Snow,'" *Robert Frost Review* (Fall 1996): 47–53.

Jost, Walter. "Civility and Madness in Robert Frost's 'Snow,'" *Texas Studies in Literature and Language* 39, no. 1 (Spring 1997): 27–64.

Miller, Lewis H., Jr. "'Snow': Frost's Drama of Belittled People," *Robert Frost Review* (Fall 1994): 47–51.

Sears, John F. "The Subversive Performer in Frost's 'Snow' and 'Out, Out—.'" In *The Motive for Metaphor: Essays on Modern Poetry*, edited by Francis C. Blessington and Guy L. Rotella, 82–92. Boston: Northeastern University Press, 1983.

"Soldier, A" (1928)

Frost presents a lance metonymically for a soldier. The soldier is a fallen lance who has been cast by governments into war. Once the soldier has fallen, he becomes "unlifted," regardless of season or time. Fallen soldiers are resources that have been used up; they are tools whose functions have been served. As a lance, the soldier is reduced to a weapon, but he also becomes more than that. He has a spirit that is shot in death "[f]urther than target ever showed or shone." George Bagby writes that "natural obstruction appears to be insurmountable, and spirit, at first glance, thoroughly defeated" (108). But the spirit of the soldier goes on even when the body is stopped short. The death of the body of the soldier catapults the spirit of that soldier forever into an afterworld.

Frost says with disappointment, "Our missiles always make too short an arc." If we think of a fallen soldier and do not think of him as being "worthy" of anything, it is because we are not looking into the distance, we are not looking "out far nor in deep." The description is a way of making the soldier's duty important even if not for the moment, even if not for the task. The soldier may have fallen because he did not make his mark, but making the mark was never entirely up to the soldier. As a weapon, he was a tool for governments, he was not his own master, and we should not forget that. The brutal deaths of soldiers have the potential to "make us cringe for metal-point on stone" and to become aware of the injustices for which we are at least partly responsible.

Frost's dearest soldier friend was Edward Thomas, who was killed April 9, 1917, in the Battle of Arras, France, in World War I. The poem dedicated to Thomas, "To E. T.," was published in Frost's previous volume, *New Hampshire*. If this poem, too, was written with Thomas in mind, it explains the great respect and faith evident in the tone, which Frost does not often express when faced with such brutal fact. In the end, as George F. Bagby writes, "the ultimate desire as intimated by the poem is to live and not die" (109).

The poem was first published as "The Soldier" in the May 1927 issue of *McCall's Magazine* and later collected in *West-Running Brook*. In 1961 Frost referred to this poem as "one kind of way of taking life about war or peace" (Cramer, 97). *See* POLITICS.

FURTHER READING

Bagby, George F. *Frost and the Book of Nature*. Knoxville: University of Tennessee Press, 1993, 107–109.

Cramer, Jeffrey S. *Robert Frost among His Poems: A Literary Companion to the Poet's Own Biographical Contexts and Associations*. Jefferson. N.C.: MacFarland, 1996.

"Some Science Fiction" (1962)

The poem was first published in booklet form as Frost's 1955 Christmas poem, without the "Envoi" quatrain. It was later collected in *In the Clearing*. The "Envoi to Hyde the Castaway of Crow Island" refers to Frost's friend Edward Hyde Cox, who lived on Crow Island, Massachusetts.

"Some Science Fiction" is representative of Frost's later poems of *In the Clearing*, where several speculations on space travel appear. The poem presents its speaker as a crotchety old man, an "Old Slow Coach," not quite receptive to or in favor of "keeping pace / With the headlong human race" as it hurls itself at space. Other people glorify science, but the speaker is skeptical and would rather wax "philosophic."

The speaker jokes that he may be "banished" for his attitudes to the "penal colony" they are likely to create on the moon. There he will humorously "go almost anywhere" with only a "can of condensed air."

The poem might be dismissed as the ranting of an old man at those who "get more nuclear" and "more bigoted in reliance / On the gospel of modern science," but this old man has a gospel of his own. Frost maintains his skill and cleverness here, but the poem is uninspired.

"Something for Hope" (1947)

The closing line of the poem is, "But spes alit agricolam, 'tis said," Latin for "Hope nourishes the farmer," an allusion to the poet Albius Tibullus'

(c. 60–19 B.C.) *Elegies*, II.vi.21. The line aptly sums up this simple poem.

The speaker reflects on the changing landscape, where trees "push / Through the meadow sweet." If the "edible grass" is crowded out, all we have to do is wait. Nothing is constant in nature, everything changes, but if we "busy" ourselves "with other things" as time passes, "the trees put on their wooden rings" and with age, or time, all good comes round. He encourages his readers to be patient and to look ahead 100 years to when the trees will have grown and can be used for lumber and the meadow will be "ready again for the grass to own."

"Hope may not nourish a cow or horse," the speaker notes, as they are incapable of hope. Hope is a human thing that can keep a farmer going. A cow or a horse will go on regardless, guided by natural instinct, as will the trees and grass of the poem. But cultivation of the land is both natural and unnatural, and sometimes farmers need more than instinct; they need hope. George F. Bagby explains that Frost expresses a faith in natural processes where "by viewing the hundred-year cycle from a perspective broader than that of any individual . . . he is able to perceive the value of each stage in the cycle" (85).

"Something for Hope" was first published in the December 1946 issue of the *Atlantic Monthly* and later collected in *Steeple Bush*. The original manuscript title was "A Living on Hope." *See also* "The LAST MOWING."

FURTHER READING

Bagby, George F. *Frost and the Book of Nature.* Knoxville: University of Tennessee Press, 1993, 84–85.

"Sound of Trees, The" (1916)

The speaker wonders about the trees whose sound "we wish to bear / Forever" more than any other sound. We welcome trees "close to our dwelling place," unlike other manifestations of nature that we tend to keep at more of a distance. The "noise" trees make when the wind passes through them is one we "suffer" until we become as fixed in our place as they are and "acquire a listening air" to what they have to say. Strangely, our "fixity" is "in our joys," which are contrasted with the description of suffering in the earlier line. The title of the poem may be "The Sound of Trees," but it speaks about the "noise" of trees. Noise is what we hear when our ears are not attuned to the sounds of nature. It is interference, like static on a radio, when we are going about our days, even joyfully. But when we "lose all measure of pace" and become accustomed to a tree's sense of time, we begin to hear what nature has to say.

Trees talk of "going" but never get away. When trees sway in the wind, they appear to be going somewhere; their constant swaying back and forth is suggestive of going and coming, over and over again. This is how they whisper of getting away and still stay. They are all talk. They grow older and wiser, accumulating rings, and eventually resolve to stay where they are, as if there were any choice in the first place. The speaker understands the trees, feeling the same sway, as his "feet tug at the floor" and his "head sways to [his] shoulder."

The trees "scare / The white clouds over them on" since they cannot move themselves. They move what surrounds them instead. The speaker, too, feels fixed and, like the trees, says that one day he "shall be gone." The question is whether he will eventually declare that he "means to stay" or will actually leave. After all, if he should "set forth for somewhere," it will be a "reckless choice."

The poet embraces stability and fixity as he reflects on the ways nature affects us and how much we are a part of it. Just as when the trunk is bigger and the tree is older, it can no longer lean or be uprooted, the more fixed we become in our "joys," the less we sway in the breezes that catch us by surprise and throw us off balance. When trees are young, they need bracing to keep them from being blown over by the wind, and so do people.

The poem offers an interesting contrast to "Tree at my Window," where again the speaker is compared to a tree. There, however, their two "heads" are contrasted: "Your head so much concerned with outer," the speaker says to the tree, "Mine with inner, weather."

The poem was first published in the December 1914 issue of *Poetry and Drama* and appeared the following year in the August 1915 issue of the *Atlantic*. It was later collected in *Mountain Interval*.

"Span of Life, The" (1936)

This couplet was first published as "The Old Dog" in *Rainbow in the Sky* (New York, 1935) before being included as part of "Ten Mills" in *Poetry* in April 1936. It was collected in *A Further Range*.

Despite its brevity, the couplet allows for multiple interpretations. The contrast is, of course, between an old dog and a new puppy. The old dog is described as barking "backward without getting up," suggesting that his bite is now his bark. He is too aged to bestir himself. He puts forth minimal effort, and his bark is uninterested. The speaker can remember when "he was a pup," when the old dog's behavior was much more physical and energetic. All that is left is the brief over-the-shoulder bark; he has no urge to move. He wants to get back to his nap.

"The Span of Life" seems to apply to the speaker himself, but the observation of the dog can apply to anyone—the title is inclusive. The commentary is not just about a particular dog but about all old dogs who have had their day.

FURTHER READING

Perrine, Laurence. "Frost's 'The Span of Life,'" *Explicator* 14, no. 6 (March 1971): 61.

"Speaking of Loyalty" (1948)

Although the talk "Speaking of Loyalty" was given at an Amherst College Alumni luncheon, Frost; Charlie Cole, the president of Amherst College; and George Whicher, a member of the English faculty, had just returned from the installation of Walter Hendricks as president of the new Marlboro College. Frost revised the recorded text of the talk for the *Amherst Graduates' Quarterly*'s August 1948 issue. For the most part the piece is unremarkable, except for what it reveals about Frost's views of loyalty, particularly to a nation.

Frost speaks of different kinds of loyalties—those to a discipline, such as chemistry, physics, geography, and history, and those to a country, such as the United States, which he identifies as "in a stronger position than chemistry, physics or history to compel loyalty." He distinguishes between a "middle-brow" and a "high-brow" loyalty. One is to one's attachments, the other to one's attractions. Frost asks rhetorically, "How do you get from an attachment to follow an attraction?" His answer: "It ought to be painful to you, it ought to be, if you're any good. It ought not to be easy. You ought not to do it cheerfully, lightly." Loyalty comes down to "belonging and belongings; belonging and having belongings." And the "sincerity of their belonging is all [one has] to measure people by."

Frost closes by saying, "You have to ask yourself in the end, how far will you go when it comes to changing your allegiance." The ultimate loyalty is to the state and the country. Frost extols American novelist Dorothy Canfield (1879–1958) for her loyalty to and pride in the state of Vermont. Frost takes pride too, even if he is a "bastard Vermonter," but, ever the nationalist, his greatest allegiance and loyalty is to the United States of America.

"Spring Pools" (1928)

"Spring Pools" is a glimpse of a change of season. The pools of water are remarkable in that reflected in them is "total sky almost without defect," even though they exist in a dark forest. The trees are foreboding outlines that not only create the darkness of the forest but "blot out and drink up and sweep away" the pools, which were created by the "snow that melted only yesterday." The pools feed the flowers beside them, which have just sprung up but "chill and shiver" in the cool temperatures of early spring. The pools do not have glory in their future; they will not become a "brook or river" but instead will be used up by the trees to "bring dark foliage on."

The trees are threatening. They are all-consuming and will "use their powers" for ill. The setup is almost a coup or a political occupation. The trees have all the power, and the scene becomes an "us versus them" situation. The tone of the poem is stark, declarative, and apocalyptic. "Let them think twice before they use their powers" the speaker says, as though there is any form of thought in natural processes. Katherine Kearns describes the poem as having the "eerie power of absolute conviction" (129) and writes that the trees "embody a hunger so voracious—or a passion so great—that it can bring ice to the boil, turn pristine winter into dark summer heat, and eradicate completely the boundaries of self by subsuming the world" (128). The speaker reads human values into his observations of nature, as is common in Frost.

While the notion is that the development of the trees from season to season will once and for all drink up the water and kill the flowers, clearly the flowers and water will return. Seasons are cyclical, but there is no vision of cyclical nature here. Instead, the poem provides a snapshot, a glimpse of one phase of a much more complicated process.

There are important connections among these natural forces. The spring pools did not come from nowhere; they came from the snow that has just melted, and they have a function. If they were not drunk, they would be excess water. Although the speaker laments the disappearance of the spring pools, the snow disappeared as well and the flowers will disappear, and the trees too, though they have a longer lifespan.

The speaker is worried about being darkened himself. And death to him could be like the darkening trees, a blotting out, drinking up, and sweeping away of what is left of him. The life-and-death cycle, as always in Frost, offers a moment of reflection on his own mortality.

The poem was first published in the April 23, 1927, issue of the *Dearborn Independent* and was later collected as the opening poem of *West-Running Brook*.

FURTHER READING

Bagby, George F. *Frost and the Book of Nature.* Knoxville: University of Tennessee Press, 1993, 58–59.

Combellack, C. R. B. "Frost's 'Spring Pools,'" *Explicator* 30 (1971): 27.

Faggen, Robert. *Robert Frost and the Challenge of Darwin.* Ann Arbor: University of Michigan Press, 1997, 18.

Kearns, Katherine. *Robert Frost and a Poetics of Appetite.* Cambridge: Cambridge University Press, 1994, 127–129.

"Star in a Stoneboat, A" (1923)

"A Star in a Stoneboat" was first published in the January 1921 issue of the *Yale Review*. It was later collected in *New Hampshire* with the dedication, "for Lincoln MacVeagh." MacVeagh, one of Frost's editors at Henry Holt and Company, was also his good friend.

The speaker imagines that a fallen star, a meteorite, has been "picked up with stones to build a wall." He opens by insisting that none interfere with his imagining by telling him that this is not the case. John H. Timmerman finds that the poem "establishes an ironic tension between imagination and practicality" and, as have others, notes similarities and allusions to "Mending Wall" (137–138).

The speaker describes the process of getting the stone-star and how the laborer who built the wall did not realize what he had. He missed much, because he was "not used to handling stars." He did not realize the stone was like a flying thing, such as those with "one large wing" and a "long Bird of Paradise's tail." The tail is the trail left by a shooting star, but "when not in use to fly" draws "back in its body like a snail." These are some of Frost's most palpable descriptions.

Halfway through the poem Frost moves from the descriptive to the philosophical, from the scene of the farmer with a loaded "old stone-boat," a wheelbarrow full of rocks and one fallen star, to a speaker who, "as though / Commanded in a dream," goes in search of a fallen star by "following walls." He does not need science or religion to reduce the universe to a manageable size. He just needs to find and hold one fallen star and let it "run off in strange tangents with [his] arm." The star will be "the prize

/ Of the world complete in any size" that he can hold in his "calloused palm," making the universe seem far less vast and making him the "compass, fool or wise." The speaker is similar to the one in "Any Size We Please" who "hugged himself for all his universe."

See SCIENCE and WALLS.

FURTHER READING

Timmerman, John H. *Robert Frost: The Ethics of Ambiguity.* Lewisburg: Bucknell University Press, 2002, 137–139.

"Stars" (1913)

The stars are unconcerned with human affairs. They "congregate" overhead as if "with keenness for our fate," but they are indifferent, having "neither love nor hate" for us. They may have the "snow-white marble eyes" of an ancient Greek statue, but they have no knowledge of our affairs; they are, after all, "[w]ithout the gift of sight."

Robert Faggen writes that "[t]he phrase 'look me in the stars' mocks our need for an overseer we can comprehend" (359). And John H. Timmerman notes that the "stars are too remote to give guidance. Like the statue of Minerva, goddess of wisdom, they bear wisdom, but it is veiled. The stars have no sight, nor a means to communicate wisdom to us" (137).

The poem was first published in *A Boy's Will* with the gloss, "There is no oversight of human affairs." Timmerman writes that the poem "embodies Frost's personal pain, first drafted as it was near the time of the death of his young son Elliott (8 July 1900)" (136).

FURTHER READING

Faggen, Robert. *Robert Frost and the Challenge of Darwin.* Ann Arbor: University of Michigan Press, 1997, 259.

Timmerman, John H. *Robert Frost: The Ethics of Ambiguity.* Lewisburg, Pa.: Bucknell University Press, 2002.

"Star-Splitter, The" (1923)

The "star-splitter" is a telescope purchased by a farmer neighbor, Brad McLaughlin, who wanted one so desperately, he burned down his "good old-timer" house to raise the money to buy one. The speaker does not endorse the idea, nor do the rest of the townspeople. They think it is a "strange thing to be roguish over," but McLaughlin argues that "The best thing that we're put here for's to see" and the "strongest thing that's given us to see with's / A telescope."

Some good old-fashioned advice is given, such as "to be social is to be forgiving" and "a house isn't sentient; the house / Didn't feel anything." The choice to sacrifice all for his passion landed McLaughlin with a job he "had to turn" to on the Concord railroad. The speaker remains unimpressed with McLaughlin's decision, even after having his own opportunity to "look / Up the brass barrel, velvet black inside, At a star quaking in the other end." The telescope is "christened" the star-splitter because it provides a view of a star split into two or three. As a farmer might, this splitting is compared to the earthly splitting of wood. The telescope splits the stars because it is not a terribly expensive one. The quaking and the splitting are a result of its being a little unsteady. A better-quality telescope would not split them, so the term *star-splitter* is also a bit derisive.

The poem closes with the speaker resolving that even after looking and looking through a telescope we know no "better where we are, / And how it stands between the night tonight / And a man with a smoky lantern chimney." We learn nothing of human affairs from looking at the stars. It is all well and good, he seems to say, to have your eye on the stars, but science has great limitations. Sacrificing everything for a glimpse at the unknown in space, when there is so much unknown here on Earth, is a foolish enterprise. After all, "Has a man . . . no rights / These forces are obliged to pay respect to?"

The poem was first published in the September 1923 issue of the *Century Magazine* and was later collected in *New Hampshire*.

FURTHER READING

Faggen, Robert. *Robert Frost and the Challenge of Darwin.* Ann Arbor: University of Michigan Press, 1997, 305–307.

Waddell, William S., Jr. "By Precept and Example: Aphorism in 'The Star Splitter.'" In *Robert Frost the Man and the Poet,* edited by Earl J. Wilcox, 115–124. Rock Hill, S.C.: Winthrop College.

Steeple Bush (1947)

Steeple Bush was first published in late May 1947 by Henry Holt and Company of New York and was dedicated to Frost's grandchildren: "For Prescott, John, Elinor, Lesley Lee, Robin, and Harold." A limited, signed edition of 751 copies also was published. The title refers to the steeplebush plant, also known as the hardhack, that grew profusely around Frost's farm in Ripton, Vermont. It also alludes to the sacredness of all nature, the steeple representing the sacred and the bush representing nature.

Jay Parini writes that Frost "understood that the critics would be looking for signs of diminishment. Indeed the signs were there; only a few of the poems in this collection were equal to his best work." One of the more balanced reviews came from the poet and critic Randall Jarrell, who wrote of "Directive" that "There are weak places in the poem, but these are nothing beside so much longing, tenderness, and passive sadness, Frost's understanding that each life is tragic because it wears away into the death that it at last half welcomes" (Parini, 369). And in many ways the poet had in truth become "half in love with easeful Death," as John Keats writes in "Ode to a Nightingale."

The poet was firmly established by the time of *Steeple Bush,* but the sensitive Frost still spent the summer fretting over the incoming reviews, which were on the whole largely unfavorable. One of the harshest came from *Time* magazine, in which the reviewer concluded that "what was once only granitic Yankee individualism in his work has hardened into bitter and often uninspired Tory social commentary" (quoted in Parini, 373).

Lisa Seale describes the volume as focusing on the social and political issues of the 1940s as well as on the challenge to original thinking in periods of national and international conflict. A large number of the poems are concerned with contemporary issues of the time and therefore lack the originality and inspiration of Frost's earlier work. The temporal allusions restrict the poems' universality and appeal, but Frost had so honed his skills by this point that he could not write an unskillful poem, simply an uninspired one.

The collection is organized into five groups of poems, the first of which is unnamed and the last four of which are "Five Nocturnes," "A Spire and Belfry," "Out and Away," and "Editorials." The first, unnamed section, includes seven poems, among which is the much-acclaimed "Directive." Described by Jay Parini as "both epitaph and poetic credo" (361), providing "a map of [Frost's] inner landscape," and by Thomas Dilworth as Frost's "most cryptic poem" (26), the poem showed that Frost had come into his own.

Poetry should not always be read autobiographically, but it is hard not see the concerns expressed in the volume as those of someone nearing the end of his life rather than of someone at the start of life. At the beginning of the volume is a mature and established Frost with "patience . . . looking away ahead" ("One Step") and trying to keep himself from "going," from being swept up in the torrential downpour of "One Step Backward Taken." He is in a position of knowledge, with the advantage of hindsight, as "Directive" demonstrates. He is also in a position to establish, in "Too Anxious for Rivers," that "'twas the effort, the essay of love."

The section "Five Nocturnes" thematically centers on one of Frost's most frequent and recognizable tropes: the night and all its implications. The poems express from various perspectives fears, hidden and not, and the individuals' desire to find safety, sometimes through manmade light and other times through one another, in a universe more vast than imaginable and darker than we would like to think. The nocturnes call to mind Dylan Thomas's poem to his aged and nearly blind father, "Do Not Go Gentle into That Good Night." Thomas was asking, almost demanding, that his father "Rage, rage against the dying of the light," his oncoming sightlessness.

The section "A Spire and Belfry," as its title suggests, concerns religion and the individual. The poet is attempting to reconcile his feelings of doubt and fear with his hope. He speculates whether "eternity / Was but the steeple on our house of life" ("Innate Helium"). He calls religious faith "Innate Helium," "a most filling vapor."

"Out and Away" is concerned with what Frost terms the "astrometaphysical," but also with being idolized and with the poet's feeling that "the play seems out for an almost infinite run," as he says in the title poem of the section. "Editorials" is focused on contemporary issues, such as the space race and war. It is nationalistic and filled with sarcasm about the state of affairs. In *The Complete Poems* (1949) Frost also appended three poems to *Steeple Bush* in "An Afterword": "Choose Something like a Star," "Closed for Good," and "From Plane to Plane," where Frost pits formal education against knowledge gained from life and work experience, a balance he was sure to have worked to create throughout his own lifetime.

While the volume does not represent Frost's most inspired work, it does reflect the insights and hindsights of an aging poet who, with a lifetime of experience, is not beyond words and still has much he hopes to impart before the dying of his light. *See* SCIENCE.

FURTHER READING

Dilworth, Thomas. "Frost's Directive," *Explicator* 58, no. 1 (Fall 1999): 26–29.

Parini, Jay. *Robert Frost: A Life*. New York: Holt, 1999.

Seale, Lisa. "'Triumphant Association': The First Group of Poems in Robert Frost's *Steeple Bush*," *Robert Frost Review* (Fall 1997): 1–16.

"Steeple on the House, A" (1947)

"A Steeple on the House" was first published in *Steeple Bush* in the section titled "A Spire and Belfry." In it the aging poet wonders, "What if it should turn out eternity / Was but the steeple on our

house of life / That made our house of life a house of worship?" His question essentially asks if the steeples on churches, and therefore churches and religious ideals themselves, are necessary to living a meaningful and blessed life.

Steeples are not portrayed as useful: We do not go "up there to sleep at night" or "to live by day," and what is more important, we would never go up there to live. This suggests that eternity and the afterlife, as represented by the steeples, are not life. They may have been designed in an effort to give meaning to the lives we are already living, but these lives are already meaningful—we do sleep at night and live by day. We do not need to have the steeple in order to have a house. We have a house already; the steeple is merely ornamental.

The closing lines read, "A spire and belfry coming on the roof / Means that a soul is coming on the flesh." Just as we attach the notion of eternity to our lives, we attach the concept of a soul to our flesh. The house of life is the structure, and we put the label of the sacred on the structure, just as we put the symbolic stamp of the soul on the body. The poem minimizes the need for soul and elevates the flesh. Ordinary life and ordinary flesh can be celebrated without religious assumptions.

The poet asks, "What if eternity wasn't magical, but life was?" He wants to keep the sacredness and specialness of life without bringing in concepts like eternity or soul. In this way he suggests that the pinnacles of our lives in this life are primary, and in comparison the concepts of eternity and the soul are of questionable significance at most.

See BELIEF.

FURTHER READING

Perrine, Laurence. "Robert Frost and the Idea of Immortality." In *Frost: Centennial Essays II*, edited by Jac Tharpe, 87–89. Jackson: University Press of Mississippi, 1976.

"Stopping by Woods on a Snowy Evening" (1923)

"Stopping by Woods on a Snowy Evening" is one of Frost's most beloved lyrics. It retains great popularity among the general public as well as among scholars. It is almost always included in anthologies and was second only to "The Road Not Taken" as the poem respondents said they most liked to read when former American poet laureate Robert Pinsky took his 1998 poll to try to identify America's favorite poem. During John F. Kennedy's campaign for president, Kennedy had a set speech, which he always ended by quoting the final lines of the poem about having promises to keep and "miles to go before I sleep." Lawrance Thompson recalls the "odd juxtaposition of the tight lyric form, with its unusual rhyme scheme, and the sprawling, discursive conversational tone of 'New Hampshire'" (238).

Frost once told his friend Reginald Cook that the poem contained all he ever knew (Parini, 212). He claimed it came to him when he went outside to look at the sun after he had been working all night on "New Hampshire." Frost said, "I always thought [the poem] was a product of autointoxication coming from tiredness" (Cook, 66). He also said of the poem, "That one I've been more bothered with more than anybody has ever been with any poem in just pressing it for more than it should be pressed for. It means enough without its being pressed," meaning, of course, that it should not be overanalyzed or overread. He said that all it means is that "it's all very nice but I must be getting along, getting home" (Cook, 64). Some readers would maintain that to them it means much more than that.

The poem is not simply a description of a natural scene but is about a person experiencing the scene. Frost once said coyly, "I guess I'm not a nature poet, I have only written two poems without a human being in them." The speaker finds himself out alone in the evening, as in so many of Frost's poems, including the opening poem, "Into My Own," in his first collection, *A Boy's Will.* But here the speaker travels by horse and carriage. On this night he stops to watch the "woods fill up with snow," and he muses "Whose woods these are I think I know." The owner of the woods has a house in the village, the speaker recalls, emphasizing that the landowner does not live in the country.

Frost wrote in "The Constant Symbol," "There's an indulgent smile I get for the recklessness of the unnecessary commitment I made when I came to

the first line in the second stanza. . . . I was riding too high to care what trouble I incurred. And it was all right so long as I didn't suffer deflection." The speaker imagines in that line that the "horse must think it queer" that he has stopped to take in the magical scene. There is no practical reason to stop between the woods and the lake on the "darkest evening of the year." The horse shakes his harness bells as if "[t]o ask if there is some mistake." The speaker is projecting onto the animal a human concern. The sound of the bells rings out in the quiet of the woods, where the only other "sound's the sweep / Of easy wind and downy flake."

The fact that the horse must think it queer points out that the workaday horse cannot be aware of the stillness and beauty of these woods. Nature is not aware of itself, and the horse, as a part of nature, is not aware of the setting. Humans, however, have a special relationship to nature. They are both inside and outside of it, but they also can step back and reflect on their relationship.

The speaker finds the woods "lovely, dark, and deep" and inviting—or, at a minimum, appealing. He seems to be content and longs to find himself lost in them, off the road, solitary. Nature often has a powerful hold on Frost's speakers, as in "The Sound of Trees," where the speaker drops his head to his shoulder as the trees sway theirs in the wind. After the private moment passes, the speaker again reminds himself of his life. He is bound, as is the woman of "The Silken Tent," to his responsibilities. He has "promises to keep" and the "miles to go" before he sleeps. The sort of sleep to which the poem alludes is the deepest of all sleeps. The speaker might be taken for a weary traveler, relishing the solitude of the woods on this dark evening when the snow, which brings a winter's death, has an opiate affect. The speaker has his moment of reflection and then snaps back to the everyday. Perhaps his attitude toward his "promises" will be affected by this deep but temporary reflection.

After reading "Stopping by Woods on a Snowy Evening," Frost ad-libbed in his lecture "On Taking Poetry," the 1955 BREAD LOAF SCHOOL OF ENGLISH address,

> Now, you see, the first thing about that is to take it right between the eyes just as it is, and that's

the ability to do that: to take it right between the eyes like a little blow and not, you know, take it in the neuter sort of. And then, you know, the next thing is your inclinations with it.

And that is how to avoid over-reading "Stopping by Woods on a Snowy Evening."

For a darker impression of a similar scene, see "Desert Places." *See also* "The ONSET" and FUGITIVE. The poem first appeared in the March 7, 1923, issue of the *New Republic* and was collected in *New Hampshire.*

FURTHER READING

Abad, Gemino H. "Stopping by Woods: The Hermeneutics of a Lyric Poem," *Diliman Review* 20 (1972): 25–40.

Armstrong, James. "The 'Death Wish' in 'Stopping by Woods,'" *College English* 25, no. 6 (March 1964): 440, 445.

Cook, Reginald L. "Frost on Frost: The Making of Poems," *American Literature* 27 (March 1956): 66.

Frank, Bernhard. "Frost's 'Stopping by Woods on a Snowy Evening,'" *Explicator* 40, no. 4 (Summer 1982): 43–45.

Hamilton, David. "The Echo of Frost's Woods." In *Roads Not Taken: Rereading Robert Frost*, edited by Earl J. Wilcox and Jonathan N. Barron, 123–131. Columbia: University of Missouri Press, 2000.

Monteiro, George. "To Point or Not to Point: Frost's 'Stopping by Woods,'" *ANQ: A Quarterly Journal of Short Articles, Notes, and Reviews* 16, no. 1 (Winter 2003): 38–40.

Parini, Jay. *Robert Frost: A Life.* New York: Holt, 1999.

Richardson, Mark. *The Ordeal of Robert Frost: The Poet and His Poetics.* Chicago: University of Illinois Press, 1997, 189–195.

Shurr, William H. "Once More to the 'Woods': A New Point of Entry into Frost's Most Famous Poem," *New England Quarterly* 47, no. 4 (December 1974): 584–594.

Thompson, Lawrance. *Robert Frost: The Years of Triumph, 1915–1938.* New York: Holt, Rinehart and Winston, 1970.

Timmerman, John H. *Robert Frost: The Ethics of Ambiguity.* Lewisburg, Pa.: Bucknell University Press, 2002, 170–173.

"Storm Fear" (1913)

Written while Frost was living with his family on Derry Farm in Derry, New Hampshire, "Storm Fear," presents the speaker trapped in his home, where "the wind works against [him] in the dark." Nature is presented as terrifying, but it can at least be temporarily kept on the other side of the windowpane. There is a struggle here, but it "costs no inward" one; there is no mention of what to make of the storm or how to contend with it.

Remaining indoors, the speaker lies awake, uncomfortable with nature and in fear of it. He recognizes his vulnerability, being only "two and a child," and finds, as the storm shouts "Come Out! Come Out!," that he cannot make his way around nature, as the speaker does in "On a Tree Fallen across the Road," or into it. Instead, he quivers where he is, afraid of the "bark" of the beastly wind and knowing that no person or god can come to his family's aid.

While nature's power is not fully realized, as the family remains protected in their home, mere physical strength is never enough to overcome nature, and as Frost's gloss on the poem when it first appeared stated, "there is no oversight of human affairs." We recognize by our very humanness how susceptible we are to nature's forces. When the drifts pile up by the door and on the road and the fire dies out, even the "comforting barn grows far away." The poem ends in uncertainty whether with sufficient will one can, if not overcome nature, at least cope with it, as his heart "owns a doubt / Whether 'tis in us to arise with day / And save ourselves unaided."

"Storm Fear" was first published in *A Boy's Will. See* HOME, THEME OF.

"Strong Are Saying Nothing, The" (1936)

In the opening of this poem, the soil is being cultivated for the spring harvest. It "gets a rumpling soft and damp" and "[t]he final flat of the hoe's approval stamp / Is reserved for the bed of a few selected seed" that the farmer hopes will generate growth.

Each man works individually. One plows the ground and the other plants the "chain of seed." There is hope for the "bloom of a plum" and more, but there is recognition that the seeds planted may not grow. They are dependent on far more than the planting. There is worry about the cold weather and there is dependence on the bees that will "come and serve its beauty aright."

The "wind goes from farm to farm in wave on wave / But carries no cry of what is hoped to be"; all hope is silent. The farmers are patient and stoical. "There may be little or much beyond the grave," a dark description of the soil bed, "But the strong are saying nothing until they see." The farmers are hopeful, as in "Something for Hope," but farming lacks certainty. There is no way of knowing before their plantings break ground just how promising the harvest will be. There is also a certain amount of superstition, as saying something, anything, may somehow jinx their opportunities.

The final lines are indicative of more than the farmer's position on the harvest, however. The reference to the soil bed as a grave equates the planting and sowing of seed to the sowing of human life. People are also optimistic that there is something beyond their earthly growth, something beyond the soil bed where their remains will be planted. But "the strong" or willful are not certain there is, and they need proof if they are to believe. The farmers have season after season of crop, yet they refrain from saying anything "until they see." The afterlife has no cycle, so the equation is not quite accurate. The strong should definitely not say anything of the afterlife, given the comparison, or if they are to say something, it should be in the negative, since season after season have indicated no bloom beyond the grave.

Frost uses the same language at the end of his lecture "Education by Poetry," which he gave at the Amherst Alumni Council Address on November 15, 1930, when he spoke of "four beliefs that [he] know[s] more about from having lived with poetry." The first is the "personal belief, which is a knowledge that you don't want to tell other people about because you cannot prove that you know.

You are saying nothing about it till you see." In this sense the farmer's belief is a personal one. He knows that the seeds are going to grow, but he cannot prove it until they actually do. This personal belief Frost also describes as the "love belief," which he says, "has that same shyness. It knows it cannot tell; only the outcome can tell." Personal belief does not apply equally to the afterlife, however, because the outcome is something no one will return to tell. A position on the afterlife applies more directly to the last belief, which is the "relationship we enter into with God to believe the future in—to believe the hereafter in." In "The Strong Are Saying Nothing" the personal belief usurps a belief in God. The uncertainty is equated with personal uncertainty. A desire for an afterlife is akin to love: A person may have a strong feeling about it, but not true knowledge, as only the outcome will tell. Frost also identifies the "national belief we enter into socially with each other, all together . . . to bring the future of the country."

The "strong" are the strong-minded, because the strong speak only after the outcome has been presented. Those who speak before they really can are not strong, as they speak without proof. They appear to be strong, but they are not; they are only foolhardy. Robert Faggen calls the poem representative of an "agnostic and stoic vision" and observes that "[m]oral strength lies not in affirmation or progress but in restraint, silence, and patience" (184–185). George F. Bagby concludes that the poem offers an "all but explicitly agnostic view of final matters" (57). The agnosticism derives from Frost's having equated a belief in God with a certain amount of foolhardiness.

"The Strong Are Saying Nothing" was first published in the May 1936 issue of *The American Mercury* and was later collected in *A Further Range*. See BELIEF.

FURTHER READING

Bagby, George F. *Frost and the Book of Nature.* Knoxville: University of Tennessee Press, 1993.

Faggen, Robert. *Robert Frost and the Challenge of Darwin.* Ann Arbor: University of Michigan Press, 1997, 184–185.

"Subverted Flower, The" (1942)

"The Subverted Flower" has been read as deeply personal. It is said to have been written about experiences Frost and his future wife Elinor had in the summer of 1892. Jay Parini calls the summer an "idyllic one" for Frost but writes about how the outings the two took together then were "often spoiled by Frost's efforts at lovemaking," which are addressed in this poem. The poem was so personal that apparently Elinor would not let Frost publish it during her lifetime (Parini, 33). It was first published in *A Witness Tree,* four years after Elinor's death.

Parini describes the poem as a "tense, compulsively rhythmical narrative, [where] a teenage boy and girl contend with strong, almost overwhelming impulses" (33). Katherine Kearns writes that the poem "becomes, in the context of Frost's ambivalence about femality/eroticism/poetry a virtual morality play, as it chokes the man with desire, depriving him of language and sending him down on all fours. Because the woman will not become the flower, the man becomes, quite literally, a beast" (105). Robert Faggen writes that the "opposition" in the poem "between *girl* and *man* indicates a difference of experience and possibly a deprecating attitude towards the emotional immaturity of women. It becomes difficult to tell from the poem the extent to which the man is bestial or to which the girl makes him so" (84–85).

While critics' interpretations differ slightly, the main thrust of their readings is the same. The poem essentially details in a highly rhythmical way the age-old story of a man's sexual advances thwarted by a nubile girl. The poem has its beauty; it is descriptive and compelling and creates sexual tension masterfully. But the dance is predictable, as are the characters.

The man has a "ragged muzzle" and "lashe[s] his open palm"; he is described as a tiger. He is rugged and strong. She has "shining hair," and he is drawn to her "neck"; she is a "puzzle." The poem draws heavily on sexual stereotypes. The girl is pursued and resists. She is the "flower" that "mar[s] a man,"

but she is not without desire herself. While she fends off the beast, who takes "flight" at the appearance of her mother, she is left with passions unsatisfied as well. And she is not entirely innocent; her mother "wipe[s] the foam / From her chin." The girl is a tigress. Her purity remains intact; she has not been deflowered. The flower of her maidenhood has been a bit subverted, however: "what the flower began / Her own too meager heart / Had terribly completed."

The "Subverted Flower" is rare as it is both highly personal and one of the most explicitly sexual among Frost's work. One might describe the poem as the "flip side" of those from his first volume, *A Boy's Will,* which tend to be more conservative in their expression.

See also the poem "MOON COMPASSES" and NATURE.

FURTHER READING

Faggen, Robert. *Robert Frost and the Challenge of Darwin.* Ann Arbor: University of Michigan Press, 1997, 84–85.

Kearns, Katherine. *Robert Frost and a Poetics of Appetite.* Cambridge: Cambridge University Press, 1994.

Morse, Stearns. "'The Subverted Flower': An Exercise in Triangulation." In *Frost Centennial Essays II,* edited by Jac Tharpe, 170–176. Jackson: University Press of Mississippi, 1976.

Parini, Jay. *Robert Frost: A Life.* New York: Holt, 1999.

Scheele, Roy. "Sensible Confusion in Frost's 'The Subverted Flower,'" *South Carolina Review,* 10, no. 1 (1977): 89–98.

Weltman, Sharon Aronofsky. "The Least of It: Metaphor, Metamorphosis, and Synecdoche in Frost's 'Subverted Flower,'" *South Carolina Review* 22, no. 1 (Fall 1989): 71–78.

"Sycamore" (1942)

Jeffrey Cramer notes that "'Sycamore' is not a Frost poem but a direct quotation from the rhymed alphabet of the *New England Primer,* a textbook first published in 1690 for children in the English settlements (124).

The quotation in the *New England Primer* was based on a section of the Bible's New Testament in which the rich Zaccheus, "chief among the publicans," seeks to see Jesus but cannot "for the press" of people, so he climbs up a "sycamore" (stet) tree to get a look. When Jesus looks up and sees Zacchaeus, he tells him to make haste in coming down, as today Jesus "must abide at thy house." Zacchaeus is received joyfully by Jesus. They go off together, as others are "murmuring" that Jesus is accompanied by a sinner. "And Zacchaeus stood, and said unto the Lord; Behold, Lord, the half of my goods I give to the poor; and if I have taken any thing from any man by false accusation, I restore him fourfold." And Jesus says, "This day is salvation come to this house forsomuch as he also is a son of Abraham. For the Son of man is come to seek and to save that which was lost" (Luke 19:1–10).

While the verse is not Frost's, the title is. And while there is little to explicate or understand about the three brief lines, it seems that given the biblical reference the poem's placement as one of the two opening poems in *A Witness Tree*, the other being "Birch," it may be meant to bear "witness" and perhaps even to save the lost.

FURTHER READING

Cramer, Jeffrey S. *Robert Frost among His Poems: A Literary Companion to the Poet's Own Biographical Contexts and Associations.* Jefferson, N.C.: MacFarland, 1996.

"Telephone, The" (1916)

Frost also writes about the telephone in "An Encounter" and "The Line-Gang," but here the telephone takes a different function. First published in an October 9, 1916, issue of the *Independent,* and later collected in *Mountain Interval,* the poem is a romantically playful dialogue between two lovers. Here the "telephone" is the flower that is used as a device to unite the two, and the conversation takes place through a kind of telepathy.

The male speaker "thinks," or at least claims, he hears his lover call him as he leans his head upon a flower bud. The head of the flower acts as the apparent earpiece to an old-fashioned telephone, designed like a tulip. Romantically he jests, "Don't say I didn't, for I heard you say—," and here his abbreviated remarks act as part of the play. The silence is a pregnant pause to permit his lover to speak. She interjects, "First tell me what it was you thought you heard," coyly intercepting his pass. He says, "[h]aving found the flower and driven a bee away," and the suggestion is that she is that flower, the bees any threat (another man or otherwise) that would interfere with his holding her "by the stalk." He says he listened and thought he heard, as he "bowed" down to the flower (also a way of deferring to and showing gentlemanly respect to the lady), "Come." His love says coquettishly that she "may have thought as much, but not aloud." "Well," he says at last, the dance complete, "so I came."

The title is unlikely for one of Frost's finest and briefest dialogues, but the carefully choreographed dance shows the poet at his most flirtatious and frolicsome. The poem is underappreciated and not often discussed, but Frost's use of the invention as a romantic device is as well choreographed, in rhyme and schema, as any of his better duets. *See* FUGITIVE.

FURTHER READING

Perrine, Laurence. "The Telephone," *Robert Frost Review* (Fall 1991): 3–4.
———. "Frost's 'The Telephone,'" *Notes on Contemporary Literature* 10, no. 3 (1980): 11–12.

"Thatch, The" (1928)

The speaker of the poem is cast out into the winter rain, either by his own doing or by his lover's. They have had a spat; they were both "[i]ntent on giving and taking pain." People are apt to hurt most the ones they most love. The speaker does not want to go far from home; a "certain upper-window light . . . was what it was all about." He wants to keep an eye out and be sure all is reasonably well, but the poem is also about "which one would win."

The light has significance. The speaker must be within view to see whether the upper window remains illuminated. The light is clearly not "what it was all about"—the conflict was about something we will not know, but it has now become about the light. The person who outlasts giving forgiveness will somehow "win" the argument. If she turns out the light, then he will go in satisfied, but he also knows the light is not likely to go out until he goes indoors. They are at a standoff. He defiantly says; "We should see which one would be first to yield."

While he is awaiting his victory in the darkness and rain, darkness that makes the world a "black invisible field," he wanders around the thatched house. As he passes by the low eaves of the house, he accidentally brushes the straw with his sleeves, causing the summer birds who had made nests in the roof to be startled and "flushed . . . out of hole after hole." While they flee their safe havens, he reflects on what he has done and feels immense grief at the fact that they will not be able to return to their nests again until "daylight ma[kes] it safe for a flyer." He has essentially cast them out into the rain; the birds and he find themselves in the same situation, and he is as responsible for theirs as for his own.

Part of the reason the speaker feels so bad is that these are summer birds and it is winter, the "rain by rights was snow for cold." He meditates on the birds' being "without nest or roost," and that is how his own "grief started to melt." The birds' position is worse than the speaker's, because he will find his way back to the light. They are left out in the cold and the rain for the rest of the evening, but he has a choice. The only thing keeping him outdoors is his pride. For them it is a matter of safety that they do not return and instead risk ending up "in mulch and mire."

The closing presents a shift in perspective and time. The shift in perspective is interesting because throughout the entire poem we are confronted with the speaker's responsibility for affecting nature. His actions were the cause of all those birds being out in the cold for the rest of the night, and he felt immense grief for it. But the last four lines offer a different perspective, showing little care about the action or inaction that affects nature. The disre-

gard of the thatched roof; the lack of attention, affects more than the roof; it affects nature. Now all of those birds are permanently homeless, not just homeless for a night.

The cottage where the events occurred has for some time been abandoned. The speaker reflects on how he is told that the cottage where he and his lover once dwelt now has a "wind-torn thatch" that goes "unmended." The thatch that sheltered the birds—as well as him and his beloved—has deteriorated. "Its life of hundreds of years has ended," and it now lets the rain that he "knew outdoors / In on to the upper chamber floors," where the light once glowed. There is a suggestion that the speaker's relationship has also ended, the speaker being permanently cast out.

"The Thatch" was first published in *West-Running Brook. See* FUGITIVE and NIGHT.

FURTHER READING

Bagby, George F. *Frost and the Book of Nature.* Knoxville: University of Tennessee Press, 1993, 157–160.
Clark, David R. "Robert Frost: 'The Thatch' and 'Directive,'" *Costerus* 7 (1973): 47–80.

"There Are Roughly Zones" (1936)

The people sit inside the house, talking about the cold outside and the wind gusts that threaten the house. But the house has proven its capacity for protection; it "has long been tried" against such threats and has remained triumphant. The people can talk of such things, calmly, with little concern for their own safety, because they are assured of their own protection. Their comfort causes the discussion to turn to the tree, which is unprotected and may "never again" have leaves. They say to one another in agreement that they will know, if it does not flourish, "that this was the night it died."

The tree is a peach that has been brought "very far north," transplanted to a place where it has no business being. It is not meant to withstand such "strength" of cold and wind. It was vulnerable to man's selfish desires in his decision to transplant the tree for his own pleasure. The speaker wonders, "What comes over a man, is it soul or mind— / That to no limits and bounds he can stay confined?" There seems to be no limitation to his self-indulgence, his self-absorption. It seems that it is in man's nature to "extend the reach / Clear to the Arctic of every living kind." The speaker finds him "so hard to teach / That though there is no fixed line between wrong and right, / There are roughly zones whose laws must be obeyed." The categorical statement is that it is in man's nature consistently to push boundaries for his own satisfaction and that he almost entirely disregards natural laws. There is an understanding that there is no absolute morality, no absolute wrong and right, but that it should not be so difficult to have a general understanding of the rightness and wrongness of certain actions.

These particular people, housed as they are, stand in judgment, as though they are not the ones who transplanted the peach tree. They feel "more than a little betrayed" by the coming together of the freezing weather and the northwest wind, which they had hoped would be at least a little on their side. The tree has no leaves and, if it is unable to withstand nature's buffets, may never have them again. They will not know for sure until spring. Despite the threats of nature, it is the threat of man that will have killed the tree should it die. If it is "destined never again to grow," the speaker concludes, "[i]t can blame this limitless trait on the hearts of men."

The morality is not between people, but between people and nature. It can be read as being about building cities in the Arctic, about dumping raw sewage into rivers and streams, about filling in the Everglades. Just as there are zones of temperature and climate, there are zones in terms of what we should or should not do to nature. Just as in "The Thatch," Frost stresses the need to be aware of how individual actions affect the natural environment.

"There Are Roughly Zones" was first published in *A Further Range*.

FURTHER READING

Bagby, George F. *Frost and the Book of Nature.* Knoxville: University of Tennessee Press, 1993, 109–111.

Jost, Walter. "Rhetorical Investigations of Robert Frost," In *Roads Not Taken: Rereading Robert Frost,* edited by Earl J. Wilcox and Jonathan N. Barron, 179–197. Columbia: University of Missouri Press, 2000.

"They Were Welcome to Their Belief" (1936)

This poem is an uncomplicated rendition of the passing of time. Grief and Care are personified, each, "overimportant," thinking it made the speaker's hair turn white. The insinuation is that grieving causes stress and care causes exhaustion, and both bring about gray hairs. But what is more accurate is that it was simply the passing of time that was the "thief / Of his raven color of hair." The passing of time is described seasonally. One snowfall after another is the marker of a year passed. With each passing year and each white roof, the speaker's hair became a "shade less the color of night / A shade more the color of snow."

The poem is not Frost at his best. It is playful and in some ways stylistically characteristic, but he might have made his point more succinctly.

"They Were Welcome to Their Belief" was first published in the August 1934 issue of *Scribner's Magazine* and later collected in *A Further Range*. The manuscript title was "The Truth of It."

"Time Out" (1942)

This sonnet functions as a sort of time out. It begins in a "pause" that makes the speaker realize that the mountain he is climbing has "the slant / As of a book held up before his eyes." He is climbing the mountain at the same angle at which he reads a book. The "text" of the mountain is its plants; he "reads" the mountain as one does a book, fingering his way through foliage rather than pages. The slope of the mountain is also similar to the angle of his head when he is deep in thought. The speaker pits these angles and tilts, slopes and slants, against "the hard and level stare / Of enemies defied and battles fought."

Nature has its place in literature, art, and philosophy; it is not a battleground. It must be read rather than fought. While the poem is not complex, what it reveals about Frost's approach to nature is telling. Nature is not necessarily something to be feared, though it may at times appear so, but it is certainly something with which to contend. Frost is interested in what nature can do for us and to us, so he is compelled to make a thorough study of it. Frost does not know quite what to make of nature at all times, so he studies it over and over, turning things this way and that. He sees nature sometimes as redemptive, at other times as injurious. His ability to see nature in almost discordant ways reveals how discerning he is about his own uncertainty. While there are various views of nature in his many poems, what is consistent throughout his work is his return to the uneasiness he feels in and about nature. He occasionally sets that unease aside and depicts a nature where he can look into the crater of an ant, his head, one imagines, tilted to one side and himself feeling relaxed and secure, but that level of comfort is the oddity in his poetry.

The closing three lines of the poem are the most complex, as they point toward questions about the transcendent. By tilting our heads as we do while climbing or reading, we find ourselves turning somewhat upward. There is a suggestion that nature, mountain climbing, reading, and battles all have to do with some form of belief and the quest for knowledge. Here there is a "gentle" but also an obstinate "air" that may be "clamored at by cause and sect," that is, what religion takes to be higher causes with transcendental assumptions. But the aim, in being obstinate, seems to resist the clamoring of religious explanations, though the poem also seems to imply that religions will be able at least to provide us with some pregnant pauses for reflection. The transcendent ends up being found in contemplating nature, in natural things by reflection, not in looking skyward or in staring down enemies in battle, or in the clamoring of "cause and sect." Nature provides the "time outs" that are most important.

The sonnet was first published in the spring 1942 issue of the *Virginia Quarterly Review* and later collected in *A Witness Tree*. In the collection it is the first poem of eight in a section that bears the same title. The manuscript title was "On the Ascent."

"Times Table, The" (1928)

The times table here is "the multiplication table of life." The farmer offers an equation in response to his mare's sigh "halfway up the pass": There is a "sigh for every so many breath / And for every so many sigh a death." The suggestion is that there are sorrows or disappointments every so often, and for every so many of them, there is a greater letdown: death. The saying he offers his mare is the same one he offers his wife.

The speaker says that though the saying is true, we cannot say it to anyone, "unless our purpose is doing harm." We do harm when we describe life as a series of sighs. If we reduce humanity's hopes, we contribute to a reduction of the human race. After all, eliminating hope will bring about the closing of roads and the abandoning of farms. It will "[r]educe the births of the human race, / And bring back nature in people's place."

People, although they die and know that they will die, do not want to be reminded of death. It is not supposed to be spoken about too openly or too often. It will happen in any case. Humans sometimes see themselves as separate from nature, and they seem to require this illusion. It is ingrained, and to dispel it would be deleterious.

The poem leaves the speaker's attitude ambiguous. He could be describing in a neutral way how humans behave, or he could be judging that humans behave this way when they do not need to. Death is, after all, natural.

Mark Richardson finds the relationship between the farmer and his wife of primary significance. Frost "describes a farmer who has devised a remarkably efficient and cruel means to crush, or at least to contain, the extravagant aspirations of his wife, a figure whom he implicitly compares to his old mare by administering the same proverb to each. It is as if the horse and his wife reside in the same bin in his imagination" (239).

The poem was first published in the February 9, 1927, issue of the *New Republic* and was later included in *West-Running Brook*.

FURTHER READING

Richardson, Mark. *The Ordeal of Robert Frost: The Poet and His Poetics.* Chicago: University of Illinois Press, 1997, 239–240.

"Time to Talk, A" (1916)

The poet is always willing to make time for talk. If a friend should call to him from the road, slowing his horse to "a meaning walk," he does not waste any time but "thrust[s] [his] hoe in the mellow ground" and goes up to the "stone wall / For a friendly visit."

There is little time for talk, visits, or friendship when the demands of country life and all the hills he has not hoed await. The irony here is that the speaker is always willing to make time for talk, even when neither he nor his friend have any. Time to talk in the country is when the horse slows to a "walk." There is not even time to inquire "What is it?" The moment may be lost. Depending on the location, human interaction can be scarce, making each meeting significant. As expressed in "The Strong Are Saying Nothing," farm life can be very solitary. But even when life makes its demands, it is important to take time for other people. John H. Timmerman describes the main idea of the poem as "communal ethics surpasses individual demands" (119).

A further twist is offered by the stone wall that figures so prominently in the NEW ENGLAND landscape. As in Frost's famous "Mending Wall," the two, however friendly they might be, still have their visit separated by a wall. There is still a limitation on how far they can go to meet each other.

The poem was first published in the June 1916 issue of the Plymouth Normal School publication the *Prospect* and later collected in *Mountain Interval. See* WALLS.

FURTHER READING

Timmerman, John H. *Robert Frost: The Ethics of Ambiguity.* Lewisburg, Pa.: Bucknell University Press, 2002.

"To a Moth Seen in Winter" (1942)

Similar to Frost's "My Butterfly: An Elegy," this is an ode to a moth. Both are reminiscent of the English romantic poet William Wordsworth's "To a Butterfly!" Frost is concerned, as he is elsewhere, with nature, transience, and the human condition.

The speaker takes his gloveless hand, warmed by his pocket, and extends it to a moth in winter as a "perch and resting place 'twixt wood and wood." The moth does not fold its wings in "repose" but keeps them spread, prepared to fly. The speaker describes the creature and wonders what type of moth it is. If only he knew the marks of moths as well as he does the marks of flowers, he would be able to tell. The moth's repose allows him a moment of reflection. He wonders what "lured" the moth "with false hope" to venture toward "eternity" and to alight on his own hand, "the love of kind in wintertime."

He asks the moth to stay and listen to him and then sets about describing its plight. He explains how its flight at this time, in this climate, is a great labor compared with the usual effort a moth puts forth. He speaks of how the moth will not find love, nor will love find it. It is well outside the human condition. But the moth is to be pitied for its "something human," the possibility that it longs for the same things the speaker does. That human thing he pities in the moth is "old incurable untimeliness," which he calls the "begetter of all ills that are." Everything depends on timing, and time is responsible for everything. The longing for love will always be untimely.

He tells the moth to take flight, to go, as he knows that having pity is not enough to change circumstances or to help. He sends it off, hoping it will fly until it can fly no more. He imagines that the moth has a knowledge he does not himself possess.

He imagines that the moth knew the hand stretched toward him would be a resting place only but would not be able to "touch [its] fate." He concludes, "I cannot touch your life, much less can save, / Who am tasked to save my own a little while."

The slightest repose and rest of a moth in the dead of winter, when it strives against time and nature to survive, has offered the speaker a moment in which to reflect on his own condition. The two struggle against the same forces: nature, time, and the long sleep of death that nature and time eventually bring. The speaker can "touch" the moth but cannot fully touch its life, not with his love or his kindness, as he cannot save the moth from the inevitable any more than he can save himself. George F. Bagby asserts that "[e]very creature, whether human being or moth, is irrevocably locked in the prison of his own yearnings, and none can reach out to touch any other with life-giving warmth." He further identifies a "barrier between poet and moth—and implicitly between man and man" (103).

The poem was first published in the spring 1942 issue of the *Virginia Quarterly Review* and later collected in *A Witness Tree*. According to Jeffrey Cramer, Frost once commented to his early biographer Robert Newdick that he composed the poem while "walking down a foggy icy mountain one thaw in March the year we were at Plymouth" and added "Not everything is as easy to date as that" (137).

FURTHER READING

Bagby, George F. *Frost and the Book of Nature.* Knoxville: University of Tennessee Press, 1993, 102–103.

Cramer, Jeffrey S. *Robert Frost among His Poems: A Literary Companion to the Poet's Own Biographical Contexts and Associations.* Jefferson, N.C.: MacFarland, 1996.

"To an Ancient" (1947)

As in "The Missive Missile," the poet addresses someone from an ancient civilization who he is "[s]orry to have no name for . . . but You." He is apologetic, bothered by the lack of familiarity. He would prefer to call the ancient by name but must rely on a neutral pronoun.

The poet explains that the ancient had two claims to immortality, the "eolith," a stone artifact, and his (or her) own bones. The "remains" were found in bits and pieces. There was no map for finding them, of course, but archeologists managed to find evidence in a brook and in a cave.

"Coming on such an ancient human trace / Seems as expressive of the human race / As meeting someone living face to face," the poet remarks. He feels well acquainted with this ancient human, even though he cannot call him by name. They are of the same kind, though separated by time. The ancient is his ancestor.

Scientists try to date when the human being lived, judging by the "silt and dust," and they consider what a "brute" he must have been. The poet is detached from such discussion. He is more concerned with his similarities to the ancient than with any differences they might have.

He remarks that while the ancient made an "eolith," a primitive form of art, his immortality could have been created by the bones that grew, "more peculiarly your own," and would "have been enough alone" for modern man to discover the ancient's existence. The art was in a sense unnecessary. While the artist may feel that his art is more his own than his bones, in a natural sense it can never be. The flesh predates the mind and creativity.

The poet closes by wondering if he could be as immortal as the ancient. He wonders if he "would go to time," would he "gain anything by using rhyme." If he were to die, would his poetry help make him immortal, or would his bones be enough to immortalize him, as were the ancient's? Just as the "Missive Missile" becomes one of Frost's own historical messages, a series of black dots, so to speak, created in his time and sent forward for all foreseeable time, so does this poem. In the "Missive Missile" the speaker is aware that his failure to read the ancient man's message will be some other man's failure to read his; he wonders if his rhymes will be discovered, or if all that will remain of him will be his bones.

The poem was first published in the December 1946 issue of the *Atlantic Monthly* before being collected in *Steeple Bush*.

FURTHER READING

Klausner, Lewis. "Frost's Claims to Immortality: The Bones of Bequest," *Southwest Review* 80, no. 1 (Winter 1995): 137–147.

"To a Thinker" (1936)

John H. Timmerman identifies "To a Thinker" as one of Frost's "more barbed poems" (131). It was first published as "To a Thinker in Office" in the January 11, 1936, issue of the *Saturday Review of Literature,* and Timmerman notes that readers quickly observed "that the first twelve lines of the poem could be read as a mockery of [President Franklin Delano] Roosevelt's increasing infirmity" (131). He also reports that the poem was run with an interview of the poet in the *Baltimore Sun* under the heading "Latest Poem by Robert Frost Versifies New Deal Is Lost." A subsequent article in the *Sun* asked "Should a poet be meddling in political affairs at all?" and an editorial in *The New York Times* was later published under the title "Poet in Politics" (Timmerman, 131). Frost denied that the poem was directed at Roosevelt, saying later that it "was aimed at the heads of the easy despairers of the republic and of parliamentary forms of government" (Timmerman, 132).

"To a Thinker" was later collected in *A Further Range,* where it was originally titled in the proofs "Our Darkest Concern." Jeffrey Cramer explains that Frost once referred to the poem as "suppressed," since it was written in the early days of the New Deal but kept from publication until "many [of the] things said in it" had "com[e] to pass" (121).

While clearly the poem is about inconsistency in relation to political opinions and positions, the commentary is decidedly critical and satirical. The poet likens swaying opinions to the sway of a walker stepping first with the left and then with the right foot. Being on the "left" or "right" is equated with being on the liberal or conservative side politically. The poem still has relevance for our elections today.

The poet says that the thinker might call such swaying "thinking," but he calls it "walking" or even "rocking." Then he contrasts a series of opposites: matter to force, content to form, crazy to norm, free to bound, sense to sound. He finds that everything has its opposite and explains that it "almost scares / A man the way things come in pairs."

The poem sways back and forth itself, conveying its ideas most pointedly. Its most biting comment is that the thinker "sway[s] with reason more or less." It is one thing to be swayed by reason, but reason "more or less" suggests something entirely different. This thinker is not a thinker at all. As the poem states in closing, "don't use your mind too hard / But trust my instinct—I'm a bard."

The thinker Frost describes is unlike Auguste Rodin's sculpted "Thinker," who does not sway at all. This thinker is more like Frost's underdog, from "On Our Sympathy with the Under Dog." His positions change as quickly as does the political climate. It is neither reason nor instinct but self-aggrandizement that causes the thinker to rock.

FURTHER READING

Cook, Marjorie E. "Dilemmas of Interpretation: Ambiguities and Practicalities." In *Robert Frost the Man and the Poet,* edited by Earl J. Wilcox, 125–141. Rock Hill, S.C.: Winthrop College.

Cramer, Jeffrey S. *Robert Frost among His Poems: A Literary Companion to the Poet's Own Biographical Contexts and Associations.* Jefferson, N.C.: MacFarland, 1996.

Stanlis, Peter J. "Robert Frost: Politics in Theory and Practice." In *Frost: Centennial Essays II,* edited by Jac Tharpe, 48–82. Jackson: University Press of Mississippi, 1976.

Timmerman, John H. *Robert Frost: The Ethics of Ambiguity.* Lewisburg, Pa.: Bucknell University Press, 2002, 131–133.

"To a Young Wretch" (1942)

"To a Young Wretch" bears the subtitle "Boethian," which refers to the Roman philosopher and mathematician Boethius. Boethius believed that evil was a necessary part of the world but the limited perspective of humans concealed this fact. Frost's poem was first published without the subtitle, in booklet form, as Frost's 1937 Christmas poem. It was also published in the December 25, 1937, issue of the *Saturday Review of Literature* before being collected in *A Witness Tree.*

The poem takes issue with the chopping down of a particular spruce tree for Christmas. The speaker addresses a "young wretch" who is as "gay" chopping down the speaker's spruce tree with his father's ax as he is going hunting with his gun and fishing with his rod. All of these "sports" entail the harming of a living thing: the death of a deer, a fish, or a tree. The speaker imagines the young man gaily walking arm and arm with the now-fallen tree, heading homeward smelling what remains of its fresh, green fragrance.

He offers that he could have purchased "as good a tree" for the boy and what "a saving 'twould have meant to [him]." He would have been able to keep his beloved spruce. But he knows that a tree "by charity is not the same" as chopping one down oneself. He says half-heartedly, "I must not spoil your Christmas with contrition." He claims he does not want to force remorse or repentance on the boy, but it is clear he does.

The woods are at odds with the boy's "Christmases." They have opposing interests, and the speaker suggests that they are to be thought of as "opposing goods." Neither is in the wrong, in this sense, and so "the war god seem[s] no special dunce," as he is "always fighting on both sides at once."

The poem closes with the speaker hoping to accept the tree's "fate with a Christmas feeling." The tree has "lost the stars in heaven" for the star placed on its top. Although he hopes to accept the tree's fate, it is clear he has not; the poem is, after all, addressed to "a young wretch." Frost makes his point with the Christmas poem: There are better ways to celebrate than making a "tree a captive in your window bay."

"To Earthward" (1923)

Frost said this lyric was written "under a plum tree" (Cramer, 80). In contrast to such a serene setting, it describes the transition from the optimism and glory of youth to the wisdom and acceptance of age. It opens with a first kiss and the overwhelming emotions of such first experiences and moves toward growing up, growing old, and becoming more practical and less idealistic. It depicts a settling down, when the speaker comes to want the jaded side of adulthood. He relishes more and more in its discontent, because it means he is living more completely, more truly.

When the speaker was young, a kiss was all he could bear, the pleasure of it was too much. Then he "lived on air" from "sweet things," moved to the "swirl and ache" from honeysuckle, and this was the beginning of the "ache[s]" of adulthood. Soon the sweetness of a kiss was not strong enough; he craved stronger sweets, the "petal of a rose" that "stung." Now, with maturity, he can have no "joy" that "lacks salt." He has turned from sweet to salty things, from pleasure to pain, from kisses to tears. Tears come from too much love, not the sweet, unencumbered, untouched love of an early kiss. Now he wants the sort of sweetness that comes with a taste of bitterness, like that of "bark" or the "burning clove." Even being "stiff and sore and scarred" is not enough hurt; he "long[s] for weight and strength / To feel the earth as rough / To all [his] length."

Love is sweeter with age because it can also be bitter. He now gains the full experience, all the pleasure and pain of life that makes sweets all the sweeter. He feels more alive and longs for it all, the good and the bad. Having survived the prick of a rose gives him strength, and feeling the earth's roughness makes him more alive.

Robert Faggen writes that the "cruelty and nihilistic longings have at bottom the pain of a wounded lover who finds comfort in some of the possibilities for survival through the loss of consciousness and a return to our biological roots" (312). But it is quite the opposite. The speaker's longings are not about nihilism but about the full embrace of life. Frost is romantic but not idealistic. He knows that life is a mixed bag, and he still wants it. Indeed, it is because it is a mixed bag that he wants it all the more.

The poem was first published in the October 1923 issue of the *Yale Review* and later collected in *New Hampshire.*

FURTHER READING

Borroff, Marie. "Robert Frost: 'To Earthward,'" In *Frost Centennial Essays II,* edited by Jac Tharpe, 21–39. Jackson: University Press of Mississippi, 1976.

Cramer, Jeffrey S. *Robert Frost among His Poems: A Literary Companion to the Poet's Own Biographical Contexts and Associations.* Jefferson, N.C.: MacFarland, 1996.

Faggen, Robert. *Robert Frost and the Challenge of Darwin.* Ann Arbor: University of Michigan Press, 1997, 310–312.

"To E. T." (1923)

Written in memory of Frost's close friend and fellow poet Edward Thomas, who was killed on April 9, 1917, in the Battle of Arras, France, in World War I, "To E. T." was first published in the April 1920 issue of the *Yale Review* and collected later that year as "To Edward Thomas" in *American and British Verse from the Yale Review* before being included in Frost's *New Hampshire.*

It opens with the speaker asleep, a book of Edward Thomas's poems spread open on his chest like a dove's wings. Thomas appears like "a figure on a tomb" in the stillness of his rest. The poems were half-read when he fell asleep, "To see, if in a dream they brought of [Thomas]." The speaker hopes to have in his dream the opportunity he missed in life to call Thomas to his face "First soldier, and then poet, and then both." The two had agreed that nothing should be "[u]nsaid" between them, yet Frost never had the chance to say this or "one thing more" that "The Victory for what it lost and gained." There was victory in the war; Thomas did not die in vain.

The poem then recounts Thomas's death and how he met the "shell's embrace of fire," and that, for Thomas, ended the war. But the war was not over yet for Frost. Now that the war has truly ended, Frost says it is "the other way." Frost's sorrow at the loss of his friend is the war that for him never ends.

When Thomas was killed in action, Frost, who had greatly encouraged him to write poetry, keenly felt the loss of his friend and the waste of war. The war had literally ended for Thomas. But by the time the poem was published, the war had in fact ended, and the German "foe [was] pushed back unsafe beyond the Rhine." Now World War I is over for Frost as well, and he confronts the realization that he will never speak of the end of the war with his late friend.

A "survivor's guilt" is hinted at in the final stanzas, as well as a sense that Frost, something of a teacher to Thomas, never quite had the opportunity to say, or at least never said, how much he appreciated Thomas's poetry. It seems that what he would like most of all is to gratify his friend and see him pleased by such admiration of his still-living words. *See* LITERARY FRIENDS AND ACQUAINTANCES.

to foreign poets: "To the Poets of Japan" and "To the Poets of Korea"

In these two pieces, written in 1957 and 1954, respectively, Frost speaks of being "national" before being "international," offering some insight into his nationalistic and conservative political stance. He explains that being national before international is akin to being "personal" before one "can hope to be interestingly interpersonal." He also suggests that we must "remember that one may be national without being poetical, but one can't be poetical without being national."

Frost is paying respect to Asian poets he has admired, reflecting that poetry, art, is what makes him think of them. Poetry bridges continents: "We aspire towards each other in the arts," he says. He qualifies that they are "not soon to be lost in each other," however, glorifying "difference" because a poet can be "nobody's repetition." He promotes being "brave about differences . . . to see them through to some real achievement." Frost is modest, admitting that he has been "slow to learn" to be international, adding that "it has not taken me all these eighty years to find out." In "To the Poets of Japan," he says that he wishes he could "read in the original the Japanese poetry [he has] admired even as it was in translation." In "To the Poets of Korea" he asserts that the "language barrier has so much to do with individuality and originality that we wouldn't want to see it removed." In "Conversations on the Craft of Poetry" (1959) Frost "guardedly" offered a definition of poetry: "It is that which is lost out of both prose and verse in translation." Here he contradicts that view. Art is a kinship in itself, transcending the barriers of difference and politics. *See* POLITICS.

"Too Anxious for Rivers" (1947)

"Too Anxious for Rivers" is contemplative and questioning: "Look down the long valley and there stands a mountain / That someone has said is the end of the world. / Then what of this river that having arisen / Must find where to pour itself into and empty?" A river may not be defenseless, but the sympathy expressed for it is evident. If the world ends or drops off on the other side of a mountain, what happens to this river of life? What might become of it? The speaker feels responsible for any river's continuance and says that he cannot "leave it to them to get out of their valleys," as we often are left to do for ourselves. He must attend the flow of life, its pouring and emptying.

Lawrance Thompson writes that philosopher Henri Bergson, in his *Creative Evolution* (1907), "had extended the Lucretian view of life as a river: the stream of everything that runs away to spend itself in death and nothingness except as it is resisted by the spirit of human beings" and there is evidence of such a view in this poem (Thompson, 300).

The river is symbolic. The speaker's sympathy is sympathy for himself and for humanity. If the world ends on the other side of that mountain, what does humanity pour itself into, where do we empty? The sympathetic "nature" of many of Frost's poems is due to the humanity that can be imputed to nature. Nature cannot be separated from human nature. We are of it, whether we choose to consider ourselves a part of it or not: "The truth is the river

flows into the canyon / Of Ceasing-to-Question-What-Doesn't-Concern-Us." We cannot cease to question; that is what it is to be human, but some questions must not be asked, cannot be answered, in that canyon, an abyss. The river concerns us because it is as much a part of nature as we are; it lives as we do. Everything concerns us. We cannot cease to be concerned any more than we can cease to question. It is not only our nature, but everything in nature, that has the capacity to affect us, and this causes us to be concerned, if not for altruistic reasons, at least for selfish ones.

Frost points out that the river itself does concern us, as the "we" in the next line suggests: "As sooner or later we have to cease somewhere. / No place to get lost like too far in the distance. / It may be a mercy the dark closes round us / So broodingly soon in every direction." Just as the river must flow into the canyon, we must sooner or later be emptied of our individual selves and flow into the canyon, like so many before us. We, too, must cease somewhere.

While the poem meditates on death, the tone is resigned. Just as the dark closes around the bird in "Acceptance" with the lines "Now let the night be dark for all of me. / Let the night be too dark for me to see / Into the future," here the poet considers whether the darkness closing in is merciful. Frost himself, according to biographer Jeffrey Meyers, was afraid of the dark and always slept with a nightlight, but here the darkness is less terrifying (24). Besides, there is "no place to get lost like too far in the distance." But the difficulty with this ironically casual report of what is to come is that it comes too "broodingly soon."

At this point the poem branches off into a discussion of how we were sprung from the earth in the first place. The contemplation of life and death grows grand as it contemplates myths of creation: "The world as we know is an elephant's howdah; / The elephant stands on the back of a turtle; / The turtle in turn on a rock in the ocean." The evocation of these myths demonstrates how a separation from nature is an illusion. If we delude ourselves into believing that we are not a part of nature and are not natural beings, we delude ourselves into thinking that we are in some way not susceptible to its forces.

Robert Faggen writes that "Frost adds an important fact to substantiate the fable of the elephant and turtle—namely, that the turtle stands 'in turn *on a rock in the ocean*' [emphasis his], a sardonic figure of the way the church of modern natural history stands on geology the way the old church of Christianity was found on Saint Peter's rock" (44).

The anxiety expressed at the beginning seeks resolution at this point. We have been confronted with possibilities in nature—with the possibility that everything may end on the other side of a mountain. Again Frost is demonstrating a process for coming to terms with such knowledge. He goes on: "And how much longer a story has science / Before she must put out the light on the children / And tell them the rest of the story is dreaming? / 'You children may dream it and tell it tomorrow.'" The questions the speaker cannot cease to ask are not answered by supernatural phenomena. He is uneasy, but he does attempt to create comfort by providing answers that explain all. There is a sort of peacefulness conveyed in the not knowing. We know that "science," or the earth's story, eventually will end and darkness will come to us, the children of the earth. But rather than fear it and imagine the worst, Frost says that what comes next is "dreaming." We are tucked away tightly in our beds as the light is put out, and we are set to slumbering in undisturbed contentment. The rest is dreaming.

At the end Frost introduces the Roman poet and philosopher Lucretius, who, like the Greek Epicurus before him, believed that fear of gods and of death caused unhappiness, so he was interested in earthly and natural, rather than divine, explanations for creation. He did not believe that any atom is brought into existence or put out of it by divine intervention. Frost suggests that while we are susceptible to nature's forces, we do not have to attribute them to otherworldly phenomena in order to come to terms with our existence. Like the birds in "Acceptance," he suggests that he is willing to let what will be simply be.

The acceptance of what will be for Frost cannot be found in assumptions that explain all in terms of supernatural forces; it can be found in the recognition that, as part of nature, we have a history and a

knowledge of nature that is internal, inherent, and natural. We are in some way linked to the "vapor" from which we came. This poem reveals why Frost is able to seek resolutions when faced with conflict. Rather than lash out at some god or controller of the universe, he recognizes the inevitability of nature's effects, knows that he can hold none accountable for them, and instead of succumbing to them, finds there is no other recourse than to persist. It is this same ability to accept our world as an unexpected happenstance that is expressed in his other poems, such as "Acceptance" and "A Leaf-Treader." And it is with a certain contentment that Frost says, "'twas the effort, the essay of love."

In "Too Anxious for Rivers" Frost, as in "On a Tree Fallen across the Road," begins with man contending with a natural roadblock and seeks to resolve the conflict in such a way as to allow for the discomfort that nature causes us to feel while creating a way to resolve those feelings of discomfort. The strength lies in our ability to accept the chaos of the natural world, accept that we are a part of it, and at the same time not despair or give in to it. Frost may present the darkness of nature, but he does not revel in it. Despite this, what he says can never quite be trusted, because there is always an undercurrent of discontent in his work. His varied views demonstrate how uncertain he is about what he is saying. He may suggest that he is accepting, but the way he puts it is not entirely believable.

Randall Jarrell says that Frost occasionally writes with a "bare sorrow with which, sometimes, things are accepted as they are, neither exaggerated nor explained away," and that is what is evident here (28).

The poem was first published in *Steeple Bush*.

FURTHER READING

Cook, Marjorie. "Acceptance in Frost's Poetry: Conflict as Play." In *Frost: Centennial Essays II,* edited by Jac Tharpe, 229–230. Jackson: University Press of Mississippi, 1976.

Faggen, Robert. *Robert Frost and the Challenge of Darwin.* Ann Arbor: University of Michigan Press, 1997, 44.

Thompson, Lawrance. *Robert Frost: The Later Years, 1938–1963.* New York: Holt, Rinehart and Winston, 1976.

"To the Right Person" (1947)

The title of this sonnet suggests that Frost did not expect everyone who read the poem to get it. What he has to say about the District Schoolhouse is critical.

He describes an institution of higher education that he at first claims to admire. The school, which is nameless, is on "[t]his side" of the Rockies and is better than any other nearby. It "has two entries for coeducation," he explains, meaning that it accepts both men and women. But he says that there is a "tight shut look to either door" and to the windows as well, and the locks seem to suggest that "mere learning" is "the devil." The students are compared to penitents who go to a confessional. They must come to school as they might remorsefully come to a superior's feet for mercy: "To make up for a lack of meditation."

Clearly the depiction is not a pleasant one, either for this school or for formal education in general, which Frost often criticized despite his being a part of it. As a child, Frost played at being sick in order to get out of going to school and he "never fit comfortably into any academic setting," referring to organized education as "never [his] taste." Frost, it seems, did not like much of anything that was organized, given the analogy to religion's penitents here (Parini, 16). Which school Frost describes is suspect, but perhaps the "right person" knows.

The poem was first published in the October 1946 issue of the *Atlantic Monthly,* at the end of Frost's prose piece "The Constant Symbol." It had the subtitle "Fourteen Lines." "To the Right Person" was later collected in *Steeple Bush* and also appeared in *The Poems of Robert Frost* (1946). *See also* "The Constant Symbol."

FURTHER READING

Parini, Jay. *Robert Frost: A Life.* New York: Holt, 1999.

"To the Thawing Wind" (1913)

Frost once said in an interview, "You know, I somehow have always written more about just that period when the backbone of winter breaks and the thaw starts. Somehow that part of spring seems to appeal to me more. No, I will not say that it appeals to me more, but I just seem to have written about it more" (Cramer, 18). Just as Frost's "My Butterfly" took its lead from William Wordsworth's "To a Butterfly!," this lyric in rhyming couplets shares the sentiments of Percy Bysshe Shelley's "Ode to the West Wind." It is another instance where Frost modeled his early work after an English romantic poet.

The speaker calls to the wind to bring the winter's thaw. He calls for the singing and nesting birds to return, for the flowers buried beneath the earth to rise and blossom. He wants a loud Southwester (The poem was first titled "To the Loud Southwester") to bring the warmth that will make the "snowbank steam." He is longing for the brown earth beneath the white snow.

The images are graphic, particularly that of the "hermit's crucifix"—the ice melting first off the windows, and then the windows themselves melting, leaving nothing but the "sticks" of the window's frame. The descriptions are intense and powerful, but the speaker still wants the storm to bring on its destruction.

The poet's home has become a "narrow stall" because he has been holed up in it for the winter. Now he wants the wind to be so strong that it bursts inside, swinging the pictures on the wall and rustling the pages of a book. Playfully he demands, "Scatter poems on the floor; / Turn the poet out of door."

The poem is brief but intense, filled with will and the power of passions. Unlike some of Frost's others, the violence in nature is goaded and then embraced, rather than feared. In "Storm Fear," the speaker is trapped in his home, where "the wind works against [him] in the dark" and nature is presented as terrifying, but here the poet shouts, "Bring it on!" He does not lie in bed concerned about protection; he is prepared to be thrust out of doors.

The poet is puffed up in "To the Thawing Wind," first published in *A Boy's Will* with the gloss, "He calls on change through the violence of the elements." Perhaps a distinction can be made between the bravado of youth and the recognition of old age, between this poem and "Storm Fear," also from *A Boy's Will* and glossed, "there is no oversight of human affairs."

FURTHER READING

Cramer, Jeffrey S. *Robert Frost among His Poems: A Literary Companion to the Poet's Own Biographical Contexts and Associations.* Jefferson, N.C.: MacFarland, 1996.

Hoffman, Tyler. *Robert Frost and the Politics of Poetry.* Hanover, N.H.: Middlebury College Press, 2001.

Stillians, Bruce. "Frost's 'To the Thawing Wind,'" *Explicator* 31 (1972): 31.

Vanderburg, Peter. "Prosody as Meaning in 'To the Thawing Wind' and 'Home Burial,'" *Robert Frost Review* (Fall 1994): 17–22.

"Tree at My Window" (1928)

This poem's primary concern is with "inner" and "outer" weather. It opens by addressing the tree that taps at the window. Lawrance Thompson explains that at the Derry Farm in Derry, New Hampshire, "Just beyond [Frost's] bedroom window grew a white birch tree with branches long enough to scrape against the house and, in wind, even against the panes of glass" (309).

This night the "sash is lowered" as if to say that the speaker's guard is down, and he requests that "there never be curtain drawn" between himself and the tree. Coming out of a dream, the tree is like a "dream-head lifted out of the ground" the "light tongues" its branches "talking aloud" against the windowpane, leaving the speaker wondering if what it shares is "profound."

He has seen the tree "taken and tossed" in the wind, and the tree has seen into his own unrest, has seen him when he was "all but lost." They have insights into each other's plights and inner turmoil, as there is only a window between them, no curtain to conceal the truth.

In the speaker's mind there exists the same sort of labyrinth of branches as in the tree. Just as the tree's branches are tossed by the wind, the speaker tosses in his bed, troubled by the branches of his

mind. Fate "put [their] heads together" to remind him of their similarities. Without a curtain drawn between the two, he will be reminded of how confused or troubled he is by looking at the tree.

Even when he is in turmoil, he can look out the window and identify with the tree, indicating that there are helpful analogies in nature even during the most difficult of times. While the tree makes a great amount of noise, the speaker can identify that the noise is similar to the confusion in his own mind, and this creates great intimacy between the two, leading to a sense of union with the world beyond his windowpane.

"Tree at My Window" was first published in the July 1927 issue of the *Yale Review* and was later collected in *West-Running Brook*.

FURTHER READING

Bagby, George F. *Frost and the Book of Nature.* Knoxville: University of Tennessee Press, 1993.

Beacham, Walter. "Technique and the Sense of Play in the Poetry of Robert Frost." In *Frost: Centennial Essays II*, edited by Jac Tharpe, 246–261. Jackson: University Press of Mississippi, 1976.

Thompson, Lawrance. *Robert Frost: The Early Years.* New York: Holt, Rinehart and Winston, 1966.

"Trespass" (1942)

"Trespass" is concerned with people having land as property and with what it means to trespass, not only property but personal space. Once the land is owned, the sense of ownership becomes territorial. While the speaker agrees that he had put up no sign, had not fenced his land, and had not insisted it not be trespassed against, he still feels somehow violated and "strangely restless" when a person of "surly freedom" makes his way onto it. He imagines the stranger having his way with the land, "opening leaves of stone," for example, or finding "specimen crab in specimen rock." He seems concerned that some object that has no "property right" will be found on his land by this other individual and that he himself will somehow lose out. The "value" he stands to lose is more about personal ownership rights than monetary ones. He simply wants acknowledgment, however little, that what he has is his.

The fact that someone else is on his land causes him to watch the clock, to count the minutes, preoccupied with how long the person is there. It becomes clear how paranoid he is when he imagines that the visitor had to "invent" coming to ask for a drink at the kitchen door. But the man's doing so calms him, because it assures him that his property is still his. He had to ask, after all, he could not just take the drink.

Of all natural things, land is one of the stranger in terms of ownership. Owning nature becomes silliness, an oddity. It is like owning a river or owning the clouds and makes little sense. He who is so concerned with ownership is made to look foolish, paranoid, and juvenile. The poem says something about how we are overly concerned with what is ours and what is someone else's and how such preoccupations have a tendency to become obsessive.

"Trespass" was first published in April 1939 in the University of Iowa's *American Prefaces* and later collected in *A Witness Tree*.

FURTHER READING

Cook, Marjorie. "The Complexity of Boundaries: 'Trespass' by Robert Frost," *Notes on Contemporary Literature* 5, no. 1 (1975): 2–5.

Schnelle, Robert. "Over the Line: Robert Frost and Trespass," *Weber Studies* 21, no. 2 (Winter 2004): 98–105.

"Trial by Existence, The" (1913)

Frost wrote in a May 4, 1916, letter to his friend Louis Untermeyer, "The day I did 'The Trial by Existence' says I to myself, this is the way of all flesh. I was not much over twenty, but I was wise for my years. I knew that it was a race between me the poet and that in me that would be flirting with entelechies or the coming on of that in me" (29). In the philosophy of Aristotle, entelechy was the condition of a thing whose essence is fully realized, a vital force that directs an organism toward self-fulfillment. Frost might have, in youth, perceived that his greatest "trial" would be becoming a recognized and esteemed poet. Although this eventually did bring him self-fulfillment, he would face other great trials.

In the opening stanza, he reflects on the bravest, who when slain, wake to find that valor reigns even in paradise, where they also find "fields of asphodel fore'er" and learn that the "utmost reward / Of daring should be still to dare." The fields of asphodel are an allusion to Greek poetry and mythology. The plant was sacred to Persephone and said to fill the plains of Hades. It was a favorite of the gods who lived in Elysium, also known as the Plain of Asphodel. The plant is also associated with death. The ancients, considering it the food of the dead, often planted it near graves. In English and early French poetry, the asphodel was the daffodil.

Soon the poem enters a mystical land where the "light of heaven falls whole and white . . . not shattered into dyes" as it is here on earth. There "angel hosts with freshness go." In this afterworld souls are gathered for "birth" and the "trial by existence named, / The obscuration upon earth." In this transcendent place, before birth souls are given the choice to live on Earth. "Those who for some good discerned / . . . gladly give up paradise." Brave and "devoted souls" choose the "trial by existence." None go without knowing there will be "good and ill / Beyond a shadow of a doubt." The souls know about "earth's unhonored things," but they "[s]oun[d] nobler there than 'neath the sun."

When God gives the choice, he reminds us that there will be no memory of the choice, "Or the woe were not earthly woe / To which you give the assenting voice." Then the "choice must be again," but it is always "still the same." God then takes the golden flower of the asphodel and breaks it, and he uses it as the "mystic link to bind and hold / Spirit to matter till death come."

The poem closes with the recognition that "'Tis of the essence of life here." We choose every aspect of our lives but lack the memory that this is so. Mark Richardson concludes that what we discover is Frost's recognition that "life holds nothing for us but what we somehow choose, though we may suffer the consequences of our choices 'crushed and mystified,' never fully conscious of our deepest resources of power and will" (215).

Frost is faithful and hopeful here. There is an optimism that our trials are purposeful and our woes meaningful. Robert Faggen writes that "Frost's use of the metaphor 'trial' is revealing in that it suggests the existence of a God as judge but one whose ultimate intentions are unclear in respect to his creations, a creator who forces us into a predicament but does not necessarily answer our demands for justice" (256). The arrangement can be seen as automatically satisfying the desire for justice, since what happens to us in this life is directly related to our choices.

Frost takes issue with God in his masques, *The Masque of Mercy* and *The Masque of Reason,* but here, earlier, he has postulated a God who takes "especial care." Faggen also notes that the title of the poem is "an alteration of the Darwinian phrase 'struggle for existence,'" which, he asserts, the "young Frost believed could dovetail with a theological belief in the value of a life of risk on earth" (255).

"The Trial by Existence" was first published in the October 11, 1906, issue of the *Independent* and later collected in *A Boy's Will. See* BELIEF and PHILOSOPHY.

FURTHER READING

Faggen, Robert. *Robert Frost and the Challenge of Darwin.* Ann Arbor: University of Michigan Press, 1997, 255–259.

Frost, Robert. *The Letters of Robert Frost to Louis Untermeyer.* Edited by Louis Untermeyer. New York: Holt, Reinhart and Winston, 1963.

Pellegrino, Joe. "Frost, Schopenhauer, and 'The Trial by Existence,'" *Robert Frost Review* (Fall 1993): 93–100.

Perrine, Laurence. "Robert Frost and the Idea of Immortality." In *Frost: Centennial Essays,* edited by Jac Tharpe, 87–89. Jackson: University Press of Mississippi, 1974.

Richardson, Mark. *The Ordeal of Robert Frost: The Poet and His Poetics.* Chicago, Ill.: University of Illinois Press, 1997, 214–215.

"Trial Run, A" (1936)

An unlikely sonnet, "A Trial Run" concerns a man-made machine called "It" that is either out for a first run or in use by the speaker for the very first time. The speaker is frightened by the power of this machine, and his fear causes him almost to say a prayer to himself. The machine, though never identified, appears to be one made for and used in war. It might be a plane, perhaps a bomber, as it "will start hair-raising currents of air." It is started when it is given the "livid metal-sap," probably fuel, and it has the capacity to make "a homicidal roar," which perhaps refers to the sound of an engine as well as the killing it would have the power to wreak. The machine will shake its "cast stone reef of floor" when it takes off, traveling at great speed. If it were to crash it would create a "thunder-clap." It is "cotter-pinned," suggesting that it is hardly held together and that one pull from the pin would have a devastating effect.

After a series of descriptions of the machine, the speaker concludes that "Everything its parts can do / Has been thought out and accounted for." He is being paradoxical. It is unclear whether he is simply unconvinced of his own statement or whether he is unconvinced but wants to be convinced of it. He perceives the machine's creators as overconfident about how well the machine is built, regardless of what it has been built to do. They are also overconfident about their ability to stop it: "when to stop it rests with you." It takes the "least touch" to set it "going round," but there is the suggestion that once it starts, it will not be stopped. Like the buzz saw of "Out, Out—," this machine could have a mind of its own or behave in a way that goes beyond the predictions of its creators.

The trial run suggests that the machine has not been used before, either by the speaker or anyone else, so he remains unsure of what it can do. While the speaker is close to prayer, the person he addresses is assumed to be confident and secure. The fear comes from uncertainty and a lack of familiarity. While there is always a chance that what we have built will do something different from what was intended, the fear also seems to stem from Frost's general concern that technology had "run away." He saw the technologies of modern life as being out of control. For Frost there always seems to be the question, "When does technological advancement stop? When is it enough?" Another reading of the title is more comprehensive. Since this is the only time that humans have existed and the only time that we have had such technology, all technology is in some sense new to us and on a trial run. Our fears, uncertainties, and concerns are therefore justified.

The poem was first published in the June 1936 issue of the *Atlantic Monthly* and was later collected in *A Further Range*.

"Triple Bronze" (1942)

Another of Frost's political poems, "Triple Bronze" addresses the question of protection and how much defense a person needs against "The Infinit[e]." The infinite represents the world and the universe as well as eternity. The speaker is told by the "Powers" that a triple bronze is necessary.

The first layer of protection is personal: "For inner defense my hide." *Hide* is used doubly, both as refuge and as skin. The "next defense outside" is the protection of a home with walls that can be made of "wood or granite or lime" as long as they are "too hard for crime / Either to breach or climb." Walls are significant in Frost's poetry. The best-known wall appears in his "Mending Wall," but walls figure prominently in other poems as well, such as "Atmosphere" and "Bond and Free." The third protection is "a national boundary," suggesting political protection.

These three levels of defense define him against the illimitable vastness, protecting what is his—his body, his belongings, and his country. He draws a parallel among the three defenses, conferred on him by nature (skin), himself (walls), and society (national borders). Though the poem's tone is playful, he seems to accept these boundaries. The concern with inner and outer defenses mirrors to some degree the inner and outer weather of "Tree at My Window."

"Triple Bronze" was first published as "Triple Plate" in booklet form as Frost's 1939 Christmas poem and later collected in *A Witness Tree*. See POLITICS and WALLS.

"Tuft of Flowers, The" (1913)

"The Tuft of Flowers" was inspired by an experience Frost had while haying at Cobett's Pond near Salem, New Hampshire. Frost considered the poem one of his best, saying that the subject was "togetherness" and that in it he "came back to people and college." He had come back to college because he submitted the poem for an assignment in his English A class at Harvard in 1897, in which he earned a "B" (Cramer, 23). In his "On Taking Poetry," a BREAD LOAF SCHOOL OF ENGLISH address in 1955, he explained that "in the old days we mowed by hand a great deal. . . . The mowing was apt to be done in the dew of the morning for better mowing, but it left the grass wet and had to be scattered. We called it—the word for it was "turning" the grass. I went to turn the grass once more."

Frost is concerned with mowing in a number of poems, including "A Late Walk," "The Last Mowing," "Mowing," and "Rose Pogonias." The speaker goes to "turn the grass once after one / Who mowed it in the dew before the sun," looks for him "behind an isle of trees," listens for his "whetstone on the breeze," and finds he is alone. The "leveled scene" becomes an opportunity for reflection. He is as alone as the mower would have been, and he declares philosophically from "within [his] heart": "all must be . . . Whether they work together or apart." There is a notion of togetherness and union both between people and between people and the natural environment.

Just as the speaker utters the phrase to himself, "[o]n noiseless wing a bewildered butterfly" passes by seeking "with memories grown dim o'er night" a flower on which to rest. The speaker's attention to the butterfly becomes a meditation, as do the ants of "Departmental" and the mite of "A Considerable Speck." Butterflies are prominent in Frost, figuring in his first poem, "My Butterfly: An Elegy," as well as "Blue-Butterfly Day," among others. George F. Bagby writes about the association of the butterfly with Psyche, or the soul, as going back to the Greeks and of Edmund Spenser's "Muiopotmos," William Wordsworth's "To a Butterfly," Samuel Taylor Coleridge's "Psyche," and John Keats's "Ode to Psyche," where psyche is not a butterfly but a dove (165).

The speaker observes the butterfly, watching it fly "as far as eye could see" and thinking of "questions that have no reply." The butterfly and the speaker are engaged in silent conversation. The butterfly's dance is its way of speaking, and its turns lead the speaker to become even more observant. He soon spots a tuft of flowers, the "leaping tongue of bloom the scythe had spared / Beside a reedy brook the scythe had bared," by having removed the grass that would have obscured it. Their having escaped the mower is described as it having "loved them thus, / By leaving them to flourish, not for us." The speaker imagines that the mower spared them not for the mower, himself, or the butterfly, "[n]or yet to draw one thought of ours to him," but from "sheer morning gladness at the brim." The mower's joy at discovering the tuft of flowers would have been enough; it would be for him.

Bagby also writes that "Frost's butterfly, like its predecessors, is a carefully crafted element of literary fiction, intended to objectify the movement of the speaker's mind" (165). It does so skillfully, demonstrating not only the dance in the speaker's mind but its movement toward conclusion. He resolves that the two had in combination "lit upon . . . a message from the dawn." The speaker is united with the mower, hearing his "long scythe whispering to the ground" as he listens to the waking birds. He no longer feels alone, finding kinship with the butterfly and the mower in this natural landscape and sensing the sort of union between humanity and nature that Walt Whitman celebrates in "Song of Myself."

The earlier phrase is repeated in the closing lines: "'Men work together,' I told him from the heart, 'Whether they work together or apart.'" The poem is almost all heart. It was first published in the March 9, 1906, issue of the *Derry Enterprise* and later collected in Frost's first collection, *A Boy's Will.* It reflects the earlier poet—its style romantic, its imagery magical—but also foreshadows much of his later work in theme and philosophy. "The Tuft of Flowers," superbly crafted and expressive, is one of Frost's most anthologized and celebrated.

FURTHER READING

Bagby, George F. *Frost and the Book of Nature.* Knoxville: University of Tennessee Press, 1993.

Cramer, Jeffrey S. *Robert Frost among His Poems: A Literary Companion to the Poet's Own Biographical Contexts and Associations.* Jefferson, N.C.: MacFarland, 1996.

Dickey, Frances. "Frost's 'The Tuft of Flowers': A Problem of Other Minds," *New England Quarterly* 75, no. 2 (June 2002): 299–311.

Fleissner, R. F. "Tufting the Host: Frost's Further Use of Wordsworth," *Notes on Contemporary Literature* 12, no. 4. (September 1982): 6–8.

Monteiro, George. "Robert Frost's Linked Analogies," *New England Quarterly* 46, no. 3 (September 1973): 463–468.

Perrine, Laurence. "Frost's 'The Tuft of Flowers,'" *Explicator* 42, no. 1 (Fall 1983): 36.

Waddell, William S., Jr. "Aphorism in Robert Frost's 'The Tuft of Flowers': The Sound of Certainty," *Concerning Poetry* 13, no. 1 (1980): 41–44.

"Two Leading Lights" (1947)

The "two leading lights" of the title are the sun and the moon. They are personified as masculine and feminine, the sun as man, the moon as woman. The speaker begins by saying that he "never happened to contrast / The two in the celestial cast / Whose prominence has been so vast" and then goes on to do just that. The sun is "satisfied with days," he says, taking a playfully earthly perspective rather than a scientific one on the movement of the sun. He says that it could "dayify the darkest realm" but "has the greatness to refrain." In this way, Frost presents the traditional role of the male as strong and powerful, as one who has the "right of eminent domain."

The moon is described in feminine terms as having "light and grace," but she is, of course, illuminated by the sun. The speaker explains that because the moon is illuminated, she has "never learned to know her place," the dark, which the "notedest astronomers / Have set . . . aside for hers." Her place is in darkness, but she does not always appear, even on clear nights. She seems dictated to by "lunatic or lunar whim" and is described as coming to the sun as the Queen of Sheba in the Old Testament made her visit to King Solomon. According to some traditions, Sheba either wed or had an affair with Solomon, eventually returning home with child, so this allusion suggests that the sun and the moon have a love affair.

"Two Leading Lights" draws a comparison between the masculine and feminine even though "[c]omparison is not her quest." But the poem can be read as antifeminist, when taken metaphorically. The moon's light comes not from the moon itself but from reflection of the sun, making the feminine moon dependent on the masculine sun and thereby secondary to it. There are nights when the moon does not appear, but these are decisions she makes on "lunatic or lunar whim," a depiction that reflects an emotional or hysterical stereotype of woman. The poem also suggests that she is coy, not always "bother[ing] to appear."

The final seven lines are of greatest significance, however. "It may be charitably guessed / Comparison is not her quest," because the moon cannot compare to the sun, nor would she want to. She has different attributes to offer. The poem closes by saying that the moon "merely" visits during the lunar changes of winter to spring, as an "irresponsible divinity / Presuming on her femininity." The bitterness of the line sounds like that of a man scorned, but in the title the lights are set not as comparisons but as equals. They each have important roles and "prominence . . . so vast."

"Two Leading Lights" was first published in a 1944 Christmas booklet of the California collector Earle J. Bernheimer and later collected in *Steeple Bush*.

"Two Look at Two" (1923)

In "Two Look at Two," two people in late afternoon or early evening make their way up a moun-

tainside. "Love and forgetting" for each other and for nature have carried them a bit farther from home than they ought to have traveled, and they will have to turn back soon if they are to make their return safely before dark.

They are halted by a wall that is "tumbled" and has "barbed-wire binding." The wall serves as a boundary. They have the "onward impulse" to keep exploring but must turn back, so they stand with "one last look the way they must not go." The land beyond the wall is the rugged sort where "if a stone / Or earthslide moved at night, it moved itself." It is treacherous ground, not fit for people, even if they had enough daylight left. The two sigh at having to give up their journey and breathe, "This is all . . . / Good night to woods." But it is not all; there is more nature to absorb before returning.

They observe a doe first, close on the other side of the wall. She does not fear them, partly, perhaps, because of the wall but also because she "seemed to think that two thus they were safe." The two people are now satisfied, having had an opportunity to delight once more in nature's beauty. But this is not all either. "What more is there to ask?" they wonder, when they are greeted by a buck who observes them standing as still as statues. "Why don't you make some motion? / Or give some sign of life?" they imagine him inquiring. "Because you can't. / I doubt if you're as living as you look," is his imagined answer. The safety of two and two makes them want to stretch out a hand, but they know it would break nature's "spell."

The moment is magical. Four of nature's creatures have met equally and unafraid: "Two had seen two, whichever side you spoke from." The two people are able to return home satisfied with what they saw: "As if the earth in one unlooked-for favor / Had made them certain earth returned their love."

Robert Faggen argues that the poem "prefigures Frost's exploration of our need for response from the world and the limited love it provides in 'The Most of It,' 'Never Again Would Birds' Song Be the Same' and 'The Subverted Flower.'" He goes on to say that

[t]his cluster from *A Witness Tree* are among Frost's best and most terrifying, which dramatize our need and ultimate failure to find our

self-love and desire confirmed by the rest of the world. They form a triptych that moves from isolation to revelations of degraded and brutal sexuality. The seeking of a model or memory of love in nature leads only to revelations of emptiness, loss, and loss of control. (77)

The poem was first published in *New Hampshire* and expresses Frost's great love for nature and a belief that we are all the Earth's children.

FURTHER READING

Bagby, George F. *Frost and the Book of Nature.* Knoxville: University of Tennessee Press, 1993.

Cook, Marjorie E. "The Serious Play of Interpretation," *South Carolina Review* 15, no. 2 (Spring 1983): 77–87.

Faggen, Robert. *Robert Frost and the Challenge of Darwin.* Ann Arbor: University of Michigan Press, 1997, 75–77.

Helphinstine, Frances. "Frost's 'Two Look at Two,'" *Explicator* 39, no. 4 (Summer 1981): 31–33.

Pack, Robert. *Belief and Uncertainty in the Poetry of Robert Frost.* Hanover, N.H.: Middlebury College Press, 2003.

Timmerman, John H. *Robert Frost: The Ethics of Ambiguity.* Lewisburg, Pa.: Bucknell University Press, 2002, 121–125.

"Two Tramps in Mud Time" (1936)

It is spring—mud time. The speaker is outside, chopping wood, not because he really has to but in order to give "a loose to [his] soul," for no other reason than that he loves the task itself. It is a day in April when the "sun is out and the wind is still," and it almost seems like the middle of May. The speaker is superstitious, believing that if he utters recognition of that beautiful spring day, a cloud will appear "over the sunlit arch" and a wind will come "off a frozen peak" and he will be squarely back in the "middle of March."

The water that in summer is all but gone and can be found only with "a witching-wand" can now be found everywhere and in every indentation of the earth, including wheel ruts and hoofprints. The moment is to be seized, because just as the clouds may soon appear overhead, at night the frost will still "steal forth," if only to "show on the water its crystal teeth."

As the speaker happily chops his wood, "two hulking tramps" come out of the woods. They are itinerant lumberjacks who judge a man by how he "handle[s] an ax." The speaker, feeling like an imposter, indirectly describes himself as a "fool." While neither the tramps nor he say anything, the tramps' continued presence enables "their logic" to fill his head. Their logic is that the speaker has "no right to play / With what was another man's work for gain." Frost, the poet-farmer, who always saw himself as a better poet than farmer, exposes his insecurities here and offers a heartfelt twist on them.

The speaker's time with the ax is "love but theirs [is] need," and they have the better claim, "agreed." But Frost declares that his "object in living is to unite / [his] avocation and [his] vocation," the way our two eyes join to give us sight. During a lecture Frost once called the poem " 'A poem against hobbies.' That is, against having a divided life" (Richardson, 27).

Frost closes with a profound statement that stretches beyond the poem: "Only where love and need are one, And the work is play for mortal stakes, / Is the deed ever really done / For Heaven and the future's sakes."

"Two Tramps in Mud Time" was inspired by an incident that occurred on Frost's farm in Franconia, New Hampshire. Frost said before reading this poem in his "Poverty and Poetry" address to Haverford College on October 25, 1937, that "few back roads are left now; mud time is going by. We used to be shut in by mud longer than by snow. All the old pleasures of mud time are nearly gone. When we first went to another farm, we helped get somebody out of the mud. But this is in memory of those good days."

Jeffrey Cramer writes that during a 1935 lecture in Colorado, Frost remarked, "A poet may be concerned with the jails, the poor-houses, the slums, the insane asylums, and wars; or, because he sees no possibility of change, he may try to find what happiness he can for himself and be cruelly happy" (103).

Reginald Cook calls the poem political but not in the "usual sense" (i.e., Democratic or Republican); instead, he feels that it is more specific in its "personal psychological approach to the problem of living one's life, and more general in its advocacy, like [Ralph Waldo] Emerson and [Henry David] Thoreau, of the higher, more conscientious individualism" (123).

"Two Tramps in Mud Time" was first published in the October 6, 1934, issue of the *Saturday Review of Literature* and later collected, with the subtitle "A Full-time Interest," in *A Further Range*.

FURTHER READING

Braverman, Albert, and Bernard Einbond. "Frost's 'Two Tramps in Mud Time,'" *Explicator* 29 (1970): 25.

Cook, Reginald. *The Dimensions of Robert Frost*. New York: Rinehart, 1958.

Cramer, Jeffrey S. *Robert Frost among His Poems: A Literary Companion to the Poet's Own Biographical Contexts and Associations*. Jefferson, N.C.: MacFarland, 1996.

Jost, Walter. "'The Lurking Frost': Poetic and Rhetoric in "Two Tramps in Mud Time,'" *American Literature* 60, no. 2 (May 1988): 226–240.

Pearlman, Daniel. "Frost and the Work Ethic: A Reading of 'Two Tramps in Mud Time,'" *Modernist Studies* 3 (1979): 61–68.

Perrine, Laurence. "'Two Tramps in Mud Time' and the Critics," *American Literature* 44, no. 4 (January 1973): 671–676.

Richardson, Mark. *The Ordeal of Robert Frost: The Poet and His Poetics*. Chicago: University of Illinois Press, 1997, 26–27.

Sears, John F. "Frost's Figures of Upright Posture." In *Robert Frost the Man and the Poet*, edited by Earl J. Wilcox, 49–59. Rock Hill, S.C.: Winthrop College, 1990.

"Two Witches" (1923)

"Two Witches" is the collective title for the two poems "The Witch of Coös" and "The Pauper Witch of Grafton." (Coös and Grafton are counties in New Hampshire.) "The Witch of Coös" was first published in the January 1922 issue of *Poetry* and later collected in *New Hampshire*. "The Pauper Witch of Grafton" was first published in the April 13, 1921, issue of the *Nation* and later collected in *New Hampshire* as well. It was inspired by a history of Sarah Weeks, found in William Little's *The History of Warren, a Mountain Hamlet Located among the White Hills, New Hampshire* (1970). Mrs. Weeks had the "very enviable reputation of being a witch" and had become "chargeable to the town of Wentworth for support as a pauper." A battle between the towns of Warren and Wentworth, where she once lived, ensued (Cramer, 71).

Titled as they are, the dramatic narratives are meant to be read as companion pieces. The first, "The Witch of Coös," tells the story of a mother and son, "Two old-believers," who live together, alone, on an isolated farm behind a mountain. The speaker spends the night with the two, who do "all the talking." The speaker's voice enters only in the opening and closing of the piece.

The dialogue between the mother and son begins with the mother talking about what "folks think a witch is." The son says that one of his mother's witch tricks is to make a table "kick with two legs like an army mule," but that is not what she is going to do to entertain this visitor. Instead she begins by talking about the dead, who are "keeping back" something. The son eerily interjects, "You wouldn't want to tell him what we have / Up attic, mother?" and thus it begins.

In the attic are "Bones—a skeleton" of a man, the son's father, Toffile, who was "killed for" his wife—or rather, the witch corrects herself, "killed instead" of her. The bones were buried in the cellar, but one night they decided to make the journey upstairs. They made their way eventually up to the bedroom, singing the old song "The Wild Colonial Boy," an Australian ballad, the refrain of which is

Come, all my hearties, we'll roam the mountains high,
Together we will plunder, together we will die.
We'll wander over valleys, and gallup over plains,
And we'll scorn to live in slavery, bound down with iron chains (Cramer, 71).

The husband and wife locked the bones in the attic, deciding that "[i]f the bones like the attic, let them have it. / Let them stay in the attic," and that is where they have been since. The wife promises her husband to "be cruel to them / for helping them be cruel once to him," by cheating on him with the man whose bones they are.

The son tries to keep the secret that he has been sworn to keep by not telling the visitor whose bones they are. But the mother says they must "[t]ell the truth for once." Besides, she decides that tonight she does not "care enough to lie" and does not "remember why [she] ever cared." The speaker verifies the name Toffile in the morning: "The rural letter box said Toffile Lajway."

The narrative acts as a campfire ghost story. Its grace lies in the description of the bones as put together "[n]ot like a man, but like a chandelier"; of the hand struck "off brittle on the floor," where "finger-pieces" slide in all directions; and of the skeleton as a "chalk-pile." The tone is both haunting and humorous, the candor of the mother suspiciously canny. It is as though the two, isolated as they are, have their greatest fun with visitors who happen along. But at the heart of the ghost story is the frightening truth of a love affair gone awry, with all the sexual jealousy, the murder of passion, and the basement burial of a television soap opera.

The second poem, "The Pauper Witch of Grafton," is reminiscent of "Provide, Provide." Here a witch woman, once a "strapping gal of twenty," was taken for bride by Arthur Amy, whom she could make do anything, including gather her "wet snow berries / On slippery rocks beside a waterfall" in the dark. Now she is being fought over by two towns, Warren and Wentworth. Neither wants the responsibility of financing her in her old age. We are reminded by her that "You *can* come down from everything to nothing," as she has. She resolves that if she had "a-known when [she] was young / And full of it, that this would be the end, / It doesn't seem as if [she'd] had the courage / To make so free and kick up in folks' faces." She says she "might have, but it doesn't seem as if. . . ."

Most of the narrative tells how she is in "double trouble" for having two towns fighting over her, but double trouble is the "witch's motto anyway." They

have confused her Arthur Amy with her husband's father, also named Arthur Amy, and this is causing part of the difficulty in resolving who is responsible. When young, her Arthur Amy had a good time calling her a witch and saying when she was out late at night that "she ain't come back from kiting yet" on her broomstick. She imagines that her husband "found he got more out of [her] / By having [her] a witch." Despite her husband's saying so, she appears to be no witch.

"The Pauper Witch of Grafton" is a reminder that anyone can fall from "great and good." The two poems may be read as companion pieces, but they are quite different in their import. This witch's tale is no campfire ghost story, as is the first, but its reality is all the more haunting.

FURTHER READING

Cramer, Jeffrey S. *Robert Frost among His Poems: A Literary Companion to the Poet's Own Biographical Contexts and Associations.* Jefferson, N.C.: MacFarland, 1996.

Faggen, Robert. *Robert Frost and the Challenge of Darwin.* Ann Arbor: University of Michigan Press, 1997, 211–215.

Kearns, Katherine. *Robert Frost and a Poetics of Appetite.* Cambridge: Cambridge University Press, 1994.

Marcus, Mordecai. "The Whole Pattern of Robert Frost's 'Two Witches': Contrasting Psycho-Sexual Modes," *Literature and Psychology* 26 (1976): 69–78.

Wallace, Patricia. "The Estranged Point of View: The Thematics of Imagination in Frost's Poetry." In *Frost Centennial Essays II*, edited by Jac Tharpe, 180–182. Jackson: University Press of Mississippi, 1976.

"Unharvested" (1936)

The sonnet begins with the "scent of ripeness" wafting over a wall. The scent causes the speaker to break from the "routine road" to follow the scent and "look for what had made [him] stall." Off the road he finds an apple tree, which had "eased itself" of its "summer load" of apples. What remains is its foliage, causing it to breathe as lightly as "a lady's fan" without the weight of the apples on its branches. The fall of the apples is equated to the biblical fall of man and the forbidden fruit of the tree of knowledge in the Garden of Eden. He describes the ground as "one circle of solid red" made from the apples, playing on the traditional use of the color red as a symbol for sin, though here the "fall" is a positive and beautiful event.

In the closing lines the speaker exclaims, "May something go always unharvested!" bemoaning the loss of innocence that comes with harvesting and wishing that something could "stay out of our stated plan." If only things more than the apples could be "forgotten and left," then "smelling their sweetness would be no theft."

"Unharvested" was first published as "Ungathered Apples" in the November 10, 1934, issue of the *Saturday Review of Literature*. It was originally 11 lines, but Frost then revised it into this sonnet, which was collected in *A Further Range*.

"Unmade Word, or Fetching and Far-Fetching, The" (1918)

"The Unmade Word, or Fetching and Far-Fetching" was a lecture Frost presented at the Brown and Nichols School on March 13, 1918. The lecture is one of Frost's freshest, partly because he is having fun, partly because he is still filled with his own youth, and partly because he is speaking of one of his favorite things: freshness in language.

Frost tells the boys not to take notes on his lecture but instead to "take the thing in as a whole," and later he will ask for an account. The title makes evident his purpose: urging the boys to make their own "unmade word[s]." He instructs them on the two types of language, spoken and written, and reminds them that the two are treated differently, the first a common vernacular language, the second a "literary, somewhat artificial style." He explains that William Butler Yeats said that "all our words, phrases, and idioms to be effective must be in the manner of everyday speech," a view that Frost himself holds. The freshness, then, is not in

the language but in the use of the language. It is in giving a "lift" to everyday words, a "metaphorical turn."

He discusses the boys' language, talking about common slang of the day such as "pill," "peach," "lemon," and "put one over on him." Frost reminds the boys that such expressions are not "allowable" in writing and that furthermore, these are "second-hand," "ready-made" words and phrases. He asks them, "Did you ever get one up?" In other words, did they ever "fetch" a word and use it figuratively? He urges them to do it but also cautions them against overdoing it. He quotes words that Ralph Waldo Emerson and John Keats "fetched" and made their own, and even one of his own fetched words from "Birches": "crazes."

Here the poet is passionate, inspired, and inspiring, both fetching and far-fetching.

"Unstamped Letter in our Rural Letter Box, An" (1947)

This "letter," collected in *Steeple Bush*, was Frost's Christmas poem in 1944. The letter (poem) is unstamped and slipped in the mailbox by a tramp to the person whose pasture he used for a "camp." The writer begins by explaining why the farmer's "dog barked all night," bringing the man to his door (it was he). The tramp describes how he was made comfortable by the "young spruce" that "made a suite of glades" and the "low-slung juniper" that was like a blanket, helping him keep "some dew out and some heat in." He says that the "place was like a city park," which is where one would typically find a vagrant such as he.

While sleeping outside that night, the tramp, being awakened by a rock that made him uncomfortable, comes face-to-face with "universal space." He then witnesses two stars joining and shooting off together and has a transcendent experience. He calls himself a "tramp astrologer" and shares how witnessing the stir of "Heaven's firm-set firmament" by the "largest firedrop ever formed" caused him to have "the equivalent, / only within." He describes how "Inside the brain / Two memories that long had lain, / Now quivered toward each other, lipped / Together, and together slipped." The bringing together of his two "minds" makes all plain to him, and he feels himself more fortunate and more informed and knowledgeable than other men, who have thought about the same "in vain."

The writer recognizes his own boastfulness and coyly asks forgiveness from his "involuntary host" by wondering whether the farmer witnessed the same and has had a similarly transcendent experience. The tramp humbly writes that "in forma pauperis," in the form of a pauper, he shares his epiphany and wonders whether they are at all similar. "Things have happened to you, yes, / And have occurred to you no doubt," he writes. He says that whereas the vision came to him from sleeping out, perhaps it came to the farmer though his hard work. He is likening himself to the farmer in part to raise his own social position a bit and in part to show that social position does not make men so unlike other men with "lesser" positions in society. In this way, Frost's usual conservative politics are less evident here than elsewhere.

The tramp also takes a playful jab, a jab that Frost, occasionally viewed as the failed farmer, seems really to be taking at himself, when he says that the farmer "went about / In farming well—or pretty well." *See* COUNTRY VERSUS CITY and STARS.

FURTHER READING

Bagby, George F. *Frost and the Book of Nature.* Knoxville: University of Tennessee Press, 1993, 161–163.
Timmerman, John H. *Robert Frost: The Ethics of Ambiguity.* Lewisburg, Pa.: Bucknell University Press, 2002. 143–144.

"U.S. 1946 King's X" (1947)

First published in the December 1946 issue of the *Atlantic Monthly,* this and other Frost poems preceded a piece by Dr. Karl T. Compton, physicist and then-president of the Massachusetts Institute of Technology, titled "If the Atomic Bomb Had Not Been Used." During World War II, the cities

of Hiroshima and Nagasaki, Japan, were destroyed by atomic bombs dropped by the United States military on August 6 and August 9, 1945. The bombs killed at least 100,000 civilians outright and many more over time. One of the primary reasons given for the use of the bomb was that it would force Japan to surrender unconditionally. Compton received a response from President Harry S Truman upon his having read the *Atlantic Monthly* article, which stated that it was the "first sensible statement" he had seen on the subject, but also that "The Japanese were given fair warning and were offered the terms, which they finally accepted, well in advance of dropping the bomb. I imagine the bomb caused them to accept the terms."

A brief political poem, "U.S. 1946 King's X" refers to that nuclear holocaust, declaring that "Having invented a new Holocaust, / And been the first with it to win a war, / How they make haste to cry with fingers crossed, / Kings X—no fairs to use it any more!" The sarcasm is biting. Frost, usually the nationalist, takes direct aim at the U.S. government, identifying the clear hypocrisy in using such an atrocious weapon of war and then declaring it unfair for future use. Defining the terms as they suit the United States is made childlike when Frost invokes "King's X," a phrase used to call truce or time out in a game of tag, and by using the phrase "no fairs," the way a child might.

"U.S. 1946 King's X" was later collected in *Steeple Bush. See* POLITICS.

FURTHER READING

Bagby, George F. *Frost and the Book of Nature.* Knoxville: University of Tennessee Press, 1993, 82–83.

"Valley's Singing Day, The" (1923)

"The Valley's Singing Day" begins with "the sound of the closing of an outside door." The closing of the door as the speaker's companion exits the house is a way of "opening the valley's singing day." The sound from the door awakens a songbird and helps him loosen the "pent-up music of over-night." Images of the morning dew are presented as "pearly-pearly" rather than the "diamonds" they will change into in the bright light of the noonday sun. The speaker is still in bed but recalls the sounds and beauty of the morning for his companion as though he were the one who, by closing the door, began the day.

The poem is a celebration of love, for one's companion, for nature, for a new day, and for the ability to speak of all of them. It is a love letter rejoicing in the quiet reserve of one who has the ability to open the valley's singing day both for her lover and for the world, but whose modesty will keep her from saying so. Such modesty causes the lover to "help [her] say" so in this poem and further indicates why he loves her so.

The poem was first published in the December 1920 issue of *Harper's Magazine* and was later collected in *New Hampshire*.

"Vanishing Red, The" (1916)

Written in the gothic spirit of Edgar Allan Poe, this poem tells the haunting tale of John, the last "Red Man," or Native, of Acton, Canada. The Miller, his murderer, is introduced with an eerie laugh, "If you like to call such a sound a laugh." The Miller recalls the incident with a sort of frightening humor, but he gives "no one else a laugher's license." The Miller is the sort of man who has the attitude of "getting a thing done with," as if what happened to John was something he needed to do. Contrarily, the speaker expresses an attitude that does not justify the actions of the Miller while claiming that we cannot really judge what happened. Instead he asserts that we "can't get back and see as he saw it," and "[y]ou'd have to have been there and lived it." It was not "just a matter / Of who began it between the two races," he says.

There is some bitter rivalry between the Miller and John, but the speaker suggests it was not just between them but between their entire races, white and red. The Miller is physically "disgusted" simply by John's "guttural exclamation of surprise" about the wheel pit. The physical reaction of the Miller suggests that the rivalry is instinctive rather than situational. The Miller feels that John is "one who had no right to be heard from" and essentially reacts with a sort of "You want to see the wheel-pit? I'll show you the wheel-pit" attitude. The Miller's invitation must have appeared benign to John, as he seems to go along willingly, without apprehension.

John is not given a name at first, only "Red Man," until the last line. Keeping him nameless allows for the objectification of the Native; Frost frequently withholds proper names until precisely the right moment. John is surprised by the technology, and because of this the Miller thinks that John is not advanced and that he himself is therefore superior to John.

The last stanza is split into two independent thoughts. The first four lines are the Miller showing John the machinery, and the last six jump to after the murder takes place. The scene has something in common with Poe's "The Cask of Amontillado." The Miller lures John down into the wheel pit and shuts him in there. When he comes up the stairs, he says something to a man eating lunch and gives the laugh that introduces the Miller at the start of the poem. What he said the man did not catch at first, but it was that "Oh, yes, he showed John the wheel-pit all right."

Race and racism are not topics often encountered in Frost. He is not often gothic, either. Frost once revealed that the story was told to him by someone from Acton, Massachusetts, and perhaps that accounts for the departure (Cramer, 59). Frost's attention to the subject matter and his approach here are surprising and partly account for the appeal of the piece. Not uncommon in Frost is the exposure of the deplorable in humanity, and that is easily found in this startling and moving depiction of "The Vanishing Red."

The poem was first published in the July 1916 issue of the *Craftsman* and was later included in *Mountain Interval. See* TECHNOLOGY.

FURTHER READING

Cramer, Jeffrey S. *Robert Frost among His Poems: A Literary Companion to the Poet's Own Biographical*

Contexts and Associations. Jefferson, N.C.: MacFarland, 1996.

Faggen, Robert. "The Rhetoric of 'The Vanishing Red,'" *Robert Frost Review* 13 (Fall 2003): 105–109.

———. *Robert Frost and the Challenge of Darwin.* Ann Arbor: University of Michigan Press, 1997, 120–122.

Hoffman, Tyler. "Robert Frost's 'The Vanishing Red' and the Myth of Demise," *Robert Frost Review* 13 (Fall 2003): 101–104.

Kilcup, Karen L. "Frost's 'The Vanishing Red': Some Further Questions and Speculations," *Robert Frost Review* 13 (Fall 2003): 110–111.

Manson, Michael L. "Trying to Find the Right Genre for Genocide: Robert Frost and 'The Vanishing Red,'" 13 (Fall 2003): 82–100.

"Vantage Point, The" (1913)

In this somewhat altered Petrarchan sonnet, the speaker says what he must do if he finds himself retreating from nature and living only among men. He goes "into his own," as he does in his poem by that title, returning to the trees. This return to and immersion in nature echoes Ralph Waldo Emerson and Henry David Thoreau, who were great influences on Frost. From his vantage point, or perspective, the speaker can see the homes and graves of men, the lives and deaths of human beings, but he has retreated from them. In this place he is "unseen." But he becomes unaware of human torments only because unseen he is more fully aware of his own attachment to nature. Here he finds comfort and can leave the concerns of life and death to another world. When his "breathing shakes the bluet like a breeze," he is similar to the loafing, leisurely Walt Whitman observing "a spear of summer grass."

In the final stanza the immersion in nature is complete: "I smell the earth, / I smell the bruised plant, / I look into the crater of the ant." This may not seem to reveal much, but it demonstrates what we may gain from nature if we can see it as a source of pleasure and contentment rather than of destruc-

tion and chaos. The speaker is his most comfortable here, smelling the earth and looking into the ant's crater. He accepts things as they are and leaves grief, for a time, on the other side of the hill, where the living and the dead reside. The speaker realizes that immersion in nature and in himself can create an ease with nature and with oneself. It is through acceptance, rather than resistance, that he can keep his fears and uneasiness at bay. But this comfort in nature is rare in Frost. Mostly he is at odds with nature more than with man, as the gloss on this poem in the first edition of *A Boy's Will* pointed out—"And again scornful, but there is no one hurt"—and usually death is not so far away as the other side of that hill. An early version of the poem had the title "Choice of Society."

FURTHER READING

Faggen, Robert. *Robert Frost and the Challenge of Darwin.* Ann Arbor: University of Michigan Press, 1997, 66.

"Version" (1962)

See CLUSTER OF FAITH.

"Vindictives, The" (1936)

An eerie poem, "The Vindictives" begins "You like to hear about gold." The suggestion is that the absent listener is greedy, and this sets the scene for the tale of greed to come. The narrative tells of a king who "filled his prison room" with "every known shape of the stuff." His captors kept asking for more, so the king kept his subjects in search, and when they "wrung all they could wring" and there "seemed no more to bring" the captors strangled the king "with a string."

"The Vindictives" of the title refers to the captured, who, when the king has been murdered, decide that "If gold pleased the conqueror, well, / That gold should be the one thing the conqueror henceforth should lack." So all join mischievously in the game of "hide-gold." The conquered "slowly and silently ag[e]" and then they, with their secrets, die. The treasure most desired, a "great thousand-linked gold chain, / Each link of a hundredweight," through their secret keeping remains hidden, the captors' greed unsatisfied.

The entire poem seems an effort to clarify a concept expressed near the end: "The best way to hate is the worst. / 'Tis to find what the hated need, / Never mind of what actual worth, / And wipe that out of the earth." It seems that Frost happened upon the idea and set about creating a poem that would support it. It is a compelling scheme and has something in common with the phrase "kill them with kindness." True vindictiveness has no appearance of being vindictive; it is subtle, underhanded, and effective. It leaves the enemy to "die of unsatisfied greed" without his knowing why. It also brings him "down to the real," which is a way of saying that it makes what matters in life more true.

"The Vindictives" was first published in *A Further Range*. While it has a few good aphorisms and some clever rhymes, it is not one of Frost's best.

FURTHER READING

Linebarger, J. M. "Sources of Frost's 'The Vindictives,'" *American Notes and Queries* 12 (1974): 150–154.

"Voice Ways" (1936)

The poem opens, "Some things are never clear," and then the poem sets about disproving the absolutist statement. The weather is clear tonight; after all, the rain cleared it. The mountains have come clearly into view and the stars are bright. The speaker says; "Your old sweet-cynical strain / Would come in like you here: 'So we won't say nothing is clear.'" The conversation occurs between the speaker and what he imagines his friend would say in response. There are different ways of voicing our ideas, "voice ways" some are sweet, some are cynical, and some are a bit of both.

The last line, from the speaker's friend, seems to miss the point of the first line of the poem. Context needs to be understood in order to gain the full understanding of an utterance. When "Some things are never clear" is uttered at the start, it is clear the speaker is not talking about the weather. But the responses are only about the weather. In a sense, when the speaker says what his friend would say at the end, he is actually reaffirming the first line of the poem, because his friend has misunderstood his thought, making his thought unclear to his friend and therefore some things are never clear.

The poem was first published in the winter 1936 issue of the *Yale Review* and was later collected in *A Further Range*.

"Waiting" (1913)

"Waiting" was first published in *A Boy's Will* with the subtitle "Afield at dusk" and the gloss "He arrives at the turn of the year." Frost once referred to the poem as "gentle" and "personal" (Cramer, 19). Written early, it is romantic and mystical. In this field at dusk, and at the edge of a summer season, "What things for dream there are."

The speaker finds himself alone, as he is so often in Frost, arriving in a field after the voices of the day laborers are gone and the day is all but done. Not a working field to him, it is a fantastical place where he can lose himself "in the antiphony of afterglow / And rising full moon." The descriptions are magical. They conjure an enchanting secret place where dream upon dream is of a bat's "pirouettes" or the "last swallow's sweep."

The speaker holds "the worn book of old-golden song," which refers to Francis Turner Palgrave's (1824–97) poetry anthology *The Golden Treasury*. He had not brought it "to read, it seems, but hold / And freshen in this air of withering sweetness." He meditates "on the memory of one absent most," his lover, "For whom these lines when they shall greet her eye." The one absent has been taken to refer to Frost's future wife Elinor and the period when she was away at St. Lawrence University, before their marriage.

What the speaker is waiting for, his beloved, is not at first apparent. The poem transcribes the heartfelt emotion of youthful love and the desperation of separation. It beautifully depicts nature, its atmosphere all aglow. But while the poem creates a skillfully cast fairyland, it ultimately lacks impact.

FURTHER READING

Cramer, Jeffrey S. *Robert Frost among His Poems: A Literary Companion to the Poet's Own Biographical Contexts and Associations.* Jefferson, N.C.: MacFarland, 1996.

"War Thoughts at Home" (2006)

Published in fall 2006 in *The Virginia Quarterly Review,* "War Thoughts at Home" was discovered by graduate student Robert Stilling. He was researching in the University of Virginia's Albert and Shirley Small Special Collections Library when he found a letter dated 1947 from Frost's friend Frederic Melcher to Charles R. Green, then the librarian of the Jones Library in Amherst, Massachusetts. The letter referred to an unpublished poem that had been inscribed in a copy of *North of Boston* that Melcher had been given by Alfred Harcourt in 1918. Stilling investigated further.

Melcher's letter to Green explained that Melcher had an "unpublished poem about the war which [had] not been reprinted," but he said that he was "not sure" that Frost "would want [him] to pass it around, even for filing purposes" (Stilling, 113). Scholars are interested in any scrap of poem a poet of Frost's stature might have left behind, but poets tend not to want to leave scraps behind. Frost had a long publishing career, and it is sensible to think that this poem, by Frost's measure, simply was not up to par. "War Thoughts at Home," lacking Frost's marked ingenuity, seems to mark no exception to such a rule. As Glyn Maxwell writes, "It sounds finished, and yet it can't be because it was never framed and shown to be finished, so it's as [François René Auguste] Mallarmé says, abandoned. Not a ruin, but abandoned. There is a house that is no more a house. Not a work in progress, because he's gone" (120).

"War Thoughts at Home" draws an analogy between the fighting of World War I soldiers in France and the "rage" of blue jays that "flash in blue feather" behind a house. The "war" of the birds takes place "[o]n the back side of the house / Where it wears no paint to the weather." It is late afternoon in early winter: "more grey with snow to fall / Than white with fallen snow." Both the time of the day and the time of year are indicative not of death itself but of the prelude to death.

The third stanza interjects a "someone," a woman who rises from her chores to observe the "flurry of bird war." Her face shows the "dim" light of winter, and her presence causes the warring birds to "cease for a space." The birds will "escape" her view "one by one," though their fight is "no more done / Than the war is in France." If only her existence could halt the war in France as it does this bird war. The cause of the fighting among birds is unidentified, making it seem purposeless, though Frost, a nationalist, would hardly have intended that inference.

The woman is reminded of the war in France: "She thinks of a winter camp / Where soldiers for France are made." She then "draws the window shade" to the birds, veiling her grief. The shade "glows with an early lamp" as she continues to keep a light burning, as a signal of hope, but the glow is at the same time an indication of desperation, as the lamp burns "early."

The woman depicted is "someone" because she could be any war bride or war mother. The sewing that she must put aside is purposeful and solitary. The poem is recognizably Frost's. The language is familiar, the form discernible. The opening two stanzas are captivating. The shift between the second and third stanzas to the woman, however, is not as typically smooth. The enjambment between the third and fourth stanzas is again an interruption. The consciousness of the birds is less believable than in other poems, such as "Acceptance." And the closing stanza, while it presents a startling image, seems to suggest a different poem altogether. There is discontinuity in the imagery, and the repetition of "Than the war is in France!" appears as filler, the exclamation mark perfunctory.

The poem was inscribed in 1918, six years after Frost published his first volume, *A Boy's Will*. It was still early in his career, but he had arrived as a poet in his second and third volumes, *North of Boston* (1914) and *Mountain Interval* (1916). He had come into his own and knew his best work, and "War Thoughts at Home" is not his best. To Frost, it apparently did not deserve further time. It is jumbled, an attempt to piece together several poems and thoughts at once. The poem is perhaps derailed because of the poet's own thoughts about the war (notably, that his close friend Edward Thomas had died the previous year, on April 9, 1917, at the Battle of Arras in France). The images are not enough to move the poem in a direction, so it becomes stuck in place.

FURTHER READING

Maxwell, Glyn. "Dead on a Side Track: On Frost's 'War Thoughts at Home.'" *Virginia Quarterly Review* 82, no. 4 (Fall 2006): 120–133.

Stilling, Robert. "Between Friends: Rediscovering the War Thoughts of Robert Frost." *Virginia Quarterly Review* 82, no. 4 (Fall 2006): 113–119.

"Waspish" (1936)

"Waspish" describes a "[p]oor egotist" who has wasplike characteristics. He stands on legs that are like "glossy wires artistically bent" and has arms as "natty wings" that "with self-assurance perk." "His stinging quarters menacingly work" at something, perhaps everything, though the poem does not specify at what.

The man is described in metaphorically precise ways. He seems to be one who puffs himself up, is overconcerned with his appearance, and is not to be entirely trusted. After all, he has stinging hind-quarters. But the keen observer, the speaker of the poem, sees through all that and avers, "he's as good as anybody going."

The man is a "poor egotist" because he is vulnerable and appears to have "no way of knowing" what his real strengths could be. That is, for all his power, there is a clear sense in which he is unaware that

these powers are useless in the face of nature. He is as good as anyone else in this respect, despite his view of himself and his insecure posturing. But he has no way of knowing this, and there is no way to tell him.

The poem was first published as "Untried" in the April 1936 issue of *Poetry* in a group of poems titled "Ten Mills" and was later collected in *A Further Range*. It was once titled "Name Untried."

Way Out, A

A *Way Out* was the only play Frost published during his lifetime. It appeared in *The Seven Arts* in February 1917 and was reprinted by Harbor Press in 1929. In *Preface to A Way Out* (1929) Frost wrote that "Everything written is as good as it is dramatic. It need not declare itself in form, but it is drama or nothing." He emphasized "the speaking tone of voice somehow entangled in the words and fastened to the page for the ear of the imagination." *North of Boston*, Frost's second book of verse, which includes some of his best dramatic narratives, including "Home Burial" and "The Death of the Hired Man," had been published only a few years before, in 1914. Frost further explained, "I have always come as near the dramatic as I could this side of actually writing a play. Here for once I have written a play without (as I should like to believe) having gone very far from where I have spent my life."

Donald Sheehy explains the connection to Frost's experiences at Ossipee Mountain in 1895. His future wife Elinor was home from college and spent the summer near Ossipee Mountain and Lake Winnepesaukee in New Hampshire with her sister Leona. Frost took a nearby cottage in order to be near Elinor, and according to Sheehy, he drew on that experience both for this play and for *The Guardeen* as well as for "The Lockless Door." Sheehy describes *A Way Out* as "an intense psychodrama of fear and identity" (43).

A *Way Out* opens in a bachelor's kitchen bedroom in a farmhouse. It is suppertime and the table is spread. Asa Gorrill, described as "in loose slippers," answers a knock at the door. He unbolts the lock, and a stranger opens the door for himself and walks in. The stranger is the first to speak. His first line is "Huh! So this is what it's like," as if to say, "this is how country folks live." He then inquires "What you afraid of?" noting that Asa "lock[s] up early." Encounters with strangers or near-strangers are frequent in Frost's poems, as are night fears of the outdoors. Encounters with strangers can be found not only in "The Lockless Door" but in "The Fear," "Love and a Question," and "The Literate Farmer and the Planet Venus," among others; the last two also begin with unexpected evening knocks at the door.

Asa explains that he is " 'Fraid of nothing," because he does not have anything anyone would want, but the stranger disagrees; he wants some of Asa's supper. The stranger is threatening, making his way around the house "as if [he] owned it" and speaking accusingly to Asa: "You're supposed to be poor then?" He wants to know what is behind a door that is nailed shut and whether there might be some money in a mattress. He assures Asa that he "shan't kill [him] anyway till [he has] something to go on," as though that were any assurance of anything. Asa stands up to the stranger, ordering him to tell him what his "business is" or to "go out." He says he has not experienced anything like this since his brother Orin died. The stranger makes fun of Asa's relationship with his brother, describing them as "keeping old-maid's hall" and as "patching each other's trousers and doing up each other's back hair." Then the title of the poem is spoken and the speaker's intentions are revealed. He was "passing this way and in trouble and [he] just thought [he'd] look in on [Asa] and look [Asa] over as a possible way out." What he needs a way out of is not yet clear and Asa does not know what he himself "might or mightn't do" to help.

The stranger is a stranger to Asa but Asa is not to him. It turns out he has heard of Asa and was not just passing by but came out of his way to see Asa because of his "reputation." Asa "popped into [his] head like an idea." The conversation turns more civilized momentarily, with Asa becoming at ease with the stranger and the stranger becoming more reasonable. But the stranger continues to be critical of Asa and the way he is living. Asa has no

cow for milk and few supplies. The only money he has to purchase anything with comes from selling eggs. The stranger is critical of Asa's life because Asa "like[s] it all" and he "shan't." Then the stranger reveals himself as a murderer on the lam. Asa is not so much shocked or fearful as he is beside himself, burying his face in his hands and groaning at the predicament.

Asa, living in the country and attempting to "keep out of things," finds himself thrust into a situation about which he has little choice. The stranger, taking control again, says that he has not quite decided what he wants Asa to do, but it is clear he does not intend Asa to have any choice in the matter. The two men have been competing since the opening of the play for control and power. Here the stranger asserts his power over Asa, insisting that if Asa does not follow along he will kill him and insisting that Asa has no choice. At the same time he insults Asa's manhood, telling him he might as well pick his head up and "be a man about it—not a wet dishrag" and later calling him a "half man" and inquiring "Does anyone know for certain you're not a woman in man's clothing anyway?"

Asa is not presented as a country bumpkin, and the stranger is not presented as a common criminal. The stranger smartly says, "it's the fashion now-a-days to hide just as near the scene of the crime as you can stay." The two are at a constant standoff, each one being more accommodating to the other than would be expected under the circumstances.

The stranger has a plan. He is considering staying on with Asa permanently, and taking turns out of the house over the years, so that folks will think only Asa lives out there and not two people. Asa is a hermit, after all, and the stranger believes he is the same hermit who was written about in a Boston paper. The stranger is trying to get a handle on Asa, trying to figure out what made him accept a life of hermiting and wondering how satisfied he is with his choice. It turns out that Asa's brother Orin was "crossed in love," and the two ended up together in the house simply by circumstance. It was not so much that Asa turned away from society and women but that society "ain't any better'n it ought to be, what with all the killing and the murdering and the whatnot," so though his circumstances did not come about through intention in the way a man goes into a church to become ordained (as the stranger inquires), the outcome is just the same.

The conversation turns philosophical as the stranger continues to speculate about Asa and what kind of a man he is, living alone. The stranger recalls reading about a fellow who had a "queer religion about inhaling from your own shoes when you took them off to go to bed so's to get back the strength lost by settling in the daytime." Asa denies having such a religion. But the stranger also talks about how the man could see the light of three cities shining at night and how he thought they "kept getting brighter and brighter attempting like to turn night into day in the face of nature." The country man thought that such bold pomposity on people's parts would eventually lead to the Lord "fetch[ing] up a storm that would wipe out those cities in a blue blaze."

The stranger turns out to be a man who does "literary reading." He wonders if Asa "like[s] the innocent woods and fields and flowers like a poem in print" and seems disappointed when he realizes that Asa is not a hermit of the poetic sort because he has not "got ideas enough to make a hermit's life interesting." That reporter for the Boston paper must not have come near enough to Asa to have gotten a good look, the stranger concludes, saying that he must have been afraid the story would be spoiled if "he came too near." The stranger wonders what Asa must say "in self-defense" to fend folks off who think that no one has a right to keep to himself as Asa does. Asa cannot recall.

Asa is tired of the examination and wonders how the stranger has "time to plague [him] so" when he is trying to "save [his] own skin." But the stranger keeps on him. He wants a sampling of Asa's handwriting. And he determines Asa is rich because he owns the pine woods, "all that timber," though he has not touched it. In that case this hermit is "just as two-faced as the next man," since he is withholding.

The scene turns sinister again as the stranger begins to reveal that his plan is to steal Asa's identity. He is going to practice his "slump" and his drawl and let his "mouth and eyes hang open." He wants to know how Asa hauls wood, how he lives, and sets about putting on Asa's jumper and overalls. Asa is not reacting. He is just explaining and deciding he will go to bed, but the stranger says, "I'm putting you to bed tonight," as if to say, "You aren't going anywhere until I tell you what's what."

When the stranger first arrived looking for supper, Asa had a pot of food all mixed together, some potatoes and string beans. Frost returns to the metaphor here, as the stranger determines that he is going to mix the two of them up like those potatoes and string beans and "see if even [Asa] can tell [them] apart." He wants to grasp Asa's hands as children do to spin round in circles and fall to the floor dizzy. It will be a game of ring-around-the-rosey gone awry. Then he wants Asa to wait to speak. He assures him that he "ain't agoing to hurt [him]—*yet*." Asa determines he is "a crazy man from a madhouse."

The stranger wants to know if Asa is a happy man, if he has anything to live for, because he claims he wants to "do this thing right when [he] come[s] into office," when he takes over Asa's identity. The stranger justifies what he is about to do by saying, "It just shows that if you won't go to life, why life will come to you." In other words, if you are going to be a hermit who retreats from life, life will come to you, even though it may be in the form of the stranger who takes your life. The stranger thinks that if Asa had just "read so much as a Sunday paper," he would have had thoughts and would have lived a more meaningful life.

The two set to spinning in circles, faster and faster, until they break apart and fall to the floor. The audience is meant to confuse the two on stage as they confuse themselves. From here on, the two characters are blurred. There is instead a first and second voice. The first says, "I know. I ain't lost track. It's you that done the crime!" The second says, "It's not!" The first says, "It is! And I'm not afraid of you any more. You've got to go. God will give me the strength to wrastle with a rascal." And that is all. The second snarls, falls backward, and faints. The first hits the second on the head and drags him out of the house.

The house is silent and empty for a bit. Then there is a knock at the door, just as at the beginning. The closing scene is made up of two voices, a "someone," "Asa," and "The Hermit." The stranger, having killed Asa, now adopts his identity. The voices are a posse looking for the stranger. The stranger passes himself off as Asa, and the curtain closes with the stranger putting himself, "Asa," to bed as he told him earlier he would.

The play is dramatically the best of Frost's three. It is suspenseful and terrifying and as complex as the best of his dramatic poems. The conversations between Asa and the stranger reveal much about Frost's view of nature, solitude, human nature, and fear. For him solitude was welcome, as it allowed time for him to be alone with his thoughts, to compose his poetry, and to engage with his learning. That is the country life Frost sought and lived. The life that Asa lives is without any of these fruits. While the stranger is a sinister, harrowing figure, he is also thoughtful and erudite. He is a murderer, but it almost seems that he deserves Asa's life, his identity, because he would make better use of the solitude. The stranger could become a hermit in the truest sense, whereas Asa is a crude hermit; his isolation has led to nothing positive, to no growth of any kind.

Frost also has the opportunity to express some of the attitudes about technology encroaching on nature that can be found in "An Encounter." The stranger's depiction of the hermit in the Boston paper who sees the city lights as in competition with nature's stars is also similar to some of Frost's poems. In "The Literature Farmer and the Planet Venus," the stars are distinguished from the artificial light as "more divine than any bulb or arc, / Because their purpose is to flash and spark, / But not to take away the precious dark."

The notion of the stranger in Frost also is compelling. There is a certain fear of strangers that runs through the body of his work but also a strange desire to welcome and accept them. The characters in his poems welcome the stranger, even when he does not deserve welcome. Here Asa can be viewed as either extremely empathetic to the stranger or extremely naive. He continues to be accommodating, and it does not always seem that he does so out of a fear for his life. Sheehy explains that "[b]ehind the melodrama of the plot, Frost is engaged in a complex study of fear and motivation" that is often evident in Frost's poems. The fear of intrusion, either by other people or by nature itself is a constant theme.

See NIGHT and TECHNOLOGY.

FURTHER READING

Kemp, John C. *Robert Frost and New England: The Poet as Regionalist.* Princeton: Princeton University Press, 1979.
Sheehy, Donald G. "Robert Frost and the 'Lockless Door,' *New England Quarterly* 56, no. 1 (March 1983): 39–59.

"Way There, The" (1958)

Frost opens playfully to his young readers with a quote from Shakespeare's *The Winter's Tale*: "Jog on, jog on, the footpath way and merrily hent the stile-a" (IV.iii.132–133). Frost found his own way to poetry through Mother Goose and often reminded his readers that they had grown up on it, too, and would find all verse familiar because of youthful attachment. Here he tells the young that they may not realize it, but they have been "gathering bits and scraps of real magic" from Mother Goose, and that those scraps cling "like burrs thrown on [their] clothes in holiday foolery"—a metaphor he often used.

He paints a scene of a mother and daughter, the little girl having hurried home excitedly with a poem in her head to share with her mother, and the mother recognizing the poem. The little girl feels betrayed: "Then why didn't you tell me?" Frost uses the anecdote as a way of getting at his purpose: to remind his reader that "poetry is said to have been invented as an aid to memory" and it is "the most unforgettable experience a man can have with words." "No poem even can describe itself," as its way with words is its own way and must be left alone.

The piece is Frost at his childlike best. It shows evidence of his relationship to his own children, as his effort to be both accessible and playful is not strained. He maintains his voice while pitching just a bit lower than usual. He closes with some commentary on "Birches" and the "companion" poem for girls, "Wild Grapes." He then says, "The way there may be from tree to tree as in this book," suggesting that reading poems is like swinging birches. He has returned to his own youth as a swinger of birches and asks the children to swing with him.

"The Way There" is an unpublished preface to what was a proposed publication of Frost's poems for young readers. The collection was to include "Questioning Faces," "Birches," "The Pasture," "Last Word of a Bluebird," "Locked Out," "Going for Water," "A Tuft of Flowers," "Dust of Snow," "Gathering Leaves," "Stopping by Woods on a Snowy Evening," "Looking for a Sunset Bird in Winter," "Spring Pools," "Blue Butterfly Day," "A Drumlin Woodchuck," "The Runaway," "A Peck of Gold," "A Time to Talk," "Blueberries," "A Minor Bird," "Lodged," "Christmas Trees," "Good Hours," "A Record Stride," "The Need of Being Versed in Country Things," "A Young Birch," "Wild Grapes," and "Mowing."

"Were I in Trouble" (1947)

See "FIVE NOCTURNES."

"West-Running Brook" (1928)

First published in *West-Running Brook* as the title poem, this narrative depicts a conversation between Fred and his wife as they meander alongside a brook. It opens with the wife inquiring which direction is north. Fred uses the direction of the brook, west, to determine which direction it is. Having used west as a determinant, the wife pronounces that she will call the brook "West-running Brook." She finds it odd that the brook runs west, since "all the other country brooks flow east / To reach the ocean," and concludes that it must be that "the brook / Can trust itself to go by contraries." She likens this to her relationship with her husband and how they can do

that with each other. She is not sure how to classify their relationship: "I don't know what we are. What are we?" she asks. "Young or new?" Fred offers in response. The wife is unsatisfied.

"We must be something. / We've said we two," she says. She determines that now that the brook has been used as a metaphor for their relationship, they will "change that to we three" and will also "both be married to the brook." She adds a romantic image of embrace, with the bridge that crosses the brook being their arms thrown over the brook and asleep beside it. She imagines eliciting a response from the brook by its "waving" to them with a "wave / To let [them] know it hears [her]." Fred is too practical for such talk and responds that the wave is a force of nature, one that has been "standing off this jut of shore / Ever since rivers . . . Were made in heaven." "It wasn't waved to us," he says forcefully. But his wife is not going to give in so easily. "It wasn't, yet it was," she says contrarily. Fred resorts to gender distinctions, telling her that if she "take[s] it off to lady-land," she leaves him and all other men outside as they "forbid" themselves to enter and he will "have no more to say." "It is your brook!" he exclaims. Again, she does not give up easily. "Yes, you have, too," she says coyly, "Go on. You thought of something." It is a playful game, and Fred does go on.

He continues with the theme of "contraries" by talking about how the "white wave runs counter to itself" and explaining that it is from that water that we were born, "long before we were from any creature." He, too, likens them to the brook, but differently. He describes it as "get[ting] back to the beginning of beginnings" and explains that it is the "stream of everything that runs away." The stream runs "seriously" and "sadly," attempting to "fill the abyss's void with emptiness," as in Frost's "Too Anxious for Rivers," in which the river "[m]ust find where to pour itself into and empty." The brook that in the woman's view was included in a loving bedroom embrace here flows beside them, over them, and between them to "separate [them] for a panic moment." It also flows with them. Fred becomes equally romantic; the brook becomes "time, strength, tone, light, life, and love." But his impression of the brook also has an edge. It is "substance lapsing unsubstantial," a "universal cataract of death." This brook is always "throwing backward on itself" in an attempt to return to "the source" that "most we see ourselves in." It is not which direction the brook runs, east or west, that determines its contrariness but its always throwing back upon itself, its desire to somehow fill the abyss with understanding. "It is from this in nature we are from. / It is most us," Fred says. The two decide to agree about both: "Today will be the day of what we both said," they resolve.

Robert Pack calls the "coordinates" of the poem "place and nothingness," which he describes as "Frost's most extensive exploration of [the] backdrop of chaos" (201). Peter J. Stanlis explains that the wife "presents a religious and idealistic view of the brook; he a scientific account of the origins of life out of matter and water. In the end they are harmonized though still distinct in what they said" (Parini, 250). Jeffrey Cramer notes that in a 1937 letter Frost "linked the poem with 'Reluctance,' 'The Tuft of Flowers' and the passage about home in 'The Death of the Hired Man' as having the 'same subject . . . [Frost's] position . . . between socialism and individualism'" (96). Robert Faggen writes that "Hyla Brook" and "West-Running Brook" "explore both the failure of nature to provide meaning and our doubts about our ability to impose meaning upon the flux" (289). He goes on to say that "[t]wo questions engender and dominate the dialogue: where are we, and who are we?" (290). Faggen also notes that in the end "[w]e are left with an uneasy sense of what will be done and whether phrases of salvation such as they have uttered can provide purpose, direction, or a justification of the future" (302).

These interpretations notwithstanding, it seems that the poem tries to paint an optimistic picture about the role of people, and lovers, in the universe and about the juxtaposition of life, love, and meaning against the backdrop of the chaos and the abyss. People are the west-running brook, the contrary to the void, and the source of meaning.

FURTHER READING

Cramer, Jeffrey S. *Robert Frost among His Poems: A Literary Companion to the Poet's Own Biographical Contexts and Associations.* Jefferson, N.C.: MacFarland, 1996.

Dietrich, R. F. "The Contrary Mr. Frost of 'West-Running Brook,'" *University of Dayton Review* 17, no. 3. (Winter 1985–1986): 83–89.

Faggen, Robert. *Robert Frost and the Challenge of Darwin.* Ann Arbor: University of Michigan Press, 1997, 288–302.

Heuston, Sean. "Frost's 'West-Running Brook,'" *Explicator* 63, no. 1 (Fall 2004): 40–43.

Hoffman, Tyler. *Robert Frost and the Politics of Poetry.* Hanover, N.H.: Middlebury College Press, 2001.

Kau, Joseph. "'Trust . . . to go by contraries': Incarnation and the Paradox of Belief in the Poetry of Frost." In *Frost: Centennial Essays II,* edited by Jac Tharpe, 99–111. Jackson: University Press of Mississippi, 1976.

Kochhar-Lindgren, Gray. "The Beginning of Beginnings: Frost's 'West-Running Brook' as a Creation Myth," *Religion and Intellectual Life* 6, no. 3–4 (Spring–Summer 1989): 220–227.

Oehlschlaeger, Fritz. "West Toward Heaven: The Adventure of Metaphor in Robert Frost's 'West-Running Brook,'" *Colby Literary Quarterly* 22, no. 4 (December 1986): 238–251.

Pack, Robert. *Belief and Uncertainty in the Poetry of Robert Frost.* Hanover, N.H.: Middlebury College Press, 2003.

Parini, Jay. *Robert Frost: A Life.* New York: Holt, 1999.

Perrine, Laurence. "Frost's 'West-Running Brook,'" *Explicator* 4 (1977): 27.

Uirak, Kim. "The Seasonal Cycle in Robert Frost's Poetry," *Arkansas Review* 5, no. 1–2 (August 1996): 81–87.

West-Running Brook (1928)

West-Running Brook was first published in New York by Henry Holt in 1928. A limited, signed edition of 1,000 copies also was published. The book was dedicated "To E. M. F." for Frost's wife, Elinor Miriam Frost. The contents were divided into six sections: Spring Pools, Fiat Nox, West-Running Brook, Sand Dunes, Over Back, and My Native Smile. In *Collected Poems* (1930) and all subsequent editions, three poems appeared in *West-Running Brook* that were not included in the initial publication: "The Lovely Shall Be Choosers," "What Fifty Said," and "The Egg and the Machine."

Made up of 39 poems in all, the book is described by Lawrance Thompson as being "as different from *New Hampshire*" as that volume had been from the previous books (313). Jay Parini explains that "Frost realized 'West-Running Brook' was exactly the right poem for the new collection, with its theme of progression by contraries" (244).

Frost was upset by some of the reviews. One of the reviewers thought that he "was an escapist, a poet out of touch with his times." Another thought that his poetry ran "counter to the consensus of opinion of the critics of all ages as well as the temper of his own era," complaining that the poems "contained nothing of industrialism." The general direction in criticism of the time was that politics had a place in poetry and that poetry must "contribute directly to the unification in imaginative terms" of culture (Parini, 267). Richard Poirier, in talking about *A Further Range* as being a better book than *West-Running Brook,* sheds some light on the politics of criticism: "Politics offered a conveniently loud and just as conveniently crude form for an attack already implicit in critical negligence. . . . [T]his was also a time when these same critics were for the most part reverential about two 'great' poets, [Ezra] Pound and [William Butler] Yeats" (238).

Thompson heralds the book for "[t]he range and variety of forms . . . heightened by the freshness of metaphors in the rhymed lyrics, by the metaphysical reach of the blank-verse title poem, and by the mingled play and seriousness of the couplets in 'The Bear'" (313). He holds that the

> new manuscript contained far more hints of [Frost's] deep religious faith than any of his other books had done. Although he remained self-consciously shy, and sometimes deceptively coy, in making direct statements concerning his metaphysical beliefs, he could not resist this artistic game of hinting at the importance to him of his puritan heritage, which he sometimes mocked and sometimes defended. (313)

Evidence of this can be found in "Bereft," "The Peaceful Shepherd," and "Sitting by a Bush in Broad Sunlight."

"West-Running Brook" is the best-known poem in *West-Running Brook,* partly because it is the title poem but largely because of its expansiveness and the degree to which it grapples with two prominent themes in his work: science and religion. While the volume does not include many of his greatest poems, it does include some, such as "Tree at My Window" and "Acquainted with the Night."

FURTHER READING

Parini, Jay. *Robert Frost: A Life.* New York: Holt, 1999.

Poirier, Richard. *Robert Frost: The Work of Knowing.* New York: Oxford University Press, 1977.

Thompson, Lawrance. *Robert Frost: The Years of Triumph, 1915–1938.* New York: Holt, Rinehart and Winston, 1970.

"[We Vainly Wrestle . . .]" (1962)

The skillful quatrain "We vainly wrestle" appears untitled near the end of *In the Clearing.* It was excerpted from an unpublished poem titled "New Grief" and reads, "We vainly wrestle with the blind belief / That aught we cherish / Can ever quite pass out of utter grief / And wholly perish." The choice of the word "vainly" in the first line and "aught" in the second line are significant, as they suggest two diverse meanings.

The first interpretation of aught is "anything," the second "nothing." Here it appears to mean both. Anything and nothing "we cherish" will ever "quite pass out of utter grief." If aught is read as "nothing," then we wrestle with the belief that things can live forever with us; we want to believe nothing is completely exterminated. Things might die, but we believe "blindly" that our memory will keep things alive or that they will perhaps survive in some other form. In this way nothing ever perishes "wholly." The first meaning of aught lends itself to a different reading. If the aught is "anything," then the opposite attitude is conveyed. Anything we cherish can pass out of utter grief and be obliterated.

The vain wrestling is between the two attitudes, whether we think that nothing will ever perish completely for us or we think that anything can completely perish for us and that nothing is safe in this way. That is why our wrestling is vain and is in vain. We only see whether something perishes in relation to ourselves. Ultimately we have no control over ourselves or it. The poem has the paradoxical function of being a message of both optimism and pessimism and an explanation of how each of these attitudes inevitably connects to our vanity. This connection of value to humanity is common in Frost and often contrasts with nature's amorality.

FURTHER READING

Kau, Joseph. "Two Notes on Robert Frost Poems: Frost's 'Version' of Zeno's Arrow and Blind Optimism in Frost's 'We Vainly Wrestle,'" *Notes on Modern American Literature* 1 (1977): 33.

"What Became of New England?" (1937)

Frost delivered "What Became of New England?" as the Oberlin College commencement address on June 8, 1937. Robert S. Newdick of the Ohio State University English Department transcribed the address from a stenographic record and published it with Frost's approval. The piece is a defense of NEW ENGLAND. Frost greets the graduating class by speaking of them and New England as "once removed."

"I never gave up willingly any love I've had," Frost says and explains that he "stand[s] on the defensive lately a good deal for New England." He says people ask him what became of New England and that he published a "little book" 20 years ago, the praise of which "cost [him] some pain," referring to poet Amy Lowell's review of *North of Boston*, which was published February 20, 1915, in the *New Republic*. "Mr. Frost's book," Lowell said, "reveals a disease which is eating into the vitals of our New England life, at least in its rural communities." Frost

also identifies a "distinguished critic" who said, "The Catholic peasantry of Europe renews itself through the ages. The Protestants, the Puritan peasantry of New England, has dried up and blown away in three hundred years." The critic to whom he refers is Ford Madox Ford (1873–1939).

The piece is a defense against these criticisms wherein Frost praises New England, beginning with its early history as the "first little nation that bade fair to be an English speaking nation." He salutes the peasant class, saying that there "were ten silversmiths in Boston before there was a single lawyer," and he reminds his audience of its short national memory: "People forget those things."

"I don't know how much of a fight you make to hang onto what's yours," he says to his young audience, insisting that the older a person gets the "harder he hangs onto what he's built into his life," partly reasoning his own way through his loyalty to New England. Frost says that the "whole function of poetry is the renewal of words, is the making of words mean again what they meant," but this is a stubbornness that resists his other comments about making words take on new meanings, new turns of metaphor, as he argues in such pieces as "The Unmade Word, or Fetching and Far-Fetching."

Frost also takes the criticism of New England as a criticism of traditional values, such as God, faith, and nationalism. He speaks of fear and jealousy as outmoded and "dismissed" words but says that the word *jealousy* is really the word *true,* a word that still lives for him. The thing New England gave most to America was "a stubborn clinging to meaning. . . . [A] purifying of words and a renewal of words and a renewal of meaning."

He speaks of disillusionment and loss: "Some people pity a person who loses his hero." He asks, "Who suffers the worst, the person who loses his hero, or the lost hero?" For Frost, New England is the hero that should never be lost or perceived as being lost.

FURTHER READING

Kemp, John C. *Robert Frost and New England: The Poet as Regionalist.* Princeton: Princeton University Press, 1979.

"What Fifty Said" (1928)

"What Fifty Said" is written from the perspective of someone who became a teacher. The speaker reflects on when he was young and what his education was like then. His teachers "were the old," and he was forced to give up "fire for form," to give up his passion in favor of channels for it. He suffered under their instruction, losing his "fire" until he was "cold." He suffered like a "metal being cast" as he learned about the past. The speaker's experience with formal education was not entirely positive, nor was Frost's, who played at being sick just to get out of going to school, though he later made a living as a teacher himself (Parini, 16).

In the second stanza the attitude toward education is more favorable, but it is also told from the vantage point of the old. The young pupil has become the 50-year-old teacher looking at his students, whom he now sees as his new teachers. He looks to the young as those who do not need to be molded but instead "cracked and sprung" like chicks hatching from their eggs. He says he has difficulty with "lessons fit to start a suture," that is, those that are designed to sew someone in. The stitches help join concepts, but they also are confining. Still, he works to suture those that are cracked, to bring together their ideas in a positive and formed way, but one that is flexible and that works to heal. A suture, in the end, is a lot more flexible than a mold, and the ending is what is most important. This teacher does not see himself as superior; he sees himself as one who is able to learn from his students as well as they from him. He goes to "youth to learn the future," rather than being forced only to "learn the past." He is as forward-looking as backward-looking.

The poem presents a distinction between the way a teacher sees education and the way a student does. The teacher sees a lecture as an attempt to connect ideas to create a uniform whole, while the student sees any constraint as like metal being cast, force and will. To the young education can be like metal being cast and fire extinguished rather than made use of. But this is something we might not learn until we are old.

Frost shakes hands with a young boy. "What Fifty Said": "Now I am old my teachers are the young." *(Courtesy Howard Sochurek / Time Life Pictures / Getty Images)*

"What Fifty Said," not originally collected in *West-Running Brook*, was added to the volume in 1930.

FURTHER READING

Parini, Jay. *Robert Frost: A Life.* New York: Holt, 1999.

"White-Tailed Hornet, The" (1936)

Appearing to be an ode to the white-tailed hornet, the poem begins by describing the hornets' nest as a "balloon / That floats against the ceiling of the woodshed." The hornet is then described as exiting its nest with the same force with which a bullet exits a gun, but it is also deemed to have more "power" than a bullet because it can "change [its] aim in flight" and because it is more "unerring." Humorously, the speaker allows that "verse could be written" about the ability of the hornet to escape his "whirling hands and arms about the head" as he defends himself from an attack, just as he writes in verse that very scene.

The poem goes on to discuss the limitations of the insect's instinct, as the speaker is surprised that the hornet cannot "recognize in [him] the exception / [he] like[s] to think [he is] in everything." The speaker, unlike the hornet, would never put the hornet's nest—this time likening it to a "Japanese crepe-paper globe"—on display as one does a "trophy." He is more humble than that. The hornet that stings him "first" and stings him "afterward," not listening to the speaker's "explanations," is not "such an execrable judge of motives" after all, because he has completely missed the mark, remaining unaware that his victim was not a threat.

The speaker decides to visit the hornet's nest. He watches the hornet attempt to capture a fly to "feed his thumping grubs as big as he is," and the hornet this time misses his mark. He swoops, pounces, and strikes, but all for nothing: "what he found he had was just a nailhead." He does it "a second time. Another nailhead." The hornet of the first stanza is now bumbling. He swoops and strikes a third time; this time it is a huckleberry. Then there interposes a fly, which "circle[s] round him in derision" and leads back to the analogy to poetry: "he might have made me think / He had been at his poetry, comparing / Nailhead with fly and fly with huckleberry: / How like a fly, how very like a fly." But the missed fly makes the speaker "dangerously skeptic" about the poetry analogy. The nailhead and the huckleberry were poetic, but a real fly would never do. The line "very like a fly" echoes Shakespeare's "Very like a whale" in *Hamlet*, where Lord Polonius and Hamlet discuss the shape of a cloud (III.iii.382).

In the closing stanza the speaker inquires,

Won't this whole instinct matter bear revision?
Won't almost any theory bear revision?
To err is human, not to, animal.
Or so we pay the compliment to instinct,
Only too liberal of our compliment
That really takes away instead of gives.

Alluding to Darwin's theory of EVOLUTION, the speaker acts troubled by the comparisons that "yield downward" to "see our images / Reflected in the mud and even dust," rather than heavenward. At one time, not long ago, we looked "stoutly upward" for comparison, "With gods and angels, we were men at least, / But little lower than the gods and angels," he recalls, alluding to the Bible, Psalms 8:5: "For thou hast made him a little lower than the angels, and hast crowned him with glory and honor." Now it is all "disillusion upon disillusion," and "[n]othing but fal-

libility [is] left us." We can no longer see our images reflected in the heavens, and now, rather than rising above our instincts, we are cursed to draw analogies of our human tendencies to the basest of creatures from this realm on Earth. And "this day's work" of observing the hornet has "made even that seem doubtful" is written tongue-in-cheek, allowing that the dangerous skeptic of the previous stanza is equally skeptical now. This is no longer an ode to a hornet but rather a place to speculate on human origins and to reflect on what comparisons really suggest when they are not left to poetry.

"The White-Tailed Hornet" was first published in the spring 1936 issue of the *Yale Review* with the subtitle "or Doubts about an Instinct." It was later collected in *A Further Range* with the subtitle "The Revision of Theories."

FURTHER READING

Cramer, Jeffrey S. *Robert Frost among His Poems: A Literary Companion to the Poet's Own Biographical Contexts and Associations.* Jefferson, N.C.: MacFarland, 1996.

Faggen, Robert. *Robert Frost and the Challenge of Darwin.* Ann Arbor: University of Michigan Press, 1997, 96–99.

Griffin, Larry D. "Frost's Syllogism in 'The White-Tailed Hornet,'" *Publications of the Mississippi Philological Association* (1994): 38–42.

Monteiro, George. *Robert Frost and the New England Renaissance.* Lexington: University Press of Kentucky, 1988, 131–135.

Perrine, Laurence. "A House for Frost's 'White-Tailed Hornet,'" *Notes on Contemporary Literature* 10, no. 1 (1980): 3.

Sokol, B. J. "Bergson, Instinct, and Frost's 'The White-Tailed Hornet,'" *American Literature* 62, no. 1 (March 1990): 44–55.

"Why Wait for Science" (1947)

In this sonnet, "Sarcastic Science" is depicted as feminine. It is a temptress who may tease but cannot follow through on what she offers. Science is also a double-edged sword. It has given us the methods by which we have created nuclear weapons and other ways to destroy the planet; it "has made things so we have to go / Or be wiped out," and yet it also would like to know "[h]ow we propose to get away from here."

There is a deep concern whether science can ever provide us with another habitable planet. The speaker is extremely skeptical about our ability to leave Earth because of the conditions that we would have to endure in order to do it, steering by rocket a distance of a "half light-year" at the "temperature of absolute zero."

Science is like religion in this sense; it has a "complacent ministry of fear." Fear is a consequence of having blindly followed science in the first place. Science gave us methods, we abused them, and now our planet is in trouble. We know not what to do, so we look once again to science, the cause of our problem and our fears, for an answer, a solution, and understanding.

At the same time the poem dismisses scientific knowledge by saying any "amateur can tell" how we will have to leave the planet, which "should be the same / As fifty million years ago we came." Facetiously the speaker asks, "If anyone remembers how that was." There are limitations to scientific knowledge. It is no surprise that we do not know how we came, given other scientific limitations. The particular answer of getting off the planet is beyond science. This amateur has a theory of how we got here, but it will hardly do. His is just a theory, he says, making equal fun of the theories of science, since they are no better than his.

No theory is going to work. Things have a natural process and progression, and trying to fast-forward or shortcut this process is nothing more than arrogance. Nature has the upper hand and is beyond our control, and flagrant dismissal of this fact will give us problems, as it did when science started to tinker with nature in the first place.

"Why Wait for Science" was first published in the November 1946 issue of the *New Hampshire Troubadour* as "Our Getaway" and later collected in *Steeple Bush. See* SCIENCE.

"Wild Grapes" (1942)

Frost once called this poem "as near being a thing written to order as I ever got." He said that "Susan Hayes Ward my first discoverer (1893) said I must write for her a girls companion piece to 'Birches' which she took to be for boys; and she would furnish me with the materials. Some years afterward to my own great surprise I found myself doing as she commanded."

Frost adopts the voice of an older woman in this poem, an oddity among his speakers. The poem begins with two questions—"What tree may not the fig be gathered from? / The grape may not be gathered from the birch?"—and sets off from there. These questions echo Matthew 7:16 of the Bible, which asks: "Ye shall know them by their fruits. Do men gather grapes of thorns, or figs of thistles?"

The speaker is a girl "gathered from a birch" who "grew to be a little boyish girl" who followed her brother about. "But that beginning was wiped out in fear" the day she swung on birches as boys do, ended up suspended from a tree bough like a grape, and "was come after like Eurydice / And brought down safely from the upper regions." Eurydice was the wife of Orpheus, whom he failed to rescue from Hades when he looked back at her and so violated the command of Pluto on their journey back to the upper world of the living. When the girl in the poem made it back to Earth safely, she began to live "an extra life." Now she has two lives: one she can "waste as [she] please[s] on whom [she] please[s]" and another, one five years younger.

The woman then retells a story of her youth, when her brother led her to a birch tree that was heavy with bunches of grapes. She recognizes the grapes from having seen them the year before, and soon there are bunches all around her, the "way they grew round Leif the Lucky's German." The reference is to the Norwegian Leif "the Lucky" Ericson, who was raised by a German and died circa 1020. He was a mariner who visited North America, possibly NEW ENGLAND but more likely Nova Scotia, which he named Vinland after the vines he found growing there. The grapes are above the girl for her to admire, but they are inaccessible.

Here, as in Frost's "Birches," the boy climbs the branches of the birch until he weighs them down to meet the earth. In this case, however, the boy throws down grapes from the tree at his sister, and she hunts for and eats them. Then, when he lowers the branches, he tells her to take hold of the tree with all her might. She grasps the tree, but the tree takes hold of her when her brother lets go, and the birch lifts her into the air. She dangles like a fish on a line. Her brother shouts for her to let go, but she holds on tight. The speaker likens it to a grip she has inherited evolutionarily from a long line of women whose wild ancestral mothers "[h]ung babies out on branches by the hands / To dry or wash or tan."

Frost paints another visual. The brother draws an analogy between the girl dangling from the birch and the grapes they have been picking from it. She is described as ripe for the plucking, but with one more stem, which makes her a little bit safer from the picker, a return to the opening metaphor of the poem.

The girl, dangling from the tree, loses her hat and shoes and still hangs on tight. Her brother urges her to let go and drop, assuring her that he will catch her when she falls. When she resists, he threatens to shake her from the tree, but she continues to hold tight. At last he decides he will get her down the way he got her up, by bending the tree's branches back down to earth.

When the girl finds her feet touching ground again, it still takes her a moment to let go, as though she were hanging on to something far greater than the birch tree. Her brother chides her that she should weigh more next time (than, perhaps, a bunch of grapes, "[e]qually with my weight in grapes") so that she "won't / Be run off with by birch trees into space."

The woman reflects that she was lifted in air not because she did not weigh anything but more because she did not know anything. She resolves that she had not "taken the first step in knowledge" and "had not learned to let go with the hands." Even with the years past, she has still not learned to let go "with the heart." It was her heart as much as her hands that held her in air, and she does not wish even in maturity to learn to let go with that any more than she did then. The poem closes with her concluding that she may still learn to live as others do, "To wish in vain to let go with the mind— / Of cares, at night, to sleep," but she has no need to learn to let go with the heart.

In many ways "Wild Grapes" is the companion to "Birches" it was meant to be. Some of the images are the same, as is the resistance to being set back down to Earth to stay. This speaker, like the one of "Birches," also seems to have wanted to "get away from earth awhile." She too seemed to want to climb toward heaven, not to it. She is cast as a different swinger of birches than the boy of the earlier poem, however. She finds herself swung by them—she is passive in her role with nature. The two share something of the heart as well. The speaker of "Birches" declares that "Earth's the right place for love" because he does not "know where it's likely to go better," and the speaker of "Wild Grapes" wants to hold onto her heart and never let go. But in many ways the image Frost presents here is traditional in respect to sex roles. The young girl is "boyish" in the first place, which explains her desire to tag along with her brother at all. Birch tree climbing is for boys, not girls, the poem makes clear at the outset. And she is dependent on her brother and described as being full of fear the day she "swung suspended with the grapes" rather than full of adventure, like the boy who was too far from town to learn baseball. Her brother must rescue her as a damsel in distress who is not in control of the situation. She is younger, but she is also the weaker and softer sex, and that depiction is evident. "Wild Grapes" is romanticized as is "Birches," but the speakers of the two poems are definitively classified according to masculine and feminine traits. The speaker of "Wild Grapes" even refers to evolutionary traits, as though she inherited her grip from her femaleness, from mothering and raising babies in the wildest of circumstances.

The two poems are companions, however. They each have heart, and the boy and girl each strive not to let go of something precious. "Birches" notably has a darker side that is not evident in "Wild Grapes" and gives it a different tone. "Birches" is also a greater composition, flawless in its execution, its choreography. "Wild Grapes" lacks the depth and bite of the other, which comes, it seems, from a speaker who is a bit more mature and experienced, but also jaded. The speaker of "Wild Grapes," while clearly grown, does not look backward from a position of old age with the same sort of disagreeable view as one whose "face burns and tickles with the cobwebs / Broken across it" and with "one eye weeping / From a twig's having lashed across it open."

The speaker of "Wild Grapes" concedes that she did not know "anything" and that she still does not want to know certain things. She is resistant to learning anything that will cause her not to go with her heart. The speaker of "Birches," in contrast, knows too much but also knows something with certainty from the heart: "One could do worse than be a swinger of birches."

Robert Pack writes,

> The old woman's gift of her story qualifies as a Frostian "momentary stay against confusion" and a respite from uncertainty—not the uncertainty about ultimate meanings or the design of a deity who may or may not exist, but the uncertainty as to whether or not anything matters, like the love of nature, the physical world itself that the imagination may perceive as being invested with symbolic richness. (76)

"Wild Grapes" was first published in the December 1920 issue of *Harper's Magazine* and later collected in *New Hampshire*.

FURTHER READING

Bacon, Helen. "For Girls: From 'Birches' to 'Wild Grapes,'" *Yale Review* 67 (1977): 13–29.

Bagby, George F. *Frost and the Book of Nature*. Knoxville: University of Tennessee Press, 1993, 114–117.

Cramer, Jeffrey S. *Robert Frost among His Poems: A Literary Companion to the Poet's Own Biographical Contexts and Associations*. Jefferson, N.C.: MacFarland, 1996.

Faggen, Robert. *Robert Frost and the Challenge of Darwin*. Ann Arbor: University of Michigan Press, 1997, 198–203.

Pack, Robert. *Belief and Uncertainty in the Poetry of Robert Frost*. Hanover, N.H.: Middlebury College Press, 2003.

Perrine, Laurence. "Letting Go with the Heart: Frost's 'Wild Grapes,'" *Notes on Modern American Literature* 2 (1978): 20.

"Willful Homing" (1942)

The speaker finds himself out alone in the winter dark. He is caught in a blizzard that "blinds him to any house." The snow is going down the neck of his shirt. The bitter cold steals his breath "like a wicked cat in bed." He cannot find his way home, so he sits in a snowdrift "[i]mprint [ing] a saddle" and determining his course. The poem ends with the conclusion that "[s]ince he means to come to a door, he will come to a door." But when he will reach a door and which door he will reach is unclear. It also ends humorously as the doorknob he turns may be "wide . . . a yard or more," suggesting that his willful homing might get him to the wrong house, and if this happens, the speaker surmises that "to those concerned he may seem a little late."

Nature's elements confuse and interfere, but this poem, unlike so many of Frost's other poems in which the individual confronts nature, makes something of a game of it. Being alone and lost in a blizzard, usually the stuff of fear and dread and death, ends up being none of these things but something to overcome, give or take a few fumblings along the way. The calmness of the traveler suggests confidence in his persistence and eventual success, and though the snow may exert force, it cannot stop the traveler from ultimately arriving at his destination. The act of our meaning something to happen ends up solidifying that action and the event. The worst that will happen is that he might arrive a yard off and a little late.

"Willful Homing" was first published in the February 26, 1938, issue of the *Saturday Review of Literature* as part of Frost's friend Louis Untermeyer's "Play in Poetry"; it was later collected in *A Witness Tree. See* FUGITIVE.

"Wind and the Rain, The" (1942)

"The Wind and the Rain" was first published in *A Witness Tree*. Jeffrey Cramer notes that the poem was likely written after Frost's wife Elinor's death in

1938. In tone it is one of Frost's darkest. It expresses deep sorrow, its message powerfully disheartened.

The poem is written in two sections. The first describes the leaves that that are blown by the wind in "season-ending" and strewn about the forest. Unlike the speaker in "A Leaf-Treader," who is sensitive to the leaves but is determined to survive and persist past their death and the cycles of nature, this speaker longs to be "drive[n] deathward too." He sings of death as he walks. "The Wind and Rain" almost builds on a recollection of that poem, which was published in Frost's previous volume, *A Further Range*.

The speaker is reminded that when "he sang of death" he was youthful, he did not yet know "[t]he many deaths one must have died / Before he came to meet his own!" And he speculates whether a child should "be left unwarned / That any song in which he mourned / Would be as if he prophesied?" suggesting that fate takes hold of our songs of suffering and loss and makes them sing true. He also draws on the need for evil in order to appreciate good when he speaks of "let[ting] the half of life alone / And play[ing] the good without the ill." The first section closes with the speaker resolving that "what is sung / In happy sadness by the young / Fate has no choice but to fulfill."

The second section takes as its subject flowers in summer "desert heat." The speaker imagines how they "contrive to bloom" even when "something in it still is incomplete." They have every intention of blooming according to the natural processes of water coming down from the mountains to "wet their feet." But even here something about this process is incomplete. The speaker then imagines what things would be like if he could have the power to control the processes. Instead of allowing the flowers to barely survive, he would rather flood them to make sure that the buds could not merely survive but thrive. He would prefer not the struggling of life but the teeming of it.

He sees the flowers "water-bowed." They lose petals in the "unsparing" flood of clouds. None seem to "care . . . for the future of the bud." The speaker likens himself again to nature, this time to the flower as he speaks of getting rained "on roots and in the mouth" and "water heavy on the head /

In all the passion of a broken drouth." The rain is as "magical as sunlight on the skin." While "no dwelling could contain" the speaker from being outside in rain, he compares the rain to "tears adopted by my eyes / That none have left to stay."

The last stanza returns to the theme of the first section, of trying to regain the passion and optimism of youth after experiencing the reality of suffering and loss. Earlier in his life, the speaker imagines himself loving the rain. But now, after all his burdens and suffering, the rain only symbolizes his tears, since he has none left to cry.

Mark Richardson writes, "In speaking of the songs of his youth, the speaker of these lines seems recognizably to be a poet" and notes that the "songs this poet sings are largely melancholy—such songs as we find, for example, in Frost's own youthful book *A Boy's Will*" (241).

The poem is complex in its expression of disillusionment. The suggestion is that we bring about our own suffering and that such suffering is necessary to living fully. In the young, the slightest emotional buffets inspire songs of death, but from the perspective of experience those earlier claims were "unworthy of the tongue."

FURTHER READING

Cramer, Jeffrey S. *Robert Frost among His Poems: A Literary Companion to the Poet's Own Biographical Contexts and Associations*. Jefferson, N.C.: MacFarland, 1996.

Richardson, Mark. *The Ordeal of Robert Frost: The Poet and His Poetics*. Chicago: University of Illinois Press, 1997.

"Wind and Window Flower" (1913)

Lovers are told to forget their love and listen instead to the tale of love between the winter wind and the window flower. He is a winter wind, on the move and the one that marks her; she is a flower that, in the end, remains silent, which, to a suitor, results in his rejection and his withdrawal.

The window flower is on the windowsill. She is safely indoors, as is the caged yellow bird who sings over her in the firelit room. The setting inside is cozy and safe. The personified wind sees her through the windowpane and falls in love. He hopes to win her and take her away with him, but the flower leans aside with nothing to say. The wind, "concerned with ice and snow, / Dead weeds and unmated birds," must move on. He gives a sigh, shakes the curtain sash, and continues onward. The time passes from noon to dark to the following morning, when the breeze is 100 miles away. The love the two have is fleeting and unfulfilled because they are opposites.

The flower dwells indoors in winter but represents a different season. He is winter; she is spring. It is a wistful love poem of youth reminiscent of Elizabethan verse. Moving and well executed, it is among the better of such poems in *A Boy's Will*. It suggests that all lovers, in some sense, feel like this. There is always something about love that cannot be bridged completely, and the speaker knows this and wants to identify. The poem may also suggest that love is never really true love, in the sense of complete unity; instead it is something that comes so close to oneness but is never complete.

"Winter Eden, A" (1928)

The speaker equates a winter garden with the biblical Garden of Eden. The one he sees is "[a]s near a paradise as it can be." In the snow all existence is lifted higher than the Earth and therefore nearer to heaven. Last year's berries shine "scarlet red" like a winter apple from Eden. In the garden is "a gaunt luxuriating beast," who can eat only the bark of the apple tree, which bears no fruit in wintertime.

Frost writes, "So near to paradise all pairing ends: / Here loveless birds now flock as winter friends." All the birds in this Eden are content in their lack of love, as were Adam and Eve before they ate of the Tree of Knowledge. They are also content with simply inspecting which buds will be leaves and which will be flowers. They do not desire the flower; they are satisfied.

Reginald Cook notes that "A spectrum of opposites is contained in this Edenic vivarium—not only atmosphere light *and* dark, but meteorological cold *and* heat, seasonal winter *and* memory of spring, biological sexual dormancy *and* seasonal mating, and even altitudinal snow depth raising the creatures heavenward in sharp contrast to the bare ground of summer" (257).

This paradise of a brief winter day ends at two in the afternoon. The vision in the alder swamp is as near a paradise as can be found in winter. The days "might seem so short" that it seems hardly "worth life's while to wake and sport" and to partake of the beauty of the garden, but the speaker's hedging "might seem" suggests that this glimpse of paradise makes it all worthwhile.

"A Winter Eden" was first published in the January 12, 1927, issue of the *New Republic* and later collected in *West-Running Brook*.

FURTHER READING

Cook, Reginald. *Robert Frost: A Living Voice*. Amherst: University of Massachusetts Press, 1974, 255–257.

"Wish to Comply, A" (1947)

"A Wish to Comply" downplays the work of Robert Andrews Millikan (1868–1953), the American physicist and educator who did research on the electron and cosmic rays in the 1920s and 1930s. Millikan won the Nobel Prize in 1923 for his famous ink drop experiment. By releasing a tiny ink drop in a specially constructed cylinder, Millikan was able to measure the charge of an electron.

The speaker initially repeats a question that the reader assumes has been asked of him, "Did I see it go by, / That Millikan mote?" and then tries to answer it. The speaker clearly lacks confidence as to whether he has seen the droplet, and he goes so far as to admit, "I rather suspect / All I saw was the lid / Going over my eye."

The poem tries to illustrate a layperson's perspective on the concepts and attitudes of scientific investigation. They may make "a good try" at seeing these things, but in the end they will miss the important aspects of science.

"A Wish to Comply" was first published in *Steeple Bush.* The manuscript title was "On Being Shown a Cosmic Ray," and the original manuscript did not include the final couplet (Cramer, 152). *See* SCIENCE.

FURTHER READING

Cramer, Jeffrey S. *Robert Frost among His Poems: A Literary Companion to the Poet's Own Biographical Contexts and Associations.* Jefferson, N.C.: MacFarland, 1996.

Sokol, B. J. "Poet in the Atomic Age: Robert Frost's 'That Millikan Mote' Expanded," *Annals of Science* 53, no. 4 (1996): 399–411.

Witness Tree, A (1942)

A Witness Tree was first published in 1942 in New York by Henry Holt. A limited and signed edition of 735 copies also was published. "Beech" and "Sycamore" were the introductory poems, followed by a table of contents that was arranged in five sections: "One or Two," "Two or More," "Time Out," "Quantula," and "Over Back." It was dedicated to his friend and secretary Kathleen (Kay) Morrison: "To K. M. for her part in it." After Elinor's death in 1938, Morrison came to Frost's aid. Frost once told Louis Mertins, "I owe everything in the world to her. She found me in the gutter, hopeless, sick, run down. She bundled me up and carted me to her home and cared for me like a child, sick child. Without her I would today be in my grave. If I have done anything since I came out of the hospital, it is all due to her" (Cramer, 123). Frost's seventh volume of poetry, *A Witness Tree,* earned him his fourth Pulitzer Prize.

The volume included a number of poems that had been written years earlier, some even decades earlier. "The Subverted Flower," which Frost had resisted publishing until after his wife Elinor's death because of the personal nature of the poem, was included, as was "The Quest of the Purple-Fringed," which had been published in 1901 as "The Quest of the Orchis." Some of the better-known poems in the volume include "The Silken Tent," "The Gift Outright," and "The Most of It." "The Gift Outright" was recited from memory at President John F. Kennedy's inauguration when the sun was too bright for Frost to read the poem he had composed for the occasion, "For John F. Kennedy His Inauguration."

William H. Pritchard calls the book "Frost's last truly significant book of verse" and notes that a "number of poems in *A Witness Tree* undoubtedly derived their dark tone from the family tragedies suffered over the decade." He finds that lyrics such as "The Silken Tent," "I Could Give All to Time," "Never Again Would Birds' Song Be the Same," and "The Most of It" stand "in the top rank of Frost's work" and notes that Frost "himself thought that some of his best poetry was contained in this book." Pritchard uses Frost's own words from "The Figure a Poem Makes" to describe how the poems of this volume "exhibit both 'how a poem can have wildness and at the same time a subject that shall be fulfilled.'"

A beech "witness tree" stood on the cover of the book. *Witness tree* was a term used to refer to the trees used by governmental surveyors as markers when Americans moved west in the mid-1800s. Some of them still stand. Frost himself moved in the opposite direction; born in SAN FRANCISCO, he moved east as a boy to NEW ENGLAND. Frost's very personal *A Witness Tree* still stands surely, serving as one of the markers of his life and achievement.

FURTHER READING

Cramer, Jeffrey S. *Robert Frost among His Poems: A Literary Companion to the Poet's Own Biographical Contexts and Associations.* Jefferson, N.C.: MacFarland, 1996.

Faggen, Robert. "Frost Biography and *A Witness Tree.*" In *The Cambridge Companion to Robert Frost,* edited by Robert Faggen, 35–47. Cambridge: Cambridge University Press, 2001.

Pritchard, William H. "Frost's Life and Career," *Modern American Poetry.* March 18, 2001. Available online. URL: http://www.english.uiuc.edu/maps/poets/a_f/frost/life.htm. Accessed February 12, 2006.

Winslow, Donald J. "The Origin of Robert Frost's 'Witness Tree,'" *American Notes and Queries* 13 (1975): 153–154.

"Wood-Pile, The" (1914)

Out walking "in the frozen swamp one gray day," the speaker pauses and faces a decision. He is not determining which road to take but rather whether to "turn back from here" or "go on farther." He determines to go farther on, as then "we shall see." What might be seen is unknown.

The speaker walks on hard snow that, for the most part, holds his weight. Occasionally a foot falls through, but his walk is not a risky one. He is surrounded by trees that are so similar to one another that he cannot use them as a guide to aid him in his journey or his return. All he can know for certain is that he is "just far from home."

He is accompanied only by a bird that is "careful" enough to leave a tree between them when he lands and to "say no word to tell [him] who he was / Who was so foolish as to think what *he* thought." If the speaker is foolish enough to imagine a bird's thoughts, then the bird is smart enough to keep him from knowing. The speaker recalls that the bird thought he was "after him for a feather," and the bird is anthropomorphized into "one who takes / Everything said as personal to himself."

The bird and speaker take leave of each other when "there was a pile of wood." The woodpile is cut, split, and measured perfectly. There are no tracks leading to or away from it, and it becomes clear that the pile is older than "this year's cutting, / Or even last year's or the year's before." A climbing clematis plant has "wound strings round and round it like a bundle." The speaker can only imagine that the one who had "spent himself, the labor of his ax" on this woodpile must live as one "turning to fresh tasks"; otherwise, how else could he "so forget his handiwork?" Instead of being used in a fireplace to keep a house warm, the cord of maple has been left to "warm the frozen swamp as best it could / With the slow smokeless burning of decay."

George Monteiro writes "that the crafted pile decays, breaking down to its elements, says much about the impermanence of man's handiwork—a point which brings us back to man's continuing quiet astonishment at the transformation of all his work—the noble and the banal—into waste and ruin" (69–70). It also suggests the impermanence of human life. The suggestion is either that he who created the woodpile has forgotten his work, an unlikely conclusion, or that, more likely, he died before appreciating the fruits of his labor.

Nature becomes a source for reflection, as always in Frost, and the speaker becomes the one "who takes / Everything . . . as personal to himself."

"The Wood-Pile" was first published in *North of Boston*.

FURTHER READING

Bagby, George F. *Frost and the Book of Nature.* Knoxville: University of Tennessee Press, 1993, 145–148.

Doreski, William. "Meta-Meditation in Robert Frost's 'The Wood-Pile,' 'After Apple-Picking,' and 'Directive,'" *Review of International English Literature* 23, no. 4 (October 1992): 35–49.

Faggen, Robert. *Robert Frost and the Challenge of Darwin.* Ann Arbor: University of Michigan Press, 1997, 263–269.

Kern, Alexander. "Frost's 'The Wood-Pile,'" *Explicator* 28 (1970): 49.

McInery, Stephen. "'Little Forms': Four Poems and a Developing Theme of Robert Frost," *Critical Review* 40 (2000): 59–74.

Monteiro, George. *Robert Frost and the New England Renaissance.* Lexington: University Press of Kentucky, 1988, 67–70.

Pack, Robert. *Belief and Uncertainty in the Poetry of Robert Frost.* Hanover, N.H.: Middlebury College Press, 2003.

Perrine, Laurence. "On Frost's 'The Wood-Pile,'" *Notes on Modern American Literature* 6, no. 1 (Spring–Summer 1982): 1.

"Wrights' Biplane, The" (1936)

This quatrain is the third in a group of poems titled "Ten Mills," most of which were originally published in *Poetry* in April 1936 and later collected in *A Further Range.* "The Wrights' Biplane" was not among the original group.

The verse refers to the American airplane inventors Orville Wright (1871–1948) and Wilbur Wright (1867–1912). The playful lines have a serious tone. While Frost calls the plane the "shape of human flight," his business is with its makers, whose recognition he feels is greatly deserved. "Time cannot get that wrong"—or should not, he says—"For it was writ in heaven doubly Wright" and visualized in the exhaust of that "First Motor Kite."

See TECHNOLOGY.

"Young Birch, A" (1947)

Frost was fond of the birch tree. In "Birches" the young boy has been swinging on them, but they also figure prominently in "Wild Grapes" and "Home Burial," as well as being referenced in "New Hampshire," "The Onset," and "Pea Brush." They are briefly mentioned in "Something for Hope" and "Good-By and Keep Cold." This is the second of Frost's poems named after the birch tree.

"A Young Birch" begins with the birch beginning to crack its "outer sheath" of "baby green" and show the white bark beneath. The poem is a tribute to the tree, singing praises to the "only native tree that dares to lean, / Relying on its beauty, to the air." The speaker suggests in an aside that perhaps it is not bravery but trust that causes the true to dare so. After all, the air when strong enough is a threat to the young tree.

The birch grows from the diameter of a cane to that of a fishing pole and then so grand that it is a thing of beauty not only meant to but sent to "live its life out as ornament." Someone who kept the brush along the wall well trimmed might have made the decision to cut the birch down too, but in sparing it that lawn worker becomes the "most efficient help" ever hired. The speaker addresses someone who does not trim bushes but is a book reader and a traveler. His land is not tended to by him. The young birch has survived through luck and persistence, not through the grace of its owner.

George F. Bagby writes that "what might otherwise be considered waste is turned into a positive virtue, a freedom from the narrow, materialistic demands of utility" (91). The young birch's owner reaps the benefits of its beauty now that it is grown, but he did not contribute in any direct way to this young birch's success any more than do we to nature's growth.

Frost was weighed down by his own wind, and ice storms too, having suffered great tragedy in his life. Perhaps he saw a likeness to himself in the tree and admired the birch most because, like him, it trusted itself to bend without breaking and somehow managed to right itself.

The poem was first published in 1946 in booklet form as Frost's Christmas poem. It was later collected as the opening poem in *Steeple Bush*.

FURTHER READING

Bagby, George F. *Frost and the Book of Nature.* Knoxville: University of Tennessee Press, 1993, 91–92.
D'Avanzo, Mario L. "Frost's 'A Young Birch': A Thing of Beauty," *Concerning Poetry* 3, no. 2 (1970): 69–70.

PART III

Related People, Places, Literary Influences, Themes, and Symbols

belief At the end of Frost's lecture "Education by Poetry" at the Amherst Alumni Council Address on November 15, 1930, he speaks of "four beliefs that [he] know[s] more about from having lived with poetry." The first is the "personal belief, which is a knowledge that you don't want to tell other people about because you cannot prove that you know. You are saying nothing about it till you see." This personal belief Frost also describes as the "love belief," which, he says, "has that same shyness. It knows it cannot tell; only the outcome can tell." The "national belief" is one "we enter into socially with each other, all together, party of the first part, party of the second part, we enter into that to bring the future of the country." And then there is the "believing [of] the thing into existence, saying as you go more than you even hoped you were going to be able to say, and coming with surprise to an end that you foreknew only with some sort of emotion." A position on the afterlife applies directly to what he identifies as the fourth belief, which is isolated as the "relationship we enter into with God to believe the future in—to believe the hereafter in."

All of the beliefs that Frost identifies are expressed in his poetry. In "The Strong Are Saying Nothing" Frost depicts the farmer as strong and hopeful when he plants seeds in the soil. He must wait to see if he will be rewarded with the fruits of his labor or if the soil bed will become a "grave" to his seedlings. The hope of the farmer is also expressed in "Evil Tendencies Cancel," which reports that the "farmers rather guess not" whether the "blight [will] end the chestnut." The belief of those who say nothing until they see is akin to hope. It is a wish for an outcome that remains unknown, and that concept of belief is quite different from Frost's approach to national or religious belief.

Frost was patriotic, and his idea of a belief in one's nation is reflected in a number of his poems. This sort of belief is not about hope or outcomes as much as it is about faith in something or support of that something. The best expression of Frost's nationalism is "The Gift Outright," his love poem to the United States. He begins with his own mythology—"The land was ours before we were the land's"—and ends with pride, speaking of the "unstoried, artless, unenhanced" country that was in a state of "becom[ing]."

Frost's position on religious belief and the afterlife is hard to pin down. He frequently appears to be an agnostic, despite his fourth belief, the "relationship we enter into with God to believe the future in—to believe the hereafter in." He is coy about his own beliefs, wavering and faltering more than a little. Even his statement of this fourth belief does not assert that he carries the belief himself. His daughter Lesley, in the introduction to Dorothy Judd Hall's *Contours of Belief*, writes that the "question being asked of late" is whether Frost had "any defined belief in an Almighty," and she concludes that Hall's "case" is so well stated "in God's favor" that she "find[s] it so easy to agree with her" (xi). But even when Frost himself insisted that he was being "orthodox" in his poetry, as in a statement he made in his *Paris Review* interview that his two masques were not "rebellious" but rather "very doctrinal, very orthodox, both of them" is, somewhat ironically, hard to believe or have faith in. A reading of the masques themselves suggests the opposite. God, after all, answers Job's questions about how he was treated by telling him that all the suffering Job endured was simply so that God could "show off" to the devil, that he was provoked almost as if by a dare. Such a depiction of God is hardly orthodox.

In "Astrometaphysical" the poet speaks directly to God, arguing that he be sent "up, not down." Such an argument, a plea, is a game, as the rhyme and the language indicate. It is for him a play, one that demonstrates that what he has witnessed thus far provides him with insufficient impressions of the afterlife and of the goodness of God to judge. Frost is always more impressed with Earth than with the unknown, which is why Earth is the "right place for love" ("Birches"). His couplet "Forgive, O Lord, my little jokes on Thee / And I'll forgive Thy great big one on me" seems indication enough.

Frost's writing is often critical of religion. He is skeptical about God, frequently presenting agnostic views because he is uncertain and untrusting, and is slightly more apt to embrace scientific approaches to existence. "Accidentally on Purpose" is cautiously Darwinian, its speaker agnostic. He does not know whose purpose the universe was, admits he has no ability to discern, and suggests that sort of speculation be left to "the scientific wits." He does not need divinity, however; all he wants is "intention, purpose, and design." In "Design" the question of an intelligent designer is raised, but again the issue remains unresolved, though the questions asked of the reader in the closing of the sonnet suggest Frost's own position: "What but design of darkness to appall?—/ If design govern in a thing so small." "The Fear of God" cautions against pride, because all seeming evidence of divine favor, under examination, turns out to be arbitrary.

In the grouping of poems titled "Cluster of Faith," there are meditations on the nature of religion, a subject that interested Frost throughout his career. In "The Trial by Existence" Frost is faithful and hopeful. There is an optimism that our trials are purposeful and our woes meaningful. He takes issue with God in his masques, *The Masque of Mercy* and *The Masque of Reason,* but here he postulates a God who takes "especial care." In "A Steeple on the House" Frost suggests that we do not need to have a steeple in order to have a house. We have a house already; the steeple is merely ornamental. The closing lines read: "A spire and belfry coming on the roof / Means that a soul is coming on the flesh." Just as we attach the notion of eternity to our lives, we attach the concept of a soul to the complexities of our flesh. The house of life is the structure, and we put the label of the sacred on the structure, just as we put the symbolic stamp of the soul on the body. Frost minimizes the need for soul and elevates the flesh. Ordinary life and ordinary flesh can be celebrated without religious assumptions. "Etherealizing" ridicules the idea of the soul without flesh when Frost writes, "A theory if you hold it hard enough / And long enough gets rated as a creed: / Such as that flesh is something we can slough / So that the mind can be entirely freed."

While Frost's views about religious belief cannot be pinned down, his views about belief generally are fairly consistent. He described himself as neither optimist nor pessimist, and "belief" then becomes a cautious hope. He is not convinced of the future either way, whether he is discussing farming, love, or God. In any case, he knows more about them all for having lived with poetry.

FURTHER READING

Hall, Dorothy Judd. *Robert Frost: Contours of Belief.* Introduction by Lesley Frost. Athens: Ohio University Press, 1984.

Kau, Joseph. "'Trust . . . to go by Contraries': Incarnation and the Paradox of Belief in the Poetry of Frost." In *Frost: Centennial Essays II,* edited by Jac Tharpe, 99–111. Jackson: University Press of Mississippi, 1976.

Pack, Robert. *Belief and Uncertainty in the Poetry of Robert Frost.* Hanover, N.H.: Middlebury College Press, 2003.

biographers   The first full-length biography of Frost was Gorham B. Munson's *Robert Frost: A Study in Sensibility and Good Sense* (1927). Frost would live another 35 years, making this early biography severely limited. Donald Greiner criticizes the work for not being "flesh[ed] out" enough. He writes that Munson "repeatedly drops hints about an event or mentions a series of topics which he discussed with Frost, but he ducks his obligations as a biographer when he omits the details of these events and topics" (20). Jay Parini describes Munson as "rac[ing] through the life and work straightforwardly, seeing Frost as a classical humanist, a man of enduring 'good sense,'" but also chides him for "working from a view of Frost already in play" (449–450). The second full-length biography was Elizabeth Shepley Sergeant's *Robert Frost: The Trial by Existence* (1960) which Greiner also criticizes as having "questionable documentation and shaky analysis" (24) and which Parini calls "an endearing profile" but criticizes for having "mistook the mask for the man" (450). The first full-length biography to appear after Frost's death was Jean Gould's *Robert Frost: The Aim Was Song* (1964), which Parini calls a "minor biography in the sentimental groove." Friend Louis Mertins's *Robert Frost: Life and Talks-Walking* (1965) soon followed.

Robert Newdick, a professor of English at Ohio University, was Frost's first identified biographer, though he chose the position for himself rather than having it selected for him by Frost. When he died unexpectedly in 1939, having written only about 100 pages, Lawrance Thompson, professor of English at Princeton, became Frost's "official" biographer on the condition that the biography not be published until after Frost's death. Newdick's work was edited by William A. Sutton and released as *Newdick's Season of Frost: An Interrupted Biography of Robert Frost* much later, in 1976. Lawrance Thompson would go on to write a vast three-volume biography, with assistance from graduate student R. H. Winnick only with the third and final volume. Thompson died in 1973, leaving Winnick to complete the work on the last book. The volumes were titled *Robert Frost: The Early Years, 1874–1915* (1966), *Robert Frost: The Years of Triumph* (1970), and *Robert Frost: The Later Years, 1938–1963* (1976). Thompson would also write *Fire and Ice: The Art and Thought of Robert Frost* (1942). Thompson established himself as Frost's most credentialed biographer, a position he held firmly until recent years.

Stanley Burnshaw's *Robert Frost Himself* (1986), Sandra Katz's *Elinor Frost: A Poet's Wife* (1988), and Jeffrey Meyer's *Robert Frost: A Biography* (1996) are more recent biographical additions.

A number of friends, in addition to Mertins, wrote accounts and memoirs of Frost, such as Sidney Cox, who wrote *Robert Frost: Original "Ordinary Man"* (1929) and *A Swinger of Birches: A Portrait of Robert Frost* (1957); Reginald Cook, who wrote *The Dimensions of Robert Frost* (1958) and *Robert Frost: A Living Voice* (1974); Daniel Smythe, who wrote *Robert Frost Speaks* (1964); and Robert Francis, who wrote *Frost: A Time to Talk* (1972). Studies of friendship can also be found in *Robert Frost and Sidney Cox: Forty Years of Friendship* (1981) edited by William R. Evans, and *Robert Frost and John Bartlett: The Record of a Friendship* (1963), by John and Margaret Bartlett's daughter Margaret Bartlett Anderson. Granddaughter Lesley Lee Francis offers intimate insights in *The Frost Family's Adventure in Poetry: Sheer Morning Gladness at the Brim* (1994). *Robert Frost in Russia* (1963), by F. D. Reeve, zeroes in on a particular period in the poet's life, as does John Evangelist Walsh's *Into My Own: The English Years of Robert Frost, 1912–1915* (1988).

Illumination of Frost's life is perhaps best taken from the poet's own words, found in his letters and interviews: *The Letters of Robert Frost to Louis Untermeyer* (1963), edited by Louis Untermeyer; the *Selected Letters of Robert Frost* (1964), edited by Thompson; Arnold Grade's *The Family Letters of Robert and Elinor Frost* (1972); *Elected Friends: Robert Frost and Edward Thomas to One Another*, edited by Matthew Spencer; and *Interviews with Robert Frost* (1966), edited by Edward Connery Lathem, are seminal. Elaine Barry's *Robert Frost on Writing* (1973) is great fun. *New Hampshire's Child: The Derry Journals of Lesley Frost* (1969) offers an intimate look.

Donald J. Greiner offers exacting criticism and analysis of letters, biographies, and memoirs in his *Robert Frost: The Poet and His Critics* (1974). The Thompson biographies, though the most extensive and detailed, have been highly criticized and devalued for the impression they left of Frost. William Pritchard writes that the Thompson biography "effected a striking change in the way people thought about Frost's character. . . . The man who had been placed on a pedestal and worshipped in schoolrooms all over America was now seen—so the presumption went—for what he had really been all along: a species of monster in human form (xi–xii). And Parini, the most recent full-length biographer of Frost, whose *Robert Frost: A Life* appeared in Great Britain in 1998 and America in 1999, writes that Thompson's biography was "driven by a mythos that distorted, rather than clarified, the material at hand" (453). A brief look at the index to the material endorses Parini's sentiments. The index is organized in such a way that bias is immediately evident. Headings such as: "Anti-Intellectual," "Baffler-Teaser-Deceiver," "Brute," "Charlatan," "Cowardice," "Escapist," "Jealousy," and "Rage" leap out at the reader. While some of Thompson's facts are historically accurate, the spin he puts on them is highly questionable.

While all of the biographies shed some light on the complex figure Frost was, Parini's recent biography emerges as the most reliable full-length text to date. In his afterword on Frost and other Frost biographers, he offers insightful and convincing commentary on those who have come before him and a clear rationale there and throughout for his own biography, "set[ting] the record straight here and there, putting in place a fresh mythos, . . . comb[ing] the facts in a certain direction but . . .

not preclud[ing] a future biographer (and there will be many) from combining the same material differently" (458). The fresh mythos Parini modestly presents is of a man who is exceedingly human, one with insecurities, passions, triumphs and tragedies, a great intellect, a gift, and sound enough judgment and character to let his own life, "like a piece of ice on a hot stove . . . ride on its own melting."

FURTHER READING

Adams, Frederick B., Jr. *To Russia with Frost*. Boston: Club of Odd Volumes, 1963.

Anderson, Margaret Bartlett. *Robert Frost and John Bartlett: The Record of a Friendship*. New York: Holt, 1963.

Barry, Elaine. *Robert Frost on Writing*. New Brunswick, N.J.: Rutgers University Press, 1974.

Burnshaw, Stanley. *Robert Frost Himself*. New York: George Braziller, 1986.

Cook, Reginald. *The Dimensions of Robert Frost*. New York: Rinehart, 1958.

———. *Robert Frost: A Living Voice*. Amherst: University of Massachusetts Press, 1974.

Cox, Sidney. *Robert Frost: Original "Ordinary Man."* New York: Holt, 1929.

———. *A Swinger of Birches: A Portrait of Robert Frost*. New York: New York University Press, 1957.

Evans, William R., ed. *Robert Frost and Sidney Cox: Forty Years of Friendship*. Hanover: University Press of New England, 1981.

Francis, Lesley Lee. *The Frost Family's Adventure in Poetry: Sheer Morning Gladness at the Brim*. Columbia: University of Missouri Press, 1994.

Francis, Robert. *Robert Frost: A Time to Talk*. Amherst: University of Massachusetts Press, 1972.

Frost, Lesley. *New Hampshire's Child: The Derry Journals of Lesley Frost*. Albany: State University of New York Press, 1969.

Frost, Robert. *The Letters of Robert Frost to Louis Untermeyer*. Edited by Louis Untermeyer. New York: Holt, Reinhart and Winston, 1963.

———. *Robert Frost on Writing*. Edited by Elaine Barry. New Brunswick: Rutgers University Press, 1973.

———. *Selected Letters of Robert Frost*. Edited by Lawrance Thompson. New York: Holt, Rinehart and Winston, 1964.

Gould, Jean. *Robert Frost: The Aim Was Song*. New York: Dodd, Mead, 1964.

Grade, Arnold, ed. *The Family Letters of Robert and Elinor Frost*. Albany: State University of New York Press, 1972.

Greiner, Donald J. *Robert Frost: The Poet and His Critics*. Chicago: American Library Association, 1974.

Katz, Sandra L. *Elinor Frost: A Poet's Wife*. Westfield: Institute for Massachusetts Studies, 1988.

Lathem, Edward Connery, ed. *Interviews with Robert Frost*. New York: Holt, Rinehart and Winston, 1966.

———, ed. *The Poetry of Robert Frost*. New York: Henry Holt, 1969.

Mertins, Louis. *Robert Frost: Life and Talks-Walking*. Norman: University of Oklahoma Press, 1965.

Meyers, Jeffrey. *Robert Frost: A Biography*. New York: Houghton Mifflin, 1996.

Munson, Gorham B. *Robert Frost: A Study in Sensibility and Good Sense*. New York: Dorham, 1927.

Newdick, Robert S. *Newdick's Season of Frost: An Interrupted Biography*. Edited by William A. Sutton. Albany: State University of New York Press, 1976.

Parini, Jay. *Robert Frost: A Life*. New York: Holt, 1999.

Reeve, Franklin D. *Robert Frost in Russia*. Boston: Little, Brown, 1963.

Sergeant, Elizabeth Shepley. *Robert Frost: The Trial by Existence*. New York: Holt, 1960.

Smythe, Daniel. *Robert Frost Speaks*. New York: Twayne, 1964.

Thompson, Lawrance. *Fire and Ice: The Art and Thought of Robert Frost*. New York: Russell & Russell, 1942.

———. *Robert Frost: The Early Years*. New York: Holt, Rinehart and Winston, 1966.

———. *Robert Frost: The Years of Triumph, 1915–1938*. New York: Holt, Rinehart and Winston, 1970.

———, and R. H. Winnick. *Robert Frost: The Later Years: 1938–1963*. New York: Holt, Rinehart and Winston, 1976.

Walsh, John Evangelist. *Into My Own: The English Years of Robert Frost, 1912–1915*. New York: Grove, 1988.

Bread Loaf School of English   The Bread Loaf Inn, a hotel not far from Bread Loaf Mountain in Ripton, Vermont, was willed by Joseph Battell, breeder of Morgan horses and newspaper proprietor, to Middlebury College. The inn included a main building and several cottages and barns. Middlebury College created on the land the Bread Loaf School Graduate School of English and offered an array of courses in literature, teaching, writing, and theater. In 1926 the first Bread Loaf Writers' Conference was held.

In December 1920 Frost wrote to Professor Wilfred E. Davison, the newly appointed head of the school, about his interest in it. Frost suggested that he

> might fit into [their] summer plan with a course on the Responsibilities of Teachers of Composition—to their country to help make what is sure to be the greatest nation in wealth the greatest in art also. I should particularly like to

encounter the teachers who refuse to expect of human nature more than a business letter. (Thompson, 161)

In 1921 Frost read at Bread Loaf for the first time. He read several of his poems and then asserted that "what Bread Loaf wanted for a teacher was an author with writing of his own on hand; one who would be willing to live for a while on terms of equality—almost—with a few younger writers. . . . In such a course, the teacher would no more think of assigning work to the students than they would think of asking him to write something for them." (Thompson, 172). Frost's theories about the school would eventually come to fruition and become the basis for the summer program.

The school was a significant mainstay in Frost's public life, and he returned each summer for many

Main house of the Homer Noble Farm, Ripton, Vermont. *(Photo by Deirdre Fagan)*

years. After his wife Elinor's death in 1938, a scholarship in her honor was established at the school. After 1939 Frost would live in proximity in the summer at the Homer Noble Farm, where "[o]ver the years, a steady stream of young writers [would make] the pilgrimage . . . and, often with their own manuscripts in hand, walk[k] along the maple-lined path to the cabin, where Frost sat in his Morris chair, usually with a glass of iced tea in hand" (Parini, 328). Frost's close friends Kay and Theodore Morrison would occupy the main house at the farm. Kay acted as Frost's manager after Elinor's death. Theodore was the director of the writers' conference from 1932–55.

Bread Loaf has counted among its faculty members such distinguished teachers and scholars as Harold Bloom, Cleanth Brooks, Reuben Brower, and John Crowe Ransom. Frost is the writer most identified with Bread Loaf, however, having returned every summer but three for 42 years. Middlebury College owns and maintains the Homer Noble Farm as a National Historic Site near the Bread Loaf campus. Nearby is the Robert Frost Trail.

FURTHER READING

"Bread Loaf School of English." Middlebury College. Available Online. URL: http://www.middlebury.edu/academics/blse/. Accessed March 22, 2006.

Parini, Jay. *Robert Frost: A Life.* New York: Holt, 1999.

Thompson, Lawrance. *Robert Frost: The Years of Triumph, 1915–1938.* New York: Holt, Rinehart and Winston, 1970.

country versus city Frost frequently contrasts city and country life. He was partial to country life and enjoyed living on farms and trying his hand at being a farmer. He was critical of technology's encroachment on nature (*see* TECHNOLOGY) and often celebrated the labors of country people, such as planting seeds, tilling land, and chopping wood. It seems that he was torn between the simple life eked out early in his life on the land and the one that he found in academia. With these two lifestyles come different types of knowledge, and Frost sometimes pits them against each other.

"The Need of Being Versed in Country Things" is concerned with just this conflict. To be versed is, if not to anticipate, at least to expect happenstance. Those not versed in country things think that nature cares about humans and other living things. Those who are versed (a nice play on words) know about the indifference of nature, that it does not respond to human affairs. The poem presents country folk as more aware than city dwellers of their position and vulnerability in relation to nature.

In "A Roadside Stand" the landscape highlights the difference in perspective between city and country people, and the country people are less vulnerable to nature than to the finances of city people. It is a quarrel over modernization in which the encroachment on nature makes the roadside stand a sad symbol of a past that is fading rapidly. The country people become dependent on city charity: "A roadside stand that too pathetically pled, / It would not be fair to say for a dole of bread, / But for some of the money, the cash, whose flow supports / The flower of cities from sinking and withering faint."

In "An Unstamped Letter in Our Rural Letter Box" the speaker is a city tramp who finds himself in the country. He sleeps in a farmer's pasture, which he finds similar to a "city park." While sleeping outside that night, the tramp, being awakened by a rock that makes him uncomfortable, comes face-to-face with "universal space," providing a city dweller's desire for relaxation and a connection to nature that is presumably absent in urban environments.

In "Christmas Trees" the city withdraws into itself. It leaves the "country to the country," but the city returns to the country to "look for something it ha[s] left behind." Frost provides an interesting twist on Christmas trees, pointing out that city dwellers still need something from the country: those trees, chopped down only to be placed in living rooms rather than to be left in the woods behind a house.

In his observances on rural life, Frost also refers to political issues, as he does in "Build Soil—A Political Pastoral" (a pastoral is a literary work that idealizes rural life), in which "Tityrus does not want to "lure the city to the country" and those who should possess the land are "only those, / Who love it."

The dramatic narrative "From Plane to Plane" offers the greatest insight into the contrast between not simply city and country life but the assumptions and stereotypes that accompany each. The poem opens with the line "Neither of them was better than the other," the colloquialism on which the entire poem is predicated. It contrasts two men working together: Dick and Pike. Pike's education comes from "having hoed and mowed for fifty years," while Dick's comes from "being fresh and full of college." The subject is the definition of work. Pike thinks of the sort of work he does as a laborer as real work and thinks of the sort of work others do as something less. Dick's academic vocabulary and his lofty examples seem patronizing to Pike, who is older and wants to be more knowledgeable. The poem narrows Dick's knowledge to what he learns in his courses, because though he is schooled, he is limited and incapable of knowing more than what others have taught him. The narrative offers Frost an opportunity to compare formal education to the education of experience. The poem says, "if they fought about equality / It was on an equality they fought," and this becomes the moral of the poem and a way of understanding the contrasting views found in Frost's poetry.

While country life often comes out on top, Frost generally does not contrast the two to prove that one is better than the other. He clearly prized both. He embraced country life but what he made of it, poetry, dispels the myth that country people and life are as simple as city people often think they are. In the end Frost reveals that to be "versed in country things" is to engage in a thorough study of his poetry. The work of knowing has just begun when we are presented with his rural complexity.

critics   Frost's first book of poetry, *A Boy's Will*, was published on April 1, 1913, by David Nutt and Company of London, ENGLAND, only days after Frost's 39th birthday. Frost had published a few poems in magazines in the United States but had not had the confidence to seek a book publisher in America. Early reviewers included Ezra Pound, who wrote in a letter to Alice Corbin Henderson, assistant of Harriet Monro of *Poetry* magazine, "Have just discovered another Amur'kn. Vurry Amurk'n,

with, I think, the seeds of grace." (128). Frank F. S. Flint also offered a favorable review. He admired Frost's "direct observation of the object and immediate correlation with the emotion—spontaneity, subtlety in the evocation of moods humour," and his "ear for silences" (Meyers, 102). Flint believed that each poem was the expression of one mood, or one emotion, or one idea. Norman Douglas of the *English Review* wrote that there was a "wild, racy flavour" to Frost's poems and that "they sound that inevitable response to nature which is the hallmark of true lyric feeling" (Thornton, 21).

Frost's second book, *North of Boston*, was published by David Nutt on May 15, 1914. One of the early reviews included Lascelles Abercrombie's unsigned review in the *Nation* on June 13, 1914, in which he wrote, "Mr. Frost certainly makes a racy use of New England vernacular. But he goes further; he seems trying to capture and hold within metrical patterns the very tones of speech—the rise and fall, the stressed pauses and little hurries of spoken language" (Thornton, 27). Edward Thomas also wrote an unsigned review for the August 1914 edition of the *English Review*, in which he said that "Within the space of a hundred lines or so of blank verse it would be hard to compress more rural character and relevant scenery; impossible, perhaps, to do so with less sense of compression and more lightness, unity, and breadth"; Thomas referred to several poems as "masterpieces of deep and mysterious tenderness" (Greiner, 77). Edward Garnett wrote in the August 1915 *Atlantic Monthly* that Frost was "a master of his exacting medium, blank verse,—a new master. The reader must pause and pause again before he can judge him, so unobtrusive and quiet are these, 'effects,' so subtle the appeal of the whole. One can, indeed, return to his poems again and again without exhausting their quiet imaginative spell" (Garnett, 40).

Henry Holt and Company of New York would publish Frost's books in the United States. *North of Boston* would be first, on February 20, 1915; *A Boy's Will* would follow in April. William Dean Howells wrote in the September 1915 issue of *Harper's* that "the earlier book [*A Boy's Will*] sings rather the most, but youth is apt to sing most, and there is strong, sweet music in them both [*North of Boston* as well]." (Thornton, 44). Amy Lowell wrote in the *New Republic,* on February 20, 1915, that "Mr. Frost has reproduced both people and scenery with a vividness which is extraordinary. Here are the huge hills, undraped by any sympathetic legend, felt as things hard and unyielding, almost sinister, not exactly feared, but regarded as in some sort influences nevertheless" (Lowell, 23).

Donald J. Greiner writes that when Frost returned to the United States from ENGLAND a "multi-edged dispute" ensued: "Some critics used Frost to comment upon the sorry state of American publishing, lamenting that native artists of exceptional merit had to find publication in a foreign country because American publishers and editors were blind and deaf to the newer movements in poetry"; others "attack[ed] Frost for his so-called British-made reputation, these critics used the poet's work as a transition to a more general argument that the American public should not patronize an American artist just because the English think well of him" (66–67).

Frost lived for nearly 60 years after the publication of his first books, and it has now been nearly a century since. He has been commented on, studied, and criticized by numerous critics over the decades, each of whom has shed light on the nuances in his work. Early critics are considered by later ones to have been naive about the tensions, contradictions, and darkness in his poetry, as Frost was considered an uncomplicated NEW ENGLAND nature poet early in his career. His simple language, use of the vernacular, and emphasis on tones and natural speech patterns made his poetry accessible and, at times, broadly misunderstood. Simplicity in language, however, did not equal simplicity in thought.

Observations of simplicity included the anonymous critic who said of Frost that "his verses do not rise above the ordinary" (Greiner, 71). In 1924 Carl Van Doren also took a reductionist view: "If Robert Frost talks as becomes a Yankee poet, so does he think as becomes one" (Vandoren, 72). The term "Yankee" stuck.

When Frost later received his third Pulitzer Prize for *A Further Range,* criticism grew more intense, as his conservative politics became more evident.

Critics batted Frost around to their own ends. Liberals and conservatives alike would let politics interfere with clear judgments of his art. Malcolm Cowley wrote in 1944,

> We have lately been watching the growth in this country of a narrow nationalism that has spread from politics into literature. . . . They demand, however, that American literature should be affirmative, optimistic, uncritical and "truly of this nation." They have been looking round for a poet to exalt; and Frost, through no fault of his own (but chiefly through the weaker qualities of his work), has been adopted as their symbol. (Cowley, 96)

Cowley reveals his own bias when he says of Frost, "He is concerned chiefly with himself and his near neighbors, or rather with the Yankees among his neighbors" and "does not strive toward greater depth to compensate for what he lacks in breadth; he does not strike far inward into the wilderness of human nature" (Cowley, 101).

The keenest of the early critics included Mark Van Doren, who wrote perceptively in the *American Scholar* in the spring of 1936 that Frost "deals . . . in indirection. The thing he seems to be talking about is never quite the thing he means to be talking about. He selects an object, an animal, a person, a life, or whatever other thing he likes, and makes it a symbol of something else which is larger or deeper than itself" (Thornton, 9). Bernard DeVoto, in the January 1, 1938, issue of the *Saturday Review of Literature,* took on the negative critics, writing that

> "Steeped in [Walt] Whitman, knowing my [T. S.] Eliot by heart as well as commentary, admiring [Edwin Arlington] Robinson as most of my colleagues once did but do no longer, I nevertheless think of Frost as the finest poet, living or dead. That, of course, is subjective; you do not prove "best" and "finest," and no one need adopt by judgment. But to ignore the attributes of greatness briefly glanced at here [in examples in his own piece] is to make a fool of yourself in public. Lovers of poetry have not committed that asininity. (Cowley, 111)

But the battle was not over. Harold H. Watt would agree with the negative criticism of Cowley and others like him in his March 1955 *American Literature* article, writing that Frost often resorts to whimsical conversation and slight, trivial editorials, keeping up the quarrel over Frost's politics (Greiner, 123–124).

As Frost neared the end of his career, the intensity of the critical wars over his poetry began to wane, and a deeper understanding and appreciation began to emerge. Philip L. Gerber writes that in 1960, George W. Nitchie's *Human Values in the Poetry of Robert Frost* and John F. Lynen's *The Pastoral Art of Robert Frost* presented two views of Frost's "central theme, the man-nature relationship." In Nitchie's view, Frost "treat[ed] nature as an incomprehensible force," and in Lynen's Frost made "of it a metaphor through which the problems confronting man may be approached, albeit obliquely" (*Critical Essays*, 10).

Beginning with Randall Jarrell and continuing through Lionel Trilling, Roberts W. French, and others, the dark side of Frost—or the "other" Frost, as Jarrell phrased it—was given much attention. It became clear that to know Frost was to apprehend the darkness in his poems as well as the light. Jarrell said that Frost's critics could only have given him such a simple, rustic reputation "from not knowing his poems well enough, or from knowing the wrong poems too well." Trilling's talk at Frost's 85th birthday celebration on March 26, 1959, at the Waldorf-Astoria in New York City jarred Frost, the audience, and Frost critics when he said, "I regard Robert Frost as a terrifying poet." Jay Parini writes that while Jarrell had "popularized" the view only a few years before, it was a "view-point substantially present in Frost criticism for several decades" (409). However, in the long battle that had been waged over Frost's poetry, this was the final defeat for many.

Philip Gerber wrote in the preface to his 1966 book on Frost, "Who and what was the real Robert Frost? Few knew or wanted to know during his lifetime, for the image was much larger and far more appealing than reality." Gerber adds, "[p]erhaps even Frost himself at last came to believe in the simple farmer-poet who had one hand clamped on the spading fork while the other was busily auto-

graphing title pages to *Complete Poems*; he was, perhaps, playing the role which had been created for him and which he had helped to lodge in the public consciousness" (*Robert Frost*, Preface). Only three years before, Reuben Brower's illuminating *The Poetry of Robert Frost: Constellations of Intention* (1963) appeared, and Richard Poirier's *Robert Frost: The Work of Knowing* (1976) would follow in the next decade, reminding readers that "Robert Frost's eighty-fifth birthday party in 1959 ha[d] since been designated 'a cultural episode,'" referring to Trilling's comments that brought to attention "certain literary antagonisms having to do with the nature of modernism and . . . demonstrat[ing] the difficulty of placing Frost's achievement within the literature of th[at] century" (Poirier, 3). Poirier went on to say that "Frost's popularity tells some essential critical and human truth about him" and that it can "be said to include terror without being itself terrified" (Poirier, 7).

In an effort to reveal the other Frost, many critics have focused on his darker poems. It is common to move from one extreme to the other: from Frost as a euphoric nature poet to Frost as an anguished nihilist. Some recent critics, such as Robert Faggen in his *Robert Frost and the Challenge of Darwin*, hover dangerously over the abyss of the latter view, but Faggen's book also identifies complexities and connections that have long been overlooked. In his introduction to *The Cambridge Companion to Robert Frost* (2001), Faggen is judicious: "If there is any truth to Emerson's aphorism 'to be great is to be misunderstood,' then Robert Frost is surely one of the greatest poets" (1).

The Cambridge Companion to Robert Frost demonstrates some of the more recent trends in Frost criticism. While the titles of the essays owe something to the old—Robert Faggen's "Frost and the Question of Pastoral," Helen Bacon's "Frost and the Ancient Muses," and Lawrence Buell's "Frost as a New England Poet"—the criticism is anything but. For example, Buell's piece opens, "To classify Robert Frost as a poet in a traditional New England vein can be dangerously misleading or entirely proper, depending on how you define your terms" (101). Other recent volumes worthy of note include John Timmerman's *Robert Frost:*

The Ethics of Ambiguity (2002) and Robert Hass's *Going by Contraries: Robert Frost's Conflict with Science* (2002).

Another recent trend in Frost criticism is the growing number of women who are now emerging as Frost scholars. Katherine Kearns, who wrote *Robert Frost and a Poetics of Appetite* (1994), is particularly notable, as is Lisa Seale, who is working on a book about Frost's public talks and readings.

Frost criticism is now more various and complex. This entry is not meant to be either a chronicle or an inventory of Frost criticism but rather an introduction to the various approaches that have been taken and where they have led the scholarship. Since the poet's death in 1963, he has been more deeply understood, more deeply studied, and appreciated more honestly by those who enjoy his work, and they are numerous.

Former poet laureate Robert Pinsky took a yearlong poll in 1998 to determine who was America's favorite poet. More than 18,000 votes were cast by participants aged five to 97, and Frost came out on top. Additionally, when participants were asked which poems they most liked to read, they most often cited "The Road Not Taken" and "Stopping by Woods on a Snowy Evening." It seems that Frost has been most loved by a public who, according to some critics, misunderstands him; with the aid of contemporary critics, perhaps the public may come to love and understand him.

FURTHER READING

Buell, Laurence. "Frost as a New England Poet." In The Cambridge Companion to Robert Frost, edited by Robert Faggen, 101–122. Cambridge: Cambridge University Press, 2001.

Cowley, Malcolm. "Frost: A Dissenting Opinion." *Critical Essays on Robert Frost*, edited by Philip Gerber, 95–103. Boston: G. K. Hall, 1982.

Faggen, Robert, ed. *The Cambridge Companion to Robert Frost*. Cambridge: Cambridge University Press, 2001.

———. *Robert Frost and the Challenge of Darwin*. Ann Arbor: University of Michigan Press, 1997.

French, Roberts W. "Robert Frost and the Darkness of Nature." In *Critical Essays on Robert Frost*, edited

by Philip L. Gerber, 155–162. Boston: G. K. Hall, 1982.

Garnett, Edward. "A New American Poet." In *Critical Essays on Robert Frost*, edited by Philip Gerber, 35–42. Boston: G. K. Hall, 1982.

Gerber, Philip L. *Robert Frost*. New York: Twayne, 1966.

Greiner, Donald J. *Robert Frost: The Poet and His Critics*. Chicago: American Library Association, 1974.

Hass, Robert. *Going by Contraries: Robert Frost's Conflict with Science*. Charlottesville: University Press of Virginia, 2002.

Jarrell, Randall. "The 'Other' Frost." In *Poetry and the Age*, 26–33. New York: Vintage, 1955.

Kearns, Katherine. *Robert Frost and a Poetics of Appetite*. Cambridge: Cambridge University Press, 1994.

Lowell, Amy. "North of Boston." In *Critical Essays on Robert Frost*, edited by Philip Gerber, 22–25. Boston: G. K. Hall, 1982.

Meyers, Jeffrey. *Robert Frost: A Biography*. New York: Houghton Mifflin, 1996.

Parini, Jay. *Robert Frost: A Life*. New York: Holt, 1999.

Poirier, Richard. *Robert Frost: The Work of Knowing*. New York: Oxford University Press, 1977.

Thornton, Richard. *Recognition of Robert Frost: Twenty-fifth Anniversary*. New York: Henry Holt, 1937.

Timmerman, John H. *Robert Frost: The Ethics of Ambiguity*. Lewisburg, Pa.: Bucknell University Press, 2002.

Trilling, Lionel. "A Speech on Robert Frost: A Cultural Episode," *Partisan Review* 26 (1959): 445–452.

Vandoren, Mark. "Soil of the Puritans." In *Critical Essays on Robert Frost*, edited by Philip Gerber, 68–75. Boston: G. K. Hall, 1982.

England In 1912 Frost resigned from a teaching position in New Hampshire to sail to England with his family. In a letter from England written on October 25, 1912, Frost's wife Elinor recounted that the previous summer they had spent "weeks trying [their] best to decide where [they] wanted to go, and gradually [they] came to feel that it would be pleasant to travel about the world a little" (Frost, 53). At age 39, Frost believed that if he had any chances left of becoming a recognizable poet he had best attempt something drastic. England was that attempt.

The family traveled on the proceeds from the sale of the Derry Farm, storing their furniture and bringing just a few books, pictures, and other belongings. Upon arrival, the Frosts lived in a cottage in Beaconsfield, Buckinghamshire, called The Bungalow, but it "lacked the full charm of rural England." Soon the family rented a home called Little Iddens in Dymock, Gloucestershire, which reminded them of the Derry Farm (Parini, 144). They would later rent a thatched-roof home near Little Iddens called The Gallows. The Frosts remained in England from September 1912 through August 1915. Frost arrived in England an unknown, came "into his own," and returned to America a poet.

When the family first arrived at The Bungalow, Frost wrote to his friend Susan Hayes Ward,

> Here we are between high hedges of laurel and red-osier dogwood, within a mile or two of where Milton finished Paradise Lost on the one hand and a mile or two of where Grey lies buries on the other and within as many rods as furlongs of the house where Chesterton tries truth to see if it won't prove as true upside down as it does right side up. To London town what is it but a run? Indeed when I leave writing this and go into the front yard for a last look at earth and sky before I go to sleep, I shall be able to see the not very distinct lights of London flaring like a dreary dawn. If there is any virtue in Location—but don't think I think there is. I know where the poetry must come from if it comes. (Frost, 52)

Like his youthful journey to the Dismal Swamp on the Virginia-North Carolina border, which connected him to his predecessors Henry Wadsworth Longfellow and Thomas More, this journey connected him to his British predecessors.

While in England Frost wrote a number of his best poems, including "Birches" and "Mending Wall," which is ironic since they are both associated with NEW ENGLAND, but he also became brave enough to solicit a publisher with a book manuscript. While he had published a handful of poems in magazines in America, he had never approached a publisher. Being out of his own country, the freedom of anonymity made him bold, and his boldness met with success. His first book, A Boy's Will (1913), was published by David Nutt of London. North of Boston (1914) also was published before he returned to the United States and began publishing with Henry Holt (see PUBLISHERS).

Frost met many significant poets while in England, including Ezra Pound, who wrote an important review of A Boy's Will; William Butler Yeats; and Wilfrid Gibson (see LITERARY FRIENDS AND ACQUAINTANCES). He also met his dear friend Edward Thomas in 1914. The two had an intense but short-lived friendship before Thomas was killed in World War I at the Battle of Arras on April 9, 1917 (see BIOGRAPHY).

Before leaving England, Frost wrote two important letters. The first was to Harold Monro, at whose bookshop Frost had met F. S. Flint, who introduced him to Pound and others. To Monro he wrote, "England has become half my native land—England the victorious. Good friends I have had here and hope to keep." The other was to Flint: "I must at least say goodbye to the man who opened England to me. You are good." Frost left England more sure of all he thought was true, returning to the open arms of America.

FURTHER READING

Frost, Robert. *Selected Letters of Robert Frost.* Edited by Lawrance Thompson. New York: Holt, Rinehart and Winston, 1964.

Parini, Jay. *Robert Frost: A Life.* New York: Holt, 1999.

Thompson, Lawrance. *Robert Frost: The Early Years, 1874–1915.* New York: Holt, Rinehart and Winston, 1966.

Walsh, John Evangelist. *Into My Own: The English Years of Robert Frost.* New York: Grove Press, 1988.

evolution Charles Darwin's (1809–82) *Voyage of the Beagle* (1839) and *The Origin of Species* (1859) had a profound impact on Western understanding of the world and the transcendent. Frost was born 16 years after the latter was published, when the fury of debates that followed the publication of the book were well under way. He first learned about Darwin from his older friend Charles Burrell, who introduced him to a number of thinkers (see LITERARY FRIENDS AND ACQUAINTANCES). The impact of Darwin's theories of evolution are expressed in a variety of ways throughout Frost's work, as he continues to turn things this way and that in his own discovery and evaluation of what it means to exist in a post-Darwinian world. Robert Faggen, in his *Robert Frost and the Challenge of Darwin,* argues that "much of the tension and power of Frost's poetry derives from his lifelong engagement with implications of science in general and Darwin in particular" (1). He also adds that "[w]ith Darwin as a prism Frost was able to view the important tenets that underlie modern science: change, indeterminacy, and relativism, all concepts that imply limits as much as freedom" (5).

This prism, as Faggen calls it, is evident in a number of poems. In "At Woodward's Gardens," as the monkeys stand "laced together" behind the bars, they react in what Faggen calls a "decidedly human way" when they exchange "troubled glances over life" (90). One puts his hand up to his nose, and Frost writes that perhaps he is "[w]ithin a million years of an idea"—a reference to the theory of evolution.

What Robert Hass calls "Frost's final word on his long struggle with evolution," "Accidentally on Purpose," postulates existence as a purposeful accident (86). "The Universe is but the Thing of things" is the opening line. Respect for the universe's vastness is highlighted in the thrice-repeated, almost liturgical "mighty." The opening stanza reflects on the universe as a series of "balls all going round in rings," making it something of a child's toy, and the second stanza focuses on our arrival, when we were but "albino monkey[s] in a jungle." With Darwin, evolution is explained, and the speaker questions whether evolution had "no real purpose till it got to us." He is concerned with our "purpose," but he says it is a mistake to believe that there was no purpose before. There must always have been a purpose, he believes, and we are that "purpose coming to a head," its culmination. The poem is only cautiously Darwinian, however. Frost does not know whose purpose the universe was, admits he has no ability to discern, and suggests that that sort of speculation be left to "the scientific wits," since Darwin himself never thought that humans were any type of "culmination" and never thought that his theory of evolution contained any vector of progress.

In "The Literate Farmer and the Planet Venus" the poet twits evolution, saying that

So much is being now expected of,
To give developments the final shove
And turn us into the next specie folks
Are going to be, unless these monkey jokes
Of the last fifty years are all libel,
And Darwin's proved mistaken, not the Bible.

The purpose and value of evolutionary traits is considered in "On a Bird Singing in Its Sleep," where the "half wakened" bird sings "halfway through its little inborn tune." The question arises whether singing half asleep has been a threat to the bird's survival and, if so, how the species could have survived. "Singing out of sleep and dream" apparently has not "made it much more easily prey." Evolution is described as traits that "come down to us so far / Through the interstices of things ajar / On the long bead chain of repeated birth."

In "Sitting by a Bush in Broad Daylight" Frost makes reference to the burning bush of the Old Testament and reflects on the beginning of all life. He asserts that if we have been watching for a long time and have never seen "sun-smitten slime / Again come to life and crawl off"—a direct reference to Darwin's theory—"We must not be too ready to scoff" at the notion. He criticizes the explanations of both religion and science: "sun-smitten slime." Although we may not feel as though we came from sun-smitten slime, this does not make it untrue. Although we no longer speak to God, this does not make it untrue that we once did. In this sense there are parallels between evolution and religion, belief and faith. And Frost presents himself as somewhere between the two extremes.

In the closing stanza of "The White-Tailed Hornet," the speaker asks,

Won't this whole instinct matter bear revision?
Won't almost any theory bear revision?
To err is human, not to, animal.
Or so we pay the compliment to instinct,
Only too liberal of our compliment
That really takes away instead of gives.

Alluding to Darwin, the speaker acts troubled by the comparisons that "yield downward" to "see our images / Reflected in the mud and even dust" rather than heavenward. At one time, not long ago, we looked "stoutly upward" for comparison: "With gods and angels, we were men at least, / But little lower than the gods and angels," he recalls, alluding to the Bible, Psalms 8:5: "For thou hast made him a little lower than the angels, and hast crowned him with glory and honor." Now it is all "disillusion upon disillusion" and "[n]othing but fallibility [is] left us."

In his prose pieces "On Taking Poetry," "Education by Poetry," and "The Future of Man," Frost also refers to Darwin. In the first he provides the example of evolution and his mother's religious distress over it: "Your idea was that God made man out of mud; the new idea is that God made man out of prepared mud. You've still got God you see—nothing very disturbing about it." In the second Frost identifies evolutionary thinking as metaphorical, and in the third he wonders whether man will become "another kind of people." Drawing on the evolutionary theories of Darwin and the anthropologists who had caused "young people" to find that there is "such an amusing distance between us and the monkeys," he asserts that the young of his day find that there "will only be another amusing distance from us to the superman," referring to the "evolutionary" ideas of philosopher Friedrich Nietzsche.

Richard Poirier writes that

Politically and intellectually, Frost tended to find evidences of "system" and its deleterious effects not in anything that has "come down" to us but in what had been more recently contrived. Darwinism, socialism, the New Deal, Freudianism were all to him the dangerous imposition of "system" upon the free movements of life. It was against these that he directed his sometimes vulgar contempt." (49)

Poirier later writes, "Frost seldom misses a chance to bring Darwinism into question, more in a teasing than a dogmatically organized way. Darwinian evolution for him implied too much linear predictability, and while it proposed the necessity of waste it was indifferent to its virtues (265). Just how Frost speaks of Darwin through his poems continues to be debatable.

While Lawrance Thompson relates that "Frost spoke with sincerity about his early delight in read-

ing and re-reading Charles Darwin's book on the famous voyage of the *Beagle* to the islands of the South Seas," he also mentions a letter Frost wrote to Sidney Cox in May 1926 about cornering some scientists at Ann Arbor on the subject of evolution. Thompson uses the letter to determine that Frost was expressing hostility toward Darwin's theories, but other interpretations can be drawn. Frost wrote, "I'm not a good debater but they are so sure of themselves in evolution that they haven't taken the trouble to think out their position. All I had to do was ask them [Socratic] questions for information. The last one led up to was, Did they think it was ever going to be any easier to be good" (284). While such comments might suggest that Frost was attacking the theory of evolution, he later said, "Sometime I'll tell you about them. I believe I'll never forget them. They just jumped off the edge. Me, I didn't have to expose myself. I was just out for information. Tell me, I'd say" (Thompson, 297). The exposure, it seems, is what it is all about.

Frost never truly exposed himself. He played all his games from both sides because it was never about choosing a side but about identifying the difficulties that lie on both sides. Robert Hass writes that

Frost convinced himself that he could meet the challenge of Darwin with only a slight remodeling of his inherited religious beliefs. The construction of a different kind of God, one partially reconfigured against Christian orthodoxy by the trial of evolution, seemed to him a likely solution to his problem. He only had to go by contraries, suspend thesis, and antithesis, extract the most congenial elements of each system, and acknowledge the limited validity of both poles without wholly sanctioning either. To Frost, Darwin had not yet dissolved the familiar comforts of organized religion, and for the moment it seemed to him that a wholly satisfactory synthesis was still possible." (46–47)

Jay Parini finds that after Burrell and Frost met, Frost "divided the world three ways in one of these pieces, into 'unquestioning followers' of religious custom, 'enemies,' and 'rethinkers'" and that he placed "himself into the 'rethinker' category," identifying with those who "follow custom—not without question, but where it does not conflict with the broader habits of life gained by wanderers among ideas" (29).

The debate continues over Frost's views on the conflict between faith and science. What is clear is that he began the debate. He was a debater, despite what he might say, only he did his debating in metaphor and he went by contraries. He denies in speech what he reveals in poetry. He denies in poetry what he reveals in speech. It might seem that he was unsure of himself, but perhaps he simply did not want to be exposed.

FURTHER READING

Faggen, Robert. *Robert Frost and the Challenge of Darwin.* Ann Arbor: University of Michigan Press, 1997.

Hass, Robert. *Going by Contraries: Robert Frost's Conflict with Science.* Charlottesville: University Press of Virginia, 2002.

Poirier, Richard. *Robert Frost: The Work of Knowing.* New York: Oxford University Press, 1977.

Thompson, Lawrance. *Robert Frost: The Later Years, 1938–1963.* New York: Holt, Rinehart and Winston, 1976.

farmer, Frost as   Frost had an early interest in farming. When he lived in SAN FRANCISCO as a boy he took it upon himself to convert a shed into a chicken coop and raise a few chicks. While a teenager, on weekends and after school he helped a man who raised chickens in Salem, Massachusetts. Frost began farming poultry later, on a rented property, after his second child, Lesley, was born. When the family moved to the Derry Farm in New Hampshire in 1900 he "devoted himself . . . to the daily rituals of farm life," working with friend Carl Burrell building coops for the chickens, picking apples and pears from the fruit trees on the land, and tending livestock (Parini, 74). The family kept the Derry Farm until 1911, and Frost's time there was his longest stint as a farmer.

Frost considered himself a bad farmer and said so on various occasions, but he embraced the lifestyle. Jay Parini writes that

> Much has been made by previous biographers of Frost's ineffectualness as a farmer. It is true that

he liked to sleep late, wasn't especially comfortable around livestock, and got sick quite often, thus having to neglect his chores but [i]n spite of this, he did keep a farm for a decade and enjoyed it. Perhaps more important, he was smart enough to fit himself into a way of life that allowed for the flexibility a writer needs in daily life. (84)

Frost celebrated farming life in both his prose and poetry. The connection became a recognizable feature of his public life and of criticisms of his work.

Between 1903 and 1905 Frost wrote a number of poultry stories and articles for the New England magazine *Farm-Poultry.* He was "fascinated by the fluffy creatures" (Lathem, 9), and when he purchased the Derry Farm, the *Derry News* reported that "R. Frost has moved upon the Magoon place which he recently bought. He has a flock of nearly 300 Wyandotte fowls" (Lathem, 11).

Frost's poetry offers various insights into farming. In "After Apple-Picking" he writes about the apple farmer who has grown heavy with sleep and is dozing off to the memory of his hard day's work. His apple barrel remains unfilled, and he is reminded of the "ten thousand thousand fruit to touch" and of the apples that "struck the earth" and "[w]ent surely to the cider-apple heap / As of no worth." He uses the farmer to speak about work left undone and about the question of worth, not only of apples, but of life. The farmer and farming life is nearly always used to some philosophical end.

In "The Code" Frost juxtaposes city and country life and people and is interested in accepted behavior among farmers. "The Code" sets protocols and behaviors among men. This embracing of tradition and accepted behaviors highlights a strange simplicity in country life, but it also casts a dark shadow over what is often assumed to be idyllic, uncomplicated rural living.

"Evening in a Sugar Orchard" depicts a romantic scene in which the sap is running and farmers are stoking the fires that will convert the sap into maple syrup. In the sugarhouse the sugaring process is under way. The speaker wants to make sure the fire keeps going, because he is enjoying the spectacle of lights across the evening sky as the sparks fly up the chimney, "[a]mong bare maple boughs," making the hill glow and enhancing the beauty of the new ("slight") moon.

"Gathering Leaves" compares the "crop" of the fallen leaves of autumn to the usual crops harvested on farms. The imagery is of leaves that escape shoveling, grasping, and loading. There is a focus on weight, highlighting the relationship between this "crop" of leaves and cash crops. "Cash crops," crops are crops that are grown for direct sale, and "cash for crops" are phrases heard frequently in rural areas. While there is great effort in gathering the leaves, the effort leads to no monetary reward. They are instead presented as antithetical to regular crops: They have bulk without weight. But there is something to be gained from harvesting the leaves: "Next to nothing for use / But a crop is a crop."

In "Build Soil—A Political Pastoral" Frost pokes fun at himself as a poet-farmer. Tityrus is described as loafing about and is asked to use his "talents as a writer" to "improve food prices" or at least "[g]et in a poem toward the next election." Meliboeus says of Tityrus: "You live by writing / Your poems on a farm and call that farming."

A reporter once said of Frost; "He is a Puritan who has fought the soil for sustenance and has fought the world for recognition as a poet. He has won success because he has fought his own emotions, digging into them and behind them, the better to strike the universal note that makes poetry out of axe-handles" (Thompson, 78). Frost makes great use of farming and country life in his poetry. He has not been called the farmer-poet for naught. He was first and foremost a poet, spent some time farming, and returned to poetry. He was a poet who made use of the material available to him, the ample material of the land and its people.

FURTHER READING

Frost, Robert. *Robert Frost: Farm-Poultry Man*. Edited by Edward Connery Lathem and Lawrance Thompson. Hanover, N.H.: Dartmouth, 1963.

Lathem, Edward Connery, and Lawrance Thompson, eds. *Robert Frost: Farm-Poultryman*. Hanover, N.H.: Dartmouth, 1963.

Parini, Jay. *Robert Frost: A Life*. New York: Holt, 1999.

Thompson, Lawrance. *Robert Frost: The Early Years, 1874–1915*. New York: Holt, Rinehart and Winston, 1966.

Florida   Later in life the Frosts began to winter in Florida, upon the recommendation of Frost's doctor. The doctor thought the warm climate would aid Frost's sometimes struggling health. Frost spent several winters at a cottage in Key West, where he met fellow poet Wallace Stevens, long associated with Key West, who wrote the well-known "The Idea of Order at Key West." The cottage in which Frost stayed is now the Key West Heritage Museum and Frost Cottage, and it holds an annual Robert Frost poetry festival in his honor. "A Drumlin Woodchuck" and "Departmental" were both begun in Key West, and Frost once referred to the ant in "Departmental" as the Key West kind, not the New England kind.

Frost also spent time in Coconut Grove near the University of Miami, where he was invited to lecture. There is a memorial stone dedicated to him on campus. In 1937 the Frosts wintered in Gainesville, Florida, where Elinor Frost died. For those who long associated Frost with NEW ENGLAND, it is disorienting that Gainesville is where Elinor suffered the series of heart attacks that abruptly took her life.

After Elinor's death Frost continued to winter in Florida. In 1940 he purchased five acres of land in South Miami, built two small houses, named the place "Pencil Pines," and cultivated a grove of fruit trees.

Frost is rarely associated with Florida though he spent a number of winters and lost his beloved there. The state had an important role in Frost's later life, and as a lover of nature who spent most of his life in NEW ENGLAND, he enjoyed the immense contrast of Florida's subtropical climate.

FURTHER READING

Muir, Helen. *Frost in Florida: A Memoir*. Miami: Valiant Press, 1995.

Parini, Jay. *Robert Frost: A Life*. New York: Holt, 1999.

form   Frost was critical of free verse, frequently saying it was like playing tennis with the net down.

He disapproved of the lack of structure and formal rhyme. He preferred to write in iambic meters, in which stressed and unstressed syllables alternate. He often wrote either rhymed verse or blank verse in pentameter (where each line contained 10 syllables in iambic meter) and chose traditional forms such as the sonnet for his lyric poems. His lyrics, though metrically precise, are also at times relaxed and conversational.

Frost had an affinity for the traditional 14-line sonnet, which he once described as "eight lines, then six lines more," the latter a turn "for the better or the worse." In "The Constant Symbol" he jokes that the "sonnet is so suspect a form" that it gets poets into corners and has "driven so many to free verse and even to the novel." But he masters the form again and again. His sonnets are often conversational, as in "A Dream Pang" and "Acceptance." They can also stun with their beauty, as does "Never Again Would Birds' Song Be the Same." In his terza rima sonnet "Acquainted with the Night," an urban narrator, very different from the usual country poet, is heard (the terza rima form demands stanzas of three lines and an interlocking rhyme pattern). Frost's "Broken Drought" is a manipulated Shakespearean sonnet, in which some of the rhymes are "eye rhymes" (words that look like they should sound alike, but do not), such as "been" and "therein." His "Bursting Rapture" and "Design" are Italian sonnets (a sonnet form with a more complicated rhyme scheme than the Shakespearean). "The Master Speed" is one of his most romantic and traditional sonnets. It was written as a wedding present for Frost's daughter Irma and her bridegroom, John Cone.

One of Frost's earliest and most romantic lyrics is "In a Vale," from his first book, *A Boy's Will.* Norman Douglas, in his review of the book in the *English Review,* wrote that there was a "wild, racy flavour" to Frost's poems and that "they sound that inevitable response to nature which is the hallmark of true lyric feeling" (Thornton, 21). Another lyric with similar effect is "The Aim Was Song" from *New Hampshire.* One of his classically lyric poems is given away by its title: "Evening in a Sugar Orchard." "Blue-Butterfly Day" is one of Frost's lesser-known lyrics, but one that should receive more attention than it does. Frost sometimes joked about lyrics and once claimed that he wrote "Fragmentary Blue" to chide his friends who wanted him to stop writing lyrics. That lyric consists of two complete sentences (Cramer).

Frost was also well known for his dramatic narratives, poems that told stories. *North of Boston* includes a great number of them and is often celebrated as his finest volume. It certainly launched his career. Frost perfected the dramatic narrative in "Home Burial" and "Death of the Hired Man." He was preoccupied with tones of speech, once having written that he could not "keep any interest in sentences that don't shape *on some speaking tone* of voice," and it is this use of tone that sets his dramatic narratives apart.

Blanford Parker identifies "three customary modes of Frostian rhetoric, the prosaic, the meditative, and the lyrical," identifying all three as appearing in the poem "Directive." Parker describes the prosaic as Frost's "chief mode for extended narrative poems"; it is "a ballast of common speech somewhere in the rhetorical mix of all but his most rarefied poems." Parker describes the meditative as illustrating "a certain moral or intellectual problem by means of a central (and often simple) event or image." He defines the lyrical not simply as the "shorter rhyming poems" but as those poems "of personal reflection and memory—a poetry of subjective realization," identifying "Happiness Makes Up in Height for What It Lacks in Length" as an "archetypal example" (179–182).

In "The Constant Symbol" Frost says "The poet goes in [to the poem] like a rope skipper," full of enthusiasm and rhythm. "If he trips himself he stops the rope" and either tries a new skip or gives up the current game. For Frost, the poet "has been brought up by ear," by what verse he has grown up on, which provides a choice of "two metres, strict iambic and loose iambic," and these are what are largely found in his verse.

In *A Boy's Will,* Frost's first book, the young poet is most influenced by traditional forms. His voice is mostly his own, but his craft is inherited, steeped in the classics and unyielding in its adherence to form. He maintained those standards throughout his career. In his later years, when he was less inspired, his mastery of his craft was still impressive. It has been pointed out that praise for his craft has been almost universal among critics, even when they have looked askance at his subjects.

Philip Gerber writes that "The simpler English metrics are admirably suited to the subjects and themes Frost presents, and Frost does select them for the majority of his poems. At the same time, within these limits, he brings to his verses an unending variety, the mark not of a primitive but of a true sophisticate" (66–67). And that he was, though for some critics this is only now becoming clear.

FURTHER READING

Abad, Gemino H. "Stopping by Woods: The Hermeneutics of a Lyric Poem," *Diliman Review* 20 (1972): 25–40.

Calhoun, Richard J. "By Pretending They Are Not Sonnets: The Sonnets of Robert Frost at the Millennium." In *Roads Not Taken: Rereading Robert Frost*, edited by Earl J. Wilcox and Jonathan N. Barron, 217–235. Cambridge: University of Missouri Press, 2000.

Chavkin, Allan. "The Ordering of the Sequence of Meditative Lyrics in Frost's *North of Boston*," *Markham Review* 10 (Summer 1981): 67–68.

Cramer, Jeffrey S. *Robert Frost among His Poems: A Literary Companion to the Poet's Own Biographical Contexts and Associations*. Jefferson, N.C.: MacFarland, 1996.

Gerber, Philip L. *Robert Frost*. New York: Twayne, 1966.

Kearns, Katherine. "Frost on the Doorstep and Lyricism at the Millennium." In *Roads Not Taken: Rereading Robert Frost*, edited by Earl J. Wilcox and Jonathan N. Barron. 32–51. Columbia: University of Missouri Press, 2000.

Maxson, H. A. *On the Sonnets of Robert Frost: A Critical Examination of the 37 Poems*. Jefferson, N.C.: McFarland, 1997.

Monteiro, George. "Robert Frost's Metaphysical Sonnet." In *Frost Centennial Essays*, edited by Jac Tharpe, 333–339. Jackson: University Press of Mississippi, 1974.

Parker, Blanford. "Frost and the Meditative Lyric." In *The Cambridge Companion to Robert Frost*, edited by Robert Faggen, 179–196. Cambridge: Cambridge University Press, 2001.

Rood, Karen Lane. "Robert Frost's Sentence Sounds: Wildness Opposing the Sonnet Form." In *Frost: Centennial Essays II*, edited by Jac Tharpe, 196–210. Jackson: University Press of Mississippi, 1976.

Thornton, Richard. *Recognition of Robert Frost: Twenty fifth Anniversary*. New York: Henry Holt, 1937.

fugitive In November 1894 the young Frost, inspired by a fear of losing his then-girlfriend and future wife Elinor, set off in a bleak mood for the Dismal Swamp, which runs along the Virginia and North Carolina border. The swamp, which has been described as a "frightening place, full of bogs and quicksand," had been regarded by poets such as Henry Wadsworth Longfellow "as a place where those who have lost hope run away from the world" (Parini, 48). Frost was then an aspiring poet who was distraught about his relationship with his beloved, his own future, and their future together. The spiritual and symbolic journey to this area connected him to his predecessors and gave him a place to embrace his quixotic emotions. In some sense the sojourn was a turning point for him. It either inspired or became material for a number of poems in which he would write about such physical and emotional journeys. The first poem of his first book, "Into My Own," draws on this harrowing and edifying experience and is the first of what might be called his fugitive poems.

In "Into My Own" the speaker retreats into nature hoping to "steal away." He cannot imagine why he "should e'er turn back, / Or those should not set forth upon [his] track," but he did, and this first poem of his first book becomes a sort of invitation to his readers to take his journeys into nature with him. He asserts that when he returns "They would not find [him] changed from him they knew— / Only more sure of all [he] thought was true," and certainly Frost used his explorations of nature to great effect in his poetry.

In "Reluctance," the last poem of *A Boy's Will*, "Out through the fields and the woods / And over the walls [the poet] [has] wended." In this instance a different conclusion is drawn:

Ah, when to the heart of man
Was it ever less than a treason
To go with the drift of things,
To yield with a grace to reason,

And bow and accept the end
Of a love or a season.

While Frost's second book *North of Boston* consists largely of dramatic narratives, his closing poem "Good Hours" presents again the fugitive on his "winter evening walk." In this instance he passes by cottages, viewing only the "shining eyes in snow" of the slits of windows. He remains walking late into the night, returning when he can see "no window but that was black." The title "Good Hours" is presumably an estimation of the value of such nightly journeys.

In *Mountain Interval,* Frost's third volume, "The Telephone" presents a speaker who is once again "just as far as [he] could walk" in nature. In this instance the journey allows for a romantic encounter, as Frost uses a flower as a literal and literary telephone to unite two people. The speaker's journey is no longer solitary. In the same volume, in "An Encounter," Frost again meditates on the telephone. The speaker, also on a journey into nature, comes face to face with a "barkless specter," a telephone pole, "Up at his shoulders, dragging yellow strands." The confrontation reminds Frost of technology's encroachment on nature. Another walk in nature in this volume can be found in "Pea Brush," in which nature is presented in one sense as innocent of and indifferent to the presence of humans, but at the same time is dominated and controlled by them. The closing poem of *Mountain Interval,* "The Sound of Trees," presents a speaker questioning the pull of nature. He "wonder[s] about the trees" and why we "wish to bear / Forever the noise of these / More than another noise." He is himself like a tree, with his "head sway[ing] to [his] shoulder."

"Stopping by Woods on a Snowy Evening" about a voice in the woods, is perhaps Frost's best-known poem. He is lured by how "lovely, dark and deep" the woods are, offering insight into a number of the poems that depict a similar setting. In "Willful Homing" the fugitive is caught outside in a blizzard in the dark. But "Desert Places," another of Frost's frequently anthologized poems, may be read as a companion to "Stopping by Woods," since it also presents a speaker with "Snow falling and night falling fast . . . / In a field" who is "look[ing] into going

past." In this instance, however, the poet pushes the symbolism much further, as if he takes the setting of the first poem and reveals it in the second.

One poem in which the speaker has been turned out of doors not for journey's sake but as a fugitive of the heart is "The Thatch," where a lover's spat has sent him "Out alone in the winter rain, / Intent on giving and taking pain." Such inner darknesses are highlighted in Frost's unusual "Acquainted with the Night." In this sonnet the fugitive is again in the rain, but he is no longer taking a country walk. Here the speaker has "outwalked the furthest city light." His inner darkness is revealed by the repetition of "I have been one acquainted with the night."

In Frost's final volume, *In the Clearing,* the poem "Away!" presents a revision of the speaker's perspective in "Into My Own." Here he is "out walking / The world desert" and has left "Good friends in town," but he is less dramatic and more playful: "let them get well-wined / And go lie down," he says. He is corrective: "Don't think I leave / for the outer dark," reminding his readers not to compare him to "Adam and Eve / Put out of the park." "Forget the myth," he says, a myth he has constructed well, "There is no one I / Am put out with / Or put out by," a mature view. He reveals that he is "urge[d] by a song" and is "bound—away!" The aging poet has rethought his earlier symbolic journey into the Dismal Swamp and knows that his last journey will hold the greatest meaning. Instead of considering returning this time unchanged from "him they knew," he says, "I may return / If dissatisfied / With what I learn / from having died."

In "Escapist-Never," also in *In the Clearing,* Frost is again corrective: "He is no fugitive—escaped, escaping," because "No one has seen him stumble looking back." The reason is that "His fear is not behind him but beside him," and he describes his "course" as a "crooked straightness yet no less a straightness." In this poem he embraces life with all his might: "He runs face forward. He is a pursuer," and his life is described as "a pursuit of a pursuit forever." He has been no fugitive; he has overcome.

Frost's "Kitty Hawk," also included in *In the Clearing,* is in two parts, which he once described as "longish." The first part presents his adventure into the Dismal Swamp. Having returned to the same area 60 years later to visit friends, Frost must have imagined his life coming full circle. He once explained that he used his own story of the Dismal Swamp to "take off into the story of the airplane" in this poem, and he described how he might have used his early experience to write an "immortal poem, but how, instead, the Wright brothers took off from there to commit an immortality." The second part of the poem he described as the "philosophical part" (Parini, 388).

Just as "Into My Own" and "Reluctance" act as bookends to his first volume, "Into My Own" and "[In winter in the woods alone]" might be described as bookends to Frost's career. The latter is the last poem of his last book, and its lack of a title suggests a lack of any need to further explain. The poet, as in "Escapist-Never," remains optimistic. He is again alone in the woods and "against the trees [he] go[es]," but he ends powerfully. He fells a tree in late afternoon in winter, "mark[ing] a maple for [his] own." He is marking where he finds himself on his life's journey, and instead of disappearing into the dark trees he makes a satisfactory single selection.

Frost ends triumphant, even if having only felled a tree. He takes with him one maple: "I see for Nature no defeat / In one tree's overthrow / Or for myself in my retreat / For yet another blow."

See also NIGHT.

FURTHER READING

Parini, Jay. *Robert Frost: A Life.* New York: Holt, 1999.

home, theme of Home is a prominent theme in Frost. As one who made a transcontinental move from the West coast to the East as a boy, took a transoceanic journey to ENGLAND for several years as an adult, wintered in FLORIDA as an older man, and lived in a number of homes in each locale, Frost knew home was not simply a place but where one belongs. In "Home Burial" it is the place for the living and the dead, but while the couple in the poem are at home, they are not at all at home with each other. In "Death of the Hired Man" Silas returns to the only home he knows to die, a place that has provided him a sense of belonging, even though by most definitions it is not his home. He

has no sense of place, no kin to return to, yet his return signals the only understanding of home to which he can in the end aspire: "Home is the place where, when you have to go there, / They have to take you in."

In the playful and political "Departmental," Frost writes movingly of returning the body of the deceased ant Jerry McCormic: "Go bring him home to his people. / Lay him in state on a sepal." For Jerry, home is not only the place where when you have to go there they have to take you in, but a place to which one must and should return. In "Desert Places" the speaker admits that he has it in him "so much nearer home / To scare [him]self with [his] own desert places," and home becomes not a place but a sense of being. This inner "home" is not always protection; it can be a frightening place.

In "Storm Fear" home is protection from what is out of doors, but it is not always reliable protection, as in "The Lockless Door," in which "with no lock to lock" the speaker is only half protected. In "Skeptic" home is much grander than our bodies or our relatives or our buildings; it is the universe that keeps us. And in "In the Home Stretch" home is something much less tangible than the arrangement of a table and chairs. It is a place where we create meaning and value, order out of chaos. As a place, it is less associated with structures and more associated with our ideas and our relationships. In "In the Home Stretch" the older couple have uprooted themselves and their "home," but they have also made a transition from the city to the country that signals a significant change in their approach to life. Their home is now, more than anything else, where they find themselves and each other.

House and home figure prominently in "The Need of Being Versed in Country Things," as does the chimney that is all that remains after a fire. "Ghost House" was inspired by "an old cellar hole with a broken chimney standing in it—what remained of a nearby farmhouse after a fire had destroyed it in 1867" (Parini, 90–91). And "The Kitchen Chimney" depicts chimneys as the cause of houses not thriving. Chimneys, made of nearly indestructible brick, are often all that remain after a fire. As such they act as a haunting and memorable symbol for the physical vulnerability of houses and the necessity of building a sense of home in the only way we truly can: by embracing nature and the universe and the natures of those who surround us, whether they are kin or friends, since chimneys only remind us that we have built our castles in the air.

FURTHER READING

Parini, Jay. *Robert Frost: A Life.* New York: Holt, 1999.

literary friends and acquaintances   Frost had a number of friends and acquaintances who could be deemed "literary." Among these were those who were helpful to his career and those whose company and intellect he simply appreciated. The friends he had of a literary bent were often not on a par with him, perhaps because of his own competitiveness. He tended to have acquaintances with those he met, such as Wallace Stevens and Edwin Arlington Robinson, rather than to become friends with them. The friends he had and most talked poetry with were often those he could mentor, such as Edward Thomas, rather than the other way around. He did not want—or, in his opinion, need—mentoring. Ezra Pound had weekly gatherings with fellow poets where they "rewrote" one another's poems. When Pound mentioned this to Frost, Frost said it sounded too much like a parlor game. He never attended a session. He frequently shared his poems before publication with friends, even forwarding them in letters. But he seems to have done so more often for the endorsement he expected to get than for criticism that might require him to make alterations.

Perhaps the most important relationship Frost had early in his career was with Pound, despite their enormous differences. Pound did not influence Frost's work, but he greatly influenced his career; they were not friends, though in a letter to John Bartlett, Frost once referred to Pound as a "quasi-friend." A major poet and critic at the time of their meeting in EN-GLAND, Pound's best-known work is his series of poems *The Cantos*, a lifelong labor. Often called a "poet's poet," Pound is known for having promoted the work of many of his contemporaries, including Frost, T. S. Eliot, and William Butler Yeats.

Frost headed to England an unknown in 1912, and it was there that he published *A Boy's Will* and

first met Pound. They were introduced through the poet Frank F. S. Flint, whom Frost had met by chance at the opening of Henry Monro's Poetry Bookshop on Devonshire Street in London. Flint told Pound about Frost, and Pound was immediately eager to meet him. He invited Frost to visit him in Kensington with a curt note that read "at home, sometimes," and several months later (just before his first publication), Frost took him up on it. Pound was eager to get hold of *A Boy's Will*, which had not yet gone to press, so their first meeting took them to the office of Frost's publisher, David Nutt, to get a copy of the book. Later that day Pound wrote a favorable review for Harriet Monro's *Poetry* magazine. To Frost's mind this review would come at a cost. Pound had asserted that Frost was yet another great artist who had been rejected by American editors and had to seek refuge and recognition in Europe. Because of this, Frost feared his career would suffer in the States, but this was not the result. Within weeks Pound introduced Frost to Yeats, and Frost's European success was assured. His American recognition would come later, but not much. Jay Parini notes that despite Pound's generosity, "[r]elations between Pound and Frost were artificial and strained, with Pound playing the teacher (though he was eleven years younger . . .) and Frost the slightly dazzled, even uncertain student" (Parini, 128). Frost never was a good student to anyone.

Pound would later move to Italy and become involved in politics. Upon his return to the United States in 1945, he would be charged with treason for broadcasting Fascist propaganda during World War II. In 1946 he was acquitted but declared mentally ill and committed to St. Elizabeth's Hospital in Washington, D.C. After a nearly two-year campaign instigated by Archibald MacLeish, Pound was released from the hospital. Frost, perhaps repaying his debt, was said by Robert Penn Warren to be the one who "almost single handedly . . . pushed [Pound's release] through" (Parini, 405). While their relationship was strained, when visited on his deathbed by Pound's daughter, Frost said, "You are a dear and so is Ezra. . . . I've never got over those days we had together. . . . Politics make too much difference to both of us. Love is all.

Romantic love—as in stories and poems. I tremble with it. I'd like to see Ezra again" (Parini, 440).

One of the most significant friendships of Frost's lifetime was that with Edward Thomas, though it was short-lived. Frost met Thomas, a critic, journalist, and poet, in a restaurant in London in 1913, and the two spent the next four years either taking long talking walks together or exchanging letters. Their families also grew close. They primarily shared interests in botany and poetry and even wrote poems to and for one another. Thomas also may have been helpful to Frost's career, having written three favorable reviews of *North of Boston*. When Thomas enlisted in the British Army and was killed in the Battle of Arras on April 9, 1917, it was a huge blow to Frost. In a letter to Helen Thomas, Thomas's wife, dated April 27, 1917, and written from Amherst, Massachusetts, Frost wrote, "I have had four wonderful years with him. I know he has done this all for you: he's all yours. But you must let me cry my cry for him as if he were *almost* all mine too." Frost also wrote, "I want to tell him that I love those he loved and hate those he hated," and "I had meant to talk endlessly with him still, either here in our mountains [in New England] as we had said or, as I found my longing was more and more, there at Leddington where we first talked of war." (Spencer, 189) He closed the letter by saying, "And I don't suppose there is anything for us to do to show our admiration but to love him forever." Frost would write a poem titled "To E. T." for Thomas and include it in *New Hampshire* (1923).

Frost encouraged Thomas to write poetry, and as Matthew Spencer has pointed out, that "encouragement was timely," as Thomas wrote his first poem in early December 1914, enlisted several months later, and died within a few short years. In the letter to Helen, Frost also wrote, "I want to tell him, what I think he liked to hear from me, that he was a poet," revealing, perhaps, a bit of remorse in not telling him sooner and more often (Spencer, 189).

Parini connects the Thomas and Frost walks with "The Road Not Taken," remarking that "One quirk of Thomas was that he often regretted the particular path he had taken," and that "Frost once

said to him, 'No matter which road you take, you'll always sigh, and wish you'd taken another'" (153). In "A Romantic Chasm" Frost writes, "I wish Edward Thomas (that poet) were here to ponder gulfs in general with me as in the days when he and I tired the sun down with talking on the footpaths and stiles of Leddington and Ryton."

An early influence on Frost was Carl Burrell, whom he met in his sophomore year of high school. Burrell was, at the time, in his mid-20s, having returned to school after supporting himself for a number of years doing odd jobs in Vermont and New Hampshire. While the Frost and Burrell relationship would often be strained, they shared an interest in books, botany, and science, and as Frost's senior, Burrell introduced him to the works of a number of authors, including Mark Twain, Charles Darwin, and Thomas Huxley, and inspired careful rereadings of works such as Henry David Thoreau's *Walden* (Parini, 24–25, 81).

Frost developed another early friendship at Dartmouth with John Bartlett, who was Frost's prize pupil. Like Frost, Bartlett married his high school sweetheart, Margaret, and the Bartletts and Frosts were lifetime good friends. The Bartletts' daughter, Margaret Bartlett Anderson, would later write *Robert Frost and John Bartlett: The Record of a Friendship* (1963). Early in his career Frost wrote to Bartlett: "You mustn't take me too seriously if I now proceed to brag a bit about my exploits as a poet" their relationship having preceded his great success (Parini, 142).

Louis Untermeyer, poet, critic, and anthologist, met Frost in April 1915 through others Frost had met early in his career, the Georgian poets Lascelles Abercrombie and Wilfrid Gibson. Theirs would be a lifelong friendship best understood through their letters, collected in *The Letters of Robert Frost to Louis Untermeyer* (1963). Parini calls their relationship "the most sustained literary friendship of Frost's long life" (164) and Untermeyer Frost's "closest intellectual companion" (288). Untermeyer would have a long talk with Frost in the days before his death.

Louis Mertins wrote a memoir of his friendship with Frost, *Robert Frost: Life and Talks-Walking* (1965), which opens, "My famous friend was dead. I call him friend, for so he had set himself down on paper many times, in that bold but infinitely graceful handwriting, which once seen could never be forgotten. Now his hand would write no more. Never again would we hold brotherly speech. His magnificent voice was silent, his warm heart stilled" (3).

Sidney Cox would also write a memoir, *A Swinger of Birches: A Portrait of Robert Frost* (1957). Cox and Frost met while Frost was teaching at the New Hampshire State Normal School in Plymouth and Cox was a teacher in the local high school. Frost took up tennis around this time, and Cox and he competed on the court. They would remain good friends and knew each other for over 40 years.

Theodore (Ted) Morrison and Kay Morrison were significant in another way. After Frost's wife Elinor's death, Kay became Frost's secretary and was essential to his career, and the three lived on the Homer Noble Farm together, Ted and Kay in the main house, Frost in the cabin out back. They made up a "family of sorts," and it is hard to imagine Frost continuing to hold himself together and maintain a career after Elinor's death without Kay, to whom his seventh volume of poetry, *A Witness Tree*, which earned him his fourth Pulitzer Prize, is dedicated: "To K. M. For her part in it." Frost once told Louis Mertins, "I owe everything in the world to her. She found me in the gutter, hopeless, sick, run down. She bundled me up and carted me to her home and cared for me like a child, sick child. Without her I would today be in my grave. If I have done anything since I came out of the hospital, it is all due to her" (Cramer, 123).

It should also be noted that Frost's favorite illustrator, his friend J. J. Lankes, created a number of woodcuts for Frost's volumes of poetry. Critics of the graphic and printing arts have observed similarities between the two artists in subject, theme, tone, and perspective. The two began corresponding in 1923 over an illustration that Lankes was to do for "The Star-Splitter." Their connection would last four decades and is studied in Welford Dunaway Taylor's *Robert Frost and J. J. Lankes: Riders on Pegasus*.

This entry is not meant to exhaust the number or kind of friendships Frost had throughout his lifetime but to identify a few that were of great significance either to his career or to his heart. In some sense it might be said that all of Frost's friendships either were or became literary as he went, as he became more and more the poet and was less often "in winter in the woods alone."

FURTHER READING

Cox, Sidney. *A Swinger of Birches: A Portrait of Robert Frost.* New York: New York University Press, 1957.

Cramer, Jeffrey S. *Robert Frost among His Poems: A Literary Companion to the Poet's Own Biographical Contexts and Associations.* Jefferson, N.C.: MacFarland, 1996.

Evans, William R. "A Literary Friendship: Robert Frost and Carl Burrell." In *Frost Centennial Essays*, edited by Jac Tharpe, et al., 504–517. Jackson: University Press of Mississippi, 1974.

Flory, Wendy Stallard. *The American Ezra Pound.* New Haven: Yale University Press, 1989.

Frost, Robert. *The Letters of Robert Frost to Louis Untermeyer.* Edited by Louis Untermeyer. New York: Holt, Reinhart and Winston, 1963.

———. *Selected Letters of Robert Frost.* Edited by Lawrance Thompson. New York: Holt, Rinehart and Winston, 1964.

Hall, Donald. *Remembering Poets: Reminiscences and Opinions: Dylan Thomas, Robert Frost, T. S. Eliot, Ezra Pound.* New York: Harper & Row, 1978.

Jackson, Sarah R. "Made in London: The Robert Frost and Ezra Pound Connection," *Worcester Review* 15, no. 1–2 (1994): 108–121.

Mertins, Louis. *Robert Frost: Life and Talks-Walking.* Norman: University of Oklahoma Press, 1965.

Meyers, Jeffrey. "An Earring for Erring: Robert Frost and Kay Morrison," *American Scholar* 65, no. 2 (Spring 1996): 219–241.

Parini, Jay. *Robert Frost: A Life.* New York: Holt, 1999.

Sokol, B. J. "What Went Wrong between Robert Frost and Ezra Pound," *New England Quarterly* 49, no. 4 (December 1976): 521–541.

Spencer, Matthew. *Elected Friends: Robert Frost and Edward Thomas to One Another.* New York: Handsel, 2003.

Taylor, Welford Dunaway. *Robert Frost and J. J. Lankes: Riders on Pegasus.* Hanover, N.H.: Dartmouth, 1996.

Thompson, Lawrance. *Robert Frost: The Early Years.* New York: Holt, Rinehart and Winston, 1966.

———. *Robert Frost: The Years of Triumph, 1915–1938.* New York: Holt, Rinehart and Winston, 1970.

———, and R. H. Winnick. *Robert Frost: The Later Years: 1938–1963.* New York: Holt, Rinehart and Winston, 1976.

Untermeyer, Louis. *The Road Not Taken: An Introduction to Robert Frost.* New York: Holt, 1951.

literary influences In the "Paris Review Interview with Richard Poirier," Frost, even when pressed by Poirier, finds it difficult, or at least pretends to find it difficult, to identify influences for his work, except what he had read, such as Latin and Greek poetry. Poirier wanted to know whom Frost admired, and the poet said coyly that he "was the enemy of that theory." Poirier hoped to find out for whom he might have felt an affinity, say, Edwin Arlington Robinson or Wallace Stevens, both acquaintances of Frost's. "I don't know who you'd connect me with," Frost said, dodging the inquiries again. He explains that he appreciates certain poems rather than the entire work of individual poets. He finds a poem he likes in an anthology and goes looking for more and finds "[n]othing. Just a couple like that and that's all." He resists influence and comparison. He has fondness for some, but that is where he wants to leave it.

Given Frost's resistance to such categorical associations, it makes most sense to look to what the poet revealed about his influences through his poetry and the books he admired. Those sources are more telling. While he dodged inquiries about how and by whom his style was influenced, he did not hesitate to say what writers and works he most respected. In the November 30, 1958, issue of the *Chicago Tribune* he offered a list of the five books that had meant the most to him: The Old Testament, *The Odyssey,* the poems of Catullus, Edward Gibbon's *The Decline and Fall of the Roman Empire,* and John Lloyd Stevens's *Incidents of Travel in Yucatan.* When asked to contribute to a volume edited by Edward Weeks, *Books We Like: Sixty-two Answers to the Question* (1936), he again listed *The Odyssey* as well as *Robinson Crusoe;* Henry David Thoreau's *Walden;* the tales of Edgar Allan Poe; *The Oxford Book of English Verse* (presumably the 1924 edition, edited by Sir Arthur Quiller Couch); *Modern American and British Poetry,* edited by his friend Louis Untermeyer; James Fenimore Cooper's *The Last of the Mohicans;* Anthony Hope's *The Prisoner of Zenda;* Rudyard Kipling's *The Jungle Book;* and Ralph Waldo Emerson's essays and poems.

Frost was well read, but these lists do not identify influences so much as interests, and his interests were various. He was particularly interested in philosophy, above all William James, and in science. During a reading he once identified the *Scientific American* as the "best magazine in the whole world," though he joked that he was "not taking subscriptions for it." He also identified Charles Darwin's *The Voyage of the Beagle* (1839) to an audience as a "better book" than Darwin's *The Origin of Species* (1859) and as one of the "best books you don't read." He also had a great appreciation for Palgrave's *Golden Treasury* (1861). But these are scattered and isolated selections.

Frost makes allusions in his poetry to the Bible, Greek and Latin poetry, English poetry (especially the romantics), American poetry, Greek and Roman mythology, Shakespeare, Ralph Waldo Emerson, Henry David Thoreau, philosophers, mathematicians, historians, inventors, sculptors, painters, and friends. He draws on American folklore and Mother Goose nursery rhymes. His allusions are as various as the books he read.

Frost's early style was marked by those who preceded him. In his "Introduction to the Arts Anthology: Dartmouth Verse," he asserts that the poet "has to begin as a cloud of all the other poets he ever read. That can't be helped," and it was the same for him. Even the title of his first book was derived from the refrain in Henry Wadsworth Longfellow's "My Lost Youth": "A boy's will is the wind's will, / And the thoughts of youth are long, long thoughts." The nod to Longfellow demonstrates the kinship Frost felt with earlier American writers who also had made the American landscape and its themes central to their work. Among these was Emily Dickinson, whom Frost admired greatly. When courting his future wife, Elinor Miriam White, during high school, he presented her with a recent posthumously published volume of Dickinson's poems. Of contemporary poets, she and Edward Rowland Sill were favorites (the second book he gave to Elinor was Sill's), as was Thomas Hardy, whom he once referred to as his "man." He shared a kinship with Edward Arlington Robinson, made all the more evident by the strain in their relationship with each other. He appreciated Wallace Stevens, whom he met in Key West, FLORIDA, and when Stevens remarked after a long evening of drinking that Frost was "too academic," Frost quipped that Stevens wrote "bric-a-brac." Frost criticized Ezra Pound and T. S. Eliot but respected them both. He mentored and was proud of Edward Thomas, his young poet friend who was killed in World War I.

Frost was influenced and was an influence, but it is difficult to nail down details. In his relationship to nature there are evidences of Emerson and Thoreau. When receiving the Emerson-Thoreau Gold Medal from the American Academy of Arts and Sciences, Frost admitted that Emerson affected him early on and that his first thoughts about his own language came from Emerson, saying: "I took Emerson's prose and verse as my illustration," and that Emerson "blended praise and dispraise of the country people of New Hampshire," as Frost himself did ("On Emerson"). But he avoided being too closely tied to Emerson. There are also hints of Hardy and Dickinson in his relationship to nature, though Hardy is more dire and Dickinson more romantic. In his "Introduction to E. A. Robinson's *King Jasper*" Frost also reveals a kinship to Robinson. They each had an ear tuned to the vernacular and to individual experience. In many respects Frost's mood is closest to Hardy's and his style to Robinson's, but Frost had such a profound influence on American poetry precisely because his own influences are hard to pin down.

Frost was not a product of his reading; he was a new American product. When he came into his own, his verse was distinct and powerful, embedding him forever in the American poetic landscape not as the influenced but as the influential.

mythology and folklore   Frost, who had a strong Latin and Greek education, at times used mythology and folklore as alternatives to creation, religion, and history. This interest was also cultivated in his childhood through his mother's bedtime stories, which were filled with fairies and spirits.

"Too Anxious for Rivers" is a questioning; a contemplation of life and death grows grand as

Frost contemplates myths of creation: "The world as we know is an elephant's howdah; / The elephant stands on the back of a turtle; / The turtle in turn on a rock in the ocean." The evocation of these myths demonstrates that the distinction between people and nature is an illusion. If people delude themselves into believing that they are not a part of nature and are not natural beings, they delude themselves into thinking that they are in some way not susceptible to its forces.

"A Never Naught Song" is in keeping with the theme that there has always been a "purpose," offering its own religious mythology when it proposes that there was never "naught," never nothing; "[t]here was always thought." The speaker imagines the Big Bang as a "burst" of matter and the bursting forth of the universe as an "atomic One." When the bang occurred, "everything was there, every single thing . . . Clear from hydrogen / All the way to men." This bang was the creation of all things; it was even the first evidence of thought. The speaker's explanation eliminates the need for the "whole Yggdrasil." The Yggdrasil is, in Norse mythology, the world tree, a giant ash that connects and shelters all known worlds. This song, then, replaces the tree myth with matter that was "[c]unningly minute" and yet possessed of the "force of thought."

"The Gift Outright" creates its own myth surrounding the history of the United States and why "the land was ours before we were the land's."

"Auspex" reflects Frost's knowledge of Greek and Roman mythology. In Greek mythology, Ganymede was a Trojan boy of great beauty whom Zeus carried away to be cupbearer to the gods. The eagle is likened to Zeus, but also to Jove. Jove, in Roman mythology, is the equivalent to Zeus, so the boy in the poem asks why his parents do not "find a barkeep unto Jove" in him. The story of Ganymede can be found in Ovid's *Metamorphoses* and in Virgil's *Aeneid*.

In "Bond and Free" Frost makes use of the story of Icarus, the son of Daedalus, who, despite his father's warning, flew too close to the sun, causing his wax wings to melt and plunging him into the sea.

In "Come In" the thrush's music entices the speaker toward the dark almost like the mythological sirens, who lured sailors to their deaths with their beautiful singing.

"The Gold Hesperidee" and "Iris by Night" both make direct references to characters of Greek mythology. In "The Gold Hesperidee" Frost refers to golden apples from the garden of the Hesperides, the daughters of the evening. Iris is the personification of the rainbow that unites Heaven and Earth and is man's messenger to the gods. In "Iris by Night" Frost refers to witnessing a rainbow at night as a strange and miraculous perception of "confusing lights." He makes the experience analogous to the legend of the Greek army's encircling and subsequent conquering of Memphis, an ancient Egyptian city, under Alexander the Great.

"Pan with Us" refers to the mythological Pan, the god of shepherds and hunters, woods, fields, and flocks.

Frost's poetry makes a number of references to folklore as well. For example, "Paul's Wife" is Frost's version of the folktale of the legendary Paul Bunyan, and "How Hard It Is to Keep from Being King When It's in You and in the Situation" has as its source a story from the 10th-century collection of folktales *Arabian Nights' Entertainments,* or *The Thousand and One Nights,* tale C, section 12, titled "Tale of the King Who Kenned the Quintessence of Things."

Frost was steeped in knowledge of the classics, and allusions appear with great frequency throughout his work; these examples are but a few. He not only appreciated and had a sound understanding of mythology, but he was himself a maker of myths. The greatest of the myths he contrived was that he was a simple and blissful NEW ENGLAND nature poet, but it is a myth that continues to warrant debunking.

FURTHER READING

Attebery, Louie W. "Fences, Folklore, and Robert Frost," *Northwest Folklore* 6, no. 2 (Spring 1988): 53–57.

Benoit, Raymond. "Folklore by Frost: 'Paul's Wife,'" *Notes on Modern American Literature* 5, no. 4 (Fall 1981): 22.

nature Frost once said in an interview, "I guess I'm not a nature poet, I have only written two poems without a human being in them." His relationship to nature stems from his preoccupation with chaos. Nature for him is often either something to be feared or something with which to contend, or both. He is interested in what nature can do for us and to us, and he is compelled to make a thorough study of it. He is never altogether at ease in a natural landscape; he goes to nature with a skeptical and slightly jaundiced eye. He finds sadness and grief there and conveys it, often with great subtlety. He sometimes scares himself half to death, as in "Desert Places" and "An Old Man's Winter Night," and one suspects the bravery is often bravado. His voice is a lonely one, his poetry a kind of singing in the dark.

In "A Leaf-Treader" he is sensitive even to the minutest manifestations of nature. He improbably but persuasively associates himself with fallen leaves, which he finds "threatening." During his autumn walk, the speaker feels that he might have with too heavy tread crushed the leaves under his weight. But if he has done so, he has not intended to, he has been "too fierce from fear."

There is a sense of both yielding to nature and exhibiting a healthy respect for it in the poem appropriately titled "Acceptance": "Let the night be too dark for me to see / Into the future. Let what will be, be." While it is not the human being who does the accepting in this poem, the human element is not trivial. Just as he does with the leaves, Frost also gives insight and understanding to the birds, though that ability is distinctly human.

In Frost's poems, people find themselves in confrontations with nature that are a cause for reflection and an opportunity for learning. Instead of depicting the effects of nature on human beings after a confrontation, Frost describes the process of working through a conflict with nature and resolving it somewhat satisfactorily. In "On a Tree Fallen across the Road" the tree has fallen to "ask us who we think we are." This random event has a significance that transcends the mere falling of a tree— just as importance was signified by the fallen leaves in "A Leaf-Treader." Here, nature is questioning human beings—an unlikely situation since nature is usually the one questioned. Nature wants to know who we think we are trying to make our way in it, who we think we are even being a part of it. We are a part of nature, yet we are intruders. We are, it seems, both in and out of our element.

Frost's "The Secret Sits" is a mere two lines: "We dance round in a ring and suppose, / But the Secret sits in the middle and knows." The answers the speaker seeks are to be found through nature in some of his other poems. Instead of attempting to disregard nature by making his way around it or heading off in some other direction, the speaker goes deep into nature in "Into My Own," the prophetic first poem of his first book, *A Boy's Will.* Growth and understanding in this case are discovered by a journey into dark trees. The poem presents many of the same images as in "On a Tree Fallen across the Road," but for a different purpose. The road is accessible to the speaker, but he avoids the openness of the road and seeks instead the darkness of the forest. His goal is to "steal away" into it, without fear and with purpose. The conflict is unstated, but the resolution sought is certainly the same. The speaker again seeks to discover what nature means for him. Upon entering the darkness, he says,

I do not see why I should e'er turn back,
Or those should not set forth upon my track
To overtake me, who should miss me here
And long to know if still I held them dear.

They would not find me changed from him
    they knew—
Only more sure of all I thought was true.

This time the will carries the speaker into nature because it holds answers, but it is only through entering nature wholly that he can find them. Indeed, there he becomes "more sure of all [he] thought was true." Knowledge and understanding are acquired, and the early intuition of things as they are becomes, at journey's end, an affirmation grounded in experience and guided by nature.

In "Acquainted with the Night" the country poet is uncharacteristically urban: "I have outwalked the furthest city light / I have looked down the saddest city lane." In "Lucretius versus the Lake Poets" Frost's idea of nature is honestly portrayed. He begins with an epigraph from Walter Savage Landor's "I Strove with None": "Nature I loved;

and next to Nature, Art." The poem closes, "The only meaning possible for Nature / In Landor's quatrain would be Pretty Scenery," but Frost knows better than that. He loves the pretty scenery, but he knows not only what it represents but what it conceals. Continually poking the mysteries at the core—in the forest beyond the trees—he turns things this way and that. What he finds is that there is no here or there in nature; there is only the process, the going, the unending exploration, the tweaking and poking and probing into the very essences of things, even when he scares himself half to death. Frost continues to take on the "Whole Goddamn Machinery."

Frost's "Into My Own" opened his first book and "[In winter in the woods alone]" closed his last. In a sense the two poems are bookends to his career. Frost, who has been taken to be a NEW ENGLAND country poet, ends with a final estimation: "I see for Nature no defeat / In one tree's overthrow / Or for myself in my retreat / From yet another blow."

Frost was a prolific writer, and his poetry that turns on nature has breadth and depth. It can be understood in a variety of ways, and its symbols and themes are constantly being rediscovered and reevaluated.

New England Frost's relationship to New England has been central to the reading of his poetry, and much ink has been spilled over its meaning. While he was San Francisco born, the landscape and people of New England captured his interest and imagination. He writes about the seasons, preoccupied largely with fall and winter, the rural people and farmers who made their living off the land, the brooks and flora specific to the region. He has a keen ear for dialect and the suggestions of intonation. He documents the stone walls that are peculiar to the landscape, and he is threatened by the 20th century's encroachment on the natural environment that was so dear to him.

Frost worked the land. His paternal grandfather had a 30-acre farm in Derry, New Hampshire, and the Frost family spent many memorable years farming there. When Frost's grandfather died, he left Frost an annuity and the use of the Derry Farm for 10 years as part of his will; after 10 years the annuity increased and the farm became his. In 1911, when Frost took a job in Plymouth, New Hampshire, he sold the farm. The sale of that farm allowed the Frosts to travel to England, where Frost began his career as a poet. The Derry Farm is now a New Hampshire State historic site that can be visited in the summertime.

The Frosts also lived on a farm in Franconia, New Hampshire, which is now the Frost Place Center for Poetry and the Arts. It includes a museum and offers summer literary programs. The family sold the home in 1920 to move to the Stone House in South Shaftsbury, Vermont, which opened a museum in 2002. The house, on seven acres, "features many Frostian associations including stone walls, birch trees, a timbered barn and some of Frost's original apple trees" (Frost Place). In 1928 the family bought a second farm, the Gulley Farm in Shaftsbury, roughly a mile from the Stone House.

In 1939 Frost bought the Homer Noble Farm in Ripton, Vermont, near the BREAD LOAF SCHOOL OF ENGLISH. Theodore Morrison and his wife Kay, then Frost's secretary, lived in the main house while Frost occupied a three-room cabin on the property. The Homer Noble Farm is situated near the Robert Frost Trail and the mountain that the Vermont state legislature named after Frost in 1955.

As Lawrence Buell writes, "To classify Robert Frost as a poet in a traditional New England vein can be dangerously misleading or entirely proper, depending on how you define your terms" (101).

The Robert Frost Stone House Museum, Shaftsbury, Vermont. "A Young Birch": "The only native tree that dares to lean, Relying on its beauty to the air." *(Photo by Deirdre Fagan)*

He notes, "The sequence of volumes that formed the basis of Frost's first *Poems* (1923) shows an initially hesitant but increasingly assertive embracement of a regional persona that was to empower, define, and by the same token delimit him" (104). In some of the most memorable photographic images of Frost he is casually dressed and surrounded by hills.

In one sense Frost is a regionalist poet, and in another he is simply a human poet. He writes about the New England landscape and makes characters of its people, but while the language he speaks may often be theirs, what he says is grander than any region. He uses the landscape as a lens through which to view the depths of the human heart. Frost's natural landscape is not equatorial Africa; it is the very root of America, but when he writes about what it is to bury the dead—including one's children, as in "Home Burial"—what he has to say travels well beyond the mountains, streams, and stone walls of New England.

FURTHER READING

Buell, Laurence. "Frost as a New England Poet." In *The Cambridge Companion to Robert Frost,* edited by Robert Faggen, 101–122. Cambridge: Cambridge University Press, 2001.

Ekins, Roger. "'At Home' with Robert Frost." In *Frost Centennial Essays,* edited by Jac Tharpe, 191–200. Jackson: University Press of Mississippi, 1974.

Frost Place. Available online. URL: http://www.frostplace.org. Accessed April 4, 2006.

Hopkins, Vivian C. "The Houses of Robert Frost." In *Frost Centennial Essays,* edited by Jac Tharpe, 182–190. Jackson: University Press of Mississippi, 1974.

Monteiro, George. *Robert Frost and the New England Renaissance.* Lexington: University Press of Kentucky, 1988.

Parini, Jay. *Robert Frost: A Life.* New York: Holt, 1999.

Robert Frost Farm State Historic Site. New Hampshire State Parks. Available online. URL: http://www.nhstateparks.com/frost.html. Accessed April 4, 2006.

Robert Frost Stone House Museum. Frost Friends. Available online. URL: http://www.frostfriends.org/stonehouse.html. Accessed April 4, 2006.

night Frost, according to biographer Jeffrey Meyers, always slept with a night-light (24). A friend, recalling Frost's terror of the dark, once said, "I would have to go into the house before him at night, to turn on all the lights. It was a thing left over from boyhood" (Parini, 49). But despite any such fears, he also was known for taking night walks alone and with his children. Perhaps the speaker of "Bravado" best couples Frost's insistence on night walks with his trepidation about the dark: "Have I not walked without an upward look / Of caution under stars that very well / Might not have missed me when they shoot and fell? / It was a risk I had to take—and took."

In Frost's poetry the figure of night often suggests a shroud of inner darkness, sadness, and contemplation in the darkest of hours. It represents the innermost loneliness, but it can also represent peace. Frost is preoccupied with things that go bump in the night, but he treats the idea in a variety of ways.

The Five Nocturnes in *Steeple Bush* thematically center on this frequent trope in Frost, expressing from various perspectives fears, hidden and not, and the human desire to find safety, sometimes through manmade light and other times through one another, in a universe vaster and darker than imaginable.

In "Design" the poet writes ominously about things that go "thither in the night," and in "On a Bird Singing in Its Sleep," which follows "Design" in *A Further Range,* he writes of a bird that makes it through the night by its singing, which has not made it "more easily a prey." In "Acceptance" we encounter birds that, "when the change to darkness in the sky" comes, think or twitter "Safe! / Now let the night be dark for all of me. / Let the night be too dark for me to see / Into the future. Let what will be, be," embracing what will come in the darkness, even if it should be death. "Once by the Pacific" follows "Acceptance" in *West-Running Brook,* and in this poem night represents not only the threat of darkness but endings, sometimes cyclical and sometimes permanent: "There would be more than ocean-water broken / Before God's last *Put out the Light* was spoken." God holds the ultimate power of darkness.

In "The Onset" a "fated night" brings "at last the gathered snow" in the "dark woods." The speaker is concerned with "that winter death" and "stumble[s] looking up and round, / As one who overtaken by the end / Gives up his errand, and lets death descend." "The Onset" follows "Stopping by Woods on a Snowy Evening" by only a few poems in *New Hampshire,* and the two can almost be read as companion pieces. In "Stopping by Woods" the "woods are lovely, dark and deep" but the traveler has "promises to keep, / And miles to go before [he] sleep[s]." Frost insisted the poem was simple and did not suggest death, but given "The Onset" and other metaphorical uses of dark woods, it is difficult to deny the suggestion, whether intentional or not.

With the night come threats not only from nature but from outsiders. Dusk often brings an unknown person knocking at a door. In "Snow" a distant neighbor, Meserve, has disrupted a couple's sleep. While Meserve does not threaten their lives or livelihood, he is an unexpected and unwanted disruption. In "Love and a Question" a "stranger c[o]mes to the door at eve" with a threat to a young marriage. "The Literate Farmer and the Planet Venus" opens with an "unexpected knocking at the door" and a traveler come to "compliment . . . on a star," and this is the "time knocking at a door did good." In Frost's play *A Way Out,* a stranger's knock at the door, or rather, rattling of the door latch and nearly forced entry, leads to annihilation: The stranger kills the homeowner Asa and adopts his identity. The play begins with the stranger saying, "Huh! So this is what it's like. Seems to me you lock up early. What you afraid of?"

Night often brings darkness not only from strangers and nature but also from within. In "Ends," for a couple who had once had "night the first, / . . . this was night the last." In "The Thatch," while the relationship is not over, the lover has been turned out of doors because of a spat to where the "world was a black invisible field." There the speaker's presence "flushe[s] birds out of hole after hole, / Into the darkness," causing him great grief for having turned them out of doors as well.

In "The Door in the Dark" darkness brings the comical, as "going from room to room in the dark"

a "slim door" gets past the speaker's guard and gives him a "blow in the head so hard" that his "native simile" is "jarred." In "Canis Major" the night is for the "Overdog," the star Sirius that "romps through the dark."

"Leaves Compared with Flowers" contrasts night and day: "Leaves by night and flowers by day." The speaker reveals that "Leaves are all my darker mood," and this impression is furthered by "Acquainted with the Night," in which the depth of the speaker's inner weather far exceeds nature's outer, and "Desert Places" where snow and night are falling fast, yet the speaker has "it in [him] so much nearer home / To scare [him]self with [his] own desert places." In "An Old Man's Winter Night" "All out-of-doors look[s] darkly in at him," and it is a combination of inner and outer weather that threatens. But despite Frost's preoccupation with night, its loneliness, its threats minor and major, and its possibilities for peace, when darkness comes he remains optimistic. "In the Long Night" he is "rest assured on eider / There will come another day." He burned a night-light and equated himself with the woman of "The Night Light," who also kept the light "Beside her attic bed at night": "Good gloom on her was thrown away / It is on me by night or day, / Who have, as I suppose, ahead / The darkest of it still to dread."

FURTHER READING

Meyers, Jeffrey. *Robert Frost: A Biography.* New York: Houghton Mifflin, 1996.
Parini, Jay. *Robert Frost: A Life.* New York: Holt, 1999.

philosophy Classically schooled, Frost was quite familiar with the Greek philosopher Plato (427?–347 B.C.) and his student Aristotle (384–322 B.C.), and a number of his poems waver as to which philosophies Frost more strongly embraced. Plato was known for articulating that the transcendent is where the realm of being exists, which contains permanent unchanging ideas and the ideal "Forms" of beauty, truth, and so forth. Aristotle disagreed with his teacher, arguing that "forms" exist only in the things themselves, as they are perceived in this world, and that a transcendental realm was not only unnecessary but also insufficient to give us real properties, values, and objects.

In "The Bear" the man "paces back and forth" like the Greeks, philosophizing and moving from "one extreme" to "the other." Frost asserts that these two extremes are the difference between "agreeing with one Greek" and "agreeing with another Greek"—the difference between agreeing with Plato or with Aristotle. By summoning the two ideas to mind, Frost plays on his own and man's constant "back and forth" and his "sway[ing] from cheek to cheek" between this world and the transcendental. Frost closes the poem with an image of man as a "baggy figure, / equally pathetic / When sedentary and when peripatetic." The term "peripatetic" derives from Aristotle's constant pacing while conducting discussions and hence is also the word for the Aristotelian school of philosophy. In "The Bear" Frost suggests that Aristotle's walking about while teaching led to no more enlightenment or satisfaction than a sedentary and baggy fellow's would.

In "A Passing Glimpse" and "Fragmentary Blue," Frost also contrasts the philosophies of Aristotle and Plato. In the first poem Frost is preoccupied with the possibility of having direct knowledge of what is real. From a train car, passing glimpses are all that the speaker can absorb. The flowers that he can view from his window "are gone before [he] can tell what they are." Indirect perceptions are all he can grasp, and reality becomes an ideal that is not quite clear: "I name all the flowers I am sure they weren't." He can gain glimpses of heaven, but it remains an ideal that eludes his perceptions. A passing glimpse does not imply a direct perception of some Platonic ideal. The poem is Aristotelian in that the speaker comes to embrace his perceptions as they present images and real objects to him, instead of attempting to view the world through an ideal and embracing his perceptions as parasitic imitations of those ideal objects. In the second poem, he resists the idea that objects in this world have value only because they are parasitic on the transcendental realm when he observes that earth becomes heaven and our wishes for blue just as easily granted by "a bird, or butterfly, / Or flower, or wearing-stone, or open eye" as by heaven.

In "The Trial by Existence" Frost considers entelechy, which in the philosophy of Aristotle was the condition of a thing whose essence is fully realized, a vital force that directs an organism toward self-fulfillment. In a letter to his friend Louis Untermeyer dated May 4, 1916, Frost wrote, "The day I did 'The Trial by Existence' says I to myself, this is the way of all flesh. I was not much over twenty, but I was wise for my years. I knew that it was a race between me the poet and that in me that would be flirting with entelechies or the coming on of that in me" (Cramer, 23).

In "Boeotian" Frost evokes Plato "toy[ing]" with the "Platonic notion / That wisdom need not be of Athens Attic." He is also playing with the word *attic*, since it is a synonym for Athens and refers to the dialect of Attica, in which the bulk of classical Greek literature was written. The poem asserts that if wisdom is practical it cannot also be transcendental, as Plato supposes, and that if it is not laconic and practical, the poet at least does not want it to be systematic, for Platonic wisdom was completely systematic. Frost seems to be pushing his assertion further by asserting that wisdom could "even [be] 'Boeotian.'"

Frost's early poem "The Demiurge's Laugh" draws on a Platonic deity, the demiurge, who fashioned the world out of chaos. He was a lesser god, a demigod, and, more literally, a worker for the people. He did not create the world but he did help build it. In the poem the speaker is hunted and haunted by the Demiurge's laugh. The poem acts as a metaphor for Frost's own doubts about the transcendent.

"Neither Out Far nor in Deep" offers a Frostian version of Plato's Allegory of the Cave. Frost criticizes "The people along the sand," who "All turn and look one way." Their single-mindedness keeps them from turning toward the land, so they turn their backs on something meaningful. The people along the sand are like those in Plato's Allegory of the Cave, who, chained inside the cave, are unable to turn their heads and are therefore unable to see anything but the shadows cast on the wall of the cave. These they take to be reality. The people in Frost's poem also mistake shadows for reality; the reflection of the standing gull on the "wetter ground like glass" seems to also be an allusion to Plato's allegory.

In his "Letter to *The Amherst Student*" Frost closes by saying that to him "any little form" he asserts on the chaos of the world is "velvet" and "to be considered for how much more it is than nothing." He adds, "If I were a Platonist I should have to consider it, I suppose, for how much less it is than everything," making it clear he is not a Platonist but an Aristotelian.

Frost's concern with value and meaning are most profoundly expressed in his two masques, *A Masque of Mercy* and *A Masque of Reason*. In *A Masque of Reason* he attempts to embrace the classic problem of value and the divine posed in the book of Job and indirectly in Plato's *Euthyphro*. Pious Job is given a tremendous amount of suffering through a bet between God and the devil. When Job asks God for an explanation, God, in the form of a whirlwind, chastises Job and explains that he is not to question God's actions. In Plato's *Euthyphro*, Socrates poses a dilemma about value and the divine in the form of a question: Is something good simply because God commands it (making it God's whim), or does God command it because it is good (making what is good independent of, and prior to, God's commands)?

In *A Masque of Reason* Frost tries to give an account of the aftermath of the book of Job, or what Job and God might have said after all the suffering and chastising played itself out. Even though there seems to be a residue of tension between Job and God, Frost provides a rather startling admission of God to Job, namely, that God was just showing off for the devil. Throughout the masque, it is important to keep Plato's *Euthyphro* in mind for the concept of value and morality.

Unlike *A Masque of Reason*, *A Masque of Mercy* is more concerned with the relationship of man to God than God to man. In *A Masque of Mercy* the concern is with how merciful God is and will be. It invokes not only Frost's usual skepticism about religion but also his criticism of the modern world that became more evident as he aged. The question of mercy is partly explored through Jonah's book in the Old Testament, where "Mercy is explicitly the subject." The questions raised are whether God can be trusted to be merciful and whether people should ever expect God to be unmerciful out of an appetite for justice. The closing line is hopeful, suggesting that all is worthwhile in the end, even the injustice that Jonah was dealt, if God's ultimate judgment is merciful: "Nothing can make injustice just but mercy."

Frost is a poet-philosopher, drawing on his immersion in the Greeks and sharing with philosophers a desire to find meaning where it is at best obscured. He scrutinizes nature with a philosophical eye, examining it this way and that and frequently venturing into it all in an effort to discern what lies there that may afford some knowledge or comprehension of what it all means. Nature becomes a metaphor for everything that we do not know and cannot know, or for everything that we will never tire of attempting to know.

FURTHER READING

Cramer, Jeffrey. *Robert Frost among His Poems: A Literary Companion to the Poet's own Biographical Contexts and Associations*. Jefferson, N.C.: McFarland, 1996.

politics Frost was known for his conservatism, and in some instances this hindered critics from appreciating him. His worry over socialism is expressed throughout "Build Soil—A Political Pastoral," in which he is wary of foreign entanglements: "We're always too much out or too much in. . . . We're so much out that the odds are against our ever getting inside again. / But inside in is where we've got to get." (Frost is also concerned with socialism in "Departmental," among other poems.)

Frost advocates tilling one's own soil, as a farmer and as a nation, when he says that we need to be national before we are international, personal before we are interpersonal, a sentiment he also expresses in prose pieces such as "To the Poets of Japan." Frost was patriotic and nationalistic, and these attitudes are best expressed in "The Gift Outright," a love poem to the nation.

In "On Our Sympathy with the Under Dog," however, the game of politics is depicted as a circus. We watch "revolving dogs," political leaders who transition as quickly as revolving doors. Politics and politicians are sometimes volatile for Frost and are often connected to wars or fighting.

"A Soldier" metonymically presents a lance for a soldier who has been cast by governments into war. A brief political poem, "U.S. 1946 King's X," refers to the nuclear conflagration that ended World War II, when the Japanese cities of Hiroshima and Nagasaki were destroyed by atomic bombs dropped by the United States on August 6 and August 9, 1945.

In "No Holy Wars for Them," published in 1947, the speaker, probably equating himself with the "puny little states" that "can only be," seems to wish that he could "wage a Global Mission" but feels in many ways powerless. All he can do is ask questions of God and hope that He intervenes before "the world's supply / Get[s] parceled out among the winning giants."

Another of Frost's political poems, "Triple Bronze," approaches the question of how much defense one needs against "The Infinit[e]." The infinite represents the world and the universe as well as eternity, the speaker asserts that protection on three levels is necessary. The first layer of protection is personal: "For inner defense my hide." *Hide* is used doubly, both as refuge and as skin. The "next defense outside" is the protection of home, with walls that can be made of "wood or granite or lime" as long as they are "too hard for crime / Either to breach or climb." The third protection is "a national boundary," providing political defense.

In 1962 Frost received the Congressional Gold Medal and was invited by President John F. Kennedy to travel to the Soviet Union as part of a cultural exchange program. The highlight of the trip was his meeting with Soviet premier Nikita Khrushchev. For Frost, whose career was affected by his politics, the trip held great meaning. He was momentarily in a key political position and spoke with Khrushchev for more than 90 minutes: The "most powerful figure in the Soviet Union had met with an American cultural icon, and they had freely talked about matters of huge cultural import" (Parini, 434). The trip to Russia was a crowning moment in Frost's life.

Frost believed in democracy and was most democratic in his poetry. He wrote in accessible prose about the haves and the have nots, about the educated and the uneducated, about women and men.

His uneducated became educated, his educated uneducated, and he at times showed a feminist side, as in "The Lovely Shall Be Choosers." While his political stance was conservative, he came from a family of staunch Democrats, and his embrace of agrarianism stemmed from his love of nature and country, as deeply expressed in "The Gift Outright."

FURTHER READING

Hoffman, Tyler. *Robert Frost and the Politics of Poetry.* Hanover, N.H.: Middlebury College Press, 2001.
Parini, Jay. *Robert Frost: A Life.* New York: Holt, 1999.

publishers Frost's "La Noche Triste," his first published poem, appeared in the Lawrence High School *Bulletin* in April 1890; a second poem, "The Song of the Wave" was published in the *Bulletin* in May. His first professionally published poem, "My Butterfly: An Elegy," was published in the November 8, 1894, issue of the *Independent.* Dr. William Hayes Ward was the editor of the *Independent,* and his sister, Susan Hayes Ward, was the managing editor. Frost called Susan his "first discoverer" (1893), and she and Frost would conduct a lifelong correspondence. Shortly before her death in 1916, Susan asked Frost to write for her a girls companion piece to "Birches," which she took to be for boys, and she would "furnish him with the materials." Frost did; he called it "Wild Grapes."

Frost printed two copies of a chapbook, *Twilight,* in 1894 and visited his future wife, Elinor, at St. Lawrence University with a copy in hand. When she received him coolly, he destroyed his own copy. The only remaining copy would be "rented" by a wealthy collector, Earle J. Bernheimer, until in financial desperation Bernheimer, to the chagrin of Frost, auctioned it for $3,500 in 1950. *Twilight* is now in the University of Virginia's Clifton Waller Barrett Library of American Literature.

Frost's first book of poetry, *A Boy's Will,* was published April 1, 1913, by David Nutt and Company of London, ENGLAND, only days after Frost's 39th birthday. Frost had published a few poems in the United States, in magazines, but had not had the confidence to seek a book publisher in America. His second book, *North of Boston,* was published by David Nutt on May 15, 1914. Frost soon learned that Henry Holt and Company of New York would publish his books in the United States. *North of Boston* was the first, on February 20, 1915; *A Boy's Will* followed in April. Henry Holt continued as Frost's publisher throughout his lifetime.

The offer by Holt to publish Frost's books in the United States was brought about by coincidence. Mrs. Holt had been given a copy of the English publication of *North of Boston* by a friend. A Vermonter herself, she was taken with the book and convinced her husband to publish Frost. Biographer Jay Parini reports that while Holt had originally imported only 150 copies of *North of Boston* from David Nutt, it soon printed 1,300 more copies, and a year later the book had reached 20,000 sales (171). Mrs. Holt also later urged Frost to move to Vermont.

Frost's first editor at Holt was Alfred Harcourt, who would leave Holt and begin his own company with Donald Brace. Frost considered going with him, but since Holt held the copyright on the poems he had already published, leaving the company would have made it difficult to put out *Complete Poems*. Frost also worked with Lincoln MacVeagh, Richard H. Thornton, and T. J. Wilson, among others. "A Star in a Stoneboat" (1923) was collected in *New Hampshire* with the dedication "for Lincoln MacVeagh," who was a good friend of Frost's.

Holt sponsored extravagant 80th and 85th birthday dinners for Frost at the Waldorf-Astoria Hotel in New York City.

Before establishing himself as a poet, Frost wrote a number of poultry stories and articles for *Farm-Poultry* and the *Eastern Poultryman*. He would continue to publish in various magazines throughout his lifetime, including Harriet Monro's *Poetry*, the *Atlantic Monthly*, the *Nation*, the *New Republic*, the *Times Literary Supplement*, and the *Yale Review*.

San Francisco   Frost is thought of as a New England poet and is rarely associated with San Francisco (or FLORIDA), but he was born in San Francisco in 1874. His early childhood was spent in the city, Napa Valley, and the California countryside. He grew up playing on the coast and watching his father swim in the Pacific Ocean. His parents were both from the Northeast, but his father's romantic view of the West brought him there upon graduation from college (he met Frost's mother on the way). Frost did not return East until his father died in 1885. He was still quite young, and those formative years in New England left their indelible impression.

Frost writes extensively about New England but rarely about the West Coast. Two of the more prominent poems are "Once by the Pacific," which reflects Frost's fears about watching his father swim in the Pacific, and "At Woodward's Gardens." The latter is titled after and set in a park that was in operation from 1854 to 1927, occupying six acres in San Francisco's Mission District. The grounds housed the largest marine aquarium in the country at the time, zoological gardens, greenhouses, and a restaurant. Another poem, "Auspex," is based on an experience "in a California Sierra," and he mentions California a number of times in "New Hampshire," but it is difficult to identify many others.

"A Peck of Gold" is significant for uniting the two regions of Frost's youth. Representing the old West and the Gold Rush, in it Frost plays on the old New England adage that we all must "eat a peck of dirt before [we] die," offering a new twist from a boy who was born and grew up partly in San Francisco. For that boy, it was "all must eat a peck of gold." Of "life in the Golden Gate" clouded by the bay's "sea-fog," the hope for gold is all the boy remembers, for it was all people "drank and ate."

In "A Poet's Boyhood," included in a brochure announcing a Frost reading to be held at the Berkeley Community Theater on November 6, 1960, in Berkeley, California, Frost, at age 86, returning to the region of his birth as an esteemed poet, recalls one of his earliest San Francisco memories: his father's role in nominating the popular Democratic candidate for the presidency in 1880, Winfield Scott Hancock, and his father's disappointment when Hancock was narrowly beaten by James Garfield.

scholars and admirers   Several organizations have been created in appreciation of Frost, among them the Frost Place, Friends of Robert Frost, the Key West Heritage House Museum and Robert Frost

Cottage, and the Robert Frost Society. The Frost Place of Franconia, New Hampshire, was Frost's 1915 mountain farmstead and is now a nonprofit center for poetry and the arts owned by the Town of Franconia. The Friends of Robert Frost is a nonprofit organization that appeals to enthusiasts of all ages who are interested in the poet's life and art and in the historic preservation of Frost's Stone House in Shaftsbury, Vermont. The Key West Heritage House Museum and Robert Frost Cottage holds a Robert Frost poetry festival each year. Frost visited Key West, FLORIDA, for several winters later in life and stayed in the cottage, enjoying the garden. The Robert Frost Society promotes scholarly discussion of the poet's life and work. It is an allied member of the Modern Language Association, and its members present papers at two annual conventions: the Modern Language Association and the American Literature Association. It

Postage stamp commemorating Frost, copyright 1974. *(Courtesy the United States Postal Service)*

also sponsors the annual peer-reviewed academic journal the *Robert Frost Review.*

science In "*Paris Review* Interview with Richard Poirier" Frost reflects that "the greatest adventure of man is science, the adventure of penetrating into matter, into the material universe." He admits having been influenced by the science of his time—Darwin, Einstein, the nuclear age, and the space race—and it is notable that many of his later poems take as their subjects questions about the nature and limitations of science. It is a subject that preoccupied him throughout his life, not only in his poetry but in his prose and public talks. Like many humanists of his time, he was deeply concerned that science, in an attempt to answer all, would dismiss and eventually destroy humanity. He knew the limitations of science well and was quick to remind his audiences of them. He knew science could not measure or otherwise quantify human emotions, the desire to create art, or more generally our simple affinity for the world we live in.

Such attitudes are expressed in "A Star in a Stoneboat," in which the speaker does not need science, or religion for that matter, to reduce the universe to a manageable size. He simply must find and hold one fallen star and let it "run off in strange tangents with [his] arm." The star will be "the prize / Of the world complete in any size" that he can hold to make the universe seem far less vast. This will make him the "compass, fool or wise," returning humanity to central importance. The speaker is similar to the one in "Any Size We Please," which is among the "Editorials" of *Steeple Bush.* In it a man whose "science needn't get him so unnerved / . . . hug[s] himself for all his universe."

There are a number of "Editorials" in *Steeple Bush* that take science as their subject. Appearing just before "Any Size We Please" is "Why Wait for Science," one of Frost's more caustic poems on the subject, though it begins by accusing science of the same: "Sarcastic Science she would like to know, / In her complacent ministry of fear." The poem speculates on the possibilities for our existence once we have managed to "ma[k]e things" on Earth "so we have to go / Or be wiped out." Possibilities are presented, such as going to another planet "by rocket / . . . Through temperature of absolute zeró." Frost suggests bitingly that "The way to go away should be the same / As fifty million years ago we came— / If anyone remembers how that was. / I have a theory, but it hardly does." He is also taking his jab at Darwinism, with which he also had a complex relationship, part admiration and part cynicism. In "Accidentally on Purpose" he takes up the same subject of existence, asking, "What purpose was it? His or Hers or Its? / Let's leave that to the scientific wits," but he resolves that "Our best guide upward further to the light" is "[p]assionate preference such as love at first sight."

"Bursting Rapture," another of the poems in "Editorials," is concerned with what "gain / Was made by getting science on the brain." The "burst" in bursting rapture will find its relief: "That's what a certain bomb was sent to be." He is referring, of course, to the threat of the atomic bomb. Frost was living at a time when it first became apparent that everything on Earth could be wiped out in minutes, not by some apocalyptic means predicted in the Bible but by human beings, and science had made it all possible.

In "A Wish to Comply" Frost illustrates the lack of significance many scientific advancements hold for the ordinary person by diminishing the work of Robert Andrews Millikan, the American physicist who did research on the electron and cosmic rays in the 1920s and 1930s. Millikan won the Nobel Prize in 1923 for his famous ink drop experiment. By releasing a tiny ink drop in a specially constructed cylinder, Millikan was able to measure the charge of an electron. Frost asks, "Did I see it go by, / That Millikan mote?" He answers, "I rather suspect / All I saw was the lid / Going over my eye." In "It Is Almost the Year Two Thousand" Frost also highlights the presumed insignificance of science, ridiculing the belief that the millennium would bring the "final golden glow / To end" existence and providing the aside "science ought to know." He writes that if this is so, "We well may raise our heads / From weeding garden beds / And annotating books / To watch this end de luxe."

In *In the Clearing,* Frost's final volume, appear the greatest number of his poems that express

concerns about science. "Does No One at All Ever Feel This Way in the Least?" reflects on the seas that have been "lost by aeroplane," since fewer people travel by ship, but this is a minor consideration compared to that of "A Reflex," in which Frost asks of his readers "Hear my rigmarole," knowing he has neared the end of his career and wanting to get in his last two cents in on the subject. He makes fun of science by juxtaposing two "experiments." In the first science sticks a pole down a "likely" or predictable hole, and the pole is bitten. In the second, science stabs, and what it stabs grabs back. Frost makes his point that science can sometimes be made to draw obvious conclusions and sets up experiments so that such obvious conclusions will be easily reached. He suggests that there is a lack of certainty in science and that it works at "holes" that we are likely to be bitten by anyway.

Frost was also preoccupied with the space race of the cold war. In "[But Outer Space]" he wonders what the fuss over space is all about, saying that "Of the popu*lace*" it remains more "popul*ar* / Than popul*ous.*" In "Some Science Fiction" he reveals himself as one who is "not keeping pace / With the headlong human race," that he has chosen instead to "sta[y] back behind" a bit and "take life at a walk / In philosophic talk." He again criticizes the race into space and the "gospel of modern science," offering himself as one who might be "banishe[ed]" to a "penal colony" on the moon for his old-fashioned views. In "Lines Written in Dejection on the Eve of Great Success" he also considers the space race and moon landings, providing something of a nursery rhyme for grown-ups. He implies that dazzling science has yet to match the beauty of the imagination. Frost's cow of the imagination jumps over moons, not onto them, as spacecraft do. He does not believe that science can overtake human dreams.

In "Quandary" he questions the adage that in order to have good we must have bad. He then satirically speaks of being "put to shame" by a "scientific book." But Frost remained a skeptic, as his poem of the same name reveals. He writes, "I don't believe I believe a thing you state. / I put no faith in the seeming facts of light." He feels wrapped in a "caul" in our universe no matter how immense it may be and despite scientific facts: "I don't believe I believe you're the last in space, / I don't believe you're anywhere near the last," he says of a star.

In his prose piece "The Future of Man," Frost speculates about where we are headed and says; "The point is that the challenge will always be there between man's originality and his law and order, his government." He then adds sarcastically, "I sometimes think the scientists have got themselves scared; they're afraid they'll run away with themselves they are so original." "They needn't worry; the executives will take care of them," he assures.

In his often-anthologized earlier poem "Fire and Ice," the poet speculates about what will bring an end to Earth. And in a sense all the poet's meditations on science can be reduced to just that. In the end science matters most in terms of how we came and how we will go, and for this we may just as easily turn to poetry as to science. *See also* EVOLUTION and TECHNOLOGY.

FURTHER READING

Abel, Darrel. "The Instinct of a Bard, Robert Frost on Science, Logic, and Poetic Truth," *Essays in the Arts and Sciences* 9, no. 1 (May 1980): 59–75.

Hass, Robert. *Going by Contraries: Robert Frost's Conflict with Science.* Charlottesville: University Press of Virginia, 2002.

stars Stars are recurring symbols in Frost's poetry. They figure in a vast number of poems, sometimes as predominant symbols. A poem by the name "Stars," included in Frost's first book, *A Boy's Will,* demonstrates his early preoccupation with them. In it he says "Those stars like some snow-white / Minerva's snow-white marble eyes." The comparison in this poem to an ancient Greek statue reveals that stars ultimately have no knowledge of human affairs since they are "[w]ithout the gift of sight," but in other poems he offers different perspectives.

Stars as a symbol of fate—as in the old adage that something is destined to happen because it "is in the stars"—are a common trope in Frost. Near the beginning of "How Hard It Is to Keep from Being King When It's in You and in the Situation," when the King and his son first flee their responsibilities, the King says "Yon star's indifference / Fills

me with fear I'll be left to my fate," and by the end of the poem the King "blames the stars" for his fate. In "Clear and Colder" the mixing of a "Witches' Weather Primer" "like fate by stars is reckoned / None remaining in existence / Under magnitude the second." Wordplay suggests fate and God in the brief quatrain "A Question," in which "A voice said, Look me in the stars / And tell me truly, men of earth, / If all the soul-and-body scars / Were not too much to pay for birth." In "Skeptic" the poet "put[s] no faith in the seeming facts of light." The question of God in "I Will Sing You One-O" offers a speaker lying awake at night listening to clocks fill their "throats" and speak to "the furthest bodies / To which man sends his / Speculation" those cosmic bodies, the constellations and stars that are "[b]eyond" where God is. The furthest stars here are cosmic specks of "yawning lenses."

In the "Five Nocturnes" in *Steeple Bush,* stars figure in four of the five poems. In "Were I in Trouble" a headlight in the night is equated with a "star fresh fallen out of the sky." In "Bravado" stars pose a threat. The speaker's walks "without an upward look / Of caution under stars" are an example of risk-taking since the stars "Might not have missed me when they shot and fell." In "On Making Certain Anything Has Happened" the speaker is a list checker in charge of "[e]very star in sight." And "In the Long Night" the lights of stars are brought to a safe place, where their falling is not a threat.

"A-Wishing Well" evokes the children's rhyme "I wish I may I wish I might," wishing for "earth another satellite." The poem is a playful version of "Twinkle, Twinkle, Little Star," written by the poet Jane Taylor (1783–1824). "A Loose Mountain" also offers a playful depiction of stars. In it the sky is a loose mountain of stars, "fiery puffs of dust and pebbles," though the speaker turns more philosophical. He mentions a Leonid, one of the falling stars of the meteor shower that recurs annually in mid-November, and speaks of meteor showers as one of nature's threats that amounts to little, though the onslaught is apparently retribution for our foolishness in embracing electricity, "artificial light," over the "sovereignty of night." In "The Literate Farmer and the Planet Venus" the stars, not the artificial lights, are a way of keeping us from being too "overtight." They interrupt the night, but they are divine. "The Milky Way Is a Cowpath" relies on the children's rhyme about the cow who jumped over the moon (Frost manipulates the same nursery rhyme in "Lines Written in Dejection on the Eve of Great Success"). In this instance he uses the Milky Way to meditate on the space race of the cold war period following World War II. Frost also uses the stars to reflect on politics in "The Peaceful Shepherd," in which the speaker imagines that if "heaven were to do it again" and the speaker were responsible for "the figures in / Between the dotted stars," he "should be tempted to forget, / I fear, the Crown of Rule, / The Scales of Trade, / the Cross of Faith."

In "Come In" the speaker is "out for stars," and in "The Mountain" too, though it is not stated as such. In "An Unstamped Letter in a Rural Letter Box" the speaker, the "tramp astrologer" has a nearly transcendent experience when he witnesses the stir of "Heaven's firm-set firmament" by the "largest firedrop ever formed," which causes him to have "the equivalent, / only within." In "On the Heart's Beginning to Cloud the Mind" the light in a house on earth as seen from the lower berth of a train is compared to a star and is a symbol for the relationship between a husband and a wife.

In "Desert Places" stars represent loneliness, but the ultimate loneliness is internal: "They cannot scare me with their empty spaces / Between stars— on stars where no human race is. / I have it in me so much nearer home / To scare myself with my own desert places." In "Lost in Heaven," appearing just before "Desert Places" in *A Further Range,* stars help us identify where we are in the universe, and when they fail, the speaker is willing to accept his "heavenly lostness" and to let it "overwhelm" him. In this instance his loneliness, while it may be "more lonely ere it will be less" (a line from "Desert Places"), it can be embraced. In "All Revelation" there is a hope that in "Bring[ing] out the stars, bring[ing] out the flowers, / Thus concentrating earth and skies," "none need be afraid of size," and we will therefore be made to feel less small when we are face to face with the universe.

In particular, the dog star Sirius, which follows Orion, is significant, lending itself to a variety of puns throughout Frost's work. In "Canis Major" the constellation Canis Major is animated and translated as "Greater Dog." The brightest star in the constellation, Sirius, is the "great Overdog, / That heavenly beast"; it is portrayed with "a star in one eye," and the speaker describes himself as a "poor underdog." In "Bond and Free" "Thought cleaves the interstellar gloom / And sits in Sirius' disc all night." "The Literate Farmer and the Planet Venus" puns on Sirius by referring to the star as the one that is "Serious by name."

Two of the more romantic appearances of stars are in "Evening in the Sugar Orchard," in which the sparks from the sugarhouse chimney are "content to figure in the trees / As Leo, Orion, and the Pleiades," and in "Fireflies in the Garden," in which, as the "real stars . . . fill the upper skies . . . on earth come emulating flies," though they were "never really stars at heart."

teaching   In the introduction to her *Robert Frost, Teacher,* Nancy Vogel writes that Frost once said, "It slowly dawned on me that my poetry and my teaching were one, and if you knew my poetry at all well, you'd see that: that every little while there was the gleam of the teacher, that there were two things working."

While Frost is associated with various colleges, he never finished as a student, and in his first 39 years he did not seem destined to teach at colleges for much of the rest of his life. Frost attended both Dartmouth College and Harvard University as a student but withdrew from both. He was not fond of formal education, and though he was a good student in the traditional sense, having been awarded a prize for excellence in classical studies his first semester at Harvard, in another sense he never was a very good student to anyone. He would accumulate more than 40 honorary graduate degrees in his lifetime, however, including ones from Dartmouth and Harvard.

In 1894 Frost taught at local schools in Massachusetts, including Methuen, where he took over an unruly class of his mother's. In 1895, he worked as a reporter for the Lawrence, Massachusetts, *Daily American* and *Sentinel* and taught in the Salem, Massachusetts, district school. After working as a poultry farmer for a number of years, he took another teaching position at Pinkerton Academy in Derry, New Hampshire, in 1906. In 1911 he taught at New Hampshire State Normal School in Plymouth before setting sail with his family for ENGLAND, where he would officially begin his career as a poet.

After returning to the United States and being published by Holt, Frost secured a position at Amherst College in 1916. He was one of the first poets to hold a position as poet in residence at a university. As Vogel explains, "his willingness to teach provided impetus to the movement for artists in residence, a movement that has subsequently brought more creative artists and professional academicians together" (2). The relationship with Amherst would likely be the most meaningful of his career. It continued throughout his lifetime, and Frost held various positions at different times.

In 1921 Frost read for the first time at the newly established BREAD LOAF SCHOOL OF ENGLISH in Vermont, which began in 1920 and is affiliated with Middlebury College. He returned each summer, and Bread Loaf would be a significant mainstay in his public life.

In 1921, also for the first time, Frost accepted a one-year fellowship at the University of Michigan. The position was renewed, and he taught again the following year. In 1923 he resigned to return to Amherst College. In 1924 he was awarded a lifetime appointment at the University of Michigan as a fellow in letters, with no teaching obligations. He resigned from Amherst to take the position. Frost stayed with Michigan until fall 1925, but he returned to Amherst College in January 1926.

In 1936 Frost became the Charles Eliot Norton Professor of Poetry at Harvard University, another meaningful moment in his career because he had attended Harvard as a student. In 1939 he accepted a two-year appointment there as Ralph Waldo Emerson Fellow in Poetry, and in 1941 he also accepted a fellowship offer from Harvard. In 1943 he became the George Ticknor Fellow in Humanities at Dartmouth College. It was as though all the colleges of his past were in a tug-of-war over him. In 1948 he left Dartmouth to resume a post at Amherst, this time as Simpson Lecturer in Literature, a position he held until his death.

Frost believed in teaching, but not the sort of rote teaching that remains common at all levels of education in the United States. He believed in "education by poetry," and his prose piece by the same name offers startling reasons for taking a thorough go at metaphor. He was an uncommon teacher. One of the more famous stories of Frost's teaching career, which many have recounted, demonstrates how creative and insightful he could be. In one of his classes on English composition, on the first day students turned in their essays, he held them up and asked if anyone was interested in having them returned after he read them. When the students in unison agreed that they did not, he dropped the handful in the wastebasket, saying, "I don't intend to become a reader perfunctory of perfunctory writing" (Vogel, 19). He wanted his students to develop the way he had.

Jay Parini offers an account from one student in a class Frost visited

> Frost began to discuss metaphors in an easy way, asking occasional questions to bring out our ideas. Gradually the evening shadows lengthened and after a while Frost alone was talking. The room grew darker and darker until we could not see each others' faces. But no one even thought of turning on the light. The dinner hour came and went, and still no one of that half score of hungry boys dreamed of leaving. We dared not even stir for fear of interrupting. Finally, long after seven, Frost stopped and said, "Well, I guess that's enough." We thanked him and left as if under a spell. (243)

FURTHER READING

Parini, Jay. *Robert Frost: A Life.* New York: Holt, 1999.
Vogel, Nancy. *Robert Frost, Teacher.* Bloomington, Ind.: Phi Delta Kappa, 1974.

technology   Frost was profoundly affected by the encroachment of technology on nature. In "Blue-Butterfly Day" the image of wheels in the final line casts a dark shadow on the intrusion of technology on what was initially an idyllic nature scene. In "An Encounter" he is preoccupied with the image of the telephone pole, a barkless tree with its "strange position of hands" that is "[u]p at his shoulders, dragging yellow strands" of wire. He is also concerned with the telephone in "The Line-Gang." In "Mowing" the technology is a simple scythe, and in "The Exposed Nest" the "new-cut hay" of the meadow is a serious threat to the now exposed "nest full of young birds on the ground."

"The Egg and the Machine" presents technology as leading either to finding better ways to destroy ourselves and others or to separating from and excluding those who fail to fall in line. In "Lines Written in Dejection on the Eve of Great Success" Frost is critical of the United States space program, bemoaning that the moon used to be the stuff of imagination, of nursery rhymes and high-flown poetry, connected to the strenuosities of imagination and the magic of stories. He ridicules how people sometimes think that technology can catch up with human dreams and imagination, a criticism he also offered on various occasions in his prose and talks, such as "The Future of Man," in which he says, "The great challenge, the eternal challenge, is that of man's bursting energy and originality to his own governance."

In "Does No One at All Ever Feel This Way in the Least?" he bemoans the sea for having been "lost by aeroplane" now that "sailors ride a bullet for a boat." One of his more perplexing poems concerned with technology is "A Trial Run," in which the speaker is frightened by the power of a machine and his fear almost causes him to say a prayer to himself. The unidentified machine appears to be one made for and used in war.

In "A Serious Step Lightly Taken" an overheated car and a view provided by a map demonstrate a historical perspective and a great shift in technology by referring first to the beginning of the country and the docking of the *Mayflower*.

In "The Vanishing Red" John's awe of technology causes the Miller to think John, a Native American, is not advanced, and the Miller's superiority further fuels his prejudice. The poem ends hauntingly with John's murder. In *A Way Out*, an equally haunting play, Frost criticizes technology's unwanted encroachment by having the stranger mention a hermit described in the Boston paper

who saw the city lights as being in competition with nature's stars.

While Frost often was critical of technology and the destruction it could engender, he also admired it. For example, he celebrated American airplane inventors in the "The Wrights' Biplane" and in "Kitty Hawk," the site of the Wright brothers' first flight.

Frost stood in awe of technology, but he knew well its limitations and cautioned against a complete embrace of it. *See also* SCIENCE.

walls Walls, though not numerous, are significant symbols in Frost's poetry. Stone walls were prominent features of the New England landscape, and many still remain. The period from 1775 to 1825 was known as the golden age of wall building. While old rail and zig-zag fences made of wood had previously been popular for fencing farms, it later became difficult to secure the necessary wood for building fences after the land was cleared. Farmers turned to using stones found on their land or even stealing or buying stone. By 1871 approximately one-third of the 61,515 miles of fencing in Connecticut was stone (Schweizer). It is no wonder that stone walls were a preoccupation of Frost's and that walls in general figured so prominently in his work.

The best-known stone wall in Frost's poetry appears in his "Mending Wall," in which he says, "Something there is that doesn't love a wall" and meditates on what is being walled in and walled out. In "Two Look at Two," two people in late afternoon or early evening make their way up a mountainside. Love for each other and for nature take the two farther from home than they ought to have traveled, until they are halted by a wall that is "tumbled" and has "barbed-wire binding." The wall also serves as a boundary.

The subtitle of "Atmosphere" is "Inscription for a Garden Wall." This poem questions the purpose of a wall by looking at the specific effects of a wall in nature. "The Ingenuities of Debt" also presents a stone wall with a message: "Take Care to Sell your Horse before He Dies / The Art of Life is Passing Losses on." This is a reminder that in the end, sand, a "serpent on its chin," is what will become of the wall, the hall, and all the rest. In contrast, in "Ghost House" walls represent permanence. "Ghost House" is one of several Frost poems that employs an abandoned house as a metaphor: The house is gone and there is little trace of it left behind, except for its cellar walls.

In "The Cow in Apple Time" a lone cow is so inspired during apple time that a wall no longer confines her, being fenced in is no different from being in an open pasture. In "Misgiving" walls provide shelter. In "Not Quite Social" "the city's hold on a man is no more tight / Than when its walls rose higher than any roof," and the allusion to fortress walls is evident. One of Frost's political poems, "Triple Bronze," questions how much protection one needs against "The Infinit[e]." The first layer of protection is personal: "For inner defense my hide." The "next defense outside" is the protection of home, with walls that can be made of "wood or granite or lime" as long as they are "too hard for crime / Either to breach or climb." In the stark "The Flood" "blood will out" and will not be held behind "new barrier walls."

"Bond and Free" draws a distinction between love and thought, heart and mind; love is described as clinging and having walls: "wall within wall to shut fear out." In "An Old Man's Winter Night" the man has "icicles along the wall to keep," reminiscent of the "promises to keep" in "Stopping by Woods on a Snowy Evening."

In "Brown's Descent (Or the Willy-Nilly Slide)" Frost evokes the childish, depicting a man who goes "'cross lots, 'cross walls, 'cross everything" sliding down a mountain. Frost also evokes folklore in "The Figure in the Doorway," in which a figure, similar to Paul Bunyan, appears so large that if he were to fall, he would reach the "further wall." In "A Star in a Stoneboat" the speaker playfully imagines that a fallen star, a meteorite, has been "picked up with stones to build a wall."

In "A Time to Talk" the farmer-poet makes time for talk. If a friend should call to him from the road, he writes, slowing his horse to "a meaning walk," he will not waste any time but will "thrust [his] hoe in the mellow ground" and mosey up to the "stone wall / For a friendly visit."

Stone walls represent work and leisure too. They are boundaries used to wall in and wall out, pastoral symbols of Frost's time that represent the poet well. He was always cagily deceptive in his poetry; he was certainly not one who did not love a wall. A wall that would not be loved for its utility could at least appeal for its beauty.

FURTHER READING

Schweizer, Corey. "The Geology of Colonial New England Stone Walls." Primary Research. 2002. Available online, URL: http://www.primaryresearch. org/stonewalls/schweizer/index.php#1. Accessed April 8, 2006.

PART IV

Appendices

CHRONOLOGY

1873
Isabelle (Belle) Moodie and William (Will) Prescott Frost, Jr., meet at Lewistown Academy in Lewistown, Pennsylvania, where they are both teaching. The two marry in March and shortly thereafter move to San Francisco, California.

1874
Robert Lee Frost, named after Confederate general Robert E. Lee, the first child of Belle and Will, is born on March 26.

1876
Belle travels east with the young Frost to Lawrence, Massachusetts, where his sister Jeanie Florence is born on June 25. The family returns to San Francisco in late November of the same year.

1879–1884
The family moves frequently between apartments and hotels and takes trips to Napa Valley and the California countryside. Frost attends kindergarten, first grade, and second grade sporadically and is otherwise schooled at home.

1885
On May 5 Will dies of tuberculosis in San Francisco. The family returns with the coffin by train to Lawrence, Massachusetts, to bury Will and live with Frost's paternal grandparents at 370 Haverhill Street. After testing, Frost enters the third grade and Jeanie the fourth.

1886
Belle moves with the children to Salem Depot, New Hampshire, and begins teaching in the district school. Frost and Jeanie enter the fifth grade.

1888
Frost passes entrance examinations and enters Lawrence High School. Belle resigns from the Salem Depot position; she soon takes a teaching job in Methuen, Massachusetts.

1889–1890
Frost finishes at the head of the class both school years. Belle is hired to teach at Methuen, and the family returns to Lawrence. Frost's "La Noche Triste," his first published poem, appears 1890; a second poem, "The Song of the Wave" is published in the Bulletin in May.

1891
Frost meets his future wife, Elinor, at Lawrence High School. His sister Jeanie is hospitalized in December with typhoid fever. Frost sits for the Harvard entrance exams, finishing seventh in English literature. He again finishes the school year at the head of his class.

1892
Frost and Elinor graduate from Lawrence High School, sharing valedictorian honors. Frost works at the Everett Mill in Lawrence as a clerical assistant. The two secretly pledge to marry. Frost enrolls at Dartmouth but leaves before the end of the term. Elinor goes to St. Lawrence College.

1893–1894
Frost teaches at local schools, including Methuen, where he takes over an unruly class of his mother's. His first poem, "My Butterfly: An Elegy," is published in the November 8, 1894, issue of the

Independent. Frost prints two copies of a chapbook, *Twilight,* and visits Elinor with a copy in hand. She responds coolly; Frost destroys his own copy and shortly thereafter begins his sojourn into the Dismal Swamp on the Virginia–North Carolina border.

1895

Frost begins work as a reporter for the Lawrence *Daily American* and *Sentinel.* He teaches at the Salem District school. Frost and Elinor marry on December 19.

1896

Frost lives with Elinor, his mother, and his sister. He teaches his mother's older students. Frost and Elinor's first child, son Elliott, is born September 25.

1897

Frost spends the summer with Elinor and Elliott in Amesbury, Massachusetts. He enters Harvard University in September and moves to Cambridge, Massachusetts. He is awarded a prize for excellence in classical studies his first semester.

1898

Frost is awarded the Sewall Scholarship for academic excellence. He again spends the summer in Amesbury. He returns to Harvard in the fall, visiting his family weekly.

1899

Frost leaves Harvard to return to Lawrence, Massachusetts. Frost and Elinor's second child, daughter Lesley, is born April 28. The family purchases a poultry farm in Methuen, Massachusetts. Belle is diagnosed with advanced cancer and comes to live with Elinor and Frost.

1900

Frost and Elinor's first child, Elliott, dies July 8 of cholera. The family moves to Frost's grandfather's farm in Derry, New Hampshire. Frost's mother dies November 2.

1901

Frost and Elinor's third child, son Carol, is born May 27. Paternal grandfather William Prescott Frost dies July 10. Frost is given an annuity and the use of the Derry farm for 10 years as part of the grandfather's will; after 10 years the annuity is to increase and the farm to become his.

1903

Daughter Irma, Frost and Elinor's fourth child, is born June 27.

1905

Daughter Marjorie, Frost and Elinor's fifth child, is born March 28.

1906

Frost takes a position at Pinkerton Academy in Derry, New Hampshire. He publishes "The Tuft of Flowers" in the Derry *Enterprise* in March.

1907

Daughter Elinor Bettina, Frost and Elinor's sixth child, is born June 18 and dies June 21.

1909

"Into My Own" appears in the *New England* magazine in May. The family moves from the Derry Farm to an apartment in Derry Village.

1911

The family sells the Derry Farm on November 16 and moves to Plymouth, New Hampshire, where Frost teaches at the New Hampshire State Normal School.

1912

Frost resigns his teaching position at the New Hampshire State Normal School. The family sails to England on August 23 to live in a cottage in Beaconsfield, Buckinghamshire. Frost prepares *A Boy's Will* and sends it to David Nutt and Company of London, which accepts it for publication.

1913

Frost attends the opening of Harold Monro's Poetry Bookshop in London and meets poet Frank S. Flint, who will introduce him to Ezra Pound. *A Boy's Will* is published April 1.

1914

The family moves to Dymock, Gloucestershire. Frost's second book, *North of Boston*, is published May 15. Frost Learns that Henry Holt and Company of New York will publish his books in the United States.

1915

On February 13 the Frost family returns to the United States, arriving on February 23, and lives on the farm in Franconia, New Hampshire. *North of Boston* is published in America on February 20. Elinor becomes pregnant and miscarries. *A Boy's Will* follows in April.

1916

Frost's third book, *Mountain Interval*, is published on November 27 by Henry Holt. Frost begins teaching at Amherst College. He also is elected to the National Institute of Arts and Letters.

1917

The family moves to Amherst. Frost teaches courses in poetry appreciation and pre-Shakespearean drama. Dear friend and fellow poet Edward Thomas is killed on April 9 at the battle of Arras in France. The family spends the summer on the farm in Franconia.

1918

Frost reappointed at Amherst College and again spends the summer in Franconia.

1919

Frost's play *A Way Out* is performed by Amherst students on February 24. He is elected president of the New England Poetry Club. Frost again spends the summer in Franconia.

1920

Frost resigns his post at Amherst and moves the family to the Stone House in South Shaftsbury, Vermont. Frost commits Sister Jeanie to the state mental hospital at Augusta, Maine, following her earlier arrest and diagnosis of insanity in Portland, Maine. Frost acts as consulting editor for Holt.

1921

Frost spends a week as "poet in residence" at Queen's University in Kingston, Ontario. He reads for the first time at the newly established Bread Loaf School of English in Vermont. In the fall Frost moves the family to Ann Arbor after he accepts a one-year fellowship at the University of Michigan.

1922

Frost is named poet laureate of Vermont by the state League of Women's Clubs. He returns to South Shaftsbury for the summer. The Michigan position is renewed for another year, and Frost returns to Ann Arbor. Christmas is spent at the South Shaftsbury farm.

1923

The *Selected Poems* are published March 15 by Henry Holt. Frost accepts an appointment at Amherst College. The South Shaftsbury farm is given to Carol as a wedding present when he marries Lillian Labatt on November 3. *New Hampshire*, Frost's fourth book, is published on November 15.

1924

Frost wins his first Pulitzer Prize for *New Hampshire*. Grandson William Prescott Frost, son of Carol and Lillian, is born on October 15. Frost is awarded a lifetime appointment at the University of Michigan as a fellow in letters, with no teaching obligations. He resigns from Amherst College to take the position.

1925

Friends throw Frost a "Fiftieth Birthday Dinner" in New York City. Frost goes to Ann Arbor to begin the appointment; he returns to Pittsfield and Elinor when Marjorie is hospitalized with pneumonia and other illnesses. He returns to Michigan in the fall.

1926

Frost returns to Amherst College in January. Daughter Irma marries John Paine Cone on October 15.

1927

Grandson Jack is born to Irma and John. Frost rents a house in North Bennington, Vermont. Marjorie spends 10 weeks at Johns Hopkins Hospital for treatment.

1928

Frost signs a new contract with Holt. Irma returns home unhappily with her son; her husband soon follows. Frost buys them a small farm in North Bennington. Frost sails for France with Elinor and Marjorie. He travels to Dublin and visits William Butler Yeats. He also meets T. S. Eliot for the first time on a visit to London to read at Harold Monro's bookstore. The family returns to America in November. In December the family buys the second farm, the Gulley Farm in Shaftsbury, roughly a mile from the Stone House. *West Running Brook,* Frost's fifth book, is published by Holt on November 19. Lesley marries James Dwight Francis in September. Shortly thereafter Frost learns that she is contemplating divorce.

1929

Granddaughter Elinor Frost Francis is born to Lesley and Dwight Francis. Frost's sister Jeanie dies on September 27 in the mental hospital.

1930

The *Collected Poems* are published by Holt. Frost is elected to membership in the American Academy of Arts and Letters. Marjorie is hospitalized in Baltimore with tuberculosis.

1931

Marjorie enters a sanatorium in Boulder, Colorado. Frost is awarded his second Pulitzer Prize for the *Collected Poems.* Lesley has a second daughter, Lesley Lee Francis, on June 20, 1931; shortly thereafter her divorce is finalized. Frost receives the Russell Loines Poetry Prize from the National Institute of Arts and Letters. He makes a visit to childhood haunts in San Francisco.

1932

Frost and Elinor move into a house in Amherst. They meet Marjorie's fiancé, Willard Fraser, for the first time in Boulder.

1933

Marjorie marries Willard Fraser in Billings, Montana, on June 3. Frost is unable to attend due to exhaustion from delivering public lectures and readings.

1934

Marjorie develops puerperal fever following complications after the birth of her daughter, Marjorie Robin Fraser, on March 16 and dies on May 2. Elinor suffers a severe attack of angina pectoris in November. Frost and Elinor go to Key West, Florida, in December for rest.

1935

Frost meets Wallace Stevens in Key West. Frost gives a lecture at the University of Miami. He returns north with Elinor in March. He and Elinor rent a house in Coconut Grove, Florida, for the winter.

1936

Marjorie's poems are published privately in a small volume titled *Franconia.* Frost lectures again at the University of Miami. He and Elinor leave Florida and head to Cambridge, Massachusetts, where he becomes the Charles Eliot Norton Professor of Poetry at Harvard University. *A Further Range,* Frost's sixth book, is published by Holt on May 20. Frost suffers from a severe case of shingles in August. Elinor and Frost spend the winter in San Antonio, Texas.

1937

Frost and Elinor return to Amherst in March. Frost wins his third Pulitzer Prize for *A Further Range.* Elinor has surgery for breast cancer in Springfield, Massachusetts. After Elinor's recovery, Frost and Elinor return to Gainesville, Florida, for the winter.

1938

Elinor dies of a heart attack on March 20 in Gainesville, Florida. Frost is devastated and is unable to attend the cremation. He remains in Gainesville until mid-April. When he returns to Amherst, he resigns his position at Amherst College, sells the Amherst house, and returns to South Shaftsbury. Kathleen Morrison agrees to be his secretary. Frost rents an apartment in Boston in October.

1939

Frost is awarded the Gold Medal by the National Institute of Arts and Letters in New York. Frost travels to Key West, Florida, for the winter and then to Cuba on his first plane trip. An expanded edition of the *Collected Poems* is published in February. He returns to Boston from Florida in late February. He accepts a two-year appointment as Ralph Waldo Emerson Fellow in Poetry at Harvard. Frost buys the Homer Noble Farm in Ripton, Vermont. He designates Lawrance Thompson his "official" biographer on the condition that the biography only appear after his death.

1940

Frost travels to Florida and shortly thereafter purchases five acres of land in South Miami. He returns to Boston in mid-March. He lives on the Homer Noble Farm for the summer. Frost visits son Carol and grandson Prescott in South Shaftsbury while Lillian undergoes surgery. Carol is depressed but Frost is assured he is stable, so Frost returns to Boston. Carol commits suicide on October 9 in Shaftsbury, and Frost returns to make funeral arrangements.

1941

Frost buys a home in Cambridge, where he will continue to live for the remainder of his life, excepting summers at the Noble Farm and winters in South Miami. Frost accepts a fellowship offer from Harvard. The urns of Elinor and Carol are buried together in a family burial plot at the First Congregational Church in Old Bennington, Vermont.

1942

A Witness Tree, Frost's seventh book, is published in April by Holt. He builds two small houses on his land in South Miami, which he names "Pencil Pines."

1943

Frost is awarded his fourth Pulitzer Prize for *A Witness Tree*; he is the first to receive the Prize four times. He becomes the George Ticknor Fellow in Humanities at Dartmouth College. He is hospitalized in December with a serious case of pneumonia.

1945

A Masque of Reason is published by Holt in March. Frost travels with Kay Morrison to Pencil Pines for the winter. Grandson Prescott is now attending the University of Miami, and he and his mother Lillian live on the grounds the remainder of the year. Irma is mentally ill, and John and Irma have separated. Her illness has similarities to Frost's sister Jeanie's.

1946

The Modern Library publishes a new edition of the *Collected Poems*. Irma stays in Ripton for the summer.

1947

Frost purchases a home for Irma in Acton, Massachusetts. Frost revisits San Francisco. *Steeple Bush*, Frost's eighth book, is published by Holt in May. Irma deteriorates and is committed to the state mental hospital in Concord, New Hampshire. *A Masque of Mercy* is published by Holt in November.

1948

Frost chooses to leave Dartmouth to resume a post at Amherst, this time as Simpson Lecturer in Literature, a position he will hold until his death.

1949

The *Complete Poems of Robert Frost* is published in May.

1950

The U.S. Senate adopts a resolution honoring Frost on his 75th birthday. (This was an error, it was actually his 76th.)

1952

Lesley marries Joseph W. Ballantine.

1953

Frost is awarded the fellowship of the Academy of American Poets. He undergoes surgery for facial skin cancer.

1954

Frost is invited to the White House. Having learned he was born in 1874, he celebrates his 80th birthday at the Waldorf-Astoria in New York. Holt publishes *Aforesaid*, a new selection of his poems. He serves as a delegate to the World Congress of Writers held in Sao Paolo, Brazil.

1955

The Vermont state legislature names a mountain in Ripton after Frost.

1957

Frost cooperates with T. S. Eliot, Ernest Hemingway, and Archibald MacLeish to have a treason indictment against Ezra Pound dropped. Frost tours England and meets W. H. Auden, E. M. Forster, and Graham Greene.

1958

Frost is invited by President Eisenhower to the White House. Again he writes in support of Pound for the dismissal of the indictment. Pound is discharged. Frost is appointed Consultant in Poetry to the Library of Congress. He receives the Emerson-Thoreau Medal of the American Academy of Arts and Sciences and delivers an address on Emerson as his acceptance speech.

1959

Frost is appointed to a three-year term as honorary consultant in the humanities at the Library of Congress. Frost celebrates his 85th birthday, again at the Waldorf-Astoria in New York.

1960

Frost testifies before a Senate subcommittee in favor of a bill to establish a National Academy of Culture. Congress passes the bill and awards Frost a gold medal in recognition of his poetry. John F. Kennedy invites Frost to read at his inaugural ceremonies.

1961

Frost writes a poem for Kennedy's inauguration, but because the glaring sun he instead recites "The Gift Outright" from memory. The Vermont state legislature names Frost poet laureate of Vermont. Frost travels to Israel and Greece with Louis Untermeyer.

1962

Frost is hospitalized with pneumonia in February in South Miami. *In the Clearing*, Frost's final book, is published by Holt, Rinehart and Winston on his 88th birthday. In August Frost is invited by President Kennedy to travel to the Soviet Union as part of a cultural exchange program. The highlight of the trip is his meeting with Soviet premier Nikita Khrushchev. Frost undergoes a prostate operation on December 10; doctors find cancer in his prostate and bladder. He suffers a pulmonary embolism on December 23.

1963

Frost is Awarded the Bollingen Prize for Poetry. He suffers another embolism on January 7. He dies shortly after midnight on January 29 in Boston, Massachusetts. A private memorial service is held in Appleton Chapel in Harvard Yard on January 31; a public service is held at Johnson Chapel, Amherst College, on February 17. Frost is buried in Old Bennington, Vermont, on June 16.

CHRONOLOGICAL LIST OF PRIZES, AWARDS, AND HONORARY DEGREES

Phi Beta Kappa Poet, Tufts University, 1915.

Phi Beta Kappa Poet, Harvard University, 1916.

Elected to National Institute of Arts and Letters, 1916.

Amherst College, M.A., 1918.

Poetry magazine Levinson Prize, 1922.

University of Michigan, M.A., 1922.

University of Vermont, L.H.D., 1923.

Middlebury College, Litt.D., 1924.

Yale University, Litt.D., 1924.

Pulitzer Prize for *New Hampshire*, 1924.

Bowdoin College, Litt.D., 1926.

New England Poetry Club's Golden Rose Trophy, 1928.

Elected to American Academy of Arts and Letters, 1930.

University of New Hampshire, Litt.D., 1930.

Wesleyan University, L.H.D., 1931.

National Institute of Arts and Letters Loines Poetry Prize, 1931.

American Academy of Arts and Letters, 1931.

Pulitzer Prize for *Collected Poems*, 1931.

Elected to St. Botolph Club, 1932.

Williams College, L.H.D., 1932.

Phi Beta Kappa Poet, Columbia University, 1932.

Columbia University, Litt.D., 1932.

Dartmouth College, Litt.D., 1933.

Book of the Month Club for *A Further Range*, 1936.

Bates College, L.H.D., 1936.

University of Pennsylvania, L.H.D., 1936.

St. Lawrence University, L.H.D., 1936.

American Philosophical Society, 1937.

Harvard University, Litt.D., 1937.

Pulitzer Prize for *A Further Range*, 1937.

National Institute of Arts and Letters Gold Medal for Poetry, 1939.

Charles Eliot Norton Professor of Poetry, Harvard University, 1939.

Ralph Waldo Emerson Fellow in Poetry, Harvard University, 1939.

University of Colorado, L.H.D., 1939.

Phi Beta Kappa Poet, Tufts University, 1940.

Phi Beta Kappa Poet, College of William and Mary, 1941.

Phi Beta Kappa Poet, Harvard University, 1941.

Poetry Society of America Gold Medal, 1941.

Princeton University, Litt.D., 1941.

Pulitzer Prize for *A Witness Tree*, 1943.

Kenyon College, Litt.D., 1945.

University of California, LLD., 1947.

Duke University, Litt.D., 1948.

Amherst College, Litt.D., 1948.

Limited Editions Club Gold Medal, 1949.

Marlboro College, Litt.D., 1950.

Colgate University, Litt.D., 1950.

University of Massachusetts, Litt.D., 1951.

Durham, England, Litt.D., 1951.

American Academy of Poets Award, 1953.

University of North Carolina, Litt.D., 1953.

New Hampshire Education Association Citation for Distinguished Service to Education, 1954.

Theodore Roosevelt Society Medal, 1954.

University of Cincinnati, LL.D., 1954.

Dartmouth College, LL.D., 1955.

University of Rhode Island, Litt.D., 1955.

Vermont legislature designates Ripton "Robert Frost Mountain," 1955.

New York University Medal of Honor, 1956.

Colby College, LL.D., 1956.

National University of Ireland, Litt.D., 1957.

Ohio State University, L.H.D., 1957.

Oxford University, England, Litt.D., 1957.

Holland Society of New York Gold Medal, 1957.

Cambridge University, England, Litt.D., 1957.

Harvard University Medal for Achievement in the Arts, 1958.

Boston Arts Festival First Annual Poetry Award, 1958.

Poetry Society of America Gold Medal, 1958.

Huntington Hartford Foundation Award, 1958.

American Academy of Arts and Sciences Emerson-Thoreau Medal, 1958.

Signet Society, Harvard University, Medal for Achievements in the Arts, 1958.

Consultant in Poetry for the Library of Congress, 1958.

Miami University (Ohio), L.H.D., 1959.

Dickinson College, $1,000 award, 1959.

Syracuse University, Litt.D., 1959.

Tufts University, Litt.D., 1959.

University of Florida, LL.D., 1960.

Hebrew Union College, L.H.D., 1960.

Boston University, Litt.D., 1961.

University of Miami (Florida), LL.D., 1961.

Windham College, Litt.D., 1961.

Vermont legislature names Robert Frost poet laureate of Vermont, 1961.

University of Detroit, L.H.D., 1962.

Edward MacDowell Medal, 1962.

Congressional Gold Medal, 1962.

University of Michigan, LL.D., 1962.

Bollingen Prize in Poetry, 1963.

BIBLIOGRAPHY OF EDITIONS OF FROST'S WORKS

Frost, Robert. *Elected Friends: Robert Frost and Edward Thomas to One Another.* Edited by Matthew Spencer. New York: Handsel, 2003.

———. *Complete Poems of Robert Frost.* New York: Holt, 1949.

———. *Frost Collected Poems, Prose and Plays.* Edited by Richard Poirier and Mark Richardson. New York: Library of America, 1995.

———. *Interviews with Robert Frost.* Edited by Edward Connery Lathem. New York: Holt, Rinehart and Winston, 1966.

———. *The Letters of Robert Frost to Louis Untermeyer.* New York: Holt, Rinehart and Winston, 1963.

———. *Prose Jottings of Robert Frost: Selections from His Notebooks and Miscellaneous Manuscripts.* Lunenburg, Vt.: Northeast-Kingdom, 1982.

———. *Robert Frost: A Collection of Critical Essays.* Edited by James Cox. Englewood Cliffs, N.J.: Prentice Hall, 1962.

———. *Robert Frost: Farm-Poultry Man.* Edited by Edward Connery Lathem and Lawrance Thompson. Hanover, N.H.: Dartmouth, 1963.

———. *Robert Frost on Writing.* Edited by Elaine Barry. New Brunswick, N.J.: Rutgers University Press, 1973.

———. *The Robert Frost Reader: Poetry and Prose.* Edited by Edward Connery Lathem and Lawrance Thompson. New York: Henry Holt, 1972.

———. *Selected Letters of Robert Frost.* Edited by Lawrance Thompson. New York: Holt, Rinehart and Winston, 1964.

———. *Selected Prose.* Edited by Hyde Cox and Edward Connery Lathem. New York: Holt, 1966.

Frost, Robert, and Elinor Frost. *The Family Letters of Robert and Elinor Frost.* Edited by Arnold Grade. Albany: State University of New York Press, 1972.

Categorical List of Frost's Works

The following works all have entries in this book.

Poems and Collections of Poems

"Acceptance" (1928)

"Accidentally on Purpose" (1962) *See* CLUSTER OF FAITH

"Acquainted with the Night" (1928)

"After Apple-Picking" (1914)

"Afterflakes" (1936)

"Aim Was Song, The" (1923)

"All Revelation" (1942)

"America Is Hard to See" (1962)

"Answer, An" (1942)

"Any Size We Please" (1947)

"Armful, The" (1928)

"Assurance" (1942)

"Astrometaphysical" (1947)

"Atmosphere" (1928)

"At Woodward's Gardens" (1936)

"Auspex" (1962)

"Away!" (1962)

"A-Wishing Well" (1962)

"Ax-Helve, The" (1923)

"Bad Island—Easter, The" (1962)

"Bear, The" (1928)

"Bearer of Evil Tidings, The" (1936)

"Beech" (1942)

"Bereft" (1928)

"Beyond Words" (1947)

"Birches" (1916)

"Birthplace, The" (1928)

"Black Cottage, The" (1914)

"Blueberries" (1914)

"Blue-Butterfly Day" (1923)

"Blue Ribbon at Amesbury, A" (1936)

"Boeotian" (1942)

"Bond and Free" (1916)

"Bonfire, The" (1916)

"Boundless Moment, A" (1923)

A Boy's Will (1913)

"Bravado" (1947) *See* "FIVE NOCTURNES"

"Broken Drought, The" (1947)

"Brook in the City, A" (1923)

"Brown's Descent (Or the Willy-Nilly Slide)" (1916)

"Build Soil—A Political Pastoral" (1936)

"Bursting Rapture" (1947)

"[But Outer Space . . .]" (1962)

"Cabin in the Clearing, A" (1962)

"Canis Major" (1928)

"Carpe Diem" (1942)

"Case for Jefferson, A" (1947)

"Census-Taker, The" (1923)

"Choose Something like a Star" (1943)

"Christmas Trees" (1916)

"Clear and Colder" (1936)

"Cliff Dwelling, A" (1947)

"Closed for Good" (1949)

"Cloud Shadow, A" (1942)

Cluster of Faith: "Accidentally on Purpose," "A Never Naught Song," "Version," "A Concept Self-Conceived," "Forgive, O Lord" (1962)

"Cocoon, The" (1928)

"Code, The" (1914)

"Come In" (1942)

"A Concept Self-Conceived" (1962) *See* CLUSTER OF FAITH

"Considerable Speck, A" (1942)

"Courage to Be New, The" (1947)

"Cow in Apple Time, The" (1916)

"Death of the Hired Man, The" (1914)

"Demiurge's Laugh, The" (1913)
"Departmental" (1936)
"Desert Places" (1936)
"Design" (1936)
"Devotion" (1928)
"Directive" (1947)
"Discovery of the Madeiras, The" (1942)
"Does No One at All Ever Feel This Way in the Least?" (1962)
"Door in the Dark, The" (1928)
"Draft Horse, The" (1962)
"Dream Pang, A" (1913)
"Drumlin Woodchuck, A" (1936)
"Dust in the Eyes" (1928)
"Dust of Snow" (1923)
"Egg and the Machine, The" (1928)
"Empty Threat, An" (1923)
"Encounter, An" (1916)
"Ends" (1962)
"Equalizer, An" (1942)
"Escapist-Never" (1962)
"Etherealizing" (1947)
"Evening in a Sugar Orchard" (1923)
"Evil Tendencies Cancel" (1936)
"Exposed Nest, The" (1916)
"Fear, The" (1914)
"Fear of God, The" (1947)
"Fear of Man, The" (1947)
"Figure in the Doorway, The" (1936)
"Fire and Ice" (1923)
"Fireflies in the Garden" (1928)
"Five Nocturnes" (1947)
"Flood, The" (1928)
"Flower Boat, The" (1928)
"Flower-Gathering" (1913)
"Forgive, O Lord" (1962) See CLUSTER OF FAITH
"For John F. Kennedy His Inauguration" (1962)
"For Once, Then, Something" (1923)
"Fountain, a Bottle, a Donkey's Ears, and Some Books, A" (1923)
"[Four-Room Shack Aspiring High]" (1963)
"Fragmentary Blue" (1923)
"Freedom of the Moon, The" (1928)
"From Iron" (1962)
"From Plane to Plane" (1949)
Further Range, A (1936)
"Gathering Leaves" (1923)

"Generations of Men, The" (1914)
"Ghost House" (1913)
"Gift Outright, The" (1942)
"Girl's Garden, A" (1916)
"Going for Water" (1913)
"Gold Hesperidee, The" (1936)
"Good-by and Keep Cold" (1923)
"Good Hours" (1915)
"Grindstone, The" (1923)
"Gum-Gatherer, The" (1916)
"Haec Fabula Docet" (1947)
"Hannibal" (1928)
"Happiness Makes Up in Height for What It Lacks in Length" (1942)
"Hardship of Accounting, The" (1936)
"Hillside Thaw, A" (1923)
"Hill Wife, The" (1916)
"Home Burial" (1914)
"Housekeeper, The" (1914)
"How Hard It Is to Keep from Being King When It's in You and in the Situation" (1962)
"Hundred Collars, A" (1914)
"Hyla Brook" (1916)
"I Could Give All to Time" (1942)
"Immigrants" (1928)
"Importer, An" (1947)
"In a Disused Graveyard" (1923)
"In a Glass of Cider" (1962)
"In a Poem" (1942)
"In a Vale" (1913)
"In Divés' Dive" (1936)
"Ingenuities of Debt, The" (1947)
"In Hardwood Groves" (1913)
"Innate Helium" (1947)
"In Neglect" (1913)
In the Clearing (1962)
"In the Home Stretch" (1916)
"In the Long Night" (1947) See "FIVE NOCTURNES"
"In Time of Cloudburst" (1936)
"Into My Own" (1913)
"Investment, The" (1928)
"[In Winter in the Woods Alone]" (1962)
"Iota Subscript" (1947)
"Iris by Night" (1936)
"It Bids Pretty Fair" (1947)
"It Is Almost the Year Two Thousand" (1942)

"Oven Bird, The" (1916)
"Pan with Us" (1913)
"Passing Glimpse, A" (1928)
"Pasture, The" (1914)
"Patch of Old Snow, A" (1916)
"Paul's Wife" (1923)
"Pea Brush" (1916)
"Peaceful Shepherd, The" (1928)
"Peck of Gold, A" (1928)
"Peril of Hope" (1962)
"Pertinax" (1936)
"Place for a Third" (1923)
"Planners, The" (1947)
"Plowmen" (1923)
"Pod of the Milkweed" (1962)
"Prayer in Spring, A" (1913)
"Precaution" (1936)
"Provide, Provide" (1936)
"Putting in the Seed" (1916)
"Quandary" (1962)
"Question, A" (1942)
"Questioning Faces" (1962)
"Quest of the Purple-Fringed, The" (1942)
"Rabbit-Hunter, The" (1942)
"Range-Finding" (1916)
"Record Stride, A" (1936)
"Reflex, A" (1962)
"Reluctance" (1913)
"Revelation" (1913)
"Riders" (1928)
"Road Not Taken, The" (1916)
"Roadside Stand" (1936)
"Rogers Group, A" (1947)
"Rose Family, The" (1928)
"Rose Pogonias" (1913)
"Runaway, The" (1923)
"Sand Dunes" (1928)
"Secret Sits, The" (1942)
"Self-Seeker, The" (1914)
"Semi-Revolution, A" (1942)
"Serious Step Lightly Taken, A" (1942)
"Servant to Servants, A" (1914)
"Silken Tent, The" (1942)
"Sitting by a Bush in Broad Sunlight" (1928)
"Skeptic" (1947)
"Snow" (1916)
"Soldier, A" (1928)

"Some Science Fiction" (1962)
"Something for Hope" (1947)
"Sound of Trees, The" (1916)
"Span of Life, The" (1936)
"Spring Pools" (1928)
"Star in a Stoneboat, A" (1923)
"Stars" (1913)
"Star-Splitter, The" (1923)
Steeple Bush (1947)
"Steeple on the House, A" (1947)
"Stopping by Woods on a Snowy Evening" (1923)
"Storm Fear" (1913)
"Strong Are Saying Nothing, The" (1936)
"Subverted Flower, The" (1942)
"Sycamore" (1942)
"Telephone, The" (1916)
"Thatch, The" (1928)
"There Are Roughly Zones" (1936)
"They Were Welcome to Their Belief" (1936)
"Time Out" (1942)
"Times Table, The" (1928)
"Time to Talk, A" (1916)
"To a Moth Seen in Winter" (1942)
"To an Ancient" (1947)
"To a Thinker" (1936)
"To a Young Wretch" (1942)
"To Earthward" (1923)
"To E. T." (1923)
"Too Anxious for Rivers" (1947)
"To the Right Person" (1947)
"To the Thawing Wind" (1913)
"Tree at My Window" (1928)
"Trespass" (1942)
"Trial by Existence, The" (1913)
"Trial Run, A" (1936)
"Triple Bronze" (1942)
"Tuft of Flowers, The" (1913)
"Two Leading Lights" (1947)
"Two Look at Two" (1923)
"Two Tramps in Mud Time" (1936)
"Two Witches" (1923)
"Unharvested" (1936)
"Unstamped Letter in Our Rural Letter Box, An" (1947)
"U.S. 1946 King's X" (1947)
"Valley's Singing Day, The" (1923)
"Vanishing Red, The" (1916)

Abad, Gemino H. "Stopping by Woods: The Herme-neutics of a Lyric Poem," *Diliman Review* 20 (1972): 25–40.

Abel, Darrel. "Frost's 'Fragmentary Blue,'" *Explicator* 48, no. 4 (Summer 1990): 270–272.

———. "Frost's 'In the Home Stretch,'" *Explicator* 45, no. 2 (Winter 1987): 37–39.

———. "Frost's 'Provide, Provide,'" *Explicator* 46, no. 3 (Spring 1988): 24–26.

———. "The Instinct of a Bard, Robert Frost on Science, Logic, and Poetic Truth," *Essays in the Arts and Sciences* 9, no. 1 (May 1980): 59–75.

———. "Robert Frost's 'Range Finding,'" *Colby Library Quarterly* 22, no. 4 (December 1986): 225–237.

Abshear-Seale, Lisa. "What Catallus Means by Mens Animi: Robert Frost's 'Kitty Hawk,'" *Robert Frost Review* (Fall 1993): 37–46.

Adams, Frederick B., Jr. *To Russia with Frost.* Boston: Club of Odd Volumes, 1963.

Allen, Margaret. "'The Black Cottage': Robert Frost and the Jeffersonian Ideal of Equality." In *Frost: Centennial Essays,* edited by Jac L. Tharpe, 221–229. Jackson: University Press of Mississippi, 1974.

Allen, Ward. "Frost's 'Iota Subscript,'" *English Language Notes* 6 (1969): 285–287.

Anderson, Margaret Bartlett. *Robert Frost and John Bartlett: The Record of a Friendship.* New York: Holt, Rinehart and Winston, 1963.

Anderson, Charles R. "Frost's 'Nothing Gold Can Stay,'" *Explicator* 32 (1964): 63.

Armstrong, James. "The 'Death Wish' in 'Stopping by Woods,'" *College English* 25, no. 6 (March 1964): 440, 445.

Attebery, Louie W. "Fences, Folklore, and Robert Frost," *Northwest Folklore* 6, no. 2 (Spring 1988): 53–57.

Bacon, Helen H. "For Girls: From 'Birches' to 'Wild Grapes,'" *Yale Review* 67 (1977): 13–29.

———. "'Getting among the Poems in Horace's Fons Bandusiae and Robert Frost's Hyla Brook," *Classical and Modern Literature: A Quarterly* 14, no. 3 (Spring 1994): 259–267.

Bagby, George F. *Frost and the Book of Nature.* Knoxville: University of Tennessee Press, 1993.

———. "The Promethean Frost," *Twentieth Century Literature* 38 no. 1 (Spring 1992): 1–19.

Baker, Christopher. "Frost's 'After Apple-Picking' as Hypnagogic Vision," *Robert Frost Review* (Fall 1994): 28–32.

Barnes, Daniel R. "Frost's 'Putting in the Seed,'" *Explicator* 31 (1973): 59.

Barron, Jonathan N. "A Tale of Two Cottages: Frost and Wordsworth." In *Roads Not Taken: Rereading Robert Frost,* edited by Earl J. Wilcox and Jonathan N. Barron, 132–152. Columbia: University of Missouri Press, 2000.

Barry, Elaine. *Robert Frost on Writing.* N.J.: Rutgers, 1974.

Beach-Viti, Ethel. "Frost's 'Mowing,'" *Explicator* 40, no. 4 (Summer 1982): 45–46.

Beacham, Walton. "Technique and the Sense of Play in the Poetry of Robert Frost." In *Frost: Centennial Essays II,* edited by Jac Tharpe, 246–261. Jackson: University Press of Mississippi, 1976.

Benoit, Raymond. "Folklore by Frost: 'Paul's Wife,'" *Notes on Modern American Literature* 5, no. 4 (Fall 1981): 22.

Bentley, Louise. "You Think the Talk Is All (Robert Frost's Poetic Conversational Power)," *Robert Frost Review* (Fall 1992): 52–57.

Berger, Charles. "Echoing Eden: Frost and Origins." In *Robert Frost,* Modern Critical Views, edited by

Harold Bloom, 147–165. Philadelphia: Chelsea House, 2003.

Bieganowski, Ronald. "Robert Frost's 'An Encounter,'" *Notes on Contemporary Literature* 10, no. 2 (1980): 4–5.

———. "Robert Frost's Sense of Choice in *Mountain Interval*," *College Literature* 11, no. 3 (Fall 1984): 258–268.

Bock, Martin. "Frost's 'The Oven Bird' and the Modern Poetic Idiom," *Texas Review* 7, no. 1–2 (Spring–Summer 1986): 28–31.

Borroff, Marie. "Robert Frost's 'The Most of It,'" *Ventures: Magazine of the Yale Graduate School* 9 (1969): 76–82.

———. "Robert Frost: 'To Earthward,'" In *Frost: Centennial Essays II,* edited by Jac Tharpe, 21–39. Jackson: University Press of Mississippi, 1976.

Bosmajian, Hamida. "Robert Frost's 'The Gift Outright': Wish and Reality in History and Poetry," *American Quarterly* 22 (1970): 95–105.

Brady, Patrick. "From New Criticism to Chaos and Emergence Theory: A Reinterpretation of a Poem by Robert Frost," *Synthesis: An Interdisciplinary Journal* 1, no. 1 (Spring 1995): 41–57.

Braverman, Albert, and Bernard Einbond. "Frost's 'Two Tramps in Mud Time,'" *Explicator* 29 (1970): 25.

Broderick, John C. "Not Quite Poetry: Analysis of a Robert Frost Manuscript," *Manuscripts* 20, no. 2 (1968): 28–31.

Brodsky, Joseph, Seamus Heaney, and Derek Walcott. *Homage to Robert Frost.* New York: Farrar, Straus and Giroux, 1996.

Brogunier, Joseph. "Frost Homage to Melville at 'The Frontiers into Eternity,'" *Melville Society Extracts* 77 (May 1989): 14–15.

———. "Walking My Dog in 'Sand Dunes,'" *Journal of Modern Literature* 16, no. 4 (Spring 1990): 648–650.

Brooks, Cleanth, and Robert Penn Warren. *Understanding Poetry.* 3rd ed. New York: Holt, Rinehart and Winston, 1960.

———. *Understanding Poetry: An Anthology for College Students.* Rev. shorter ed. New York: Henry Holt, 1950.

Brophy, Robert. "A Frost Poem on Jeffers," *Jeffers Studies* 3, no. 1 (Winter 1999): 14–15.

Brower, Reuben A. *The Poetry of Robert Frost: Constellations of Intention.* New York: Oxford University Press, 1963.

Brown, Terrence. "Robert Frost's *In the Clearing*: An Attempt to Reestablish the Persona of 'The Kindly Grey Poet,'" *Papers on Language and Literature* 5 (1969): 110–118.

Bruels, Marcia F. "Frost's 'Out, Out—,'" *Explicator* 55 no. 2 (Winter 1997): 85–88.

Buell, Laurence. "Frost as a New England Poet." In *The Cambridge Companion to Robert Frost,* edited by Robert Faggen, 101–122. Cambridge: Cambridge University Press, 2001.

Burnshaw, Stanley. *Robert Frost Himself.* New York: George Braziller, 1986.

Calder, Alex. "Robert Frost: North of Boston." In *A Companion to Twentieth Century Poetry,* edited by Neil Roberts, 369–380. Oxford: Blackwell, 2001.

Calhoun, Richard J. "By Pretending They Are Not Sonnets: The Sonnets of Robert Frost at the Millennium." In *Roads Not Taken: Rereading Robert Frost,* edited by Earl J. Wilcox and Jonathan N. Barron, 217–235. Cambridge: University of Missouri Press, 2000.

Cappeluti, Jo-Anne. "For Once, Then, Something: The Sublime Reality of Fictions in Robert Frost," *Robert Frost Review* (Fall 1993): 86–92.

Carroll, Rebecca. "A Reader-Response Reading of Robert Frost's 'Home Burial,'" *Text and Performance Quarterly* 10, no. 2 (April 1990): 143–156.

Carter, Everett. "Frost's 'Design,'" *Explicator* 47, no. 1 (Fall 1988): 23–26.

Cawthon, W. U., and Tom Fitzpatrick. "Frost's 'A Servant to Servants,'" *Explicator* 53, no. 3 (Spring 1995): 163–166.

Challender, Craig. "Robert Frost's Strategies of Syntax in Selected Letters, 'The Silken Tent,' and 'The Gift Outright,'" *South Carolina Review* 19 (Summer 1987): 19–28.

Charney, Maurice. "Robert Frost's Conversational Style," *Connotations: A Journal for Critical Debate* 10, no. 2–3 (2000–2001): 147–159.

Chavkin, Allan. "The Ordering of the Sequence of Meditative Lyrics in Frost's *North of Boston,*" *Markham Review* 10 (Summer 1981): 67–68.

Claassen, Jo-Marie. "Robert Frost's 'Build Soil': A Modern Text Based on an Ancient Mode, the

Pastoral," *Theoria: A Journal of Studies in the Arts, Humanities, and Social Sciences* 65 (October 1985): 1–13.

Clark, David R. "Robert Frost: 'The Thatch' and 'Directive,'" *Costerus* 7 (1973): 47–80.

Clarke, Peter B. "Frost's 'Mending Wall,'" *Explicator* 43, no. 1 (Fall 1984): 48–50.

Coakley, John. "T. S. Elliot's 'Mr. Apollinax' and Frost's 'Demiurge's Laugh,'" *Explicator* 45, no. 1 (Fall 1986): 42–45.

Cohen, Allen Carson. "Robert Frost's Anthropods," *American Entomologist* (Summer 1999): 70–72.

Collins, Michael. "A Note on Frost's 'Love and a Question,'" *Concerning Poetry* 8, no. 1 (1975): 57–58.

———. "Poetry and Empiricism: The Example of Three Poems," *Crux: A Journal on the Teaching of English* 16, no. 1 (January 1982): 21–27.

Combellack, C. R. B. "Frost's 'Spring Pools,'" *Explicator* 30 (1971): 27.

Conder, John J. "'After Apple Picking': Frost's Troubled Sleep." In *Frost: Centennial Essays*, edited by Jac L. Tharpe, 171–181. Jackson: University Press of Mississippi, 1974.

Cook, Marjorie. "Acceptance in Frost's Poetry: Conflict as Play." In *Frost: Centennial Essays II*, edited by Jac Tharpe, 229–230. Jackson: University Press of Mississippi, 1976.

———. "The Complexity of Boundaries: 'Trespass' by Robert Frost," *Notes on Contemporary Literature* 5, no. 1 (1975): 2–5.

———. "Dilemmas of Interpretation: Ambiguities and Practicalities." In *Robert Frost: The Man and the Poet*, edited by Earl J. Wilcox, 125–141. Rock Hill, S.C.: Winthrop College, 1990.

———. "The Serious Play of Interpretation," *South Carolina Review* 15, no. 2 (Spring 1983): 77–87.

Cook, Reginald. *The Dimensions of Robert Frost*. New York: Rinehart, 1958.

———. "Frost on Frost: The Making of Poems," *American Literature* 27 (March 1956): 66.

———. *Robert Frost: A Living Voice*. Amherst: University of Massachusetts Press, 1974.

Cooper, David D. "Looking beyond the Picture: Robert Frost's 'For Once, Then Something,'" *Robert Frost Review* (Fall 1993): 47–49.

Coulthard, A. R. "Frost's 'Mending Wall,'" *Explicator* 45, no. 2 (Winter 1987): 40–42.

Cowley, Malcolm. "Frost: A Dissenting Opinion." In *Critical Essays on Robert Frost*, edited by Philip Gerber, 95–103. Boston: G. K. Hall, 1982.

Cox, Sidney. *Robert Frost: Original "Ordinary Man."* New York: Holt, 1929.

———. *A Swinger of Birches: A Portrait of Robert Frost*. New York: New York University Press, 1957.

Cramer, Jeffrey S. *Robert Frost among His Poems: A Literary Companion to the Poet's Own Biographical Contexts and Associations*. Jefferson, N.C.: MacFarland, 1996.

Crane, Joan. "Robert Frost's 'Kitty Hawk,'" *Studies in Bibliography: Papers of the Bibliographical Society of the University of Virginia* 30 (1977): 241–249.

Crannell, Kenneth C. "A Metrical Analysis of Robert Frost's 'The Hill Wife." In *Studies in Interpretation*, edited by Esther M. Doyle, et al. 99–114. Amsterdam: Rodopi, 1977.

Cunningham, John. "Human Presence in Frost's Universe." In *The Cambridge Companion to Robert Frost*, edited by Robert Faggen, 261–272. Cambridge: Cambridge University Press, 2001.

Cureton, Richard D. "Temporality and Poetic Form," *Journal of Literary Semantics* 31, no. 2 (2002): 37–59.

D'Avanzo, Mario L. "Frost's 'A Young Birch': A Thing of Beauty," *Concerning Poetry* 3, no. 2 (1970): 69–70.

———. "Frost's 'Departmental' and Emerson: A Further Range of Satire," *Concerning Poetry* 10, no. 2 (1977): 67–69.

———. "Frost's 'Sand Dunes' and Thoreau's Cape Code," *Notes on Contemporary Literature* 10, no. 5 (1980): 2–4.

———. "How to Build a Chimney: Frost Gleans Thoreau," *Thoreau Journal Quarterly* 9 (October 1977): 24–26.

Davis, Charles G. "Frost's 'An Old Man's Winter Night,'" *Explicator* 27 (1968).

DeFalco, Joseph M. "Frost's 'Paul's Wife': The Death of an Ideal," *Southern Folklore Quarterly* 29 (1965): 259–265.

Dell, Roger D. "Three Separate Leaves from Robert Frost's Derry Years: A Note and Transcriptions," *Studies in Bibliography: Papers of the Bibliographical Society of the University of Virginia* 36 (1983): 229–232.

Dickey, Frances. "Frost's 'The Tuft of Flowers': A Problem of Other Minds," *New England Quarterly* 75, no. 2 (June 2002): 299–311.

Dietrich, R. F. "The Contrary Mr. Frost of 'West-Running Brook,'" *University of Dayton Review* 17, no. 3 (Winter 1985–1986): 83–89.

Dilworth, Thomas. "Frost's Directive," *Explicator* 58, no. 1 (Fall 1999): 26–29.

Doreski, William. "Meta-Meditation in Robert Frost's 'The Wood-Pile,' 'After Apple-Picking,' and 'Directive,'" *Review of International English Literature* 23, no. 4 (October 1992): 35–49.

———. "Robert Frost's 'The Census-Taker' and the Problem of Wilderness," *Twentieth Century Literature* 34, no. 1 (Spring 1988): 30–39.

Doyle, John Robert, Jr. *The Poetry of Robert Frost: An Analysis.* New York: Hafner Press, 1962.

Dubinsky, James. "War and Rumors of War in Frost," *Robert Frost Review* (1995): 1–22.

Edwards, C. Hines, Jr. "Frost's 'Dust of Snow,'" *Notes on Contemporary Literature* 12, no. 2 (March 1982): 3–4.

———. "'Neither Out Far nor in Deep': Frost's Use of a Traditional Metaphor," *West Georgia College Review* 21 (May 1991): 7–10.

Edwards, Margaret. "Animal Anthropomorphism in the Poems of Robert Frost." In *Frost: Centennial Essays II,* edited by Jac Tharpe, 236–245. Jackson: University Press of Mississippi.

Ekins, Roger. "'At Home' with Robert Frost." In *Frost Centennial Essays,* edited by Jac Tharpe, 191–200. Jackson: University Press of Mississippi, 1974.

Elder, John. "The Poetry of Experience," *New Literary History* 30, no. 3 (Summer 1999): 649–659.

Emerson, Ralph Waldo. *Collected Poems and Translations.* Edited by Harold Bloom and Paul Kane. New York: Library of America, 1994.

———. *Ralph Waldo Emerson Essays and Lectures.* New York: Library of America, 1983.

Evans, Ivor H. *Brewer's Dictionary of Phrase and Fable.* Centenary ed., revised. New York: Harper & Row, 1981.

Evans, William R. "A Literary Friendship: Robert Frost and Carl Burrell." In *Frost: Centennial Essays,* edited by Jac Tharpe, et al., 504–517. Jackson: University Press of Mississippi, 1974.

Evans, William R. ed. *Robert Frost and Sidney Cox: Forty Years of Friendship.* Hanover: University Press of New England, 1981.

Faggen, Robert, ed. *The Cambridge Companion to Robert Frost.* Cambridge: Cambridge University Press, 2001.

———. "Frost Biography and *A Witness Tree.*" In *The Cambridge Companion to Robert Frost,* edited by Robert Faggen, 35–47. Cambridge: Cambridge University Press, 2002.

———. "The Rhetoric of 'The Vanishing Red,'" *Robert Frost Review* 13 (Fall 2003): 105–109.

———. *Robert Frost and the Challenge of Darwin.* Ann Arbor: University of Michigan Press, 1997.

Feaster, John. "Robert Frost's 'The Code': A Context and a Commentary," *Cresset* 55, no. 7 (May 1992): 6–10.

Finger, Larry. "Frost's Reading of 'The Road Not Taken,'" *Robert Frost Review* (Fall 1997): 73–76.

Finnegan, Sister Mary Jeremy. "Frost Remakes an Ancient Story." In *Frost: Centennial Essays,* edited by Jac L. Tharpe, et al., 389–397. Jackson: University Press of Mississippi, 1974.

Fleissner, Robert F. "Frost's Ancient Music," *Paideuma: A Journal Devoted to Ezra Pound Scholarship* 13, no. 3 (Winter 1984): 415–417.

———. "Frost's 'Fireflies in the Garden,'" *Explicator* 39, no. 4 (1981): 26–28.

———. "Frost's 'Moon Compasses,'" *Explicator* 32 (1974): 66.

———. "Frost's 'Once by the Pacific,'" *Explicator* 40, no. 4 (Summer 1982): 46–47.

———. "Like Pythagoras' Comparison of the Universe with Number: A Frost Tennyson Correlation." In *Frost: Centennial Essays,* edited by Jac Tharpe, 207–220. Jackson: University Press of Mississippi, 1974.

———. "Markin' the Frost Line: On Robert Frost and Edwin Markham," *South Carolina Review* 16, no. 2 (Spring 1984): 120–124.

———. "Sub Rosa: Frost's 'Five-Petaled' Flower," *Colby Literary Quarterly* 20, no. 4 (December 1984): 206–224.

———. "Tufting the Host: Frost's Further Use of Wordsworth," *Notes on Contemporary Literature* 12, no. 4 (September 1982): 6–8.

————. "Whose 'Road Less Traveled By'? Frost's Intent Once Again," *Robert Frost Review* (Fall 1999): 22–26.

Flory, Wendy Stallard. *The American Ezra Pound.* New Haven: Yale University Press, 1989.

Francis, Lesley Lee. *The Frost Family's Adventure in Poetry: Sheer Morning Gladness at the Brim.* Columbia: University of Missouri Press, 1994.

————. "Robert Frost and the Child: *Mother Goose* and "The Imagination Thing," *Massachusetts Review* 45, no. 2 (Summer 2004): 256–268.

Francis, Robert. *Frost: A Time to Talk—Conversations and Indiscretions.* Amherst: University of Massachusetts Press, 1972.

Frank, Bernhard. "Frost's 'Stopping by Woods on a Snowy Evening,'" *Explicator* 40, no. 4 (Summer 1982): 43–45.

Frattali, Steven V. "Frost's Critique of Humanism: A Rereading of 'Directive,'" *Robert Frost Review* (Fall 1994): 94–100.

Freedman, William. "Frost's 'The Pasture,'" *Explicator* 29 (1971): 80.

French, Roberts W. "Robert Frost and the Darkness of Nature." In *Critical Essays on Robert Frost,* edited by Philip L. Gerber, 155–162. Boston: G. K. Hall, 1982.

French, Warren. "'The Death of the Hired Man': Modernism and Transcendence." In *Frost: Centennial Essays III,* edited by Jac Tharpe, 382–401. Jackson: University Press of Mississippi, 1978.

Fowler, James. "Frost: The Poem Mistaken," *Publications of the Arkansas Philological Association* 23, no. 1 (Spring 1997): 41–47.

Frost, Carol. "Frost's Way of Speaking," *New England Review: Middlebury Series* 23, no. 1 (Winter 2002): 119–133.

Frost, Lesley. *New Hampshire's Child: The Derry Journals of Lesley Frost.* Albany: State University of New York Press, 1969.

Funkhouser, Linda Bradley. "Acoustic Rhythm in Frost's 'Dust of Snow,'" *Language and Style: An International Journal* 14, no. 4 (Fall 1981): 287–303.

Gage, John T. "Rhetoric and Dialectic in Robert Frost's a Masque of Reason," *Pacific Coast Philology* 17, no. 1–2 (November 1982): 82–91.

Garnett, Edward. "A New American Poet." In *Critical Essays on Robert Frost,* edited by Philip Gerber, 35–42. Boston: G. K. Hall, 1982.

Garrison, Joseph M., Jr. "'Our Singing Strength: The Texture of Voice in the Poetry of Robert Frost,'" In *Frost Centennial Essays,* edited by Jac L. Tharpe, et al. 340–350. Jackson: University Press of Mississippi, 1974.

Gentry, Marshall Bruce. "Five Poems and One: Frost's 'The Hill Wife,'" *Conference of College Teachers of English Proceedings* 48 (September 1983): 110–115.

George, William. "Frost's 'The Road Not Taken,'" *Explicator* 49, no. 4 (Summer 1991): 230–232.

Gerber, Philip L. ed. *Critical Essays on Robert Frost.* Boston: G. K. Hall, 1982.

————. *Robert Frost.* New York: Twayne, 1966.

Goede, William. "The 'Code-Hero' in Frost's 'Blueberries,'" *Discourse* 11 (1968): 33–41.

Gould, Jean. *Robert Frost: The Aim Was Song.* New York: Dodd, Mead, 1964.

Gowler, Steve. "Frost's 'In Hardwood Groves,'" *Explicator* 40, no. 3 (Spring 1982): 48.

Gozzi, Raymond D. "Frost's 'The Gift Outright,'" *Explicator* 41, no. 3 (Spring 1983): 44–45.

————. "Lowell's 'The Cathedral' and Frost's 'Happiness Makes Up in Height for What It Lacks in Length,'" *Explicator* 45, no. 3 (Summer 1987): 28–30.

Grade, Arnold, ed. *The Family Letters of Robert and Elinor Frost.* Albany: State University of New York Press, 1972.

Greider, Josephine. "Robert Frost on Ezra Pound, 1913: Manuscript Corrections of 'Portrait D'une Femme,'" *New England Quarterly* 44 (1971): 301–305.

Greiner, Donald J. *Robert Frost: The Poet and His Critics.* Chicago: American Library Association, 1974.

Griffin, Larry D. "Frost's Syllogism in 'The White-Tailed Hornet,'" *Publications of the Mississippi Philological Association* (1994): 38–42.

Gwynn, Frederick L. "Analysis and Synthesis of Frost's 'The Draft Horse,'" *College English* 26, no. 3 (December 1964): 223–225.

Haddin, Theodore. "Surfaces and Depths: The Metonymic Wells of Thoreau and Frost," *Publications of the Mississippi Philological Association* (1985): 40–49.

Hall, Donald. *Remembering Poets: Reminiscences and Opinions: Dylan Thomas, Robert Frost, T. S. Eliot, Ezra Pound.* New York: Harper & Row, 1978.

Hamilton, David. "The Echo of Frost's Woods." In *Roads Not Taken: Rereading Robert Frost,* edited by Earl J. Wilcox and Jonathan N. Barron, 123–131. Columbia: University of Missouri Press, 2000.

Hancher, Michael. "'Sermons in Stone': An Explication of Robert Frost's Poem 'A Missive Missile,'" *Centrum* 2, no. 1 (1974): 79–86.

Hansen, Tom. "Frost's Fire and Ice," *Explicator* 59, no. 1 (Fall 2000): 27–30.

Hass, Robert. *Going by Contraries: Robert Frost's Conflict with Science.* Charlottesville: University Press of Virginia, 2002.

Haynes, Donald T. "The Narrative Unity of *A Boy's Will,*" *Publications of the Modern Language Association of America* 87, no. 3 (May 1972): 452–464.

Hays, Peter L. "Frost and the Critics: More Revelation on 'All Revelation,'" *English Language Notes* 18, no. 4 (June 1981): 283–290.

———. "Robert Frost 'Happiness' Line in FWBT?" *Hemingway Newsletter* 16 (June 1988): 2.

Heaney, Seamus. "Above the Brim." In *Robert Frost, Modern Critical Views,* edited by Harold Bloom, 201–218. Philadelphia: Chelsea House, 2003.

Heath, W. G. "The Scholar and the Poet in Robert Frost's 'The Mountain,'" *Gombak Review* 2, no. 2 (December 1997): 97–107.

Helphinstine, Frances. "Frost's 'Two Look at Two,'" *Explicator* 39, no. 4 (Summer 1981): 31–33.

Henderson, Harold G. *An Introduction to Haiku.* New York: Doubleday & Co., 1958.

Heuston, Sean. "Frost's 'West-Running Brook,'" *Explicator* 63, no. 1 (Fall 2004): 40–43.

Hill, William Thomas. "'Oh Years Ago—Ten Thousand Years': The Sound of Sense and Iconography in 'A Cliff Dwelling' by Robert Frost," *Gakuen* (August–September 1995): 36–43.

Hines, Edward C., Jr. "Frost's 'Once by the Pacific,'" *Explicator* 39, no. 4 (Summer 1981): 28–29.

Hoffman, Tyler. *Robert Frost and the Politics of Poetry.* Hanover, N.H.: Middlebury College Press, 2001.

———. "Robert Frost's 'The Vanishing Red' and the Myth of Demise," *Robert Frost Review* 13 (Fall 2003): 101–104.

Holland, Norman N. *The Brain of Robert Frost.* New York: Routledge, 1988.

Hollander, John. "Robert Frost's Oven Bird." In *Sewanee Writers on Writing,* edited by Wyatt Prunty, 80–91. Baton Rouge: Louisiana State University Press, 2000.

Hopkins, Vivian C. "The Houses of Robert Frost." In *Frost: Centennial Essays,* edited by Jac Tharpe, 182–190. Jackson: University Press of Mississippi, 1974.

Hornedo, Florentino H. "All the Difference: Frost's 'The Road Not Taken,'" *Unitas: A Quarterly for the Arts and Sciences* 75, no. 3 (September 2002): 490–495.

Iadonisi, Richard A. "(In)Felicitous Space: The Interior Landscape of 'Snow,'" *Robert Frost Review* (Fall 1996): 47–53.

Ingebretsen, Edward J. "'Design of Darkness to Appall': Religious Terror in the Poetry of Robert Frost," *Robert Frost Review* (Fall 1993): 50–57.

———. "Robert Frost's 'The Pasture' and Wendell Berry's 'Stay Home': Figures of Love and the Figure a Poem Makes." In *His Incalculable Influence on Others: Essays on Robert Frost in Our Time,* edited by Earl J. Wilcox, 81–88. Victoria, British Columbia: University of Victoria Press, 1994.

Irwin, W. R. "The Unity of Frost's Masques," *American Literature: A Journal of Literary History, Criticism, and Bibliography* 32, no. 3 (November 1960): 302–312.

Isaacs, Elizabeth. *An Introduction to Robert Frost.* Denver: Swallow, 1962.

Isitt, Larry. "Dark Climber: Robert Frost's Spiritual Ambivalence in 'Birches,'" *Robert Frost Review* (Fall 1994): 13–16.

Jackson, Sarah R. "Frost's 'The Master Speed,'" *Explicator* 51, no. 1 (Fall 1992): 33–35.

———. "Made in London: The Robert Frost and Ezra Pound Connection," *Worcester Review* 15, nos. 1–2 (1994): 108–121.

Janzen, J. Gerald. "Reassessing Frost's Fair Impression and His Mistrust," *Religion and Literature* 20, no. 3 (Autumn 1988): 71–87.

Jarrell, Randall. "The Other Frost." In *Poetry and the Age,* 28. New York: Vintage, 1955.

———. "To the Laodiceans." In *Poetry and the Age,* 88–91. New York: Vintage, 1955.

Jost, Walter. "Civility and Madness in Robert Frost's 'Snow,'" *Texas Studies in Literature and Language* 39, no. 1 (Spring 1997): 27–64.

———. "Lessons in the Conversation That We Are: Robert Frost's 'Death of the Hired Man,'" *College English* 58, no. 4 (April 1996): 397–422.

———. "'The Lurking Frost': Poetic and Rhetoric in 'Two Tramps in Mud Time,'" *American Literature* 60, no. 2 (May 1988): 226–240.

———. "Ordinary Language Brought to Grief: Robert Frost's 'Home Burial,'" In *Ordinary Language Criticism: Literary Thinking after Cavell after Wittgenstein,* edited by Kenneth Duaber and Walter Jost, 77–114. Evanston: Northwestern University Press, 2003.

———. "Rhetorical Investigations of Robert Frost." In *Roads Not Taken: Rereading Robert Frost,* edited by Earl J. Wilcox and Jonathan N. Barron, 179–197. Columbia: University Press of Missouri, 2000.

Kann, David. "Deadly Serious Play: Robert Frost's 'Design,'" *University of Hartford Studies in Literature: A Journal of Interdisciplinary Criticism* 14, no. 1 (1982): 23–32.

Katz, Sandra L. *Elinor Frost: A Poet's Wife.* Westfield: Institute for Massachusetts Studies, 1988.

Kau, Joseph. "Frost's 'Away!': Illusions and Allusions," *Notes on Modern American Literature* 7, no. 3 (Winter 1983): 17.

———. "'Trust . . . to go by Contraries': Incarnation and the Paradox of Belief in the Poetry of Frost." In *Frost: Centennial Essays II,* edited by Jac Tharpe, 99–111. Jackson: University Press of Mississippi, 1976.

———. "Two Notes on Robert Frost Poems: Frost's 'Version' of Zeno's Arrow and Blind Optimism in Frost's 'We Vainly Wrestle,'" *Notes on Modern American Literature* 1 (1977): 33.

Kearns, Katherine. "Frost on the Doorstep and Lyricism at the Millennium." In *Roads Not Taken: Rereading Robert Frost,* edited by Earl J. Wilcox and Jonathan N. Barron, 32–51. Columbia: University of Missouri Press, 2000.

———. *Robert Frost and a Poetics of Appetite.* Cambridge: Cambridge University Press, 1994.

———. "The Serpent's Tale." In *Robert Frost,* Modern Critical Views, edited by Harold Bloom, 179–180. Philadelphia: Chelsea House, 2003.

Kemp, John C. *Robert Frost and New England: The Poet as Regionalist.* Princeton: Princeton University Press, 1979.

Kern, Alexander. "Frost's 'The Wood-Pile,'" *Explicator* 28 (1970): 49.

Ketterer, David. "The Letter 'Y' in The Road Not Taken,'" *Robert Frost Review* (Fall 1997): 77–78.

Kilcup, Karen L. "Frost's 'The Vanishing Red': Some Further Questions and Speculations," *Robert Frost Review* 13 (Fall 2003): 110–111.

———. "Something of a Sentimental Sweet Singer: Robert Frost, Lucy Larcom, and 'Swinging Birches,'" In *Roads Not Taken: Rereading Robert Frost,* edited by Earl J. Wilcox and Jonathan N. Barron, 11–31. Columbia: University of Missouri Press, 2000.

Klausner, Lewis. "Frost's Claims to Immortality: The Bones of Bequest," *Southwest Review* 80, no. 1 (Winter 1995): 137–147.

Kochhar-Lindgren, Gray. "The Beginning of Beginnings: Frost's 'West-Running Brook' as a Creation Myth," *Religion and Intellectual Life* 6, no. 3–4 (Spring–Summer 1989): 220–227.

Kozilkowski, Stan. "Frost's 'After Apple-Picking' and God's Judgment," *Robert Frost Review* (Fall 1997): 39–43.

Lakritz, Andrew. "Frost in Transition." In *Roads Not Taken: Rereading Robert Frost,* edited by Earl J. Wilcox and Jonathan N. Barron, 198–216. Columbia: University of Missouri Press, 2000.

Lathem, Edward Connery, ed. *Interviews with Robert Frost.* New York: Holt, Rinehart and Winston, 1966.

———. *The Poetry of Robert Frost.* New York: Henry Holt, 1969.

Lehmberg, P. S. "Companion Poems in Frost's *A Further Range,*" *Literary Criterion* 11, no. 4 (1975): 37–44.

Lentricchia, Frank. "The Resentments of Robert Frost." In *Out of Bounds: Male Writers and Gender(ed) Criticism,* edited by Laura Claridge and Elizabeth Lanland, 268–289. Amherst: University of Massachusetts Press, 1990.

———. *Robert Frost: Modern Poetics and the Landscape of Self.* Durham, N.C.: Duke University Press, 1975.

Levay, John. "Frost's 'Directive,'" *Explicator* 52, no. 1 (Fall 1993): 42–44.

Linebarger, J. M. "Sources of Frost's 'The Vindictives,'" *American Notes and Queries* 12 (1974): 150–154.

Linneman, William R. "Robert Frost's 'New Hampshire': A Most Jestful State," *Studies in American Humor* 6 (1988): 52–60.

Locklear, Gloriana. "Frost's 'Out, Out—,'" *Explicator* 49, no. 3 (Spring 1991): 167–169.

Loreto, Paola. "A Man in Front of His God, a Man in Front of Himself: The (Post)Modernity of Robert Frost's *A Masque of Reason*," *Robert Frost Review*, (Fall 1999): 27–39.

Lowell, Amy. "North of Boston." In *Critical Essays on Robert Frost*, edited by Philip Gerber, 22–25. Boston: G. K. Hall, 1982.

Lynen, John F. "Du Côté de Chez Frost." In *Frost: Centennial Essays*, edited by Jac Tharpe, 562–594. Jackson: University Press of Mississippi, 1974.

———. *The Pastoral Art of Robert Frost.* New Haven: Yale University Press, 1960.

Mansell, Darrel, Jr. "Frost's Range-Finding," *Explicator* 24 (1966): 63.

Manson, Michael L. "Trying to Find the Right Genre for Genocide: Robert Frost and 'The Vanishing Red,'" 13 (Fall 2003): 82–100.

Marcus, Mordecai. *The Poems of Robert Frost: An Explication.* Boston: G. K. Hall, 1991.

———. "Robert Frost's 'Bond and Free': Structure and Meaning," *Concerning Poetry* 8, no. 1 (1975): 61–64.

———. "The Whole Pattern of Robert Frost's 'Two Witches': Contrasting Psycho-Sexual Modes," *Literature and Psychology* 26 (1976): 69–78.

Marks, Herbert. "The Counter Intelligence of Robert Frost." In *Robert Frost, Modern Critical Views*, edited by Harold Bloom, 554–578. Philadelphia: Chelsea House, 2003.

Matterson, Stephen. "'To Make It Mean Me': Narrative Design in *North of Boston*." In *Rebound: The American Poetry Book*, edited by Michael Hinds and Stephen Matterson, 45–55. New York: Rodopi, 2004.

Maxson, H. A. *On the Sonnets of Robert Frost: A Critical Examination of the 37 Poems.* Jefferson, N.C.: McFarland, 1997.

McClanahan, Thomas. "Frost's Theodicy: Word I Had No One Left but God." In *Frost: Centennial Essays II*, edited by Jac Tharpe, 112–126. Jackson: University Press of Mississippi, 1976.

McCoy, Joan D. "Frost's 'The Armful,'" *Explicator* 47, no. 1 (Fall 1988): 21–23.

McInery, Stephen. "'Little Forms': Four Poems and a Developing Theme of Robert Frost," *Critical Review* 40 (2000): 59–74.

McPhillips, Robert T. "Diverging and Converging Paths: Horizontal and Vertical Movement in Robert Frost's *Mountain Interval*,'" *American Literature* 58, no. 1 (March 1986): 82–98.

Mertins, Louis. *Robert Frost: Life and Talks-Walking.* Norman: University of Oklahoma Press, 1965.

Meyers, Jeffery. "An Earring for Erring: Robert Frost and Kay Morrison," *American Scholar* 65, no. 2 (Spring 1996): 219–241.

———. *Robert Frost: A Biography.* New York: Houghton Mifflin, 1996.

Micelli, Pauline. "Frost Misread: The Road Not Taken," *Occident* 103, no. 1 (1990): 275–278.

Michaels, Walter Benn. "Getting Physical," *Raritan* 2, no. 2 (Fall 1982): 103–113.

Miller, David L. "Dominion of the Eye in Frost." In *Frost: Centennial Essays II*, edited by Jac Tharpe, 141–158. Jackson: University Press of Mississippi, 1976.

Miller, Lewis H. Jr. "Design and Drama in *A Boy's Will*." In *Frost: Centennial Essays*, edited by Jac Tharpe, 351–368. Jackson: University Press of Mississippi, 1974.

———. "'Snow': Frost's Drama of Belittled People," *Robert Frost Review* (Fall 1994): 47–51.

Monteiro, George. "Frost's Hired Hand," *College Literature* 14, no. 2 (Spring 1987): 128–135.

———. "Frost's 'Quest for the Purple-Fringed,'" *English Language Notes* 13 (1976): 204–206.

———. "History, Legend, and Regional Verse in Frost's 'Directive,'" *New England Quarterly* 75, no. 2 (June 2002): 286–294.

———. *Human Values in the Poetry of Robert Frost.* Durham, N.C.: Duke University Press, 1960.

———. "A Pre-publication Version of Robert Frost's 'November,'" *Robert Frost Review* (Fall 1991): 5–6.

———. *Robert Frost and the New England Renaissance.* Lexington: University Press of Kentucky, 1988.

———. "Robert Frost's Liberal Imagination." In *Roads Not Taken: Rereading Robert Frost*, edited by Earl J.

Wilcox and Jonathan N. Barron, 153–175. Columbia: University of Missouri Press, 2000.

———. "Robert Frost's Linked Analogies," *New England Quarterly* 46, no. 3 (September 1973): 463–468.

———. "Robert Frost's Metaphysical Sonnet." In *Frost: Centennial Essays*, edited by Jac Tharpe, 333–339. Jackson: University Press of Mississippi, 1974.

———. "Robert Frost's Solitary Singer," *New England Quarterly* 44, no. 1 (March 1971): 134–140.

———. "To Point or Not to Point: Frost's 'Stopping by Woods,'" *ANQ: A Quarterly Journal of Short Articles, Notes, and Reviews* 16, no. 1 (Winter 2003): 38–40.

Moore, M. Shawn. "Robert Frost's 'The Pasture': Poem and Metapoem," *Virginia English Bulletin* 36, no. 2 (Winter 1986): 49–51.

Morrissey, L. J. "'Mending Wall': The Structure of Gossip," *English Language Notes* 25, no. 3 (March 1988): 58–63.

Morse, Stearns. "'The Subverted Flower': An Exercise in Triangulation." In *Frost: Centennial Essays II*, edited by Jac Tharpe, 170–176. Jackson: University Press of Mississippi, 1976.

Muir, Helen. *Frost in Florida: A Memoir*. Miami: Valiant Press, 1995.

Muldoon, Paul. "The End of the Poem: 'The Mountain' by Robert Frost," *American Poetry Review* 30, no. 1 (January–February 2001): 41–46.

———. "Getting Round: Notes towards an Ars Poetica," *Essays in Criticism* 48, no. 2 (April 1998): 107–128.

Munson, Gorham B. *Robert Frost: A Study in Sensibility and Good Sense*. New York: George H. Doran, 1927.

Murray, Keat. "Robert Frost's Portrait of a Modern Mind: The Archetypal Resonance of 'Acquainted with the Night,'" *Midwest Quarterly* 41, no. 4 (June 2000): 370–384.

Nathan, Rhoda. "'Perfect and Upright?' Frost's Fidelity to Hebrew Scripture in a Masque of Reason," *Studies in the Humanities* 19, no. 1 (June 1992): 58–67.

Newdick, Robert. *Newdick's Season of Frost: An Interrupted Biography of Robert Frost*. Edited by William A. Sutton. Albany: State University of New York Press, 1972.

Nietzsche, Friedrich. *The Gay Science*. Translated by Walter Kaufmann. New York: Vintage, 1974.

Norwood, Kyle. "The Work of Not Knowing," *Southwest Review* 78, no. 1 (Winter 1993): 57–73.

O'Donnell, William G. "Talking about Poems with Robert Frost," *Massachusetts Review* 39, no. 2 (Summer 1998): 225–250.

Oehlschlaeger, Fritz. "Robert Frost's 'The Pasture': A Reconsideration," *CP* 16, no. 2 (Fall 1983): 1–9.

———. "Two Woodchucks, or Frost and Thoreau on the Art of the Burrow," *Colby Literary Quarterly* 18, no. 4 (December 1982): 214–219.

———. "West toward Heaven: The Adventure of Metaphor in Robert Frost's 'West-Running Brook,'" *Colby Literary Quarterly* 22, no. 4 (December 1986): 238–251.

Oster, Judith. *Toward Robert Frost: The Reader and the Poet*. Athens: University of Georgia Press, 1991.

Pack, Robert. *Belief and Uncertainty in the Poetry of Robert Frost*. Hanover, N.H.: Middlebury College Press, 2003.

Parini, Jay. *Robert Frost: A Life*. New York: Holt, 1999.

Parker, Blanford. "Frost and the Meditative Lyric." In *The Cambridge Companion to Robert Frost*, edited by Robert Faggen, 179–196. Cambridge: Cambridge University Press, 2001.

Paton, Priscilla M. "Robert Frost: 'The Fact Is the Sweetest Dream That Labor Knows,'" *American Literature* 53, no. 1 (March 1981): 43–55.

PBS.org. "Secrets of Easter Island." Available online. URL: http://www.pbs.org/wgbh/nova/easter/ civilization. Accessed June 30, 2006.

Pearce, Donald. "The Secret Ministry of Frost," *Robert Frost Review* (Fall 1993): 59.

Pearlman, Daniel. "Frost and the Work Ethic: A Reading of 'Two Tramps in Mud Time,'" *Modernist Studies* 3 (1979): 61–68.

———. "A Political Satire Unveiled: Frost's 'Neither Out Far nor In Deep,'" *Agenda* 17, no. 2 (1979): 41–63.

Pellegrino, Joe. "Frost, Schopenhauer, and 'The Trial by Existence,'" *Robert Frost Review* (Fall 1993): 93–100.

Perrine, Laurence. "The Dilemma in Frost's 'Love and a Question,'" *Concerning Poetry* 5, no. 2 (1972): 5–8.

———. "Frost's 'An Empty Threat,'" *Explicator* 30 (1972): 63.

————. "Frost's 'Design,'" *Explicator* 42, no. 2 (Winter 1984): 16.

————. "Frost's 'Dust of Snow,'" *Explicator* 29 (March 1971): 61.

————. "Frost's 'Gathering Leaves,'" *CEA Critic* 34 (1971): 29.

————. "Frost's 'Iris by Night,'" *Concerning Poetry* 12, no. 1 (1979): 35–43.

————. "Frost's 'I Will Sing You One-O,'" *Explicator* 34 (1976): 48.

————. "Frost's 'New Hampshire' 1–60," *Explicator* 29, no. 3 (Spring 1981): 38–39.

————. "Frost's 'Nothing Gold Can Stay,'" *Explicator* 42, no. 1 (Fall 1983): 38–39.

————. "Frost's 'Once by the Pacific,'" *Explicator* 41, no. 3 (Spring 1983): 44.

————. "Frost's 'Pod of the Milkweed,'" *Notes on Modern American Literature* 5 (1980): 5.

————. "Frost's 'Revelation,'" *Explicator* 42, no. 1 (Fall 1983): 36–38.

————. "Frost's 'The Fear': Unfinished Sentences, Unanswered Questions," *College Literature* 15, no. 3 (1988): 199–207.

————. "Frost's 'The Mountain': Concerning Poetry," *Concerning Poetry* 4, no. 1 (1971): 5–11.

————. "Frost's 'The Rose Family,'" *Explicator* 26 (1968): 43.

————. "Frost's 'The Span of Life,'" *Explicator* 14, no. 6 (March 1971): 61.

————. "Frost's 'The Telephone,'" *Notes on Contemporary Literature* 10, no. 3 (1980): 11–12.

————. "Frost's 'The Tuft of Flowers,'" *Explicator* 42, no. 1 (Fall 1983): 36.

————. "Frost's 'West-Running Brook,'" *Explicator* 4 (1977): 27.

————. "A House for Frost's 'White-Tailed Hornet,'" *Notes on Contemporary Literature* 10, no. 1 (1980): 3.

————. "Letting Go with the Heart: Frost's 'Wild Grapes,'" *Notes on Modern American Literature* 2 (1978): 20.

————. "The Meaning of Frost's 'Build Soil.'" In *Frost: Centennial Essays*, edited by Jac Tharpe, 230–235. Jackson: University Press of Mississippi, 1974.

————. "Misreadings of Frost's 'Silken Tent,'" *Notes on Modern American Literature* 9, no. 1 (Spring–Summer 1985): 3.

————. "On Frost's 'The Wood-Pile,'" *Notes on Modern American Literature* 6, no. 1 (Spring–Summer 1982): 1.

————. "Provide, Provide," *Robert Frost Review* (Fall 1992): 33–39.

————. "Robert Frost and the Idea of Immortality." In *Frost: Centennial Essays II*, edited by Jac Tharpe, 87–89. Jackson: University Press of Mississippi, 1976.

————. "Robert Frost's 'Provide, Provide,'" *Notes on Modern American Literature* 8, no. 1 (Spring–Summer 1984): 5.

————. "Robert Frost's 'The Hill Wife': Evidence, Inference, and Speculation in the Interpretation of Poetry," *College Literature* 10, no. 1 (Winter 1983): 1–15.

————. "The Sense of Frost's 'The Self-Seeker,'" *Concerning Poetry* 7, no. 1 (1974): 5–8.

————. "The Telephone," *Robert Frost Review* (Fall 1991): 3–4.

————. "'Two Tramps in Mud Time' and the Critics," *American Literature* 44, no. 4 (January 1973): 671–676.

Peters, Joan D. "Education by Poetry: Robert Frost's Departure from the Modern Critical Edition," *South Carolina Review* 21, no. 1 (Fall 1988): 27–37.

Poirier, Richard. "Choices." In *Robert Frost*, Modern Critical Views, edited by Harold Bloom, 43–61. New York: Chelsea House, 1986.

————. *Robert Frost: The Work of Knowing*. New York: Oxford University Press, 1977.

Poland, Peter. D. "Frost's 'Neither Out Far nor In Deep,'" *Explicator* 52, no. 2. (Winter 1994): 95–96.

Pritchard, William H. *Frost: A Literary Life Reconsidered*. New York: Oxford University Press, 1984.

————. "Frost's Life and Career." Modern American Poetry. Available online. URL: http://www.english.uiuc.edu/maps/poets/a_f/frost/life.htm. Accessed June 30, 2006.

Quinn, M. Bernetta. "Symbolic Landscape in Frost's 'Nothing Gold Can Stay,'" *English Journal* 55 (1966): 621–624.

Rea, John A. "Language and Form in 'Nothing Gold Can Stay,'" *Robert Frost: Studies of the Poetry*, edited by Kathryn Gibbs Harris, 17–25. Boston: Hall, 1979.

Reed, Richard. "The Animal World in Robert Frost's Poetry." In *Frost: Centennial Essays II,* edited by Jac Tharpe, 159–169. Jackson: University Press of Mississippi, 1976.

Reeve, Franklin D. *Robert Frost in Russia.* Boston: Little, Brown, 1964.

Reichert, Victor. "The Faith of Robert Frost." In *Frost: Centennial Essays,* edited by Jac Tharpe, et al., 415–426. Jackson: University Press of Mississippi, 1974.

Richardson, Mark. "Frost and the Cold War: A Look at the Later Poetry." In *Roads Not Taken: Rereading Robert Frost,* edited by Earl J. Wilcox and Jonathan N. Barron, 55–77. Columbia: University of Missouri Press, 2000.

———. "Frost's 'Closed for Good': Editorial and Interpretive Problems," *Robert Frost Review* (Fall 1996): 22–35.

———. "Frost's Poetics of Control." In *The Cambridge Companion to Robert Frost,* edited by Robert Faggen, 197–219. Cambridge: Cambridge University Press, 2001.

———. *The Ordeal of Robert Frost: The Poet and His Poetics.* Chicago: University of Illinois Press, 1997.

Rogers, William E. "Mysteries in Frost," *Furman Studies* 32 (December 1986): 53–64.

Rood, Karen Lane. "Robert Frost's Sentence Sounds: Wildness Opposing the Sonnet Form." In *Frost: Centennial Essays II,* edited by Jac Tharpe, 196–210. Jackson: University Press of Mississippi, 1976.

Rooke, Constance. "The Elusive/Allusive Voice: An Interpretation of Frost's 'A Servant to Servants,'" *Cimarron Review* 38 (1976): 13–23.

Rosen, Kenneth. "Visions and Revisions: An Early Version of Robert Frost's 'Our Doom to Bloom.'" In *Frost: Centennial Essays,* edited by Jac L. Tharpe, et al., 369–372. Jackson: University Press of Mississippi, 1974.

Rosenblatt, Louise M. "The Poem as Event," *College English* 26, no. 2 (November 1964): 123–128.

Rotella, Guy L. "Metaphor in Frost's 'Oven Bird.'" In *Robert Frost the Man and the Poet,* edited by Earl J. Wilcox, 19–30. Rock Hill, S.C.: Winthrop College, 1990.

Sanders, Charles. "Frost's 'Skeptic,'" *Explicator* 40, no. 3 (Spring 1982): 47–48.

Sanders, David Alan. "Frost's *North of Boston,* Its Language, Its People, Its Poet," *Journal of Modern Literature* 27, no. 1–2 (Fall 2003): 70–78.

———. "Looking through the Glass: Frost's 'After Apple-Picking' and Paul's 1 Corinthians," *Robert Frost Review* (Fall 1996): 12–22.

———. "Revelation as Child's Play in Frost's 'Directive.'" In *Frost: Centennial Essays II,* edited by Jac Tharpe, 267–277. Jackson: University Press of Mississippi, 1976.

Saunders, Judith P. "Frost's 'Once by the Pacific,'" *Explicator* 39, no. 4 (Summer 1981): 29–31.

Savoie, John. "A Poet's Quarrel: Jamesian Pragmatism and Frost's 'Road Not Taken,'" *New England Quarterly* 77, no. 1 (March 2004): 5–24.

Scheele, Roy. "Sensible Confusion in Frost's 'The Subverted Flower,'" *South Carolina Review* 10, no. 1 (1977): 89–98.

Scheick, William J. "Frost's 'October,'" *Explicator* 62, no. 2 (Winter 2004): 96–98.

Schiffbauer, Judith P. "Three Poems by Robert Frost: A Jamesian Reading," *Kentucky Philological Review* 8 (1993): 46–52.

Schnelle, Robert. "Over the Line: Robert Frost and Trespass," *Weber Studies* 21, no. 2 (Winter 2004): 98–105.

Schutz, Fred C. "Frost's 'The Literature Farmer and the Planet Venus': Why 1926?" *Notes on Contemporary Literature* 4, no. 5 (1974): 8–11.

Scott, Mark. "Andrew Lang's 'Scythe Song' Becomes Robert Frost's 'Mowing': Frost's Practice of Poetry," *Robert Frost Review* (Fall 1991): 30–38.

Seale, Lisa. "'Triumphant Association': The First Group of Poems in Robert Frost's *Steeple Bush,*" *Robert Frost Review* (Fall 1997): 1–16.

———. "War and Peace: Robert Frost and the United Nations Meditation Room," *New England Quarterly* 77, no. 1 (March 2004): 108–114.

Sears, John F. "Frost's Figures of Upright Posture." In *Robert Frost the Man and the Poet,* edited by Earl J. Wilcox, 49–59. Rock Hill, S.C.: Winthrop College, 1990.

———. "The Subversive Performer in Frost's 'Snow' and 'Out, Out—.'" *The Motive for Metaphor: Essays on Modern Poetry,* edited by Francis C. Blessington and Guy L. Rotella, 82–92. Boston: Northeastern University Press, 1983.

Seib, Kenneth. "Robert Frost's 'Neither Out Far nor In Deep,'" *Contemporary Poetry* 1, no. 2 (1973): 28–29.

Sell, Roger D. "Two Unpublished Plays: *In an Art Factory, The Guardeen*," *Massachusetts Review* 26, nos. 2–3 (Summer–Autumn 1985): 265–340.

Sergeant, Elizabeth Shepley. *Robert Frost: The Trial by Existence*. New York: Holt, Rinehart and Winston, 1960.

Sheehy, Donald G. "The Poet as Neurotic: The Official Biography of Robert Frost," *American Literature* (October 1986): 393–409.

———. "(Re)Figuring Love: Robert Frost in Crisis, 1938–1942)," *New England Quarterly* (June 1990): 179–231.

———. "Robert Frost and 'The Lockless Door,'" *New England Quarterly* 56, no. 1 (March 1983): 39–59.

Shurr, William H. "Once More to the 'Woods': A New Point of Entry into Frost's Most Famous Poem," *New England Quarterly* 47, no. 4 (December 1974): 584–594.

Slakey, Roger L. "Frost's 'Moon Compasses,'" *Explicator* 37, no. 1 (1978): 22–23.

Smith, Evans Lansing. "Frost's 'On a Bird Singing in Its Sleep', 'Never Again Would Birds' Song Be the Same,' and 'The Silken Tent,'" *Explicator* 50, no. 1 (Fall 1991): 35–37.

Smythe, Daniel. *Robert Frost Speaks*. New York: Twayne, 1966.

Sohn, David A., and Richard Tyre. *Frost: The Poet and His Poetry*. New York: Holt, 1967.

Sokol, B. J. "Bergson, Instinct, and Frost's 'The White-Tailed Hornet,'" *American Literature* 62, no. 1 (March 1990): 44–55.

———. "Poet in the Atomic Age: Robert Frost's 'That Millikan Mote' Expanded," *Annals of Science* 53, no. 4 (1996): 399–411.

———. "What Went Wrong between Robert Frost and Ezra Pound," *The New England Quarterly* 49, no. 4 (December 1976): 521–541.

Squires, Radcliffe. *The Major Themes of Robert Frost*. Ann Arbor: University of Michigan Press, 1963.

Stanlis, Peter J. "Robert Frost's Philosophy of Education: The Poet as Teacher," In *Roads Not Taken: Rereading Robert Frost*, edited by Earl J. Wilcox and Jonathan N. Barron, 78–104. Columbia: University of Missouri Press, 2000.

———. "Robert Frost: Politics in Theory and Practice." In *Frost: Centennial Essays II*, edited by Jac Tharpe, 48–82. Jackson: University Press of Mississippi, 1976.

Steward, Garrett. "Dust of Snow," *Robert Frost Review* (Fall 1993): 60–61.

Stillians, Bruce. "Frost's 'To the Thawing Wind,'" *Explicator* 31 (1972): 31.

Stone, Edward. "'Other 'Desert Places': Frost and Hawthorne." In *Frost Centennial Essays*, edited by Jac Tharpe, et al., 275–287. Jackson: University Press of Mississippi, 1974.

Stott, William. "'Living Deeper Into Matter': Robert Frost's 'Kitty Hawk' and the Creation of Nature," *North Carolina Literary Review* 12 (2003): 46–56.

Sullivan, D. Bradley. "'Education by Poetry' in Robert Frost's Masques," *Papers on Language and Literature: A Journal for Scholars and Critics of Language and Literature* 22, no. 3 (Summer 1986): 312–321.

Summerlin, Charles Timothy. "The Romantic Absolute in Frost's 'Home Burial,'" *Robert Frost Review* (Fall 1994): 53–57.

Sutton, Betty S. "Form as Argument: Frost's 'Lesson for Today,'" *Fu Jen Studies: Literature and Linguistics* 18 (1985): 81–96.

Taylor, Welford Dunaway. *Robert Frost and J. J. Lankes: Riders on Pegasus*. Hanover, N.H.: Dartmouth College Library, 1996.

Thomas, Ron. "Thoreau, William James, and Frost's 'Quest of the Purple-Fringed': A Contextual Reading," *American Literature* 60, no. 3 (October 1988): 433–450.

Thorson, Robert J. The Stone Wall Initiative. Available online. URL: http://stonewall.uconn.edu. Accessed June 29, 2006.

Thompson, Lawrance. *Fire and Ice: The Art and Thought of Robert Frost*. New York: Russell & Russell, 1942.

———. *Robert Frost: The Early Years*. New York: Holt, Rinehart and Winston, 1966.

———. *Robert Frost: The Years of Triumph, 1915–1938*. New York: Holt, Rinehart and Winston, 1970.

Thompson, Lawrance, and R. H. Winnick. *Robert Frost: The Later Years, 1938–1963*. New York: Holt, Rinehart and Winston, 1976.

Thoreau, Henry David. *Henry David Thoreau: Collected Essays and Poems.* Edited by Elizabeth Hall Witherell. New York: Library of America, 2001.

Thornton, Richard. *Recognition of Robert Frost: Twenty-fifth Anniversary.* New York: Henry Holt, 1937.

Timmerman, John H. *Robert Frost: The Ethics of Ambiguity.* Lewisburg, Pa.: Bucknell University Press, 2002.

Tomlinson, Sandra W. "Frost's 'Draft Horse,'" *Explicator* 42, no. 4 (Summer 1984): 28–29.

Trachtenberg, Zev. "Good Fences Make Good Neighbors: Frost's 'Mending Wall,'" *Philosophy and Literature* 21, no. 1 (April 1997): 114–122.

Trilling, Lionel. "A Speech on Robert Frost: A Cultural Episode," *Partisan Review* 26 (1959): 445–452.

Turrill, Charles Beebe. "Woodward's Gardens." The Virtual Museum of the City of San Francisco. Available online. URL: http://www.sfmuseum.org/hist9/woodward.html. Accessed June 29, 2006.

Uirak, Kim. "The Seasonal Cycle in Robert Frost's Poetry," *Arkansas Review* 5, nos. 1–2 (August 1996): 81–87.

"Unsigned Review of *A Boy's Will.*" In *Robert Frost: An Introduction*, edited by Robert A. Greenberg and James G. Hepburn, 45–52. New York: Holt, Rinehart and Winston, 1961.

Untermeyer, Louis. *The Road Not Taken: An Introduction to Robert Frost.* New York: Holt, 1951.

Vail, Dennis. "Frost's 'Ghost House,'" *Explicator* 30 (1971): 11.

———. "Frost's 'Mowing': Work and Poetry," *Notes on Contemporary Literature* 4, no. 1 (1974): 4–8.

———. "Point of View in Frost's 'The Peaceful Shepherd,'" *Notes on Contemporary Literature* 4, no. 5. (1974): 2–4.

Vanderburg, Peter. "Prosody as Meaning in 'To the Thawing Wind' and 'Home Burial,'" *Robert Frost Review* (Fall 1994): 17–22.

Vandoren, Mark. "Soil of the Puritans." *Critical Essays on Robert Frost.* Edited by Philip Gerber. Boston: G. K. Hall, 1982. 68–75.

Vogel, Nancy. "A Post Mortem on 'The Death of the Hired Man.'" In *Frost Centennial Essays*, edited by Jac Tharpe, et al., 201–206. Jackson: University Press of Mississippi, 1974.

Von Frank, Albert J. "Frost's 'The Gift Outright,'" *Explicator* 38, no. 1 (1979): 22–23.

———. "'Nothing That Is': A Study of Frost's 'Desert Places.'" *Frost Centennial Essays*, edited by Jac

Tharpe, et al., 121–132. Jackson: University Press of Mississippi, 1974.

Waddell, William S., Jr. "Aphorism in Robert Frost's 'The Tuft of Flowers': The Sound of Certainty," *Concerning Poetry* 13, no. 1 (1980): 41–44.

———. "By Precept and Example: Aphorism in 'The Star Splitter,'" In *Robert Frost the Man and the Poet*, edited by Earl J. Wilcox, 115–124. Rock Hill, S.C.: Winthrop College, 1990.

Wakefield, Richard. "Robert Frost's 'In the Home Stretch': The Renewal of New England," *Robert Frost Review* (Fall 1999): 45–61.

Wallace, Patricia. "The 'Estranged Point of View': The Thematics of Imagination in Frost's Poetry." In *Frost: Centennial Essays II*, edited by Jac Tharpe, 180–182. Jackson: University Press of Mississippi, 1976.

Walsh, John Evangelist. *Into My Own: The English Years of Robert Frost.* New York: Grove Press, 1988.

Warner, Stephen D. "Robert Frost in the Clearing: The Risk of Spirit in Substantiation." In *Frost Centennial Essays*, edited by Jac Tharpe, 398–411. Jackson: University Press of Mississippi, 1974.

Watterson, William Collins. "Gerontion as Jokester: Humor and Anxiety in Robert Frost's 'Directive,'" *Robert Frost Review* (Fall 1992): 59–67.

Weltman, Sharon Aronofsky. "The Least of It: Metaphor, Metamorphosis, and Synecdoche in Frost's 'Subverted Flower,'" *South Carolina Review* 22, no. 1 (Fall 1989): 71–78.

West, Michael. "Versifying Thoreau: Frost's 'The Quest of the Purple-Fringed' and 'Fire and Ice,'" *English Language Notes* 16 (1978): 40–47.

Westbrook, Perry. "Abandonment and Desertion in the Poetry of Robert Frost." In *Frost: Centennial Essays II*, edited by Jac Tharpe, 291–304. Jackson: University Press of Mississippi, 1976.

Wilcox, Earl J., and Jonathan N. Barron, eds. *Roads Not Taken: Rereading Robert Frost.* Columbia: University of Missouri Press, 2000.

Will, Norman P. "Robert Frost's 'Beech': Faith Regained," *Notes on Modern American Literature* 6, no. 1 (Spring–Summer 1982): 2.

Winslow, Donald J. "The Origin of Robert Frost's 'Witness Tree,'" *American Notes and Queries* 13 (1975): 153–154.

Wolosky, Shira. "The Need of Being Versed: Robert Frost and the Limits of Rhetoric," *Essays in Literature* 18, no. 1 (Spring 1991): 76–92.

INDEX